D1546609

WITHDRAWN
TOURO COLLEGE LIBRARY
Kings Hwy

The Way
Jews Lived

ALSO BY CONSTANCE HARRIS

Portraiture in Prints (McFarland, 1987)

THE WAY JEWS LIVED

Five Hundred Years of Printed Words and Images

Constance Harris

Foreword by Shalom Sabar

TOURO COLLEGE LIBRARY
Kings High
WITHDRAWN

McFarland & Company, Inc., Publishers

Jefferson, North Carolina, and London

KH

LIBRARY OF CONGRESS CATALOGUING-IN-PUBLICATION DATA

Harris, Constance.
The way Jews lived : five hundred years of printed words
and images / Constance Harris ; foreword by Shalom Sabar.
p. cm.
Includes bibliographical references and index.

ISBN 978-0-7864-3440-4
illustrated case binding : 50# alkaline paper

1. Art, Jewish. 2. Judaism and art. 3. Jews—History.
4. Judaism—History. I. Title.
N7415.H36 2009 704.03'924—dc22 2008036564

British Library cataloguing data are available

©2009 Constance Harris. All rights reserved

*No part of this book may be reproduced or transmitted in any form
or by any means, electronic or mechanical, including photocopying
or recording, or by any information storage and retrieval system,
without permission in writing from the publisher.*

On the cover: *Solomon Hirschell*, 1803 engraving
by W. Holl, after a painting by Benjamin Barlin;
background and border ©2008 Shutterstock

Manufactured in the United States of America

*McFarland & Company, Inc., Publishers
Box 611, Jefferson, North Carolina 28640
www.mcfarlandpub.com*

10/10/10

Acknowledgments

This book would have been an impossible task had not a number of scholars and institutions generously helped along the way. They lent me their expertise and gave me hours of their precious time.

It is a pleasure to offer them my very sincere appreciation: Todd Endelman, Tal Gazani, Eric Goldstein, the late Joseph Gutmann, Tara Hitchcock, Michael Hittleman, the Israel Museum, Eric Chaim Kline, George Krevsky, Steven Lowenstein, Darin Margules, Maud Mandel, Tobey C, Moss, Suzanne Specter, Irvin Ungar, Steven Weil—and Shalom Sabar, who was my first mentor and who graciously wrote the Foreword. A very singular thanks to Jeffrey Blutinger, who waded through all the chapters with infinite patience. Nichole Julian organized the bibliography. Rena Small photographed some of the illustrations. Nicola McGee helped with the computer. Chris Haun was invaluable.

Many of the prints included here were gifted to the Special Collections Library of the University of Michigan as "The Jewish Heritage Collection Dedicated to Mark and Dave Harris," where they received far better conservation and preservation there than I was able to provide. A subsequent exhibition and catalogue in 2005 showcased a selection of these prints as well as Jewish books and artifacts.

For her grace and warmth, I am indebted to Peggy Daub, the head of the Special Collections Library, who allowed me to impose on her for more time and space than she probably bargained for. She and her staff made me a part of their team and provided a computer and a comfortable window view in the library's reading room. Thank you all for consideration and thoughtfulness: Angela Balla, Kathy Beam, Kathleen Dow, Elliot Gertel, William Gosling, Julie Herrada, Eileen Heeran, Thomas Hogarth, Leyla Lau Lamb, Erica Lehrer, William Lovick, Mei-Ying Moy, Harriet Teller, Marcy Toon, and Shannon Zachary. A particular note of appreciation to Franki Hand, Margaret Reyes, Morgan Jones, Jamie Tanner, and Benjamin Johnson who chased reference books and scanned prints with good humor and a special brand of niceness.

My son Stephen tirelessly walked me through mazes of computer aberrations. To him, my daughter-in-law, Ruth, and my grandsons, Dave and Mark, I dedicate this study of Jewish history and art with the hope that it will be transmitted MiDor leDor—From generation to generation.

Table of Contents

Foreword

by Shalom Sabar

The study and research of Jewish art is a late-comer in the two disciplines associated with it—Jewish studies and art history. When the various fields of Jewish studies were defined by the scholars of the nineteenth century German movement, *Wissenschaft des Judenthums (Science of Judaism)*, Jewish art was not one of them. At the time, the leading authorities of the new discipline believed that this aspect of Jewish life was not worthy of serious research. Moreover, the common belief had been that Judaism denies images and that one should not even question whether Jewish art ever existed. Art historians commonly accepted this view and belittled the role of the visual in Jewish life and practice. Some noted Jewish scholars agreed, including the well-known connoisseur of Italian Renaissance art, Bernard Berenson, who wrote: "Israel through the ages has manifested nothing essentially national in the plastic arts, neither in antiquity, nor through the Middle Ages, nor today.... The Jews, like their Ishmaelite cousins the Arabs ... have displayed little talent for the visual, and almost none for the figurative arts" (Bernard Berenson, *Aesthetics and History in the Visual Arts,* New York, Pantheon, 1948, 162, 164). Another influential Jewish authority, Sigmund Freud, even found ulterior motives for the supposed lack of visual perception among Jews: "The prohibition against making an image of God ... signified subordinating sense perception to an abstract idea; it was a triumph of spirituality over the senses..." (Sigmund Freud, *Moses and Monotheism*, New York, Vintage Books, 1939, 144).

Freud and others writing at the time, however, either were unaware of or simply neglected to examine the rich physical remains and visual heritage of Jews living under Christianity in Europe or under Islam in the East. The fact is that in nearly every Jewish society attractive objects and illustrated manuscripts were produced. True, these objects and manuscripts were not created as "works of art" to be admired for their inherent aesthetic qualities, but rather as functional artifacts; their images generally served to enhance liturgical usage and meaning within the Jewish realm. Though the "image" in Judaism is indeed secondary to the "word," some of the best craftsmen and folk artists in Europe and Islamic lands created the fine Judaic *objets d'art* currently preserved in Jewish museums and private collections.

The involvement of Jews in the visual arts, as minor as it may have been, led to hitherto little-known cultural and aesthetic interactions and relationships with the host societies. Undoubtedly, to a certain degree, the dominant artistic styles, designs, and aesthetic principles influenced local Jewish communities. Particularly in Europe, Jewish patrons often commissioned non–Jewish craftsmen to create their ceremonial objects, illuminate their manuscripts,

1

or produce printed images pertaining to Jewish life, rituals, and practices. These images reveal how the Jews and their culture were perceived and understood (or misunderstood) by their contemporaries.

A category of its own is the image of the Jew and Judaism in Christian European art. This topic reflects the complex attitudes of Christianity and the West towards Jews who lived among them. The Jews were not just another religious minority, but deeply connected with the origins and foundations of Christianity. The visual references to them are thus not limited to realistic depictions of people or ceremonies—which, in fact, did not appear before the late Renaissance and Baroque periods—but are expressed through multifaceted visual themes and symbols. Thus, for example, in Medieval Christian art selected Old and New Testament events and characters provided many opportunities to convey the "Jewish image" and the attitude towards Judaism. A typical example is the scene of Cain murdering his younger brother Abel, which was taken as prefiguring the crucifixion of Jesus or the younger religion by the older. Therefore, Cain, whose offering was symbolically rejected by God, and was condemned to become a "ceaseless wanderer on earth" (Gen. 4:12), became in Christian eyes a prototype of the Jew, and was thus depicted with typical "Jewish features."

In like manner, Jews and Judaism are represented in allegorical and symbolical representations—e.g., the blindfolded and humiliated Synagoga juxtaposed with victorious and proud Ecclesia. In addition, anti–Jewish popular legends and myths gave rise to numerous folk as well as "high" works of art, especially in German-speaking lands. Numerous woodcuts and copper engravings depict, for example, popular blood libel stories—e.g., the famous 1475 blood libel of Simon of Trent. Others documented, in great detail, the legend of the Jewish desire to obtain and torture the host—representing the body of Jesus (an extremely popular motif in German art, but also known from a work by an Italian master, the Urbino predella of Paolo Uccello, 1468).

As times changed and new ideas emerged, the depiction of Jews in Christian art followed new trends, and occasionally even helped to shape them. The interest of some leading Italian Renaissance humanists in the Hebrew language, Jewish philosophy, and Kabbalah, led Bernard Gozzoli to include the Jewish scholar Rabbi Elijah del Medigo among the respected cortege of the Medici family in his fresco of the *Procession of the Magi* (Florence, Palazzo Medici-Riccardi, 1459). This attitude continued in subsequent centuries; even in Germany one finds a relatively positive image of Judaism in contemporary visual art. Thus, despite some anti–Semitic overtones in books about Jews written by sixteenth to eighteenth century German Hebraists, their images often feature authentic Jewish ceremonies and rituals with curious ethnographic details—at times unavailable from any other written or visual source. This attitude culminated in the Dutch "Golden Age," when leading artists such as Rembrandt and Emanuel de Witte, and noted printmakers such as Romeyn de Hooghe and Jan Luyken, depicted favorably, even admiringly, the life of contemporary Jews, especially members of the affluent and acculturated Portuguese community. Rembrandt went one step further, using Jewish models and Hebrew inscriptions to enhance the authenticity and humanity of his work.

The present book is dedicated to the Jewish image in periods of major transitions in Jewish history. Considering a single medium, that of the printed image, Constance Harris examines the many ways in which Jews of Europe and America perceived themselves and the ways they were viewed by others. Printed images, whether woodcuts, copper engravings, etchings, or lithographs, have been widely accessible, relatively inexpensive, and were produced not only by distinguished masters, but also by many less-known or even anonymous craftsmen. Accordingly, they represent wide social and cultural phenomena as well as a broad range of opinions. The medium also accommodated the needs of pre–Emancipation European Jews who would not represent themselves through figurative paintings or forbidden three-dimensional objects.

Hebrew printing flourished in the capitals and many small cities of Europe; practically every Jewish home had some Jewish books. Their illustrations were disseminated from Italy and Holland to Poland and Turkey as well as the New World, and were even imitated by the Jews of India, Morocco, and Iraq.

The present book, therefore, is doing an important service—assembling and discussing for the first time under one cover a wide spectrum of printed images pertaining to Jewish life as seen through the eyes of Christians and Jews during the last five hundred years.

Shalom Sabar is a professor at the Hebrew University of Jerusalem.

Introduction

This is the story of survival and a history of adaptation. It is a five-hundred-year overview of visions, prejudices, persecutions, and triumphs recounting and depicting the Jewish experience in many of the countries in which Jews lived. Half a millennium and more, of course, tells less than half its chronology. As unfolded in the Bible and interpreted in the Talmud, Judaism evolved from homeless tribes into a kinship that found its ultimate significance in a moral and spiritual relationship with God, and in the conviction of progressing from a landless community to a life force in their own country.

After Five Books of stories, poetry, legal codes, songs, and reproofs—what Heinrich Heine called the whole drama of humanity—the Torah ended on a hopeful note. Although Moses was not destined to enter it, the Promised Land was bequeathed to the children of Israel. From their conquest of Canaan to the establishment of the First Temple—from its destruction and the Babylonian Exile after 586 B.C.E. to the homecoming and rebuilding of the Sanctuary—from the subjugation by Greece to the revolt against Hellenism and the establishment of an independent state—from the vassalage of Judea by Pompey to the heroic but unsuccessful resistance at Masada—from the ravage of the Second Temple by the Roman army in 70 C.E. to wanderings and martyrdoms—from the crematories of Europe and a revived Israel to one in painful transition—Jewish history has embodied success and bitter failure.

While religious, ethnic, and racial hatred have beset all of mankind, in length of time and relentlessness of purpose no other people have endured the unhappy fortunes of the Jews. But their history transcends a recital of pain and lamentation. They gave the world unique ethical systems. Their Sabbath day of rest and study gifted a society that knew weeklong drudgery and endless toil. Their festivals, rituals, and customs offered more than legislation, more than aesthetics; they inculcated tradition and cultural continuity and offered opportunities to alleviate the bad and savor the good. Mainstream Judaism historically denied magical practices or human sacrifices, restricted slave ownership, regulated the tillage of the soil, and limited the collection of debts. Marriage and divorce laws were more liberal than many religious and civil codes elsewhere. It was possible for women to be financially secure and active when other cultures diminished their roles. Hospitality was enjoined, the rights of the poor were stressed, while the mandate to love—or at least respect—one's neighbor was obligatory. Jews taught the pleasures of marriage and family, recognizing the need to rejoice in the body as well as to elevate the mind—for had not the Babylonian rabbi Abba Areca decreed that "a man will have a demerit in his record on Judgment Day for everything he beheld with his eyes and declined to enjoy"?

Over time, Jewish culture interfaced with medieval Islam and Christendom, sometimes as colleagues, often as dissenters. Over time, Jewish communal life developed with rabbinic scholarship and the interpretation of Talmudic laws. It partnered with the rich Muslim civilization but eschewed its concentration on philosophy and science. It grappled with the social and economic forces that anticipated the destructive power of the Crusades, which ironically intensified religious commitment and brought northern European populations into an Ashkenazi orbit. In the wider world, Jews played a relatively small role among Europe's petty rulers who were busy elsewhere dealing with the collapse of feudalism, fragmented political jurisdictions and disruptions in the production of goods and services. As a tentative capitalism and banking system based on urban trade and industry emerged, agricultural economies broke down, land ownership began to move from the concentrated power of Church and State to vassals and tenant farmers, while the resentful peasant class remained stuck at the bottom of the social system. Within this environment, some Jews moved to other lands, securing financial and personal advantages through their internal and worldwide family networks, although they remained as "others," outsiders inside alien communities.

But they were neither invisible nor ignored. Following their expulsion from England, central Europe, and the Iberian Peninsula, the end of the fifteenth century found them seeking refuge in Holland, Italy, Turkey, and eastern Europe. They had become involved with the printing press and printmaking, inventions which brought their books, faces, troubles and customs to the attention of their Renaissance and Reformation neighbors.

Although history and art are inevitably intertwined, this book is neither a detailed history of the Jews nor a full survey of Jewish art. Rather, it scans Jewish events and culture as Jews have perceived themselves and as they have been perceived by others through works on paper. The focus is on the seminal, anecdotal, or descriptive elements, with technical process and connoisseurship in subordinate roles. While some of the prints and books discussed here were produced by skilled masters, others are by less known, or unknown, practitioners. Together, they represent a small selection of the documents that have molded popular Jewish opinion precisely because they were popular and accessible to rich and poor, simple and sophisticated alike.

It is at this point that our narrative begins, with each entry recalling a moment in the way Jews lived.

1

Jewish Art:
In the Beginning...

What constitutes Jewish art? Is it a sentimental print of a rabbi absorbed in the holy books? Is it a depiction of life in Europe's former ghettos, of the American immigrant experience, or even images of the Holocaust? Does it include any work with Jewish significance regardless of the nationality of its maker, or only work by someone born a Jew? Do such items appeal equally to all, or does a Jewish component influence or distort the viewer's critical judgments? Is the art Jewish where the intent is malevolent? Was the concept of a Jewish art credible during the period when Jews lacked a state of their own? Has Israel produced Jewish or Israeli art? These questions, including the problem of whether such a category actually exists at all, are complex and confusing.

Stephen Kayser, former director of the Jewish Museum in New York, said that wherever art is applied to Judaism, the result is Jewish art. Others have broadened the definition to something that imparts Jewish symbolic and spiritual meaning, enhances Jewish feelings, conveys Jewish ideals and kinship, or comments on Jewish events. The Jewish historian Franz Landsberger claimed that the "individual character of the artist, as well as his national and social background, are expressed in his art. That is why we turn to works of art in order to understand the character of a race or a people."

Barnett Newman said that his abstract works were intended to convey a Jewish mystical approach to divinity. Hermann Struck defined Jewish art as something intrinsic to Jewish artists, something symbolic of their values, something unavailable to non–Jews. Peter Krasnow claimed that "the Jewish artist produces an essentially Jewish art, independent of subject."

Some commentators believe that the traditional emphasis on values and societal responsibility has penetrated the psyche of Jewish artists; even when specific Jewish subject matter is lacking, the theme of social justice imparts a Jewish element. Others reject the presumption that moral or aesthetic sensibilities have been bred into the peoplehood, if only unconsciously, suggesting that Jewish descent alone is no longer relevant. Art critic Harold Rosenberg thought that "while Jews produce art, they don't produce Jewish art." "The more an artist tries to be "Jewish," wrote Ben-Zion, "the less his work will have creative value."

Not all Jews developed Jewish sensibilities or saw themselves as Jewish spokesmen simply by reason of their ancestry. Some deliberately avoided Jewish identification or were drawn to alternative topics, preferring to be defined in the spirit of their times and to be remembered for the quality, rather than the religious expression, of their work. Meaningfulness for them existed not to instruct or indoctrinate, but to communicate whatever they considered aesthetically or personally valid in imaginative and unconditional terms.

Jewish art did not develop as a universally coherent phenomenon. In its early years, it borrowed from the many environments where Jews lived, often provoking charges that Jews distorted the talents of others or were freeloaders lacking innovation and originality. Yet, their efforts embodied some unique qualities that not only were quite separate from those of their host country but varied creatively among themselves. Certainly, Ashkenazim and Sephardim in Amsterdam, or Jews in Rome and Venice, employed different artistic languages. In countries such as Afghanistan, Yemen, Morocco, and Iran, Jewish tastes and styles differed from those of the West, and at times from each other.

Other than questions of intent or significance, there are controversial issues relating to the Second Commandment: "Thou shalt not make any graven (or sculpted) image, or any likeness of anything that is in the heaven above, or that is in the earth below, or that is in the water under the earth: Thou shalt not prostrate thyself to them, nor serve them" (Exodus 20:4, 5; Deuteronomy 5:8). It is commonly assumed that the fear of paganism, as expressed in idol or cult worship, was the motive of the commandment, rather than any intrinsic objections to art; limitations were instituted against forms that imitated nature, such as human figures (Deuteronomy 4:16) or the golden calf which confronted Moses when he offered the Law to the desert exiles (Exodus 32:19). The concern that pagan beauty would supplant biblical beauty was real; the power of images was believed to suppress the voice of a single god. But, as the threat of idolatry and the influence of foreign cultures began to wane, strictures against the visual arts were relaxed. By the third and fourth centuries C.E., some rabbis were already amenable to decorative synagogue architecture, ornamental ceremonial objects, and figurative paintings and mosaics. Artistic expression was constrained, however, in delineations of the Jewish God. Although the Bible describes God as imparting His likeness to man (Genesis 1:27), traditional Jewish artists generally have not depicted the forbidden face. Moses reminded Israel that while God's voice could be heard, His appearance could never be known; the concept of God's immateriality or invisibility was fundamental (Deuteronomy 4:12). "Paganism sees its gods," wrote the nineteenth century Jewish historian Heinrich Graetz, "Judaism hears Him." Christianity, too, saw its God, but not from the same perspective. At the time of the High Renaissance, Michaelangelo and Raphael, among others, reflected the sixteenth century humanistic dictum that *man* is the measure of all things, and felt no compunction in representing God as a burly fellow with a well-developed musculature and snowy beard; their symbolism was clearly more anthropomorphic than transcendent or supernatural.

The development of Jewish plastic arts was further curtailed because of concerns that art, as an adjunct to the permissible pleasures of life, would foster materialistic attitudes, that Jewish spirituality and morality might be subverted into a sensually oriented life, and that an emphasis on man's creation of the perishable could undermine and demean God's creation of the eternal. According to these views, the search for beauty in the manual arts was in conflict with higher ethical values, recalling Anchises' comments to his son in Virgil's *Aeneid*: "Others, no doubt, will better mold the bronze to the semblance of soft breathing, or draw from marble the living countenance; and others plead with greater eloquence, or learn to measure better than we, the pathways of the heavens and the risings of the stars: Remember, Roman, to rule the people under law, to establish the way of peace, to battle down the haughty, to spare the meek. Our fine arts, these, forever."

However, according to the Victorian painter George Frederick Watts, a culture committed to ethics or a philosophy dedicated to reason need not disown aesthetics: "Art, in partnership with altruism, may kindle all that is best and noblest in humanity," he wrote. "In the future it may speak with the solemn and majestic ring in which the Hebrew prophets spoke to the Jews of old, demanding noble aspirations, condemning in the most trenchant manner private vices, and warning us in deep tones against lapses from morals and duties." Few contemporary scholars would endorse such views, holding that art in itself is neutral, neither ethical nor unethical; that whether it prompts worthiness or worldliness, or whether it is useful or harmful, rests with the viewer.

Certainly, there were no scriptural assumptions that beauty in art would displace the beauty of holiness. Hiddur Mitzvah, which derives from Exodus 15:2—"This is my God and I will glorify Him"—affirms Jewish sensibilities through its ritual objects. The Talmud later expanded on this injunction: "Make a beautiful sukkah in His honor, a beautiful lulov, a beautiful shofar, beautiful tsitsis, and a beautiful Scroll of the Law, and have a skilled penman write it with fine ink and a fine reed, and wrap it in beautiful silk" (Sabbath 133b). With this motivation, the biblical artist embellished his world as a means to sanctification and worship.

Craftsmanship is recorded very early in the Bible when the silver, gold, and copper of the Tabernacle, as well as the menorah, incense altar, cherubim, and vestments of the High Priest, are offered for the delight and glory of God—and, no doubt, for the pride and gratification of His people (Exodus 25–28). Jewish artists make their first appearance when Bezalel and Oholiab receive the "wisdom, understanding, and knowledge with which to do all manner of work of the engraver and of the dexterous workman" (Exodus 35:30–35). They were charged not only with the teaching, but with transmitting moral values, the Hebrew word for teaching connoting both ethics and learning. Later we are given a great deal of information about the construction of the Temple in the tenth century B.C.E. As in the story of Noah's Ark, God assumes the role of architect; we learn how it was made, but we know very little about how it actually looked. What we do know is that King Solomon imported the Phoenician worker Hiram, son of a Jewish mother, to design and build the Sanctuary as a national center for prayer. Working with thirty thousand Israelites and one hundred fifty thousand Canaanites, he fashioned a pair of massive bronze columns to stand at its entrance. Two winged cherubim guarded the Ark of the Covenant, twelve bronze oxen supported a basin large enough to accommodate two thousand bathers. Hewn stones and carved and engraved floral motifs graced the building along with a show-bread table, candlesticks, and household vessels all adorned in pure gold for the Most Holy Place, the House of the Lord (I Kings, 5:15–7:51; II Chronicles: 2–4).

The oldest known biblical manuscripts were discovered in 1947 by shepherds along the Dead Sea at Qumran; more were found fifteen years later in caves north of Jericho. The scrolls appear to date from the third century B.C.E. to about 68 C.E., and are neatly written and carefully ruled; clearly the scribes took pride in turning out attractive texts. No doubt these are not unique specimens. The Palestinian Talmud mentions a family of "artists" from shortly before this period, indicating that Jews were knowledgeable in the preparation of manuscripts (Meg. 71d). That there was no shortage of reading matter can be deduced from Ecclesiastes' complaint that "of making many books there is no end" (Kohelet 12:12).

Jewish coins dating from the Hasmonean period identified the current high priest and were decorated with anchors, stars and vine leaves (135–37 B.C.E.). No forbidden images appear on them. During the war against Rome (66–70 C.E.) shekels were issued bearing the words "Holy Jerusalem." After the destruction of the Second Temple and Jerusalem in 70 C.E., coins were stamped featuring the victors Titus and Vespasian on one side, the vanquished Jew on the reverse, marked "Judaea Capta: Judaea Captured." Titus then erected the famous arch which stands to this day close to the Roman Forum bearing on its inside wall a relief of the menorah being carried away on the shoulders of Jewish prisoners. From 132 to 135 C.E. under the leadership of Bar Kokhba, coins were struck bearing the slogan "For the freedom of Jerusalem."

The significance of a synagogue excavation in the 1920s and '30s in the Roman garrison town of Dura-Europos can hardly be exaggerated. Originally built in 245 C.E. on the Euphrates River in present-day Syria, its thirty surviving wall paintings are wonderfully preserved. While some of the motifs, such as shells representing life emerging from the sea, originated in Roman art, others, such as the pomegranate, by tradition bearing six hundred thirteen seeds, stands for the number of commandments incumbent on all Jews. The panels are covered with biblical scenes and human forms, as well as menorahs, lulavs, and etrogs, symbols evoking the harvest festival of Sukkot. God's immateriality or invisibility is strictly maintained—only His hand is visible. As there is no known earlier narrative work of this importance or continuity, it is possible that Byzantine Christian biblical cycles some two hundred years later may have had their sources in Jewish antecedents, given the frontal aspect of the figures, symmetrical arrangements, flat perspective, and otherworldly facial expressions in the Dura paintings. The image of a man with a scroll, possibly Joshua or Moses, bears a surprising similarity to future depictions of Jesus, although both could have stemmed from Roman originals. Since the synagogue was built in a provincial town, its decorations may have followed from more sophisticated works in major Jewish centers, although nothing else of its scale has been found. It is also possible that because its very remoteness precluded the presence of captious authorities, it was indeed an isolated development.

The first known examples of art from ancient Palestine were third and fourth century C.E. synagogues in Hammat, Tiberias, built in the Hellenistic style and unearthed in 1920 and 1961–63. Ornamental mosaic floors include the names of its Jewish artists or builders, as well as depicting ritual items and a zodiacal wheel with the personification of the four seasons, alluding, perhaps, to man's voyage through time. Excavated in 1929, the mosaic floor of a sixth century synagogue in the present-day Israeli kibbutz of Beth Alpha discloses the binding of Isaac along with God's hand indicating His mediation in human affairs. Zodiac signs, the seasons of the year, the Ark and other synagogue accouterments fill the upper area of the pavement.

From the seventh through the ninth centuries there is a break in the chronology and few examples of Jewish artisanship have survived. That period witnessed the Muslim conquest of Arabs and Jews, when rules against decoration became more stringent. Islam enforced Second Commandment figural prohibitions, interpreted Christian worship of religious imagery as polytheism, and believed that God's word is best expressed through calligraphy and geometric decorative patterns. The pope rejected those views, getting around the commandment by declaring at the Second Council of Nicaea in 787 that inasmuch as God had addressed only the Israelites on the subject, others were surely exempted. The Church recognized very early that centrally controlled art could be instrumental in shaping religious attitudes, and accordingly spent vast sums commissioning great cathedrals filled with instructive paintings and statues.

When a ninth century Cairo synagogue was demolished in 1763, some two hundred thousand worn fragments of illuminated manuscripts bearing God's name were recovered in its storeroom or genizah after lying intact and unsuspected for almost a thousand years. (Jewish law forbids the destruction of sacred material.) Brought to the attention of the scholar and founder of Conservative Judaism, Solomon Schechter, in 1891, the collection yielded remarkable texts, including Maimonides' handwritten response, much of the original Hebrew Book of Ben Sira, dedications to artists' patrons, and nonfigural designs embodying verses from Isaiah. The patterns ranged from early Roman and Hellenistic examples through Byzantine, Moorish, and classical styles, varying greatly in quality and effect. Some are crude and stiff, others delicate in workmanship; some richly embellish the vellum with heavy coloring and gold leaf, others are lightly outlined in ink and filled with contrasting pigments.

After the eleventh century, animal and bird pictures, as well as those of the Ark, the Tablets of the Law, and other religious symbols began to appear in illuminated manuscripts for home prayer. But when religious paintings on interior synagogue walls were introduced, Maimonides, fearing that they might hinder concentration, closed his eyes during services. However, another authority, Rabbi Ephraim ben Isaac of Regensburg, decided that since the pictures did not encourage sacrifices or idolatry, he could withstand their charms with his eyes open. (Some Polish, German, and French synagogues, particularly after the sixteenth century, permitted animal representations on walls and ceilings. Although almost no synagogues today display murals with human images, Wilshire Boulevard Temple in Los Angeles, inspired by the Dura excavations, in 1929 commissioned a figurative biblical cycle by Hugo Ballin for its sanctuary.)

By the end of the fourteenth century, Jews were producing crafts for Jewish and Christian use, although at times they farmed out their orders to Christian artisans; a fifteenth century volume of Maimonides' code of Jewish law, the Mishnah Torah, was obviously designed by a non–Jew who decorated it with horses and knights in resplendent armor! The manufacture of leather book bindings and some ceremonial objects for the Church was monopolized by Spanish Jews until 1415, when it was prohibited by Pope Benedict XIII. Polish law, on the other hand, allowed Jews to organize shops in which metal work—pewter for the poor, copper or silver for the rich—was created for home and ritual use. Permissive Moorish rule in the Near East and North Africa found Jews engaged in manuscript production, coin minting, stone masonry, wood carving, weaving, glass making, dyeing, and embroidery. Yet, because Jews needed a settled and stable environment to produce significant artistic achievements, it was a long time before they made important contributions. Nevertheless, their considerable involvement in the manual arts is evident from the expressive verses that live on in the Yom Kippur service. Basing his similes on the prophetic writings of Jeremiah (18:6) and Isaiah (64:7), the anonymous poet lyrically evoked the concept of God molding the Jewish nation, and compared His hands to those of the skilled workmen who supplied local populations with their daily needs:

> Like clay in the hand of the potter
> Who expands it or contracts it at will ...
>
> Like stone in the hand of the cutter
> Who grasps it or smashes it at will ...
>
> Like iron in the hand of the blacksmith
> Who forges or destroys it at will ...
>
> Like an anchor in the hand of the sailor
> Who holds it or casts it at will ...
>
> Like glass in the hand of the blower
> Who shapes it or dissolves it at will ...
>
> Like fabric in the hand of the embroiderer
> Who designs it evenly or unevenly at will ...
>
> Like silver in the hands of the silversmith
> Who adulterates or purifies it at will,
> So are we in Your hand, O God—
> Remember Your covenant and disregard our iniquity.

But of all the crafts in which enterprising Jews took part, none compared to their handwritten and meticulously embellished books. While for most people book art was secondary, for the Jews it was central. They concentrated chiefly on their inner world—Torah, Talmud, and holiday texts. In their spiritual introspection, in their lack of physical security and political significance and in their wandering existence, Jews focused on books. Their most imaginative efforts were reserved for the Haggadah, history's first and greatest paean to freedom and liberty. Recited for over two thousand years during the Passover Seder, it is a collection of bib-

lical and Talmudic excerpts, psalms, blessings, and instructions for eating special foods, cul-
minating in the symbolic arrival of the Messiah. Possibly the earliest surviving specimens, dating from about 1000 C.E., were the fragments found in the Cairo genizah. By then its basic
form was set, although later generations attached questions and answers designed to pique
children's curiosity and songs to keep them awake or tickle their imaginations. Originally part
of the Siddur, it was issued separately sometime between the eleventh and thirteenth centuries.
Since it was used in the home rather than the synagogue, it could be figuratively illustrated—
and by the mid–fourteenth century was often lit with bright pigments and gold leaf that shim-
mered across the page.

The Sarajevo Haggadah, a Spanish manuscript from the first quarter of the fourteenth
century, turned up in 1894 in Bosnia, Yugoslavia, when a young boy in a Jewish school brought
it to his teacher, hoping that its sale would aid his impoverished family. Other than the fact
that it was censored by Giovanni Dominico in Italy in 1609, its location for six hundred years
is unknown; perhaps it traveled eastwards with a Jewish family following the Spanish expulsion of 1492. It is thought to be of Jewish workmanship, in part because the sequence of its
sixty-two biblical scenes reads from right to left as in Hebrew books, and because of the artist's
familiarity with midrashic legends, presumably unknown to most Christians. The figurative
art reveals classical influences as well as the elongated shapes and flat perspective of International Gothic design. Most of its miniatures derive from the Pentateuch text and the Seder
rituals; almost more interesting are the contemporary images disguised as biblical events:
Joseph's burial is in the guise of local funerary rites, the Tower of Babel as local architecture.
Designed to inform and charm their readers, illustrated Haggadot became one of the best
sources of information about Jewish customs, costumes, furnishings, and family life for later
historians.

Early books still exist because, unlike gold or silver objects which were melted down in
troubled times, parchment leaves had no commercial or intrinsic worth. They did, however,
have great personal and sacred value—any manuscript containing God's name always ranked
among a community's most cherished possessions. The Talmud actually exempts scribes and
those who buy and sell holy works from reading certain prayers and wearing phylacteries
(Sukkah 26a). "If you keep a box of books in your bedroom," we are cautioned, "place it at the
head, not at the foot of your bed." But since only the wealthiest members of the congregation
could afford them, the humble majority had to rely on access to very limited synagogue collections, or on occasional private generosity. "They who lend books to students," wrote Judah
the Pious, "merit the same share in the world to come as do the students themselves."

Unfortunately, after generations of copying and recopying manuscripts and illustrations,
errors crept in. Hand-drawn material simply was not able to meet community needs because
the process was too slow and duplicates could not be reproduced with sufficient accuracy; faster
and more precise methods were needed to provide inexpensive, uniform, exactly repeatable
images and texts. A remedy arrived in Europe in the early fifteenth century with the inventions of printmaking. By modifying the ancient arts of woodcutting and engraving on metal,
printmakers were able to derive multiple copies of an artist's work by inking and transferring
designs onto paper with absolute fidelity. The craft at first served Christian needs through the
sale of religious images along pilgrimage routes. Vying for popularity were printed playing cards
which provided a bit of relaxation from the serious business of salvation.

Not until the invention of the camera in the first half of the nineteenth century would
there be such radical changes in the transmission of art. Printmaking made it possible for the
first time in the Western world to illustrate and disseminate a wide range of passing events.
Unlike unique drawings or paintings only accessible to the few, inexpensive prints enabled
almost anyone to accumulate pictorial information. They constituted a revolution in percep-

tion, enlarging every aspect of general and technical knowledge, while their reproductive capacity provided a fundamental breakthrough in the spread of clear explanatory diagrams, maps, and art works. Much of what we know about how our predecessors looked and lived survives in the prints that recorded their traditions and shaped their ideas and attitudes. Prints that described or denigrated scenes of daily Jewish observances and holiday celebrations, that depicted their costumes and worldly goods, that paraded everyday faces and forms, or that illustrated a text, provided much of the visual documentation of Jewish life. Voltaire, who hardly believed in God, remarked that even the Deity "loves a collection of prints which bestow immortality to the human race."

Looking at pictures was not the only form of entertainment. More and more people were now learning to read, spurring the next great opportunity for human progress. Many centuries earlier, Socrates had complained that the invention of writing made serious erosions on the intellect and psyche. He reported that the Egyptian god Thamus castigated Thoth, the god who invented letters, for a discovery that "will create forgetfulness in the learners' souls because they will not use their memories." He continued, "Writing gives your disciples not truth, but only the semblance of truth; they will be hearers of many things and will have learned nothing; they will appear omniscient and will generally know nothing; they will be tiresome company, having the show of wisdom without the reality." Nevertheless, printed books, even more than the manuscripts against which Socrates fulminated, permitted almost anyone to learn from inexpensive texts and to carry them anywhere—a boon to the peripatetic Jew. As mechanical alternatives to handwritten material, they were newly available to anyone who required accurate standardized type, offering literary, scientific, artistic, and religious texts in quantities never before imagined. Soon all kind of secular and religious material—as well as anti–Jewish and proselytizing tracts—targeted the Jewish market. However, the profusion of publishing houses, along with the development of a literate and independent mercantile class, contributed to the loss of Church control over what could or could not be issued.

At first, the printing business was not open to Jews since they could not enter Christian guilds. But by the sixteenth century, in spite of intense resistance Jews began to organize guilds for their own artisans. They served as readers or editors in Christian firms and as agents of their own presses. Nevertheless, much of the early work pertaining to Jewish life was done by Christians, sometimes with reasonable accuracy and sentiments, more often with cruel distortions. Negative texts, however, were not limited to those born as Christians; bitter and vindictive apostate Jews also created works of irreparable harm.

In the heyday of seventeenth and eighteenth centuries, Jewish lifestyles, traditional customs, and ceremonies were treated sympathetically or were depicted with ludicrous or disagreeable caricatures. Some Protestant artists created visual encyclopedias of normative Judaism, implying that Catholicism wasn't the only authentic religious option, and that other beliefs were equally valid expressions. The Enlightenment, with its mix of rationalism, emancipation, and nationalism extending over the eighteenth and nineteenth centuries, prompted Jews and Gentiles alike to reevaluate their attitudes towards the dramatic rise of anti–Jewish attitudes. Concentrating on issues of identity and community, Jewish writers and artists came into their own, counterbalancing past hurts through provincial, nostalgic or romantic incarnations of shtetl life. But by the early years of the twentieth century, with a growing involvement of Zionism and a closer examination of political and social realities, they began to offer a greater variety of themes within a modern Jewish consciousness and a wider worldview. Only a few decades later, the Nazi grip shut down almost every avenue of Jewish aesthetics and communication, exploiting the worst excesses of racial fanaticism. The post–Holocaust period found Jews integrated into the global art community, adopting pluralistic attitudes in both abstract and representational styles.

   Because Jewish material was periodically destroyed in pogroms and wars, and because folk art was neither highly esteemed nor preserved, much has been erased from the collective memory. But the supply of prints and books that remains conjures up an entire Jewish culture and history—in its accomplishments and in its determination to exist.

2

The Fifteenth Century: Printmaking and Printing Begin

"May God bless copper, burin, pen and all the tools of reproductive printing, so that once good things are in existence, they may be saved from oblivion by countless images." This benediction by Johann Wolfgang von Goethe commented on the sweeping transmission of culture that marked the end of the European Middle Ages when printed texts and pictures began to replace works written and drawn by hand. The abundance of printed material suddenly made knowledge accessible to almost anyone who could read, and permitted the rapid development of science, industry, architecture, and aesthetics.

Francis Bacon wrote that the introduction of printing (along with gunpowder and the compass) "changed the whole face and state of things throughout the world ... inasmuch that no empire, no sect, no star seems to have exerted greater power and influence in human affairs." Thomas Carlyle listed gunpowder, printing, and Protestantism as his candidates for the most significant accomplishments of Western culture. When James Boswell quoted a "gentleman who maintained that the art of printing had hurt real learning, by disseminating idle writings," Samuel Johnson replied: "Sir, if it had not been for the art of printing, we should now have no learning at all, for books would have perished faster than they could have been transcribed." And Thomas Jefferson, in a letter to John Adams in 1823, wrote that "the light which has been shed on mankind by the art of printing has eminently changed the condition of the world."

Yet the techniques which produced those marvels may have been in use in ancient times. Those who wish to read into Job 19:23 the first attempt at printing may recall the verse

> O, that my words were now written!
> O, that they were printed (inscribed) in a book:
> That with an iron pen and lead
> They were graven in a rock forever.

All the same, printed books as we know them made their debut in the middle of the fifteenth century in Germany; those that date from before 1501 are known as incunabula or cradle books. Johann Gutenberg is generally credited with the invention of casting metal type in small individual molds or punches and developing oil-based inks to insure sharply defined lettering. His forty-two-line Bible, 1455–1456, was finely printed in dark ink in two columns with wide margins. It appeared in an edition of perhaps two hundred copies; less than fifty are extant. Gutenberg financed his business in part through Jewish loans, hired a Jewish typographer, and bought his typefaces from Jews, which indicates that Jews were already involved in the trade. There are references as early as 1444 in the French city of Avignon to Procopius Waldvogel, a Christian metalsmith, who contracted with Davin de Caderousse, a Jewish dyer, to "make, and when made, to render and deliver to the said Jew twenty-seven movable Hebrew letters cut in iron ... and also to supply him with the machine made of wood, tin, and iron." In exchange, de Caderousse agreed to show Waldvogel how to dye fabrics and to keep to himself the secret of printmaking. (The dyeing industry was largely a Jewish one.) Probably cut rather than cast type was used, but if any books were produced by them, none have survived.

In 1464, a number of Gutenberg's printers, having found themselves on the losing side of a political rivalry, moved to France, Holland, and the Iberian Peninsula. Two of the emigrants, Conrad Sweynheym and Arnold Pannartz, went to Rome, bringing the art of printing to Italy. They likely shared their quarters with Obadiah, Manasseh, and Benjamin, Jewish typographers who had fled expulsions in Germany. Sometime between 1469 and 1472 they published several Hebrew books. Possibly the first was Rashi's *Commentary on the Bible*, or *Perushe ha-Torah*, a thirteenth century biblical commentary by the Spanish rabbi Moses ben Nachman (Nachmanides), one of the leading talmudists of the Middle Ages. Although the book had no illustrations, its colophon was decoratively printed in the shape of a wine goblet. Another of their early books was *Teshuvot She'elot ha-Rashba* (*The Responsa of Rashba*), based on the writings of the thirteenth century rabbi of Barcelona, Solomon ben Abraham Adret. They also produced the first midrashic and talmudic dictionary: the twelfth century *Arukh* (*Lexicon*) by Nathan ben Jehiel. That book facilitated the move of scholarship from the Babylonian rabbinical schools which had closed in the eleventh century to the Jewish communities of central Europe.

Pious rabbis believed that the printing of sacred works was a divine craft and that such books would be among the greatest wonders of the heavenly world. But even in this world, the enormous value of the printing press was clear. Congregants anywhere could pray from identical standardized texts, while many rituals and religious principles achieved uniformity during this period. Economic conditions were becoming good enough to sustain a moderately wide distribution of Hebrew editions. More and more people availed themselves of the religious materials, parables, allegories, and folktales that were published and collected for those hours when the eye and mind sought entertainment or spiritual guidance.

In the early 1400s, artist-printmakers learned how to create exactly repeatable images by drawing designs on blocks of wood and collaborating with carpenters or *formschneiders* who cut away the parts that were to appear white; the raised lines were then inked and pressed onto paper. However, the first known *dated* woodcut appeared in the ninth century not in the West but in China. It depicted the Buddha; an accompanying text expressed the hope that it would be freely and universally distributed. It was printed on fibrous matter, a two-thousand-year-old Chinese invention which remained a closely guarded secret until the middle of the eighth century when Arab armies captured some knowledgeable prisoners who disclosed the mystery. European manufactured paper was probably developed in Greece in the eleventh century and in Spain in the twelfth, where it was immediately picked up by Jewish craftsmen. Because they had been forced to become peddlers of used clothing and old rags, they were linked to the manufacture of paper, its main ingredient. Their contributions were soon noted by Peter, the Abbot of Cluny, in his *Adversus Judaeos* (*Against Jews*), c. 1140, when he decided that humble paper was unfit for Christian manuscripts. Nevertheless, he added, any article derived from rags was an appropriate choice for the degenerate Talmud. Notwithstanding this rebuke, Jews established one of the earliest paper mills in Europe in Aragon, Spain in 1273, turning out smooth, low-cost material as an alternative to scarce and expensive vellum and parchment. It opened the way for printmaking and large-scale book production.

Few fifteenth century prints have been preserved because they were not thought to have lasting value. Nevertheless, those that have survived have played significant roles in history, and in particular, Jewish life. During periods of political and religious threats such as the Spanish and Portuguese Inquisitions, printmakers kept Jewish issues before the public. Beginning in 1478, the examination of heretics aimed at imposing theological unity and protecting the Church from contamination by unbelievers through the uprooting and punishment of Jews as well as Muslims. Mobs, urged on by the fanatic Dominican confessor to the queen, Tomás de Torquemada, tore through one town after another looking for the Jewish "Christ killers," desecraters of the Host, and collectors of Christian blood. Despite occasional moderating papal intercession, impassioned friars forcibly baptized thousands of Jews. In 1481, six New Christians in Seville were charged with insincerity and impenitence, but because the Inquisition kindly forbade direct bleeding, untold numbers were whipped, tortured, strangled, laid on the pyre and cremated. Festive crowds gathered in town squares for these occasions, while printmakers busied themselves recording the proceedings. In the anonymous *Auto-da-fé* (*Act of Faith*), a crowd gawks at the wretched prisoners and takes bets on whether priests might be successful in last-minute conversions (Ill. 2:1). Pope Sixtus IV believed the excesses had gotten horrifyingly out of hand, acknowledging that "the lust for wealth more than zeal for the faith" motivated the atrocities.

Thirty thousand Jews were killed by other means—disease, banditry, starvation—and perhaps one hundred thousand more were deported from Spain in 1492, forced to tramp across dirt roads towards Portugal under an oppressive July sun or to board ramshackle overloaded boats from which many were drowned. Columbus watched the leading intellectuals, financiers, and professional figures sail by and noted their exodus in the opening lines of his diary: "In that same month in which their majesties issued the edict that all Jews should be driven out of the kingdom and its territories, they gave me the order to undertake, with sufficient men,

Ill. 2:1. *Auto-da-fé*. Woodcut. c. 1480.

my expedition of discovery to the Indies." There is some circumstantial evidence that although Columbus' parents had settled in Genoa, Italy, they were of Marrano descent; all his extant papers were written in Spanish, his favored signature was Colon, a traditional Jewish name (he never referred to himself as Columbus). His first journey, delayed by a day possibly because it was Tisha b'av, a time of Jewish mourning, was largely financed by a loan from a baptized Jew, Luis de Santangel, comptroller-general to the Spanish majesties. It was he who received Columbus' initial report of the great adventure to the American continent. Although the ostensible goal of the Inquisition was not greed but Jewish conversion, the debts, confiscated property, and profits from the sales of Jewish booty went to the pope and the Crown. It was part of that hoard which paid for Columbus' voyage. Isabella managed to keep her famous jewels.

Many Jews remained in Spain as sincere New Christians, prospering beyond their expectations, but they were always suspected of Jewish sympathies and hated for their successes. Others returned to Judaism after fleeing to Italy, Antwerp, Holland, North Africa, and the Ottoman Empire, where their talents were better appreciated and where they lived in relative safety. Thanks to their international relationships, they became active in the promotion of trade, boosting their host countries' economies as well as their own. It is said that Turkish Sultan Bayazet II, the only ruler to invite the exiled Jews, wondered why Ferdinand was considered a wise king "since he made his country poor and ours rich."

Portugal offered five years of limited toleration, but in 1497 King Manuel I withdrew that courtesy in exchange for a profitable marriage to Ferdinand and Isabella's daughter. Since a union with a country harboring Jews could not be tolerated, it presaged further disaster. Forced conversions were imposed, but not the option of escape. Unabated proselytizing and grisly forms of retribution soon made a bitter end to Judaism's Golden Age. The objectives of Church and State had been accomplished. Spain and Portugal were as clean of Jews as brutality could make them. (Although Jews were permitted to return to Spain in 1869, the original Edict of Expulsion was not lifted until 1968.)

Things were occasionally better in parts of Europe. Mainz, Krakow, Strassbourg, Lucerne, and Vienna herded Jews into separate, but unlocked, quarters where they lived between onslaughts. Brandenburg, Rottenburg, and Saxony expelled but did not officially molest them. A few towns in Germany and Bohemia were open, although alternately receptive and abusive. England was effectively closed from the fourteenth century until well into the seventeenth. France had ejected and confiscated the property of declared Jews in 1306, but nine years later Louis X, realizing that his economy was suffering, invited them back. But it was only a twelve-year reprieve, after which they were again obliged to leave. Those who refused were pursued and destroyed, along with their Jewish books and other possessions. The *Massacre of Jews*, a woodcut in Jean Mielot's *Miracles de Notre Dame*, 1456, documented the harsh days of medieval France (Ill. 2:2). Newly immigrant Jews in Italy aroused stormy reactions among their settled co-religionists who feared that greater numbers would exacerbate anti–Jewish feelings; potential economic rivalry, no doubt, compounded those motives. On the whole, Jews fared best in Italy. Its tolerance bore fruit in their contributions to the economy, publishing having a considerable share in the prospering environment. Segregation, however, at first voluntary for reasons of defense and to maintain an intimate community was, by 1516, compulsory in Venice.

Italy was established as the center of Jewish printing following the editions of Obadiah, Manasseh, and Benjamin. In 1475, Abraham ben Isaac ben Garton introduced the first *dated* Hebrew book in the southern town of Reggio di Calabria. An eleventh century biblical commentary by Rashi, the acronym of Rabbi Shlomo Yitzhaki, it combined midrashic homilies with ethical teachings. It was printed at least six times in the fifteenth century, more than any other religious work. Other than fragments, only a single copy remains, and even that, in the

Ill. 2:2. *Massacre of Jews*. Woodcut. From *Miracles de Notre Dame* by Jean Mielot, 1456

Palatine Library in Parma, is incomplete. Without Rashi's explanations, various texts, including the Talmud, would be far more obscure.

In 1475, Meshullam Cusi, a physician and former scribe, published Jacob ben Asher's authoritative fourteenth century rabbinic code, *Arba'ah Turim* (*Four Columns*), the title referring to the four rows of jewels on the High Priest's breastplate (Exodus 28:17). The work, a systematic analysis and summary of Jewish laws in France, Spain, and Germany, settled various controversial issues surrounding halakhic rulings. In an original and creative colophon, the printing press itself proudly addressed the reader:

> Wisdom am I, and crown of all science,
> Hidden am I, a mystery to all.
> Without a pen-stroke, my imprint stands evident—
> Without a scribe, a volume appears!
> One moment, in which ink pours over me
> Without guide lines, and every word stands straight.
> Do you wonder at the stalwart Deborah
> Who ruled with the pen of the scribes -
> Had she been aware of my power
> She would have made of me a crown for her head.

Another edition, in 1493, was published by David and Samuel ibn Nachmias. The first Hebrew work to appear in the Ottoman Empire, it became the basis for Joseph Caro's later code, *Shulchan Aruch* (*Prepared Table*.) The first of only two Hebrew incunabula issued during the lifetime of their authors was *Nophet Tzuphim* (*Drippings of the Honeycomb*), c. 1475. Written by Judah bar Jehiel (Messer Leon), a Mantuan rabbi, physician, and philosopher, it exalted the Jewish prophetic teachings over Greek and Roman scholarship. He projected humanistic Renaissance attitudes onto the Hebrew Bible by suggesting that the grammar, philosophy, and literature of Aristotle, Cicero, and Quintilian had their inception in Israel and could successfully be adapted to conform with the Torah. The book, a rare secular undertaking in Hebrew, may have been the cause of a noisy fight between Judah and Rabbi Joseph Colon, a traditionalist who objected to linking pagan authors with sacred texts. After unsuccessful attempts to resolve matters peacefully, the Duke of Mantua threw both disputants out of his territories. Abraham ben Solomon Conat, a Mantuan scholar and physician, had printed the book, as well as several other exemplary works from 1474 to 1476, using a distinctive Hebrew type based on his own handwriting. His wife, Estellina, was one of many Jewish women who were employed as typesetters and printers in family businesses. She published *Behinat Olam* (*Investigation of the World*) by Jedaiah Bedersi, congratulating herself in the colophon, "I, Estellina, wrote [i.e. printed] this book." Conat marveled at what had been achieved "with many pens without the intervention of miracles."

What perhaps did seem like a miracle to a German family in 1454 was the permission, granted by the Duke of Milan, to settle in the northern town of Soncino. (Smaller cities were favored by Jewish printers since they generally avoided the prying authorities in major centers.) In gratitude for its hospitality, they adopted its name as their own. Samuel ben Moses, the patriarch of the clan, then established the largest Hebrew printing house in Europe. His son, Israel Nathan, his grandson Joshua Solomon, and his great-grandson, Gershom, together published more than one third of the one hundred sixty known incunabula Hebrew books, as well as a large number in Italian and Latin.

Soncino's press began in 1483 with the Babylonian Talmud tractate *Berachoth* (*Blessings*), although Joshua Solomon did not publish it until February of the following year. Therefore, his edition of Solomon ben Judah ibn Gvirol's poem *Mivchar ha-Peninim* (*Choice of Pearls*), a longing for communion with God and the salvation of the Jewish people, takes pride of first place, having seen the light the previous month. Other Soncino books soon followed. *Sefer ha-Ikkarim (Book of Principles)* by Rabbi Joseph Albo, based on the precepts of Maimonides' thirteen articles, came out in 1485; missing in most extant copies are three pages expunged by papal censors because they were thought to contain anti–Christian passages. In 1413, Albo had been forced into a rigged dialogue with an apostate rabbi in the presence of Pope Benedict XIII during an abortive attempt to convert Jews. The disputation lasted almost two years and sixty-nine sessions; its conclusion, which surprised no one, was that Christianity alone possessed the key to religious truth. Albo, alarmed that Jewish principles were being challenged on rational grounds, determined to reinforce vacillating beliefs by insisting that God's existence, His revelations at Mt. Sinai, and His provisions for rewards and punishments constituted a credible philosophic platform for the divine laws. Proudly aware of its contribution to Jewish scholarship, the book's colophon paraphrased Isaiah's famous lines, "Out of Zion shall go forth the Law, and the word of the Lord from Soncino."

There was reason to be proud. Soncino texts were produced with the best ink, paper, and workmen available, and particularly those under the direction of Gershom, were artistically designed and carefully edited with the highest aesthetic and intellectual values. When he was short of cash or because Jews were not always able to afford his wares, he became the first Jewish printer to publish non–Hebrew books, including an anti–Jewish work, Petrus Galatinus' *De Arcanis Catholicae Veritatis* (*Concerning the Secrets of Catholic Truth*). Jewish scholars were shocked, fearing that exposure to Christian polemics would result in lapses in Jewish commitment. Joseph Caro later criticized "those who compose and edit and print [such books], leading the multitude into sin."

Tehillim (*Psalms*), probably printed in Bologna in 1477 by Meister Joseph and his son,

Hayyim Mordecai, was accompanied by the commentary of David Kimchi who explained at the end of Psalm 72 that Jesus could not have been the Messiah because there was no peace during his lifetime; copies were heavily censored by papal authorities, and later by Jewish publishers, who wanted to avoid trouble. Because of its many errors, a finer and more complete version was imperative. Bologna led the way again in 1482. An Aramaic translation, *Targum Onkelos*, was printed at the side of the Hebrew texts, while Rashi's commentary framed the top and bottom of the pages, a typesetting style that was widely imitated in later editions.

Once basic Hebrew books were available, it was time to think about publishing the complete Bible. That was accomplished by the Soncinos in 1488 with the help of Abraham the Dyer, known as "a workman whose equal in Hebrew typography does not exist in the whole world"—faint praise, since Hebrew typographers could be counted on the fingers of one hand. A framed border decorated with birds, animals, and cupids was borrowed by Joshua Solomon from Francesco Tuppo's 1485 edition of Aesop's *Vita et Fabulae* (*Life and Fables*) (Ill. 2:3). Although some authorities disapproved of the secular designs, most rabbis didn't seem bothered by the startling appearance of little pagan love gods. The first word, "*Bereshit*" (*In the beginning*), was cut in large woodblock characters by a friar of Bologna, Francesco Griffo, inventor of the style known as italic. Unfortunately, his other activities weren't as laudable; for the murder of his son-in-law, he is said to have ended up on the gallows.

An improved third edition of the Bible, published in Brecia in 1495 by Gershom, was issued in a small easily transportable format, the printer stating in his epilogue, "so that it may be with every man night and day to study therein, that he may not walk four ells without the Bible, but that he may have it by him and that he may read it when he lies down and when he rises up night and day just as he carries about him his phylacteries." (It was the basis for Martin Luther's German translation in the following century, a pivotal contribution to the Protestant Reformation.)

In 1491, Gershom issued the first printed and illustrated work in Hebrew—a rhymed group of parables, mythical tales, and puns, *Mashal haKadmoni* (*The Fable of the Ancients [or Easterners]*). Based on lost thirteenth century drawings by the Spanish poet, kabbalist, and physician Isaac ben Solomon ibn Sahula, its eighty woodcuts depict humans and animals engaged in scientific, grammatical, and philosophical discussions. In *Teaching the Lion*, the denizens of the forest instruct the noble but unlearned king of the beasts about human experiences, messages that would have been dangerous in a less symbolic form (Ill. 2:4). Some authorities considered the prints—probably by Jewish artists—a violation of the Second Commandment. Nevertheless, the blocks, sustained by the energy and vigor of the knife work, served as prototypes for future draftsmen who used and reused the designs. For those who could not read, such pictures were instructive and entertaining. For those who could, the stories, mostly of Arabic and midrashic derivations, taught a simple morality under the guise of legends. Folktales were not to be despised, a rabbinical scholar pointed out, for "with a penny candle one may find a gold coin."

"I saw fit to illustrate it," Sahula wrote, "in order to develop understanding, to hold the interest of children, and to bring peace to those in great pain.... And perhaps their hearts will be freed from deceitful books by heretics and Epicureans." He probably had in mind Hebrew translations of popular secular books such as *The Voyages of Sinbad the Sailor*, which attracted many Jewish readers. He surely would have been startled had he known that another version of his masterwork was offered in about 1545 with a new set of illustrations, some of which were highly erotic. That edition, printed in Venice by Meir Parenzo, is rarely found intact because the questionable woodcuts were frequently removed, both by the pure in heart and by those with other agendas. Gershom printed another illustrated work, *Sefer ha-Machberot* (*Book of Verses*), also in 1491, by the medieval poet Immanuel ben Shlomo of Rome. It was likewise

Ill. 2:3. *Woodcut Border*. From an Italian Bible

Ill. 2:4. *Teaching the Lion.* **Woodcut. From** *Mashal haKadmoni (The Fable of the Ancients)*, **1491**

considered forbidden fruit because of its sensual imagery. Joseph Caro banned it, but Moses Isserles later came to the rescue, ruling that it could be read—but only in Hebrew.

Joshua Solomom was able to issue about four books in Naples in 1491, shortly before the expulsion of Jews from nearby Spain overwhelmed that community. By the time its press was closed down, it had published David Kimchi's *Sepher ha-Sharashim (Book of Roots)*, a lexicon which greatly facilitated the application of grammatical rules and helped to revive Hebrew as a literary language. The Soncino dynasty endured well into the next century, setting up presses in various Italian and other cities. From about 1526 to 1528, when censorship and competition undid them, they picked up work in Greece and Turkey, and then in Constantinople from 1530 to 1547 when anti–Jewish attacks finally forced them out. Gershom's colophon from a Rashi commentary on the Bible printed in Bologna in 1525 offers a glimpse into the human side of the business: "Said the youngest of the printers and pupils, the son of Moshe Soncino [Gershom's grandson, Gershom ben Eliezer, the last Soncino printer]: Since I have become old and weak, I have despaired of printing any more, neither in Hebrew, Greek nor Latin ... yet the people around me ... have begged me to do this Rashi commentary on the Torah, saying that all those printed or written by hand hitherto are faulty.... Even though it is a big burden and although I am upon my sickbed all day, for I had fallen ill, I summoned up strength saying 'time to do the work of the Lord....'"

Gershom ben Eliezer ran a press in Cairo from 1557 to 1562, the first of its kind in the Middle East. Altogether, Soncino books helped to create unity and conformity both in personal religious observance and in formal ceremonial worship. Their formats and typography became so ingrained that later editors believed it would be almost sacrilegious or disrespectful to alter them. Among the important innovations they developed was Sephardic-style lettering to accommodate Jews who had fled from the Iberian Peninsula and North Africa. They also published various editions of talmudic commentaries known as Tosaphot, comparing them with earlier works of Rashi. Had the family not gathered such material, many important manuscripts would have been lost.

The Soncinos were not without serious competition. From about 1486 to 1492, a German Jew, Joseph ben Jacob Gunzenhauser, his son Azriel, and a group of financial backers and skilled workers operated a prestigious publishing house in Naples. The initial book from their press was the first printed Hebrew edition of Mishlei (Proverbs). Their *Ha-Kanon (The Canon)*, 1491, written by the eleventh century Arab physician and philosopher Avicenna, was noted for its extremely fine typography and illustrated woodcut charts. For several hundred years it was the standard medical text in Europe, and the first and only printed scientific book translated into Hebrew in the fifteenth century. Other rival publishers included Isaac ben Judah ibn Katorzi, who had an important Hebrew press in Naples, and Manuel Aldo, a non–Jewish Italian humanist who adopted a typeface similar to Gershom's, causing some unpleasant feelings.

Naples boasted a prosperous Jewish population of about forty thousand until 1493 when the Spanish expulsion reverberated in many of the Italian towns which had formerly been hospitable. In 1494, the city was invaded by French armies under Charles VIII. A plague, which devastated the area, was blamed on the Jews although they suffered equally with the Christian community. Hebrew printing came to an abrupt end; an exodus began to more receptive Italian cities, as well as to Morocco, Turkey, and Egypt. Because authorities were ignorant of its potential, Jews were permitted to take their strange-looking typefaces to other lands. Although Sultan Bayazet had forbidden printing by Muslims, he had no objections to Jewish practitioners so long as they refrained from employing Arabic lettering. Over two hundred years had to pass before Muslims permitted the use of Arabic characters (but not for religious works). That printing equipment was obtained from Jewish sources in 1727.

The first known Spanish publication was a 1476 Rashi commentary on the Pentateuch printed in Guadalajara by Soloman ibn Alkabez, who turned out some twenty other titles from 1476 to 1482. Following that, a Hebrew Bible was published in 1486 or 1487 by the physician and scholar Eliezer ben Abraham ibn Alantansi and his wealthy partner, Solomon ben Maimon Zalmati in Hijar, Spain. An elegant metalcut frame with delicate patterns of tendrils, fruits, flowers, and stylized animals enclosed the Song of Moses (Exodus 15) (Ill. 2:5). Its Christian designer, Alfonso Fernandez de Cordoba, had been sentenced to death in absentia in Valencia for operating a printing shop with Jewish connections. Even though he was also involved in the production of Christian books, and even though he also worked for non–Jewish printers, the mere association with Jews was enough to bring down the fury of the Inquisition.

The frame appeared again in 1489 in the first printed commentary on David Abudraham's fourteenth century *Sefer Abudraham (Abudraham's Prayer Book)* from the Lisbon press of Rabbis Samuel Zorba and Eleazer ben Jacob Toledano when that city became for a short time a nucleus of Jewish culture noted for its accurate texts and variety of typefaces. It was the first dated book in Portugal, printed six years before any non–Hebrew work. (There does exist, however, a single copy of a 1487 Pentateuch on vellum from "Taro," an unknown city, unless it was a misprint of Faro. That could indicate an even earlier date for Hebrew printing in Portugal.) Abudraham examined the customs connected with prayer, he said, because "they varied from one country to another and most people don't understand them, nor do they understand the

Ill. 2:5. *Metalcut Frame*. From a Spanish Bible, c. 1486

correct reasons for the ritual procedures." (Unfortunately, the passage of five hundred years has not eliminated that problem.)

The peripatetic frame was then brought to Constantinople and was reprinted there in worn condition between 1505 and 1509 by David and Samuel ibn Nachmias. And when North Africa became the next haven for Hebrew printers, the border was used in Fez in 1516 by Portuguese exiles Samuel ben Isaac Nedivot and his son, Isaac, in their edition of Abudraham's work; the first book of any kind to be printed in Africa, it provided Moroccan Jewry with rabbinic commentaries.

    Jews also introduced printing in two of the three Portuguese cities that had presses—Lisbon and Leiria. Samuel de Ortas and his sons founded a publishing concern in Leiria where, in 1492, they produced the first of their four known works, *Mishlei*, complete with commentaries.

Ill. 2:6. *Woodcut Border.* **From** *Arba'ah Turim (Four Columns)*, **1495. Woodcut by Abraham de Ortas**

Their 1495 edition of Asher's *Arba'ah Turim* included somewhat crude woodcut borders and Hebrew letters, presumably created by de Ortas' son, Abraham. Its animal figures were derived from *Pirke Avoth* (*Sayings of the Fathers*): "Be strong as a leopard, light as an eagle, fleet as a deer, and brave as a lion in performing God's will" (5:23) (Ill. 2:6). In 1496, the only Spanish incunabulum published in Portugal was de Ortas' edition of *Ha-Hibbur ha-Gadol* (*The Great Treatise*) by Abraham ben Samuel Zacuto, the Jewish court historian and astronomer to Kings John II and Manuel I; his high-ranking position was not high enough to prevent his banishment in 1497 when he refused the king's order to convert. De Ortas published an abridged version of *Ha-Hibbur* by Zacuto's pupil, the Jewish scientist Joseph Vecinho, who translated it into Latin and Spanish as *Almanach Perpetuum*, a perpetual astronomical calendar. Its reliable navigational and astronomical information helped guide Vasco da Gama, who had a Jewish interpreter when he visited India, and used Zacuto's and Vecinho's improved astrolabe in his attempt to open a new sea route to India. It also proved a life-saver to Columbus on his last trip to Jamaica in 1504 when he took advantage of its prediction of a moon eclipse to trick frightened natives into feeding his malnourished crew. (Mark Twain cribbed the incident in *A Connecticut Yankee in King Arthur's Court.*) Columbus' own annotated copy of the book is preserved in a Seville museum.

In 1929, the last King Manuel wrote a history of publishing in his country, *Early Portuguese Books*, acknowledging that "the Renaissance found Portugal ready to receive its impetus because the ground had already been prepared by its learned Jews." He didn't mention how much more Portugal might have benefited had not thousands of Hebrew works been destroyed by its Inquisition, or if its Jewish population, which had existed there for at least a thousand years, had not been subjected to exile, forced conversions and worse.

Other than books, single illustrated sheets, generally spontaneous in expression, intimate in quality, and relatively low in cost, were available to entertain or divert the citizenry. One of the earliest surviving examples with Jewish interest is a pair of Passover woodcuts without text probably printed in Venice about 1480 (Ill. 2:7). These fragments, discovered in the late nine-

Ill. 2:7. *Passover Scenes*. Woodcuts, c. 1480

הַזֶּה כָּל יְמֵי חַיֶּיךָ לְהָבִיא לִימוֹת הַמָּשִׁיחַ

בָּרוּךְ הַמָּקוֹם שֶׁנָּתַן תּוֹרָה לְיִשְׂרָאֵל

בָּרוּךְ הוּא כְּנֶגֶד אַרְבָּעָה בָנִים

דִּבְּרָה תוֹרָה אֶחָד חָכָם וְאֶחָד רָשָׁע וְאֶחָד

תָּם וְאֶחָד שֶׁאֵינוֹ יוֹדֵעַ לִשְׁאֹל :

חָכָם מַהוּ אוֹמֵר מָה הָעֵדוֹת וְהַחֻקִּים

וְהַמִּשְׁפָּטִים אֲשֶׁר צִוָּה

אֱלֹהֵינוּ אֶתְכֶם אַף

Ill. 2:8. *Passover Seder*. Woodcut, c. 1490

teenth century in the Cairo Genizah, introduced the tradition of printed pictures of customs connected with the cycle of holidays. The artist, most likely a Christian, depicted the Seder table with six elders responding to the questions of a child, as well as pictures of the slaughter of the sacrificial lamb and the brushing of its blood on a doorpost according to biblical injunctions (Exodus 12:7). It is not known whether the pictures were once part of a Haggadah or whether they were printed independently. If they were originally Haggadah illustrations, they are the prototype of over a thousand illustrated editions in over two dozen languages from almost two hundred places where Jews have lived.

Printed Haggadot were at first bound into books rather than issued separately. A Haggadah was included in Maimonides' *Mishneh Torah* in a Rome edition of 1480, in a Soncino edition of 1490, a Soncino Siddur of 1486, and a Machzor of 1486 begun in Soncino but published in Cassalmaggiore. This last featured illustrations of rabbits and the first printed picture of a matzo and the bitter herb maror. The earliest known separately printed Haggadah, surviving in a unique copy in the National and University Library in Jerusalem, is a twelve page double-columned edition without illustrations or vowel marks, probably published in Guadalajara, Spain in 1482 by Solomon ibn Alkabez. Because scholars are unable to estab-

lish the date or place or origin of the first known printed *and* illustrated Haggadah, three nations claim that honor—Spain before 1492, Portugal before 1496, and the Ottoman Empire, between 1503 and 1515. Unfortunately, only eight pages, containing seven pictures, remain. One depicts four seated figures inviting "all those who are hungry to enter and eat" (Ill. 2:8).

Illustrated material from the non–Jewish press often focused on Jews. A salvation history by Johann Schnitzer, *Der Seelen-Wurzgarten* (*The Soul's Herb Garden*), 1483, featured *Five Jewish Elders Debating* (Ill. 2:9). They are identified by their pointed or funnel-shaped hats topped with a knob; such hats, as well as round badges sewn on their clothes, first took on humiliating connotations after 1215 when the pope made them mandatory. The scholars share a single book since printed works were still relatively expensive. While the artist avoided anti–Jewish facial caricatures, the text made sure to point out Jewish errors and ignorance. Other prints appearing at about the same time often depicted hostile disputes between Jews and Christians relating to clashing messianic issues. (Christian "scholars" were often apostate Jews.)

Ill. 2:9. *Five Jewish Elders Debating*. Woodcut. From *Der Seelen-Wurzgarten (The Soul's Herb Garden)*, 1483. By **Johann Schnitzer**

The perception of money-hungry Jews was a very popular theme. *Bauer und Stadte beim Jüdischen Geldverleiher (Farmer and Townsman at the Home of a Jewish Moneylender)* appeared in Hans Foltz's *Die Rechnung Kolpergers von dem Gesuch der Juden. (Kolperger's Bill of the Petition of the Jews)*, 1491 (Ill. 2:10). The interest of the Nuremberg woodcut lies in the glimpse of the pawnbroker's living quarters; its offensiveness in the accompanying text which describes the shiftless Jew as a parasite sponging off his Christian patrons. The artist was not able to keep the cradle from appearing to fall forward, but he compensated for his awkwardness with a few well-placed black highlights. In addition to household scenes, distinctive fifteenth century Jewish clothing styles apparently were curious enough to be featured two centuries later in A. Wurfel's *Historische Nachrichten (Historical Reports)*, 1755, showing the outfits worn for Sabbath services in Nuremberg (Ill. 2:11).

**nach dem vñ iüdiſch liſtiẞeyt
yr furſeẞt gar on all arbeyt
mit gäẞer faulẞeit ſich zu nern**

Ill. 2:10. *Bauer und Stadte beim Jüdischen Geldverleiher (Farmer and Townsman at the home of a Jewish Moneylender)*. Woodcut. From *Die Rechnung Kolpergers von dem Gesuch der Juden (Kolperger's Petition Bill of the Jews)*. By Hans Foltz, 1491

A contemptuous image, *Das Grosse Judenschwein (The Large Jewish Pig)*, c. 1465, by Claus, a German woodcutter, shows a group of Jews gathered around the taboo animal (Ill. 2:12). The pig is incongruously fitted with a cow's udders and a boar's tusks, suggesting an irrational connection between the Jews' rejection of swine's flesh and their irrational rejection of Christianity. The Jew facing backwards comments on absurd behavior, while the turbaned figure and the long-nosed man portray absurd rabbis. Seven young men cavort around the animal, variously fondling, sucking, and addressing the pig's anus. The banderole reads: "Look, dear people, how I treat our mother." One boy encourages another to lick the tail: "Suck hard, dear brother of my heart, then I'll blow in her ass." The bottom inscription explains that "because we do not eat roast pork, we have yellow looks [we are cowardly and wear yellow clothes]. And thus we are lustful and our breath stinks." The border of the garment on the tail-sucking boy is decorated with pseudo–Hebraic lettering, a device often used by those unfamiliar with the language.

Goethe remembered frightening childhood emotions on seeing this image at a bridge in Frankfurt together with a blood libel of a Christian boy being tortured. "It took a long time before I attempted to go there alone," he wrote in his 1811 autobiography. "Although modern people had a better opinion [of Jews], yet the very large picture ... bore extraordinary witness to their discredit because it had not been made as unruly amusement, but at the public expense of authorities." He also commented on the appearance of the Jewish street, was repelled by its dirty multitude and disagreeable language, but admired the way Jews stuck to their customs and observed that the pretty girls liked to flirt with Christian boys.

Stereotypical Jewish features showed up in books, tapestries, paintings, and church fur-

Ill. 2:11. *Fifteenth Century Clothing Styles.* From A. Wurfel, *Historische Nachrichten (Historical Reports),* **1755**

Ill. 2:12. *Das Grosse Judenschwein (The Large Jewish Pig).* Woodcut by Claus, c. 1465

nishings. Large hooked noses, prominent lips, dehumanized behavior, and devil-like features often defined Jews in a range from unattractive to repulsive. Such images, widely circulated in anti–Jewish tracts by Franciscan and Dominican friars among others, inflamed the population and succeeded in denigrating the Jewish community. In 1475, a monk, Bernardino de Feltre, devised a ritual-murder accusation involving Simon who supposedly was kidnapped and killed for his blood. Thanks to the recently invented printing press, the notorious case was widely publicized throughout much of western Europe. Albertus Duderstat's *Geschichte des zu Trent ermordeten Christenkindes (The Story of Trent's Murdered Christian Children)*, 1475, recounted the story in twelve full-page woodcuts: The sinister deed accomplished, the Jews proceed with their gruesome plan until they are discovered. Simply outlined illustrations dealt graphically with forced circumcision (Ill. 2:13), blending the child's blood into Passover foods, tearing Christian flesh, and finally, the torture of the perpetrators (Ill. 2:14). After their teeth were ripped out by pliers they were burned; two who converted were strangled. Simon was beatified. (In 1965 the Vatican reversed his "martyrdom.")

Iniquitous Jews also found their way into another book, *Contra Perfidos Judeos (Against Treacherous Jews)*, printed by Konrad Fyner in 1475. A longer version, *Stern des Meschiah (Star of the Messiah)*, appeared two years later, the first German book to contain examples of Hebrew printing. Its author, Peter Schwartz (Petrus Nigri), a Dominican preacher (and possibly an apostate Jew), not only elicited an imperial decree forcing Jews to attend his conversionary sermons, but confiscated their belongings as well. Schwartz declared that these flawed people would be denied a place in the next world, and he apparently saw no harm in harassing them in this one. Those who could read were treated to a popular analysis of the Jewish personality:

> The Jews have been punished severely from time to time. But they do not suffer innocently. They suffer because of their wickedness, because they cheat people and ruin whole countries by

Ill. 2:13. *Forced Circumcision.* **Woodcut. From** *Geschichte des zu Trent ermordeten Christenkindes (The Story of Trent's Murdered Christian Children),* **1475. By Albertus Duderstat**

their usury and secret murders, as everyone knows. That is why they are so persecuted and not innocently. There is no people more wicked, more cunning, more avaricious, more impudent, more troublesome, more venomous, more wrathful, more deceptive and more ignominious.

Another woodcut from Fyner's workshop, *Legenda Sanctorum* (*Golden Legend*), 1481, depicts the Jewish physician Ephraim at the bedside of St. Basil, the fourth century archbishop of Caesarea. Despite the law which forbade Jews from ministering to Christians, they were in great demand. Kings and popes alike were willing to overlook their prejudices in the sickroom.

A broadside dating from about 1480 described the Host desecration which allegedly was perpetrated in 1478 in the town of Passau, Bavaria (Ill. 2:15). Twelve woodcuts traced the

Ill. 2:14. *Torture of Alleged Perpetrators.* **Woodcut. From** *Geschichte des zu Trent ermordeten Chris-tenkindes (The Story of Trent's Murdered Christian Children),* **1475. By Albertus Duderstat**

story—the stealing and selling of wafers, stabbing and burning them to draw Christ's blood, apprehension of the quarry, and the employment of creative methods of torture. In the final image, priests kneel in congratulatory prayer as the synagogue is converted into a church. The extortion of large fines as well as the appropriation of Jewish property were the usual incentives for these acts.

The fears and distrust that the Church harbored for all outsiders found their way into a Spanish book, *Fortalitium fidei Contra Judaeos* (*Fortress of the Faithful Against Jews*), 1460. Its author, Alfonso de Espina, was a Franciscan monk and a converted Jew whose accusations of blood libels and desecrations of the Host incited support for the Inquisition. He is shown among satanic monsters who take on the ominous characteristics of Jewish witches and devils (Ill. 2:16). While the pagan and the dissenter, alternately mild-mannered or dangerously armed, are also enemies of the Revealed Faith, their eyes are open; they are not as culpable as

Ill. 2:15. *Host Desecration.* Woodcut, c. 1480

the Jews who, wearing blinders, are determined not to see Christian truth, and were therefore rightly liable to persecution. The devil, astride an intimidating creature, patiently awaits their doom. To the simple-minded believer, such works carried a persuasive message: alien people were evil.

As the Renaissance peaked, a more sophisticated middle class began to emerge, and dread of the stranger slowly abated. Concepts about Jews began to shift from religious hostility to resentment based on Jews' perceived undeserved wealth. Some Jews were tax collectors, having been drafted by the nobility to help finance wars, living styles, and community infrastructures. Since the peasants and lower burgher classes paid in good part for these amenities but received few benefits in return, they naturally interpreted Jewish commercial dealings in the worst possible light. Nevertheless, as revenue poured into government coffers, discontent subsided for a moment. (A moment only. Massacres in the seventeenth century and later, deriving in part from such tax collecting, destroyed vast numbers of Jews.)

Christian pilgrimages for piety and pleasure were becoming less hazardous and more comfortable as roads were repaired and better policed. While armchair trekkers could only conjure up visions of faraway places, financially able and better-educated townsmen discovered the pleasures and broadening power of travel. Dean Bernhard von Breydenbach of Mainz, repenting of his youthful excesses, determined to put his spiritual life in order by undertaking a religious mission to Palestine. Combining atonement with entrepreneurship, he invited a local draftsman, Erhard Reuwich, to join him in producing an illustrated journal of their trip, the *Peregrinatio in Terram Sanctam* (*Travels in the Holy Land*). Published in 1486 by Johann Fust and his son-in-law Peter Schoffer, who had acquired Gutenberg's by now bankrupt business, it was the first printed travel guide and the first illustrated printed book to include the artist's name and to portray different nationalities, animals, and buildings.

Ill. 2:16. *Supernatural Monsters.* **Woodcut. From** *Fortalitium fidei contra Judeos (Fortress of the Faithful Against Jews).* **By Alfonso de Espina, 1458–1459**

Ill. 2:17. *Jewish Moneylender.* **Woodcut by Erhard Reuwich. From** *Peregrinatio in Terram Sanctam (Travels in the Holy Land)* **by Dean Bernhard von Breydenbach, 1486**

Reuwich didn't neglect the Jewish community, which was visited in 1483–1484. One of his woodcuts depicts a well-fed Jewish moneylender exacting payment from a lean and hungry Christian client (Ill. 2:17). The accompanying passage described the "four hundred Jews in Jerusalem who persist in great error and disbelief," concluding that "they are intertwined and knotted up with many errors which they firmly believe, as anyone will know who reads the foolish fables in the Talmud." For those who had not yet read it, he helpfully supplied a Hebrew alphabet along with the names of the letters. The chatty text and depictions of all manner of people and places turned out to be an enormously successful project, going through thirteen editions in thirty-six years.

But the best selling non-biblical book of the fifteenth century was Hartmann Schedel's *Liber Chronicarum (Nuremberg Chronicle).* Published in 1493 and printed by Anton Koberger, the most prominent bookseller of the time, it passed the biggest scoop of the century—Columbus' voyage. The Chronicle begins with the biblical account of creation and ends in 1490, shortly after the Jews were expelled from Nuremberg; it was profusely illustrated with six hundred forty-five woodcuts that were used and reused eighteen hundred nine times. Jews are shown with the degrading badge on their garments. Included were pictures of well-poisoners and blasphemers of Jesus—to which crimes they "confessed," and a gruesome depiction of flames licking their flesh for "their evil actions," i.e., profanation of Hosts (Ill. 2:18).

Another of the woodcuts portrays a group of Jews extracting blood from a Christian child who is placed in a crucifixion pose. Wilhelm Pleydenwurff, Michael Wolgemut, and possibly even the young Albrecht Dürer contributed to the *Chronicarum.* If Dürer did indeed supply some of the illustrations, they lack the expertise of his earlier woodcut of 1492, *St. Jerome Cur-*

Ill. 2:18. *Burning Jews.* Woodcut. From *Liber Chronicarum (Nuremberg Chronicle).* By Hartmann Schedel, 1493

ing the Lion (Ill. 2:19). The saint, who diligently studied Hebrew with a convert and met with Jewish teachers for over twenty years, is shown with books in Latin, Greek, and Hebrew—the languages of scholars—opened to the first verse of Genesis. None of this, however, prevented ill-natured remarks from slipping into his writings: "The Jews ... seek nothing but to have children, possess riches, and be healthy. They seek all earthly things, but think nothing of heavenly things."

Books of Jewish interests were published in about seventeen cities in Spain, Portugal, and Italy. Approximately one hundred seventy-five such books, including several that are incomplete, survive; others may have been burnt or otherwise destroyed. (This compares to approximately thirty-five thousand non–Jewish books extant.) Some of the finest books in all of Europe were produced by Jewish printers because their materials were the best to be had, their letters were poured from molds that had been crafted in great detail, and their texts were often surrounded by aesthetically appealing large margins. Editions were typically small—perhaps three hundred copies of each title—since costs were high, the machinery was difficult to operate, and good paper was relatively scarce. Nevertheless, the significant output of the Hebrew presses confirmed Isaiah's prediction that "the earth shall be full of the knowledge of the Lord" (11:9).

All kinds of printed works were proudly displayed in private and public collections. Some connoisseurs, however, regarded their artistic quality as provincial and weak—and many undoubtedly were. The Florentine humanist Angelo Politian lamented that "now the most stupid ideas can in a moment be transferred into a thousand volumes and spread around." And

Ill. 2:19. *St. Jerome Curing the Lion.* **Woodcut by Albrecht Dürer, 1492**

the biographer of Federigo da Montefeltro of Urbino declared that while the duke's collection, including Hebrew manuscripts, was all of "faultless beauty, written by hand on parchment and adorned with miniatures, he does not have a single printed book. He would have been ashamed to own any."

Had the philosopher and the duke seen the best examples of the Hebrew presses, they might have been ashamed not to.

3

The Sixteenth Century:
Let There Be Books

Life for most people in the sixteenth century was vexatious and grim. War, pestilence, religious convulsions, and economic shoving matches absorbed their strength and ravaged their lands. Nevertheless, in spite of hardship and privation, great periods of exploration and colonization in the New World invigorated commerce and expansionism in many parts of Europe. Growing communities were turning away from a semi-agricultural base, medieval feudalism broke down, and secular ideas challenged faith and authority.

Men began to regard themselves, rather than the Church, as the center of their world. This was the herald of the High Renaissance and the beginning of the modern age, marking the rebirth of classical ideals and scholarship. Hebrew was taught in Italy's universities, accenting the intellectual ferment and appreciation of religious literature. Christians translated the works of famous rabbis into Latin in order to study Jewish life and to facilitate conversions. Jews deciphered papal manuscripts in order to understand, and where necessary, refute certain Catholic doctrines. Reciprocity and animosity coexisted as did parallel humanistic interests. Ecumenism, however, was slow and irregular with alternating bouts of persecution and limited tolerance.

Venice was emblematic of the alternating advantages and debilities. Jews had been singled out as economic scapegoats by Pope Julius II after Church and European armies overturned Venice's landward claims in 1510. They were blamed by the lower clergy, among others, for the severe financial disruptions that followed. While the city became a haven for displaced Jews with the influx of Spanish and Portuguese refugees in the decades after 1492, they were often subjected to resentment and religious fanaticism. Still, the Inquisition never took hold in Venice. Its government was run by doges, powerful lay rulers who operated somewhat independently of the Roman papacy; its population was not only affluent, but intellectually lively. Its synagogues were magnificent; its yeshivot diligent. Although their numbers never exceeded five thousand, Jews were so useful as middlemen, consumers, and taxpayers that they could not be disregarded. The authorities protected them, as well as other foreign entrepreneurs, as Shakespeare noted in *The Merchant of Venice*: "For the commodity [privilege] that strangers have with us in Venice, if it be denied, will much impeach the justice of this state, since that the trade and profit of this city consisteth of all nations" (Act III, scene 3).

Trade and profit notwithstanding, compulsory separation between Christian and Jew had been imposed in 1516 in Venice, the first city in Europe to establish a locked ghetto. Bricked-up windows and high walls were mandated to shield Christians from brazen Jewish eyes: "It is highly absurd and improper that the Jews, condemned by God to eternal slavery because of their guilt, should, on the pretext to dwell in our midst, show such ingratitude to Christians as to insult them for their mercy, and presume to mastery instead of the subjection that beseems them...." However, in spite of crowded, inadequately ventilated and filthy conditions, the ghetto encouraged cultural life and a sense of entitlement within the Christian community, minimized the lure of conversion, prepared Jews for urbanization in major cities, and fostered interactions with the Christian world through an active printing press and lively economy. Its gates were closed at night and on major Christian holidays, but open during business hours; the authorities knew better than to compromise its benefits to the public treasury.

Northern Italy, which had been under French domination, was invaded by the Spanish who substituted one style of tyranny for another. In Rome, a great plague flared up and overwhelmed the population. Before the city could recover, it was sacked in 1527 by Charles V leading Spanish and Protestant German armies. Bloody massacres and economic stagnation did not subside until the city was rebuilt by Sixtus V towards the end of the century. The Church, now challenged by the loss of its cultural and religious dominance, began shunting heretical Jews from one papal state to another in a frantic effort to reestablish its jurisdictions. But because they were vital to the economic health of the area, a few towns were forced to grant immunity from expulsions. Immunity, however, did not translate into acceptance.

Some popes, notably Leo X who had approved the printing of the Hebrew Bible and Talmud, were conciliatory to the Jews. Julius III was personally liberal, forbidding forcible baptism and extending certain residence permits to Marranos, but he yielded to the reactionary Cardinal Caraffa and authorized the burning of the Talmud in 1553 and the censoring of Hebrew works a year later. Caraffa, having become Paul IV, zealously promoted the Counter-Revolution by burning the Talmud and censoring Hebrew books. He restricted the number of synagogues to one per town and prohibited Jews from engaging in the rag trade; other than moneylending, it had been almost the only occupation permitted them. He ghettoized Jews in Rome and Ancona, an important Jewish shipping and market center in 1555. A year later, twenty-five Marranos were burned in Ancona and hundreds more were attacked or imprisoned. The yellow badge, the funny hat, the shoddy coat and dress, and Christian sermonizing became mandatory. Robert Browning, in his nineteenth century poem, *Holy Cross Day*, evoked those times:

> By the torture, prolonged from age to age,
> By the infamy, Israel's heritage,
> By the ghetto's plague, by the garb's disgrace,
> By the badge of shame, by the felons place,
> By the branding tool, the bloody whip,
> And the summons to Christian fellowship....

(Browning added a postscript: "Pope Gregory XVI [officiated 1831–1846] abolished this bad business of the Sermon." But not until 1885 was the forced segregation of the ghettos eradicated in Italy.)

Pius V banished Jews from all his territories except Rome and Ancona. He oversaw confiscations and burnings of Jewish books in Cremona, a center of scholarship, later mitigating that decree after a persuasive two-hour Latin discourse by an emissary from the Italian Jewish community, Avtalyon Modena. Gregory XIII inherited the papacy in 1572, protected Rome's ghetto from attacks, made concessions to Jewish moneylenders, helped ransom Jewish prisoners, and relieved Jews from wearing the hated badge when on business trips. Yet he insisted on compulsory missionary sermons and in 1581 empowered the Inquisition to charge Jews with profanation and other violations.

In Spain, baptized Jews remained under the repressive grip of the Inquisition; their forced

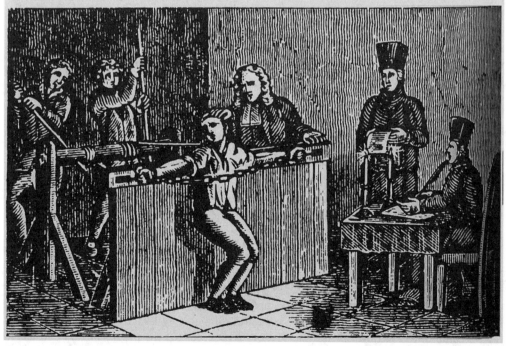

Ill. 3:1, 3:2. *Victims of the Spanish Inquisition*, c. 1505

conversions were never entirely trusted. Although professing Jews were gone from the Iberian Peninsula, in 1506 a group of conversos determined to conduct a clandestine Passover Seder. King Manuel II had waived persecution for ten years to those who had converted in 1497, but Dominican friars were not satisfied. After they preached fiery sermons on Easter Sunday calling on worshippers to kill the Jews, a massacre, popularly known as "The Slaying of New Christians," erupted. While some of the assailants were caught and executed, it didn't help the two thousand to four thousand dead victims. Engravings of *The Spanish Inquisition*, c. 1506, depicted various forms of torture that awaited those suspected of Judaizing (Ill. 3:1; Ill. 3:2).

Spain's domination extended beyond its borders to the Low Countries under the repressive rule of Charles V's son, Philip II. The Protestant north (Netherlands) and the Catholic south (Belgium) responded in 1567 with an uprising that lasted almost forty years, although north and south were soon attacking each other. But once freed from Spanish oppression, Holland adopted tolerant religious attitudes, making that country a haven for Spanish and Portuguese refugees, many of whom threw off the "false Christian" disguise and reaffirmed their lives as Jews.

Northern Europe was beginning to achieve economic coherence as overseas expeditions demanded more systematic credit and banking arrangements. The Church was forced to recognize those lucrative possibilities and to abolish the rules that denied its own members the right to charge interest on investments. This concession, together with lower tax rates for Christians, meant that most Jews lost their fiscal advantages, and with that, claims they once had on kings or nobles. Moneylending had long been condemned by the Church as a sin fit only for sinful Jews, but Pope Leo X recognized that the gains to his coffers outweighed the transgression and reversed the three-hundred-year-old ruling. (It is an irony that Christian moneylenders—including Shakespeare's father, who reportedly was twice charged with violating usury laws—often imposed higher fees than Jews, such as Shylock in *The Merchant of Venice*, and were as cordially hated.)

Exclusions, interconnected Christian culture, and overzealous religious piety all boded ill for Jews who were more and more perceived as different and alien. In an unsettled business climate, they faced growing antagonism and mob violence. Charges of Host desecrations and thefts of sacred chalices were raised in Germany in 1510, resulting in the burning of thirty-eight Jews; thirteen others were sentenced to other brutal forms of death. Unable to live comfortably, they learnt to live shoddily. Barred from more desirable occupations, they turned to peddling and pawnbrokery.

The Church, increasingly subjected to a loss of its autonomy and influence, faced dissident philosophical and theological rumblings from a variety of abuses that were becoming louder and more insistent. It responded by persecution, but not by reform. The papacy had adopted a presence more in keeping with royalty than religion, ignoring accusations of power struggles and corruption that were shaking its political organization and weakening its spiritual health. In 1517, a German monk named Martin Luther was asked to confirm the credibility of the sale of indulgences—remissions of sins for a fee. He refuted them as clerical immorality, further denouncing Catholic policies such as celibacy, monasticism, veneration of saints, dependence on the priesthood for salvation, and belief in a mystical papacy. Although Luther declared that the Church was incapable of economic, religious, or political self-reform, he had not planned to launch the Protestant Reformation. Yet his radical views changed the medieval European spirit into one which broke the unanimity of Western Christendom. Luther's ideas owed their widespread influence to the printing press which rapidly disseminated his works across Europe in spite of Church censorship. A collision resulted between those who wished to maintain the status quo and those who demanded the creation of a more liberal denomination.

Turning his attention to the Jews, his *Sermon von dem Wucher* (Sermon on Usury), 1520, with an ill-featured caricature of a moneylending Jew, opened a disastrous period for Jews (Ill. 3:3). He followed it in 1523 with *Dass Jesus Christus Ein Geborener Jude Sei* (*That Jesus Christ Was Born a Jew*), suggesting that if Jews were treated more sympathetically many would convert. But they weren't and they didn't. Furious, he provoked fresh enmity with other tracts such as *Von den Juden und iren Lugen* (*Jews and Their Lies*), 1543, whipping up hysteria, inciting mobs to tear out Jews' tongues, destroy their books, and drive them into forced labor. "Their synagogues should be set on fire and whatever remains should be covered with dirt so that no one may ever see a cinder or stone of it. Also, their homes should be destroyed—all for the honor of God and Christianity so that God can see that as Christians we have not knowingly tolerated or approved their lying, cursing, and blaspheming." Below the title of the book, a woodcut by Lucas Cranach depicts a Jew with horns and an abacus as an instrument of the devil and a usurer (Ill. 3:4). Jews who had had reasonably amiable relations with their neighbors, became "an evil affliction," unwelcome trespassers, poisoners of wells, ravagers of maidens, and murderers of Christian children. His writings stoked anti-Jewish feelings for centuries and were resurrected by Hitler to rationalize genocide.

Luther was not alone. The popes were desperate to silence heresies. The Jews' continued resistance to proselytism, as well as the jealousy aroused by a few successful financiers, resulted in harsh, restrictive policies and expulsions. Although they were no longer accused of deicide by more enlightened people, they nevertheless were perceived as a threat to Church unity; it was suggested (with some justification) that they had encouraged the Reformation.

France had exiled its Jews in the fourteenth century, but by 1550 covert refugees from Portugal found their way to Bordeaux regions when Henry II permitted "New Christians" to settle there. However, cut off from organized religious influences, before long most melted into the local culture and were lost to Judaism.

England was Catholic until 1534 when Henry VIII was excommunicated for marrying Anne Boleyn in defiance of the pope's refusal to grant him a divorce from Catherine of Aragon, the daughter of Ferdinand and Isabella. Three years earlier, the

Ill. 3:3. *Sermon von dem Wucher (Sermon on Usury),* **1520. By Martin Luther**

Ill. 3:4. *A Jew with Horns and an Abacus*, 1543. Woodcut by Lucas Cranach

king had called on an Italian rabbi to provide him with biblical justification for the dissolution of his marriage. Perhaps Henry had been aware of a copy of the talmudic tractate on divorce in the royal library. (Rabbi Rafael Peglione rejected the appeal.) The ecclesiastical censure resulted in the establishment of a separate national religion, the Church of England, as well as the breakup and confiscation of monastic property which reverted to the king and his wealthy subjects. Beginning in 1558 under the reign of his daughter, the Protestant Elizabeth, the country experienced its greatest development, but because Jews had been banished at the end of the thirteenth century, the few crypto–Jews who had gained entry could not participate, and they, too, disappeared into the surrounding environment.

In Russia, Jews, who had had the right to live where they chose, suddenly found themselves banned from the entire country because the Orthodox Church panicked over their perceived influence. In 1545, during the reign of Ivan the Terrible, devastating persecution wrecked the property of the few who remained. Eighteen years later many of those who refused baptism were rounded up and drowned.

Turkey was busy expanding its empire, first in the Muslim east against Persia, and then in the west, primarily against Hungary and Austria. In 1517, it won control of Palestine from Egypt, and some twenty years later began rebuilding the walls of Jerusalem. Jews gratefully rekindled ties with the Holy Land, revived expectations of the Messianic Age, and enjoyed unaccustomed economic, political, and religious liberties. They established a famous yeshivah in Salonika in 1520, and were welcomed—or tolerated—as consummate businessmen useful in developing a much-needed middle class. About one hundred thousand Jews lived in the Ottoman Empire, supporting forty-four synagogues in Istanbul alone. Dona Gracia Mendes Nasi, a wealthy Portuguese converso, fled there in 1553 to escape the Inquisition. With her large resources, she supported important institutions of Jewish learning and led the Jewish community in a failed boycott of the papal state of Ancona when those who reverted to Judaism were being tortured and burned. Her son-in-law Joseph Nasi and daughter Reyna followed her example, developing her commercial and diplomatic activities, and establishing Hebrew printing presses from 1578 to 1600. Nevertheless, when intrigues and corruption involved the country in economic difficulties towards the end of the century, the family's influence could not prevent Jews and "Jewish money" from being charged with debasing the coinage.

Interlocking kinship relationships, participation in international trade, and increased social and political acceptance moved Jews toward a wider diaspora. While most families remained in the Old World, a few migrated to the New. As early as 1508, the bishop of Cuba complained to his superiors in Spain that practicing Jews as well as New Christians were showing up in Havana even though they were forbidden unto the fourth generation to live in Spanish territories. The Inquisition reached Mexico City in 1528 when two suspected backsliders became fuel for an *auto-da-fé*. An engraving by Palacio from *El Libro Rojo* (*The Radical Book*), 1590, demonstrated methods of torture applied to Francisca Carvajal (Ill. 3:5). In 1596, eight members of her family were consigned to the flames; two other relatives, a sister and a daughter, were burned alive in 1601 and 1649.

In some areas of the Americas, Jews were accepted and prospered. They founded the plantation system and the sugar industry in St. Thomas, importing Negro slaves to work the soil. Hernando Cortez' conquest of Mexico in 1519 introduced so many New Christians that they supposedly outnumbered Catholics until the Inquisition caught up with them. Things were better in non–Catholic North America, where Jews did not have to live as apostates. In 1584, the first known English-speaking Jew, Joachim Gaunse, arrived at Roanoke Island, Virginia, hoping to find commercially viable mineral deposits. Finding none, he stayed only a few months and returned to England where, as a secret Jew, he helped develop that country's copper industry. In 1589, having been asked by the Reverend Richard Curteys if he believed that Jesus was

Ill. 3:5. *Torture of Francisca Carvahal*, 1590. Engraving by Palacio. From *El Libro Rojo (The Radical Book)*

the son of Almighty God, he replied that if God were truly almighty, he had no need for a son. He was charged with blasphemy, but no reprisals were made. Nothing further is known of him.

Although most countries hoped that the Jewish presence could be eliminated or at lest contained, opportunities existed to reinvigorate religious studies. A new interest in the Hebrew Bible, including polyglot editions, had been generated by the rise of Protestantism and humanism. One of the by-products of expanded scholarship was the rapid advance in printing and printmaking which made research and learning widely available.

Fine examples of printed books and images pertaining to Jews had been produced in the fifteenth century, but the sixteenth saw even greater clarity, design, and creativity. Beginning in 1504 and continuing for seventeen years, the brothers David and Samuel ibn Nachmias brought out seventy Hebrew books in Turkey, strengthening that country's extraordinary commitment to Hebrew studies. Among their important editions was *Pirkei Avoth, Rosh Amanah* (*Pinnacle of Faith*) defending the belief in Redemption while opposing certain Maimonidean theories, and Isaac ben Judah Abrabanel's commentaries on the Haggadah. Abrabanel was a distinguished religious philosopher and former statesman in the Spanish court of Ferdinand and Isabella, honored by Christians as well as Jews as a Renaissance humanist. But after a futile attempt to head off the deportations of 1492, he fled to Naples where he served its royal family as a diplomat and friend until that city was attacked two years later by Charles VIII's army, which destroyed his home and library and ravaged its Jewish population. He ended his life in Venice.

Constantinople also produced the first printed edition of *Menorat ha-Ma'or* (*Candlesticks of Light*), 1514, by the fourteenth century author Isaac Aboab, who argued that the homiletic passages in rabbinic literature possessed a merit equal to the Talmud. It was translated into several languages other than Hebrew so that Jews everywhere could relate to its message. In 1519, Solomon ben Mazal Tov printed the first work on customs, particularly as practiced in the south of France, stressing their foundation on Jewish law. Likewise published in Constantinople, it was based on *Ha-Minhag* (*The Guide*), a thirteenth century handbook by the French scholar Abraham ben Nathan of Lunel, which provided information on synagogue rituals that would otherwise have been lost. Gershom Soncino, along with his son Eliezer and many other Jews who had experienced both the disastrous Sack of Rome in 1529 and the pressures of the Catholic Counter-Reformation, also found their way to the Ottoman Empire where they remained under the tolerant government of Sulayman the Magnificent.

In Salonika, Greece, the large population of Jews who had been expelled from German cities relied on an Ashkenazi prayer book printed from 1551 to 1555 by the presses of Solomon and Joseph Jabez. Solomon moved to Istanbul where he continued printing, while Joseph remained in Salonika to prepare a commentary for an edition of the Psalms published in 1571. The production of an entire Talmud by the brothers was unsuccessful, but together or alone they printed several tractates and forty authoritative responsa and commentaries. During the sixteenth century, well over a hundred books came off Ottoman Hebrew and Ladino presses, including more than forty Soncino editions, as well as Greek, Spanish, Arabic, and Persian translations of biblical, scientific, and literary works. Among other Salonika settlers were Eliezer ben Isaac Ashkenazi and his son Isaac who, during a disturbance in their hometown of Prague, prudently took their presses to Greece in 1575, where they issued about fifteen books. They then moved on to Safed and brought out Hebrew commentaries on the Book of Esther and the Song of Songs. Four other books by that family followed between 1577 and 1587, the first Hebrew publications in the Holy Land, and the last for two hundred fifty-four years. (The Israeli government would later honor Eliezer with a postage stamp depicting one of his title pages.)

Propelled by the emergence of these and other learned works, conventional information and perceptions underwent basic restructuring; new ideas struggled to break out of old molds. Among the humanists who studied the Hebrew Bible in its original language was Conrad Pellicanus whose *De modo legendi et intelligendi Hebraeum*, Strasbourg, 1504, was one of the first Hebrew grammars published by a Christian. Thomas Anshelm's grammar and dictionary, *Liber de rudimentis Hebraicis*, 1506, published in Pforzheim, Germany, was compiled by the Gentile scholar Johannes Reuchlin, a specialist in Hebrew philology and Kabbalah; it was paginated from right to left as in Hebrew. Anshelm also published Reuchlin's treatise on Hebrew accents and spelling, *De accentibus et orthographia linguae Hebraicae*, in 1510 in Alsace, another impressive addition to the study of linguistics. It followed rabbinical guidelines, as well as Greek and Latin sources, and initiated the printing of biblical Hebrew musical cantillation, a contribution to the glorification of God through song. The notes were arranged from right to left (Ill. 3:6).

Reuchlin and other Christian Hebraists moved biblical scholarship away from medieval theology, awakened Europe to a greater appreciation of rabbinic studies, and promoted equal rights for Jews based on Roman canon law. When quarrels between Jews and Christians broke

Ill. 3:6. *Hebrew Musical Cantillation, 1510.* From *De accentibus et orthographia linguae Hebraicae (Concerning Accents and Spelling of the Hebrew Language).* **By Johannes Reuchlin**

out in Germany over the credibility of the Talmud and other sacred books, Reuchlin became involved in a dispute with an apostate Jewish butcher, Johannes Pfefferkorn, a thief who had earlier won his prison release by converting to Christianity. Pfefferkorn, knowing little or no Latin and not much more Hebrew, attached himself to a group of Dominican friars who published inflammatory Latin diatribes in his name, claiming that the Church required the conversion or expulsion of Jews and destruction of the blasphemous Talmud. His familiarity with rabbinic lore and kabbalistic mysticism, though marginal, gave him credibility in the Chris-

tian world. Twisting the material into unnatural contexts, the friars made the case that talmudic Judaism had developed away from biblical theology, and in so doing, surrendered much of
its "authenticity." When Pfefferkorn obtained the consent of Emperor Maximilian, lover of erudition and patron of Dürer, to make a bonfire of Jewish writings in 1509, Reuchlin successfully
opposed the vandalism. A woodcut, *Pfefferkorn and Reuchlin*, 1516, shows the antagonists in bitter confrontation, with Pfefferkorn lifting the flag of the Christian faith, while Reuchlin is
depicted as a two-tongued demagogue and traitor to Christian values. For a decade or more, a
deluge of books and pamphlets descended on Europe on both sides of the controversy in one
of the earliest efforts, along with Luther's, to woo public opinion via the printing press.

Reuchlin enlisted the help of Erasmus who called Pfefferkorn "a criminal Jew who had
become a criminal Christian." But he protected Jewish books with greater zeal than he championed Jews, believing that they were "captives of the devil" who deserved mass expulsion
because of their collective guilt of deicide. Yet he defended the Talmud as "not being composed for every scoundrel to tread on with unwashed feet and then claim he knew it thoroughly." Appointed by Maximilian to a commission to investigate the charges and to scrutinize
Jewish literature for signs of heresy, Reuchlin reached the conclusion that Hebrew books should
be spared since the Church and state protected Jewish customs which were not considered
heretical, and because the Kabbalah revealed Christian prophesies and presented a rational
basis to secure Jewish conversions.

By 1516, Maximilian, persuaded by liberal humanists, resisted Dominican pressure and
prohibited the expulsion of the Jews. Thanks mainly to Reuchlin, the debate subsided, but not
until he was accused by the Inquisition in Cologne of undermining Catholicism and promoting a "reformed" Christianity. Although Hebrew was ultimately validated as an important academic discipline worthy of a place beside Latin and Greek, the victory came too late for
Reuchlin; his works were placed on the proscribed Index in 1520, two years before he died.
But the day had passed when the Church might arbitrarily command wholesale obedience.
His books were impossible to suppress, and contributed significantly to the rise of Protestantism and interest in Hebrew scholarship.

Salomon de Rossi, an honored composer at the court of the Duke of Milan, published
polyphonic liturgical harmonies for the synagogue and sonata forms for the general public,
thus establishing cultural ties with the outside Christian community. One of the few Jewish
musicians who refused conversion as the price of success, his unexpected "modern" works owed
something to church music, but then, as he pointed out, church music owed its origins to the
Temple services in Jerusalem. His relative, Azariah de Rossi, no less a phenomenon, was the
greatest exponent of philosophy and Hebrew literature in the latter part of the century, defining
contemporary Jewish criticism and theories that tied Jewish to non–Jewish references works
from the classical period. His prodigious history, *Me'or Enayim* (*Light of the Ey*es), 1573–1575,
among other things, described the 1570 earthquake in Ferrara. He interpreted midrashic legends, not always as literal truths, but rather as folktales designed "to induce a pleasant state
of mind among readers." He argued that the so-called classical works attributed to the Jewish
philosopher Philo, who lived at the time of the Second Temple, actually originated in the
medieval period and could not therefore be trusted as reliable. He questioned the dating of
the creation story, reasoning that neither the ancient scholars nor the Bible itself made claims
that the calendar began with Genesis. His critical analysis reflected the spirit that enlivened
humanism—abominations to some rabbis who prohibited anyone to own or read the book; others merely banned its study to anyone under the age of twenty-five. Although he eliminated
some of the objectionable material in a revised edition and begged pardon of the authorities
(they forgave him), two hundred years had to pass before his wide knowledge and keen mind
were fully appreciated in the Enlightenment of the eighteenth century.

The French press's contribution to scholarship was its Hebrew and Greek grammar, *Grammatica hebraica et graeca*, published in 1508 by François Tissard, who had studied Hebrew in Italy. Following a visit to a synagogue in Ferrara to get a first-hand look at the arcane world of Jewish culture, he announced that he didn't much care for it. "One might hear a man howling, another braying, another bellowing," he wrote. "Such a cacophony of discordant sounds do they make! Weighing this with the rest of their rites, I was almost brought to nausea." Luckily his queasiness diminished through the ministrations of his Jewish teacher, whose lectures presumably were less jangling to his ear.

France's first complete Hebrew Bible, one of the most beautiful of its kind in the sixteenth century, was published from 1539 to 1544 by Robert Estienne, a classical scholar and printer of Hebrew, Greek, and Latin works for Francis I, who encouraged its publication. Unusual in its small format, approximately four inches high and two and a half inches wide, it was particularly welcome to itinerant Jewish merchants who were required to study and observe religious precepts "when sitting in their house and when walking by the way" (Deuteronomy 6:7). During the king's reign, some forty towns were able to support printing presses, bur after his death in 1547, Estienne, who had published some works deemed "heretical," was threatened with an *auto-da-fé*. Sensibly, he took his equipment to Geneva and gifted that city with meticulous editions.

Johann Froben established Basle, Switzerland, as a center for Hebrew printing, issuing a Psalter in 1516 together with two Christian Hebraists, Conrad Pellikan and Sebastian Munster. The first Hebrew religious book edited by non–Jews, it, too, was small enough to slip into a pocket. From 1534 to 1535, Munster oversaw the first translation of the Hebrew Bible into Latin, specifically for the Protestant community. Froben's grandson, Ambrosius, published an important Talmud, 1578–1580, under the supervision of the Jewish editor Israel Zifroni. Catholic monks censored many of its passages and eliminated the Avodah Zarah tractate on idolatry, but it wasn't enough. A papal bull issued in 1592 prohibited Talmud production once more. Zifroni then sought work in one town after another, including places forbidden to Jews. Fearful of revealing the cities where his books originated, one of his title pages bore only a vague clue: "Printed by Zifroni where he lives."

Samuel ben Isaac Nedivot and his son Isaac published fifteen Hebrew works over a period of six years in North Africa, using typefaces brought from Portugal. Their *Sefer Abudraham*, 1516, was notable for its talmudic and rabbinic commentaries. In spite of harassment by Spanish authorities in Fez who went out of their way to restrict the importation of paper, their colophon gloats over the "numberless books printed for all to study and read." It was the first book of any kind printed in Africa.

In an effort to escape grievances, particularly in Germany, many Jews had moved to Polish cities and towns where they were encouraged by the Crown to develop a mercantile class. Although they didn't entirely escape conflicts, their troubles were mitigated because of less economic competition. Important contributions to Hebrew printing were made by the Halicz brothers, who set up the first Hebrew press in Krakow in 1530 under a license from King Sigismund I, but when they converted to Christianity in 1537, Jews refused to buy their books. The king perceived the rejection as a personal affront and forced the community to purchase the entire output. They bought it and destroyed it, but they weren't without Hebrew works for long. The first printing of a Talmud tractate appeared in Lublin in 1559 following its burning in Italy on orders of the Inquisition. Another press was organized in 1569 by Isaac ben Aaron Prostitz who brought machines and a proofreader from Italy. Happily, he and his family remained Jewish and prosperous, publishing some two hundred Hebrew and Yiddish books during the fifty years' license period granted them by Sigismund II.

In Antwerp, Estienne, Froben, and Christopher Plantin made up the great trio of north-

ern Europe's Christian printers. Plantin worked for Philip II of Spain under the naive impression that he would be compensated for his efforts, but when the king defaulted, he almost lost
his business. However, he managed to pioneer elaborate title pages, publish a highly esteemed
eight-volume polyglot Bible between 1568 and 1572, and a two-by-four-inch Bible in 1574.
Copies were sold throughout Europe and North Africa, both to Christian scholars and to Jewish communities. But in spite of Plantin's prominence, he was unable to protect his Christian
editor, Arias Montano, from the toils of the Inquisition when that gentleman unfortunately
expressed some Jewish sympathies.

Knowledge of Hebrew lagged in England although the theologian Roger Bacon had been
an avid student of the language in the thirteenth century. He believed that all human wisdom
emanated from the Jewish God through the Hebrew Bible, and that God's word could not be
adequately conveyed through translations. But his enthusiasm and research came to nothing.
Interest evaporated and consequently Hebrew printing in England was delayed. The first example of a few words in Hebrew type was the polyglot *Oratio de laudibus et utilitate trium lin-
guarum Arabicae, Chaldaicae and Hebraicae* (*Essay on the Usefulness of Three Languages—Arabic,
Aramaic, and Hebrew*) by Robert Wakefield, chaplain to Henry VIII and professor of Hebrew
at Cambridge and Oxford Universities. Printed by Wynkyn de Worde in 1524, it was a crude
production using primitive wooden blocks, but it showcased Wakefield's grasp of rabbinic studies and medieval Hebrew literature.

The only Bibles in England were in Latin and that was the way the Catholic hierarchy
wanted it; once people could read and judge the Scriptures for themselves, the Church's absolute
authority would be challenged. When Willam Tyndale, an open reformer, decided to print
one in the English language, the Church forbade the attempt, forcing him to escape to Germany. There, after many hardships, his translation of the entire Pentateuch directly from the
Hebrew was printed in Marburg by Hans Luft in 1530. Many copies were smuggled into
England, many were burned. Tyndale didn't fare any too well himself. Accused of undermining the monarchy and branded a heretic, he was hunted down in the Netherlands, strangled,
and burned at the stake in 1536. Of his entire edition, only one complete version survives, now
housed in the British Museum.

The first lengthy Hebrew text in England was *Daniel and His Chaldic Visions...*, London,
1596, by the Protestant theologian Hugo Broughton. His goal, to produce a good English translation of the Bible, prompted him in 1597 to publish a letter "to the learned nobility of England"
on the subject, but his difficult personality stood in the way of realizing the project. When a
committee was set up to implement such a translation, one that was not "corrupt" and would
be "answerable to the truth of the Original," Broughton's overtures were rebuffed. Other scholars were then chosen to prepare the King James Authorized Version of 1611; much of its language originated with Tyndale.

But interesting and impressive as all this material was, the finest Hebrew works of all were
issued in Italy—mostly by Christian presses in Venice, Mantua, Rome, and Livorno. Christian Hebraists turned to the Venetian printer Aldus Manutius who produced the first Hebrew
grammar in 1501, *Introduction perbrevis in linguam hebraicam* (*Brief History of the Hebrew Language*). In both its Greek and Latin editions some Hebrew words were printed from wood-
blocks. Together with subsequent grammars and vocabularies, these books laid the groundwork
in the Christian West for the development of serious Hebraic study in universities, legal circles, and bibliographic scholarship.

Fifteen years later a polyglot Psalter, the earliest multilingual version to be printed with
the original Hebrew text, and containing translations into Latin, Greek, Arabic, and Aramaic,
was published in Genoa by Bishop Agostino Giustiniani, a student of Oriental languages
and professor of Hebrew in the College de France (Ill. 3:7). The entire production was con-

ceived and created by Christian editors, type designers, and printers. Its interlinear glosses were invaluable for the comparative study of European languages, scriptural materials, and for seeking christological references. Of particular interest is Psalm 19, Verse 5: "And their words are gone out to the end of the world." According to Giustiniani, it was the first reference to America in a Jewish literary work: "By his wonderful daring," he commented, "Christopher Colum-

Ill. 3.7. *Polyglot Psalter with Translations into Latin, Greek, Arabic, and Aramaic, 1516*

bus, the Genoese, has discovered another world and a new congregation of Christians...." With the pride of a fellow Genoan, Giustiniani added a biography of the famous sailor, but although the Psalter was dedicated to Pope Leo X, most copies of the book were destroyed because of Christian resistance to its Hebrew scholarship and, it was said, on complaints of inaccuracies by Columbus' son.

Venice's Jews, although ghettoized, were generally protected. The cultural, banking, and trading capital of Europe, with an affluent population and a recuperating business cycle, Venice flourished as its sea power expanded. A brisk market attracted merchants who sold fine quality paper at a reasonable cost, while the comparatively liberal government encouraged the fledgling publishing industry and the immigration of skilled printers from Germany and other northern cities. Therefore, by 1512 the time was ripe for Daniel Bomberg, a Christian printer originally from Antwerp, to set up the first fully functioning publishing house for Hebrew books in Venice. Up-to-date machinery boosted production, while his promotional techniques guaranteed him ready customers all over Italy, Europe, and the Ottoman Empire. One of his Jewish assistants, Abraham de Balmes, a physician and author of a Hebrew grammar, *Mikneh Avram* (*The Flock of Abraham*), 1523, remembered Bomberg as one whose "deeds shine like the splendor of the sky." He was highly regarded by some rabbis, too, who spoke of him as a "righteous Christian," although others labeled him an opportunist who cynically exploited a burgeoning market. Still another verdict was reached by Gerardus Veltvyck, the German ambassador to Constantinople and an apostate whose anti–Jewish works Bomberg also published. He claimed that the printer was a zealot who hoped to expose Judaism's hidden and corrupt values. Bomberg said he simply wanted to produce the books "on which the entire structure of Christianity rests."

He dominated the field for over three decades, preempting what until then had been the almost exclusive domain of Gershom Soncino. All the basic Hebrew texts came from his workplace—two hundred twenty-two remarkably fine books, mostly pioneer editions. Bomberg used the best materials, hired competent Jewish and formerly Jewish typographers and readers, and helped arrange for his Jewish employees to come and go from the ghetto without their humiliating yellow hats—although they still had to submit to lock-ups each night. One of his prominent Jewish editors, Elijah Levita, author of Hebrew and Yiddish grammars, dictionaries, and stories, taught such Christian humanists as Sebastion Munster and Cardinal Egidio de Viterbo, at whose home he was a guest for at least a decade and who helped establish a Hebrew press in Rome in 1518.

Bomberg developed the still current layouts and pagination for the Talmud, a system borrowed from the Vulgate. His four volume *Mikra'ot Gedolot* (*Multi-Commentary Bible*), 1516–1518, with the Aramaic Targum and various rabbinic glosses, helped renew biblical studies which had lost ground to the Talmud and Kabbalah. It was edited by the monk Felix Pratensis, a Jewish convert who suggested the project and secured the copyright. Felix also wrote a Latin dedication to Pope Leo, who had encouraged its production in a moment of Renaissance enlightenment. Not surprisingly, it was rejected by the Jews who wanted nothing to do with an apostate editor or a papal endorsement, but it was prized by King James scholars who used it as a source for their own translations. When it sold out, even finer second and third editions appeared in 1524–1525 and 1546–1548 with references to both Pratensis and the pope omitted; papal authorities were not pleased and ordered the destruction of several tractates. It remains, however, the standard, perhaps the finest, rabbinical text ever produced. Jacob ben Hayyim wrote:

> When I explained to Bomberg the advantage of the Massorah, he did everything in his power to search for it in all countries, and praised be the Lord we obtained as many of the massoretic books as could possibly be got. He was not backward, and his hand was not closed, nor did he draw back

his right hand from producing gold out of his purse to defray the expenses of the books and of the messengers who were engaged to search for them in the most remote corners and in every place where they might possibly be found.

Leo also gave Bomberg a monopoly for his greatest accomplishment, the printing of the complete Talmuds, the Babylonian, 1519–1523, followed by the Palestinian, 1523–1524. (Until that time individual tractates only had been published by the Soncino family beginning in 1483.) Rabbi Chiyyah Meir ben David, judge of the Venetian Jewish court, functioned as editor, Israel (Cornelio) Adelkind, presumably a convert to Christianity and for many years Bomberg's most valued associate, designed the pages and served as master printer. Together they provided exceptional technical skills for the Aramaic and Hebrew texts. Jacob ben Hayyim supervised the 1525–1528 reissue of the Rabbinic Bible, so famous for the distinctness of its printing that it became the exemplar for all later editions. Unfortunately, Jacob, too, defected to Christianity. His name was then excised with the hope that the Lord would "place his soul in a bag full of holes" (Haggai 1:6). Nevertheless, the complete Talmuds were now readily obtainable to world Jewry. They turned out to be landmarks in the typography of Hebrew book art, featuring, among other innovations, one of the early title pages in a Hebrew book, a gate "welcoming" the reader. The composition, which remained popular for over two centuries, was often embellished with twisted columns representing the Holy Temple and with Moses and Aaron serving as "guides."

In 1548, the Venetian Senate issued a charter barring further Jewish participation in printing or publishing. Although enforcement of the law was fairly lax because capable Jewish typesetters and proofreaders were necessary for Christian scholarship to function, many Jewish editors and printers were forced out of business. Some two dozen Gentile publishers stepped into the vacancy, forcing Bomberg into financial difficulties in spite of—or perhaps because of—his attention to detail and his insistence on correcting "mistakes and purifying the style until the works are as refined as silver and as pure as gold."

Continuous rivalry among publishers eventually provoked a disaster that jeopardized Hebrew literature and ended the "golden years" of Hebrew printing. A pair of Gentile publishers, Alvise Bragadini and Marco Antonio Giustiniani, brought charges of unfair competition and offensive anti–Christian passages in each other's editions of Maimonides' Mishneh Torah. Persuaded by hostile apostates (including two grandsons of Elijah Levita) that the book was heretical, Pope Julius III was under severe pressure from the fanatic Dominican order to "purify the Church." Anxious to counteract the perils of the Reformation, he ordered its destruction together with twelve thousand copies of other "blasphemous" Hebrew works. Rounded up from printing establishments as well as from Jewish and Christian homes, they disappeared in a huge bonfire at the Campo dei Fiori that lit up the streets of Rome on Rosh Hashanah, September 9, 1553. To add to the festivities, Cornelio da Nomtakino, a former monk who had become a Jew, was placed among the flaming books. The spectacle drew general applause, said an eyewitness, but it was "echoed back with the sighs and tears" of Jewish onlookers. On the Sabbath day in the following month, a pyre at Venice's San Marco Cathedral ignited countless more Jewish books, including copies of Bomberg's Talmuds and Bibles. A papal nuncio standing nearby spoke of the "fine blaze," but Abraham Rapa, a Jewish proofreader at Bragadin who also witnessed the burning, fasted on its anniversary for the rest of his life.

Similar cremations were reenacted in other Italian cities—Rome, Padua, Bologna, Ravenna, Mantua, Ferrara, even Crete. Since editions were small to begin with, hardly any Hebrew works in pristine condition remain from these areas. Some scorched books were later found, plucked from the flames at what cost or by whom we will never know. Those Jews who watched the conflagration were perhaps consoled by the traditional legend that only the paper disappears when holy books are burned—the letters fly up to heaven.

The technique of breaking a people's spirit by the destruction of their literature wasn't new. Julius might well have remembered that more than a thousand years before his own time, the pagan emperor Diocletian had attempted to destroy Christianity by purging its "abominable scriptures." Shakespeare, too, was aware that a civilization might be debased through the loss of its written history. He wrote in *The Tempest* (Act III, Scene 2)

> ... thou mayst brain him,
> Having first seized his books, or with a log
> Batter his skull, or stab him with a stake
> Or cut his throat with thy knife. Remember
> First to possess his books, for without them
> He's but a sot.... Burn but his books.

Pleadings and payoffs limited some of the burnings, while from 1554 to 1563 Venice's Hebrew works experienced heavy censorship. Only a single prayer book was published in 1560, of which very few copies survive through an apparent oversight. Strictures were so tight that, after the Bomberg editions and one by Giustiniani, 1546–1551, not one complete Talmud was printed in Italy in the sixteenth century, nor was it even permissible to own one. In 1564, the Council of Trent published its *Index Librorum Prohibitorum* which barred "the Talmud, its glosses, annotations, interpretations, and expositions" although some censored editions were allowed. If the Jews feared the Church, the Church clearly had a bad case of paranoia regarding the Jews.

When Venice once again permitted publication of Hebrew books, it no longer had a monopoly or its former excellence. The Bragadin firm, however, scored a coup with the 1564 edition of Joseph Caro's Sephardic collection of earlier talmudic codes, the *Shulchan Aruch* (*Prepared Table*). Moses Isserles of Krakow then added the Ashkenazic viewpoints in *Ha-Mappah* (*The Tablecloth*), 1569–1571, thus providing a universally accepted version. Because inconsistencies in religious customs brought on by centuries of disruptions in Jewish life had created a certain amount of confusion surrounding ceremonial rituals and observances, these codes not only kept traditions intact, but provided practicing Jews with uniform and stable directives wherever they lived.

Giovanni di Gara, having bought out Bomberg's press, published over one hundred Hebrew works from 1565 to 1609, often in collaboration with Bragadin. Among his innovations was the introduction of tables of contents and indexes, but because he was forced to use Christian typesetters, his editions suffered from their inferior skills. Although it was again difficult for Jews in the printing industry, in 1574 Meir Parenzo, working for the Bragadin press, was able to reprint the Mishneh Torah, the prototype for future editions. Parenzo, the only Jew who independently published Hebrew books in Venice, included his printer's mark, a lush Venus standing on a seven-headed Hydra wearing nothing but a smile and a crown (Ill. 3:8). Racy pictures sold widely then as now. A verse from Psalm 45:12, "the king desires thy beauty," provided the tenuous connection. Complete copies of the book are rarely found, since many of the original owners carefully removed the unseemly page—for what purpose, they didn't say. Venus, as the queen of love, and Venice, as the queen of polity, had, of course, always been linked as fixed stars in heavenly space. Fanciful "trade-marks" in Hebrew books sometimes included pagan images that had their source in Renaissance humanism. As portents of good luck or fortune they found their way into religious texts and even into synagogue decoration. But by the end of the century, Venetian exuberance had unfortunately worn thin. Political and economic decline signaled the winding down of the High Renaissance and the end of the myth of the ideal State.

Jewish erudition and proofreading had deteriorated to such an extent that Christian presses in Cremona, Mantua, and smaller Italian localities were able to compete successfully. After 1589, those in power demanded ever-stricter controls over texts. Although an exception was made for the Kabbalah because Christian theologians felt it was a key to the understanding of their own faith, and because it was thought to confirm the existence of the Trinity, few Hebrew books escaped the attention of Venetian censors, many of whom were so ignorant that they often obliterated non-controversial material. With bitter irony, an Italian Jew commented that Boccaccio's bawdy *Decameron* was apparently considered a worthier moral and ethical model than Jewish holy works.

Two Marrano printers, who had lived in Portugal and Spain under the Christian names Duarte Pinhel and Jeronimo de Vargas, found refuge in Ferrara under the relatively tolerant rule of Duke Ercoli. They reverted to their Jewish names, Abraham Usque and Yom-Tov ben Levi Athias, and initiated Spanish and Portuguese translations of

Ill. 3:8. *Printer's Trademark*: *Venus*, 1574–1575, by Meir Parenzo. From *Mishneh Torah*

literary and religious Hebrew books for conversos, hoping to revive an interest in Judaism. Their Spanish edition of the entire Hebrew Bible, published in 1553 in separate editions for Christians and Jews, was so influential that it was reprinted in the seventeenth and eighteenth centuries in Amsterdam. In the translation of Isaiah 7:14 in the Christian version, the Latin word *virgen* (virgin) was conveyed as the Hebrew *alma* (young woman). Actually, the Hebrew word for virgin is *betoolah*. The verse has traditionally caused antagonistic feelings between those who wish to read christological interpretations into the Hebrew word and those to whom such interpretations are both anathema and incorrect. In an effort to put off censorship by the Inquisition, the Jewish edition offered the Spanish *moca* (young woman), in place of *alma*. Readers were free to choose according to their own preferences.

The woodcut frontispiece of the Bible displayed the image of a storm-tossed ship with a broken mast, a metaphor for the broken, but resolute, Spanish refugees fleeing the Inquisition. The printer's mark included a prayer for deliverance: "My soul waits for the Lord and in His Word do I hope" (Psalm 130:5). But that hope was dashed in 1555 when the forces of the Counter-Reformation became more active and the Spanish edition was suppressed. The ruling duke then withdrew his protection and the press was shut down. Meanwhile, on the northern side of the Alps, Hebrew printing was launched with a Jewish book never intended for Jewish use—an illustrated Haggadah of 1512. It was published in Latin in Frankfort during the Pfefferkorn-Reuchlin debates by a humanist Franciscan friar, Thomas Murner, for the benefit of Christian scholars who might wish to counter Pfefferkorn's savage description of the "blind Jews celebrating their Easter." Murner's brother, Beatus, illustrated its six roughly drawn

Ill. 3:9. *Kiddush Ceremony*, 1512. Woodcut by Beatus Murner from *Haggadah*

woodcuts, possibly derived from non–Jewish sources. The Kiddush ceremony, the four cups of wine, and the covered matzot on the table are all correctly depicted (Ill. 3:9).

Haggadah images typically center on four kinds of representation: those which explain the text, those to guide the leader, those depicting Seder preparations and the Seder service, and biblical scenes which have some connection with the Passover tradition. The Haggadah was one of the very few outlets possible for artistic expression within the narrow limits imposed by Jewish tradition.

Prague was the first northern city to print Hebrew books specifically for Jewish consumption, leading off with the Ashkenazi *Seder Tefillot* (*Prayer Book*), 1512, in which the Star of David served as the printer's mark. Two years later, Gershom Katz (ha-Cohen) helped produce a pamphlet, the *Zemirot u-Birkat Ha-mazon* (*Song Book, Grace After Meals*), with a woodcut illustration of a father offering the Kiddush (Ill. 3:10). The women wear stylish head-dresses held in place with chin straps; the men sport flat barrettes and wide collars. Such informal pictures were tacked up on walls as examples of local fashions or as warm evocations of holiday observances. As with most ephemera, only a few copies remain, defying extinction.

Ill. 3.10. *Kiddush Ceremony*, 1512. Woodcut. From *Zemirot u-Birkat Ha-mazon (Song Book, Grace After Meals)*

The community in Prague boasted one of the wealthiest Jews in Europe, Mordechai Meisel, whose charitable activities steamrolled an assortment of building projects including the still surviving Meisel Synagogue, which so impressed Rudolph II that he declared it off limits to his officers and exempted it from taxes. But Jewish Prague was distinguished most of all for the first complete printed, dated, and illustrated Haggadah that can reasonably assigned to Jewish craftsmen. Produced in 1526 by Gershom Solomon Kohn Katz and his brother Gronem, it is one of the finest of the thousands that exist and is arguably among the best of any sixteenth century printed and illustrated books. By combining Renaissance and German Gothic architectural and costume elements, and featuring sixty woodcuts alongside the margins as well as the first printed Yiddish song, it set the style and format for many later Haggadah illustrations, typography, and well-balanced pages.

Hayyim Shahor is the artist generally credited with the convivial images derived from fifteenth century and earlier non–Jewish sources. Following the biblical admonition "Thou shalt say unto thy sons...." he represented the famous "boys" in one of its three borders: the Wicked Son appears as a soldier while his younger Simple brother seems mentally defective. Surely such illustrations captured the imagination of the children, while the seniors noted the architectural elements (portrayed as Egyptian buildings) and enjoyed the picture of a three-generational family gathered around the Seder table. The presence of women at the ceremonial meal dates from about the thirteenth century, when they routinely joined the males and shared in the recitations. Perhaps it was not altogether a coincidence that Jewish women had already established Hebrew presses and even served in medical, financial, and theatrical professions. Early feminists may have complained about a woodcut showing the man of the house pointing at his wife with one hand while holding the plate of bitter herbs in the other. Since almost every tradition corresponds to a biblical or midrashic statement, this illustration can be related either to Proverbs 5:3,4, in which the "strange" woman is as "bitter as wormwood," or to the occasionally misogynous Ecclesiastes 7:26—"And I find more bitter than death the woman whose heart is snares and nets."

Four standing figures that were possibly designed for a Christian Bible decorate the Haggadah's crowded northern-style borders; the white on a black ground contrasts with the black letters on white paper, dramatizing the effect. Adam and Eve, while flawed as humans, are there presumably because they started the whole story. Samson, removing the gates of Gaza (Judges 16:3), and the apocryphal Judith, holding her avenging sword and the head of the villainous General Holofernes, were heroes who had saved their people and hopefully would rescue them again in the days of the Messiah. Collectively the images remind God to "pour out Thy wrath on the nations that have not known Thee ... pursue them in anger and destroy them," an understandable, if bitter reproof, given the murderous Crusades when the lines were presumably written (Psalms 69:25, 79:6). Similar themes were occasionally incorporated in prayers during the troubled Passover season. The artist, however, in hopeful expectation, tucked in an image of Elijah entering Jerusalem on a woebegone donkey to announce the advent of the Messiah (Zachariah 9:9) (Ill. 3:11). Symbolizing the redemption of the Jews on whose behalf he will appear, the doors of Jewish homes were thrown open during the Seder in anticipation of his arrival. Unhappily, he was (and is) inexplicably detained.

On a lighter note, the Haggadah introduced a barely clad long-haired woman: "...thou camest to excellent beauty; thy breasts were fashioned, and thy hair was grown; still, thou wast naked and bare" (Ezekiel 16:7). It was a somewhat ambiguous manner of expressing a spiritually, if not physically, undeveloped Jerusalem. (Perhaps Shahor's and Meir Parenzo's equally exposed ladies were intended to demonstrate God's creation of humankind in Her own image.) A 1556 Haggadah included some Yiddish instructions and notations, along with a depiction of a horned Moses, a misunderstanding by the Vulgate translators who confused the similar Hebrew words for "horn" and "emanating light." Shahor (or, more likely, a Christian artist) may be excused on the grounds that the Midrash (as well as Hans Holbein the younger and Michelangelo) had made the same inference. The Had Gaddya song was included for the first time in a Prague Haggadah of 1590, although it dates back to the fourteenth or fifteenth century and may have originally been an independent work. Intended perhaps as a metaphor for the eventual victory of the Jews under the watchful eye of God, it is as long-winded as *The House That Jack Built*.

While expulsions and restrictions hindered the production of most Hebrew books in Italy, Haggadot had freer scope. In 1545, Giustiniani published the first Venetian example with the commentary of Isaac Abrabanel and a printer's mark representing the Temple. After Venice, Mantua's press was the busiest. The artist of its 1560 Haggadah copied the angular Northern Gothic typography of the 1526 Prague version, but added an Italianate twist to the new marginal woodcuts and floral borders. Illustrating the verse "Your ancient fathers dwelt beyond the river" (Joshua 24:2), Abraham takes on a southern flavor as he rides by in a gondola—in the Prague edition he is rowed in an ordinary boat (Ill. 3:12). For the first time in a printed edition, matzo baking was illustrated. The mixing of the dough was paired with the mixing of the sexes. Permission for this extraordinary coupling was derived from Psalm 148:12: Men made the holes, women rolled out the batter, the old with the young, the virgins with the bachelors. (However, when the 1609 edition appeared, no women were to be seen and no explanation was offered for their removal.) There was also a picture of Jewish mothers helplessly witnessing Pharaoh's order to drown their first-born sons. Published by the Christian Giacomo Ruffinelli in collaboration with Isaac ben Samuel Bassan, it was the only Hebrew book printed from wood blocks, the first illustrated Haggadah with a title page, and the prototype for later Italian illustrated editions. Depictions of the Four Sons were included. Its woodcut

Ill. 3:11. *Woodcut Border* by Hayyim Shahor, 1526. From *Haggadah*

Above: Ill. 3:12. *Abraham in a Gondola.* From Mantuan Haggadah. 1560. *Below:* Ill. 3:13. *Jewish Astronomer,* 1528. Woodcut. From *Tabule Perpetue (Perpetual Calandar)*

of a fool "who said in his heart, 'there is no God'" (Psalm 53:2) was taken from Holbein's *Historiarum Veteris Instrumenti Icones (Images from the Old Testament)*, 1537–1538, but the artist converted the disbeliever into the unenlightened "son who does not know how to ask questions." Michelangelo's Jeremiah, last seen on the Sistine Chapel ceiling, showed up with the addition of a pointed Jewish hat as the Wise Son in the 1568 reissue printed by Joseph Shalit ben Jacob Ashkenazi at the Filippon press. And when Giovanni Di Gara printed the Venice Haggadah of 1599, the figure appeared as the young Talmudic scholar Rabbi Eleazar ben Azariah, who in one night grew a beard so long and white that he was deemed worthy to serve as the head of a school. It is one of only twenty-five printed Haggadah editions known from the sixteenth century, since most of the demand was still being met by handwrit-

ten specimens. By contrast, during that same period, almost two thousand volumes in Hebrew, Yiddish, and Ladino were published, in addition to many prints of Jewish interest, fueling an unprecedented surge of scholarship and graphic art.

Interest in Jewish customs and manners never flagged. A Belgian woodcut from the *Tabule Perpetue (Perpetual Calendar)*, 1528, Louvain, depicted a bearded Jewish astronomer participating in an examination of the heavens with his Christian colleagues (Ill. 3:13). A book of engravings, *Sacri Romani Imperii Ornatu (Apparel of the Holy Roman Empire)* by C. Rutz,

Ill. 3:14. *Kapparot Ceremony*. Woodcut. From *Book of Customs*

1588, illustrated fashions sanctioned for Frankfort's Jews. Fearful of arousing jealousy, the rabbinate as well as the local authorities governed the length of sleeves, collars, and cloaks, the amount of fur and lace trimmings, prohibited the wearing of jewelry except on certain festivals, and banned silk shoes at any time. Women looked so plain that they were sometimes mistaken for nuns. A woodcut from a Venetian book of customs accurately portrayed the Kapparot ceremony in which sins are symbolically transferred to a fowl on the eve of Yom Kippur (Ill. 3:14). Yet another image, *Judaeus Mercator Patavinus* (*Jewish Peddler of Padua*), engraved in 1594, demonstrated that Yiddish was still the communal language as the street seller calls out "*Was welt ier geben?*" (*What do you offer?*) (Ill. 3:15).

Anti-Jewish printed material was continuously turned out by artists who were experts at spreading trouble. Scurrilous pamphlets by Pfefferkorn, one beginning *Ich heys ein buchlyn* (*I'm called a booklet*), and another, *Libellus de Judaica Confessione* (*Confession of the Jews*), were drafted in 1508 under the auspices of the Dominican friars of Cologne. With insulting texts and incoherent images, such as a Kapparot scene, ritual bath, and matzo preparation all jumbled together, other illustrations, including a Tashlich service during Rosh Hashanah when sins are cast off into a body of water, were correctly described (Ill. 3:16). The woodcut, however, shows the congregants with veiled eyes, indicative of their blindness to Christian truths. By heaping derision on rituals connected with the High Holidays, the prints successfully promoted hysterical attitudes against Jews. The prints were subsequently plagiarized in an inferior version, *Der gantz judische Glaub ...* (*The Whole Jewish Faith...*), Augsburg, 1530, by Antonius Margaritha, a Hebrew professor in Augsburg and Leipzig and a rabbi's apostate son. The book, accusing Jews of treason, parsimony, and offending Christianity, was discredited and the author banished by Charles V following a disputation between Margaritha and the Jewish scholar Joselmann of Rosheim. But it accomplished its aim since its ravings were disseminated by Luther and reprinted by others well into the eighteenth century.

Degrading pictures of Jews kept Jew-hatred alive and well. A woodcut, *Der Ander Teil* (*The Other Part*) by Hans Frutenbach from Ulrich Tengler's *Laienspiegel* (*Mirror of the Layman*), Augsburg, c. 1509, portrays a Jew with the mandatory badge on his sleeve, kneeling and placing a holy book on the ground, both forbidden practices (Ill. 3:17). It depicts the humiliating *More Judaico* (*According to Jewish Custom*), a ritual oath dating back to Christian courts perhaps as early as the fifth century and lingering in some areas until the nineteenth. Jews were often required to stand on a pig's skin, to wear nothing much more than a haircloth, and to solicit horrific punishments on themselves for swearing falsely in lawsuits with Christians: "May my descendants be cursed ... may I grope along the wall like a blind man ... may the earth open up and swallow me."

Another woodcut, in the form of a playing card by the German illustrator Hans Leonard Schauffelein, presented a Jewish seducer of a Christian woman. He appears to be on good terms with a pig, a badge, and a money purse, but the artist, not convinced that such details were sufficiently odious, made his point doubly clear by incorporating the symbol for the Two of Acorns, the least desirable card in the deck.

Brought on in part by such prints, a climate of foreboding spread across Protestant northern Europe. As religious upheavals, wars, and social and economic agitation intensified, sorcery, demonological notions, and the occult were increasingly evoked by credulous persons. Jews already had a reputation for magical arts, including fortune telling, amulets, love potions, and dybbuks. (Walter Scott condemned the lovely Jewess Rebecca to the pyre because her familiarity with unguents and herbs implied a knowledge of witchcraft; of course, it took a Christian knight, Ivanhoe, to retrieve her honor.)

The notorious manual *Pharetra catholicei fidei* (*Quiver of Catholic Faith*) described "worthless" Jews and other renegades as tools of Satan "repulsed of God." Such publications encouraged animism, hag-like nudity, and other infernal images as source material for artists. Hans Baldung Grien of Strasbourg was among the printmakers who were fascinated by the macabre and supernatural.

Ill. 3:15. *Judaeus Mercator Patavinus (Jewish Peddler of Padua),* 1594

Tashlich

Ill. 3:16. *Tashlich.* Woodcut, 1508. From *Libellus de Judaica Confessione (Confession of the Jews)*

Der ander tail

℃ Aber an enden da die judiſchait nicht wonhafft/noch die pücher
für zů brin gen ſein / mag man die vorberürten wort des gepotts in
hebreyſcher oder teütſcher ſprach/dem juden ſchriftlich oder mündt
lich fürlegen oder jn ſelbs laſſen verleſen.Sein hand darauf/oder
an ſein pruſt legen/vnd den ayd wie vor ſteet/thůn.

Ill. 3:17. *Der Ander Teil (The Other Part).* Woodcut by Hans Frutenbach. c. 1509. From *Laienspiegel (Mirror of the Layman)* by Ulrich Tengler

Ill. 3:18. *Jewish Moneylender and a German Peasant.* **Woodcut, 1531. From an edition of Cicero's** *De Officiis*

His woodcut *The Witches' Sabbath*, 1510, displays an assortment of symbolic paraphernalia scattered in the foreground, while an urn with mysterious markings belches out a malevolent brew. Some scholars have suggested that the writing was a form of pseudo–Hebrew relating to the juxtaposition of evil spirits and Jewish life. A faked knowledge of the Hebrew language was sometimes introduced in artworks, associating Jewish wisdom with magical powers.

Another derogatory woodcut from an edition of Cicero's *De Officiis* (*On Obligations*), 1531, depicted a Jewish moneylender and a German peasant with the borrower asking, "Please, Jew, give me cash against a promissory note and leave what I owe you to my judgment" (Ill. 3:18). The pseudo–Hebrew characters on the skirt of the Jew identify him for those unable to read the German caption, and reminds them that Jews grow rich from poor Christians. Although loan contracts were regulated by the local rulers and rates of interest were fixed, Jews had little or no recourse from conniving debtors.

Jost Amman, a facile and prolific woodcut artist working in Frankfort and Nuremberg, chose subject matter ranging from the Bible to the fable of Reynard the Fox. He illustrated the poet Hans Sachs' description of the various social classes and trades that constituted

Der Geltnarr.

Ein Geltnarr so werd ich genannt/
On ruh ift mein hertz/mund vnd hand/
Wie ich nur groß Gelt vnd Reichthumb
Vnverschempt liftig vberfumb/
Mit dem Jüdenfpieß thu ich lauffn/
Mit Wucher/dufffätzn vnd verfauffn/
Bin dcct darbey fehr genauw vnd farck/
Ich fpar das gut vnd fiiß das arg.

Ill. 3:19. *Der Geltnarr (The Money Fool).* Woodcut by Jost Amman. From *Eygentliche Beschreibung aller Stander auf Erden—aller Kunste und Handwerker (The Correct Description of All Ranks, Arts, and Trades on Earth)* by Hans Sachs, 1568

sixteenth-century life in *Eygentliche Beschreibung aller Stander auf Erden— aller Kunste und Handwerker (The Correct Description of All Ranks, Arts, and Trades on Earth)*, 1568. Among Amman's one hundred thirteen woodcuts is *Der Geltnarr (The Money Fool)*, in which a Jew grasps his money bags and turns away from an imploring petitioner, explaining "I practice [excessive] usury when I sell and make contracts" (Ill. 3:19). "It is not for nothing that I am called a Jew," reads yet another comment: "I lend only half the money against a pledge. And if the pawner cannot redeem it in time then I get that as well. In this way I ruin the loose-living mob that wants only to feast, to gorge, and to drink. Yet my trade does not diminish since I have many brothers just like me."

Other than Shahor, the names of only a few sixteenth century Jewish printmakers are known, but almost nothing of their work. Moses da Castellazzo, the son of German rabbi Abraham Sachs, was an Italian painter and printmaker who made biblical woodcuts for which he was awarded a copyright in Venice in 1521, but they have not been traced. Andrea Marelli, probably Jewish, worked in Rome from 1567 to 1572, where he is said to have published engravings for a Purim Megilla. David de Laude, the first known Italian Jewish engraver of whose prints we have a record, prepared large maps for Antonio Campi's *Cremona Fidelissim Citta (The Faithful City of Cremona)* in 1582. They are exceptionally well delineated, with an attractive foldout chart decorated with putti and calligraphy; portraits of famous personalities as well as of the ruling worthies of Milan enhance this historical record.

Woodcuts, at first the only means of producing inexpensive pictorial information, were capable of enormous numbers of impressions. But their inherent disadvantages—coarseness and general roughness of form—deterred connoisseurs who preferred hand-painted manuscripts. So when engravings and etchings were developed with the potential for more graceful forms, abundant detail, and the illusion of light and atmosphere, they tapped a new audience who

Ill. 3:20. *Bookplate for Wilibald Pirckheimer*. Woodcut, c. 1510. By Albrecht Dürer

believed they embodied a higher order of beauty. Woodcuts, despite their directness and imme-diacy, were demoted to secondary functions—more as folk art for the lower classes. (In twen-tieth century Germany they regained their status as prints of choice.)

While most illustrators were minor or anonymous craftsmen, a few of the leading artists in Germany and Italy discovered that printed images could be as memorable as paintings. When someone of the stature of Albrecht Dürer signed his prints with a distinctive mono-gram (and urged his wife to sell them at nearby fairs), he acknowledged their financial and artistic potential. He had learned engraving techniques from his father, and woodcutting from Michael Wohlgemut in whose studio he "suffered greatly" from fellow students. But he enjoyed a close relationship with Wilibald Pirckheimer, who was born to a noble family and educated as a gentleman's son. In about 1510, Dürer presented his friend with a woodcut bookplate declaring that "the beginning of wisdom is the fear of God," inscribed in the three languages of scholars, Hebrew, Latin, and Greek (Psalm 111:10) (Ill. 3:20). Bookplates provided a bit of immortality in a fragile world—a means for the literate classes to distinguish themselves from ordinary folks. Erasmus had called Pirckheimer "the chief glory of Germany." One of his glo-ries was the petition he signed to expel Nuremberg's Jews.

Among those influenced by Dürer was Hans Burgkmair the Elder, whose decorative prints borrowed classical Italian ele-ments. His woodcut *Die Drei Guten Juden* (*Three Good Jews*), 1516, was part of a series of nine notables (pagan, Jewish, and Christian), but the figures of Joshua, King David, and Judah Maccabee were secular interpre-tations of sixteenth century sol-diers. The ubiquitous medieval Jewish hat crowns Maccabee, the hero of the Chanukah story (Ill. 3:21).

Another of Dürer's disciples, Albrecht Altdorfer of Regens-burg, was a painter, printmaker, and builder. In his late thirties he became politically involved with the city's Outer Council and participated not only in the harassment and expulsion of its eight hundred Jews but oversaw the confiscation of the debts owed to them and the ruination of their synagogue because of an alleged disparagement of the Virgin. His architectural skills came in handy for an etching made at the time of its destruc-

Ill. 3:21. *Die Drei Guten Juden (Three Good Jews)*. Woodcut, 1516. By Hans Burgkmair the Elder

tion in 1519—*The Interior of the Regensburg Synagogue* (Ill. 3:22). An inscription noted that the devastation properly reflected God's will. For the first time in a print, a building is presented through the observant eyes of a working architect. The beautifully proportioned Romanesque columns enclosing an early Renaissance bimah and the rendering of lambent light and receding perspective infuse the etching with more than topical interest. The synagogue, which had served the Jews for about three hundred years, was torn down in two hours. Altdorfer then piously joined in the removal of its five thousand gravestones, some of which he used to pave the area around his home. When a workman who had been injured during the demolition unexpectedly recovered, a miracle was declared, calling for the erection of a church on the destroyed site. In its honor, Michael Ostendorfer, a local artist, designed the woodcut, *Pilgrimage to the Church of the Beautiful Virgin*, 1520. Disparaging the "superstitious" synagogue, he sketched in the broken remnants of Regensburg's once Jewish homes. Thousands of souvenirs citing the "victory against the Jews" were sold, including these memorial prints.

Ironically, in 1535, three years before he died, Altdorfer was ordered by the Council to carry a belated letter of contrition to Ferdinand I, the occasionally tolerant ruler of Austria, who had complained that the outrage against the Jews deprived him of their financial support. William Ivins, the first print curator at the Metropolitan Museum of Art, wrote in *Prints and Books*, 1971, that he would have liked to know Altdorfer "intimately and familiarly, since he was so obviously such a nice person.... One is sure of his gently whimsical attitude toward life ... and of the great tenderness that accompanied his comprehension of human motives." One man's tenderness is another's pain.

Other followers of Dürer were Hans Sebald Beham and his brother Barthel, known as the Little Masters because of the size of their engravings. Their themes, biblical, mythological, and allegorical, were large in scope, however. A woodcut bookplate attributed to Hans Sebald, *Coat of Arms of Hector Pomer*, 1525, was designed for the Nuremberg patrician with the inscription "To the pure all things are pure" in Hebrew,

Ill. 3:22. *Interior of the Regensburg Synagogue.* Etching, 1519. By **Albrecht Altdorfer**

Ill. 3:23. *Coat of Arms of Hector Pomer.* Woodcut, c. 1520. Attributed to Hans Sebald Beham

Latin, and Greek (Titus 1:15) (Ill. 3:23). Barthel's bookplate, 1530, for Hieronymus Baumgartner, Dürer's patron, reflects Ecclesiastes 3:1, "To everything there is a season," referring to the brevity of life.

The Hopfer family of Augsburg is credited with developing the technique of etching on paper from its earlier origins on armor and guns. Daniel Hopfer may have been the first to ink and print an etched plate even before 1513, the year of the earliest dated etching. In one of his prints a Jewish hat appears on a banner in a crucifixion scene. When symbols often spoke louder than words, it was immediately recognizable as a stereotype of the culpable people. An etched portrait by Daniel's son, Jerome, of a Wittenberg professor, Johann Boeschenstain, represents the sitter as a stern and resolute scholar (Ill. 3:24). Its Hebrew printed matter is drawn from the Psalms, "I will thank God as befits his Justice and will sing the name of the Lord most High" (7:18), a conventional enough invocation. But the remaining selection, "I know, oh Lord, that your rulings are just; rightly have you humbled me" (119:75), suggests tantalizing questions. What distressing act might have been responsible for those penitent lines?

A woodcut, *Christ at the Cross Adored by Paul Weidner and His Family,* 1559, is by Donat Hubschmann, a printmaker active in Leipzig and Vienna (Ill. 3:25). One would hardly guess that the subject, a physician and rector of Vienna University, was born Asher Judah ben Nathan Ashkenazi. Following his conversion to Catholicism in 1558, he wrote *Loca praecipua Fidei Christianae (Chief Texts of the Christian Faith)* to proclaim the validity of his adopted religion. The Renaissance cult of individuality was expressed by showing that, not only could a human being share a platform with the heavenly host, but that he could be depicted equal in size to his savior. However, God wasn't entirely displaced; His centrality was confirmed by the inclusion of a verse chosen from Isaiah in Latin and Hebrew—"For the Lord is our Judge, The Lord is our Lawgiver, The Lord is our King; He will save us" (33:22).

Having one's portrait taken whetted the appetite of Jews as well as of Christians since men and women persuaded themselves that posterity would be interested in how they looked. As a way of keeping memories of loved ones fresh, or as preserving images of individuals conspicuous for either good or bad, portraits were cherished and displayed. Jews had the problem of deciding whether or not portraiture defied the Second Commandment, but determined that since prints were not as pretentious as paintings nor as three-dimensional as sculptures, religious compliance could be sustained. Clothing was yet another element of close examination. The way people dressed—or were forced to dress—characterized who they were and how they lived. Jews could not always adapt their wardrobes to local standards; they had to contend with special rules mandated both by rabbinic and local authorities. Obligatory modest or conservative attire was imposed and the length of beards was regulated, with violations punishable by forfeiture of garments,

Ill. 3:24. *Johann Boeschenstain.* Etching, c. 1520. By Jerome Hopfer

Ill. 3:25. *Christ at the Cross Adored by Paul Weidner and His Family.* Woodcut, 1559. By Donat Hubschmann

Left: Ill. 3:26. *Der gelb geckl (The Yellow Fop).* Woodcut. *Right:* Ill. 3:27. *Medico guido (Jewish Doctor).* Etching, 1568. From *Les quatre premiers livres des navigations ... Orientales (The First Four Books of Oriental ... Navigations).* By H. de Nicolay

a hundred lashes, or loss of property. For his portrait, Jobst Mellern, a gentleman from Prague, decked himself out in a Jewish fur hat, a traditional sleeveless cloak bearing the Jewish hallmark, and a well-endowed money bag; he is clearly a bit vain of the total effect. The artist, with more than a touch of malice, inscribed the print *Der gelb geckl* (*The Yellow Fop*), indicating both cowardliness and affectation (Ill. 3:26).

Since Jews worked in trade and craft industries and occasionally served as influential diplomats, administrators, and honored physicians, illustrations in Christian books introduced more and more material about these interesting people to the general reader. The famous Sephardi physician Moses Hamon, whose patients included Sulayman the Magnificent, appeared in an etched portrait, *Medico guido* (*Jewish Doctor*) in the first illustrated book to include Ottoman Jewry, *Les quatre premiers livres des navigations ... Orientales* (*The First Four Books of Oriental ... Navigations*) by H. de Nicolay, 1568 (Ill. 3:27). Jews were credited with "exceeding all other nations [in] the knowledge which they have in language and letters, Greek, Arabian, Chaldee and Hebrew...." As a mark of royal esteem, Doctor Hamon was entitled to a red hat rather than the yellow turban which differentiated non–Muslims from Turks. *Donna guida d'Adrianopoli* (*Jewish Woman of Adrianople*), seen in the same book, was permitted to show a bit of hair, though otherwise her charms were well concealed (Ill. 3:28).

A small number of privileged *Hofjuden* or Court Jews, acting as advisers and bankers to central European princes, rose to high social and political positions. Most of them, like Lippold of Prague, a Jewish minter and court factor, served honorably as buffers between their own people and the nobles for whom they worked. When his protector, the elector Joachim II of Brandenburg, died suddenly, Lippold was accused of poisoning him, and was tortured until he "confessed." Whether he was actually guilty of murder was never established, but in the portrait engraving *Execution of Lippold*, 1573, he is drawn and quartered in the presence of an enthusiastic crowd after refusing conversion (Ill. 3:29). As a collective punishment, Jews were then banished from the city. A portrait of the unhappy victim quietly and sadly contemplating his fate was included at the bottom of the print. It is unlikely that he was comforted by the heavenly presences of Justice and Moses keeping an eye on the ax man's grisly work.

The converso physician Amatus Lusitanus had a very different memorial. A portrait engraving indicating his dignity and

Right: Ill. 3:28. *Donna guida d'Adrianopoli (Jewish Woman of Adrianople)*, 1568. From *Les quatre premiers livres des navagations ... Orientales (The First Four Books of Oriental ... Navagations)*. By H. de Nicolay. *Below:* Ill. 3:29. Detail from *Execution of Lippold*. Engraving, 1573

prestige was conveyed by a profile image and Roman toga-like cloak (Ill. 3:30). Amatus, originally from Portugal, moved to Antwerp in 1533 following threats against the Jewish community. He was appointed to the faculty at the University of Ferrara, became a practicing Jew,

turned down an offer to serve as court physician to the king of Poland, and attended Julius III, the pope who had sanctioned the burning of the Talmud in 1553. He was a medical adviser to several monasteries, and a famed writer on anatomy, internal medicine, and emotional illnesses. After the election of the anti–Jewish pope Paul IV in 1555, he was arrested, fled to Muslim Salonika stripped of "my gold, silver, royal clothing, and, most important, my library and manuscripts." There he was remembered with the lines, "He who so often recalled the breath well-nigh gone from the dying, and was, therefore, beloved by kings and people, lies far from the land of his birth...."

Not all doctors received such gracious encomiums. Roderigo Lopez, the Portuguese New Christian physician to Queen Elizabeth, had the honor of sitting for the

Above: Ill. 3:30. *Amatus Lusitanus.* Engraving, c. 1555. *Below:* Ill. 3:31. *A Thankfull Remembrance of God's Mercie.* Engraving, 1594

first portrait to be engraved in England, but esteem turned to disgrace when he was accused by the Earl of Essex of attempting to poison the sovereign. It was once thought that Shakespeare had Lopez in mind for the character of Shylock, although Lopez's fate was even more unhappy than that of the moneylender: He was hung, drawn, and quartered in 1594, proclaiming, it is said, that he loved the queen "as well as he loved Jesus Christ." The crowd had the last word: "He is a Jew!" Though he meddled in areas outside his field of expertise, history has since acquitted him of the treachery. But not everyone was convinced of his innocence. George Carleton, Bishop of Chichester, affixed the doleful Latin caption, "Traitors end on the rope," to another portrait of the physician in *A Thankfull Remembrance of God's Mercie* (Ill. 3:31). Medical careers could be more perilous for practitioners than for their patients.

The sixteenth century was a period like many others, of splendor and prosperity coexisting with inglorious war and degrading clashes of religious faith. The proliferation of bigotry and of unsavory texts and pictures was acutely painful to the Jewish community, but it surely found immense satisfaction in the ready and almost unlimited access to their sacred books— fastidiously edited and beautifully printed.

4

The Seventeenth Century:
The Old World and the New

European history in the seventeenth century can readily be split down the middle. It was dominated in its first half by the Thirty Years' War (1618–1648), the culmination of religious dissensions that originated a hundred years earlier with the Reformation. In its second half, it introduced a prodigious development of art and literature, witnessed the fragmentation of the German states, the rise of absolutism, and another round of hostilities. It pitted Protestants against Catholics in an unholy struggle that left both sides in ruin and changed almost nothing at all. Europe remained divided, with each side hell-bent to rid the world of popery or heresy. The last war to be begun over theological issues, it was the first to be ended by a secular assembly that shook off Church jurisdiction.

France survived the war moderately well, flowering and fading under Louis XIV. In his pursuit of glory, the king confused the glitter of his court with the radiance of the planets; he became *le Roi Soleil*, and left his stamp for better or worse on all of Europe. Hoping to extend France's boundaries, regulate protectionist tariffs, and overcome Dutch trade advantages, he invaded Holland in 1672. In desperation, the Dutch opened the dikes and flooded the land. France was forced to withdraw. When Louis finally realized that his wars were destroying the country and that Europe had turned against him, he became resigned to peace, and in 1697 concluded a humiliating treaty with Holland, Spain, and England. He lived on until 1715, securing the Spanish throne for his grandson, but sacrificing a million lives along the way and losing control of the seas. The Sun King had set.

In perversity or folly, he had called for indictments against Protestant Huguenots and expulsion of France's forty thousand Jews. His mercantilist minister Jean Baptiste Colbert successfully argued that the latter would be a dangerous option because "commerce is almost entirely in Jewish hands," and that economic advantages should supersede religious prejudices. As a devout Catholic Louis desperately wanted to convert the powerful Protestant minority whose political and religious strength and power he feared. Outside of France, however, he was tolerant to the Jews in the French Caribbean Islands when in 1671 he advised its governor, M. de Baas: "Having learned that the Jews who have settled in Martinique and in the other islands where my subjects live have had considerable expenses for the cultivation of the land, and that they are still usefully defending their towns, I write to inform you that I wish them to enjoy the same privileges as others there; they are to be given full freedom of conscience." He was careful to add that, of course, they must not offend the local Catholics.

Jews in Bayonne and Bordeaux in southwest France had already been granted the right to live there, although most of them soon dropped their ties to Judaism. Jews in the Lorraine area lived there legally after 1648, the first time since 1394 when they were expelled by Charles VI that they were accorded the privilege. Grateful for their contributions to commerce and trade, the government allowed them to regulate their own religious institutions and even welcomed them as agents to reverse the economic decline. Nevertheless, their conditions were troublesome—land ownership, tax relief, and membership in Christian guilds were favors earned chiefly through bribery. However, Jewish guilds began to provide opportunities for their own members—with the stipulation that half an hour each day would be spent learning to write.

While the continent was wrestling with religious and military adventurism, England was developing a parliamentary system of government. Queen Elizabeth died in 1603 after a reign that produced Shakespeare, commercial expansion, and naval superiority. She had ruled with a headstrong power that postponed but could not avoid civil war. By mid-century, Calvinists (in England called Puritans), and members of the Church of England (known to lean to Catholicism), were battling over religious and political issues as well as control of Church wealth; the Catholics supported the king while the Puritans supported Parliament, which Charles I had arbitrarily bypassed. Parliament rebelled. Charles insisted on his divine rights. In 1649, he paid with his head for his recalcitrance.

His death was followed by the eleven-year rule of Oliver Cromwell, who restored the country to power by suppressing challenges from Ireland and Scotland and engaging in a successful war with the Dutch, but he undermined its health through religious and moral despotism. He united the Puritan government under the stern principles of the Hebrew Bible, permitted Catholics to hold services but only in their own homes, and facilitated the resettlement of Jews who had not lived there openly for over three hundred years: "They are people," he said, "who God chose and to whom He gave His law." But his motivation was their ultimate conversion; as he pointed out, Christians couldn't preach to the Jews "if we will not tolerate them among us." He was aware, of course, that the few New Christians secretly living in England could, together with their Dutch co-religionists, draw trade away from his bitter rival, Holland. The possibility of their return, however, unleashed the usual talk of Jewish lust for Christian blood, of plans to convert the populace, and of Jewish encroachment on England's commerce.

Fear of Jews was pervasive. William Hole's woodcut of a knife-wielding Jew, on much the same mission as Shylock, appeared in Thomas Coryat's travel book *Crudities*, 1611 (Ill. 4:1). "Fly from the Jews, lest they circumcise thee" reads the inscription. (The "pound of flesh" was a common euphemism for genitals.) The distinguished printmaker, William Faithorne, upon hearing that incoming Jews would purchase

Ill. 4:1. "Fly from the Jews, lest they circumcise thee." Woodcut by William Hole, 1611. From *Crudities* by Thomas Coryat

St. Paul's Cathedral, warned of the danger in his 1656 engraving of Cromwell's chaplain, Hugh Peters, a defender of Jewish interests. He included the church in the background, together with the derisive caption "Let [rent] it out to ye Jews."

In 1660, the English, finally tired of the overdose of asceticism and a "godly" England, restored the monarchy under "Merrie" Charles II, initiating a period of frenzied hedonism as well as intellectual zest. Charles remembered the Jews who had helped him to return and whom he viewed as a bulwark against Protestant incursions. After 1664, when he permitted them open residency, the community felt secure enough to appoint its first rabbi and optimistic enough to pursue avenues for increased social and political equality. But once again the Jews were accused of disrupting economic development at home, as well as upsetting the balance of trade between England and her American colonies, where, it was believed, they had formed a conspiracy to appropriate the tobacco market. Cooler heads, mindful of Jewish financial usefulness, ignored the charges and granted them religious freedom. In 1685, James II became king, but the people, alienated by his Catholicism, demanded a sober Protestantism. Parliament deposed James four years later and imported William and Mary from Holland to share the throne, thus assuring a Protestant dynasty to England. The move was made possible thanks in part to a no-interest loan of two million florins from Isaac Suasso, a Dutch Jew. In 1694, that money helped to finance a coalition against France. A balance of power now prevailed in Europe.

While England was mending itself, Germany was sinking from the mayhem of the war. It lagged in literature and science (Leibniz was the exception), led in superstition and witch burning, lost its land-based traffic to Portugal's ocean-going routes, and watched helplessly as its neighbors, backed by national monarchies, gained control of the Baltic trade. The Holy Roman Empire was in shambles as over three hundred chopped-up states declared their own sovereignty. Protestants and Catholics, about equally divided in numbers, were united in mutual distrust of Jews whom they blamed for the economic decline and viewed as foreign elements despite their lengthy residence in the area. Particularly in the first half of the century, Jews suffered from impoverishment, forced emigrations, Christian sermons, and punitive taxes to support standing armies and military campaigns. Their few rights were circumscribed, their every activity, from walking and talking to buying and selling, dictated by city fathers.

The tensions between upper-class German families and the heavily Jewish lower-class tradesmen provided the spark that enabled Vincent Fettmilch, a disgruntled pastry cook, to persuade local guild members and small merchants to purge Frankfort of its four thousand Jews. During synagogue services in August, 1614, he and his followers attacked the Judengasse (Jewish quarter), compelling the women and children to find refuge in the cemetery. For two days, pillaging and looting were uncontrolled. Some thirteen hundred victims were rounded up, their property was destroyed, debts owed them were canceled, they were escorted to the gates of the city, and expelled. Hundreds of books and Jewish ceremonial objects were confiscated or lost in spite of ransoms that had been paid for their protection; very few have survived. The chaos had a crippling impact on Hebrew and Yiddish publishing. It took two years to restore order and permit the central government to seize control from the "Commission of Citizens." Although Fettmilch, who styled himself as the "New Haman," met the same fate as the Old Haman, many restrictions against the Jews persisted.

The incident attracted wide attention. *The Plunder of the Ghetto Following the Fettmilch Riots,* an etching by H. Merian, found its way into J.L. Gottfried's *Historische Chronica* in 1642, a topic still of interest twenty-eight years after the fact (Ill. 4:2). Other prints of the time depicted "many injuries sustained by both sides," or showed a crowd in the town square giving its undivided attention to the execution of Fettlmilch and his associates. But bad as it was, it signaled a new attitude—the perpetrators were disciplined. The Jews were indulged because

Ill. 4:2. *Plunder of the Ghetto Following the Fettmilch Riots*. Etching by H. Merian, 1642. From *Historische Chronica* by J. L. Gottfried

of their trading connections in Europe and the Indies, and valued because they enriched the culture, supported the area's growing capitalism, and enabled cities, such as Fürth and Frankfort, to rival the best of the Empire.

Nevertheless, whenever Jewish affairs threatened Christian interests, Jewish life was not a healthful choice. Among those who had settled in Austria was Franz Engelberger, a Jewish embezzler who had converted to Christianity in hopes of winning a pardon. He later retracted his testimony, claimed that he desecrated the Host, and asked to die as a Jew. A Viennese mob would have none of it. A 1642 engraving shows him strung up by the heels and stoked over a flame for retracting his conversion. A second victim is dragged to the ax, while a third is about to meet his end on a gibbet.

In 1670, the wise Elector of Brandenburg offered a few dozen rich Jews the privilege of settling in Berlin in order to enhance the economy. At about the same time, the unwise Austrian emperor, Leopold I, decided to placate his Spanish-born wife, who believed that heaven had punished them with the loss of their first child for tolerating a Jewish presence. He then capped a long history of abuse by expelling his Jews and relieving himself of debts owed them. He swore never to readmit them, but was unprepared for the disorder that followed. Strapped for hard cash, he renounced his oath, swallowed his pride, and extended an invitation to moneylenders and financiers such as Samuel Oppenheimer to return as Court Jews. These privileged individuals were exempted from laws against usury, permitted to live outside the Jewish quarter, to discard the hated Jewish badge, and to dress quite like any Christian gentleman, as Oppenheimer's portrait, engraved by I. A. Pfeffel and C. Engelbrecht in 1690, demonstrated (Ill. 4:3). Oppenheimer reorganized the banking system and raised enough capital to wage a successful war against Turkey's Muslim forces. In gratitude, Leopold permitted the printing of the Talmud in 1695. Money talked.

Spain was handicapped by demented kings. The country had long since been emptied of Jews, but that didn't stop the government from delivering more than two dozen Judaizers to the stake. Portugal's Inquisition was even harsher. Hundreds of New Christians were burned in person or in effigy, thousands were "reconciled" with various penalties or fled to other parts of the world where mistreatment was usually limited to curbs on political and economic activities.

During much of this period, all manner of tracts, commentaries, and kabbalistic books were imported from Venice and Amsterdam to eastern European centers where they supplied yeshivot with the means to raise rabbinical education to high levels. But Torah and Talmud were no protection against violence. For three years, beginning in 1648, Jews faced a disaster as great as any they had known since the Iberian expulsions and Inquisition. Cossack mobs led by Bogdan Chmielnicki terrorized Catholic Polish and

Ill. 4:3. *Samuel Oppenheimer.* Engraving, 1690. By I. A. Pfeffel and C. Engelbrecht

Lithuanian landlords and clergy and their Jewish agents and leaseholders who had been employed as stewards and tax collectors; entire Polish communities faced utter ruin. Over seventy-five thousand Jews were massacred or reduced to serfdom, a quarter of the population in that part of the world. Witnesses described the slaughter of children in front of their parents and the suturing of live cats in the bellies of pregnant women. Invasions by Russian and Swedish forces obliterated much of what was left of Polish-Lithuanian Jewry. Refugees fled west, permanently reversing their eastward direction and substantially enlarging their presence in Germany, western Europe, and eventually in America.

The tragedies intensified interest in sixteenth century eschatological themes as well as in mid–seventeenth century kabbalist prophecies that predicted the imminent arrival of the Messiah and the return of the scattered Remnant to the Holy Land. Many an unhappy and beleaguered Jewish family, convinced that the horrors they experienced were proof of an impending apocalypse, dreamed that the Redemption was close at hand. It only remained for the gifted and personally charming, but psychologically unstable, thirty-nine-year-old Shabbatai Zvi to seize the public credulity in 1665, declare that he indeed was the Redeemer, ready to light the way—a way that had been prepared by Nathan of Gaza, who settled on Shabbatai as its incarnation. An engraving, *King of the Jews,* by Johannes Meyfsens, featured the redeemer's splendid mustache and a feather in his cap (Ill. 4:4).

Although condemned by some community leaders for challenging rabbinic jurisdiction, rejecting parts of religious beliefs, and some Torah laws, Shabbatai successfully mobilized

Le Vray Portraict de SABETHA SEBI Roy des Juifs n... n la ville de Smirne en Asie augé de 40 Ans

Ill. 4:4. *Shabbatai Zvi, King of the Jews.* **Engraving, c. 1665. By Johannes Meyfsens**

thousands of impassioned adherents from among all classes of Jews—including large numbers of conversos—who believed in his mission to release divine sparks from sin and heal the world. Betting houses and stockbrokers took odds on the validity of his claims. Gifts were lavished on him. Benedictions were printed in his honor as he wandered from the Turkish port city of Smyrna (Izmir) where he was born, to Salonika, Cairo, and into Jerusalem. His claims of mystical intuition even led some Christians who placed their faith in the Zohar to conclude that a miraculous revelation would occur in 1665 when he would return to Jerusalem (where the Messiah was scheduled to make his first appearance), and proclaim the approach of the Redemption. An engraving, *Shabbatai Zvi, The Great Betrayer and False Messiah, King of the Jews,* in *Tikun ha-Keriah,* a 1666 Dutch prayer book, recorded him enthroned in grandeur, guarded by lions, protected by an angelic host, exuding royal authority with all the panoply accorded to divinity, and entertaining his followers with royal prodigality (Ill. 4:5). In the colophon, the publisher, David de Castro Tartes, established the date as the first year in the new era. Shabbetai apparently never doubted that the Sultan of Turkey (and ruler of Palestine) would be dethroned, after which he planned to conduct all of Israel to the Promised Land. Instead, his popularity so alarmed the Turkish court that he was shackled by arms and legs and stowed in a castle to contemplate his indiscretions. Other prints showed him being crowned with a laurel wreath and anointing his disciples; depending on one's politics, they were sneered at or lovingly passed from hand to hand. Offered the option of death or conversion to Islam, he considered the alternatives and chose the latter. Surfacing publicly as Aziz Mehmed Effendi, and graced with a fourth wife, he took up his new duties as royal doorkeeper. Reviled by many for steering Jews to Mohammed, he was revered by others as a martyr who alone understood God's mysteries.

The anguish of most Jewish communities predictably resulted in apostasy, spiritual disintegration, and a turn to "authoritative" Hasidism in the next century.

On the whole, Turkish Jews had a relatively autonomous and comfortable existence although as non–Muslims they paid excessive taxes. They developed well-organized banking, trading, military and tax brokering interests following the Spanish and Portuguese influx. Although Jewish women were criticized for ostentatious display of jewelry and clothing, nothing kept the Jewess in la Chapelle's mid-century engraving from proudly displaying her finery (Ill. 4:6). She dwarfs Istanbul in the background, an indication of the secure and self-esteeming life deemed possible in the Ottoman Empire at the time. But by 1683, Turkey had lost its preeminence through disastrous wars and a stumbling economy, and Jewish life suffered from renewed intolerance and the loss of its important publishing houses.

Ill. 4:5. *Shabbatai Zvi, the Great Betrayer and False Messiah, King of the Jews.* Engraving, 1666. From *Tikun ha-Keriah (Dutch Prayer Book)*

The sense of well-being in other communities, however, was aided by the proliferation of treasured Hebrew and Yiddish books, although Jews were hampered or prohibited from securing licenses. Among the lucky publishers were the sons of Abraham Ashkenazi of Damascus, who, in 1605 and 1606, were able to print the first three books of the Bible. In 1661, the Athias firm in Amsterdam engaged Johannes Leusden, a Calvinist professor of Hebrew, together with a Jew, Samuel de Cazeres, to edit a Spanish translation of the Bible in order to familiarize Spanish Marranos with their heritage. It had originally been printed in 1553 in Ferrara by Abraham Usque, but it evidently was still necessary, after one hundred and eight years, to continue their re-education and to encourage their studies of post-biblical Judaism. In 1679, Athias' translation of the Bible into Yiddish was welcomed by the Ashkenazim. A decade earlier, Isaac ben Judah

Ill. 4:6. *Jewess*. Engraving by la Chapelle, c. 1650

Loeb Yuedels of Prague had received permission to operate a Hebrew publishing company in Sulzbach, which issued many well-received books, including the Zohar, 1684, and a Machzor, 1699. The press functioned until the mid–nineteenth century.

Most publishing houses that printed Hebrew books were owned by Christians. Bibles, commentaries, grammars, and philosophical texts such as Johannes Buxtorf the Elder's anti–Jewish *Synagoga Judaica*, 1603, revived charges that Jews had been well-poisoners; the presumption of their guilt still hung over their descendants. He attempted to discourage the Protestant perception of Judaism as authentically biblical, commenting that Jewish practices were illogical, superstitious, and unethical. He included an engraving of a Jew swearing an oath, his right hand on a Hebrew Bible and his feet on a dead pig (Ill. 4:7). The German Hebraist and master of Yiddish, Johannes Christoph Wagenseil, apparently was sincere in wishing to protect Jews from forced baptisms and charges of ritual murder, but nevertheless wrote anti–Jewish tracts and demanded conversions. His *Tele Ignea Satanae* (*Fiery Darts of Satan*) in 1681, featured anti–Christian works by Jewish authors and exhorted rabbis to leave scholarly research to those better qualified—Christians.

One area in which Gentiles and Jews shared a mutual interest was having their portraits taken, preferably while they were alive, or to be remembered by their friends after they were gone. The posthumous image of the Christian scholar, Simon de Muis, professor of Jewish history and literature at the Royal College of Paris, was engraved in 1649 by Michel Lasne, one of the best artists money could buy (Ill. 4:8). He focused on the dignity, richness of tone,

Ill. 4:7. *Jew Swearing an Oath.* Engraving, 1603. From *Synagoga Judaica* by Johannes Buxtorf the Elder

and depiction of character that exemplified seventeenth century French portraiture. "Who is like him as a teacher?" reads the Hebrew inscription. "Happy is the man who has lived with the Torah, guiding his pupils towards the creator. He has passed away, but his teachings go on."

In Italy, Jews continued to face persecution and expulsions, occasionally mitigated by bribes. Yet, they were fortunate, particularly in the port cities of Pisa and Livorno (Leghorn) where their merchants were tolerated, and in their relatively easy economic association with the Christian population. Venice's synagogues drew many Christian visitors who were surprised by the simple facades (possibly to discourage looters), but were astonished by the magnificent interiors. While ghetto life was often degrading, the community not only took pride in these temples but in their fine printed books as well. A 1603 Haggadah tackled a problem inherited from the earlier Prague and Mantuan examples of 1526—how to depict an almost naked lady and still remain within the bounds of decorum. A personification of sinful Jerusalem "playing the harlot" unfortunately experienced a noticeable indignity. Beset by prudish or unappreciative connoisseurs, the editors removed her breasts, presenting her as a him, although the text clearly refers to a full-bodied woman: "Thou did increase and grow up, and achieved excellent beauty: thy breasts were fashioned and thy hair grown; yet thou was naked and bare" (Ezekiel 16:7).

Another unique image, also not dependent on the Prague model, was the 1609 Venetian Haggadah. A glimpse into an Egyptian bedroom illustrated the touching Midrash of a couple who remained apart so as not to conceive children during the time when Pharaoh ordered the drowning of newborn boys (Ill. 4:9). Among its other attractions were decorative architectural borders, modishly dressed Seder participants in thirteen little genre pictures indicating the order

מִי כָּמוֹהוּ
מוֹרֶה

אַשְׁרֵי הָאִישׁ שֶׁלּוֹ תוֹרָה   הָיְתָה תָּמִיד כְּחַיּוֹת חוֹרָה
מוֹרֶה תַלְמִידָיו לְנָצְרָה   עָלֶיהָ פַּת נַם־נִשְׁמְרָה

of the Passover service, and depictions of the Ten Plagues, making an appearance in a Haggadah for the first time. Giovanni da Gara printed it for the Jewish publisher Israel ben David Zifroni, who may also have prepared its woodcuts. With unprecedented Ladino, Judeo-Italian, and Yiddish translations (printed in Hebrew characters), it was readily accessible to each community. Having sold out rapidly, it was followed by a second edition twenty years later with Rabbi Leone da Modena's explanatory remarks, pointing out that while "it already includes pictures to delight the eye, how much better it is now to include commentaries to delight the spirit." One of thirty-seven known Haggadot printed in the seventeenth century, its initial letters contained depictions of the Four Sons: The Wise Child studies a religious tract—a lamb at his side suggests his peaceful and settled judgment; the youngest son simply plays with his hobby horse, too young to be concerned with the proceedings. The

Above: Ill. 4:8. *Simon de Muis.* Engraving, 1649, by Michael Lasne. *Below:* Ill. 4:9. *"Egyptian" Bedroom.* Woodcut, 1609. *Venetian Haggadah*

Haggadah established a Venetian format that remained essentially unchanged for a hundred and fifty years. Unfortunately, it was the last hurrah of Italian Hebrew book production. Hebrew publishing became a victim of censorship and mutilation. Because Jewish printers elsewhere were better able to provide complete or unexpurgated editions, the great current of Venetian Jewish printing dwindled to a trickle, barely surviving until 1810, when even the trickle dried up.

Venice's Sephardim adopted somewhat freer approaches to rituals than their Ashkenazi brothers who remained under the more rigid influence of their German-born rabbis. Among those who carved out a more liberal attitude was the offbeat Modena, who started out as a child prodigy and grew up to be a silver-tongued rabbi and renowned scholar. His sermons charmed Jew and Gentile alike, but his compulsive gambling exasperated the authorities almost to the point of excommunication. He settled his losses at the card table or betting parlor whenever his oratorical skills brought in enough small change; denouncing his vices in public, he continued to indulge them in private. Yet his sins were fewer than his misfortunes, for he supported a widowed daughter, cared for an insane wife, and outlived four of his five children—one, a teenager, was hanged for teasing Christian neighbors.

He chronicled his hard times in *Hayye Yehuda* (*Life of Judah*). Not only his personal history but much of what is known about Italian Jewish life in the waning years of the Renaissance can be found in his autobiography, a rare undertaking in his generation. Somehow, he found the time to serve as director of a music and drama academy, teacher, author, editor, translator, proofreader of Hebrew works, bookseller, merchant, and a variety of other activities. His *Historia de'riti hebraici* (*History of Jewish Rites*), 1637, was the first important book by a Jewish author to present the Jewish tradition to Christians, and was meant to "defend my poor much oppressed nation," and help readers resist the Buxdorf's polemics. Commissioned by an English nobleman for presentation to King James I of England, who was interested in comparative religion, it alternately attacked and defended rabbinic Judaism and Jewish superstitious beliefs. Because he worried about censorship at home, he chose to publish the *Riti* in Paris; he revised it in 1638 in a Venice edition, but "there were still a few things in it which I was afraid might not find favor with Christians." The book contained "four or five forcible expressions which the Inquisition had forbidden to be uttered, or even written or printed. I cried aloud in terror that all Jews would suffer for it if the material became known in Rome.... But Gaffarelli [a scholar who had charge of printing the manuscript in France] had been careful to strike out the passages I had feared...." It was not an idle fear. Three years earlier, his grandson and two associates had been "thrown into a dark dungeon and the house sealed up" for printing another of his books, *Bait Judah* (*House of Judah*), an indiscretion which had been reported to officers of the Inquisition. "After fifteen days of effort they were permitted to go out from darkness to light, but kept in the prison where they remained for sixty-six days, and I came daily in great distress and incurred great expense. Finally, by God's mercy, they were acquitted by the Criminal Court." The printing business in Italy was no place for the faint-hearted.

The *Riti* was translated into Latin, Dutch, English, German, and French. The title page introduced him bare-headed because, he explained, head coverings were neither rabbinicly nor talmudicly mandated (Ill. 4:10). Most Jews, he noted, only adopted that custom as a perceived sign of respect. Gossips murmured that he held a dim view of many Orthodox traditions. He would have been pleased to know that his judgments helped to lay the foundations for the Enlightenment of the eighteenth and nineteenth centuries, but in his epitaph he expressed the bitter conviction that he would soon be forgotten: "Here he lies buried, hidden and lost."

A Dutch version of the book, *Kerk-Zeeden send Gewoonten die huiden in gebruik Zijn onder di Jooden* (*Customs in Use Among the Jews*), 1683, was illustrated with four engravings by a Christian artist, Jan Luykens. Among its scenes is the halitzah ceremony, *Weigering van des*

Broeders Weduwe te Trouwen (*Refusal of Marriage by a Man to His Brother's Childless Widow*) (Ill. 4:11). This procedure, meant as a public humiliation, takes place when a brother-in-law refuses to marry his brother's widow so that she may bear children and carry on the family name. The widow spits on the ground and removes the unwilling gentleman's shoe while reciting "so shall be done to the man who will not build his brother's house."

While dislocations all over Europe had created extraordinary upheavals for everyone, with time almost everyone was able to rebuild from the rubble. Jews, however, did not always have that option, and when their backs were against the precipice, they did what they had often

Ill. 4:10. *Rabbi Leone da Modena.* **Engraving, 1637. From** *Historia de'riti hebraici (History of Jewish Rites)*

Ill. 4:11. *Halitzah Ceremony.* Engraving by Jan Luykens, 1683. From *Kerk-Zeeden send Gewoonten die huiden in gebruik Zijn onder di Jooden (Customs in Use Among the Jews)*

done before—they gathered their families and goods and moved to more hospitable areas. Time and politics were on their side when they found toleration in Amsterdam. Because of its high level of tolerance as well as its access to secular and rabbinic learning, Amsterdam was viewed as the "The New Israel," opening its borders in unprecedented generosity not only to the urbane conversos from Spain and Portugal, but, following the Chmielnicki massacres in 1648, to their less sophisticated and impoverished cousins from eastern Europe. The city developed a unique and respectful relationship with its Jews, even acquiring a Jewish nickname, *Makeem* (*The Place.*) For a while, there was friction between the Sephardi and Ashkenazi refugees. They dressed differently, spoke differently, ate differently, and prayed separately. But the community soon obliged both groups; in 1675, the first Jewish newspaper, the Ladino language *Gazetta de Amsterdam*, reported general international items. It was followed by the Yiddish *Dinstagishe und Fraytagishe Kuranten*, 1686 and 1687, carrying specific Jewish news.

The Protestant Dutch declared themselves the "spiritual descendants of the ancient Israelites," reverently crediting their good fortune to divine intercession. This proved to be of great benefit to the Jews in Holland's larger cities, where they received favorable treatment. Freedom of trade and industry as well as certain privileges were accorded, but sexual relations with Christians and printing the Talmud were prohibited. Although Jews were still barred from all professions other than medicine and were not admitted to the guilds, within fifty years the financial competence of the Sephardim was such that the king of Denmark tried to lure them with offers of greater religious freedom. But they honored their debt to the Dutch and used their substantial interests in the Dutch West India and Dutch East India Companies to snatch some of the Indian trade from the Portuguese fleet. That bonus helped propel Holland to world leadership in trade and finance, as well as in the tobacco, diamond, and printing industries.

Societal differences in Holland produced a rabbi very different from the Italian Leone da Modena. Whereas a secular Renaissance tradition had encouraged religious deviation in Modena, Manasseh ben Israel, born into a Portuguese New Christian family, was content to stay within conventional Jewish systems of belief. He and his parents had fled Lisbon's Inquisition for Amsterdam's liberal environment where, at age seventeen, he wrote his first work, an unpublished Hebrew grammar, *Safah Berurah* (*A Clear Diction*). At eighteen, he was already widely respected in both Jewish and Christian circles, and his lectures, which he could deliver in several languages, were attracting broad audiences. No less a dignitary than Queen Henrietta Marie of England had made a point of stopping by his synagogue in 1642, where she allowed that she was charmed by his sermon, composed expressly in her honor.

At twenty-two, he founded the first Hebrew press run by a Jew in Amsterdam, proudly establishing his "independence of Bomberg." He was active from 1627 to 1655, publishing over seventy works in five languages, many directed at non–Jewish readers. Amsterdam, the wealthiest city in Europe, reigned as the Jewish book capital of the world for the next two hundred years, supplying texts as far away as America and India. However, even in that benevolent community, undercurrents of anti–Jewish feelings persisted, particularly in the narrow Calvinist establishment, where the Church council in 1651 prohibited Manasseh from printing his books in the Dutch language because they would offend pious Christians.

Ill. 4:12. Joseph Delmedigo. Engraving by Willem Delff, 1629. From *Sefer Elim*

Manasseh's new typefaces and his inclusion of authors' portraits were well received and emulated by other publishers. Among his popular works was the *Sefer Elim*, 1629, describing a place where the Israelites camped on their way to Sinai. Its thirty-seven-year-old author was Joseph Delmedigo, whose haggard face was engraved for the frontispiece by Willem Delff (Ill. 4:12). The book, with numerous astronomical and mathematical illustrations, was unique in Hebrew scientific work before the modern period. It was written as a response to a series of questions posed by a Karaite, Zerah ben Nathan of Troki, who, in common with members of his sect, rejected the Oral Law. Delmedigo, who was suspected of moving dangerously close to heresy, applied his reasoning as mathematician, physician, rabbi, pupil of Galileo, literary critic and skeptic, to the reconciliation of science and faith. He accused "ignorant" rabbis of neglecting secular education, derided printers who neglected the best classics in favor of current works, and criticized contemporary authors whose wretched literary styles, he declared, consisted mainly of recycling each other's ideas.

In 1645, Manasseh printed the first fully illustrated Hebrew book in the Netherlands, Isaac Tyrnau's *Minhagim*, a compilation of religious rites and customs featuring traditional images. But in spite of his success as a publisher, his overriding passion was to hasten the arrival of the messianic age and to resettle a professing Jewish community in England. Almost four hundred years had passed since their expulsion, years that included the spectacular cultural growth of the Elizabethan period, the defeat of the Spanish Armada and consequent supremacy of British sea power, the challenge to divine right over which Charles I lost his throne and his head, and the era of Oliver Cromwell.

In a letter to the Lord Protector of England, Manasseh shrewdly pointed out that the prophecies in Deuteronomy 28:64 and Isaiah 11:12 precluded the return of the Messiah until the dispersion of the Jews had reached "from one corner of the earth to the other." Since England was synonymous with "corner of the world" (Angle-Terre), the Second Coming awaited only the admission of Jews. Manasseh had been impressed by reports of a Portuguese New Christian merchant, Antonio de Montezinos, that an Indian guide in South America had identified himself as a descendant of the biblical tribe of Reuben. If the lost Ten Tribes of Israel had indeed surfaced in the New World, then surely it was Manasseh's duty to inform the English government that the arrival of the Kingdom of God was imminent, and only its intransigence was holding up the event. To that end, the rabbi composed the *Esperança de Israel* (*Hope of Israel*) in 1650, had it translated into English, dedicated it to Parliament, reminded its members that God and the world were watching, and, at Cromwell's invitation, betook himself to London in 1655. He reminded the Council of State in his *Humble Address* that the fourth quarter of the earth had yet to readmit Jews who would be an asset to the country.

The religious potential of the rabbi's theories should have been irresistible to the millenarian Puritans who assumed that the Jews would finally acknowledge Jesus. While the Protestant emphasis on the Hebrew Bible led to greater sympathy for the Jews, the monetary advantages that they secured to the Dutch were certainly not overlooked. The economic clout of the small number of New Christians who had secretly settled in England was known to be impressive. Yet the council's response was to rehash tales of Jewish lust for Christian blood, to charge that Jews would attempt to convert the populace, encroach on England's commerce, and take over the churches.

Manasseh had attempted a rationale to overcome such fears in his *Vindiciae Judaeorum* (*Vindication of the Jews*) published in 1656, but he died soon after, unaware that Cromwell would bypass Parliament—and public opinion—and permit the Jews to quietly, but unofficially, return. The resettlement did not attract the large numbers anticipated by Manasseh, but nevertheless, it was mostly free of intolerance and allowed the establishment of a cemetery and a Sephardi congregation in Creechurch Lane in 1657. When the community outgrew that building, it moved to Bevis Marks where an elegant structure was dedicated in 1701. A number of Ashkenazi Jews from Amsterdam, Poland, and Germany organized their own synagogue in 1690 in Duke's Place at the east end of the city; it was later known as the Great Synagogue. (In 1941 it was destroyed by German bombs.) About five hundred Jews, many of them impoverished, now made their homes in England.

Manasseh's efforts on behalf of his co-religionists no doubt were gratifying, but his natural modesty turned away tributes. Nevertheless, in 1663 he was honored with a portrait by his friend and neighbor Rembrandt van Rijn, who was impressed by his unpretentiousness and sincerity. The artist made his home within the Jewish community of Amsterdam, and at times chose his models from among his acquaintances there. By capturing the spiritual quality of whatever his theme, by frequently depicting his secular subjects as neither beautiful nor young,

Left: Ill. 4:13. *Manasseh ben Israel.* Etching, 1636. By Rembrandt van Rijn. *Right:* Ill. 4:14. *Manasseh ben Israel.* Etching, 1642. By Salom Italia

his biblical characters as neither timeless nor heroic, or his Jews neither as Christ-killers nor penitent New Testament figures, he broke with Gothic and Renaissance standards of representation. His patrons did not always understand or admire his work, or that its excellence lay in the mystery of intuition and the mastery of unforced and expressive lines which aimed at inspiring devotion and piety through a greater appeal to the senses.

The artistry in Rembrandt's etching of Manasseh, 1636, is almost hidden in the clarity and openness of its method (Ill. 4:13). (The identity of the sitter is based on comparative material.) An early biographer had described the rabbi as "of medium stature and inclined to be stout ... his plain but presentable dress inducing an attitude of reverence justified by his venerable deportment." Rembrandt apparently caught that quiet reserve, missed by Salom Italia in his 1642 etching of the rabbi which lacked softness and natural harmony (Ill. 4:14). Coming from a family of printers in Italy who had fled to Amsterdam the previous year, Salom, the most famous Jewish engraver of the time, found ample work, specializing in portraiture, decorative religious documents, and calligraphy. Manasseh may have preferred Salom's portrait over Rembrandt's; in any event, he used it in some copies of the *Esperança de Israel* and *Nishmat Hayyim* (*On the Immortality of the Soul*), 1652, and presented it to his family and friends. So much for rabbinic connoisseurship.

In the upper right corner of the print is a candle and an excerpt from Psalm 119: 105, "Thy word is a lamp unto my feet, and a light unto my path." The Latin text urges the viewer to contemplate the fine qualities in the rabbi's face. In the upper left, Italia included Manasseh's motto from his printer's mark, "By our wanderings we seek," along with a sketch of the Wanderer. (The story of the Wandering Jew is said to have originated in a medieval English legend in which Ahasuerus, a Jewish shoemaker from Jerusalem, was damned to roam the world eternally because he mocked Jesus on his way to the crucifixion. The figure first appeared in a print in a German chapbook and reappeared regularly in literature and art for the next three

Left: Ill. 4:15. *The Great Jewish Bride.* Etching, 1635. By Rembrandt van Rijn. *Right:* Ill. 4:16. *Ephraim Bonus.* Etching, 1648. By Rembrandt van Rijn

hundred years. Its first English representation was in a woodblock title page, *The Wandering Jew Telling Fortunes to Englishmen,* 1640.)

In Rembrandt's etching of 1635, commonly known as *The Great Jewish Bride,* the presumed newlywed is thought to be holding a ketubbah or marriage license in her left hand (Ill. 4:15). The title was given by later scholars who assumed that the portrait fixed on the moment when an unmarried Jewish woman would be shorn of her flowing hair following the wedding ceremony. Others guessed that she represents Queen Esther carrying a petition to the king to save the Jews of Persia.

As the artist's sense of volume and drama replaced his earlier open linear designs, his vivid contrasts, dense shadows, and jagged strokes explored the newer Baroque style. In 1648, these qualities showed up in the etched portrait of the Jewish scholar and physician Ephraim Bonus (Ill. 4:16). In addition to his medical duties, Bonus was an editor of Joseph Caro's *Shulchan Aruch* (first printed in Venice in 1565) and a co-founder of the *Or Torah* (*Light of the Torah*) school in 1656. Dignity and stability are established in the print through the implied vertical of the panel above his hat and extending to the right hand and balustrade. Bonus, lost in contemplation, is invested with all the humanity and sympathy of Rembrandt's maturity. Robert Browning's poem *Fra Lippo Lippi,* addressed to that fifteenth century painter, might as easily apply to Rembrandt:

> Make them forget there's such a thing as flesh.
> Your Business is to paint the souls of men—...
> Give us no more of body than shows soul!

Jan Lievens, an early friend of Rembrandt's, also etched Bonus' portrait, but he chose body over soul, reason and ease over mystery, modeling his efforts on the aristocratic style of the contemporary London-based Flemish painter Anthony van Dyck (Ill. 4:17). Bonus holds his hat in his lap so that his skullcap is visible. Costume and column share equal billing with the face, unfortunately detracting from the intensity and penetration of the features. But

Lievens' design suggests that the Jew measures up, that he matters to himself, and that he is esteemed in the community.

A Rembrandt etching generally known as *Jews in the Synagogue*, 1648, was associated in the eighteenth century with a "temple in perspective which seems to be a synagogue" (Ill.

4:18). Since no synagogue resembling it has been discovered, and no ritual paraphernalia is visible, it may simply be a depiction of a group of Jewish tradesmen in front of an unknown building; the clothing is of Polish style. But Rembrandt was offering a mood rather than a literal description, inviting us to share a moment of quiet sociability among Amsterdam's Jews. His pairs of standing men on the left and right establish a foreground, but it is the enigmatic man with his back to the viewer who is the principal element in the picture. Perhaps that isolated figure represents Rembrandt himself in his disillusioned middle years, or perhaps a lonely Jew, thrust from who knows where into an unfamiliar and unsettled environment.

Other artists, too, were busy interpreting Jewish life. Matthaeus

Above: Ill. 4:17. *Ephraim Bonus*. Etching, c. 1650. By Jan Lievens. *Below:* Ill. 4:18. *Jews in the Synagogue*. Etching, 1648. By Rembrandt van Rijn

Above: Ill. 4:19. *Passover.* Etching, 1620–1630. From *Icones Bibliae (Biblical Pictures)*. By Matthaeus Merian. *Below:* Ill. 4:20. *A Woman Kindling Sabbath Candles.* Woodcut, 1663. From *Philologus Hebraeo-Mixtus (A Philologist of Hebrew and Other Languages)*. By Johannes Leusden

Merian's *Icones Bibliae* (*Biblical Pictures*), 1625–1630, became a standard source for art, dear to Jews and Christians alike. The book was snapped up all over Europe; Goethe remembered it fondly from boyhood days. Merian had appropriated designs from the sixteenth century German artists Hans Sebald Beham and Hans Holbein the Younger; such copying was common among artists who depended on each other for popular images. Merian's etching *Passover*, after Holbein, records the long-tailed hood and sleeveless cloak worn by Ashkenazi Jews from the sixteenth through the eighteenth centuries (Ill. 4:19). The print illustrates the passage from Exodus 12:11 in which, on their last night as slaves, Jews were enjoined

to eat "in haste with loins girded, sandals on your feet, and staff in your hand," ready to leave at a moment's notice.

Johannes Leusden was interested in the relationship of Hebrew texts to the New Testament. He clarified certain doubtful Hebrew and Christian wording and introduced the system of numbering the verses in a Hebrew Bible published in Amsterdam by the Athias press in 1666. It included a tribute to Joseph Athias' father, who had been roasted alive as a Judaizer

Above: Ill. 4:21. *Cleansing of Dishes.* Woodcut, 1663. From *Philologus Hebraeo-Mixtus (A Philologist of Hebrew and Other Languages).* By Johannes Leusden. *Below:* Ill. 4:22. *Tonsio Judaica (Jewish Haircut).* Etching, 1682. From *Philologus Hebraeo-Mixtus (A Philologist of Hebrew and Other Languages).* By Johannes Leusden

in Cordova the previous year. In the belief that a proper understanding of Jesus necessitated a proper understanding of Jewish rites and customs, Leusden's *Philologus Hebraeo-Mixtus (A Philologist of Hebrew and Other Languages),* 1663, offered thirteen two-and-a-half-inch-square woodcut illustrations of Jewish ceremonies. Such pictures explained Jewish life to the Christian world. The print of a woman kindling Sabbath candles suggested the question, Why women rather than men? (Ill. 4:20). Other than the obvious conclusion that women are usually at home at the prescribed time, Leusden discussed the Midrash that Eve attacked Adam for initially refusing the forbidden fruit. Because of this sin, the sun was forever destined to shine less brightly; if, however, her female descendants were to become instruments of light, the sun would renew its brilliance. Another of the distinctive little pictures depicts the cleansing of dishes in preparation for the Passover holiday (Ill. 4:21). Leusden indicated that the Halacha prohibits the immersion of several dishes together in a pot because water must reach every possible point of contact. The popularity of the book encouraged a second Utrecht edition in 1682 containing an anonymous set of eight new etched plates. Among them is *Tonsio Judaica (Jewish Haircut),* a scene in a well-stocked barbershop (Ill. 4:22). Personal grooming, among other activities, was religiously prescribed during the Lag B'omer holiday, following Passover. It marked the end of the Omer mourning period, when certain prohibitions, including shaving, the cutting of beards, weddings, and entertainments, were lifted. During Simchat Torah, a happy celebrant appears in *Festum Laetitiae Legis* (*Festival of the Rejoicing of the Law*), eager to perform the mitzvah of supplying the town's children with goodies (Ill. 4:23).

One of the most engaging books of the time, because it focused on the Jewish interest in medical and scientific studies, was the *Alphabeti vere Naturalis Hebraici* (*Natural Hebrew Alphabet*), 1667, by Franciscus Mercurius van Helmont, a Belgian physician with an interest in language arts (Ill. 4:24). Its engravings by F. Franck instructed deaf-mutes how to master phonic skills through the mouthing of Hebrew letters. It attracted enough interest to be translated thirty years later into Dutch.

An unprecedented memoir by Glueckel of Hameln, a businesswoman and mother of a dozen children, described the lives and times of central Europe's influential merchants and privileged financial agents, as well as the Chmielnicki massacres and the fallout in the wake of the Shabbetai Zvi scandal. She began writing in 1690 following the death of her husband "in the hope of distracting my soul from its grief." The work covered both the difficult and happy events in her town where Jews survived with few rights or privileges, but where she found fulfillment in arranging the marriages and fortunes of her enormous progeny. Copies of the manuscript were passed from hand to hand by generations of family and townsfolk until it was published in 1896.

Not all books fared as well. Miguel de Barrios' *Imperio de Dios en la harmonia del mundo* (*The Power of God in Earthly Harmony*), was rejected in Amsterdam because an allegorical portrait of his family engraved by Christian van Hagen after a painting by Aaron de Chaves included women and children, subject matter

Top: Ill. 4:23. *Simchat Torah (Rejoicing of the Law).* Etching, 1682. From *Philologus Hebraeo-Mixtus (A Philologist of Hebrew and Other Languages).* By Johannes Leusden. *Bottom:* Ill. 4:24. *Hebrew Phonic Skills.* Engraving, 1667. From *Alphabeti vere Naturalis Hebraici (Natural Hebrew Alphabet).* By Franciscus Mercurius van Helmont

TOURO COLLEGE LIBRARY

Ill. 4:25. *Allegorical Family Portrait.* **Engraving by Christian van Hagan, c. 1673. From** *Imperio de Dios en la harmonia del mundo (The Power of God in Earthly Harmony).* **By Miguel de Barrios**

not deemed lofty enough to appear in a poetic translation of the Bible (Ill. 4:25). It was finally published in Brussels, probably in 1673, where more liberal minds reigned. Chaves, a Sephardi colleague of Jan Lievens, then took advantage of the relaxed conditions in England and became the first Jewish artist permitted to work there; his painting of Moses and Aaron flanking the Ten Commandments, 1675, was placed in London's Creechurch Lane synagogue in defiance of traditional practices which shunned figurative images.

As the European economy grew, Jews participated to a greater extent in the financial affairs of urban centers. While most never made it to the top, a lucky few were able to enjoy some of the perks that wealth provided, including the opportunity to invest freely in the art market, to become art patrons and to commission or purchase works that might be displayed in their homes. Collectable prints to hang on walls or to cherish between the covers of books became the newest rage. Although these prints were well done, their linearity could not render shading in uninterrupted gradation of tones as could paintings. It fell to Ludwig von Siegen to overcome that difficulty in 1642 with the invention of mezzotint engraving. It was particularly suitable for portraits, such as Peter Schenck's study of the Dutch Sephardic calligrapher Jacob Gadelle, who was widely admired by both Christians and Jews, as attested by a flattering inscription (Ill. 4:26).

Many of the best prints and books came from Holland where, in spite of some restrictions, Jewish artists were able to function. Benjamin Godines, a calligrapher, editor, and printmaker, engraved a frontispiece for the *Me'ah Brachhot* (*Hundred Blessings*) in 1687 (Ill. 4:27). Published by the Gentile Albertus Magnus, it memorialized the martyrs of the Inquisition, included commandments and benedictions involving the five senses, gave instructions for building a mikvah, supplied a Haggadah with a recipe for charosis, and offered benedictions for the purchase and circumcision of slaves.

Ill. 4:26. *Jacob Gadelle*. Mezzotint, c. 1645. By Peter Schenck

From 1645 to 1708, a non–Jewish artist, Romeyn de Hoogh, etched twenty illustrations of Dutch Jewish life, among which is *Hof van den Baron Belmonte* (*House of Baron Belmonte*), c. 1675 (Ill. 4:28). It is a clear expression of affluence, although a generous exaggeration of the building's size. But it was no accident. Printmakers knew how to please the proud balbatim whose wealth often surpassed that of some Christians. Another of his etchings, *Hof van Isaac de Pinto* (*The Home of Isaac de Pinto*), 1675, showed off the splendid horses, elegant carriages, and nattily dressed Jews who graced the neighborhood (Ill. 4:29). The family, neighbors of Rembrandt, decorated the building with such enthusiasm that the local powers chided them for its pretentiousness.

Amsterdam's *Jooden Tempel* (*Synagogue*), 1663, having outgrown its space, was replaced in 1672 by a more imposing structure, the first permitted to be larger than a house. De Hooghe, possibly an eyewitness to its dedication, etched *Den Tempel der Jooden tot Amsterdam* (*The Jewish Synagogue of Amsterdam*), 1675, depicting its floor plan, a view of the exterior, and, in the side roundels, the community's grateful recognition of its Spanish and Portuguese benefactors (Ill. 4:30). While the print re-created the festivities on earth, the cloud-borne figures, proclaiming that "freedom of worship upholds the Republic," participated in the celebration as it was surely observed in heaven. The visitor today finds the sanctuary almost unchanged—the celestial scene regrettably only an illusion, but the great brass chandeliers still hang in place holding a total of six hundred thirteen candles, one for each of the commandments undertaken by Orthodox Jews; nowadays, only on Simchat Torah, when the yearly reading of the Pentateuch is completed and begun anew, are all the tapers lit. (Other than during World War II, it has been in continuous use. Spared from Nazi destruction thanks in part to its designation as an international monument, it was renovated in the 1990s and has remained one of the great tourist attractions of the city.)

The Ashkenazim, meanwhile, had prospered to the point where they were able to begin

Ill. 4:27. *Me'ah Brachhot (Hundred Blessings)* **Engraving, 1687. By Benjamin Godines**

Above: Ill. 4:28. *Hof van den Baron Belmonte (House of Baron Belmonte).* Etching, 1675. By Romeyn de Hoogh. *Below:* Ill. 4:29. *Hof van Isaac de Pinto (House of Isaac de Pinto).* Etching, 1675. By Romeyn de Hoogh

Ill. 4:30. *Den Tempel der Jooden tot Amsterdam (The Jewish Synagogue of Amsterdam)*. Etching, 1675. By Romeyn de Hoogh

construction of their own Great Synagogue in 1670, facing its Sephardi neighbor on the Hout-gracht Canal. In 1710, Adolf van der Laan provided an etching, *A Prospect of the Portuguese and High German Jews Churches at Amsterdam*, which offered both communities an equal opportunity for crowing. (In 1943, the Germans closed the synagogue and broke up its galleries for firewood. Since restored, it now serves as a museum.)

To some non–Jews, Jewish lifestyles were interesting, even appealing; to others they were distasteful. John Evelyn, an English diarist who visited Holland in 1641, wrote admiringly that "their ceremonies, ornaments, lamps, laws and schools afforded matter for my wonder and inquiry." However, Samuel Pepys, another English diarist, noted after visiting a London synagogue that he was appalled "to see the disorder, laughing, sporting, and no attention, but confusion in all their service, more like brutes than people knowing the true God." Such a "disgraceful" service was unthinkable to someone brought up in the decorous Church, but for a Jew the synagogue was more than a house of worship—it was a meeting place where one could encounter both God and one's neighbors on the most intimate and informal terms.

Talmud study, poetry, music, occasional dancing and theatrical performances, as well as more mundane activities, enhanced the lives of many Europe's Jews. Pictures of their customs were often evocative of well-being, gracious living and faithful devotion to God. Purim festivals celebrated the victory over wicked Haman. The holiday always provided an opportunity to cut loose and drown care; drinking to the point where Mordechai and Haman were con-

Ill. 4:31. *Jewish Burial Ground Near Amsterdam*. Engraving, 1670. By Abraham Blooteling

fused was an established tradition. Sorrow, finding its inexorable way into the final parting which every generation must reenact, was recorded as well. Abraham Blooteling engraved the Jewish burial ground near Amsterdam, 1670, after Jacob van Ruisdael's painting (Ill. 4:31). De Hoogh's etching *Gedenk Plichten op de Graven* (*Mourning Over the Grave*) is a moving tableau of a casket delivered by barge through the famous canals (Ill. 4:32).

A very different area of tragedy imposed itself into the worldly affairs of Amsterdam—the corroding impact of medieval and Renaissance philosophy on Jewish theology. Jews had achieved a good measure of religious security in Holland; rarely in history had the prospects for peace and harmony been so attainable. Yet the community was wrestling with a fear that worldliness would lead to godlessness. For the true believers, challenges to piety had to be suppressed. Secularism based on reason could not be tolerated if Jewish life, as it was traditionally practiced, was to survive. The problem, already present in the skepticism and rationalism of Delmedigo and Modena, erupted in the heresies of Uriel Acosta and Baruch Spinoza.

Acosta's family were Marranos, but he reverted to a Judaism that accepted the Bible, not the Talmud, as the repository of truth. He denied the immortality of the soul which, he claimed, expires with the body. He championed a "natural" religion that stressed love, as opposed to a "revealed" Judaism that fostered enmity. Both Christians and Jews found his theories unacceptably deviant. He was arrested, isolated, and excommunicated by the Jewish community in 1624 under humiliating circumstances. Sixteen years later, still unable to bear the ridicule and contempt, he went home and shot himself.

Spinoza was born in Amsterdam to an influential Marrano family and studied under Manasseh ben Israel and the best Hebrew teachers available. It is said that although he was modest in most things, he was proud of his curly hair, full brows, and soulful eyes. He was drawn to classic Renaissance paganism, rejecting such Jewish doctrines as chosenness, the divinity of

Ill. 4:32. *Gedenk Plichten op de Graven (Mourning Over Graves).* **Etching, 1675. By Romeyn de Hoogh**

the Bible, the immaterial nature of God's body, and the eternal vital force. He spoke of a universal God that manifests itself, not beyond the limits of man's scope, but through nature alone—clearly heretical in an almost two-thousand-year-old Judaic-Christian creed. He envisioned a government empowered to resolve conflicting civil and religious laws, but the rabbis could not allow a system that permitted either man or the state to determine religious truths. It wasn't their only concern. They were worried that Christians would condemn freethinking if it appeared to be condoned by Jewish authorities. Dutch liberalism might be real, but it was nevertheless conditional.

In 1656, from the pulpit of the synagogue, the rabbinate ordered Spinoza barred from every Jewish contact; he was twenty-four years old. The excommunication did not prevent him from pursuing his theories—"Ceremonies do not add to blessedness," he said. "When I saw that all the things I had feared, and which feared me, had neither good nor bad in them except as they affected the mind, I determined to inquire whether there might be anything which was truly good and able to communicate in goodness." Arriving at a negative conclusion, he lost his faith but believed he had found reason. He never formally converted, although he was buried in a church grave; an alienated Jew, he was neither close to his own religion nor officially a part of any other. Perhaps only Holland could have produced a person such as Spinoza.

An anonymous engraved portrait that caught his somewhat quizzical air was included in his *Opera Posthuma* (*Posthumous Work*), 1677, published by his friends in the year of his death (Ill. 4:33). Shortly after, the book was banned for blasphemy. His message—"Perfect liberty to philosophize is compatible with piety"—was disseminated far beyond the small circle of Dutch critics, where it sowed the seeds for the eighteenth century Enlightenment.

It is an irony of history that all the writings of the great philosopher reached fewer Jews than the prints of a little-known Christian proselyte to Judaism. Abraham ben Jacob, a former Protestant preacher, had emigrated to Amsterdam from Germany and found work among Jewish printers; drawn to their religious lifestyle, he converted to their faith in 1689. His famous Amsterdam Haggadah of 1695, adapted from Merian's *Icones Biblicae*, was the first to use detailed and elaborate engravings rather than "primitive" woodcuts to illustrate the Passover text. One measure of its lasting influence is its version of the Four Sons, for the first time placed together within a sin-

Ill. 4:33. *Baruch Spinoza.* Engraving, 1677. From *Opera Posthuma (Posthumous Works)*

gle frame (Ill. 4:34). They actually have no internal coherence or religious symbolism at all. The Wise Son, an elderly man with upraised arm, the Simple Son leaning on a staff, the Son who doesn't know how to ask as a tiny figure with one arm up and the other outstretched, are derived from Merian's *Life of Hannibal*. While the Hebrew text says nothing about the Wicked Son as a soldier, that image was based on Saul's anointment by Samuel in Merian's *Sacred and Profane History*.

This Haggadah, published by the Amsterdam press of Moses Kosman ben Eliah Gomperz, contained the first printed map of the Holy Land, which Merian based on a 1590 chart by Christian von Adrichom. Its technical achievements were proudly saluted on the second title page:

> A spirit of knowledge and fear of God caused the exalted person of Abraham, son of Jacob our father, to draw and cut and engrave with tools upon a sheet of copper, when previously the forms were cut in wood, and there was no beauty. Everyone will now see with their own eyes that the elegant forms engraved in copper possess the same superiority that light has over darkness, and will rejoice forever over this innovation of craftsmanship by an artist known for all time as a practiced craftsman of the highest skill and ability in the art of drawing and engraving seals, plans, models, and pictures of everything in heaven and earth.

But, the inclusion of King David kneeling to the Holy Spirit unmistakably revealed the artist's non–Jewish origins and his dependence on Merian's *The Pharisee and the Publican* (Ill. 4:35). However, several objectionable images were Judaized in later printings, and the book won an enormous following throughout the world as a paradigm of folk art; later editions appeared in 1712, 1781, and 1810.

פירש אברבנאל   ה   הגדה

רָשָׁע מַה הוּא אוֹמֵר מַה הָעֲבוֹדָה הַזֹּאת לָכֶם לָכֶם
וְלֹא לוֹ וּלְפִי שֶׁהוֹצִיא אֶת עַצְמוֹ מִן הַכְּלָל כָּפַר
בְּעִקָּר וְאַף אַתָּה הַקְהֵה אֶת שִׁנָּיו וֶאֱמָר לוֹ בַּעֲבוּר זֶה
עָשָׂה יְיָ לִי בְּצֵאתִי מִמִּצְרָיִם לִי וְלֹא לוֹ אִלּוּ הָיָה שָׁם לֹא
הָיָה נִגְאָל:

תָּם

שֶׁאֵינוֹ יוֹדֵעַ לִשְׁאוֹל   תָּם   רָשָׁע   חָכָם

צוּרַת אַרְבָּעָה בָנִים דִּבְרֵי תוֹרָה

Ill. 4:34. *Four Sons.* Engraving by Abraham ben Jacob, 1695. *Haggadah*

Ill. 4:35. *King David Kneeling to the Holy Spirit.* Engraving by Abraham ben Jacob, 1695. *Haggadah*

Isaac Da Fonesca Aboab, brought to Holland as a child from Portugal, was, descended from a family of scholars and writers, remembered as the first rabbi to serve in the Western Hemisphere. Thanks to the colonial expansion that Holland's prosperity had made possible, he joined a small band of adventurous Jews, taking ship in 1641 for the Dutch (formerly Portuguese) colony of Recife (Pernambuco), Brazil. Beginning in 1630, it was the only South American community in which practicing Jews could settle, although two years earlier a small number of Marranos had arrived in Barbados, the easternmost island of the West Indies. By the time Aboab reached Brazil, earlier immigrants had already built a synagogue and were active in the sugar and timber industries. After five years of a good life there, he wrote a thanksgiving poem, "*Zekher asiti le-nifla'ot El*" (*I made a remembrance of the wondrous deeds of God*), the first known Hebrew printed work in the New World.

Until Portugal forcibly retook Recife in 1654, its Jewish population of fourteen hundred was large enough to organize a separate army unit which was obligingly exempted from military duties on the Sabbath. But when the relentless Inquisition was reestablished, most Jews, including Aboab, packed up their lives and fled back to Amsterdam, but not until they, as well as the Dutch Protestants there, had suffered terrible destruction and famine.

"Volumes would not suffice to tell of our miseries," Aboab wrote. "The enemy covered field and wood, searching here for booty and there for life. Many of us died, sword in hand, others from starvation; they now rest in the cold ground. We survivors faced death in every form; those accustomed to fine things were glad to have moldy bread to appease their hunger."

After a hapless attempt to defend Recife, the Jews sold most of their possessions for a pittance and left Brazil in sixteen ships. Fifteen of the boats returned safely to Holland; one, carrying four men and nineteen women and children, lost its way. The Jews headed to West Indian islands but were turned away by Spanish authorities as they attempted to pass through Jamaica and Cuba. Almost penniless after being captured by Spanish pirates who confiscated their belongings and planned to sell them into slavery, they were rescued by a passing French ship on the way to New Amsterdam, a village with population of less than a thousand. Held hostage by its captain when their few remaining goods proved insufficient to pay their fare, they depended on compassionate New Netherlanders who bought up their meager items and returned them to the "big and little Jews"; the captain was unhappy with the proceeds. A stalemate dragged on for almost two months. When the impasse was resolved at last, the Jews fell into the hands of the New Amsterdam governor, Peter Stuyvesant. He didn't want them. On September 22, 1654, he wrote to the Amsterdam Chamber of the Dutch West India Company about his unexpected, unwelcome, and insolvent visitors:

> The Jews who have arrived would nearly all like to remain here, but learning that they (with their customary usury and deceitful trading with the Christians) are very repugnant ... we pray for ourselves and also for the general community of your worships, that the deceitful race, such hateful enemies and blasphemers of the name of Christ, be not allowed further to infect and trouble this new colony....

The chamber, which included a number of prominent Jews, replied: "After having weighed the matter, we observe that this would be somewhat unreasonable and unfair ... because of the large amount of capital which they (the 'Jewish Nation') have invested in the shares of this Company."

With the admonition that they be responsible for the "poor among them," the Jews were granted permission to stay, but not to maintain a synagogue; services were restricted to private homes, where the Shearith Israel Congregation was formed in 1654, the first in North America. They could not buy land or trade along the stockade *waal* (later, Wall Street), which secured the colonists from Indian raids. Almost immediately the refugees applied to Stuyvesant for a small piece of land as "a burying ground for their nation ... inasmuch as they did not wish to bury their dead in the common [i.e. Christian] burying ground." On February 22, 1656, they were assigned "a little hook of land," the first Jewish cemetery in America. Where it was located is lost to history. What is known is that additional property near the Bowery, approximately fifty-two by fifty feet, was bought by the community in 1682; presumably the earlier plot was by then occupied. Fifty years later this little ground, too, was filled, and in 1729, it was enlarged enough to serve for another century. Only Trinity Churchyard predates it by twenty years.

The refugees had been greeted by the only two Jews, Jacob Barsimon and Salomon Pietersen, who had come temporarily from Holland as traders and elected to remain. They were followed by a small number of their brethren in 1655, including five well-to-do Sephardim in the fur and tobacco trades. But there were no rabbis, no Jewish schools, no Jewish social groups to bind them. For a while they had a Torah, brought by a later arrival, Abraham de Lucena; he reclaimed it in 1663 when he returned to Amsterdam for lack of a minyan. And, because no Hebrew works were printed in America until the middle of the eighteenth century, they had no prayer books other than what they may have carried with them.

After a period of loneliness and economic disappointments, most went back to Amsterdam; a few took off for the Caribbean where commercial interests beckoned. Only one Jew of whom we have any known history stayed behind. Asser Levy had arrived with the boatload from Recife, but by 1664 he was a wealthy burgher fighting for the privilege of lending money (which helped build the Lutheran Church), selling liquor (a third of all businesses were reputed to be grog shops), and opening his own butcher establishment (where he was exempted from slaughtering pigs). He petitioned unsuccessfully for the privilege to serve in the militia "like other burghers," but was offered instead the privilege to depart whenever he pleased. Ultimately, he bought his own home—probably the first Jew to do so in North America—demanded and won the right to protect his property, and served on a jury that acquitted Stuyvesant of withholding funds from a former Dutch West India Company employee. A practicing Jew till the end, at Levy's death several cherished old books and ritual objects for Sabbath observance were found among his possessions.

Perhaps at one time he owned a copy of the first significant North American publication in the English language—the *Bay Psalm Book*, published in 1640 in Cambridge by Stephen Daye, the "American Gutenberg," just twenty years after the *Mayflower* Pilgrims landed. Accompanying Psalm 119 was the entire Hebrew alphabet, a particular boon to Governor William Bradford of the Massachusetts Bay Colony, who was determined to learn Hebrew in order to facilitate conversations with God and the angels when he met them. Richard Mather, Boston's first preacher, wrote the preface and introduced five words in specially cut Hebrew type, but on the whole, the book was only a mediocre work, an inauspicious debut for Hebrew printing in America. It appeared in an edition of seventeen hundred; perhaps ten are extant.

Nevertheless, it established a distinctly Hebrew spirit in the colonies, was "faithfully translated into English metre" directly from the Hebrew by Mather, Thomas Welde, and John Eliot, the chief ministers in the Bay Colony. Richard's grandson, Cotton Mather, the leading scholar of the day, was so fascinated by the Jews that he adopted the title of rabbi and donned a skullcap as a tribute to the "Kingdom of Christ." He spent the years from 1693 to 1700 writing a Jewish history interpreted through the Puritan spirit—"One of the greatest works that I ever undertook in my life." He hoped it would speed conversions. As far as is known, only one candidate showed up, a meager reward for his troubles.

The first printed Bible in America was published in 1661, not in English, but in the Algonquin language. It was conceived by Christian missionaries in the hope of converting the Indians. Two years later John Eliot produced a Mohawk translation of which four hundred sixty-four verses were from the Hebrew Bible and one hundred twenty-six from the New Testament. Among Eliot's admirers was Johannes Leusden, who in 1688 dedicated his own Hebrew and English edition of the Psalms to the man who "preached the word of God to the Americans in the Indian tongue." Although Eliot guessed correctly that the Indians had arrived in America via Asia, he apparently believed, as did Manasseh ben Israel, Cotton Mather, Roger Williams, and William Penn, that because Indians shared some common customs with Jews, they were descendants of the Lost Tribes of Israel. Eliot offered that information to the English reverend Thomas Thorowgood, who had already heard it from John Durie, the chaplain to the Princess of Orange, who had in turn received it from Manasseh ben Israel. Thorowgood then wrote a pamphlet in 1650, *Jews in America, or Probabilities that The Americans are of that Race..., and earnest desires for effectual endeavors to make them Christians.*

In 1658, a Jewish settlement is thought to have come to Rhode Island under the protection of Roger Williams but, if so, it disappeared by 1700. In 1695, a small group arrived in Charleston, South Carolina, but they, too, were unsuccessful in establishing a toehold, leaving no known trace. At the time there were about two hundred Jews in America, most living along the Atlantic coast, working as tailors, watch-makers, soap-makers, farmers, shippers, and Indian traders. When British forces captured New Amsterdam in 1664, they renamed it New York; one of the first directives from London was to enable "...all persons of what Religion soever, quietly to inhabit within ye precincts of your jurisdiction...." Among those persons were Jews who settled mainly in port cities where they found work, expanded the boundaries of religious pluralism, and organized synagogues along the way.

Meanwhile, once back in Amsterdam, Rabbi Aboab pursued a busy career, participating

Ill. 4:36. *Isaac Da Fonseca Aboab*. **Engraving by Aernout Nagtegaal, 1685**

in the trial that condemned his former student Spinoza, joining the followers of Shabbeti Zvi, founding a religious school, and urging the construction of the Amsterdam Synagogue in 1675. Like a number of other seventeenth century scholars, he amassed a fine library of classical and philosophical works, including some four hundred Hebrew books. In 1685, at the age of eighty, the rabbi sat to Aernout Nagtegaal for an engraved portrait (Ill. 4:36). The inscription reads, "Engraved with a pen of iron and lead, the form of a man still living, Isaac; to the last day in honor, he will stand and live before God." Some of his detractors accused the rabbi of superstition and a weak will, but at least one Christian admirer, the Jesuit preacher, Antonio Vieira, compared him favorably to Manasseh ben Israel: "Manasseh says what he knows, Aboab knows what he says."

Perhaps the rabbi occasionally looked back to his earlier years and wondered whether his efforts had made any contribution to a permanent Jewish presence in the Americas. But surely he could never have guessed that from such humble beginnings would emerge, not only a new fork in the road of Jewish history, but the largest and most active Diaspora community in the world.

5

The Eighteenth Century: Enlightenment, Emancipation

The Age of Enlightenment opened on the continent with battles royal. Occasional treaties of peace interrupted the hostilities until intrigue or opportunism renewed the tugs of war. The Age of Enlightenment also generated a passion for critical observation and a conviction that reason and experience would promote universal happiness. War and learning were perennial; universal happiness was frustrated, among other things, by the unequal balance of power in western and central Europe. Many unresolved issues of the seventeenth century lingered—authoritarianism versus principles of equality, theology versus skepticism. The Enlightenment questioned entrenched institutionalized values and dogma, attacked what it considered religious superstition, but not deism or religious faith. It juxtaposed humanist morality and intelligence with environment and nurture, favored the separation of church and state, and fostered the application of rational law in its approach to the social sciences and human progress. The Enlightenment coexisted with Emancipation, which conferred independent legal status to specific groups and alleviated political and communal disabilities within recognized bounds. It was propelled by the democratic ideals of pre-revolutionary America and France—a demand to extend rights and privileges "according to the spirit of the times."

The Jewish Enlightenment or Haskalah, spanning the mid–eighteenth century to the last quarter of the nineteenth, adopted some Western social, philosophical, and literary conventions, frowned at mysticism and Kabbalah, and made an effort to retain Jewish principles and identity outside the strict conformity of the ghetto. The mechanistic order of the universe was rejected in central and eastern Europe where Orthodox beliefs resisted liberal modifications. Jewish Emancipation signified the removal of certain impediments and the acknowledgment that Jewish citizenship and equality were inherent rights, not community judgments. It was unevenly distributed at the pleasure of individual rulers, and generally contingent on abandonment of what was perceived as clannishness and irrelevant mores. Once Jews undertook to "improve" themselves, blessings would flow: religious tolerance, social approval, economic parity, lowered taxes, access to a cosmopolitan culture, citizenship, and trade and agricultural advantages.

The Enlightenment and Emancipation moved slowly but deliberately across Europe. England enjoyed the most favorable situation largely due to its comparatively tolerant property-owning middle-class. It experienced order at home, avoided bloodshed on its soil, and engaged in successful wars on the continent. Parliament encouraged low taxes and free trade to stabilize and protect the rapidly expanding empire. Huge profits accrued from the sale of

American furs, employment rose with improved textile and industrial machinery, and steam power transformed mining and metal smelting industries. Agriculture discovered better ways to grow food, while railroad construction and shipbuilding speeded the delivery of goods and services around the world.

For England's native-born Jews, many equable arrangements already existed—they were citizens, they could live with few restrictions, work mostly where and how they chose, and were exempt from unfair taxation. The Act for Suppressing Blasphemy, passed in 1698, had given them freedom to practice their religion. Courts often ruled in their favor, and the fact that they numbered only about nine thousand meant they had fewer opportunities to step on English sensibilities or to threaten the economic or social equilibrium.

On the other hand, they were aliens, legally barred from holding civil, military, or other offices, unable to become educators, lawyers, or members of Parliament. Foreign-born Jews who would not take the oath "according to the usages of the Anglican Church" faced barriers in land purchases, special duties, and the right to engage in colonial trade. Religious scholarship and practice was lax. Agrarian interests collided with improved techniques and efficient mechanization. Poverty and hunger, licentiousness and disease, child labor and gin hangovers were direct challenges, as was the noxious slave trade that hauled millions of Africans to American plantations. Parliament's arrogant grip on elective representation pushed the case for greater democratic participation, not as an option, but as an obligation.

The problems were exacerbated by the arrival of more and more economically depressed central European Jews who often wound up in unrespectable occupations—begging, hawking cheap odds and ends, or trading in second-hand clothes. Not far behind came the usual sprinkling of criminals, prostitutes, and other offending types, many of whom were the predictable products of poverty and deprivation. Serious efforts were made to bolster tradition, rectify inappropriate behavior, provide jobs, and set examples of desirable etiquette.

For all that, many English Jews were optimistic about the future. Skilled craftsmen, petty merchants, small-time financiers and speculators eventually formed strong middle- and upper-class communities. Because the need for religious services was a high priority, a group of Dutch Sephardim bought property and built London's Bevis Marks Synagogue outside the city limits. (Jews could not buy land within.) Completed in 1701, it was situated on a side street so as not to offend a passing crowd. An engraving, copied after a watercolor by the Jewish artist Isaac Mendes Belissario, recalled the Amsterdam prototype they had left behind (Ill. 5:1). The proliferation of synagogues that followed was not matched with a parallel flowering of scholarship or strict religious observance. An attempt to open a prayer group close to the Ashkenazi Duke's Place—Great Synagogue was thwarted with the result that a breakaway membership formed the Hambro congregation in 1726. Half a century later, the New Synagogue opened, likewise with dissident members of the Great Synagogue. The Western Synagogue evolved at about the same period in an outlying area. These offshoots developed their own brand of worship, although eventually they cooperated in common areas of concern. Some catered to poorer Jews occupied with basic subsistence and maintaining order on quarrelsome streets, others to the rich who were often accused of preferring business to Talmud, mistresses to wives, mansions to modest dwellings. Those in between moved as quickly as they could along the road to status and excess.

They read the latest books, including English translations of Moses Mendelssohn and other Jewish writers, and commissioned paintings of themselves by the best people, many of which were translated into prints. Johann Jacob Schudt noted in *Jüdische Merkwürdigkeiten* (*Jewish Curiosities*), 1714–1718, "There is no doubt that many Jews had their portraits done." While Joshua Reynolds and Thomas Gainsborough focused on England's upper circles, the Jewish artist David Estevens found work among Jewry's aristocrats. He painted England's only important Jew-

Above: Ill. 5:1. *Bevis Marks Synagogue.* Engraving, c. 1705. After watercolor by Isaac Mendes Belissario. *Below:* Ill. 5:2. *David Nieto.* Mezzotint, c. 1728. By James McArdell

ish intellectual, the revered Haham of Bevis Marks, David Nieto with a Protestant wig and collar, a well-stocked bookcase, a world globe, and a sample of his manuscripts. James McArdell used it as a basis for a posthumous mezzotint, probably in 1728 (Ill. 5:2). Nieto had pursued careers in medicine, linguistics, and literature, arguing in favor of compatibility between Judaism and science and championing converso interests with a power that helped restrain Portuguese inquisitors. He authored the first serious Jewish work printed in England, *Matteh Dan* (*Dan's Rod*), 1714, in Spanish, Spanish-Hebrew, and Hebrew editions, validating the Oral Law to Marranos reluctant to acknowledge its authority. His response to an archbishop who attempted to affirm the credibility of the New Testament by misinterpreting Hebrew sources was widely admired.

A prosperous and respected Jewish community inclined the Whig party toward broadening civil and commercial privileges to a small number of well-to-do foreign-born Sephardim. Naturalization legislation, popularly known in 1753 as the Jew Bill, was immediately opposed by Tories who claimed that poor Ashkenazim fleeing from Germany and eastern Europe would manipulate laws, endanger commercial dominance, and destroy Anglican homogeneity. Cries were raised that British Christians would end up "tilling and toiling for Jewish landlords," that England would be a Jewish state within a hundred years, and that Jews would help Catholics undermine the Established Church and return the Stuart line to the English throne. Emotions ran so high that a production of *The Merchant of Venice* was cancelled because anti–Jewish reactions might provoke violence.

The bill immediately caught the attention of satiric artists, who churned out dozens of prints deriding or spoofing the proceedings: *The Dreadful Consequences of a General Naturalization, The Jews' Triumph,* and *England's Fears Set Forth.* Folks were alerted to the *Jew Naturalized* astride a pig urging the public to "Buy My Pork"—the Judensau theme had been imported from the continent (Ill. 5:3). *The Grand Conference of the Jew Predominant* represented Samson Gideon, a wealthy loan agent who had raised large sums to help the government rebuild its finances, bribing a devil to gain support for the bill (Ill. 5:4). Jews presumably would then be in a position to turn Parliament into a Jewish high court, seize the lands of the impoverished gentry, and force circumcision on unwilling males. In *A Good and a Bad Spirit,* a cleric is mortified to learn that Jewish money controls the nation's affairs. The caption, raising the charge of deicide, reads in part: "As JUDAS did for pelf betray our Lord/ Grant Heav'n that [Jews] may meet their just Reward!" Still another print, *A Prospect of the New Jerusalem,* depicts an affluent devil conspiring with "Christ's natural enemies, the Jews," to purchase St. Paul's Cathedral and transform it into a synagogue (Ill. 5:5). The natural enemies, however,

Ill. 5:3. *The Jew Naturalized.* Engraving, 1753.

Ill. 5:4. *The Grand Conference of the Jew Predominant.* **Engraving, 1753**

were more often burdened with constraints which precluded such acquisitions. Rather than buying up churches, most peddled through small towns where locals sneered at their boxes, beards, and black coats.

The bill was withdrawn after six months, but the offensive caricatures bred lasting negative consequences. The trouble was that Jews were not Christians. They were not even regular Englishmen. What they were, of course, were political and economic rivals, handy objects for humorous or demeaning lampoons. Aided by a free press, conspicuous exaggeration became an acceptable way to express ridicule. It was popular because its message—some people are insiders, some are outsiders—was simplistic and easily understood. It was insidious because numbers of Jews decided that they had no future in that environment and converted.

Young children as well were exposed to the narrow views of their elders. John Newbery's mid-century *Mother Goose Melody*, which included the popular rhyme *The Goose That Laid the Golden Egg*, was a lesson in Jewish taunting. Yet what could be more innocuous than the nonsense verses?

> Old Mother Goose,
> When she wanted to wander,
> Would ride through the air
> On a very fine gander.
>
> This is her son Jack,
> A plain-looking lad,
> He is not very good,
> Nor yet very bad ...

Ill. 5:5. A Prospect of the New Jerusalem. Engraving, 1753

It turns out that that Jack had found a golden egg which he sold to a "rogue of a Jew/Who cheated him out of/The half of his due." It is possible that the lines hit an enlightened nerve. Later versions in English and American editions adjusted the words "To a rogue named New," "To a rogue in red shoes," "To a merchant untrue," and "To a rascally knave" who gave poor Jack less than half its worth.

While every group and everyone's predilections or mannerisms were open to prejudice, the negative image of Jews was intensified. Their "otherness" was belabored in ever more repellent slovenly appearance, sexual perversions, gluttony, and greed. Nor were bankers or brokers immune, although as well-groomed and decorous as any proper citizen; they were shown with fine clothing and behavior, but "speaking" with an outlandish Yiddish accent. The point was that rich Jews embarrass polite society as surely as poor ones sap its strength. Book illustrations, penny sheets, and prints were useful to channel the frustrations that prompted one group to look down on another perceived as less worthy of merit or respect.

From where was this calculated distortion acquired in the rational Age of Enlightenment when religious inclusion was viewed as consistent with a logical mind? Perhaps one answer is that Realism, then current in art as well as in social standards, endorsed literal or cynical depiction—the world seen through unromantic, even unflattering eyes. It was, therefore, only a small step towards representing ethnic types according to "truthful" images: Jews as usurers, despoilers of Christian maidens, and deputies of the Devil.

Satire, cynicism, and the bleaker side of the Industrial Revolution found recognition in London thanks to one of the most inventive masters of the genre. William Hogarth was not just another clever artist, but England's first great native-born painter and engraver to describe and interpret the ways of a wayward world. He was able to get away with poking the underbelly of a society he believed to be hopelessly decadent because the relatively democratic government permitted a relatively open political climate to artists and authors. A born storyteller, he addressed his subjects as a "dramatic writer—my picture is my stage, and men and women my players...." He carried his point by painting six theatrical episodes of *A Harlot's Progress* and then, to reach a wider audience, engraving the set in 1732. In the first scene, Moll Hackabout, an ingénue just off the farm, falls into the snares of a disreputable procuress. An unattractive wealthy Jew ogles her suggestively from a doorway. In the next plate, *The Quarrel with Her Jew Protector*, she kicks over a table in order to distract him from the stealthy exit of her Christian lover (Ill. 5:6). Hogarth underscored the unsavoriness by linking a monkey's features and turn of the head to that of the Jew.

He included two biblical paintings in the background as additional reference points. In one, Jonah experiences the transient benefit of a gourd's shelter (Jonah 4:6). In the other, Uzzah dies because he touched the Ark of the Covenant (2 Samuel 6:6). If Moll and the Jew had only heeded the lessons on the wall, she would have realized the fragile nature of her protector's custodianship, and the profligate Jew would have learned the price of pursuing the forbidden. The heavy-handed moral was obvious by the end of the drama—Moll dies after a sad and dissolute life; scriptural justice prevails. Her "progress" ends in deceit and death. The series reverberated throughout London and was translated into a number of theatrical performances with Beau Mordechai as a stock Jewish rascal being tricked out of his mistress. The *Harlot* plates drew attention to the bleak life endured by many imperiled or unsuspecting women and led to the founding of Magdalen Hospital for prostitutes in 1758.

Hogarth's prints were plagiarized to such an extent that he sought and won copyright privileges for himself and others in 1709, a law still known by his name. (Possibly the earliest attempt to protect authors was made in 1599 by a Jewish doctor, Paul Rici, for a translation of a medieval work by a Muslim physician, Abul Kasim.) Having received legal protection for his work, Hogarth engraved *A Rake's Progress* in 1735, a series centered around the vices of the

Ill. 5:6. *The Quarrel with Her Jew Protector*. Engraving, 1732. From *A Harlot's Progress* by William Hogarth

rich and the craze for gambling: Tom Rakewell betrays the girl who loves him, marries an older woman for her money, loses her fortune, and comes to a bad end in a madhouse. Scene 6 takes place in Hell, an actual gaming room where one of the players haggles with the ubiquitous Jewish moneylender. In Hogarth's world—and in this case, the real world, too—punishment was inevitable. The building was destroyed by a fire.

Hogarth was a champion, as he understood it, of England's ultranationalism; he felt that the country should not be contaminated by non-Englishmen—Catholics or Jews. During the time of the Jew Bill, he engraved an Election series, of which *Humors of an Election Entertainment* was the first plate. A bearded effigy reading "No Jews!" represented Hogarth's sentiments as well as those of many of his fellow citizens. A detail of the next plate, *Canvassing for Votes*, included a Jewish peddler displaying bits of jewelry to a pair of ladies (Ill. 5:7). As their men look on, there is a hint that the wily Jew is denigrating the integrity of the ballot by offering trinkets as a bribe. Although women couldn't vote, their influence could be counted on, given appropriate incentives.

Jewish manners—or lack of them—were easy butts for the wicked etching needle of Thomas Rowlandson. He was a fine and careful draftsman, a master of line when he chose; otherwise his figures are more bizarre or preposterous than Hogarth's, his exuberance coarser. Unlike Hogarth's judicious earnestness, his caricatures were personal and comic; his high-spirited and bawdy images targeted pomposity more than sin. He found his subject matter wherever an amusing, provocative, or pornographic scene suggested itself. His shameless gentlemen, blowzy ladies, and outlandish old-timers were mostly good-natured spoofs of royalty, social climbers, and frauds, but he also included peddlers, moneylenders, blasphemers, and libertines—often parodies of well-known baptized Jews.

Sexual depravity and the deflowering of Christian maidens were among his pet themes.

Ill. 5:7. *Canvassing for Votes*. Engraving, 1753. Detail from *Humors of an Election Entertainment* by William Hogarth

Ill. 5:8. *The Rabbi Turn'd to a Christian*. Etching, 1722. By Thomas Rowlandson

The Jew Rabbi Turn'd to a Christian, 1772, illustrates what happens when a lascivious Jew, who was expected to know better, tempts an innocent lass with a bag of gold (Ill. 5:8). Perhaps even more than the lady, a smirking devil on the wall is aware of the imminent loss of her virtue. Rowlandson portrayed rich old Jews and scapegrace young men with equal relish. *Money Lenders*, 1784, reveals a pair of cautious fellows bargaining with the decadent Prince of Wales over a deed or bond (Ill. 5:9). They clearly are not strangers to their spendthrift client who in reality was a sad burden to the king. The print implied that many aristocrats were beholden to Jewish money-lenders. The easy camaraderie between Israelite and patrician marks a development in the status of the Jews, a turn of events unlikely before the Enlightenment period.

Moneyless Jews were equally tempting laughing stocks. (Somehow Jews were always too rich or too poor.) As they began to arrive on English shores in greater numbers towards the end of the century—there were some fifteen thousand by then—most became itinerant vendors. In *Too Many for a Jew*, 1785, Rowlandson depicted one such hapless character, no match for a group of larcenous children who, by distracting his attention with a few tossed coins, snatch a trifle from his box (Ill. 5:10). *Ladies Trading on Their Own Bottom*, 1799, an etching with an indelicate title, was presumably by Rowlandson (Ill. 5:11). Its unappetizing lecher offers money-bags to a pair of eager prostitutes; on the same theme, an anonymous etching, *A Jewish Merchant with Christian Flesh*, likewise was not calculated to win the Jews much public affection (Ill. 5:12). For those elements of the English population who saw the Jew as a boor, the impression that Jews were the dregs of decent society was validated.

Other eye-catching Jewish vices as well were given visual form. A mezzotint by Robert Sayer, *Jews Receiving Stolen Goods*, 1777, reported on the increase in criminal activity of Jewish burglars, pickpockets, gang members, and shady street traders (Ill. 5:13). Four disreputable fences, "members of the tribe," take advantage of a soldier's disability by cheating him on the worth of some filched objects. The artist suggested the disparity between Jewish haves and Christian have-nots by highlighting an expensive screen in the swindler's home. The dog can't be bothered to watch the proceedings; having witnessed this scene so often, he has come to resemble his master, wig and all. The escalating crime rate encouraged synagogue personnel to work with the police in identifying individuals buying and receiving stolen merchandise— "the foreign miscreants who stain our religion by calling themselves Jews."

MONEY LENDERS.

Above: Ill. 5:9. *Money Lenders*. Etching, 1784. By Thomas Rowlandson. *Below:* Ill. 5:10. *Too Many for a Jew*. Etching, 1785. By Thomas Rowlandson

Above: Ill. 5:11. *Ladies Trading on Their Own Bottom.* Etching, 1799. Presumably by Thomas Rowlandson. *Below:* Ill. 5:12. *A Jewish Merchant with Christian Flesh*

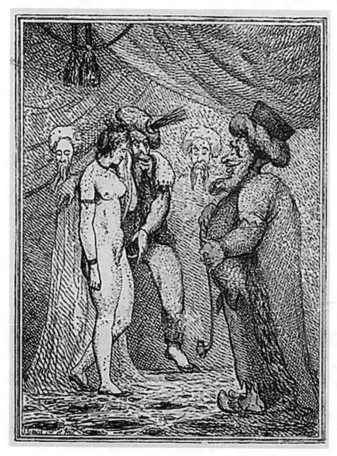

Luigi Schiavonetti, an English-based Italian artist, produced prints of street life after Francis Wheatley's *Cries of London*, 1793–1797. The fifth plate in the series, *Water-Cresses, Come Buy My Water-Cresses*, contributed to the familiar theme and variations: the Jew is morally corrupt, he has no interest in the child's soup-greens, but is inflamed when they are offered by a buxom lass—a message that had more to do with venery than vegetables (Ill. 5:14).

Ridicule of Jews, stereotyped not only as thieves and philanderers but as physical cowards, commonly led from minor street brawls to serious violence. Times were changing, however, and Jews were learning to fight back. A newspaper reported that a Jewish orange-seller, arrested for attacking a burly porter, declared, "Jews larns in their own defense ... we are so

Jews receiving Stolen Goods.

Ill. 5:13. *Jews Receiving Stolen Goods.* Mezzotint, 1777. By Robert Sayer

CRIES OF LONDON. NO. 5, 'WATER-CRESSES, COME BUY MY WATER-CRESSES.'

Ill. 5:14. *Water-Cresses, Come Buy My Water-Cresses.* **Engraving. From** *Cries of London,* **1793–1797. By Francis Wheatley**

exposed to insult that ve're obligated to pitch in as vell as ve can." They put on boxing gloves, won grudging respect, and turned what had been haphazard hits and misses into a professionally regulated sport. This pugilistic miracle was due to the exertions of Daniel Mendoza, who, as a child, protected his interests with his fists in the alleys of Jewish London. He later attracted public attention with a dramatic victory over Richard Humphries, the incumbent champion of the ring. J. Grozer popularized the fifty-minute contest with an aquatint after Rowlandson, *The Jewish Boxer Daniel Mendoza,* 1789 (Ill. 5:15). Children risk life and limbs hanging from

Ill. 5:15. *The Jewish Boxer Daniel Mendoza.* Aquatint, 1789. By J. Grozer

trees, grownups watch in nervous anticipation. Grozer and other artists who admired Mendoza refrained from depicting the "Light of Israel" with exaggerated caricature-type features, perhaps suggesting that bigotry, as well as Humphries, was taking a beating. Mendoza pummeled his way through "thirty-three pitched battles, most of them with antagonists far superior to me in strength and size." Though only five feet seven inches tall and one hundred sixty pounds, he refined jab-and-run techniques into a science and filled his memoirs with training methods.

All England took to Mendoza the Jew, as he called himself, to its heart. Crowds of twenty thousand fans turned out for his matches, particularly from 1792 to 1795 when he was the champion of all England. A rare exception was a great nobleman, Lord Althorp, himself a boxer, who claimed that he had seen Mendoza "knocked down for the first five or six rounds by Humphries, and seeming almost beaten until the Jews had got their money on, when a hint being given, he began in earnest and soon turned the table." But such sneers weren't typical. Members of the royal family and other dignitaries attended his bouts and lauded him with honors and respect. Songs and medals celebrated his talents. Eventually he opened a school where he taught the secret of his skills and helped some of his Jewish students win honors in the prizefighting profession.

A different sort of character was Richard Brothers, a retired Christian naval officer who announced that he was the messiah since he and James, the brother of Jesus, shared the word "brother[s]." He explained that the Ten Lost Tribes of Israel, together with the Tribes of Abraham and Isaac, had sprouted miraculously on British soil—hence the word *Berit-Ish* (Man of the Covenant.) As another son of God, he had been delegated by his Father to lead His subjects to their homeland. Brothers' millenarian book, *A Revealed Knowledge of the Prophesies and Times: The Restoration of the Hebrews to Jerusalem by the Year of 1798,* made a great splash when it came out four years before the promised date. Cartoonists had a field day with the prophet. James Gillray depicted him *Conducting the Elect to the Promised Land* over the body of George III, whose death he demanded, presumably because the king resisted his scenario (Ill. 5:16). After arranging the mummified body of his wife in his parlor, he declared that since the French Revolution was ordained by God, Britain must end hostilities with France. He was tossed into an asylum for the criminally insane, an action that hardly daunted his many admirers, who founded the British-Israelite movement in his honor.

Another eccentric was Lord George Gordon. Born into an aristocratic Protestant family, he converted to Judaism after leading anti–Catholic riots in 1780. Excommunicated from the Church of England, he practiced strict Orthodoxy, sharply criticizing those of his disciples who were less meticulous. For condemning the British government's treatment of convicts and libeling Marie Antoinette for other indiscretions, he landed in a commodious London jail where he held regular services with a *minyan* of ten Polish Jews and gave formal dinner-dances attended by a number of royal princes. He was concerned about the proper length of a Jewish beard, and indeed his own was long and handsome, eventually extending to his waist. A mezzotint, *Lord George Gorden,* from about 1788 shows it descending to the halfway mark. When a friend offered to visit him in prison, he declared that only Jews with suitable beards would be admitted. The poor fellow was advised to "tarry until thy beard is grown." Which he did. Gordon died in prison, becoming a "Martyr of Freedom" to his followers. One of the many

Ill. 5:16. *Conducting the Elect to the Promised Land.* Etching, c. 1794. By James Gillray

Ill. 5:17. *The Birmingham Moses*. Etching, 1787

caricatures of the "lunatic apostle," as Horace Walpole called him, is an etching, *The Birmingham Moses*, 1787, which includes a pair of attacking dogs and weather vane to indicate the fluctuation of his beliefs (Ill. 5:17). Part of the caption reads:

> To Law & Presbyters he bid adieu,
> To save his Soul and Body in the Jew;
> And wonder not he stole to mis-believers,
> Since they of stolen things are oft receivers....

Poisoned pens remained on the cutting edge of social commentary through much of the second half of the eighteenth and well into the nineteenth century as the vices and foibles of an upstart Jewish middle-class permeated literature as well as art. Thomas Bridges' novel *The Adventures of a Bank-Note*, 1770, introduces a garrulous old lady who can hardly believe that the Patriarchs were Israelites since the Bible never mentions their selling "a black lead pencil, or a roll of hard pomatum, or a pair of sleeve buttons in their lives." Richard Sheridan's comic opera *The Duenna*, 1775, diverted its audience with Isaac, an unscrupulous Jew; however, two years later he presented Moses in the *School for Scandal* as an honest man. Tobias Smollett was likewise ambivalent—Isaac Rapine in his *Adventures of Roderick Random*, 1748, was bad. Joshua Manasseh in *The Adventures of Ferdinand Count Fathom*, 1753, was good.

Society and culture were very different across the Channel. King Frederick I of Prussia immediately raised Jewish taxes when he began his reign in 1701. Twelve years later, his heir, Frederick William I, put some of those winnings to advantage by setting his country on sound fiscal and military principles, structuring an oppressive dictatorship, and maintaining an equivocal relationship with his Jews. In 1714, he limited the number of their households and restricted their inheritance rights. Sixteen years later, he accommodated Christian guilds by preventing Jewish merchants and artisans from peddling small items or working in handicrafts (except seal engraving and gold embroidery, where Jews had established a monopoly.) He denied Rabbi Mirels permission to print the Talmud, but allowed publication of other Hebrew works. He encouraged Jewish craftsmen and merchants to develop his economy and allowed them to build the Heidenreutergasse Synagogue in Berlin when that city had only about one thousand Jews; it was said that he attended its dedication on Rosh Hashanah eve. An etching by A. B. Goblin, 1744, forgivably exaggerated the building's great size and grand interior, but no amount of elaborate appointments could hide the fact that the sanctuary was built below street level because synagogues could not be taller than local churches.

His son, Frederick II (the Great) was a capable administrator and military genius who spoke of all his countrymen as members of "the damned human race." Nevertheless, he wrested legions of that race from Austria and Poland during his reign from 1740 to 1786, pausing occasionally to impose restrictive measures and heavy taxes on "tolerated" Jews, and to exile Danzig's Jewish community from Prussian lands. His anti–Jewish laws were described by Honoré de Mirabeau, French revolutionary leader and champion of the Jews, as "worthy of a cannibal." Yet legend tells us that when he inquired of his wise men if there was any proof of God's existence, they suggested that it was the survival of the Jewish people. Salomon Bennett, a Jewish printmaker who had complained bitterly of the inequities suffered by German Jews, engraved a posthumous portrait of the cannibal, *Frederick II of Prussia*, 1797. The print was awarded a government prize.

Like other progressive rulers, Frederick developed industrial and commercial markets for which he needed competent leaders; he found many of them among the secular Jewish bankers, physicians, and scholars to whom he offered inducements to settle in Berlin and other German cities. There they were protected as "useful" administrators, providing him with marketing and other benefits as he moved the country towards a modern capitalist economy. Once in positions of influence and power, these Court Jews shaved their beards, adopted wigs, dressed in the height of fashion, and socialized with broad-minded Gentiles. Living a dual existence as privileged outsiders immune from general taxation and the threat of expulsion, they were still subject to many impediments. By and large, they served as advocates to the great mass of "useless" Jews, enabling many of them to remain within the fold during the difficult journey from exclusion to civil equity.

Joseph Oppenheimer (Jud-Süss) was such a Court Jew. A financial wizard, he enriched the pockets of the Catholic Duke of Wurttemberg, stirring up enormous resentment in the Protestant opposition party. He came to an inglorious end with the sudden death of his patron and was hanged on charges of embezzlement and consorting with Christian women. Offered his life on condition of baptism, he refused, grew a traditional beard and renounced his secular lifestyle in favor of strict religious observance. A mezzotint by J. J. Baumgartner in 1738, the year he was hanged, depicts him in a fine costume and wig (Ill. 5:18). The pulley, chain, and devils, however, pointed to his sad fate. "When a great gentleman abuses good fortune with bad counsel," reads the inscription, "as this impudent Jew Süss Oppenheimer did, when avarice and insolence also accompany voluptuousness, he must, like Haman, finally come to the gallows." An anonymous engraving, *Galgen des Joseph Süss Oppenheimer* (*Gallows of Joseph*

Ill. 5:18. *Joseph Oppenheimer*. Mezzotint, 1738. By J. J. Baumgartner

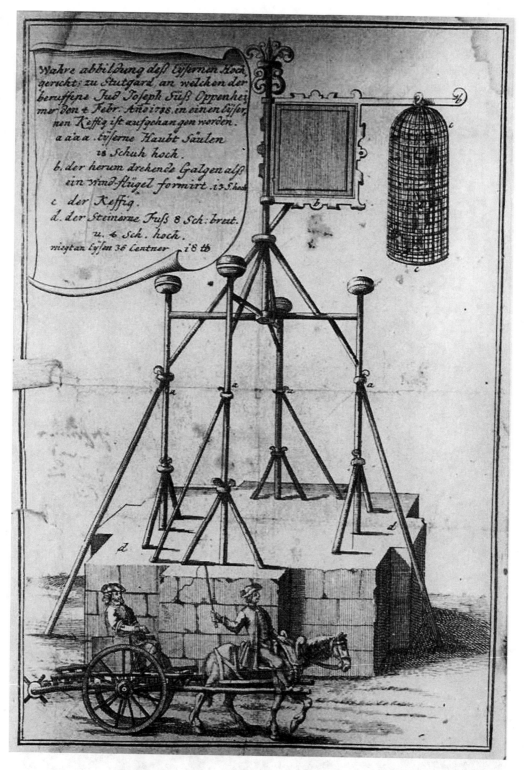

Ill. 5:19. *Galgen des Joseph Süss Oppenheimer (Gallows of Joseph Süss Oppenheimer)*. Engraving, 1738

Süss Oppenheimer), 1738, shows him conveyed to his execution in an open carriage and then dangling in a birdcage over the main street in Stuttgart (Ill. 5:19). (According to an old wives' tale, birds were explicit references for sexual depravity.) Motivated by the thousands who attended the spectacle—including a representative group of his alleged mistresses—engravers around Europe hawked pictures of his downfall. Anti-Jewish cartoons, prints, and books equated him with Satan and celebrated his end. To his fellow Jews, he was a martyr.

It is ironic that Frederick may have been an unwitting patron of the Jewish Enlightenment through his toleration of diverse religious opinions and his concessions to Court Jews who quickly absorbed the new rationalist spirit. In spite of himself, he was impressed by the reputation of the most influential member of the Berlin Jewish community, Moses Mendelssohn, whose metaphysical treatise won the top prize from the Prussian Royal Academy of Sciences against such competitors as Immanuel Kant. Frederick denied his election as a member. Mendelssohn attempted to find rational proofs of God's existence and the immortality of the soul. He stressed Judaism's link to ethical values, epitomizing the highest values of the Berlin Enlightenment. In the 1750s he founded the first Hebrew periodical, the short-lived *Kohelet Musar* (*The Preacher of Morals*), and in 1788, launched the first successful Hebrew magazine, *Ha-Me'assef* (*The Assembler*), catering to Haskalah enthusiasts with prose, poetry, science, history, and biographies, all to help Jews participate in the world outside the ghetto. Berlin's salons, dominated by brilliant Jewish women, were enlivened by the best and brightest cosmopolites. Mendelssohn's home was open to the best and brightest scholars and men of influence. He was an observant Jew who attempted to reconcile rabbinic and modern ideals, an uphill task considering that while he believed the Talmud was divinely revealed, certain of its doctrines were not. He translated the Bible into German, hoping to promote religious faith through a reasoned focus, but traditional voices complained that he opened the door to assimilation and secular culture and violated talmudic law.

His fame attracted Daniel Chodowiecki, a prolific etcher of German manners and occasional aspects of Jewish life such as the *Kleiderhandler* (*Clothing Hawker*), 1780 (Ill. 5:20). In 1774, he engraved an ex-libris for Mendelssohn's friend, David Friedlander, who in 1786 translated the earliest "reformed" prayer book into German. A willingness to "adapt the spirit and aims of Mosaic law to our times and our custom," took Friedlander to the edge of baptism, and all of his family across.

Mendelssohn's great companions were the Lutheran clergyman John Casper Lavater and the playwright Gotthold Lessing, whose *Nathan der Weise* (*the Wise*), 1779, was modeled on Mendelssohn. It was a plea against prejudice, implying among other things, that Jews had a right to humane treatment, and that Christians, Muslims, and Jews shared equally valid monotheistic religions—heretical notions which caused the play to be banned for several

Ill. 5:20. *Kleiderhandler (Clothing Hawker)*. Etching, 1780. **By Daniel Chodowiecki**

Ill. 5:21. *Fanciful Portrait of Moses Mendelssohn, John Casper Lavater, and Gotthold Lessing.* Etching, 1856

years and led to rumors that wealthy Jews had paid Lessing to write ecumenically. However, enlightened as he was, Lessing agreed with Lavater that Christianity was superior, Judaism inferior; the Christian character in his play charged Jews with fostering bigotry through their claims of chosenness. Lavater called on Mendelssohn to convert, asserting that Judaism was not germane to current times. The challenge spurred Mendelssohn to defend his "oppressed people" in his celebrated *Jerusalem*, 1783, in which he defended both rationalistic Judaism and ceremonial practices. So successful were his arguments that Lavater apologized, but the emotional strain on Mendelssohn brought on a collapse from which he never fully recovered. A fanciful portrait of the three was etched in 1856 based on a Moritz Oppenheim painting; such a meeting never actually took place, but the image survives as a celebration of enlightened mutual respect and fellowship despite polarities of opinion (Ill. 5:21). Mendelssohn died in 1786, unsuccessful in merging his intellectual approach to Jewish continuity with a strict adherence to Jewish law, and never knowing that most of his family, including the composer Felix Mendelssohn and the painter Philipp Veit chose to live as practicing Christians. While the Enlightenment envisioned new possibilities, the denial of permanent social and civil rights for Jews closed off real chances to advance careers, leading Anton Mengs and Edward Bendemann, the first internationally recognized artists of Jewish origin, to convert.

Frederick's archenemy was Austria's Maria Theresa, who ruled the divided and heterogeneous Hapsburg dominions; their destinies were locked in punitive battles which she unsuccessfully launched against his military machine. She blamed some of her troubles on her Jewish subjects after false reports of political disloyalties. She then banished the entire

Jewish population of Prague. "Dreadful indeed is their departure in the bitter cold," reported a Catholic rector of the university. Dreadful, too, was the disarray in the imperial treasury following the loss of their financial and industrial skills. Quietly, the accusations of treason were dismissed and the exiles were invited back. The event was possibly the first time in history that groups of organized Jews, as well as several rulers in central and western Europe, were able to coordinate effective clout against her harsh decrees. In 1754 she intervened on behalf of Mantuan Jews, over whom she ruled, when they were attacked at the gates of the ghetto: "No one may molest, disturb, harm or mistreat Jews," she ordered, "under penalty of imprisonment."

Prussia, Russia, and Austria set their sights on the Polish kingdom, which, encumbered by insecure borders and troubled by internal disturbances, was no match for their aggression and was soon obliterated. When Polish Galicia, with its large Jewish population, came under her control in 1772, Maria Theresa found herself with the largest Jewish population in Europe. Her animosity towards alien heretics was stinging: "There is no worse plague for the state than this nation because its deceitfulness and usury bring us more harm than good." That opinion didn't prevent her from using Jewish talent and money to help provision her armies and build her palaces and factories—in which no Jews were permitted to work.

Jewish talent and money, of course, were absolutely necessary, something that Maria Theresa's son and heir Joseph II noticed since they largely managed his country's finances. He encouraged their support by issuing an Edict of Toleration in 1781—the beginning of civil rights for German Jews. It abolished humiliating and oppressive laws such as the poll tax and Jews' Badge, but imposed marital regulations in order to curb the birth rate. Yiddish and Hebrew were forbidden in most public documents in order to promote assimilation. Universities were opened to Jews, but ghettos remained closed. Jews were inducted into the army, but kept from high office. A dress code which confined fancy apparel and even phylacteries to weddings was repealed in 1781, although prosperous individuals had already gotten around most sumptuary laws. The ladies, of course, had kept their silks and satins, possibly because the authorities shrank from thwarting the fair sex and their must-have fashions. The few concessions were welcome, but they resulted in accelerated assimilation and a loss of traditional cultural patterns.

At the suggestion of Mendelssohn, Christian Wilhelm Von Dohm, an enlightened Prussian historian and political theorist, attempted to improve the situation of Alsatian Jews with his influential treatise *Über die bürgerliche Verbesserung der Juden* (*On the Civic Improvement of the Jews*), 1781. He recommended a shift from their traditional commercial affairs to livelihoods in which they could be more "useful and productive," i.e. working the land. He acknowledged that Jewish "shortcomings" were the result of persecution and religious intolerance by the Christian world, but suggested that through the removal of trade and other restrictions, their strengths—intelligence, perseverance, and aptness—could be reinforced, while their weaknesses—superstitions, exclusiveness, and excessive love of money—could be modified. The expectation, of course, was that Jews would abandon their Jewish identity, align themselves with the state, and participate in the Christian world. Many Jews, as well as Gentiles, applauded his efforts.

Unlike central European Jews, those further east remained politically and economically insignificant. Access to professions and education was severely limited. Business dealings from which they were excluded, craft guilds from which they were denied membership, and compulsory "gifts" for which there were no constraints at all reduced many to indigence and subjected them to the whims of local rulers. The radical idea that the political and social status of Jews might be open to permissive legislation was unthinkable to the czarist regime which maintained rigid class and social privileges not available to Jews. Emancipation for Russian Jews would have to wait.

The Scandinavian Jewish community dates from 1774, Sweden having decreed in 1726 that Jews, drifters, and tinsmiths shall "be driven out of the Nation, never to be tolerated there." Yet when King Gustav III needed a seal engraver, he turned to German Jews, Europe's ablest die-makers. Aaron Isaac was selected but turned out to be a problem. Mr. Isaac would not come unless the king invited nine additional Jews to form a *minyan*. Permission granted, ten men, along with their families, settled in Stockholm. A former red-light district later made room for a thousand-seat synagogue.

Frederick VI came to the Spanish throne in 1746 amid inadequate attempts to modify the still active Inquisition against New Christians. That year, Francisco Goya, the country's first great etcher and satirist and one of Europe's greatest artists, was born. He focused on the intemperance of the Spanish and French wars and the cruelties of the Inquisition, which targeted a variety of free-thinkers as well as Jews. His *Los Caprichos* (*Whims*), 1796–1798, attacked the abuses of Church authority. Plate 14 from that series, *Que sacrificio* (*What a Sacrifice*), was an uncharacteristic anti–Jewish image—a physically repulsive foppish, heavy lipped, deformed figure—unexpected from this artist of liberal sensibilities. A young girl, "sold" to an elderly, over-eager Jewish suitor, cringes from any contact with him by placing her hands over her genitals. The twenty-third plate, *Aquellos polbos* (from a proverb expressing "See the Result"), depicts a cleric preaching to a heretic (probably, but not explicitly Jewish) wearing the fearful cone-shaped corozo and yellow sambenito (Ill. 5:22). During Goya's lifetime almost a thousand souls, most of whom were accused of being secret Jews, were condemned; seventy-five went to the stake. If the dissident repented with sufficient humility, he might be dragged through the streets in triumph, "disciplined" by a hundred lashes, or, if lucky enough to avoid the flames, strangled.

Ill. 5:22. *Aquellos polbos (See the Result)*. Etching, c. 1797. From *Los Caprichos (Whims)*. By Francisco Goya

Pre-revolutionary France was home to forty thousand Jews, over thirty thousand of whom were Yiddish-speaking Ashkenazim in Alsace-Lorraine and Paris; others lived in Spanish- and Portuguese-speaking areas in the South. Most couldn't participate freely in commerce and industry; many feared that their children would be secretly baptized. Nevertheless, they found a measure of security as moneylenders by helping economic development along trade routes. J. Lebas' etching, *Sabbath Eve Celebration*, 1722, caught a rare pleasant moment in the life of its pious Jews—the mother lights a hanging lamp, the father recites Kiddush, the children and guests offer a blessing, a servant prepares to serve dinner (Ill. 5:23).

Liberal voices were beginning to be heard. A dynamic middle-class began its protests against the repressive state. Radical philosophers such as Jean-Jacques Rousseau, François-Marie Voltaire, Denis Diderot, and Charles Montesquieu were

Ill. 5:23. *Sabbath Eve Celebration*. Etching, 1722. By J. Lebas

concerned with human rights, but not all were concerned with Jewish rights. Montesquieu was the most pro–Jewish of the lot. His *Lettres Persanes* (*Persian Letters*), 1721, and *De l'Esprit des Lois* (*On the Spirit of Laws*), 1748, made early appeals for toleration of the Jews. Diderot, compiler of the influential thirty-five volume *Encyclopedia*, 1751–1780, raised his distinguished voice against them, citing their ignorance and cupidity. But it was Voltaire who helped lay the groundwork for the virulent anti–Jewish sentiments that gained respectability. "The Jews are nothing more than an ignorant, barbarian people," he wrote in the *Dictionnaire philosophique*, 1757, "who combine the foulest greed with a terrible superstition and an uncompromising hatred of all the peoples who tolerate them and at whose cost they enrich themselves." A rebuttal was published five years later by the Jewish philosopher and political economist Isaac Pinto in his *Apologie pour la Nation Juive* (*Apology for the Jewish Nation*): "Is the damage caused by the pen less harmful than the flames...? What can this unhappy people expect from the mob, when barbarian prejudices are even shared by the most famous genius of our enlightened time?" Voltaire acknowledged receiving a copy of the work but was unmoved.

William Blake in *The Commonplace Book* remonstrated with the religious skepticism or ambivalence of the enlightened philosophs:

> Mock on, Mock on Voltaire, Rousseau:
> Mock on, Mock on: 'tis all in vain!
> You throw the sand against the wind,
> And the wind blows it back again.
>   And every sand becomes a Gem
> Reflected in the beams divine;
> Blown back they blind the mocking Eye,
> But still in Israel's path they shine.
>   The Atoms of Democritus
> And Newton's Particles of light
> Are sands upon the Red sea shore,
> Where Israel's tents do shine so bright.

In 1784, Louis XVI initiated a human rights program, dictated by political necessity as well as by liberal Christian voices. Jews, who had been paying dearly for the privilege of living where they were told, were relieved of some inequities and taxes, but land ownership was still out of the question. Count Mirabeau in his essay *Sur Moses Mendelssohn, sur les reforme politique des juifs....* (*On Moses Mendelssohn and the Political Reform of the Jews ...*), 1787, indicated that many benefits would accrue to France with the granting of full civil rights to its Jews. Two years later, the Catholic Abbé Henri Grégoire proposed that Jews should be westernized, made useful, and incorporated into the nation's culture. In his prize-winning *Essai sur la regeneration physique, morale, et politique des Juifs* (*Essay on the Physical, Moral, and Political Reformation of the Jews*), he declared that "the Jew is born the same as we.... If he has faults, Christian society is responsible. In their place would we not be worse?" What had seemed hopelessly unattainable was now almost within reach as reforms were initiated. Christian guilds became secular craft unions, and Jews operated their own tailoring, goldsmithing, shoemaking and other businesses in relative peace. Extortions, lootings, and forced baptisms were mitigated as progressive Frenchmen examined the guidelines of independence and equality. For Jews, this meant equal, not "special" rights, rights due by nature, not by sufferance.

France needed to centralize and harmonize its relationship with all its subjects. But the stubborn Jews stuck out. They couldn't be absorbed in their present condition, weren't about to abandon their religious faith, wouldn't become invisible, resisted being spruced up, and declined to "improve" themselves as a prerequisite to entering mainstream life. An anonymous pamphlet, *Les Juifs d'Alsace doivent être admis au droit citoyen actif?* (*Should the Jews of Alsace Be Granted Equal Citizenship Rights?*), 1790, described them as "foreign and un-French in their total demeanor, unworthy of being granted civil rights." The engraved frontispiece urged them to renounce usury and to take up "useful or serviceable" occupations such as handicrafts, farming, fiddling, cobbling, and carpentry, all depicted on a clothesline of acceptable vocations (Ill. 5:24).

The president of the Constituent Assembly, Comte Stanislas de Clermont-Tonnerre, recognized that respect for France's Jews and support for their Emancipation was validated by the Declaration of the Rights of Man—providing they suppressed their peoplehood and discarded their traditional distinctiveness: "To Jews as individuals, everything; to Jews as a nation, nothing.... There must be no nation within the nation." He believed the Jews would be amenable to assimilation—and they were; otherwise they faced expulsion.

Quittez un vil trafic, renoncez à l'usure,
à l'industrie
Aux arts ~~et aux métiers~~ joignez l'agriculture.
Stellt Wucher und Betrug, und schnödes Schachern ein,
handwerck, Kunst, Ackerbau, mus euer Nahrung sein.

Ill. 5:24. *Frontispiece.* **From** *Les Juifs d'Alsace doivent être admis au droit citoyen actif? (Should the Jews of Alsace Be Granted Equal Citizenship Rights?* **Engraving, 1790**

Eventually the political and social pressures worked. Jews were rewarded for adapting loyally to the French language and culture. Sephardim, mostly from Bayonne and Bordeaux, were emancipated in 1790; Ashkenazim from Alsace, Lorraine, and Metz a year later under the terms of the Revolution. This was an enormous step; it recast them into a social as well as a religious agency, a decisive concept in Jewish communal history.

Ashkenazi Jews expected that the high-minded directives of the Revolution—which they had supported with money, manpower, and prayers—would apply to them as well. They didn't count on the opposition of conservative Sephardim who, having already achieved a measure of prosperity and acceptance, blocked their emancipation for a year on the grounds that they were socially and culturally inferior; only "well-born productive Sephardi Jews" were worthy. Nevertheless, on September 27, 1791, French Jews were given full citizenship for the first time since the Roman Empire.

France had faced more serious issues than its relationship with Jews. In 1789, after generations of corruption and an intransigent Church, an overburdened and rebellious people mounted the barricades in bloody rebellion. The flags of Liberty, Equality, and Fraternity were unfurled, symbols of civil, moral, and religious justice for a free citizenry. But those ideals didn't live up to their promise. Hungry mobs defied the monarchy, the aristocracy, and the Church, initiating the Reign of Terror that guillotined thousands of men and women, including the king and queen. Religious institutions were not exempt—churches and synagogues were as willfully vandalized as landed estates. By 1794, the immediate goals of the Revolution lay in ruins with an economy in collapse and a ruthless political leadership exhausted. When it seemed as if nothing could moderate the alienation and disillusion, Napoleon Bonaparte pulled together the demoralized country, suppressed further violence, averted a civil war, established himself as dictator—and remembered the Jews. It was reported that during his botched 1799 Egyptian campaign, he urged the "rightful heirs to claim the restoration of your privileges among the population of the universe which had been shamefully withheld for thousands of years."

Among the rulers of this complicated world was Peter the Great, who had stepped onto its stage as czar of all Russia in 1721. He flexed unexpected military prowess in his drive towards Western culture and westward expansion. Having studied European civilizations (including the art of engraving), he imported experts in modern technology and science, initiated reforms in health care, introduced printing presses, and embroiled his country in twenty years of war. Russia was living off an impoverished peasant economy, modern factories were few, and secret police and punitive taxes inhibited well-being and hindered growth. Peter the Great was brutal when opposed, especially by the Church which he believed undermined his programs. Nor did he hold a brief for the useless Jews, although when they attempted to gain permission to settle in his lands, he reportedly said that he would pity them were they to live long among Russians. After he died in 1725, the country marked time under three different empresses, all of whom issued decrees banishing Jews and seizing their property. In 1762, Catherine II (the Great), picking up where Peter left off, undertook grandiose schemes to expand and consolidate the empire. When Poland was partitioned in 1772, and again in 1793 and 1795, she agreed that the tens of thousands of Jews she suddenly acquired "shall be left in the enjoyment of all those liberties with regard to their religion and property which they now possess." Notwithstanding those conciliatory words, before long, clashes erupted between Russian and Jewish merchants in Austria and Galicia. In 1791, she capitulated to Russian tradesmen, acceded to claims of special privileges by upper-class citizens, and limited Jews to the Pale of Settlement, an area between the Black and Baltic Seas made up mostly of former Turkish and Polish lands. Her earlier enlightened sympathies degenerated into repression of her Jewish subjects who were deemed "unfit for admission into civil society."

Nevertheless, Jewish artists found occasional opportunities to employ their skills in her lands. Catherine graciously sat for her portrait by Michael Johann Lowe; perhaps she was unaware the he had once been Moses Samuel. In 1760, when the court wished to commemorate Peter's 1709 victory over Sweden's Charles XII, the Jewish mint engraver, Samuel Juden was hired to produce a celebratory coin. But any real attempt at a Russian-Jewish national art would be delayed for almost another hundred years.

In general, where Jews lived determined how they lived. While the Enlightenment and Emancipation prospered in the West testing traditional Orthodoxy, eastern European Jews, who were little touched by Western thought, trusted that their own systems would strengthen cohesiveness and ensure religious integrity. Under the guidance of Israel Ba'al Shem Tov, the founder of Hasidism, they stressed God's omnipresence in all of nature along with the belief that meditation, amulets, ecstatic visions, joy, and spiritual purity, rather than either halachic or secular learning, were the path to the Almighty. Although he never published a statement of those principles, his disciple Rabbi Yaakov Yosef ben Zevi ha-Kohen Katz communicated his teachings in *Toldot Ya'akov Yosef* (*The Offspring of Yaakov Yosef*), 1780. It was received with exaltation by his followers and with deprecation by Lithuanian mitnagdim who branded it as heretical and delusional. In an uncharacteristic instance of book burning under Jewish auspices, it was destroyed under the direction of Elijah ben Solomon Zalman, the Gaon or eminence of Vilna who not only demanded the elimination of Hasidic literature but the excommunication of its proponents who he believed undermined communal authority.

Struggles over religious meaning and significance took on a painful urgency, weakening rabbinic authority in some areas and separating traditionalists who clung to strict Torah precepts from the maskilim who sought justification for Jewish life in its ethical mission to serve as a "light to the nations." The split, which renewed messianic fervor, became the talk of Jewish intellectual circles in Europe. Two uncompromising scholars, Jacob Emden and Jonathon Eybeschuetz, fought tirelessly over whether the latter was or was not a follower of Shabbetai Zvi. Emden directed his almost paranoid fear of the Shabbetains at Eybeschuetz, a dabbler in the murky depths of the Kabbalah. He founded his own private press and ran off pamphlets and books on the subject, some of which were banned and burned. Eybeschuetz swore great oaths in the synagogue that the contents of certain anti–evil-eye amulets for pregnant women which he may—or may not—have written (and which Emden had deciphered) were entirely innocent of subversive content. A portrait of Eybeschuetz, etched by Elimelekh Rose in 1770, was widely dispersed to his followers, who were reminded to keep their teacher's image before their eyes (Isaiah 30:20) (Ill. 5:25).

Congregants chose up sides in the free-for-all that ranged from curses "for which there is no cure" to appeals to the king of Denmark, who urged everyone to calm down. Scholars argued the points long after the rabbis' deaths. Current opinion holds that Eybeschuetz might have been a Shabbetain—or he might not. Those who like to think that the apple doesn't fall far from the tree point to his son Wolf, whose modest admission that he was the genuine messiah closed down his father's yeshiva. But then, Wolf also believed he was the Baron von Adlerstal.

One result of these squabbles was that many Jews began to move as far as they could from both Hasidism and Messianism, distancing themselves from the word "Jew" which, in their judgment, carried derisive or negative connotations; "members of the Mosaic faith," or "Israelites" seemed more felicitous. Released from the pressure to conform, they turned into avid purchasers of secular works such as Tobias Smollett's *The Adventures of Ferdinand, Count Fathom*, 1753, which portrayed a charitable Jew, and a Yiddish version of Daniel Defoe's *Robinson Crusoe*, 1764. Because Defoe referred to religious and biblical topics, authorities were apparently reconciled to Jewish readership, although his earlier *Roxana*, 1724, had introduced an evil Jew. (Having read a Hebrew version of *Crusoe* as a young boy, Eliezer ben Yehuda claimed that it sparked his development of a secular Hebrew language in early Palestine.) Jean-Baptiste Racine's *Athalie* was translated by a Jew, David Franco Mendes, in 1770. Such books enriched the lives of enlightened Jews and helped bring them into the nineteenth century mainstream. More and more considered themselves permanent members of the countries in which they lived, rather than exiles from Eretz Yisrael. Religious traditions and influences were displaced by a Judaism that emphasized the prophetic over the rabbinic heritage. Congregations began to build synagogues outside the ghettos in local architectural styles. Seating was arranged in formal rows in imitation of neighboring churches. Decorum was urged. Proud members chose to pray in elegant buildings and to celebrate holidays such as Passover with artistically printed books for home use.

Fine-looking Haggadot, therefore, continued to be offered, sometimes with fresh illustrations, mostly still in imitation of the Amsterdam publication of 1695. In 1712, a revised version was printed by Solomon ben Joseph Proops with plates that were probably engraved by Abraham ben Jacob, the artist of the 1695 edition. It boasted a new frontispiece with a copy of Merian's *Moses and the Burning Bush*. It also added engravings copied from the influential Venetian Haggadah of 1609, illustrating the order of the service, the Ten Plagues, and the Seder participants in contemporary dress (Ill. 5:26). It became the exemplar of many Haggadot down to the present time.

For some reason, a Haggadah published in Offenbach in 1722 reverted from engraved illustrations to more "primitive" woodcuts, still based on Abraham ben Jacob's prototype but also picking up on some of Merian's designs. A 1768 Haggadah from Amsterdam also featured woodcut illustrations in which the wine cups are large enough to test sobriety. The Berlin Haggadah of 1785 and the Offenbach reprint of 1795 were transliterated with Hebrew letters into German rather than Yiddish in deference to Joseph II's Edict of Toleration. (The line between German and Yiddish in Hebrew script is not always clear.) It was expected that as soon as Jews became accustomed to Gothic German printing, Hebrew characters would be consigned to oblivion. It didn't happen.

The earliest English Haggadah was translated and published in 1770 by Alexander Alexander, the first Jewish printer in London. It was designed with Hebrew and English on confronting pages, and was prepared for both Ashkenazi and Sephardi readers, one with Yiddish songs, the other with Ladino instructions. Although the translations were mediocre at best, they supplied English-speaking Jews with understandable texts. Seeing the book through production had been an uphill fight because Sephardim had insisted that only Ladino be used. All in all, two hundred thirty-four known editions of the Haggadah were printed in the eighteenth century,

Ill. 5:25. *Jonathon Eybeschuetz.* **Etching, c. 1770. By Elimelekh Rose**

Ill. 5:26. *Frontispiece. Moses and the Burning Bush.* Haggadah. Presumably by Abraham ben Jacob. Engraving, 1712

most of them in Germany and Austria, most of them still overworked copies of the Amsterdam and Venice originals. As Enlightenment offerings, they enhanced cultural and educational integration and afforded swifter assimilation.

Religious texts, as well as Haggadot, were unifying objects of spiritual and intellectual delight. Christian and Jewish firms from Fez to Damascus and from London to Vilna met the needs of a growing pool of educated and willing-to-be-educated buyers of study materials, including replacements of innumerable plunders, deportations, and burnings of thousands of pictures and texts. The non–Jewish Oxford Clarendon Press produced the first all–Hebrew Bible in England in 1750. David Nieto's son, Isaac, published a Ladino Siddur, *Orden de las Oraciones de Ros-ashanah y Kippur*, 1740, to accommodate London's Sephardim during the High Holidays. A problem arose in 1765 when Sephardi authorities prohibited the English translation of a Siddur; the manuscript had to be sent to New York for publication. Since no such restraints existed there, it was welcomed by the few members who built the Spanish and Portuguese synagogue Shearith Israel on Mill Street in Lower Manhattan in 1730. An anonymous *Evening Services for Rosh-Hashanah and Yom Kippur,* 1761, was attributed to Isaac Pinto, a learned New York patriot and merchant, written for the colony's three hundred Sephardi Jews. He said that "Hebrew is imperfectly or not at all understood" in the colonies.

Jüdische Merkwürdigkeiten (Peculiarities of the Jews), 1714–1718, by Johann Jacob Schudt, which purported to interpret religious writings and to present historical documentations of Jewish life, appeared after a fire destroyed the Frankfort ghetto in 1711. Along with its descriptive passages of contemporary Jewish life in various parts of the world, it repeated a number of anti–Jewish fictions, including the *Judensau* preoccupation and blood libels. He noted that "nowadays many Jews no longer looked much different from the general population ... except that on the Sabbath and holidays one sees with surprise that precious materials are worn by the women." He was less inclined to admire the men, arguing that walking sticks, swords, and pistols adopted by emancipated Jewish dandies should be outlawed items since they were causing disturbances and envy.

He was indebted to Johann Andreas Eisenmenger's *Endeckes Judentum (Judaism Unmasked)*, 1700, which outdid almost any previous work with its anti–Jewish bias. After learning that three Christians had converted to Judaism, he determined to prevent future heresy by calling attention to Jewish "errors," uncovering negative references to Christianity in Jewish works, and rehashing the stories about well-poisonings and blood libels. The Jewish community hoped to suppress the book with a large bribe, but was unsuccessful. That the slander went beyond the limits of even the unsympathetic government was confirmed by the order of Emperor Leopold I to quash the entire output. Nevertheless, editions were published in 1711 and 1741. Reprinted over and over in German and English versions, it corrupted Christian attitudes for over two hundred years.

Jüdische Augen-Gläser (Jewish Eye-Glasses), 1741–1743, by Elias Roblik, was an anti–Jewish production by a Czechoslovakian Catholic who studied Hebrew in order to help unknowing Jews see the truth through Christian spectacles. Basing his work on Eisenmenger's *Endeckes Judentum*, and buttressing it with various Hebrew texts and plates, he added a caricature of an elderly Jew with large eyeglasses and a larger nose contemplating a scale weighing Jesus on one side, the Talmud on the other. Jesus came out on top.

Hebrew printing in Amsterdam was energized by the Athias family. They published many important titles including an edition of the Mishnah Torah, 1702; its colophon noted that "This great and noble book was completed at the behest and in the printing establishment of the fine young man, Immanuel, the son of the honored elder Joseph Raphael, the son of the martyr Abraham Athias, who was burned at the stake [in 1667] for the glorification of the blessed name of God in the city of Cordoba." Following the Athiases, and possibly related, was Abraham ben Raphael Hezekiah, who published actively from 1728 to 1740. Joseph Dayyan and Moses Frankfurter, who served as religious judicial officers, printed Talmuds and Bibles from 1724 to 1727 for the Ashkenazi trade. Naphtali Herz combined duties as a physician and printer, and was, with his son-in-law, famous for a number of well-received books. But Solomon ben Joseph Proops and his family led all the Amsterdam printers from 1704 until the middle of the nineteenth century. His Minhagim of 1707 contains Yiddish explanations of religious observances illustrated with woodcuts copied from Leusden's *Philologus Hebraeo-Mixtus* of 1663. Proops' books for daily and holiday services were handsome publications, but he is particularly remembered for *Simchat haNefesh (Joy of the Soul)*, 1723, an uplifting ethical work in Yiddish primarily for women, and for the first Hebrew sales catalogue, *Apirion Shelomoh (The Palanquin of Solomon)*, 1730. The latter included advertisements of books in his stock, a boon to later collectors and bibliographers. His sons, Joseph, Jacob, and Abraham, followed his lead, publishing the first edition of the Bible in Hebrew and Spanish, 1762. It was commissioned by Abraham Mendes Castro, a resident of Curaçao in the Dutch West Indies, because there weren't enough copies there for students; it was the first Hebrew book to be paid for and used by Jews on the American continent.

A fascinating addition to Hebraic literature is a classic encyclopedia of medical and natural sciences, *Ma'ase Tuvia (Tuvia's Works)*, 1707–1708, by Polish-born Tuvia ben Moses Cohen, who was educated in the great capitals of Europe and became a savant in Jerusalem and a royal physician in Turkey. One of the earliest works of its kind, it summarized known scientific information, defending Harvey's theory of blood circulation but deriding Copernicus as the "first-born of Satan." Illustrated with the author's portrait, a world map, experiments in physics, astronomy, and medicine, as well as philosophical, geographical, gynecological, botanical, and theological issues, it featured a remarkable engraving comparing the human body to the structure of a building—the eyes analogous to windows, the nose-opening to an attic, the stomach to a kitchen, the lungs to a furnace, the urethra to a fountain (Ill. 5:27). Since autopsies were permitted under Jewish law only to save a life, few people knew how the body operated; the print made anatomical order clear and understandable. It served an additional purpose as well, stressing the relevance between the individual and the modern world. At a time when secular Jewish works were frowned on, it was acceptable because intellectual rabbinic scholarship had begun to move towards a scientific and religious synthesis, and because it was printed in Hebrew. (Most medical treatises by Jews were published in Latin.)

The production of fine editions in central and eastern Europe had fallen sharply although the readership potential was large—three quarters of a million Jews occupied the area, far more than in any other part of the world. Because the best Jewish publishers had difficulties in obtaining necessary licenses and because local authorities controlled what could or could not be published in their own spheres of influence, many books had to be imported from other sources. Presses in a few small cities were allowed, but neither Krakow nor Lublin was able to contribute substantially to the book trade. Competition and rivalry left no option to the major publishers but to pare down expenses and cut corners in order to bring out needed works. There were only two Hebrew publishing houses in France—the first, organized in Metz in 1764, the second a year later in Avignon (the Sephardim lacked their own printing facilities). Since publishers in Amsterdam had already established successful outlets in France, the local efforts lagged, although some rabbinic and other books were issued. Some texts, however, such as the Talmud, were printed in sufficient quantity to service the many yeshivot opening in Poland, Russia, and the Ukraine. "Let us hail the printers," wrote Rabbi Jeseph Teomim in the introduction of his *Pri Megadim (Choice Fruits)*, Frankfort, 1785, "for were it not for the art of printing in these difficult times, Israel would have forgotten the Torah." French prints, however, were a people's art, some of which depended on anti–Jewish stereotypes or legends.

Woodcuts of the *Juif-Errant* (*Wandering Jew*) "sighted" in 1784 in Avignon were among the images that stirred up hostility by perpetuating the medieval folktale of the Jew condemned to walk the earth until the Second Coming (Ill. 5:28).

In some smaller cities in Italy, Jews lived under relatively lax conditions. Rome's Jewish

Ill. 5:27. *The Human Body Likened to a Building.* Engraving, c. 1707. From *Ma'ase Tuvia (Tuvia's Works).* By Tuvia ben Moses Cohen

Ill. 5:28. *Le Juif-Errant (Wandering Jew).* **Woodcut, 1784**

Ill. 5:29. *A Jewish Girl Dressed for Her Marriage Ceremony*. Engraving, 1768. By J. White

community, however, was under severe restraints. During the pontificate of Benedict XIV, 1740 to 1758, the ghetto was dispossessed of thirty-eight cartloads of books; Clement XIV in 1775 and Pius VI in 1793 followed through with conscientious zeal, hoarding the finest examples for Vatican libraries. Many of these volumes were temporarily removed to Paris when Napoleon conquered Italy in 1797.

The Ottoman Empire was no longer a happy place for Jews. Years of graft, heavy tax burdens, the breakdown of political and social order, and the disintegration of army discipline tore at the structure of Turkish rule. Jews, who had received a generous welcome following the Spanish and Portuguese Inquisition, and were rewarded for helping the government defeat the Persian army in the seventeenth century, increasingly became targets for oppression in the eighteenth. They were censured for extravagant lifestyles and threatened with extermination. Those living near mosques were forced to sell their homes and belongings for a pittance to Muslims so as not to defile the neighborhood. Jewish houses had to be built lower than those of Turks. Even the shape and color of hats and shoes was regulated. Trade between Jews and Muslims was severely limited, but because many luxury products were manufactured by Jews, Jewish women agents were permitted to offer gold and other precious articles to the virtual prisoners in the harems of the Topkapi Palace. In 1727, Istanbul became the first city in a Muslim country to establish a printing press; its master printer was a Jew.

In *A Jewish Girl Dressed for Her Marriage Ceremony*, engraved in 1768 by J. White, the subject is draped in an ermine robe (Ill. 5:29). An upper-class Turkish bride was often a vision of unbridled luxury, but finery was restricted to indoor display. Even women's street clothing was exceedingly modest because rabbis as well as governmental officials stipulated that splendid Jewish clothing aroused feminine jealousy. An engraving from M. Guerdevillle's *Atlas Historique*, 1719, displayed a *Juife de Smyrne* (*Jewess of Smyrna*) dressed up and covered down. Nevertheless, she apparently flouted sumptuary prohibitions with a pearl collar and a headdress embroidered with gold and silver threads.

The liberalized climate in Amsterdam, and later in Germany, continued to generate interest in colorful or exotic conventions. Printmakers kept busy supplying the demand. Voltaire, who hardly believed in God, remarked that even the deity "loves a collection of prints after the great masters, an enterprise most useful to the human race, which multiplies at little cost the merits of the best artists ... which would perish without the help of engravings." German Jews of all classes—those of comparative comfort and

Ill. 5:30. *Die Judin nach der synagog gehend (Jewess on Her Way to the Synagogue)*. Etching, 1700. By Christian Weigel

those who remained at the bottom of the economic or social ladder but with tough spirits. Christian Weigel's etching of 1700 *Die Judin nach der synagog gehend* (*Jewess on the Way to the Synagogue*) has her hair concealed as befit a married lady, her neck modestly encircled in a stiff ruff and her body hidden under a long cloak (Ill. 5:30).

Poor "idlers" or peddlers sometimes made up a *minyan*, shared a more fortunate neighbor's meal, and occasionally even sold a few items. The engraving of a Jewish beggar depicted such a "merchant" who dreamt of making a fortune—or at least a living (Ill. 5:31). A few actually did make it, but most struggled under difficult conditions in ghettos such as Augsburg, depicted most flatteringly (Ill. 5:32).

Paul Christian Kirchner found more realistic scenes. His *Jüdisches Ceremoniel* (*Jewish Ceremonies*), 1716, included factual illustrations of Nuremberg's Jewish culture, but its text was frequently inaccurate and biased. Among the thirty etchings by J. G. Puschner, *Die Geschehene Copulation* (*Wedding*) surveys a wedding party where guests rejoice and the groom steps from the canopy to break a glass against a marriage stone imbedded in the synagogue wall (Ill. 5:33). The custom has a number of interpretations; its origin lies in the legends of demonology, but it is generally construed as a memorial to the destruction of the Temple. Weddings were traditionally held in the home or the synagogue courtyard. (Not until the early nineteenth century, when the Orthodox rabbi

Ill. 5:31. *Jewish beggar*

Samson Raphael Hirsch, decided to perform the ceremony in the sanctuary, was this custom abrogated. The change brought charges of aping Christian practices.)

Schlachten und Zübereitung der Speisen (*Slaughter and Preparation of Food*) demonstrated the binding of cattle, the specially sharpened knives, the hole in the ground to catch blood, the dressing of the carcass, and in the rear, the examination of a chicken for signs of bruises or sickness which would render it unfit (Ill. 5:34). Ethical practices applied to animals as well as to humans: they must be treated kindly, permitted to rest on the Sabbath, fed properly even if it means postponing the owner's meal, and slaughtered with as little pain as possible.

Neumonds Gebeth ausser dem Tempel (*Blessing the New Moon Outside the Synagogue*) is particularly effective as a glittering night scene lit by heavenly bodies above and earthly tapers below (Ill. 5:35). Though the ritual performed when the moon is newly visible may have originated in early nature worship, it was transmuted into a hymn to God who monthly renews His light over Israel. (Since women's bodily cycle is tied to the lunar calendar, some modern feminists have re-imagined the ceremony into a spiritual union with the Creator.)

Well-to-do Jews in Amsterdam found their celebrations and rituals mirrored in the etch-

Above: Ill. 5:32. *Ghetto in Augsburg. Below:* Ill. 5:33. *Die Geschehene Copulation (Wedding).* Etching by J. G. Puschner, 1716. From *Jüdisches Ceremoniel (Jewish Ceremonies)* by Paul Christian Kirchner

Ill. 5:34. *Schlachten und Zubereitung der Speisen (Slaughter and Preparation of Food).* **Etching by J. G. Puschner. From** *Jüdisches Ceremoniel (Jewish Ceremonies),* **1716. By Paul Christian Kirchner**

ings of a Protestant printmaker who had fled religious persecution in Catholic France. Bernard Picart settled in Holland, requiting that country's hospitality with his ecumenical set *Ceremonies, moeurs, et coutumes religieuses de tous les peuples du monde* (*Ceremonies, Habits, and Religious Customs of All the People in the World*), 1723–1743. It featured two hundred sixty-one plates, twenty of which have become icons of Jewish life-cycles. By reportedly depicting actual individuals, he lent the etchings a unique verisimilitude. While he derived many of his ideas from earlier Minhagim, his own reportorial skills detailed a scrupulously authentic and sympathetic record of Dutch Ashkenazi and Sephardi society, still largely unknown to the Christian world. The text by Italy's Leone da Modena, later translated into several languages, was intended to demonstrate, especially to the Catholic Church, not only that all faiths were valid, but that all "agree in several things, share the same principles of a good part of mankind, and follow the same path." The etchings depicted Jewish rites of passage from birth to death, along with holiday rituals and festivities. Hardly a volume of Jewish history or art omits one or more of his delightful evocations of Jewish life.

L'Examen du Levain (*The Search for Leaven*) depicts the custom still enacted in traditional homes before Passover—the mother places bits of unleavened bread for the father and children to discover and dispose of, the cleansing of household utensils, the scrubbing of cabinets and furnishings (Ill. 5:36). The rituals remind Jews that because of their hasty retreat from Egypt there was no time for dough to rise; in commemoration, all leavened products are removed from the home for eight days. In a companion print, *Le Repas de Pacques* (*The Passover Seder*), Picart himself joins a Marrano family and their servant at the table (as a Christian his Chris-

Ill. 5:35. *Neumonds Gebeth ausser dem Tempel (Blessing the New Moon Outside the Synagogue)*. Etching by J. G. Puschner. From *Jüdisches Ceremoniel (Jewish Ceremonies)*, 1716. By Paul Christian Kirchner

L'EXAMEN du LEVAIN &c.

A. La Maitresse de la maison, qui met du PAIN LEVE en divers endroits, afin que son Mari qui en fait la recherche en trouve.

Above: Ill. 5:36. *L'Examen du Levain (The Search for Leaven).* Etching, 1723. From *Ceremonies, moeurs, et coutumes religieuses de tous les peuples du monde (Ceremonies, Habits, and Religious Customs of All the Peoples in the World).* By Bernard Picart. *Below:* Ill. 5:37. *Le Repas de Pacques (The Passover Seder).* Etching, 1723. From *Ceremonies, moeurs, et coutumes religieuses de tous les peuples du monde (Ceremonies, Habits, and Religious Customs of All the Peoples in the World).* By Bernard Picart

Le REPAS de PAQUES
chez les
JUIFS PORTUGAIS.

A. le Marié donnant l'Anneau à la Mariée, tous deux sous le Talod.
B.B. les 2. Maraines de la Mariée.
C.C. les 2. Parrains du Marié.

CEREMONIE NUPTIALE
des
JUIFS ALLEMANDS.

D. le Rabin. ✱ le derriere de la Sinagogue.
E. le Chantre tenant la Bouteille pour faire Boire les Époux.
F. deux garçons avec des Batons ornez qui marchent devant les Mariez.

Ill. 5:38. *Copulation (Ashkenazi Wedding)*. Etching, 1723. From *Ceremonies, moeurs, et coutumes religieuses de tous les peuples du monde* (Ceremonies, Habits, and Religious Customs of All the Peoples in the World). By Bernard Picart

tian head is uncovered) (Ill. 5:37). His presence was seen by some as a refutation of blood libels associated for centuries with the holiday. He indicated few Passover symbols; families who still feared the Inquisition often partially concealed them and even excluded children who might create suspicion by their appearance late at night. Images of the Seder hardly exist in Christian art; it was a touchy subject which most artists avoided, fearing connotations of the Last Supper.

In the *Copulation* (*Wedding*) scenes, the Ashkenazi ceremony is set outdoors to be witnessed by the heavens, and the Sephardi is indoors, providing the family an opportunity to display its handsome possessions (Ill. 5:38; Ill. 5:39). The Ashkenazim proudly flourish beards and their own hair. Sephardi gentlemen mostly sport wigs and clean-shaven chins. Not too much has changed over time: musicians play, food is passed, relatives are gathered, the happy couple hopes for the best.

Death, too, was included in Picart's overview of Jewish life. A mourner faints with grief; family and friends chant consolatory psalms, a skull monitors the proceedings (Ill. 5:40). The *Acafoth ou les sept tours autour du cercuëil* (*Procession or Seven Circles Around the Coffin*) probably originated as a barrier to evil spirits hoping to snatch the soul of the deceased. The practice fell away in the nineteenth century with the borrowing of subdued Protestant funeral parlor conventions.

Among Picart's other prints of Jewish interest were five engraved title pages for a six-volume Spanish-Hebrew Bible published in Amsterdam in 1726, the only Hebrew book that he

A.le Marié cassant le verre.
B.la Mariée veillée.
C.C. les 2 personnes servant de Baraines a la Marié.

CEREMONIE NUPTIALE
des
JUIFS PORTUGAIS.

D.D. les 2 Personnes servant de Parrains au Marié.
E. le Rabin. F. les Chantres.
G.Celui qui écrit les Aumônes que les Assistans promettent.

Ill. 5:39. *Copulation (Sephardi Wedding)*. Etching, 1723. From *Ceremonies, moeurs, et coutumes religieuses de tous les peuples du monde (Ceremonies, Habits, and Religious Customs of All the Peoples in the World)*. By Bernard Picart

illustrated. Depicting the darker side of the Jewish experience, he etched relapsed New Christians marching to the Inquisition's flames in the sanbenito or penitent's tunic. More horrific is his drawing of a *Place of Torment and Types of Torture*, engraved in the nineteenth century by S. P. Jacobs (Ill. 5:41).

His designs were replayed over and over by other engravers. The German theologian Johann Christoph Georg Bodenschatz compiled his own book of customs, *Kirchliche Verfassung der heutigen Juden, sonderlich derer in Deutschland (Summary of Current Religious Customs Among German Jews)*, 1748–1749, objectively and accurately reporting Jewish religious practices for German readers. The text as well as the plates were by-products of the two-way communication between Christians and Jews in the Enlightenment years. While several of the thirty etchings designed by G. Eichler and Johann Conrad Muller and engraved by G. Nusbiegel were derivative, the elaborate Baroque frames of curved and asymmetrical scrollwork were original conceptions.

Italian contributions are less known. Giuseppi Vasi's portfolio *Magnificenza di Roma (Magnificence of Rome)*, 1752, featured the *Piazza di Pescaria (Fish Market)* in the Jewish quarter where housewives gathered to gossip and shop under the watchful eye of the Church of St. Maria. A 1784 etching by Giovanni del Pian shows a draped casket (with meaningless Hebrew letters) being lowered to a gondola for burial in the Jewish cemetery on Lido Island (Ill. 5:42). A gracefully posed gondolier adds to the Italian setting. A dwarf holds an alms box,

Les ACAFOTH *ou les sept tours, autour du* CERCUEÏL.

Above: Ill. 5:40. *Les Acafoth ou les sept tours autour du cercueïl (Procession or Seven Circles Around the Coffin).* Etching, 1723. From *Ceremonies, moeurs, et coutumes religieuses de tout les peoples du monde (Ceremonies, Habits, and Religious Customs of All the Peoples in the World).* By Bernard Picart. *Below:* Ill. 5:41. *Place of Torment and Types of Torture.* Nineteenth century engraving by S. P. Jacobs after Bernard Picart drawing

Above: Ill. 5:42. *Funeral Casket Lowered to a Gondola.* Engraving, c. 1784. By Giovanni del Pian.
Below: Ill. 5:43. *Purim Masked Ball.* Etching, 1780. By Caspar Jacobsz Philips

signifying that "charity (righteousness) saves from death" (Proverbs 10:2; 11:4). (Dwarfs were associated with invoking the spirits of the dead.)

Although mainly intended for the souvenir market, these prints furthered communications between Christians and Jews by way of the social reporters who witnessed and documented their lives and habits: Dom Augustin Calmet, Friederich Albrecht Christiani (a converted Jew), Pieter Tanjé, William Hurd, A. Joels, Caspar Jacobsz Philips, and C. F. Fritschius. Philips' *Purim Masked Ball*, 1780, included a wicked Haman and fashionably turned-out revelers (Ill. 5:43). Hurd's *Mikvah (Ritual Bath)* from his six-volume *Oude en Tegenwoordige Staat en Geschiedenis van alle Godsdiensten* (*Universal History of Religious Rites, Ceremonies, and Customs*), 1781–1785, depicts an integral aspect of ghetto life, perhaps second only to synagogue attendance, that marks the occasion when women immerse themselves before marriage and after menstrual periods and childbirth for spiritual cleansing (Ill. 5:44).

Across the Atlantic Ocean, approximately two hundred and fifty Jews were living in America in 1700. Judah Monis, an Italian or Algerian-born Jew who may have been a rabbi, converted to Christianity in 1722, thus becoming eligible to teach the Hebrew language at Harvard College. Students studied it one day a week for a full three years; those who planned to become ministers were required to read the Hebrew Bible in its original form. Failing to find an adequate textbook, Monis wrote *Dickdook Leshon Gnebreet* (*Hebrew Grammar*) in 1735, the first of its kind in America and the first American publication, other than the 1640 *Bay Psalm Book*, to contain Hebrew type.

In 1730 American Jews were given the right to hold civic office and to worship freely and

HET BAD DER HOOGDUITSCHE JOODEN, TE AMSTERDAM.

Ill. 5:44. *Mikvah (Ritual Bath)*. Engraving. c. 1781, by William Hurd. From *Oude en Tegenwoordige Staat en Geschiedenis van alle Godsdiensten* (*Universal History of Religious Rites, Ceremonies, and Customs*)

openly—but only in private homes. After that date, Shearith Israel inaugurated public services; the majority of its congregants were central and east European Ashkenazim. Contrary to its own laws, in 1740 England naturalized American Jews after a seven-year residency and allowed them to eliminate the Christological references in legal proceedings. Indeed, the few Jews hardly troubled the courts. Most worked peacefully in the trades they knew best—tailoring, shoe, candle, soap, and clockmaking. Trailblazers, they helped colonize the Eastern Seaboard as merchants, exporters, and plantation owners; a few became importers of African slaves. Some were adventurous drifters for whom the New World represented escape from European poverty. Some thought their religion was onerous or a handicap and deliberately avoided observance of traditional ceremonies. Others conscientiously tried to model their lives after the Orthodox traditions they had left behind, although it was almost impossible to maintain proper kashrut or other observances at the frontier since there were no rabbinical establishments to oversee rituals, synagogue affiliations, or Judaic study. A rabbi might have been hired from the nearby West Indies, but there didn't seem to be any compelling reason to do so; instead, a hazzan or shochet officiated when necessary.

In 1733, a boatload of poor English Jews financed by their more prosperous brethren arrived in Savannah, the first group to settle in the South. A year later they formed a congregation. As others gradually joined them, the usual tensions and bickering broke out between Sephardim and Ashkenazim; a local minister chastized them by claiming their mutual persecutions outweighed Christian invective. Charleston's Jews prayed in each other's homes until they established the Sephardi Kahal Kadosh Beth Elohim Congregation in 1749. Fifty-five years later the city's four hundred Jews dedicated the synagogue building, the second oldest in America. Solomon Carvalho's lithograph of its interior is all that survived following a destructive fire in 1838. (It was restored in 1840.) The first Jew to hold elective office, Francis Salvador served in South Carolina's Provisional Congress in 1775. He was also the first Jewish victim of the American Revolution—scalped by Cherokee tribesmen under British command. The first American synagogue building was the Georgian-style Touro, dedicated in 1763 by Newport's wealthy Sephardi ship owners and manufacturers. In order that members could face toward Jerusalem, it was built on an angle to the street. Israel established the Rodeph Shalom congregation in 1795, a break-away group from Philadelphia's Mikvah, and the first Ashkenazi synagogue in America. Most Jews defined themselves according to voluntary synagogue membership rather than conforming to separate denominational groups.

Lay figures provided a certain amount of leadership or influence. David De Isaac Cohen Nassy's *Observations on the Cause, Nature, and Treatment of the Epidemic Disorder Prevalent in Philadelphia*, 1793, was the first medical treatise by an American Jewish physician to deal with the ravages of yellow fever. David Franks and his cousin Isaac held high posts in the diplomatic service. Haym Salomon, the Revolutionary patriot who raised a quarter of a million dollars for Washington's destitute army as a broker and commission merchant, contributed twenty-five percent of the cost of Congregation Mikva Israel in 1782. "There is very little Yiddishkeit in Philadelphia," he observed, adding that Jewish learning was considered unimportant and that anyone who wished to study Hebrew would be advised to stay in Europe. The chance to provide a chair in Hebrew studies at the college of Rhode Island (later Brown University) was refused by otherwise charitable Jews such as Aaron Lopez, Newport's leading merchant, who amassed a fortune with ships that carried goods back and forth to the distant Falkland Islands and the African coast.

Nevertheless, all was not lost. Lopez's son-in-law, Uriah Hendricks, was so pious that he refused to attend synagogue services during a visit to Newport because the Torah portion was read from a printed book instead of a handwritten scroll. A young soldier volunteered to perform his watch duty on weeknights so as to be relieved from that obligation on the Sabbath.

Some prominent businessmen closed their shops rather than desecrate holy days. And Isaac Pinto, who wrote that "Hebrew is imperfectly or not at all understood," is thought to have produced an English translation of the evening High Holiday service in New York in 1761. Five years later his name was attached to an expanded translation for the country's three hundred Sephardim. It was the first North American prayer book written by a practicing Jew for "the improvement of many of my Brethren in their Devotion." Benjamin Gomez, the first Jewish bookseller and publisher in the colonies, produced twenty-two titles of religious and secular interest. In 1794, he reprinted Joseph Priestly's *Letters to the Jews*, a conversionary attempt by the English minister and scientist, and followed it with *Letters to Dr. Priestly* by David Levi, the first Jew to write tracts in the English language defending Jewish interests.

Europe had not forgotten the colonies. France and England played for high stakes in the French and Indian War which dragged on from 1754 to 1763. For the lucky winner it meant possession of American commerce, control of the lucrative fur trade, and the opportunity to exploit the rich lands beyond the Alleghenies. The ultimate English victory secured English culture and language to much of North America, but the victors exacted a painful accounting. American businesses were forced to trade exclusively with English firms, and to absorb import duties, stamp taxes, and currency restraints. Redcoats and colonists angrily taunted each other until the Boston "massacre" in 1770 in which five American "radicals" died. The English wouldn't or couldn't back down. William Pitt, who gave his name to the Pennsylvania city of Pittsburgh, declared to the House of Lords that "this is the mother-country, they are the children; they must obey, and we prescribe." The children threw a tea party in 1773, goading the mother-country into confrontation. "The die is now cast," George III wrote bitterly to Lord North, "The Colonies must either submit or triumph." On July 4, 1776, the Continental Congress declared three million Americans independent of England. Perhaps two thousand were Jews. Benjamin Franklin, John Adams, and Thomas Jefferson chose a seal for the new nation—Moses delivering the Israelites from bondage. The design was rejected.

While the Founding Fathers championed equal political rights for minorities, Jews were occasionally still slandered or discredited. In 1737, they were accused of securing a New York Assembly election through their votes and were disenfranchised. Having killed Jesus, a Puritan lawyer charged, they never should have been allowed to vote at all. Cemeteries were vandalized, conversionary efforts blossomed. Benjamin Nones, a Revolutionary War patriot, was assaulted in a Federalist publication for being a Jew, a Republican, and poor. A Jewish funeral procession was attacked in South Carolina in 1743. In 1762, Pennsylvania and Rhode Island barred Jews from holding public office or voting, a prohibition that held until the Revolutionary War.

Thomas Paine, author of the widely read Revolutionary pamphlet, *Common Sense* 1776, used the Bible as his authority to characterize hereditary monarchy as "one of the sins of the Jews." He did not believe in the creed practiced by Jews, but he felt the same way about the precepts of Christianity and Islam; his church, he declared, was his own mind. Jewish, Christian or Turkish religious expression "appear to me no other than human inventions set up to terrify and enslave mankind and monopolize power and profit." Another pamphlet presumably by Paine, distributed anonymously in 1784, declared: "We see these people [Jews] eternally obtruding themselves ... what are we to expect but to have Christianity enacted in a capital heresy, and the synagogue to become the established church?"

Among other problems, the young government had to deal with bank-note forgery; very harsh measures were imposed on those who transgressed. In a print *A Counterfeiter in Pillory* 1764, a guilty engraver has his ear cut off and receives twenty lashes. Sure enough, there is a Jew at the proceedings, identified by his medieval hat. As it was unlikely that the engraver had ever seen a colonial Jew in such a headpiece, he probably copied the image from an old print.

Since no Jew had been a party to the crime, there was no reason to drag the fellow in—no reason except that a Jew was somehow naturally included in the context of swindling or deception. The Jewish stereotype had arrived in the new world.

Yet, most Jews found themselves far better off than at any time in their history. However, in 1788, Rabbi Isaac Cordoba of Jamaica, concerned that they were too comfortable, wrote the first original essay on the topic in the New World, warning that the Enlightenment might bode ill as well as good. It was subsequently published in Philadelphia in 1791 and in Richmond thirteen years later, indicating an awareness that Jewish traditions were weakening.

Myer Myers, the first important Jewish artisan in America, was a prominent silver- and goldsmith who created synagogue ritual objects and fine metalwork for the general community in addition to serving as president of the Shearith Israel Congregation. The native-born painters Charles Willson Peale and Gilbert Stuart were patronized by wealthy Jews, Peale having executed three Jewish portraits, and Stuart, who was "indebted to Jewish clients," twelve. Some of their compositions were based on imported English mezzotint engravings used as prototypes for poses and arrangement of clothing. But the editor of an illustrated Bible apologized to his readers in 1791, asking that "a proper allowance be made for works engraved by artists who obtained their knowledge in this country." Nevertheless, they were in steady demand, many being sold at auction in New York in 1797 by Isaac Moses, a Jewish merchant and patriot.

Congress recognized that religious openness was making impressive strides and decided to encourage a political system based on Judeo-Christian principles. In 1782, it arranged for Robert Aitken, a Philadelphia printer, to publish a fourteen-hundred-page Hebrew and New Testament Bible. "Resolved," read the document, "that the United States in Congress assemble and approve the pious and laudable undertaking of Mr. Aitken ... and recommend this edition of the Bible to the inhabitants of the United States." When Moses Mendelssohn heard about it he worried that an "endorsement of an established religion" could be an ominous step. Congress evidently rethought the proclamation and rescinded it twelve years later.

A peace treaty was ratified in 1783 whereby Britain recognized American independence. Among its defenders were about one hundred Jewish soldiers, blockade runners, suppliers of weapons and essential goods, and bill-brokers. Sore points remained. The American economy was largely dependent on the sales of tobacco, cotton, and the black human beings who wrested the crops from an obstinate soil. Already there were indications that the widening separation between pro- and anti-slavery interests would shape America's future. On the positive side, the Constitution, ratified in 1789, included Article VI, one of the loftiest provisions in any governmental statement concerning sectarian tolerance: "No religious test shall ever be required as a qualification to any office or public trust." Two years later, the First Amendment of the Bill of Rights added that "Congress shall make no law respecting an establishment of religion, or prohibiting the free exercise thereof."

Benjamin Franklin was among those who vigorously promoted America's ideals: "Tyranny is so generally established in the rest of the world," he wrote while serving as an envoy in Paris, "that the prospect of an asylum in America for those who love liberty gives general joy, and our cause is esteemed the cause of all mankind." Although he was too ill to attend, two years before he died in 1790, he arranged a July 4th celebration in which the clergy of different Christian denominations walked arm in arm with the rabbi of the Jews. The year before, Moses Seixas, president of Newport's Jewish community, was invited to Washington's inaugural. In 1790, he wrote to the president expressing gratitude to "a government which to bigotry gives no sanction." Washington repeated the phrase in his gracious reply: "It is now no more that toleration is spoken of as if it was by the indulgence of one class of people that another enjoyed the exercise of their inherent natural rights. For happily the government of the United States, which gives to bigotry no sanction, to persecution no assistance, requires only that they who live under its protection should demean themselves as good citizens.... May the children of the stock of Abraham, who dwell in this land, continue to merit and enjoy the good will of the other inhabitants, while everyone shall sit in safety under his own vine and fig tree, and there shall be none to make him afraid."

Faith Jews had at the beginning of the century, faith and legitimate hope they had at its end.

6

England in the Nineteenth Century: The Industrial Revolution Challenges the Politics of Equity

At the beginning of the nineteenth century England was sharply divided by extremes of wealth and want. Rich landowners and poor farmers shared a country that labored strenuously to maintain a growing population. Entrepreneurs and gentry pushed their way up the class structure at the same time that devastated workers remained at the bottom. Although group pressure slowly imposed new pecking orders, the aristocracy clashed with an aggressive bourgeoisie in an effort to keep its fixed divisions intact and its charmed circle closed to Catholics, Dissenters, Jews, and paupers. Tories, determined to preserve the status quo, bumped heads with Whigs intent on promoting parliamentary, educational, and fiscal reforms.

Admiral Nelson's victory at Trafalgar in 1805 gave the island control of the waters, enabling it to expand in a surge of nationalism and imperialism. But the economic insecurity following the boom years of the war, as well as the budding Industrial Revolution, generated unforeseen difficulties. Those who had produced the country's goods in cottages or independent shops faced ruin as power-driven machinery replaced hand tools. Small farmers and craftsmen were forced to abandon grazing lands and villages for overcrowded towns where exploitive conditions bred terrible hardships. Shabbily built housing quickly turned into shabby slums.

Although much of this rural agitation only marginally affected the twenty-six thousand urban Jews, associated problems spilled over to the community. Disease, polluted factories, unholy working hours, and class enmity infiltrated London's East End, where large numbers of immigrants had settled. When expectations of improvements failed, many of the newcomers left for America; those who stayed met a moderate anti–Semitism. It was certainly nothing like that in Europe, but the perception remained that Jews were too alien, too pushy, too numerous, or too unprincipled. Undoubtedly some were no better than they should be, but harping on notions of vulgar or offensive characteristics kept them on the fringes of polite society rather than as part of its core. Neither wealth, position, nor philanthropy could move them from the outside to the centrality of the English experience.

But conversion might. The London Society for Promoting Christianity Among the Jews, founded in 1809, welcomed Jews who hoped to rid themselves of Jewish debilities or who held a dim view of Judaism. Only a few hundred were recruited, however—and those came at a considerable cost to the organization. One observer wrote, "'Tis true 'tis strange, and strange 'tis true,/Cash *buys* but cannot *keep* a Jew."

Although some of the converts recanted, it was a painful episode for the community.

The scenario wasn't entirely bleak. On the plus side, liberal policies influenced by the ideals of the French and American revolutions began to sway public and governmental positions. Some personal freedoms were extended, some previously closed doors were opening. England's Jews had a share in the wonders that made the country a paradigm of all that was tasteful, cultivated, and sophisticated. Thanks to the railroads, ready access to outlying towns and large metropolitan areas provided new social and business opportunities; peddling declined as small shops prospered. Philanthropic agencies stepped in to spruce up depressed areas and the chronically poor. Reorganized mercantile systems, advances in science and health care, and upgraded educational and vocational prospects all promised a better life.

Ill. 6:1. *A Lyoness.* Etching, 1801. By James Gillray

That life was documented by the caricaturists who recorded the foibles—and occasional virtues—of the omnipresent Jews. English society found these worthies amusing, English artists doted on them; the tasteless appropriation of the best English fashions was always good for a smirk. Jews were famous or ridiculous or both—objects for printmakers who could make or break a reputation with a felicitous caption or a telling line. Jews eager to appear before the world as social equals were skewered instead as social climbers. To judge by James Gillray's 1801 etching of Polly de Symons, *A Lyoness,* Jewish ladies didn't always know what to keep in or what to let out (Ill. 6:1). An etching, *Mrs. Judith Levy, the Rich Jewess Usually Called the Queen of Richmond Green,* 1803, shows the lady dipping into her snuff box, likewise the butt of nouveau riche humor (Ill. 6:2). A generous do-gooder, she paid for the renovation of the Great Synagogue in 1790 following the example of her father, Moses Hart, who had defrayed its cost in 1722. Nor were Jewish gentlemen spared. Richard Dighton's etching of Pellegrin Travers showed the old fellow preening as *A Fashionable Jew TRAVERSing the Steyne at Brighton,* c.1805; an intimate of the Prince Regent, in time he not only became postmaster-general but a Christian as well (Ill. 6:3). From his elegant wig to his bow-tied boots, *Abrm. Goldsmid Esq.,* brother of the celebrated Polly, defined the too well-groomed, too well-fed, too upwardly mobile Ashkenazi Jew in Dighton's etching of 1806 (Ill. 6:4). But sartorially acceptable or not, he was a greatly admired philanthropist—note his bundle of charitable subscriptions. He and his brother Benjamin made generous military loans which helped defeat the French at the end of the previous century. A friend of Admiral Nelson, he lavishly hosted an assortment of royals and elegant courtesans in his home; unhappily, he committed suicide in 1810 when the col-

Left: Ill. 6:2. *Mrs. Judith Levy, the Rich Jewess Usually Called the Queen of Richmond Green.* Etching, 1803. *Right:* Ill. 6:3. *A Fashionable Jew TRAVERSing the Steyne at Brighton.* Etching, 1805. By Richard Dighton

lapse of the financial market wiped out the family fortunes. Benjamin followed suit two years later.

Solomon Hirschell, Chief Rabbi of the Great Synagogue as well as of Britain's Ashkenazi congregations overseas, was pleased to sit for a painting by Frederick Benjamin Barlin that celebrated his fine figure, fur hat, and smart robe; the imposing image was subsequently engraved by W. Holl in 1803 (Ill. 6:5). Solomon Bennett, an immigrant Jewish artist, also engraved his portrait but scolded him for overweening pride and slackened religious standards: "I have often seen Jewish picture-dealers, furniture sellers, and cloth merchants of pretended piety attend public sales on the Sabbath day, all without blushing before the Christian community ... and yet our pious Grand Rabbi never rebukes them ... because they would look upon him with a frown." In 1808, Levi Alexander, son of the first Jewish printer to work in England, included the engraving in a pamphlet, *The Axe Laid to the Root; or Ignorance and Superstition Evident in the Character of the Rev. S. Hirschell.* Alexander was upset because the rabbi had permitted a rival printer, E. Justin, to use the portrait in a recently published Siddur. However, Alexander eventually overlooked the rabbi's ignorance and superstition and added the portrait nine years later to his own Siddur, *Interpreting Tephilloth or Daily Forms of Prayers.*

Joshua Van Oven, a pillar of the Ashkenazi community, had a better reputation. An esteemed physician and advocate for the Jewish poor, he promoted a plan to curb crime that was aban-

Left: Ill. 6:4. *Abrm. Goldsmid Esq.* Etching. 1806. By Richard Dighton. *Right:* Ill. 6:5. *Solomon Hirschell.* Engraving, 1803. By W. Holl, after a painting by Benjamin Barlin

doned because the Sephardim refused to cooperate with the less worthy Ashkenazim. He helped found the Jews' Hospital in 1807 and the Jews' Free School in 1817, improving the lot of the needy, frustrating the conversionary missions, and meriting the accolade beneath the 1815 stipple engraving by T. Blood: "May God preserve him for he brings glory to his community; to his friends he is a jewel and a crown" (Ill. 6:6). The doctor is presented with great dignity, a model of the modern Jew—his face clean-shaven, his temples fashionably embellished with curly locks. It was because of people like Oven and the Goldsmids that the editor of *Guide to Knowledge* in 1832 defined Jews as honest, kind, industrious, and extraordinarily charitable individuals—though "uncouth in their beards and time-worn in their clothes, they were rarely beggars." Eastern European dress had appeared on London streets with the influx of Polish refugees, but many of them were already exchanging their homely Jewish garments for anglicized models. Uncouth beards and time-worn clothes had long since disappeared from affluent Jewish neighborhoods.

But whether they were depicted as prosperous merchants or as lowly hawkers, prints of their activities had a wide appeal. An anonymous mezzotint, *Moroccan Peddler*, 1800, shows an indigent man with his tray of ribbons and scissors; he was immediately stamped as a Jew since Muslims seldom traveled abroad (Ill. 6:7). Thomas Rowlandson's *Rhubarb Seller*, 1820, depicting a crafty fellow selling a widely used Moroccan purgative, was included in the artist's *Characteristic Sketches of the Lower Orders* (Ill. 6:8). *Old Clothes to Sell* by A. Courcell has a Jewish pitchman offering a batch of cast-off clothes (Ill. 6:9). He is a familiar figure to the master of the house, an article of wonder to a little boy, and an object of misgivings to a dog. Regularly topped by two or three hats, Jewish hucksters frequently appeared in illustrated booklets describing various trades. They were essential to local economies until the Industrial Revolu-

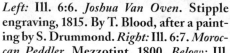

Left: Ill. 6:6. *Joshua Van Oven.* Stipple engraving, 1815. By T. Blood, after a painting by S. Drummond. *Right:* Ill. 6:7. *Moroccan Peddler.* Mezzotint, 1800. *Below:* Ill. 6:8. *Rhubarb Seller.* Etching, 1820. By Thomas Rowlandson. From *Characteristic Sketches of the Lower Orders*

tion made factory goods affordable in the second half of the century.

Rowlandson zeroed in on almost every type of common or absurd figure. His etching *Jew Broker,* 1801, depicting an overwrought money-lender, is a rehash of Shylock's wrathful "Let him look to his bond" (Ill. 6:10). The artist placed the broker at the Great Synagogue in Duke's Place; since he lived in that area himself, he was familiar with its daily life. His etching *Family Quarrels or the Jew and the Gentile,* 1803, was based on a stage production by Thomas Dibdin starring the leading tenor of the day, John [A]Braham (Ill. 6:11). Although always identified as a Jew, Braham was one of the public figures who traded heritage for fame. The play, featuring a demeaning script about Jewish prostitutes and peddlers, attracted groups of noisy protesters whose "barbarous howls" were roundly criticized in the press. The Jew, belting out an elaborate arpeggio with the musical notation "Allegro Squekando," is almost undone by his exertions, but is cheered on by a couple of large-nosed fans calling out in

RHUBARB.

a Yiddish accent, "Mine Cod, how he shing." Charles Incledon, a virile embodiment of John Bull, responds gracefully to his claque's demand for an "Encore."

Rowlandson chose the heavily Jewish Houndsditch area for an 1808 aquatint underscoring Jewish moral delinquency—*Get Money Money still, And then let Virtue follow, if she will* (Ill. 6:12). An 1812 etching, *Raising the Wind* (i.e. seeking funds), pairs a straitened nobleman and his patrician dog with "little Isaacs" who dubiously examine the young man's assets. A picture on the wall of a miser greedily weighing his coins suggests that the wealth of Christians typically passes into Jewish pockets. His bawdy etching *Humours of Houndsditch or Mrs. Shevi in a Longing Condition*, 1813, introduces a lascivious fellow ogling milady as her inhibitions lose ground

Ill. 6:9. *Old Clothes to Sell.* By A. Courcell

to an insatiable love of pork—a swipe at what many Christians believed were relaxed attitudes at best, or sodomy at worst (Ill. 6:13). Her friend can hardly wait to be diverted with the pig, while an apoplectic old Jew offers a five-pound reward for the recovery of stolen hogs;

perhaps he, too, has a prurient interest in the animals. The perception that Jews harbored sexual fantasies and wish fulfillment about pigs again revived images of the sixteenth century German *Judensau.*

Boxing was a different sort of pastime where skill spoke louder than appetite. It had become a fashionable Jewish exercise as well as a source of protection from rowdy street gangs. Rowlandson was presumably the etcher of *Boxing Match for 200 Guineas,* 1810, in which the Jewish pugilist Samuel Elias, with less discretion than valor, humbled a bodyguard of King George IV after forty-nine rounds (Ill. 6:14). Ten thousand spectators turned out to cheer or boo their man. Dutch Sam, as he was known in honor of his birthplace, was an English hero, undefeated until he was almost forty, having by then fought over one hundred matches and reputedly inventing the "upper cut." Unfortunately,

Above: Ill. 6:10. *Jew Broker.* Etching, 1801. *Below:* Ill. 6:11. *Family Quarrels or the Jew and the Gentile.* Etching, 1803. Both etchings by Thomas Rowlandson

he was as adept with the bottle as he was with his fists and soon died from too many celebrations.

George Cruikshank, the most prolific of English satirists, was generally harsher than Rowlandson, although his work as a book illustrator was necessarily defined by the writers he represented. His biting etchings for a variety of authors mirrored something of the attitudes

Ill. 6:12. *Get Money Money still, and then let Virtue follow, if she will.* Aquatint, 1808. By Thomas Rowlandson

Ill. 6:13. *Humours of Houndsditch or Mrs. Shevi in a Longing Condition.* Etching, 1813. By Thomas Rowlandson

Ill. 6:14. *Boxing Match for 200 Guineas*. Etching, 1810. Presumably by Thomas Rowlandson

towards the country's Jews. Twelve plates for Edgar Taylor's translation of Grimm's fairy tales, originally known as *German Popular Stories*, c. 1823, included *The Jew in the Bush*, evil from his greasy head and ugly features to his menacing body. In 1839 Cruikshank etched twenty-seven plates for William Harrison Ainsworth's novel *Jack Sheppard*, among which is *Jonathan Wild Throwing Sir Rowland Trenard Down the Well-hole* (Ill. 6:15). It combined the skillful lighting of a horror movie with the thrill of a murder story as the unfortunate Sir Rowland is about to get his comeuppance. The grisly mood is punctuated by a conniving Jew beaming a torch into the dim interior.

Cruikshank's etchings ridiculed English politics as well—in vain did George IV pay him to be "shown no more in immoral situations"—but it was as Charles Dickens' favorite illustrator that he is best remembered. His more benign etchings for *Sketches by Boz*, 1836, included *Monmouth Street*, where Moses sold hats, a tailor stitched, boots were purchased, neighbors chatted, and children played the games that children play (Ill. 6:16). Some of his best work was prepared for *Oliver Twist*, 1838, the story of a poor youth lured into the clutches of a notorious Jewish thief and corrupter of young boys. Dickens no doubt planned the novel as an appeal against the Poor Laws and child labor, yet he invested Fagin with every ill-looking stereotype—a miserly satanic nature, mangy aspect, and a foul smell. The artist went a step further, extending Fagin's nose beyond the author's already vivid description. One of the four scenes in which he appeared, *Fagin in the Condemned Cell*, is an oppressive image with dark walls lit by a few rays of light from the barred window (Ill. 6:17). Cruikshank captured the agitation of the pickpocket tearing his fingernails, and ably rendered the textures of metal, fabric, and stone. Although Dickens designated other characters by their names, he referred to Fagin some three hundred times as "The Jew"—an insistent reminder page after page of the cupidity of his race. Having been charged by a Jewish reader, Mrs. Eliza Davis, with "a great wrong," he expressed regret but added that any Jews who might complain were "a far less sensible, a far less just, and a far less good-tempered people than I always supposed them to be ... I have no feeling towards the Jews but a friendly one." He pointed out that the book was replete with

Ill. 6:15. *Jonathan Wild Throwing Sir Rowland Trenard Down the Well-hole.* **Etching by George Cruikshank, 1839. From** *Jack Sheppard* **by William Harrison Ainsworth**

Christian villains about whom no one seemed to object, and that "it was unfortunately true of the time to which that story refers, that that class of criminal almost invariably was a Jew."

But Dickens didn't forget Mrs. Davis' reproach, atoning for Fagin in his last complete novel, *Our Mutual Friend*, 1864. The hero, Mr. Riah, an honorable and compassionate Jew, is almost too good to be human. Yet he is a blunt realist. Men "take the worst of us as samples of the best," he says bitterly. "They take the lowest of us as presentations of the highest; and they say 'All Jews are alike.'" Marcus Stone engraved these plates, giving Jews an exception-

Ill. 6:16. *Monmouth Street*. Etching by George Cruikshank, 1836. From *Sketches by Boz* by Charles Dickens

Ill. 6:17. *Fagin in the Condemned Cell.* **Etching by George Cruikshank, 1838. From** *Oliver Twist* **by Charles Dickens**

ally sympathetic appearance in accordance with Dickens' declaration, "There cannot be kinder people in the world."

Most publishers dealing with books of Jewish interests were concentrated in London with subsidiary outlets in the university towns of Oxford and Cambridge. Although the fare was limited, readership was broad. When news of Napoleon's attentions to Jews reached England, *The Transactions of the Parisian Sanhedren*, 1807, was immediately snapped up. The rapidity with which information was disseminated unsettled everyone from the slippery politician to the gossip columnist, from the all-fired journalist to the neutral annalist; the word-smith ruled. The Scottish poet and journalist James Montgomery spoke in the proud voice of the press:

> "The Press!—What is the Press?" I cried;
> When thus a wondrous voice replied:
>
> "In me all human knowledge dwells;
> The oracle of oracles,
> Past, present, future, I reveal,
> Or in oblivion's silence seal;
> What I preserve can perish never,
> What I forego is lost forever."

Because publishers were concerned with rising prices, they were always on the lookout for cheaper ways to ply the public with books and pictures. New methods of binding, together with mechanized steam power adapted for printing type, kept expenses down and speeded manufacturing up. The processing of smoother continuous sheets of paper made clearer and more detailed prints possible. Although many books included costly lithographs, less expensive engravings, etchings, and wood-engravings flooded the market in quantities unseen before or since. Newspaper and magazine readership soared, driven by the extraordinary variety and amount of material as well as the reduction of the stamp tax to a penny.

On January 1, 1823, the first—though short-lived—Anglo-Jewish newspaper, *The Hebrew Intelligencer*, appeared, followed by a variety of similar publications both in London and in outlying communities. None featured pictures. But by 1841, *Vanity Fair*, *Punch*, *The Graphic*, *The Illustrated News*, and *The Illustrated London News* began printing items of Jewish interest.

Vanity Fair and *Punch* specialized in political satire or serious issues. In its Jewish material it concentrated on caricatures of tailors and old-clothes men. *The Graphic*, *The Illustrated News*, and *The Illustrated London News* were mainly interested in events of the day, along with the doings of wealthy Jews.

Among the newsworthy articles following the Napoleonic wars were stories that alien Jewish infiltrators had overwhelmed the island, but agitation over their presence subsided as it became clear that most Jews in England were native-born. The issue of legal and social impediments to Jewish civil rights now became a steady theme: In *Jewish Disabilities*, c.1830, a lithograph in *The Illustrated News*, an unnerved Christian minister clutching a Bible reacts with disbelief to a Jewish upstart who proposes that the House of Commons be a house of inclusion: "Is it not Written, Your Nation shall be a scab a scorn a spitting; and would You sit

Ill. 6:18. *Jewish Disabilities*. Lithograph, c. 1830

Ill. 6:19. *Reformers of the 19th Century.* Lithograph, c. 1830. By J. Davis

in the House of C....s?" (Ill. 6:18). The big-bellied Jew (i.e. Lionel Rothschild) who views the House of Commons as fair pickings, responds in Yiddish accent—"Mine goot friend, it <u>ish</u> possible to sit there midout spoiling your Propheshie." Fears that Jews would de–Christianize the nation were still alive.

But Jews had before them the examples of Emancipation in France as well as the gains won by English Catholics in 1829, and they weren't about to abandon efforts on their own behalf. Bills for the repeal of certain handicaps were launched and defeated again and again beginning in 1830. When Sir Robert Grant introduced a civil rights motion, Sir Robert Inglis opposed it. J. Davis, the first Jewish political satirist in England, published a lithograph that year, *Reformers of the 19th Century*, dedicated to Sir R. Ingle-ass wearing the head of a donkey (Ill. 6:19). Despite political and economic pressures by conservative elements, by 1831 Jews at last received the Freedom of the City of London, which enabled them to engage in retail trade. Petitions from liberal Christians carried the signatures of twenty-six hundred prominent merchants and professional men—"a most important testimonial in favour of the Jews," declared a member of Parliament, "because it was from the great body of those among whom they resided."

One of those favored Jews was Moses Montefiore, knighted by Queen Victoria when he became sheriff of London in 1837; she said she was pleased to do "what I think quite right." A stockbroker, observant Jew, and industrialist, he was lauded for his efforts on behalf of oppressed Turkish, Moroccan, Romanian, and Russian Jews. When the twenty-fifth anniversary of the consecration of the Western Synagogue took place in 1851, Montefiore's tall figure

Ill. 6:20. *Consecration of the Western Synagogue.* Wood-engraving, 1851

appeared behind the ninety-year-old Rabbi Abraham Belais in a wood-engraving in *The Illustrated London News* (Ill. 6:20). The inscription noted that "the procession, followed by boys and girls from the charity-schools connected with the congregation, then advanced until it arrived at the ark, during which the leader and choir sang 'Blessed be he, who cometh in the name of the Lord....' Offerings towards repairs and decorations were then announced, among which was the sum of fifty pounds given by Sir Moses Montefiore.... The galleries were exclusively occupied by elegantly dressed ladies." Among the elegants was the baronet's wife, the former Judith Cohen. Their marriage had united prominent English Ashkenazi and Sephardi families for the first time. Lady Montefiore, whose "enthusiasm for everything that is noble," wrote her husband, "and [whose] religious faith sustained me in my career," in 1846 compiled the earliest English-language kosher cookbook and manual on personal home care, to raise scholarship funds. In spite of her family's objections to the participation of women in synagogue worship, she established her commitment to equality by frequently attending services. Feminist activities were organized by the Jewish Ladies' Benevolent Loan Society and the Ladies' Visiting Society, the first women-oriented charities in England. The groups worked diligently to care for eastern European and other Jewish girls, some of whom had been recruited as prostitutes.

For the upper classes it was a time of vitality, dynamism, and expansion. For the recent east European immigrants it was a time of hard work in retail and small manufacturing trades. But as financial and commercial opportunities opened up, some fortunate Jews were able to move from the unwholesome East End to more salubrious neighborhoods. They built splendid religious palaces and never seemed to tire of the engravings and etchings that showed these houses of worship to advantage. Judging by the large number of synagogue prints that appeared in the general press, the public must have taken a considerable interest in them. A wood-engraving, *The New Synagogue in Great St. Helens,* 1841, showed off the building created by David Mocatta and John Davies, Jewish and Christian architects respectively in the employ-ment of Nathan Rothschild; it more than fulfilled his vision (Ill. 6:21). *London Interiors* mag-azine in 1841 declared that it "eclipses every one of our modern churches." This was hardly an exaggeration; its Romanesque-style windows and arches were copied by synagogues through-out the world. When the North London Synagogue, designed by the Jewish architect Hyman

Ill. 6:21. *The New Synagogue in Great St. Helens.* Wood-engraving, 1841

THE FEAST OF TABERNACLES AT THE NORTH LONDON SYNAGOGUE—THE READER TAKING
THE PALM BRANCH

Ill. 6:22. *The Feast of Tabernacles at the North London Synagogue—The Reader Taking the Palm Branch.* Wood-engraving, 1872

Collins, celebrated Sukkot in 1872, *The Feast of Tabernacles at the North London Synagogue—The Reader Taking the Palm Branch,* a "curious and somewhat picturesque scene," was engraved for *The Graphic* (Ill. 6:22). A description of the service noted that "With the increase of synagogues in this country, our Jewish brethren have been enabled to participate more largely than heretofore in the more important ceremonies enjoined by their creed." *The Consecration of the Central Jewish Synagogue,* 1870, was pictured with its rich Moorish ornamentation in a wood-engraving in *The Illustrated London News* (Ill. 6:23).

The Bevis Marks Synagogue, however, became the scene of a troublesome event and a serious challenge to the Jewish community. One of its members, Isaac D'Israeli, author of the popular *Curiosities of Literature,* 1791, was elected as warden but declined the honor on the grounds that he wasn't consulted and that Judaism had little meaning for him. Fined forty pounds for noncompliance, he refused to pay, and upon the death of his Orthodox father, left the congregation. Although he remained within the fold, he converted his five children to Christianity and wrote critically about the Jews in *The Genius of Judaism,* 1833, urging rejection of the Talmud and Jewish "superstitions," but keeping traditions in terms of the Enlightenment. His son, Benjamin Disraeli (he dropped the apostrophe), was baptized at age twelve, in 1817, thus making him eligible for the high offices he later held in the British government. Although he was a bona fide Christian, he was regularly referred to as "the Jew," and always acknowledged his heritage with pride. It is said that when he was taunted by the Irish leader Daniel O'Connell in 1835 as a descendant of "miscreant" Jews, he replied, "I admire your scurrilous allusions to my origin.... Yes, I am a Jew, and when the ancestors of the right honourable

THE CENTRAL JEWISH SYNAGOGUE, GREAT PORTLAND-STREET.

Ill. 6:23. *The Consecration of the Central Jewish Synagogue.* Wood-engraving, 1870

gentleman were brutal savages in an unknown land, mine were priests in the temple of Solomon." (A similar statement has been attributed to Judah P. Benjamin, the Confederate secretary of state.)

Disraeli's early travels to Palestine inspired a number of his novels. *David Alroy*, 1833, set in the twelfth century, deals with messianism and efforts to restore Jerusalem to the Jews: "You ask me what I wish," the author-hero remarks. "My answer is the Temple, all we had forfeited, all we have yearned for ... and our ancient customs." A lithograph of the handsome young author the following year by his friend Alfred D'Orsay hinted at his keen sartorial interest (Ill. 6:24). He was known to turn up in pink trousers and embroidered waistcoat, with a carefully tended ringlet curling down his forehead. But outward vanity never obscured the brilliant mind or his determination to make England the greatest nation in the world. In 1844, he wrote of an ambitious political leader in *Coningsby*, who may have been an idealized version of Lionel de Rothschild—and himself. In *Tancred*, 1847, he campaigned for Jewish national independence and challenged the

Ill. 6:24. *Benjamin Disraeli*. Lithograph, 1834. By Alfred D'Orsay

Christian Church to acknowledge its Jewish roots. He scolded lapsed Jews "ashamed of their race and not fanatically devoted to their religion," affiliated himself with the struggle to remove impediments involving religious oaths, and supported the return of Jews to the "land of their fathers." But as did many leaders of the time, he viewed Judaism more as a racial concept than as a divine revelation.

He became prime minister in 1868 and again in 1874, taking his seat in Parliament "on the true faith of a Christian." As head of the Conservative Party, and with the financial backing of the Rothschilds (once denigrated by the queen), he bought up shares of the Suez Canal Company in 1875 when the Khedive of Egypt found himself in need of ready cash. In so doing he not only gave England control of the coveted route to India but designated Victoria empress of the continent. "It is just settled, you have it, Madam," he wrote her in triumph. He was rewarded with the title of Earl of Beaconsfield. A *Punch* cartoon that year, *Mose in Egito* (*Moses in Egypt*), by Sir John Tenniel, shows him in sly cahoots with the Sphinx as he holds the Key of India (Ill. 6:25). His dandified appearance and aggressive politics made him the focus of so many caricatures that the magazine eventually published over one hundred examples from 1843 to 1878; only a few satirized him as a Jew.

At least part of the interest in Jews was derived from the long and remarkable existence of the House of Rothschild. Over the years, the London branch of the family, led by Nathan Meyer, had provided loans that helped defeat Napoleon, expand the textile industry, save the Bank of England, and finance the purchase of the Canal. He regularly parked himself next to a column at the Royal Exchange picking up and transmitting financial gossip to his European family. Legend has it that carrier pigeons, winging confidential news back and forth across the Channel, provided him with the fastest method of communication then known, enabling him

Above: Ill. 6:25. *Mose in Egito (Moses in Egypt)* Lithograph, 1875. By Sir John Tenniel. *Below:* Ill. 6:26. *N. M. Rothschild, Esq.* Lithograph, 1817

to outmaneuver his competitors. An early caricature, *N. M. Rothschild, Esq.*, 1817, presents him with an amiable expression, an admirable belly, and a fiscal document in hand (Ill. 6:26). It was drawn by William Makepeace Thackeray, famed author of *Vanity Fair*, who doubled as an artist with an occasional anti–Jewish bite. Nathan wasn't happy with the likeness, although it satisfied his brother Solomon, who commented, "I hope our children, my Anselm and your Lionel, are also the butt of such caricatures, if, with God's help, they also reach a respected place in society." Sir Nathan became the first Jew in the House of Lords in 1885, seated by amendment of the Christological oath.

Lionel was Nathan's eldest son. A lithograph, *Baron Lionel de Rothschild*, c. 1840 (his title was courtesy of the Austrian emperor), shows a young man attired as finely as any gentleman in the realm (Ill. 6:27). He was the first Jew-

Left: Ill. 6:27. *Baron Lionel de Rothschild.* Lithograph, c. 1840. *Right:* Ill. 6:28. *Sir David Salomons.* Wood-engraving, 1855

ish member of Parliament, elected to the House of Commons in 1847, but in spite of raising the style quotient, was denied admission since he could not take the required oath. In his autobiography, Henry Adams, an American diplomat stationed in England, acknowledged being impressed by the Rothschild elegance: "In its best days, Victorian society had never been 'smart.' ... Fashion was not fashionable in London until the Americans and the Jews were let loose."

In 1851, Sir David Salomons, an ardent fighter for Emancipation, was elected to the House of Commons, with no better luck than Lionel. He took his rightful seat, but his services as the first Jewish sheriff and alderman notwithstanding, was ceremoniously removed because he too refused to take the oath. *The Illustrated Times* ran a laudatory story along with a wood-engraved portrait when he was elected Lord Mayor of London in 1855 thanks to an act of Parliament passed ten years earlier which enabled Jews to hold municipal offices without the official requirement (Ill. 6:28). However, in spite of the *Times'* stamp of approval, the celebrated novelist Nathaniel Hawthorne, when a guest in Salomons' home in 1856, described his "repugnance" towards his host's race. The *Times* later featured an illustration of the Great St. Helen's Synagogue, of which Sir David was a member, on the occasion of its reopening after having been partially destroyed by a fire. A long and patronizing description of the service followed, as the reporter "looked upon the living, breathing Jews as a strange anachronism in the present day, having no single thing in common with us but the one fact that they were men, as we are." He then expressed the generally ambivalent attitude towards Jews: "However strongly we, as Christians, may denounce the Jew's religion as an error; however ardently we may wish that his belief, like his nationality, were no more, but that he were connected to a better faith, still ... we must in some degree respect it. Pity him if you will; convert him if you can; but do not mock his worship."

Ill. 6:29. *Baron Rothschild at the Table of the House of Commons.* Wood-engraving, 1858

Not until 1858 were Jews finally permitted to take oaths of office according to Jewish requirements. No longer excluded from Parliament, Lionel Rothschild took his seat in the House of Commons, an occasion honored by *The Illustrated London News* with a wood-engraving (Ill. 6:29). He distinguished himself during his sixteen-year tenure by never rising to make a speech. In 1881, a full-page wood-engraving, *The Wedding of Lionel's Son Leopold to Mlle. Marie Peruga* in the Central Synagogue appeared on the cover of *The Graphic* (Ill. 6:30). The ceremony brought out the country's bluest blood, including members of the Sassoon family and the Prince of Wales, who presented a silver ewer and basin to the couple. The building, with its "lofty campanile" rising four stories high, became something of a local attraction by its royal association.

Jews caught both positive and negative attention from some of England's greatest writers. The economist David Ricardo consistently argued for full Jewish advantages although he was a proselyte. His *Principles of Political Economy and Taxation,* 1817, was acclaimed as an important contribution to monetary policies. Karl Marx's *Das Kapital,* 1867, composed during long hours in the British Museum, demanded the overthrow of existing bourgeois social orders through proletarian dictatorship and Communism. In spite of the fact that many Jews like himself were victims of discrimination and poverty, Marx, living in desperate straits in England, could see them only as profiteers.

In the early years of the century, when over-wrought emotionalism defined the Romantic period, George Gordon, Lord Byron, perhaps its greatest spokesman, wrote admiringly of the Bible, but not of religion. In 1815 he obliged his friend Isaac Nathan, cantor, composer, and music instructor to Princess Charlotte and George IV, by grouping some of his most famous poems under the title *Hebrew Melodies,* which Nathan set to old Jewish tunes. But Byron did not love the Jews. Although one of the five proto–Zionist poems, *O Weep for Those...* included the lines "The wild dove hath his nest, the fox his cave, Mankind their country, Israel but the grave," he later "damned the *Hebrew Melodies*" and "cursed the Tribes to boot." He excoriated the Rothschilds for bringing down Napoleon's empire for what he perceived was their own benefit: "On Shylock's shore behold them stand afresh, To cut from Nations' hearts

Ill. 6:30. *The Wedding of Lionel's Son Leopold to Mlle. Marie Peruga.* Wood-engraving, 1881. From *The Graphic*

their proud pound of flesh." But while he was repelled by Jews, making many demeaning references to them in his crowning work, *Don Juan*, he apparently was also superstitious, for when Nathan gifted him with Passover matzos, he hoped they would act as a "charm against the destroying angel ... and a fearful looking form of judgment."

In 1867, Matthew Arnold wrote an appreciative tribute to Hebrew culture, *On Heine's Grave*, although he remarked that Jews were "petty unamiable people ... without science, without art, without charm." William Wordsworth's feelings were softer. His poems *For the Wandering Jew*, 1800, and *A Jewish Family*, 1828, expressed sympathy for the injustices they suffered. Sir Walter Scott's Rebecca emerged as an entirely good woman in *Ivanhoe*, 1820, a novel which pitted upright Jews against cruel Christian knights. Her character reputedly was based on Washington Irving's recommendation of Rebecca Gratz, founder of benevolent societies and Jewish schools in America. The father of Scott's Rebecca, Isaac of York, was also drawn as a noble character, but with a more ambivalent pen. Algernon Charles Swinburne's *On the Russian Persecution of the Jews* empathized with the pogrom victims.

Sir Isaac Lyon Goldsmid, nephew of Abraham and Benjamin, was knighted in 1841, the first professing Jew to become a baronet. He worked untiringly for Jewish Emancipation, the abolition of slavery, and penal reform. The nondenominational University College of London, which he helped found, was the first school to offer academic degrees to Jews in 1837. Robert Cruikshank didn't like it. His 1825 etching *The Political Toyman* caricatured one of its proponents, Lord Henry Brougham, wearing a model of the proposed building on his head, while the "puppet," Goldsmid, dangled from his belt, along with several other liberals who insisted that there were not to be "any religious tests or doctrinal forms which would oppose a barrier to education of any sect among His Majesty's subjects." Goldsmid was unfazed. He responded by hiring the poet Hyman Hurwitz as a Hebrew instructor at the university.

Samuel Taylor Coleridge claimed in *Table Talk*, 1830, that he once addressed an old-clothes man seated opposite him in a coach: "Son of Abraham! thou smellest ... thou art offensive ... thou stinkest foully...." But since the fellow admitted those sins and apologized, we may assume that Coleridge had a legitimate point. He was something of a Hebrew scholar, helping Hurwitz translate a Hebrew poem in memory of Princess Charlotte into English. Writing to his publisher, he commented, "Mr. Hurwitz is ... an extraordinary character. A Jew, not more by birth than by conviction, not merely honest and strictly conscientious, but even delicately and honorably so, liberal in all his principles and opinions and of all the religious men I have known, perhaps most deserving the name of philosopher." Jews' College opened in 1855 as a rabbinical training ground, but in spite of Hurwitz's eminence, until 1871 Oxford and Cambridge allowed Jews only to matriculate, not to graduate. That year the Anglo-Jewish Association was formed to "obtain protection for those who may suffer in consequence of being Jews, and to advance the social, moral and intellectual welfare of Jews of Eastern Europe and elsewhere."

Sir Francis Palgrave was a handsome, aristocratic-looking scholar and the father of Sir Francis Turner Palgrave, anthologist of the *Golden Treasury of the Best Songs and Lyrical Poems in the English Language*, 1861. He was a Cohen at birth until he took his Christian mother-in-law's maiden name in order to please his wife. He didn't impress Henry Adams, however, who said that Palgrave was the only great English historian who was un-English—"and the reason for his superiority lay in his name, which was Cohen, and his mind which was Cohen also...." His mother-in-law, Mrs. Dawson Turner, etched his portrait in 1823 after a painting by Thomas Phillips, a member of the Royal Academy (Ill. 6:31).

William Blake, a creative engraver and poet, hated the Jewish God "Old Nobabaddy" who "farted and belched and coughed and said I love hanging and drawing and quartering every bit as well as war and slaughtering." The Hebrew Bible, parts of which he idealized and engraved with an extraordinarily powerful vision, nevertheless exemplified "the wickedness and deceit of the Jews ... as well as their "human beastliness in all its branches."

As a young woman in 1848, George Eliot (Mary Ann Evans) wrote that "everything specifically Jewish is of a low grade," and "almost all their history is utterly revolting." But ten years later, during a tour of Jewish Prague, Naples, and Amsterdam with her longtime companion George Henry Lewes, she became more sympathetic to the situation of European Jewry, and began a study of Hebrew and the Talmud. In 1858, she composed a proto–Zionist novel, *Daniel Deronda*, which at times confused culture with race or ethnicity, yet dealt sensitively with the disillusion accompanying the secularization of the Enlightenment. Her prediction of a utopian Palestine where all Jews would settle—"the vision is there, it will be fulfilled"—ran counter to the preferences of most middle-class English Jews, who were tolerably happy and had no burning desire to relocate. The premises of the book, while inspiring a number of Hebrew writers, were derided by many critics, prompting her to repeat its nationalist themes in *The Modern Hep-Hep*, 1878. Her point of view, however,

Ill. 6:31. *Sir Francis Palgrave*. Etching, 1823. By Mrs. Dawson Turner after a painting by Thomas Phillips

did not coincide with that of George DuMaurier, author and illustrator of *Trilby*, 1894, in which the Jewish Svengali appeared as a member of an inferior race—a horrible "incubus ... a dread, powerful demon" who mesmerized and corrupted the innocent Gentile heroine.

A few Jewish novelists enjoyed recognition. Aside from Disraeli's works, Grace Aguilar's *Vale of Cedars*, posthumously published in 1850, was a somewhat cloying story of virtuous Spanish Marranos. The foremost Anglo-Jewish writer was the native-born Israel Zangwill, whose struggles to reconcile old country observances with new country freedoms appeared in his autobiographical *Children of the Ghetto: A Study of a Peculiar People*, 1892, and in the satirical *King of the Shnorrers*, 1894. Typical of his urban tales, they were enormously successful among Jews and Gentiles on both sides of the Atlantic. On the other hand, he occasionally indulged in self-denigration and resented being known as a "Jewish" novelist; he considered himself an Englishman. It is thought that he was influenced by Amy Levy, whose novel *Reuben Sachs*, 1888, described the worldly upper-class life of English Jews in unflattering terms. Despair or regret led to her suicide soon after its publication.

John Kitto's *Pictorial History of Palestine and the Holy Land with a Complete History of the Jews* appeared in 1844 in London with five hundred wood-engravings, an important addition to the genre. A young Scottish artist, David Roberts, found a lucrative specialty based on his travels to the Middle East from 1838 to 1839. His drawings and watercolors were translated by his friend Louis Haghe into a six-volume set of two hundred forty-eight tinted lithographs, published in London from 1842 to 1849 as *The Holy Land, Syria, Idumea, Arabia, Egypt, & Nubia*. The introduction carried a tribute to Jews; one of its plates, *Polish Jews Embarking from Jaffa After a Visit to the Holy Land*, is expressive in its fore, middle, and distant grounds (Ill. 6:32). The prevalence of beautifully illustrated works encouraged the well-to-do to make their way to alien and exotic places. For those who could only dream of long-distance excursions,

Ill. 6:32. *Polish Jews Embarking from Jaffa After a Visit to the Holy Land*. From *The Holy Land, Syria, Idumea, Arabia, Egypt, & Nubia*, 1842–1849. Lithograph by Louis Haghe after a drawing by David Roberts

the collections were a welcome addition to a sociable evening, providing some of the very few available pictures of faraway countries, although, in truth, they were vastly romanticized.

But not many Jews were able to travel to distant lands. In the heyday of the Victorian golden age perhaps twenty percent of the community required subsidies from the Jewish Board of Guardians to provide financial aid and social services. More familiar than views of Palestine was a wood-engraving, *The Old Clothes Market in Petticoat Lane,* c. 1860, depicting the dilapidated area where torn goods were unloaded for mending and resale, kosher meat and fried fish were bought for Shabbat dinners, hungry children dreamed of stuffing themselves with penny delights, boys and girls diverted themselves with covert flirting, and a colorful assortment of less than respectable individuals plied their unsavory trades (Ill. 6:33).

The Industrial Revolution, for all its energy and technological power, abetted the degrading urban poverty that Dickens described and that many worthy Victorians took for granted. In 1873, the French printmaker Gustave Doré, on one of his visits to the East End, produced a series of etchings, *A Pilgrimage*, which included a number of stereotyped Jewish subjects such as butchers, rag merchants, and a half-blind panhandler, *Mendicant Juif a Londres* (*Jewish Beggar in London*). In another print, he recorded "endless swarms of ragged children ... and the doorways in which Jewish butchers lounge—fat and content." Fat they may have been, but probably not very content. As late as 1897, *The Illustrated London News* featured Francis W. Lawson's wood-engraving *The Soup Kitchen for Poor Jews* on its cover, emphasizing large noses as well as hot meals (Ill. 6:34). For the young man whose fingers protruded from torn gloves, or the group patiently waiting their turn for a meal, there was little in the way of comfort other than what was undertaken by benevolent organizations and reformers. Government action to control runaway industrial development lagged.

Ill. 6:33. *The Old Clothes Market in Petticoat Lane.* Wood-engraving, c. 1860

Cause for alarm loomed with the meltdown in the Russian economy and the assassination of Czar Alexander II in 1882. Blame for those disasters was automatically settled on the Jews, launching a series of murderous pogroms. *The Illustrated London News* printed a wood-engraving, *Meeting at Guildhall on Behalf of the Jews of Russia,* 1890, remonstrating against the persecution (Ill. 6:35). In the same year a cartoon in *Punch* introduced Pharaoh's ghost admonishing the czar not to raise his sword against his Jewish subjects: *Forebear! That weapon always wounds the hand that wields it.*

But Alexander did not forbear. Whole communities fled to Germany, France, and England's already overcrowded East End. One hundred thousand Jews from Russia and eastern Europe descended on English cities, adding to the sixty-five thousand already struggling for decent homes and enough food. Complaints were heard of cut-throat marketing, unpalatable sweatshops, and criminal behavior, as well as of foreigners with strange clothing, manners, and languages who were unable to blend smoothly into well-bred English society. However, even though Lord Rothschild feared that "we have a new Poland on our hands," many of the refugees were absorbed. They had the Yiddish language in common, shared many Old World customs, and established synagogues, religious schools, cemeteries, mikvas, kosher markets, and trade unions. For information they read *The Jewish Chronicle,* for entertainment there was the Pavilion Theatre, for English literacy there were teachers, for spiritual needs there were rabbis, for affairs of the heart there were dancehalls, for misbehaving there were gaming houses and worse.

Jewish artists had already begun to make a name for themselves. Solomon Alexander Hart's paintings *Elevation of the Law,* 1830, and *Rejoicing of the Law in the Ancient Synagogue of Leghorn,* 1850, were widely reproduced in postcards and prints. He was the first Jew to be appointed as a full member of the Royal Academy in 1840, and later became a professor of painting and a librarian. These great honors, however, were tempered when he was once introduced to some friends in what was apparently considered an appropriate manner: "This is Mr. Hart whom we have just elected Academician. Mr. Hart is a Jew, and the Jews crucified our Saviour, but he is a very good man for all that..."

The siblings Abraham, Rebecca, and Simeon Solomon were likewise important painters, the latter much admired by his fellow Pre-Raphaelites Sir Edward Bourne-Jones and Dante Gabriel Rosetti. They were followed by Solomon Joseph Solomon who worked well into the twentieth century painting portraits of the choicest personages in Jewish and English society, including Israel Zangwill, Solomon Schechter, and the queen. In the 1850s and 60s, Simeon's print port-

Ill. 6:34. *The Soup Kitchen for Poor Jews*. Wood-engraving, 1897. By Francis W. Lawson, from *The Illustrated London News*

folio *Jewish Ceremonies* became the first such body of work since the eighteenth century etchings of Jewish rituals—and his were created by a Jew. Unlike those of his predecessors, however, his images projected low spirits and apathy. His painting, *The Scrolls of the Law, 1865,* was a model of religious observance, but his open homosexuality and alcoholism placed him on the wrong side of Victorian morality; cast out by family and friends, he died a derelict in a London workhouse.

Positive as well as negative factors regulated the community. Gala philanthropic affairs,

Ill. 6:35. *Meeting at Guildhall on Behalf of the Jews in Russia.* Wood-engraving, 1890

promoted for the have-nots and enjoyed by the haves, always called up the handsomest dandies and loveliest Jewish butterflies in London. But, as *Harper's Bazaar's* 1872 wood-engraving *The Jews' Infant-School Ball* pointed out, it was not only an occasion for dancing, it was an example of "the spirit of charity which especially characterizes the Hebrew community.... If Christian charities were proportionately as extensive and as well organized, the misery which disgraces our great cities would soon be considerably lessened" (Ill. 6:36).

Unlike the English artists who caricatured the gross side of Jewish life, James Abbot McNeil Whistler, an expatriate American, etched a homely scene in London's run-down East End, *Clothes-Exchange*, 1887 (Ill. 6:37). While it lacked the finish that was generally admired, its qualities of dissolving light and broken lines captured the essence of the ordinary. His wife described the neighborhood in her diary with its "small traffic and bustle where hundreds of dealers of cast-off clothing used to assemble after their morning rounds, picking up whatever they could hope to sell for shillings and for pence." In 1899, Whistler included the atmospheric *Jews' Quarter* in his etched scenes of Amsterdam neighborhoods, which he considered one of his best works.

Lucien Pissarro, the son of Camille and a Gentile mother, moved to England where he founded the Eragny Press in 1896 and produced, among his other editions, sentimental prints illustrating the biblical books of Ruth and Esther. He married a Jewess, of whom he made a lithographic portrait, and raised a printmaker daughter, Orovida.

As in every country where Jews found themselves, the Haggadah enjoyed an honored status. It was one of the few important liturgical works prepared in England before the last two decades of the century when presses responded to the flood of Jewish immigration; until

Ill. 6:36. *The Jews' Infant-School Ball.* **Wood-engraving, 1872. From** *Harper's Bazaar*

then most material for Jewish use was imported from the continent. A London example of 1806 printed by Levi Alexander took its familiar prints from earlier non–Jewish sources, but it filled a need since it appeared with an English translation. In 1813, Alexander published a Sephardic Haggadah in Hebrew and Spanish, catering to those who revered the traditions of

Ill. 6:37. *Clothes-Exchange*. Etching, 1887. By James Abbot McNeil Whistler

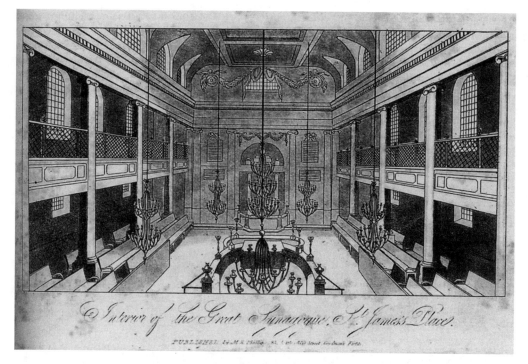

Ill. 6:38. *Interior of the Great Synagogue, St. James's Place.* Haggadah, 1831

pre–Inquisition Spain; its illustrations were borrowed from the 1806 edition. An Ashkenazi Haggadah, printed in 1831, edited by Isaac Levi with Hebrew and English on facing pages, featured an engraved frontispiece, *Interior of the Great Synagogue, St. James's Place* (Ill. 6:38).

Perhaps the most unusual Haggadah ever printed appeared on August 17, 1840, in the London *Times.* When a number of Jews were charged with the murder of a Franciscan friar in Damascus, Syria in order to obtain his blood for Passover use, the *Times* responded by printing most of the Haggadah in its regular columns. To the chagrin of those who still believed the old canard, there was absolutely no mention of Christian blood being drawn for ritual purposes. Whether or not that evidence changed any minds was not recorded, but the article created international support for the imprisoned Jews. Sir Moses Montefiore immediately went to Egypt (which ruled Syria) where his reputation and the implied backing of the English government won the release of all but one victim, who had died under torture, and one who, unable to cope with the pressure, converted to Islam.

The first Reform Haggadah appeared in London in 1842, rather than in Germany where the movement was born. The English non-rabbinic edition was part of a two-volume Siddur which grew out of disagreements within the Bevis Marks community over proposed changes in the services. When a dissenting group broke away in 1840 forming the liberal West London Synagogue of British Jews, they eliminated certain Passover traditions such as the four cups of wine, charoses, and the afikomen on the grounds that they were not biblically mandated. The Haggadah never caught on. David Nieto's warnings in the previous century against the rejection of the Oral Law were hastily invoked by alarmed conservative elements. For their trouble, the rebels were stigmatized as non-professing Jews and excommunicated by Rabbi Hirschell, although that ban was later removed. The Reform movement never really caught on either, mainly because there was no urgent desire to do so. Anglo-Jews were, after all, quite conventional in their habits, satisfied with a few cosmetic changes—and with assurances that their services were more genteel, less Gentile than those of German Reform.

Jews of the Commonwealth countries such as India developed their own customs since they matured at a distance from conventional centers. According to tradition, Jews known as B'nai Israel had settled there in biblical times, unaware of later traditions until the end of the eighteenth century when Jewish arrivals from Cochin and other cities brought them up-to-date. Together with co-religionists from the Malabar coast and neighboring communities, they built a synagogue in Bombay in 1796 and published a Hebrew grammar in 1832 in Marathi, the indigenous language. The first Hebrew press in India was established in Bombay in 1840 by Eleazar ben Aaron Saadiah Iraqi haCohen, who probably cast his own type. His business, which lasted until 1856, compared favorably with the best that Europe had to offer at that period. The first Indian Haggadah appeared in Calcutta in lithography in 1841 when the Jewish population there was not much over one hundred. It was translated into Arabic "so that common folks, women and children, would be able to understand the miracles." The 1846 lithographed Marathi Haggadah was a copy of the Amsterdam version of 1712, but the Haggadah of 1874, printed in the city of Poona with lithographic illustrations of men and women making Seder preparations in native costumes, was entirely original—the ladies, tastefully attired in pearls and saris, squat on the floor in Hindu style, remembered to tuck a few flowers in their hair (Ill. 6:39). The publishers, Moses Jacob Talker and Aaron David Talker, carefully pointed out the community's strict adherence to religious law and rituals.

India was home to a gifted Anglo-Indian Jewish family which had arrived from Baghdad in 1834. Its most distinguished member was David ben Sasoon, an observant Jew and generous philanthropist. His gift to the Industrial and Reformatory Institution was acknowledged in *The Illustrated London News* with a wood-engraving of the school, designed for "juvenile delinquents arrested by the police and the encouragement of apprenticeship among the working class...." He established synagogues in Bombay and Poona, endowed educational scholarships, developed profitable textile and tobacco businesses, and encouraged the publication of Hebrew liturgical works.

Ill. 6:39. *The Ladies Squat on the Floor Hindu Style.* Lithograph, Poona Haggadah, 1874

When the Anglo-Jewish Historical Exhibition opened in London's Royal Albert Hall in 1887 following its Paris showing in 1878, it stirred up enthusiasm for cultural and religious artifacts. Joseph Jacobs and Lucien Wolf prepared the catalogue, which listed over twenty-six hundred items. It was the first time that Judaic antiquities, paintings, engravings, caricatures, and books were displayed in England, although none were by Jewish artists; most were portraits of well-known Anglo-Jewish individuals. No local Hebrew printing was included. Nevertheless, it introduced the serious study of Jewish art, encouraged collectors, and went a long way to instill pride and cultivate self-esteem. Its impact on both Jewish and Gentile visitors led to the publication of the *Jewish Quarterly Review* in 1889; five years later the Jewish Historical Society of England was founded, opening previously untapped avenues in art and historical research. The Chief Rabbi of England, Hermann Adler, commented on the potential for art influencing the perception of Jews as they moved through history: "Had there been less mystery about our religious observances," he said, " there would perhaps have been less prejudice, certainly greater freedom from foul aspersions."

By the end of the century, Jews were fairly well integrated into the English mainstream. The poor were moving up, the middle class got richer, the upper class commanded the very best places in society. Scholarship, too, gained an honored place. Rabbi Solomon Schechter pieced together manuscript fragments brought to England from the Genizah of the ancient Fostat Synagogue in Cairo. During his travels to Egypt, he collected large numbers of specimens documenting over a thousand years of Mediterranean Jewish life, shipped them to England, and presented the lot to the Cambridge University Library. The treasures, which had survived because of the dry atmosphere, contained parts of Ecclesiasticus (its Hebrew version previously thought to be lost). In 1899, he published the second century B.C.E. *Wisdom of Ben Sira*, an apocryphal work that changed and enlarged the scope of biblical research. "Having spent nearly fifty years on the study of Jewish literature and Jewish history," he wrote, "I am deeply convinced that we cannot sever Jewish nationality from Jewish religion."

His research coincided with notable alterations in English manners. Life became less formal. Like their Christian neighbors, Jewish men traded chin-tickling neckcloths for collars and ties, high silk hats for bowlers. Their ladies gave up hoops and crinolines for slim skirts and advertised their nether regions with bustles that poked out like a shelf. Inventions and new modes of communication such as the telegraph and the postal system transformed daily activities. Electric lights were already brightening shops and homes. Steam-powered carriages reached speeds of twenty miles per hour, but horse-coach and locomotive interests in 1896 effectively blocked their development. It didn't much matter, because the Daimler automobile with an internal combustion engine fueled by gasoline was introduced that same year.

England's Jewish population now stood at one hundred eighty thousand, thanks to the large inflow from Russia and eastern Europe, although after about 1830 there was considerable emigration to America. Having overcome most disabilities without serious impediments and been granted full Emancipation in 1871, English Jews were confidently Anglicized and Jewishly connected. By and large they prospered and were ready to play leading roles in service to their country. Because their civil rights were acknowledged, most did not feel politically threatened or embarrassed by their religious observances. Given that situation, they generally eschewed Reform affiliation, although some Orthodox customs lapsed. Most kept their cultural identities and contributed to activities that they believed enhanced their influence in the Christian world and respect in their own.

Yet misgivings began to replace the spirit of tolerance and communal good will. Anti-Jewish sentiments were spreading. Disraeli's alleged anti–Christian policies were said to favor Jewish financial interests. Jewish leaders were accused of manipulating business contracts. Jewish moneyed men were elbowing their way into too many proper English homes, Jewish moneyless men were turning the East End into crime-ridden mini–Jerusalems. Jews were responsible for unemployment. Jewish working-class immigrants and reprobate thugs looked bad, smelled bad, and weren't English. Offensive Jewish material by the well-known writers Anthony Trollope, Thomas Carlyle, and William Makepeace Thackeray negatively shaped English attitudes and influenced its politics. By the time the English Zionist Federation was born in 1899, the decline of liberalism, as well as the rise of nationalism and its partner anti–Semitism, was unmistakable—not as inimical as in parts of Europe, but still unmistakable.

7

France in the Nineteenth Century: The Rule of Napoleon and the Rise of Zionism

At the beginning of the nineteenth century France was in almost total disarray with much of its traditional social order shattered. It had started out as a largely agricultural and handicraft society. It ended up with a highly commercial economy, a progressive technology, and streamlined transportation and communication capabilities. Liberal secular interests and the prosperity created by cultural achievements and international trading vied with labor and anarchist unrest. In literature, science, music, and art, the country reached an efflorescence of intellectual and imaginative energy. A sense of hope, infused by the promises of the Revolution and never entirely lost, was propelled by optimism and escapism, and gradually began to lift its spirit. France, if not as splendid as it once had been, was nevertheless *à la mode*.

But the road had not been easy. Once the extremities of the Reign of Terror ended, the government faced a new set of challenges: monarchy versus republicanism, aristocracy versus the common man, inequality versus equality before the law, and a propertied bourgeoisie versus the propertyless proletariat. To the great discomfort of the nobility and the Church, their lands began to pass to the middle class. The peasant majority, denied a reasonable share of the spoils, labored for a pittance under oppressive circumstances with continuing bitterness between opposing factions. When it seemed as if France had sunk almost too low ever to raise her head among the family of Europe, Napoleon Bonaparte pulled the country together in a political dictatorship.

Napoleon's impact on French Jews was lasting. He had begun a serious relationship with them in 1801 when, mindful of the ideals of 1789, posterity's judgment, and possible benefits, he decided "to govern men as the great majority of them wish to be governed ... [I plan] to revive among the Jews ... the sentiments of civic morality that unfortunately have been lost during long centuries of degrading existence." He granted them existence as a nation among the nations with "the unlimited natural right to worship Yehovah in accordance with your faith, publicly and in likelihood forever."

By suppressing the radical press and revving up a public relations machine, the politically astute emperor found an effective way to heighten his credibility, glorify his person, and win approval for his ecumenical programs. An engraving, *Religious Liberty*, 1802, shows him extending a hand of fellowship to a Catholic, Jew, Quaker, Protestant, Buddhist, Greek, Mexican, Muslim, and idolater while exhorting them to love the government under which they live (Ill. 7:1).

Ill. 7:1. *Religious Liberty*. Engraving, 1802

Ill. 7:2. *Napoleon the Great Re-establishing the Religion of the Israelites*. Engraving, 1806. By François-Louise Couche

But beneficent words and cosmopolitan images were not adequate to cope with the threats of violence that in 1806 plagued the nerve center of French Jewry, Alsace-Lorraine. Some twenty thousand Ashkenazim, comprising more than half of all French Jews, had lived in that agricultural countryside because, prior to the Revolution, they had been denied the privilege to live in cities. After 1791, they were allowed more freedom of movement, but most preferred to stay close to the small towns in which they and their parents' parents were born—among their neighbors but not of them. While they gained certain civil rights, their religious autonomy was curtailed. Mainly they suffered because the pre-industrial economy often brought impoverishment, forcing moneylenders to charge high interest rates. Creditors balked.

The vexing situation prompted Napoleon to freeze all debts owed to the Jews for one year—depriving them of all income—while he convened an assembly of one hundred twelve Jewish notables in 1806. Their job was to investigate and respond to twelve basic issues, including intermarriage with Christians (it was permitted), polygamy (it was prohibited), divorce (it would require a civil act), the taking of interest (it would be subject to civil law), and the compatibility of Jewish and French laws (they could get along). Having thus secured the compliance of the Jewish leadership, he commissioned prints which he believed would underscore his influence or power. François-Louise Couche's engraving, *Napoleon the Great Re-establishing the Religion of the Israelites*, 1806, likens him to Moses offering the rules under which Jews will henceforth live (Ill. 7:2). Mount Sinai rises in the distance, the Temple vessels reappear. Oozing authority with every gesture, Napoleon animates the sunken but responsive Jewish spirit. Not lost on the wide and persuadable audience was the symbolism of his Christ-like posture and the holy men kneeling at his feet. Rabbi Joseph David Sinzheim, president of the

Ill. 7:3. *The Grand Sanhedrin.* Engraving, 1807

Sanhedrin, or Jewish "Supreme Court," along with two representatives of the Jewish people, make obeisance to the new leader.

Napoleon considered himself an agnostic but believed that a disciplined system of theology was necessary to tame men's preferences for lawlessness and insubordination, and that dutiful submission to religion would maintain tradition, family, social order, and the moral authority of government. In 1807 he summoned seventy-one delegates drawn from the group who had participated in the Assembly of Notables to serve as a religious tribunal modeled on ancient prototypes. Forty-five eminent rabbis and twenty-six laymen, appearing with and without beards or head coverings and wearing the clerical robes of their Christian colleagues, were asked to take a stand between commitment to their tradition and their obligations as French citizens. An engraving, *The Grand Sanhedrin,* 1807, depicted the assembly, formally seated in a hall of classical proportions, trading the concept of peoplehood and communal autonomy for secular state supervision and, presumably, a normative civil status (Ill. 7:3). Against charges of lax patriotism, usury, and existence as a "nation within a nation," the Sanhedrin agreed to define French Jews as Frenchmen who happened to be born into the Mosaic faith, affirmed that Jews would follow laws regulating interest rates, accept civil marriage and divorce, and adopt cooperative attitudes towards their fellow citizens—all implications that their heritage was somehow faulty, and that their public and private spirit was suspect. "Nowadays," they declared, "Jews no longer constitute a nation, since they have had the honor of being accepted into the body of the Great Nation in which they see their political salvation." Jews received that honor with prayers of gratitude for Napoleon, whom they looked upon as their savior. He is said to have boasted that the Sanhedrin was a useful tool that would open the purses of Jewish Europe and win him political loyalty, and indeed it did. From the first, he hoped that the Jewish clannishness and inbreeding which kept them distinct would melt and that Jews would become integrated into agriculture and crafts. He told one of his ministers, the Count Jean-

Ill. 7:4. *Digestion du budget, travail administratif, politique, moral et surtout economique (Digestion of the Budget, Administrative, Political, Moral and Above All, Economic).* Lithograph, 1832. By Jean Gerard, known as Grandville

Baptiste Champagne, that assimilation was necessary "so that Jewish blood may lose its specific essence." In many ways Napoleon got what he wanted. When the question was posed to the Notables as to whether French Jews would willingly defend the fatherland, they responded in a single voice: "To the death!"

Napoleon was to be the messiah. France, not Israel, was to be their home. As he shrewdly anticipated, once the Jewish community was reorganized according to consistories or government supervised guidelines it began to lose its cohesiveness as a separate culture. Lay and religious leadership was reduced to funding charitable institutions, supervising religious requirements, and to accommodate spiritual needs. As opposed to eastern European Jewry, which clung to rabbinic control of its internal affairs, French rabbis abdicated their authority as a fixed judiciary.

After appearing sympathetic to Jewish concerns, in 1808 Napoleon made a U-turn, presumably to protect Christian economic interests. He again annulled debts owed to Jews and enforced restrictions which denied them many of the rights they thought they had secured in Alsace and Lorraine. These Infamous Decrees, to be in force for ten years, almost bankrupted the community. They played into the hands of social reformers such as François Marie Charles Fourier, who commented that since commerce was the source of all evil, and Jews were the "incarnation of commerce," it followed that the Hebrews constituted history's most despicable nation.

Napoleon's obsessive wars ended in humiliating defeat when Waterloo finally put an end to his dreams of expansion. By 1815, his remarkable career was over. Although France more or less resumed its former borders, the fallout demoralized the nation and undermined the democratic reforms that were the legacies of the French Revolution. Having lost their new privileges, the Jewish community hardly knew how to cope. Conversion appeared to be an alternative to confusion, an option followed by scores of Jews, including many of its leaders. Nevertheless, as a by-product of Napoleon's victories, ghetto walls had come down in Europe's cities, some civil rights were granted, some vocational options were conceded.

A newly activist French middle-class now demanded a republican-style government with greater economic, social, and democratic progress. In a protest against what he saw as political corruption, Jean Gerard (Grandville) created a stinging lithograph, *Digestion du budget, travail administratif, politique, moral et surtout economique* (*Digestion of the Budget, Administrative, Political, Moral and Above All Economic*), 1832 (Ill. 7:4). It included a Jew, among other unworthy citizens, who, it was claimed, sucked the labor of poor workers and passed the spoils via a tube to the aristocrats' secret stash. Grandville viewed himself as a champion of the disenfranchised; the government viewed him as dangerous and often censored his output.

The restoration of the monarchy under the reactionary kings Charles X and Louis Philippe lasted until revolutions again tore up the continent. Insurrections from 1830 to 1848 resulted from working-class unrest, suffrage inequities, weak leadership, graft, and economic reprisals against the outspoken liberal press. Along the way, German and English inroads on French commerce created unemployment and economic uncertainties. Socialist and capitalist theories, advocating either collective or private ownership of goods, crossed paths and squared off against each other. However, under Napoleon III's constitutional republic, Paris was modernized and rebuilt, health and environmental standards were updated, great medieval buildings were restored. But the Socialist passions and nationalistic fervor which had prompted the rebellions were contagious and soon radiated over much of Europe. From 1848 to the Franco-Prussian War of 1870, amid class struggles, right-to-work issues, and quarrels over the candidacy to the Spanish throne, France lost its dominant role in Europe to the German Empire and was forced to surrender Alsace and Northern Lorraine; Jews there not only feared Prussian control over their ways of life, but induction into the hated German army. Anti-Jewish rioting again erupted, still based on feared competition. "We haven't time to hate one another," declared Victor Hugo. Few people heard.

Nevertheless, the French economy expanded, and with it, fiscal and social changes which benefited Jews. In 1846, the hated oath More Judaico was finally retracted, and in 1859 a rabbinical seminary was able to open in Paris. Having by then increased their population to almost one hundred thousand through a high birth rate and a stream of immigrants, French Jews at last found themselves generally free of official discrimination with wider educational opportunities for Jewish primary and trade schools, as well as access to the civil service and army. But because they still could not join craft guilds, most continued as small traders, peddlers, and moneylenders in the poor and crowded neighborhoods of Paris. Thanks to the new railroads, some took the high road to outlying districts, becoming successful shopkeepers and even owners of a few acres in the countryside. Some found a musical awakening. *La Juive (The Jewess)*, 1835, and *Les Contes d'Hoffman (Tales of Hoffman)*, 1881, by Jewish composers Jacques Halevy and Jacques Offenbach, challenged Europe's best. And in spite of some social barriers, a few became active in public life, wore clothing as fine as the Christian family next door, and named their children after Christian saints.

High on the agenda was the preparation of religious texts. Rabbi David Drach, son-in-law of the Grand Rabbi of France, produced the first Haggadah translation into the French language in 1818—with unpredictable results. Most of the copies were destroyed when he became a Roman Catholic four years later and published conversionary pamphlets and Hebrew poems dedicated to the pope and cardinals. In spite of his example, a Metz Haggadah appeared in 1821, followed by Paris editions in 1869 and 1873. The first prayer book to be rendered into French, *Rituel des Prières Journalienes* (*Daily Prayers*), was printed in Metz in 1827 with a vernacular translation by Joel Anspach, the brother of a high-ranking jurist.

The Levy and Alcan publishing families in Metz and Paris offered works by the finest Jewishly intolerant writers of the day, Honoré de Balzac and Ernest Renan, as well as by the broader-minded Alexandre Dumas. A conservative Jewish monthly, *L'Univers Israelite*, served as the voice of the chief rabbinate from 1844 until 1940, when it was silenced. An opposing journal, *Les Archives Israelites de France*, edited by Isadore Cahen, promoted a liberal agenda from 1858 until 1935. Cahen was instrumental in alerting the world to the secret baptism of an Italian Jewish child, Edgar Mortaga; the Church refused to return him to his parents. The affair galvanized protests—unsuccessful despite international pressure—and led to the founding of the first modern defense agency, Alliance Israelite Universelle in 1860. Its mandate was to "work everywhere for the Emancipation and the moral progress of Jews," to develop educational opportunities and benefits for Jews living under French rule as well as outside the country, and to act as a stimulus for Jewish revival. Non-Jews immediately dubbed it as an overarching Jewish attempt to control Europe's politics and economies.

Yet the Jewish community believed that France was home and not a way-station on the road to Eretz Yisrael. It built houses of worship in which congregants could gather publicly and in peace. C. de Lasleyrie's lithograph *Vue intérieure d'une synagogue* (*Interior of a Synagogue*), c. 1810, presumably in the city of Nancy, displays an eclectic assortment of attendees— some bearded, others clean-shaven, some sporting turbans or stylish tall hats, while others, members of Napoleon's Grand Army, wear military dress (Ill. 7:5). In 1822, the six or seven

Ill. 7:5. *Vue intérieure d'une synagogue (Interior of a Synagogue).* Lithograph, c. 1810. By C. de Lasleyrie

thousand Jews of Paris established the incongruously named synagogue Rue Notre-Dame de Nazareth (*Street of Our Lady of Nazareth*), with seating for a thousand people. Massive columns support the women's gallery and the imposing span over the Torah niche. But as its condition deteriorated, it was abandoned in 1850, and it was replaced twenty-four years later with the five-thousand-seat Rue de la Victoire Synagogue. A lithograph demonstrates the accomplishments of its Jewish architect, Alfred Aldrophe, who used newfangled cast iron in its Romanesque-Byzantine construction, and, in a bow to assimilation, designed a splendid rose window, luminous under an enormous vaulted roof (Ill. 7:6). The congregation had hoped to locate the building in a more auspicious neighborhood, but it was said that Empress Eugenie refused approval in deference to her confessor—possibly a Jewish convert—so as not to discomfort any good Christians. Nevertheless, it attracted sight-seers from all parts of Paris. In previously undreamed acts of self-assurance or presumption, Jews erected synagogues in other cities that were not only large and imposing, but that almost, but not quite, resembled churches.

Some Jews demanded that Sabbath and Holy Day liturgies should reflect the looser rituals already in place in Germany. Compromises were introduced. Among the reforms were shorter and more decorous services and the use of an organ (on condition that it would be played by a non–Jewish musician). Some congregations omitted the Jewish prayer "Next Year in Jerusalem" to dispel any suggestion that they rejected allegiance to France. With marginal amiability, Orthodox and modernist groups went their own ways.

By mid-century, guild restrictions were largely eliminated. As the demand for descriptive pictures increased, the door was opened to Jewish artists. Alphonse Levy arrived in Paris from Alsace at a young age, studied with the well-known French painter and teacher Jean Leon Gerôme, but chose to evoke the rural customs and ceremonies of his former home in gently humorous prints. Some were visual substitutes for Daniel Stauben's *Scenes de la vie juive en Alsace* (*Scenes of Jewish Life in Alsace*), 1857–1859. Wrote its author, "It will not be long before these last vestiges of our ancient traditions will crumble, the way all vanishes with age. That is why I have been so eager to retain on paper at least the most characteristic traits of our Alsatian Jewish country life, while it still lasts." Levy, in partnership with Stauben, remembered accurately and preserved those memories. He focused on Jewish peasants rather than on scholarly or middle-class Jews, fitting the shtetl rather than the assimilated mold. Occasionally they embodied all the earmarks of eccentric or even offensive stereotypes. Certainly, the idealized and romantic evocations of Frankfurt's well-to-do Jews by his German counterpart, Moritz Oppenheim, carried greater appeal than Levy's humble images, but his *Hozen* (*Bridegroom*) summoned by a matchmaker (Ill. 7:7), and *Matzah Gnebflich* (*Matzo Balls*) (Ill. 7:8), both c. 1890, were unabashed love songs to the Jews of his home town.

Most images of Jews, however, were still seen through Gentile eyes such as those of Eugène Delacroix. In 1829 he furnished illustrations for Sir Walter Scott's *Ivanhoe*, one of the first novels to treat the Jewish experience sympathetically. Delacroix's interest in the Jews dated to the time shortly after France annexed Algiers in 1830. In spite of its need of Algeria's wheat, France had not paid for grain deliveries owed to the Jewish Bacri and Busnach families. A fight erupted between the Muslim representative and the French consul. The former struck the latter with a fan, which the French regarded as justification—along with other economic and territorial issues—for three years of blockades and war. The brouhaha ended with the French conquest of Algeria, its wheat allotment only partially paid by Louis XVIII. An offer to accompany a French diplomatic mission there opened a remote world to Delacroix, providing him with a fascinating glimpse into its colorful lifestyle. By the time he returned to France he had internalized the classical beauty of North Africa, along with contrasting the "noble simplicity" of Moroccan dress with "our ridiculously tight shoes, constricted clothes, and pitiful corsets."

He found his Jewish subjects in the mellahs or neighborhoods where he sketched and later

Ill. 7:6. *Rue de la Victoire Synagogue*, Lithograph. c. 1874

Above: Ill. 7:7. *Hozen (Bridegroom).* Etching, c. 1890. *Below:* Ill. 7:8. *Matzah Gnebflich (Matzo Balls).* Etching, c. 1890. Both etchings by Alphonse Levy

etched *Juive d'Alger* (*Algerian Jewess*), 1833; its shimmering lights show off a richly clothed bride (Ill. 7:9). The artist was not, of course, present, since young women were traditionally isolated with their friends and maids, but the costumes and customs engaged his interest and he recorded the image as it was described to him by a Jewish guide, Abraham ben Chimol. Memories of the visit still lingered five years later when he painted *La Noce Juive au Maroc* (*The Jewish Wedding in Morocco*), showing a young couple descending from their apartment into a courtyard to enjoy the performance of a sultry dancer. A clever arrangement of horizontal, vertical and diagonal lines provided a sense of depth, while the panoramic view offered a ringside seat. The painting aroused considerable attention with its sug-

gestion of easygoing abandon; its translation into a wood-engraving soon appeared in a French newspaper, bringing the tableau to thousands of readers who never could have seen either the original work, the occasion that inspired it, or the culture it represented (Ill. 7:10).

The Paris *haut monde* was charmed by the exotic Algerian lifestyle. Perhaps influenced by Delacroix's success, in 1853 François-Claudius Compte-Calix prepared twenty hand-colored engravings for *Le Keepsake de Costumes* which were published in the fashion magazine *Les Modes Parisiennes*. Society ladies, including several in the Jewish community, copied the styles for their lavish masquerade balls. The embroidered gown of the *Jeune fille juive d'Alger* (*Young Jewess of Algeria*) might well have been the star of the season (Ill. 7:11).

Above: Ill. 7:9. *Juive d'Alger (Algerian Jewess).* Etching, 1833. By Eugène Delacroix. *Below:* Ill. 7:10. *La Noce Juive au Maroc (The Jewish Wedding in Morocco).* Wood-engraving, c. 1839, after a painting by Eugène Delacroix

Perhaps because they were viewed as alien or colorful, Jewish events fascinated many Parisians. Every society marriage was exhaustively reported and depicted in the gossip sheets with parties as lavish or elegant as money could buy, or for which the families were willing to plunge themselves into debt. A wood-engraving by Haenen, *Marriage Israelite (Jewish Wedding)*, 1886, featured the bride, a vision in the dressmaker's finest effort, with the gentlemen appropriately decked out in tallit and tails (Ill. 7:12).

After a wedding, the next order of business in the Jewish lifecycle is the Bris or ritual circumcision of the male child. *Festin Juif (A Jewish Celebration)* by C. Motte from Lessore and Wyld's *Voyage Pittoresque dans la Régence d'Alger (Picturesque Voyage in the Algerian Regency)*, 1835, illustrated Moorish-style religious observances (Ill. 7:13). The men and women's headdresses must have made a remarkable impression on the Jewish folks back home in Paris.

Soon it is time for the young boy to begin his bar mitzvah studies. A nervous child is put through his paces as his classmates whisper

Ill. 7:11. *Jeune fille juive d'Alger (Young Jewess of Algeria).* Engraving, 1853. By Francois-Claudius Compte-Calix. From *Les Modes Parisiennes*

among themselves in Emile Vernier's 1872 lithograph after Edouard Brandon's painting *L'Examen (The Examination)* (Ill. 7:14). There is a hint of assimilation in a large wall map, which signifies that secular education was now included in the curriculum. The Jewish artist Edouard Moyse studied with French masters and exhibited at the salons. He focused on contemporary Jewish life by redefining images away from older traditions, and his portraits of rabbis described intellectual and animated features. Both he and Brandon offered spiritual values and themes, appealing not only to secularized Jews, but to the general public who might admire dignified or understated versions of Jewish life.

Among non–Jewish artists, Henri Daumier was one of the most powerful and experimental of the nineteenth century. An all-time master of lithography, he produced some four thousand satirical scenes, many puncturing middle-class morality, lampooning the political regime, and ridiculing censorship and governmental abuses. He kept the conscience of France alive in unforgettable prints that appeared two or three times a week for many years in Charles Philipon's periodicals, *La Caricature*, a weekly which flourished from 1830 until it was suppressed in 1835 for attacks on the king, and *Le Charivari*, a daily in operation for over a hundred years beginning in 1832, likewise subject to occasional repression. But after harsh fines and a thirteen-month prison sentence, he gave up political barbs aimed at Louis-Philippe and turned his attention to the perils of human nature. From 1840 to 1842 he worked on a lithographic series, *Les Bohemiens de Paris* (*Parisian Bohemians*), which included a Jewish *Marchand d'Habits* (*Old Clothes Seller*) (Ill. 7:15). Even before the Revolution of 1848 forced the problems of the labor class to the attention of the public, Daumier saw the worker as a defining element in the

Ill. 7:12. *Marriage Israelite (Jewish Wedding)*. Wood-engraving, 1886. By Haenen

Above: Ill. 7:13. *Festin Juif (A Jewish Celebration).* By C. Motte. From *Voyage Pittoresque dans la Régence d'Alger.* By Lessore and Wyld. *Below:* Ill. 7:14. *L'Examen (The Examination).* Lithograph, 1872, by Emile Vernier after a painting by Edouard Brandon

Ill. 7:15. *Le Marchand d'Habits (Old Clothes Seller)* Lithograph, c. 1841. By Henri Daumier. From *Les Bohemiens de Paris (Parisian Bohemians)*

Ill. 7:16. *Your Purse or the Whip!* Lithograph, 1855. By Henri Daumier

embryonic democratic movement towards egalitarianism. Although he generally avoided commenting on international events, he was concerned enough in 1855 to portray Czar Nicholas I as a bully demanding money of his Jewish subjects: *Your Purse or the Whip!* (Ill. 7:16).

He specialized in caricaturing Parisian types, including a pair of famous Jews. Isaac Adolphe Crémieux was a prominent lawyer and public official who fought successfully for the repeal of the More Judaico, helped free Jewish prisoners accused of blood libel in Damascus in 1840, served as minister of justice in the provisional government in 1848, co-founded the *Alliance Israelite Universelle*, facilitated laws abolishing slavery in French colonies, and, in 1870, secured French citizenship for Algerian Jews. Daumier acknowledged his good deeds, but was disturbed by his features: "If only he could improve his face, this great spokesman for improvement would lack nothing for his happiness." He then gave posterity a sample of the poor fellow's appearance in an 1858 lithograph (Ill. 7:17). Achille Fould, the first Jew to sit in the Chamber of Deputies, three-time minister of finance, banker, politician and member of the prestigious Academy of Fine Art, was another of Daumier's lithographic subjects from that period (Ill. 7:18). Although he evidently cut a more appealing figure than Monsieur Crémieux, "He couldn't find anything better to do than to adopt his favorite position—crossing his arms." This was directed at the gentleman's reputed reluctance to deal decisively with political affairs. Daumier jabbed at almost everyone who came within his range, but he avoided anti–Jewish overtones. He was a master who inspired almost every illustrator that followed or was his contemporary. Poverty and blindness overtook him in his sixties, finally stifling his lithographic crayon.

Left: Ill. 7:17. *Isaac Adolphe Crémieux.* Lithograph, 1858. *Right:* Ill. 7:18. *Achille Fould.* Lithograph, c. 1858. **Both by Henri Daumier**

Gustave Doré could describe dramatic events with such effect that his admirers never seemed to tire of the ten thousand images carrying his name. Unable to fill the demand himself, he employed more than three dozen highly skilled technicians who, depending on one's point of view, enhanced or ruined many of his drawings. His series of twelve woodcuts, *Le Juif Errant* (*The Wandering Jew*), 1856, illustrating Pierre Dupont's poem, was yet another rendition of the mythical character fated to wander the earth forever because he had rebuffed Jesus on his way to Calvary. True to form, the Jew hugs a money pouch to his breast as he plods

unswervingly past a specter of the Cross—
"Too late he feels, by look, and deed, and
word, How often he has crucified his Lord."
Four years earlier, in a meaner spirit, the
grossness of his lithograph *The Jew in
Search of a Final Resting Place* anticipated
the ridicule that exploded later in the Dreyfus Affair (Ill. 7:19).

Doré was a year younger than the
Sephardic Jew Camille Pissarro, who was
born to Marrano parents who had settled
in the French West Indies in 1824. Perhaps
the most consummate and intellectual
craftsman of the Impressionist school, he
was the first internationally acclaimed Jewish artist as well as the first major Jewish
artist to enlist in the post–Emancipation
secular art movement. His primary concern
was to work quickly in order to capture
what he called "the spontaneity of sensation"—impulsive notations hinting at effects rather than spelling them out in detail.
By the time he arrived in Paris in 1855, an
etching revival was well under way as a re-

Ill. 7:19. *The Jew in Search of a Final Resting Place.*
Woodcut, 1852. By Gustave Doré

action to formal reproductive engravings of the eighteenth century. Set in motion by such
artists as Delacroix, Millet, Daumier, and Corot, a new experimental approach to printmaking was developing, freer in line, more original in concept, more economical in draftsmanship,
concentrating on the balance of reflected light and shadow in atmospheric elements.

Pissarro barely had any Jewish education or identity, preferring to think of himself as a
universal man whose Socialist and anarchist principles freed him from his religious heritage.
Because of his interest in Impressionism, which exalts nature rather than man and generally
ignores religious themes, he was able to choose neutral subject matter and compete on an equal
basis with Gentile artists. Once embarked on his career, he married a Christian woman who
had been a servant in his mother's home, a hardworking, sharp-tongued mate who never really
understood his single-minded passion for art nor adjusted to a life of extreme poverty. Recognition came mainly from his colleagues who admired his skills and appreciated the many personal kindnesses which made him a beloved figure among them. His lifelong interest in
impoverished and powerless peasant workers grew out of his perception of the injustices of the
Industrial Revolution, a point of view shared by his literary contemporaries Charles Dickens,
Gustave Flaubert, and Emile Zola. It may be that his championing of such causes, his yearning for an ideal humanity, and his sympathy for the poor and oppressed were characteristics
that expressed whatever latent Jewishness remained from his upbringing. He exemplified the
assimilated Jew who nevertheless couldn't entirely escape his lineage, at one time blaming "a
matter of race" for his lack of success.

Discouraged by the lack of popular interest in his painting, he turned his hand to various etching and lithographic techniques beginning in 1863, producing almost two hundred
prints of luminous exteriors, countrywomen quietly tending their geese, and weary laborers
going about their daily grind. His feeling for abstract design influenced such masters as Paul
Cézanne and Paul Gauguin and, through them, much of the simplicity and experimentation

Ill. 7:20. *Camille Pissarro, par lui-même (Self-Portrait)*. Etching, 1890. Ill. 7:21. *Lucien*. Etching, 1890. By Camille Pissarro

of the twentieth century, particularly in printmaking. "At the moment," he remarked with some exaggeration in 1897, "prints are the exclusive interest here; it is a mania, the young artists no longer do anything else."

His etching and drypoint, *Camille Pissarro, par lui-même* (*Self-Portrait*), 1890, executed when he was almost sixty years old, harks back to Rembrandt's psychological studies (Ill. 7:20). Although by then a recognized master, he represented himself as a humble peasant in tonalities ranging from very light to dark grey. His white hat contrasts sharply with the background, as does the white beard above the black coat. Very little of the face is visible, but the solemn eyes have a watchful look behind the half-glasses. The 1890 etching of his son Lucien who lived in England and was himself an artist, is almost a "Jewish" portrait in its rabbinic presence; it was the father's only work of that genre (Ill. 7:21).

Pissarro feared that bourgeois capitalism, with its attendant disruptions in traditional methods of agricultural and manufacturing systems, would impede economic life and the inchoate struggles of the labor movement. His philosophy was developed in great part by those who were convinced that Jewish financiers had been instigators in the Revolution, and were ruining France by promoting big business to the disadvantage of the small merchant class. Anti-Jewish sentiments had become more frequent after France's defeat in the Franco-Prussian War of 1870, even as the Rothschilds openhandedly paid a five billion gold franc indemnity demanded by Germany. The anti–Jewishness inherent in the anarchism Pissarro espoused became explicit in the stereotypes which appeared in posters, prints, and illustrated books, but it was evidently not enough to offend him, for he made twenty-eight repellent drawings as gifts for his Jewish nieces in 1889 or 1890. Unpublished until 1972 as *Les Turpitudes Sociales* (*Social Degenerates*), they featured beak-nosed bankers worshipping the golden calf. Some apologists have suggested that his anarchism demanded that he reject his middle-class background, that he was simply naive, or that anti–Semitic images were so ingrained in the French psyche that the personification of greedy capitalists could only be transmitted effectively by such means. While Pissarro explained that he had meant to represent all exploiters, in those sketches he depicted only Jews. In a letter to Lucien in 1891 he declared that "artists could work with absolute freedom only if they were rid of the terrible constraints of Mssrs. Capitalist, collector-speculators, and dealers." Jewish specialties, all.

Nevertheless, when the Dreyfus Affair exploded in 1894, he was deeply affected, outraged both by the injustices perpetrated by the military and Church, and because it brought out unsuspected waves of anti–Jewishness in those he had regarded as his friends. Cézanne, Renoir, and above all, Degas, whom he called "a ferocious anti–Semite," broke with him simply on the basis of his ancestry. "What can be in the minds of such intelligent men that makes them so foolish?" he asked. He never denied being a Jew, but was at odds with all organized religions as being restrictive and inhibitive. "The frightened bourgeoisie," he wrote, "surprised by the immense clamor of the disinherited masses, by the tremendous demands of the lower classes, feels that it is necessary to bring the people back to superstitious beliefs. Hence the bristling of religious symbolism." He congratulated Zola on his powerful pro–Dreyfus stance but apparently lost interest in the case once the prisoner was offered and accepted a pardon. During the period of the trial, however, he sent relevant editions of newspapers to Lucien in London and was so preoccupied with its outcome that his wife charged him with neglect: "Doubtless the Zola Affair takes all your time so you can't write to me. That interests you much more than your family!"

The growth of nationalism narrowed tolerance for the outsider Jews whose mobility in moving from one level of social or political participation to another still faced impediments or full barriers. It aggravated the struggle for equal participation and ultimately fed into the Dreyfus case. In part a rebellion from, or escape to, a "rational" scientific notion of society, it based its viewpoint on "natural" or bred-in-the-bone principles. Therefore, when the perception that Charles Darwin's *Origin of Species*, 1859, and *Descent of Man*, 1871, attributed "natural selection" rather than the Creator to physical and mental abilities and debilities, some racists seized on that theory and suggested that an intrinsic "biological inferiority" would—and should—replace "Jewish spiritual degradation" and cause Jews to disappear. And further, since acquired characteristics such as baptism or conversion could not be inherited, anti–Semites explained that nothing, neither emancipation nor assimilation could—or should—wipe clean the taint of Jewish blood. In 1881, the first avowedly anti–Semitic newspaper, *L'Anti-Juif*, initiated attacks based, not on the religious component of Judaism, but on Jewish heritage alone.

Some of the reasoning behind this attitude originated with Fourier's disciple Alphonse Toussenel, whose *Les Juifs, rois de l'époque* (*Jews, Kings of the Century*), 1844, linked Jews and money in an unholy alliance—"contemptible moneylenders, parasites who live off the labor of others." It was followed by Pierre Leroux's work of the same name two years later, Joseph Gobineau's *Essai sur l'inégalité des races humaines* (*Essay on the Inequality of the Human Races*), 1853 to 1855, the rantings of Henri Gougenot Mousseaux, author of *Le Juif, le judaisme et la judaisation des peuples chrétiens* (*The Jew, Judaism, and the Judaization of Christians*), 1886, and a much respected essay on race and religion by Renan in 1883, as well as that author's five-volume *Histoire du Peuple d'Israel* (*History of the Jewish People*), 1887 to 1893. Between them they raised questions of "ethnic purity," suggested that race was the ultimate power which impelled or motivated society, that Aryans were genetically superior and physically more attractive, and that while Jews were innocent of deicide, their deficits were, by nature, immutable. Even as they believed those ideas were on solid scientific grounds, their arguments found their way into emotional nationalist theories surrounding the Dreyfus case, and ultimately into Nazi ideology.

Anti-Semitic fervor grew exponentially. Edouard Drumont's book, *La France Juive* (*Jewish France*), 1886, had already revealed that Jews avoided agricultural labor, were materialistic and morally lax, and had discovered nothing of value themselves although they were masters at exploiting the inventions and labor of Christians. Not only did they develop sinister intrigues to infiltrate and debase the highest reaches of the government, but, *mon Dieu*, they murdered

Christian children at Passover! The absurd allegations didn't prevent the book from selling over a hundred fifty thousand copies in French and German editions, an unprecedented number at the time (and ten times that many in reprints since). Drumont, the self-styled "rabbi of anti–Semitism," followed it in 1892 with a lithograph *Savonnage infructueux* (*Fruitless Soaping*) in the daily tabloid, *La Libre Parole* (*Free Speech*), demanding that the "repulsive" Jews be deported (Ill. 7:22). He then disclosed that Jews like Dreyfus were merely cogs in a vast plot working for Jewish financiers. He appeared bursting out of its front page gloating over the condemned traitor Dreyfus—*A bas les Juifs* (*Down with the Jews*.) It wasn't an uncommon sight to see ladies twirling parasols on which those words were printed.

Well-known writers of the time, including Balzac and Apollinaire, jumped on the Drumont bandwagon. Even Emile Zola portrayed a greedy but charitable banker in somewhat anti–Semitic terms in his novel, *L'Argent* (*Money*), 1890, although another figure in the book maintained that all people, including Jews, were equal (but not necessarily worthy of social inclusion). While Jews had typically been cast as peddlers, usurers, or fornicators in the seventeenth and eighteenth centuries, by the nineteenth they frequently appeared as Rothschild-like power brokers. The anti–Semitic novelist Alphonse Daudet unintentionally complimented Jewish leadership skills, writing in 1892, "Already masters of finance, of administration, dictating arrests to judges, they will definitely be the masters of France the day they command the army. Rothschild will make himself commander of plans for mobilization." In 1899, Charles Huard, together with his caption writer, Jean Mably, prepared a lithographic poster to publicize *En Israel* (*In Israel*), a book dedicated to Drumont that reinforced messages of capitalist disorder and hate (Ill. 7:23).

While anti–Semitic groups busied themselves about Jewish campaigns to loot businesses and organize riots, manual and industrial laborers banded together to improve their circumstances. One result was that working-class radicalism and repression of trade unionism developed into physical clashes between a powerful elite and powerless underlings. Théophile-Alexandre Steinlen's lithograph *La grève des Juifs* (*The Jewish Strike*), 1898, reflected Jewish involvement in the social upheaval (Ill. 7:24).

The revival of acute anti–Semitism led to a collision between military figures and advocates of civil honor, a collision in which France became bogged down in the defining event of French social and political history. The assimilated well-to-do family of Alfred Dreyfus had lived in Alsace-Lorraine until the loss of that territory in the Franco-Prussian War drove them and other Jews to France. The German occupation of his homeland induced him to enlist in the French army, where he achieved the rank of captain and the distinction of being the only Jew on the General Staff. In 1894 he was convicted of treason for allegedly turning over confidential military documents, supposedly written in his hand, to the hated Germans. "I am innocent," he cried, "*Vive la France!*" He was sentenced to life in prison on Devil's Island. The trumped-up charges, based on anti–Jewish prejudice and intense nationalism, led to his public degradation on January 5, 1895, in the crowded courtyard of the Ecole Militaire, the "West Point" of France. He was stripped of his rank, the buttons of his uniform were torn off and his sword was broken in two. Pictures of his humiliation, *Le Traitre* (*The Traitor*), made the front page of every paper in town including *Le Petit Journal* and *The Graphic* (Ill. 7:25). To make sure that he didn't swim back to France from the coast of South America, as soon as the sun went down he was chained to his bed in a hut surrounded by an eight-foot high double stockade. He endured that life for five years, fighting off a breakdown and thoughts of suicide.

Among the onlookers at the degradation was Theodor Herzl, a Jewish Viennese journalist on assignment to cover the story. While Dreyfus himself apparently was puzzled by the mob's shouts of "Death to the Jews," Herzl, appalled that *all* Jews were being condemned even

Ill. 7:22. *Savonnage infructueux (Fruitless Soaping)*, 1898. From *La Libre Parole (Free Speech)*

Above: Ill. 7:23. *En Israel (In Israel)* Lithograph, 1899. By Charles Huard and Jean Mably. *Below:* Ill. 7:24. *La grève des Juifs (The Jewish Strike)* Lithograph, 1898. By Theophile-Alexandre Steinlen

before the trial had begun, angrily noted that bigotry had raised its head "in republican, modern, civilized France, a hundred years after the Declaration of the Rights of Man." He claimed that it was the turning point of his life. He abandoned the idea of "a great movement for the free and honorable conversion of Jews to Christianity" and determined instead to find a political solution—not necessarily religious or cultural—for the Jewish problem. He believed that the Dreyfus Affair forever closed a chapter of vain expectations, that neither assimilation, Emancipation, nor isolation were viable answers to life as a minority community. Disappointed that Napoleon's Sanhedrin and other measures had secured neither true equality nor tolerance, he declared, "I have become a Zionist and all my efforts are directed towards Palestine."

At the time of the trial, newspapers in France were multiplying like rabbits. Because of relaxed censorship laws in 1881, two thousand publications were already on the streets flashing the latest bulletins. New steam engines capable of printing the exceedingly fine lines of wood-engravings enabled the reproduction of drawings by photo-mechanical processes at the rate of twenty-five thousand copies per hour. Fast trains shipped the news across the length and width of France to the largest audiences in history; they were one of the most powerful instruments for social change. Their wide circulation turned the Affair into a media circus, guaranteeing an enormous readership and creating a unique forum for public debate. Artists suddenly became court reporters, while politicians took on the role of journalists. Dreyfusards, who championed the ideals of the Revolution, and anti–Dreyfusards, who supported the army, the Church, and the government, were locked in furious battle—sometimes with words and images, sometimes with fists and guns. The mass-circulation publications achieved transcendence through its famous and infamous writers and artists, many of whom lent their talents to the controversy. They chose up sides and attacked each other with stirring or irresponsible articles and sympathetic or virulent prints. The Affair was fought in the press as thoroughly as on the streets or in the courts; it was resolved as much through journalism as through the legal system.

Among the prominent artists supporting Dreyfus were Paul Signac, Théophile-Alexandre Steinlen, Claude Monet, Mary Cassatt, and Edouard Vuillard; the authors Victor Hugo, Bernard Lazare, Alexandre Dumas fils, Anton Chekhov, Marcel Proust, George Sand, Mark Twain, and Anatole France; the composer Edvard Grieg; and the reigning actress Sarah Bernhardt, daughter of a Jewish mother though baptized as a Catholic. Many illustrators also rooted for Dreyfus and Zola. Henri-Gabriel Ibels, Leon Couturier and others pointed out that the great threat to France was not the Jews but the collusion of the Church and the military. Ibels' *Est-ce une Croix ou un Sabre?* (*Is It a Cross or a Sword?*), 1898, regarded the animosities as a plague that was tearing France apart (Ill. 7:26). On the other hand, that year the Jesuit paper *Catholic Civilization* reminded France that Judas Iscariot was of the same race as Jews, that Jewish treachery had a very long history, and that it was necessary to abrogate the legacy of the Revolution.

At the climax of the court case, Zola challenged the evidence against Dreyfus. In a passionate letter that appeared in Georges Clemenceau's newspaper, *L'Aurore*, January 13, 1898, he charged the War Office with falsifying evidence and accusing high-ranking individuals of a cover-up. Two hundred thousand copies of the paper were snapped up. Anatole France called the letter "a moment in the conscience of mankind." Others characterized Zola's intervention as the decisive moment in the transition from government by an inner circle of corrupt military administrators to a system of political accountability. But Zola, who wrote that the "hunting down of 'dirty Jews' ... disgraces our epoch," was found guilty himself of libeling the army and was forced to escape to England where he remained for a year while the case attracted international interest.

The Swiss-born Félix Vallotton contributed his talents to the liberal periodical *Le Cri de*

Ill. 7:25 *Humiliation of Alfred Dreyfus*. Wood-engraving, 1895.

Ill. 7:26. *Est-ce une Croix ou un Sabre? (Is It a Cross or a Sword)?* 1898. By Henri-Gabriel Ibels

Paris (*Paris Cries Out*), founded in 1896. His photomechanical print *L'Age du Papier*, which appeared on its cover just ten days after Zola's editorial, indicated the enthusiasm with which the middle-class in particular responded to the profusion and power of the media (Ill. 7:27). The news of the day had become the talk of the town, and most of the news and the talk were heavily anti–Semitic, including that of the prominent Catholic paper *La Croix*, established in 1883 with the blessings of Drumont and royalist interests; it explained, among other facts, that Jews, in cahoots with Freemasons, had been responsible for the Revolution. A year later, Vallotton created a lithograph for an album of twelve prints honoring Colonel Marie-Georges Picquart, the army's chief of intelligence who discovered the forged letter and became convinced that it implicated the German spy Major Ferdinand Esterhazy as the real culprit. "Dreyfus is innocent!" Picquart shouted at the trial, a shout that reverberated in the dreams of the prime minister, Félix-Jules Meline, who nevertheless remained pro-military, indifferent to the fact that Picquard suffered solitary confinement for sixty days because of his efforts to reopen the case.

Although in 1896 it was proved that the incriminating handwriting belonged to Esterhazy, few anti–Dreyfusards were convinced. But the demand for a retrial could not be ignored. When Dreyfus returned in 1899 he was a broken man, smaller than his friends remembered him, white-haired and bowed. His prison sentence was reduced to ten years although he was again found guilty of treason, "with extenuating circumstances." Clemenceau observed in *L'Aurore*: "Extenuating circumstances indeed! ... France is now a country with no security either for liberty, life, or the honor of her citizens.... Many people exclaim 'Why should it concern us whether Dreyfus was judged aright or not! After all, he is only a Jew!'"

Under political duress in 1899, Dreyfus reluctantly accepted a presidential pardon rather than exoneration. "It means nothing to me without honor," he wrote. It took seven years for the farce to be resolved, during which time Zola had died, some said in questionable circumstances. In 1906, the High Court finally admitted that Dreyfus had been convicted by "error and wrongfully," but refused to reverse its verdict, claiming that exoneration was unnecessary. He rejoined the army and served during World War I, receiving the French Legion of Honor medal. He died in 1935 in his beloved Paris, spared the news that his granddaughter, Madeleine Levy, who fought for France in the resistance movement of World War II, was caught by the Nazis; she now lies among the ashes at Auschwitz.

French radio and television stations well into the 1970s were forbidden to make references to the Dreyfus Affair. Another decade had to pass before an attempt was made to erect a statue of Dreyfus at the site of his public humiliation; in 1985, after arguments that it would inflame public opinion, it was decided to place it instead in the Tuileries Gardens where the pleasurable surroundings might induce a more benign mood. And it took another ten years before the army finally declared him innocent.

Decades of conservative clericalism, labor unrest, anarchist disturbances, and political and economic scandals had demanded a scapegoat, and Dreyfus came along just in time. He was stigmatized as one of too many Jews whose presence disrupted an otherwise homogeneous society. During this period, Church, military, and royalist leaders not only kept themselves busy denouncing Dreyfus but, by association, all Jews as evil and satanic figures obsessed with money. Much of the country turned against the Jews although physical violence was minimal, and that mainly in French Algeria (which found Drumont worthy to sit in its parliament.) Yet, for all the bombast, the Dreyfus case might have ended up as no more than a relatively minor incident. Actually, it failed to disrupt the status of Jews, many of whom found life in France better than was possible elsewhere. It became instead a critical transition in French history as citizens were forced to examine the roles of virtue, honor, and justice in their nation. If the Affair in the end accomplished nothing else, it effectively finished off the monarchists

Ill. 7:27. *L'Age du papier (The Age of Paper)*, 1898. By Félix Vallotton

and resulted in the final separation of Church and State. Control of the army and navy passed from a small clique of officers into more competent hands, signaling a democratic and effective organization.

Some of Dreyfus' early enemies, particularly the anarchists, were finally convinced of his innocence, but, viewing themselves as fellow sufferers, remained ambivalent because the "bourgeois Jew" had received international sympathy while the volatile economic situation and the lack of social reforms seemed to go unnoticed. Industrialization had been steady but slow coming to France, resulting in poor wages for most workers while permitting huge profits for aggressive businessmen. Some of these capitalists were Jewish, a fact widely exploited by the radical element as well as by the Church. Perhaps the best known of the artists who shared those beliefs was Jean-Louis Forain, who merged a devout Catholicism and an equally devout belief in the army and the unity of France with an uncanny ability to catch facial and bodily expressiveness. Influenced in his art as well as in his politics by Degas, he made a reputation as a Jew hater, recognizing that he could combine acid illustrations with his political views. In 1889, the same year that Paris opened its World's Fair, plugged in newfangled electric lights, and celebrated Alexandre Gustave Eiffel's thousand-foot-high engineering miracle, he began publication of *Le Fifre*, an illustrated four-page newspaper which railed against what he called social corruption. Corruption, for him, meant a capitalist—by definition a pitiless Jew—protecting his ill-gotten gains from the starving poor.

Drumont had tied anti–Semitism to the bribery charges against several Jewish businessmen, who had illegally raised funds in the '80s and '90s for the Panama Canal, originally a French undertaking. He undercut his own credibility, however, when it was revealed that he was guilty of taking loans from one of the malefactors. An illustration, *Panama scandale*, by Comtesse Sibylle Martel (known as Gyp or Bob), depicts Cornelius Herz, one of the prominent Jews who were involved, manipulating a puppet Parliament while a dog urinates on France, the helpless police bite the dust, sacks of money lie nearby, and France weeps as the Tree of Liberty is hung with filthy creatures (Ill. 7:28).

Forain and Russian-born Emmanuel Poire, known as Caran d'Ache, made common cause as editors of the scurrilous weekly journal *Psst...!* From February 5 until September 16, 1898, when Dreyfus was again found guilty, they supplied anti–Jewish cartoons exacerbating an already polarized atmosphere. In one example, a rich Jew becomes a walking phallus, propositioning an innocent ballerina—"Wouldn't you like to live on my income?" Forain produced thousands of equally entertaining illustrations, such as *Le Pon Badriote*, an intentional misspelling of *Le Bon Patriot* (*The Good Patriot*), in which Zola is shown posting his famous letter in an outhouse (Ill. 7:29). Yet another of his efforts depicts a Jewish auctioneer raising his hammer: "We are selling the flag," a reference to Dreyfus' "selling" military secrets.

Echoing Forain, Caron d'Ache in 1898 again laid the responsibility for the Revolution of 1789 on Jewish financiers who, he charged, profited on the backs of the wretched peasantry. A master of scatology, his contribution to propriety was represented by *Coucou, le voila* (*Boo, There He Is*): Zola rising from a toilet, a take-off on the Dreyfusard theme of Truth Rising from a Well (Ill. 7:30). In 1892, at the height of the scandal, *Le Petit Journal* featured a huge golden calf being worshipped by Jews. A dozen or more clever illustrators, including Adolphe Willette and Alfred Le Petit, portrayed Jews as aliens and money-grubbers intent on bleeding France and delivering her to the enemy. They depicted Jews as rats devouring the nutriment of France while the government nodded off. Even after the Dreyfus retrial in 1899, the lithographer V. Levenpeu published a series of fifty-one posters under the title *Musée des Horreurs* (Freak Show). French and Jewish public figures were shown with their faces grafted onto monstrous animals. Zola—*Le Roi des Porcs*—(*King of the Pigs*) smears France with his feces while perched on a stack of his own loathsome books (Ill. 7:31). Dreyfus was transformed into *Le*

Ill. 7:28. *Panama scandale*, c. 1890. By Comtesse Sibylle Martel, known as Gyp or Bob

Traitre! (*The Traitor*), a grotesque modern-day Hydra (Ill. 7:32). Though his body is pierced by a sword, the "monster" continues to hatch vipers from his head, endlessly spreading venom. A year passed before the Ministry of the Interior decided that enough was enough and put an end to the series.

While the League for the Rights of Man supported Dreyfus, reactionary forces rallied around ultra-rightist groups that identified Jewish interests with nefarious international organizations, one of which, *La League des Patriots*, attempted to weaken the incipient Third Republic in order to reestablish the monarchy. As usual, Jews were the sacrificial offerings, accused of usurping the government, controlling the economy, encouraging Socialism, promoting atheism, and undermining Catholicism. Its leader, Paul Deroulede, attempted to seize power after the Esterhazy forgery was disclosed, but spent ten years in exile instead for his efforts. In 1899, the hubbub reached the New York magazine *Puck*, which gleefully depicted Deroulede as an exploding frog astride a symbol of anti–Semitism in a lithograph aptly titled *Poof*. Under the satisfied gaze of a French citizen, the slogan *Vive la Republique* announces hopes for a revitalized France.

Almost everyone had taken sides in the Dreyfus case. Count Henri Marie Raymond de Toulouse-Lautrec apparently did not, evidently believing that high birth and wealth permitted a certain amount of detachment or at least neutrality. The whole world knows the story of the crippled genius who burned out his syphilitic and alcoholic life at the age of thirty-seven in the brothels and dance halls of Montmartre. He was heir to an aristocratic family in 1864, and his life spanned the end of the Romantic period to early twentieth century Modernism. The final decade of the century that witnessed his most important work coincided with the coming of the machine age and its stormy reordering of society. The ferment and excite-

Ill. 7:29. *Le Pon Badriote (The Good Patriot)* c. 1898. By Jean-Louis Forain

Coucou, le voilà!

La Vérité sort de son puits.

Ill. 7:30. *Coucou, le voila (Boo, There He Is)*. 1898. By Caron d'Ache

ment, the perversions and glamor of "vulgar" traits, the quest for innovative subject matter and styles, partnered with receptive audiences, all seduced him. Guided by professional master printers, he moved lithography from stark black and white images to explosions of color. Large posters with cut-off images and vigorous diagonals suddenly appeared, their iconography borrowed from the unusual perspectives made possible by the new portable cameras, the work of Degas, and Japanese woodcut prints. As Daumier had rescued lithography from its commercial overtones, so Lautrec gave artistic credibility to lithographic posters, promotional material, menus, and even book and song-cover designs, eloquently capturing the spirit of the day and exploring every facet of his surroundings.

From time to time he depicted Jewish types, either on commission or drawn from the crowds that passed before his retentive eye. One of his acquaintances—he mingled with both Jews and known anti–Semites—was Victor Dobrisky, a Polish immigrant who in 1892 wrote the novel *Reine de Joie* (*Queen of [Libidinous] Pleasure*) under the pen name Victor Joze. Lautrec created a theatrical-looking lithographic advertisement for the book, whose popularity was heightened by its anti–Semitic and sexual overtones (Ill. 7:33). It tells the story of a beautiful young demimondaine and a salacious old Jewish banker, Baron de Rozenfeld, whose fatuous and indiscreet behavior contrasts sharply with the cool demeanor of her Gentile friend. The anti–Semitic figure was clearly modeled on Baron Alphonse de Rothschild, who attempted to impound the book and the illustration but was unable do it. So much for Jewish clout over the press.

Among the Jews whom Lautrec admired (and whom his ultra-conservative Catholic family abhorred) were his early supporters Thadée and Misia Natanson. Supposedly Lautrec had a crush on her, as did half of their artistic circle. He portrayed her in an Art Nouveau lithograph in 1895 ice-skating across an advertisement for her husband's influential Dreyfusard journal, *La Revue Blanche* (Ill. 7:34). Yet that close relationship did not prevent him two years later from drawing a pair of disembodied heads with exaggerated Jewish features on the lithographic cover of another of Victor Joze's anti–Semitic novels, *La Tribu d'Isadore (Isadore's Tribe)*, 1897 (Ill. 7:35). Lautrec may have believed that he was merely recording reality; some have questioned his objectivity. But racially motivated or otherwise, the sweeping diagonal of the buggy rider, the floating Jewish caricatures, and the cropped horse are brilliant examples of his ability to coordinate a variety of design elements—motifs well ahead of their time.

Ever walking both sides of the line, Lautrec next accommodated his friend Henri Fleury, publisher of a group of Clemenceau's ingenuous stories about eastern European Jews, *Au Pied de Sinai (At the Foot of Sinai)*, 1898. His Jewish characters, realistic depictions of the types seen around the Jewish neighborhoods in Paris, suggest fragile, almost quivering images, but were

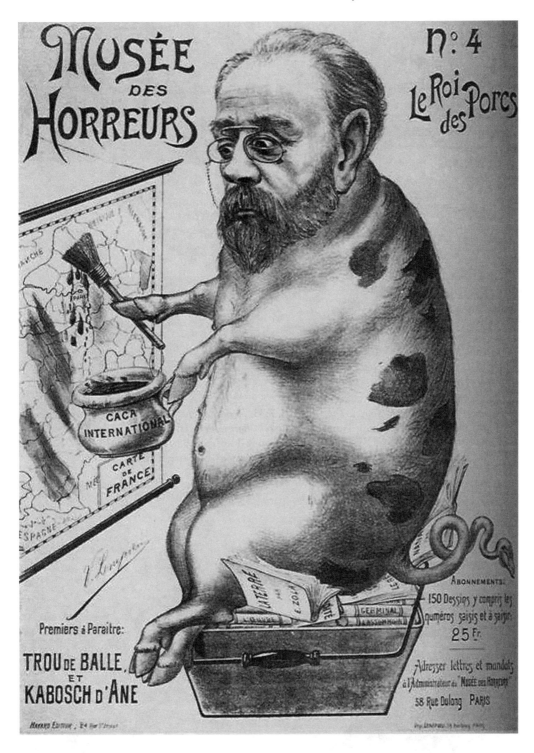

Ill. 7:31. *Le Roi des Porcs (King of the Pigs).* Lithograph, 1899. By V. Levenpeu. From *Musée des Horreurs (Freak Show)*

Top left: Ill. 7:32. *Le Traitre! (The Traitor!)* Lithograph, 1899. By V. Levenpeu. From *Musée des Horreurs (Freak Show). Top right:* Ill. 7:33. *Reine de Joie (Queen of [Libidinous]Pleasure).* Lithograph, 1892. By Henri de Toulouse-Lautrec. *Bottom left:* Ill. 7:34. *La revue blanche (White Revue).* Lithograph, 1895. By Henri de Toulouse-Lautrec. *Bottom right:* Ill. 7:35. *La tribu d'Isadore (Isadore's Tribe).* Lithograph, 1897. By Henri de Toulouse-Lautrec

well adapted to the rather acerbic text. Clemenceau, the future prime minister of France, was an advocate of human rights and empathetic to Jewish aspirations, yet his tales hover between pro- and anti–Jewish viewpoints. *La Loge—Le Baron Moise (Baron Moses in the Theater Box)*, tells of a rich man who sought redemption through starvation but found madness instead. The parallel between Moise's predicament and Jesus' suffering for mankind was, of course, antithetical to Jewish theology. For another tale, *Les Juifs Polonaise, Carlsbad (Polish Jews in Carlsbad)*, Lautrec provided a portrayal of a weary Ashkenazi Jew bowed down by too many years of adversity.

Socialist-humanitarian policies and the impact of world opinion curtailed public anti–Semitism, although the Vichy-Nazi role during World War II proved that it was not forgotten. Yet France's Jews emerged with a dynamic sense of self and a belief that an era of inventiveness and originality was just around the corner. Yiddish-speaking villagers were molded into French-speaking middle-class citizens for whom traditional observances often became marginal. Yiddish never died out but it faded as successive generations gave it up for the language of the street and schools. Jews organized charitable and self-help activities, sponsored the Society of Jewish Studies, developed liberal rabbinic institutions, and published important historical treatises, commentaries, and secular and liturgical material.

They forgave readily, were devoted to their country, and trusted that their commitment was reciprocated. And while they relearned the old lesson that the pen and printed image could and did produce a vicious legacy, many understood that the Enlightenment had largely succeeded, and that artists and much of the press had operated powerfully in the interests of human dignity. Although the immigrant Jews who arrived after the Dreyfus Affair tended to be suspicious of republican commitment, the telling words of the Yiddish community *"leben vi got in Frankraykh"* (*living like God in France*), underscored the expectation that the country would live up to the promise of the Revolution.

8

Central Europe and Russia in the Nineteenth Century: Modern Anti-Semitism

The situation for German Jews was worrisome. The Frankfurt Judengasse (Jews' Street) which had twice burned to the ground—in 1711 and again in 1796—rose once more, as grim and oppressive as ever. A wood-engraving, c. 1805, depicted the long curved road where some ten thousand people were crowded into a few hundred houses (Ill. 8:1). In his memoirs, published in 1811, Goethe, who lived in the city, described the scene as he remembered it as a young man: "The cramped space, the filth, the swarming masses, the unpleasant accents, all together made the most distasteful impression...." The Rothschilds, its most famous residents, were one of perhaps a dozen families boasting a mercantile golden touch, but its general population still feared the wolf at the door.

The Industrial Revolution initiated commercial dislocations and depressed markets as hand and animal strength gave way to steam power and the machine. Abrupt changes in manufacturing techniques and rapid transformations in the social, economic, and political climate shunted millions of peasants from the countryside to the cities. Slums sprouted up, followed closely by all the vexing disturbances that accompany large population movements. Severe droughts in 1816 caused prices to rise and jobs to fall. Desperate for a scapegoat, the frightened middle and upper classes placed much of the blame on Jewish fiscal intrigues. Disgruntled individuals called for violence, and violence was what developed. The *Hep! Hep!* storm (possibly standing for the Crusader slogan *Hierosolyma est perdita—Jerusalem is lost*) swept through towns and cities in 1819 with homicidal fury. The engraving *Plundering the Frankfurt Ghetto*, 1819, shows looters ramming through a helpless village, methodically taking lives and vandalizing property (Ill. 8:2).

Jews were able to keep some of the rights granted by Napoleon although academic positions, military promotions, and civil service employment were still dependent on conversion. Some five thousand defectors opted for that route, hoping for economic benefits, wider social inclusion, or access to Western ideology. What generations of brutality had not accomplished, apostasy, assimilation, and intermarriage nearly did, especially in business, science, and the arts. Most of Moses Mendelssohn's descendants adopted Christianity as the "religious form most acceptable to the majority of civilized human beings." Gustav Mahler, Ludwig Börne, and Heinrich Heine were among those who, ruefully at best, bought the "entry ticket to European society." While for many the desired positions were realized, the tickets for others were never honored. Jew haters still called them Jews.

Obsessive nationalism continued to resist foreign cultures or "undesirable" elements. Germanness was inextricably bound up with a Christianity that automatically excluded the internationalist Jews, who, unfenced by political borders and defying chauvinism, were obvious examples. They were not only outsiders with their own identity, language, and religious traditions, they were obtrusive merchants, tradesmen, and entrepreneurs. While a few were successful moneylenders and pawn brokers, most were indigent peddlers who had exchanged their carts and stalls for small retail shops.

Ill. 8:1. *The Street of the Jews*. Wood-engraving, c. 1805

Hepp ! Hepp !

Ill. 8:2. *Plundering the Frankfurt Ghetto.* Engraving, 1819

All were anathema to the Protestant theologian Bruno Bauer who, in *Die Judenfrage (The Jewish Question)*, 1843, declared that the problem was unsolvable without conversion, citing the "Jewish national spirit" and Jews as members of an "extraneous community ... incompatible with the requirements of general Emancipation." Judaism was just not ready for political legitimacy. The baptized Karl Marx, whose father converted after being denied permission to practice law because of his religion, was descended from a rabbinic family, but had as little use for his new faith as for his old, declaring that formulated beliefs were the "opiate of the masses." He saw in the bourgeois Jew a dangerous catalyst in the class struggle, a symbol of economic and capitalistic potency and greed. His essay *Zur Judenfrage (On the Jewish Question)*, 1843, asked "What is the secular basis of Judaism? Self-interest. What is the worldly cult of the Jew? Huckstering. What is his worldly god? Money."

Marx's opinions were driven in part by the small number of Jews who had become successful. He ignored the fact that most Jews were still burdened with oppressive taxes and civil restrictions. While they achieved some freedoms in the revolutions of 1830 and 1848 and the Constitution of 1849, it was not because the government experienced a softening of conscience, but rather because insurrections were costly and the granting of a few privileges was perceived as a reasonable exchange for Jewish loans; actually, most of the mandated civil rights were no more than wishful longing. Uprisings exacerbated the issues of nationalism, ethnicity, and economic and political prerogatives, topics which were soon translated into prints. *Habts Acht! (Attention!)*, a caricature by the Viennese Joseph Lanzedelli, portrayed a profit-loving band of Jews insisting on equal rights for themselves, while their crowned leader denies equal rights to a helpless Christian (Ill. 8:3). Another, *Die Herausgemanzipirten Juden* (*Newly Emancipated Jews*), depicted a group of soldiers holding a flag with a dead rabbit—a reference to cowardice (Ill. 8:4).

With no certain remedy for the problems of unemployment or equitable recognition, many Jews responded with their feet. By 1857, some fifty thousand, young and old, had gone to America, departing where possible with Torah scrolls and precious religious objects. Twenty years later, as another hundred thousand followed, a bit of doggerel encouraged them to "Hurry to freedom's land, free from prejudice, hate, and jealousy, free from the noose and the tyrant. A better day awaits you, my brothers, so consider and hurry."

But for those who remained, prejudice, jealousy and hate barely let up. It didn't help when Richard Wagner, under a pseudonym, published *Das Judenthum in der Musik* (*Jewry in Music*), 1850, belittling the compositions of Felix Mendelssohn, Jacques Offenbach, and Giacomo Meyerbeer as trivial and shallow. Nineteen years later he republished it, this time proudly adding his name. The liberal community was appalled, but that hardly fazed him. His *Bayreuther Blätter* (*Bayreuth Pamphlets*), 1878, called for racial purification and targeted Jewish financiers and brokers as well: "The demons who cause mankind's downfall ... should be burned." It is ironic that a Jewish actor, Ludwig Geyer, might have been his father; his mother never made it clear. But his widow, daughter, and son-in-law were among Hitler's staunchest fans. Hitler, in turn, became one of Wagner's staunchest fans.

Some Jews, even without conversion, were able to move up commercial ladders, taking

Ill. 8:3. *Habts Acht!* (*Attention!*), c. 1840s. By Joseph Lanzedelli

von Schamschele Parch componirt   *Ged b C Horegschj in Wien*

Ill. 8:4. *Die Herausgemanzipirten Juden (Newly Emancipated Jews)*, c. 1840s

advantage of a few relaxed laws. Although numbering only about one percent of the population, they built and controlled coal and iron industries. Railroads grew under their leadership,
while advances in electronics, shipping, retail trade, banking, law, and medicine likewise owed
much to the Jewish community. Artistically inclined Jews expressed their aptitudes, secular or
otherwise, through craft guilds and art schools. Galleries hung their works alongside those of
their Christian colleagues and sold them to Jewish collectors. Wolf Heidenheim composed liturgical works beginning in 1800 in the Frankfort area, and was considered an accurate and scholarly editor of religious texts. Two sets of printers and dozens of rabbis fought over protective
monopolies in the publication of the Talmud.

There were a few successful Jewish printmakers. The Polish Michel Plonski, working in
the style of Rembrandt, etched *Juif d'Amsterdam* (*Jew of Amsterdam*), c. 1800, in the rough dress
of a burly farmer (Ill. 8:5). Despite its debt to the master, the print stands on its own, particularly in the unyielding bulldog stance of the Jewish peasant—he may be someone's hireling,
but he's no man's slave. Moses Samuel Loewe (who in a career move changed his name to
Michael Johann Lowe), produced a set of engravings in 1806 featuring the leaders of the
Enlightenment, *Bildnisse jetzt-lebender der Berliner Gelehrten* (*Current Pictures of Berlin Scholars*). Goethe praised that work. In 1808, Heinrich Bendix's mezzotint portrait *Aaron Beer*
showed the cantor and composer of liturgical melodies with a fashionable tricorn hat on his
head and a sheet of Hebrew music in his hand (Ill. 8:6).

Upper-class Jews, by dress and by design, were stepping into a more cosmopolitan world. A mezzotint portrait, *Fanny von Arnstein*, 1804, represented a daring challenge to the proprieties—neither pulpit sermons nor raised eyebrows deterred this woman of the world from displaying her curls or flaunting her bare arms (Ill. 8:7). Her salons, and those of other popular hostesses, drew the pick of Viennese society and set the tone for every tastemaker, Christian or Jewish. While Jewish men were often portrayed either as dandies or as country bumpkins, surely no one could quarrel with the snappy dresser in the wood-engraving *The Jews' Quarter*, 1887. He would not have embarrassed the most elegant fashion plate in Fanny's circle (Ill. 8:8).

Ill. 8:5. *Juif d'Amsterdam (Jew of Amsterdam)*. Etching, c. 1800. By Michel Plonski

Left: I:ll 8:6. *Aaron Beer*. Mezzotint, 1808. By Heinrich Bendix. *Right:* Ill. 8:7. *Fanny Von Arnstein*, Mezzotint, 1804

Moritz Daniel Oppenheim was the first professing Jewish artist to be widely acclaimed, the first to step out of the ghetto and build an eminent career based on Jewish integration into modern life, the first to portray Jews as members of a dignified enlightened tradition "worthy" of Emancipation. But because he refused to deny his religion, he lost the top art award at the academy in Rome. "Attempts to convert me succeeded only in making me more pious," he declared. "Our frequently dismal synagogues have affected me more deeply than the splendor of St. Peter's." His attitude and achievements helped to mitigate Jewish negative attitudes towards art, and sizably influenced the next group of Jewish genre painters.

His *Return of the Jewish Volunteer*, 1833, with its politically significant theme of Emancipation, signaled a major shift in the way Jews were customarily depicted; the suggestion now was that patriotic young soldiers, in service to Germany against Napoleon, should be regarded with respect. The family acknowledges the process of assimilation, although the military cross on the young man's uniform subtly warns against it. Prints after Oppenheim's *Bilder aus dem Altjüdischen Familienleben* (*Scenes of Traditional Jewish Family Life*), 1865, were enormously popular. Among them, the *Bar Mitzvah Boy Delivering a Sermon* not only testified to emerging manhood but validated the unbroken continuity of his heritage (Ill. 8:9). Such heart-tugging images, idealizing the Orthodox community, appealed to observant as well as secular or converted individuals who retained sentimental memories of their youth. Oppenheim's citified German Jews were climbing the economic and social ladders into banking, the professions and trade, in sharp contrast to Alphonse Levy's countrified yokels at the same period in Alsace.

Maurycy Gottlieb picked up Oppenheim's intimate style, but outdid him in decorative settings, lavish costumes, and the natural arrangements of his figures. His working lifetime was only seven years, but he produced a masterpiece, *Jews at Prayer on the Day of Atonement*, 1878, which included a self-portrait at age twenty-two, images of his parents, and his fiancée who, it was said, broke his heart when she called off their engagement. Influenced by the spir-

VIENNA: THE JEWS' QUARTER.

Ill. 8:8. *The Jews' Quarter*. Wood-engraving, 1887

Ill. 8:9. *Bar Mitzvah Boy Delivering a Sermon*, 1865. Moritz Daniel Oppenheim. From *Bilder aus dem Altjüdischen Familienleben (Scenes of Traditional Jewish Family Life)*

itual and psychological qualities of Rembrandt, the melancholy painting carried a prescient Hebrew prayer "for the salvation of the late Maurycy Gottlieb's soul." He died just one year later. Tuberculosis robbed him of fulfillment; the Nazis almost finished the job, destroying many of his works, some of which survive only in expressive reproductive prints.

Polish life, too, had it chroniclers. Leon Hollaenderski's *Les Israelites de Pologne* (*The Jews of Poland*), 1846, is descriptive of the life he led and fled before settling in France, but he kept the history and memories of his birthplace alive in an engaging book filled with engravings, among which *Le Juif de Varsovie et sa femme* (*The Warsaw Jew and His Wife*), revealed the charms of an up-to-date family (Ill. 8:10). However, *Polish Jews in the Ghetto at Vienna*, 1873, an anonymous wood-engraving in *The Illustrated London News*, documented a less fortunate scene (Ill. 8:11). The accompanying text reads, "They start in the world with a small stock of ready money, but with all the more shrewdness; and by opening an old curiosity shop, or clothes shop, they manage, through strenuously acting upon the principle of the largest possible profits

Ill. 8:10. *Le Juif de Varsovie et sa Femme (The Warsaw Jew and His Wife).* Engraving, 1846. By Leon Hollaenderski. From *Les Israelites de Pologne (The Jews of Poland)*

and the quickest returns, to gain such wealth as must excite the envy of the less energetic and less cunning, if not more scrupulous, Christian brethren."

Isador Kaufmann began his career as a history painter, but after settling in the Hungarian ghetto, he concentrated on such subjects as self-reliant eastern European Jews in their best Sabbath clothes. They were intended to recapture memories of shtetl life—memories he didn't actually share, having come from a bourgeois background. His painting *A Visit from the Rabbi* so appealed to Emperor Franz Josef that he purchased it for Vienna's Museum of Fine Art. Prints made from this and other works after his death spread his fame throughout the Jewish world well in the twentieth century.

One of the first modern Jewish artists was the Dutchman Josef Israels—modern because, like Camille Pissarro, he broke with academic conformity and concentrated on what he called "the atmosphere of the life of ordinary people and of the underprivileged." He took his cue in part from Rembrandt's portrayals of Jews; indeed, his countrymen honored him with an entire room opposite that of his great mentor in Amsterdam's Rijksmuseum. A humanitarian by instinct, an Orthodox Jew by upbringing and conviction, he painted evocations of the Jewish spirit in *The Son of an Ancient People*, 1889, and *A Jewish Wedding*, 1903. His etched *Self-Portrait*, along with that of *Mrs. Israels*, were rare examples of Jewish subject matter in his prints.

Homey or casual views were always relished, perhaps even more than formal or stylized scenes. An engraving, *Machitonim Tanz (In-law's Dance)* shows the parents of a happy couple expressing joy—or perhaps relief—at the marriage of their children. *The Rabbil Presides Over a Divorce* shows, with some humor, the official end of a marriage (Ill. 8:12). *The Geese Market in Krakow before Passover*, 1869, by the German etcher William Unger, portrays a typical holiday scene. The Danish Jew Joel Ballin recorded a comfortable middle-class family in his *Mother and Child*, an etching from about 1830 (Ill. 8:13). Denmark had established a good relationship with its Jews. They enjoyed civic, but not full political rights, a bonus which arrived in 1849. However, in a period of academicism and rationalism, many of these works were hesitant and anecdotal. The artists were pathfinders, still at the beginning of a journey which would not lead to sophistication and maturity until the next century. Challenged to

POLISH JEWS IN THE GHETTO AT VIENNA.

Above: Ill. 8:11. *Polish Jews in the Ghetto at Vienna.* Wood-engraving, 1873. From *The Illustrated London News. Below:* Ill. 8:12. *The Rabbi Presides Over a Divorce,* c. 1850

Rozwód przed Rabinatem.
„Get" Ehescheidungsprozeß vor dem Rabbinate.

Ill. 8:13. *Mother and Child.* Etching, c. 1830. By Joel Ballin

harmonize spiritual ideals with cultural and national goals, they struggled in a time of major societal transitions. But they were more than simple genre artists—they were a Jewish presence in the arts, archivists in the preservation of their own history.

Meanwhile, halfway across the world, the Ottoman Empire, which had been a haven for Marranos at the end of the fifteenth century, instituted some prohibitions after many years of tolerance when rumors of blood libels and other slanders created trouble. Nevertheless, once the government permitted the settlement of foreign Jews, its Jewish population, third only to those of Russia and Austria-Hungary, grew to approximately a third of a million souls, some of whom became quite prosperous. In a mid-century lithograph, the *Juive de Constantinople* (*Jewess of Constantinople*), inhabiting the dream-world of high society, looks like a million lira in a lace headdress and gown (Ill. 8:14). However, the female working class, seen in a lithograph, c. 1830, *Jewish Women of Izmir, Whitewashing*, labored under harsher circumstances, enjoying few of the benefits enjoyed by their more fortunate sisters (Ill. 8:15).

As styles of apparel differed, so did styles of worship. When activist rabbis in Germany rejected some of the obligations or legalisms of Orthodoxy which they believed were authored by men, not the deity (although divinely inspired), they endorsed what they viewed as a revision or corrective branch of Judaism. The Reform movement modified or eliminated a number of basic tenets, stressed morality and systematic investigation over traditional ideology, and hoped to increase access to a secular society and to rescue ambivalent Jews who were looking with conversionary interest at the Church. It excised references to a Messiah, the reestablishment of the Temple, and restoration of the Jewish people to Zion; the mission of the Diaspora became central. Head coverings, prayer shawls, kosher foods, and laws of marital purity were out; mixed choirs, mixed seating, German hymns, and an abbreviated liturgy were in. Rabbis demanded decorum from their congregants, delivered sermons in the regional tongue, and modeled their vestments on those of their Christian colleagues. Israel Jacobson incorporated organ music and vernacular prayers in the first Reform temple in 1810 in Seesen, and in the second in 1815 in Berlin. Modern secular scholarship was included in the religious training offered by Leopold Zunz, who pioneered the *Wissenschaft des Judentums (The Science of Judaism)* and edited its journal, *Zeitschrift für die Wissenschaft des Judenthums (Journal for the Science of Judaism)*, 1822. In 1835, Abraham Geiger published the first issue of the *Wissenschaftliche Zeitschrif für jüdische Theologie (Scientific Journal of Jewish Theology)*, defining the parameters of Reformism and

JUIVE DE CONSTANTINOPLE

Ill. 8:14. *Juive de Constantinople (Jewess of Constantinople)* Lithograph, c. 1850 emphasizing the need to pursue and interpret individual spiritual values. Samuel Holdheim spoke of a constantly evolving ethical Judaism and the obsolescence of nationalist elements. For all that, the rabbis were wary. "Suicide is not Reform," advised Zunz. And even fifty years later, Rabbi Caesar Seligmann warned that "the denial of the Talmud is the erasing of twenty-five hundred years of Jewish history."

Orthodoxy fought back, offering creative modifications of its own within permissible guidelines in order to counter what it saw as the threat to Jewish unity and coherence. The historian Heinrich Graetz, author of the eleven-volume *History of the Jews*, 1853–1878, based his defense of divine Judaism on the validity of its spiritual affinity throughout all of history. He denied the tenets of Reformism, expressed adverse opinions of its proponents, and thought that Christian anti–Semitism alone was the chief factor in molding Jewish history. However, possibly because he lacked a rigorous academic background, he turned a blind eye to the impact of

Ill. 8:15. *Jewish Women of Izmir, Whitewashing*. Lithograph, c. 1830

social, cultural, and economic forces. Isaac Bernays and his disciple Samson Raphael Hirsch asserted that what Jews needed was to reform themselves rather than to reform Judaism. They declared that a neo–Orthodoxy could accommodate itself to modernity and develop a synthesis between rabbinic and secular cultures within "the spirit of the times." Israel Hildesheimer opened seminaries that combined Jewish and Western ideals and raised the level of rabbinic studies; emphasis was centered on Torah principles in concert with the hard-won gains of the Emancipation. Jacob Ettlinger, established the German-language journal *Der Treue Zionwachter* (*The True Guardian of Zion*) in 1845, with a Hebrew supplement to promote Orthodoxy and Orthodox scholarship in light of the challenges of Reform. And mediating between these widely differing attitudes, Zacharias Frankel, an early exponent of secular education, spearheaded a compromise: the Conservative movement, "maintaining the integrity of Judaism simultaneously with progress." Despite their theological differences, all parties united in the battle for religious and political freedoms which they argued were natural rights.

While denominational observances ranged over the widest extremes and interpretations, a sense of optimism, perhaps never before so hopefully experienced, was recognized. Many communities, believing that they were no longer menaced by destruction or confiscation, undertook the erection of revival-style synagogues and temples that no longer had to camouflage their height to avoid rising above neighboring churches and that were large enough to hold thousands of worshippers. An eclectic—and sometimes chaotic—assortment of architectural elements drawn from Gothic, Romanesque, Greek, Baroque, and above all, Moorish prototypes, were often reproduced from pattern books filled with engravings of standard or classical specimens.

A wood-engraving of Cologne's Glockengasse Synagogue, built between 1856 and 1861, displays Moorish horseshoe arches matched with a Gothic rose window (Ill. 8:16). (The building was destroyed by the Nazis on Crystal Night, November 9–10, 1938, along with two hundred eighty other magnificent and humble synagogues.) A wood-engraving of Berlin's Moorish Oranienburg-erstrasse Synagogue, 1855–1866, constructed of cast iron and brick, proudly displayed an interior of great proportions and brightness (Ill. 8:17). (It was heavily damaged by Allied bombing during World War II, but was reconstructed in the 1950s by the East German government.) One of the largest European temples was the Dohany in Budapest. A wood-engraving suggests the lavish décor, although the budget necessitated limits on silver and gold ornamentation (Ill. 8:18). The organ, however, was sufficiently magnificent to attract performances by Liszt and Saint-Saëns.

Ill. 8:16. *Glockengasse Synagogue.* Wood-engraving, c. 1862

Ill. 8:17. *Oranienburgerstrasse Synagogue.* Wood-engraving, c. 1866

Ill. 8:18. *Dohany Synagogue*. Wood-engraving, c. 1850

But if Jews thought that religious diversity or physical signs of achievement would stem the resurgence of mudslinging, they were very much mistaken. A few authors, such as Franz Grillparzer and Otto Ludwig, wrote positive stories during this period of strong German nationalism, but most books encouraged negative attitudes. The inflammatory novel *Biarritz*, written in 1868 by Hermann Godsche under the pseudonym Sir John Retcliffe, claimed that the Jews were laying plans to enslave the world; it influenced Germany's court chaplain Adolf Stoecker, who founded the Christian-Social Workers' Party in 1878. He asserted that Jewish successes in business, as well as resistance to conversion, were contrary to the German spirit, and that Jewish blood carried a destructive force. He played on the twin fears of a Jewishly imposed Capitalism and a Jewishly imposed Marxism, "working from both sides to bring down the present political and social order." Anti-Jewish demonstrations, boycotts, attacks on Jewish institutions, and a proliferation of anti–Semitic books and organizations soon followed.

Although the term Semite (from Shem, son of Noah) originally was limited to describing people from southwestern Asia, the Semitism of the Jews was irrationally associated with moral corruption and was disparagingly contrasted with the Aryan (from Sanskrit, "noble"), Indo-European or Nordic heritage. Language groupings were converted into racial groupings, promoting the notion that cultural traits were revealed through speech and lineage. Since the Germanic Aryan race alone held the formula for political, social, and commercial revitalization, to be "for" a debased people was illogical; to be anti–Semitic was to safeguard the future of higher breeds. Because theological arguments against Jews were hardly respectable in the rational nineteenth century, racist doctrines were trotted out. No longer could conversion eradicate the stigma of Yiddishism or Hebraism. Expulsion of Jews and suppression of their social and political "domination" became valid and even logical solutions when "inferiority" itself was the justification for hatred and persecution.

Anti-Jewishness, therefore, was no longer an appropriate expression. Anti-Semitism better suggested "scientific" truth based on deficient ancestry. The term first came into the language in 1867 when it was used in a pamphlet, *Der Sieg des Judenthums über das Germanentum* (*The Victory of Judaism Over Germanism*) by Wilhelm Marr, a journalist who founded the Anti-Semitic League that year to prevent the fatherland from being "taken over" by Jews. Marr then raised enough money from like-minded members to publish the *Zwanglose Antisemitische Hefte* (*Incidental Anti-Semitic Tracts*) in 1881.

With the unification of Germany following victory in the Franco-Prussian War of 1871, the economic and social situation of many Jews improved—but just for a moment. They did achieve Emancipation with access to the professions and cultural life, but when inflation and bankruptcy loomed in 1873, the victory proved hollow. As usual, a Jewish conspiracy was blamed, this time for urging national self-determination and a democratic constitutional government. Although civil rights were eventually secured, a heavy price was exacted: Jews were held responsible for the riots and looting that followed the economic panic and depression that lasted until 1879. Some ten thousand Jews—along with thirty thousand Russian and Austro-Hungarian Poles—were expelled in 1885 and later by the first chancellor of the German empire, Otto von Bismarck; it was a way of dealing with the illegal mass immigration to Germany that had begun in 1881. Hundreds of thousands began another exodus to the West.

Jews who had benefited from newly competitive opportunities found themselves more and more on the receiving end of an anti–Semitism that was harsher and meaner than anywhere in Europe. While printmakers elsewhere exhibited bigoted and spiteful images, they were usually directed to specific individuals or conditions. It was the competent Germans who disgorged new levels of animosity. An etching, *Israelchen hat einen Dukaten verschluckt* (*Little Israel*

Ill. 8:19. *Israelchen hat einen Dukaten verschluckt (Little Israel Swallowed a Ducat).* Etching, 1820

Swallowed a Ducat), 1820, titillated its audience with a scatological image, but it was actually a commentary on the perception of money-hunger (Ill. 8:19). The text describes a child who swallows a gold piece after watching his family ogling it. He soon becomes the center of attention on the dining-room table where the first order is the recovery of the coin by means of purgatives and an enema. Only when the ducat is passed are joy and well-being restored.

Fecal humor aside, mercenary traits could always be dragged into service. The Rothschild family continued to be singled out as the personification of avarice and self-indulgence. *Die Generalpumpe* (*The General Creditor*), a lithograph of 1848, shows the great world powers humbly under Jewish despotism (Ill. 8:20). A diadem clapped on a Rothschild head is composed of debts owed by the leading states of Europe: Jewish money manipulating and holding the Gentile economy in hock. Labeled the "incarnation of a financial system that covers and dominates the entire globe," Rothschild rises from a sack of coins, literally too big for his breeches. Another print showed a rapacious Rothschild enthroned on a pile of money extracted from his creditors. Kings, nobility, churchmen, a jackass, and an emaciated beggar all kneel at his feet handing over jewels, a crown, and two bottles of liquid assets; the pickings never looked so irresistible and no doubt the old Jew would soon be wallowing in the booty.

Not to be outdone, the Viennese magazine *Kikeriki* followed suit. A satiric cartoon, *Das Grösste Getreide-Wucherthier der Welt* (*The Greatest Profit-making Animal of the World*), 1862, needed little commentary; it was generally understood that Jews were taking over the world through speculations in the grain market (Ill. 8:21). Enlightenment notwithstanding, once freedom of the press became a reality, the door was open to material other than money-love or superstition. As in some other European examples, exaggerated postural and facial patterns were based on the projection of the Jew as profiteer, profligate, capitalist, and as lascivious defiler

Ill. 8:20. *Die Generalpumpe (The General Creditor).* Lithograph, 1848

Ill. 8:21. *Das Grösste Getreide-Wucherthier der Welt (The Greatest Profit-making Animal of the World)*, 1862. From *Kikeriki*

Ill. 8:22. *Im Privatkontor (In the Private Office)*. Wood-engraving. By Daniel Greiner

of Christian maidens. Whole series of indelicate prints such as Daniel Greiner's wood-engraving *Im Privatkontor* (*In the Private Office*) were spawned (Ill. 8:22). Rich old Jews were paired with credulous young women. Male and female, Jews were represented practicing their "favorite sin." A Jewish woman, asking a Christian for help, falls not on her knees, but on her back. Pornography reached a pungent high as Jewish noses were transformed into phalluses and Jewish ladies were shown willingly spreading their legs for non–Jews.

By rendering Jews as evil-natured or disreputable, it was understood that they had no place in a decent community, and that social equality was not only unwise, but an insult to the political and economic equilibrium. Reichstag member Hermann Ahlwardt used Marr's arguments to describe Jews as "beasts of prey." Addressing that august chamber that year, he said, "We wouldn't think of going as far as have the Austrian anti–Semites in the Federal Council and to move that a bounty be paid for every Jew shot or to decree that he who kills a Jew shall inherit his property. What we want is a clear and reasonable separation of the Jews from the Germans. An immediate prerequisite is that we slam the door and see to it that no more of them get in." Fifty-one representatives out of a total of two hundred eighteen voted with him.

Jews weren't to get in, but they were urged to get out. A wood-engraving, *The Jews Leave Germany*, 1895, showed Jewish riffraff shuffling along with their ill-gotten possessions while the Rothschilds drive out in an elegant carriage, indifferent to their co-religionists' distress. Much of the support for the removal of Jews came from small shopkeepers, artisans, farmers, and others who weren't able adapt to modernity and graduate to bourgeois status.

The proliferation of anti–Semitic texts encouraged government-backed epidemics of abusive procedures. Jacob Brafman's *Book of the Kabal*, 1869, August Rohling's *The Jew According to the Talmud*, 1871, and *The Talmud Unmasked: The Secret Rabbinical Teachings Concerning Christians* by Father Justin Bonaventura Pranaitis, 1892, which anticipated the 1905 forgery *The Protocols of the Learned Elders of Zion*, all became best sellers.

Something had to be done to protect Jewish interests and counteract anti–Semitism. The search for its psychological, economic, and social roots eventually led to the Zionist movement. The Israelitische Allianz of Austria, first organized in 1873, and the Central Union of German Citizens of the Jewish Faith, established twenty years later, undertook defense programs to discourage violence, to coordinate legal and welfare agencies wherever they were needed, to form labor unions for the improvement of working conditions, and to strengthen Jewish solidarity. Prompted by the Russian pogroms of 1881 (when that word entered the English language), Leon Pinsker, an Odessa physician, founder of Hovevei Zion (Lovers of Zion), and former assimilationist, published a pamphlet in Berlin the following year, *Autoemancipation—A Warning to His Fellow People from a Russian Jew*. In it he urged Jews to seek a homeland as the only answer to persecution. Neither assimilation nor enlightenment would work. Emancipation from their alien situation might—preferably in Palestine with the acquisition of land as its immediate goal and agriculture as its base. Jew hatred, or Judophobia, as Pinsker termed it, was an intractable pathological issue. "To the living, the Jew is a corpse," he commented, "to the native, a foreigner, to the homesteader, a vagrant, to the proprietary, a beggar, to the poor, an exploiter or a millionaire, to the patriot, a man without a country, for all, a hated rival."

However, many leaders repudiated the Zionist cause as too extreme. Baron Maurice de Hirsch and Baron Edmond de Rothschild protested that Jews were too scattered and disorganized to unite on the issue. Reform and Orthodox authorities rejected the summoning of a Zionist Congress on the grounds that Jewish nationalism was an inconsistency. Discouraged but unfaltering, Theodor Herzl endorsed Pinsker's solution in *Der Judenstaat* (*The Jewish State*), 1896, demanding an end to the "Jewish problem" through the creation of a safe political entity. The first Congress was convened in Basel in 1897 with one hundred ninety-seven representatives from seventeen countries agreeing to launch Zionist organizations in dozens of communities—many of which survived until silenced by the Nazis. In addition to Zionism, which promoted Palestine as the Jewish national home with Hebrew as the national language, the Bund, a Yiddish-oriented secular labor party, was organized to establish a Socialist regime and improve Jewish life within Russia.

While some Russian and other eastern European Jews had already immigrated to Palestine, they faced there not only dwindling funds but the unsympathetic Turkish government which controlled the area and placed restrictions on buying and improving property. Lawrence Oliphant, among other Christian supporters, unsuccessfully attempted to persuade the sultan to allow a reasonable life for the settlers, but they were left with the choice of bribing corrupt administrators or of packing up and going home. Sneered the Russian illustrator Frederick Villiers in a 1901 cartoon, *While Russians Visit the Holy Land, the Jews Themselves Take Good Care Not to Stay There* (Ill. 8:23).

Italy had its own story. Following the defeat of Napoleon in 1815, Pope Pius VII reinstated the Inquisition. An etching by Samuel Valentine Hunt, *The Ghetto, Rome*, includes the

While Russians visit the Holy Land, the Jews themselves take good care not to stay there. Our illustration shows Jewish emigrants on an Atlantic liner going to the "land of the free" to blossom out in time as twisters of the Lion's tail

Ill. 8:23. *While Russians Visit the Holy Land, the Jews Themselves Take Good Care Not to Stay There,* 1901. By Frederick Villiers

local church in the background, evidence that Jewish and Christian neighborhoods were just a stone's throw from each other (Ill 8:24). An image of the Virgin monitored the daily comings and goings in the Jewish quarter. To those who lived within its borders, the ghetto bore a fearful air, horribly crowded, dirty, and foul-smelling. Although the number of its residents grew, the authorities would not permit any enlargement of its borders; existing buildings were forced to add unstable upper levels vulnerable to collapse and fire. The outlook was dim, although, as Von Guise pointed out in a lithograph, *Das Innere Synagogue in Rome* (*Interior of the Synagogue in Rome*), c. 1823, a quiet atmosphere was possible during those periods when the congregants were left undisturbed to practice their rituals (Ill. 8:25). Most of the men were dressed and barbered according to the best European taste, and many details of the synagogue were accurately described. But the print had an additional agenda. It mocked what was perceived as a want of dignity and self-respect. Services were indeed unruly, but unruliness was a time-honored tradition in the synagogue which also functioned as a community center and public forum. (According to the Babylonian Talmud, at the Great Synagogue of Alexandria the noise was so great that it was necessary to hold up a flag to let the back know when to say "Amen.") In another lithograph that year, *Die Bekehrung der Juden in Roma* (*The Conversion of the Jews in Rome*), Von Guise showed Jews being subjected to baptism and mandatory attendance at proselytizing sermons where friars policed the ceremonies (Ill. 8:26). In 1870, when the papal regime fell, Pope Nicholas III abolished the ghettos as well as the compulsory edict which had been in force since 1278.

Carnival time had never been much fun for Jews. Practical jokers went about in costumes and disguises, planning amusing sports that forced half-naked Jews to crawl along the streets

Ill. 8:24. *The Ghetto, Rome.* Etching. By Samuel Valentine Hunt

Above: Ill. 8:25. *Das Innere Synagogue in Rome. (Interior of a Synagogue in Rome).* Lithograph, c. 1823. By Von Guise. *Below:* Ill. 8:26. *Die Bekehrung der Juden in Roma (The Conversion of the Jews in Rome).* Lithograph, c. 1823. By Von Guise

Ill. 8:27. *L'ebreo dento la botte roroato dalla plebaglia. (The Jew Inside a Barrel Rolled by a Mob.)* **Etching, 1823. By B. Pinelli**

with jeering riders on their backs; better yet was tucking a town elder into a barrel lined with nails and pushing it down a steep Roman hill. B. Pinelli etched the diversion in *L'ebreo dento la botte roroato dalla plebaglia* (*The Jew Inside a Barrel Rolled by a Mob*), 1823 (Ill. 8:27). Only spoilsports complained when the amusement turned fatal. Another carnival etching, *Jewish Masks at Carnival Time*, depicted a pair of outlandish characters dressed in Sabbath coats and prayer shawls grasping financial statements in lieu of prayer books (Ill. 8:28). The Jews of Florence lived under a more benign authority. French armies had freed them from the ghetto in 1800; Grand Duke Leopold II conferred equality in 1848. At that point, Italy was united, and its Jews were able to choose where to live without assaults or conversionary pressures. Florence got its turn to shine with the construction of a magnificent Moorish-style domed synagogue in 1882, visited, its congregation boasted, by the king himself. By the close of the century the city's level of Jewish wealth and culture outstripped its sister communities.

Such achievements were beyond hope in eastern Europe. Following the partition of Poland in 1795, Russia acquired most of that unfortunate land and its multitude of Jews. Czar Alexander I addressed the "Jewish Problem" in 1802, ultimately determining that education would be available in Russian, Polish, or German, but not in Yiddish or Hebrew. Jews could not live where they chose or employ Christians or sell alcoholic beverages to the peasants, a main source of their income. Beginning in about 1812, Russia's Jews, mostly craft workers, innkeepers, and tradesmen, were expelled to areas annexed from Poland in the westernmost part of the country, the Pale of Settlement, a region larger than France. By 1880, about half of all the Jews in the world lived in that area.

Active presses promoted both religious as well as secular books. From 1801 until 1835 publishers in Slavuta and Vilna vied for the rights to promote their own editions. The disputes led to bitter rabbinic court hearings where very large amounts of money hung in the balance, to say nothing of the reputations of the Hasidic editors on one side and their Lithuanian counterparts on the other. The czar finally declared the issue moot with his order to close down all Hebrew presses in Russia; only a few exceptions were obtained through bribes and the promise of additional censorship. The rivalries nevertheless persisted for much of the century. In the decades from 1825 to 1855, Nicholas I promulgated some six hundred harsh laws intended to speed assimilation and acculturation, including placing children in Christian schools, censoring Jewish books, banning wigs for married women and ear-locks and traditional Jewish clothing for religious men. Forced conversions were achieved through mandatory army service that conscripted boys as young as twelve and kept many in servitude for twenty-five years. Parents pauperized themselves to rescue their sons from kidnappers or "snatchers." Young men mutilated themselves to escape the loneliness and torture of army life. The Jews fought back with their only weapons—fasts and prayers.

Nicholas' successor, Alexander II, who served from 1855 to 1881, was cognizant of enlightenment values. He permitted an interval of moderation during which some onerous laws were rescinded. Serfs were freed in 1861 and "useful" Jews were given opportunities to "improve" themselves. Restrictions on craftsmen were relaxed, directives for military services were eased, and possibilities for higher education in medical and governmental fields became available. Prints showing Jews in normative home settings also indicated the lessening of tensions. T. Pauli's album of lithographs, *The Peoples of Russia*, 1862, included for example *Rabbinic Jews Comfortably Dressed in Traditional Jewish Clothing* (Ill. 8:29). A woodcut, *Polish Jews*, by K. A. Savitsky, 1877, shows an intimate domestic scene: here, Mama knits, Papa holds a tool of his trade, and Junior scratches his head for lice. Such genre prints acquainted readers with Jews as they were beginning to be viewed as normal members of society.

A few wealthy or educated Jews belonging to merchant guilds were able to reside outside the Pale and organize local councils. Even some collaboration between Jewish and Russian intellectuals was possible. But none of that was acceptable to one of Russia's greatest authors, Feodor Dostoevski. He exacerbated anti–Jewish feelings in *Crime and Punishment*, 1866, and became even more reactionary in the 1870s during the closing years of his life. He declared that only Russia and the Orthodox Church, filtered through the ideals of Christian brotherhood, held the keys to moral and ethical virtue.

But Jews believed that they could be worthwhile citizens and even patriotic solders. During the Crimean War, the czar visited Jewish troops on the eve of Yom Kippur in 1877. A lithograph of

Ill. 8:28. *Jewish Masks at Carnival Time.* Etching

Ill. 8:29. *Rabbinic Jews Comfortably Dressed in Traditional Jewish Clothing.* Lithograph, 1862. By T. Pauli. From *The Peoples of Russia*

that event depicts the makeshift synagogue where he observed the services (Ill. 8:30). Jews bought the print and were proud to display it. Acculturation and inclusion seemed possible, but it was not to be. Radicals demanded immediate changes in Russian affairs after the assassination of Alexander in 1881. His efforts to moderate some of the problems had been too few and not soon enough. Agricultural and industrial interests had suffered enormous dislocations as the old feudal economy made way for one based on a monetary system. Freed serfs who left farms for cities found the transition difficult. Burdensome new taxes condemned many to penury. Those whose lives were challenged wasted no time making the case that Jewish gains were responsible for their troubles. The Orthodox Church wasn't far behind, insinuating that Jews were corrupting Holy Russia. Predictably, bloodbaths broke out in over one hundred fifty towns—against "economic exploitation by the state within a state."

Needing a scapegoat to explain away the economic turndown, Alexander III, who ruled from 1881 to 1894, responded by tightening his father's liberalism through the "temporary" May Laws of 1881. These limited residence rights, placed quotas on enrollment of Jews in schools and professions, forced half of Moscow's Jews from their homes, and then presided over massacres and riots to divert attention away from internal governmental weaknesses. In his attempts to regulate a uniform religious and linguistic culture, he antagonized racial minorities such as the Poles and Finns, but the Jews bore the greatest suffering. Unlike the discriminatory practices against Jews in western and central Europe, anti–Jewish activities in Russia were concretized in administrative policies and abetted by officials, the police, and the army. The head of the ministry in charge of church affairs, Konstantin Pobedonostsev, predicted that definitive Russification would take place only when one-third of the Jews converted, one-third died, and one-third left the country.

Cartoonists and illustrators, mirroring his sentiments, produced large numbers of demeaning prints which encouraged the exodus of more than two and a half million Jews to Amer-

Captions under the lithograph (right to left):

1. RELIGIOUS SERVICE BEFORE THE CZAR ON THE PREVIOUS DAY OF ATONEMENT.

2. PUNISHMENT OF DEATH FOR DENIAL OF FAITH.

THE RUSSIAN-TURKEYISH WAR. "PLEWNA"

3. TEMPORARY SYNAGOGUE FOR THE DAY OF ATONEMENT.

4. BRIDGE OVER THE DANUBE.

Above: Ill. 8:30. *Jewish Troops on the Eve of Yom Kippur.* Lithograph, 1877. *Below:* Ill. 8:31. *Peddler's Wagon.* Etching, 1883. By E. Z. Krasnushkina

Ill. 8:32. *In Prison*. Lithograph, c. 1890

ica, as well as a small number to Palestine between 1881 and 1914. E. Z. Krasnushkina's 1883 etching *Peddler's Wagon*, with its scrawny horses and dilapidated travelers, hardly accorded with description of Jews as exploiters of commerce and industry (Ill. 8:31). And only Jews were targeted in the lithograph *In Prison*, c. 1890, although a variety of swindlers regularly duped peasants into selling their belongings under the pretext of taking them to America (Ill. 8:32). Those who managed to leave suffered greatly in the process. A wood-engraving from *The Illustrated London News*, 1891, depicted the sad partings in the *Expulsion of Jews from St. Petersburg at the Baltic Railway Station* (Ill. 8:33). (Because of suppression of information within Russia, European and American presses became the best sources of facts and data.)

An English wood-engraving, *Russian Refugees in Vienna*, reported on the Jewish flight from terror-stricken areas. Few Russian Jews had passports; most depended on smugglers to obtain passages to the West and ultimately to America. Even so, they were frequently turned down on the ground that too many had already overburdened available relief systems. While some international efforts on their behalf were eventually undertaken, diplomatic realities being what they were, no country was willing to risk Russia's trading or political clout. A hail of murderous pogroms together with financial backlashes ensued.

In June of 1881, *The Illustrated London News* printed a wood-engraving, *Assault on a Jew in the Presence of the Military at Kiev* (Ill. 8:34). Mobs of young men with hammers and other weapons attacked a neighborhood here or a business establishment there while onlookers and the police watched the destruction of Jewish homes and workplaces. The English poet Algernon Charles Swinburne dramatized the situation in a sonnet calling on Jesus to heed the tragedies, *On the Russian Persecution of the Jews, 1882:*

> O son of man, by lying tongues adored,
> By slaughterous hands of slaves with feet red-shod
> In carnage deep as ever Christian trod
> Profaned with prayer and sacrifice abhorred

Above: Ill. 8:33. *Expulsion of Jews from St. Petersburg at the Baltic Railway Station.* Wood-engraving, 1891. *Below:* Ill. 8:34. *Assault on a Jew in the Presence of the Military at Kiev.* Wood-engraving, 1881. Both from *The Illustrated London News*

ASSAULT ON A JEW IN THE PRESENCE OF THE MILITARY, AT KIEV.

And incense from the trembling tyrant's horde,
Brute worshippers or wielders of the rod,
Most murderous even of all that call thee God,
Most treacherous even that ever called thee Lord;
Face loved of little children long ago,
Head hated of the priests and rulers then,
If thou see this, or hear these hounds of thine
Run ravening as the Gadarean swine,
Say, was not this thy Passion, to foreknow
In death's worst hour the works of Christian men?

The American artist Thomas Nast provided an even more direct indictment in his wood-engraving in *Harper's Weekly*, 1882: *Live and Let Live in Russia.—"Your Money, Jew, or Your Life!" The Cry for Ages* (Ill. 8:35). The whip, the fire, the fear tell the story. Other papers, such as *Die Illustrierte Zeitung* of Leipzig printed articles and wood-engravings showing Jews escaping from pogroms; with their homes gone, their belongings looted, relatively few Jews did escape. London's *Punch* featured a scathing wood-engraving in 1891, *The Alarmed Autocrat—Czar of All the Russians*, showing his retreat from the presence of a battered and tattered Jew being detained by two burly officers. *"Take him away! He frightens me"* (Ill. 8:36).

Things had not always been so bad for Russian Jews. *The Illustrated Times* in 1856 had pictured an agreeable *Jews' Walk in the City of Odessa* (Ill. 8:37). "Odessa can only boast of one public walk, and this is situated in the best part of the town and near to the harbor. Every Saturday this walk is crowded by the Israelitish inhabitants, who constitute a large proportion of the entire population, and who, with their families, pass the greater portion of the day under the cool shade of the chestnut and lime trees, with which the walk is freely planted." The first Hebrew papers, *HaKarmel* and *HaMelitz,* and the weekly Russian periodical *Razsvet* had debuted in 1860 as Enlightenment publications. And in 1874, a wood-engraving, *Football in the Jews' Market, St. Petersburg,* in *The Illustrated London News*, depicted a seemingly untroubled group of young people enjoying a friendly game (Ill. 8:38). The text described the marketplace, which "contains, besides a wonderful medley of Jews' odd merchandise, a large collection of live birds and pet animals. There are nearly five thousand stalls in these two markets...."

The reprieve during the reign of Alexander II was predicated on Jewish assimilation, but most Jews were more interested in Emancipation. Either way, they did achieve some access to secular life, including permission to band together in Moscow and St. Petersburg art schools. The landscape painter Isaac Levitan and the stage and costume designer Leon Bakst met with success, perhaps because they

Ill. 8:35. *Live and Let Live in Russia—"Your Money, Jew, or Your Life!" The Cry for Ages*. **Wood-engraving, 1882. By Thomas Nast**

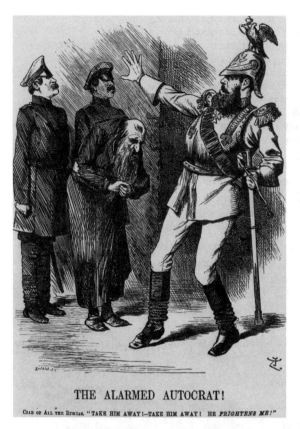

THE ALARMED AUTOCRAT!

Czar of All the Russias. "TAKE HIM AWAY!—TAKE HIM AWAY! HE *FRIGHTENS ME!*"

eschewed Jewish themes in their compositions. Others, like the sculptor Mark Antokolsky and painter Samuel Hirschenberg, expressed themselves through cultural and social Jewish subject matter (sometimes critically), in hopes of establishing an eastern European Jewish aesthetic and securing sympathy for the harassed Jews. Large numbers of magazines and illustrated albums occasionally included prints of everyday Jewish life. *Russian Money-Changers*, c. 1840s, a lithograph by G. D. Mitreuter, included a pair of merchants—one Russian, one Jewish—amicably negotiating a bit of private business in the Kremlin neighborhood. A collection of lithographs from 1843 by L. A. Bielousov included a convivial *Jewish Pub* where Jews and Ukrainians share a glass of vodka or tea (Ill. 8:39).

So why the change? Why did Russia set out to destroy its own countrymen? As always, the increased visibility

THE JEWS' WALK, CITY OF ODESSA, RUSSIA.

Above: Ill. 8:36. *The Alarmed Autocrat—Czar of All the Russians*. Wood-engraving, 1891. From *Punch. Below:* Ill. 8:37. *Jews' Walk in the City of Odessa*. Wood-engraving, 1856. From *The Illustrated Times*

Ill. 8:38. *Football in the Jews' Market, St. Petersburg.* Wood-engraving, 1874. From *The Illustrated London News*

and competition of Jews were causes for alarm. They threatened the newly emancipated serfs who felt that the intruders were profiting from whatever meager reforms they believed were rightfully theirs. The worse their own situation, the more bitterly they resented Jewish success. Suspicion, distrust, and rivalry, of course, clouded their attitudes. Would it help if they knew more about Jews? Count Leo Tolstoy thought it was a fair question. "What is a Jew?" he asked. "Let us see what peculiar kind of a creature a Jew is, which all the rulers and all the nations have together and separately abused and molested, oppressed and persecuted, trampled and butchered, burned and hanged—and in spite of all this is yet alive. What is a Jew, who has never allowed himself to be led astray by all the earthly possessions which his persecutors constantly offered him in order that he should change his faith and forsake his own Jewish religion? [The Jew] is the spring and fountain out of which all the rest of the peoples have drawn their beliefs and the religions. The Jew is the pioneer of liberty.... The Jew is the pioneer of civilization." In many ways the Jews *were* pioneers. It was a hard lesson for Russians to understand or accept.

While Tolstoy was somewhat carried away, it was true that many Jews had of necessity learned to bear up under alienation. When options were few, they turned to their religious and cultural support systems that represented the continuity and coherence of their lives. Under difficult circumstances they involved themselves and each other in a close and closed community, not the least of which was their Yiddish and Hebrew books and papers, which aroused nationalistic sentiments as well as pride among many young Jews. Among the literary output was the Polish-Yiddish *Dostrzegacz Nadwislanski* which appeared in the first decades of the century and *Der Beobachter an der Weichsel* (German with Hebrew lettering), which had a short run from 1823 to 1824. Alexander Tsederboym added a lively Yiddish supplement, *Kol Mevaser*, to his weekly Hebrew newspaper, *HaMelitz*; it ran for eleven years beginning in 1862, initi-

Ill. 8:39. *Jewish Pub*. Lithograph, 1843. By L. A. Bielousov

ating a modern Yiddish literary outlet for such authors as Mendele Moicher Seforim and
Shalom Aleichem. The first Hebrew daily newspaper, *HaYom*, began publication in St. Peters-
burg in 1886. The weekly *Der Yid*, 1899 to 1902, was the first Zionist periodical circulated in
Russia.

Internationally known works also became available, signifying the new ease. Between
1860 and 1900, poetry, children's stories, and literary criticism, as well as works by Shakespeare,
Hugo, Dumas, Emerson, and Scott were among some three thousand titles translated into
Hebrew, Yiddish and Russian. An expanding interest in Talmud and Hasidism provided a mis-
cellany of books on almost every subject. Religious material topped the list, but the twenty-
eight-volume *Universal Encyclopedia* was not far behind. Itinerant booksellers fanned out to
inflate the market, working the streets independently of big shops, though often living pre-
cariously. The poet Wladyslaw Syrokomla memorialized such a man: Tolstoy would have
respected him.

> With his back to the wall
> Stands a grey-bearded Jew, dressed in rags.
> Blood-shot, filmy eyes, senility written on his face,
> An old book under his arm. This is the doyen of the booksellers!
> Don't laugh at him! It is almost fifty years
> Since he took up his place by this wall
> And offered pamphlets and trash to the passers-by.
> In exchange for a copper coin, he gave golden learning.

Abraham Mapu wrote the first modern Hebrew novel, *Ahavat Ziyyon* (*Love of Zion*), 1853. Published in Vilna, it was a runaway success in more than a dozen editions and almost as many translations. Yet he lamented that although young people love books they don't buy them. Shtetl Jews remained suspicious of secular literature; city-bred Jews, closer physically and emotionally to the sources of Emancipation and cultural integration, were often indifferent to traditional works. Mapu fought a long battle with the Orthodox community, which objected to his liberal orientation and satiric tone. Although his works were set in the biblical period and employed a biblical style, they were inspired by Enlightenment principles and were important contributions to the Zionist movement. His modernist outlook influenced later writers of Hebrew literature in their own explorations of the natural world.

A series of forty-five pamphlets, *Sifrei Agura* (*Penny Books*), 1889, was successfully published by Ben Avigdor, whose company, Tushiyah, was the precursor of twentieth century Hebrew publishing in Odessa. To him must go the credit for raising both the income and the morale of dozens of Jewish writers. Books by non–Jewish authors, some partly sympathetic, some offensive, were available as well. Joseph Pennell, an American etcher and close friend of Whistler, wrote and illustrated an account of his visit to eastern Europe, *The Jew at Home, Impressions of a Summer and Autumn Spent with Him*, 1892. What seemed to irritate him most was that the Russian Jew maintained his centuries-old appearance rather than conforming to Western styles of haberdashery, hairiness, or hygiene (Ill. 8:40).

Back-to-back Talmud editions appeared in 1864 and 1866. The Viennese court printers Joseph Hrazchansiky and Anton Schmidt published Siddurs, Bibles, and five important Talmud editions in mid-century. The Widow and Brothers Romm, who printed Mapu's novel, turned out hundreds of Yiddish and Hebrew titles, including fine editions of the Babylonian and Palestinian Talmuds. A German translation of *Berachoth*, the first tractate of the Talmud, was published in Berlin in 1842 by Dr. E. M. Pinner, who dedicated it to Czar Nicholas I, the "great monarch, rich in deeds, and high-minded protector of every pure aspiration." To the Jews he was popularly known as Haman II. Perhaps Pinner had hoped to placate him; if that was his motive, it was, unfortunately, futile.

While the Zionist movement urged the teaching of spoken Hebrew as an affirmation of national identity, by contrast, the Socialists supported the study of Yiddish and suggested that Jews seek cultural, rather than political, autonomy. Mark Warshawsky's Yiddish song *Oifen Pripitchik* (*At the Fireplace*) exhorted children to "understand that this alphabet contains the tears and weeping of our people. When you grow weary and burdened with exile, you will find comfort and strength within the Jewish alphabet." Secular Yiddish education grew during the Enlightenment period. The child was groomed to take his place as a citizen in the modern Jewish intellectual and professional worlds of medicine, law, science, art, and music. Many bankers, industrialists, builders of railways, founders of sugar and textile factories, manufacturers of clothing and shoes, emerged from the Yiddish experience.

Only a few interesting Haggadot were produced during the nineteenth century in central and eastern Europe; presumably readers didn't object to the repetitions of earlier models. In most homes, each Seder participant now had his or her own copy, which made the publishers happy. An early example appeared in 1819 in Ostrog, Russia, repeating the engravings of

THE RUSSIAN JEW.

Ill. 8:40. *The Russian Jew*, from *The Jew at Home, Impressions of a Summer and Autumn Spent with Him*. Etching, 1892. By Joseph Pennell

Ill. 8:41. *Jews at the Seder Table.* **Engraving, 1864. Trieste Haggadah**

the Amsterdam versions in woodcuts. Also of interest, but only as an eccentric curiosity, is the Berlin Haggadah of 1830 in Hebrew and Yiddish, notable for its Christian proselytizing—"to rouse the hearts of Jewish children to seek the path of salvation." A Hebrew-German version in 1840 with commentaries by Samson Raphael Hirsch was of particular value to the Orthodox community. The only truly innovative Haggadah of the century was produced in 1864 in Trieste, Italy, by Joshua Cohen and Abraham Hayyim Morpurgo. Here was a non-derivative edition, larger in size than most, no longer totally dependent for its illustrations on either Venice or Amsterdam prototypes. Of the fifty-eight engravings by K. Kirchmayer, the most startling depicts Moses kneeling before the disembodied face of God in the burning bush, a singular apparition in a Hebrew book published and edited by Jews. While most of the plates were based on earlier images, the participants around the Seder table are shown in contemporary dress, looking alert, and interacting in a lively way (Ill. 8:41).

All in all, the nineteenth century in central Europe and Russia (like those before and after) witnessed the highs of scholarship and the lows of prejudice and fear. Efforts to build progressive societies never faltered. Conservative or reactionary interests never slept. Repressive policies and pogroms in the Old World led more than three million Jewish immigrants to the New. Of those that remained, six hundred thousand were in Germany, two million in Austro-Hungary, and five million in Russia. Most of them probably hoped that their children and grandchildren would be able to live in those lands in peace and prosperity—at least from time to time.

9

America in the Nineteenth Century: Immigration and Liberation

Thomas Jefferson, the "Man of the People," took office on the new Democrat-Republican ticket in 1801 after Alexander Hamilton swung the tied vote away from Aaron Burr. The election was seen as a triumph of the Declaration of Independence and majority rule over government by the privileged class. The capital moved from Philadelphia to the District of Columbia, still undeveloped and beset with yellow fever and cholera; amenities were lacking, and members of Congress had to scramble to find housing. With the push towards the frontier, Native Americans were expelled, the social system based on slavery was expanded, and forests were turned into cities. Some settlers prospered and built homes filled with gracious, imported furnishings; more lost everything to Indian raids and an unyielding wilderness.

Out of a total population of about five million, Jefferson became president of some two thousand Jews. Early in his administration, he reappointed Reuben Etting as United States Marshal for Maryland, although according to that state's constitution Jews were prohibited from holding public office. (Washington had originally appointed Etting to the post in 1791.) When he named Solomon Nones as consul to Portugal, he may have wondered how that Inquisition government would respond to the presence of an avowed Jew. In his later years Jefferson urged Jews to pursue secular information "to keep pace with the advances of time" and to become "equal objects of respect and favor." (He acknowledged, however, that he was "little acquainted with the liturgy of the Jews or their mode of worship.")

Jefferson's predecessor, John Adams, also kept up with Jewish issues. Taking up his pen against Voltaire's jaundiced views, he wrote to Judge Francis Adrian van der Kemp in 1808: "How is it possible this old fellow should represent the Hebrews in such a contemptible light? If I were an atheist and believed in blind eternal fate, I would still believe that fate had ordained the Jews to be the most essential instrument for civilizing the nations.... They have given religion to three-quarters of the globe and have influenced the affairs of mankind more and more happily than any other nation, ancient or modern." At the same time, he admitted that he "found it very hard work to love most of them."

His distant relative Hannah Adams, the first professional woman writer in America, authored the *History of the Jews from the Destruction of Jerusalem to the Nineteenth Century* in 1812, the first book on the subject of Jews in America. Although generally accurate and sympathetic, it was not altogether comforting since, as an associate of the Society for the Promotion of Christianity Among the Jews in America, she advocated the conversion of religious Jews. (The irreligious were dismissed as lost causes, although she worried that their lack of faith might infect weak-minded Christians.) Other self-appointed missionary groups, such as the American Society for Meliorating the Condition of the Jews, imposed their own agendas, notwithstanding that in 1820 in all America there were barely three thousand members of that wicked race. In his anti–Semitic tract disarmingly named *Israel's Advocate*, the society's founder, the apostate Joseph Frey, complained that Jews not only resisted conversion but refused to relocate to communities where brainwashing could be administered. That no such communities ever existed evidently didn't deter him or the others who took his evangelical movement seriously.

Rebuttals such as "*A defense of Judaism against all adversaries, and particularly against the insidious attacks of Israel's Advocate*" appeared in 1823 in *The Jew*, the country's earliest periodical of its kind, published by Solomon Henry Jackson, the first Jewish printer in New York. Jackson, possessing both English and Hebrew type fonts, produced the first printed Hebrew and English Siddur in America for Sephardi congregations in 1826, and in 1845 became the first American Jew to publish the Hebrew Bible in an English translation, giving American Jews an alternative to the King James version. He committed the power of the press to warding off intolerance and ignorance, hammering away at deceptive readings of the Hebrew Bible and challenging the missionary zeal of the Society for the Conversion of Jews until that organization effectively surrendered. *The Jew* tried to combat conversionary efforts, but its efforts were short-lived, 1823 to 1825.

There were other accounts of Jewish life as well as conversionary arguments. Isaac Gomez, scion of a famous family, collected a few uplifting tales for his *Selections of a Father for the Use of His Children*, 1820, the first children's book by an American Jew. An amusing satire, *Gotham and the Gothamites*, by Samuel Judah, a popular but critically discredited playwright and self-hating Jew, appeared three years later, needling some of New York's choicest worthies. Litigation being a conditioned reflex, he was promptly sued for defamation and clapped into prison. Luckily, he enjoyed enough poor health to gain his release, whereupon he became counsel to the New York Supreme Court.

In politics, Joel Hart was elected to the New York State Senate; David Emanuel (possibly baptized), became governor of Georgia in 1802; and, in the same year, Simon Levy received his degree as part of West Point's first graduating class. Myer Moses and Chapman Levy of South Carolina, respectively, served in that state's House and Senate. David Levy Yulee of Florida was the first Jewish United States congressman, elected to the Senate in 1841; Lewis Charles Levin made it to the House of Representatives three years later. Rebecca Gratz, a Philadelphia philanthropist and early feminist, founded the Female Hebrew Benevolent Society in 1819, a Sunday school system for Jewish children, and the Jewish Home and Orphan Asylum in 1838. A renowned beauty, she sat for Thomas Sully among other famous artists, and was reputed to be the model for the heroine in Sir Walter Scott's *Ivanhoe*. Although she spoke out against conversion, such was the spirit of the times, that there were no Jews among her descendants.

The first known Jewish school or Talmud Torah was established in New York in 1808. Some non–Jewish scholars began to study Hebrew as part of a general renewed religious zeal. Particularly useful was the first Hebrew dictionary to appear in America: Samuel Pike's 1802 reprint of a 1766 London edition, *A Compendious Hebrew Lexicon Adapted to the English Language and Composed Upon a New Commodious Plan to Which Is Annexed a Brief Account of the Contribution and Rationale of the Hebrew Tongue*. Clement C. Moore, an Episcopalian minister and professor of Hebrew, compiled his own *Compendious Lexicon of the Hebrew Language* in 1809. (He was probably not the author of the poem beginning "Twas the Night before Christmas," although he took credit for it. That honor apparently belongs to a Boston farmer, Major Henry Livingston Jr.)

An American edition of the Psalms, *Liber Psalmorum Hebraica*, with verses in Hebrew and Latin, was issued by the Harvard College press in 1809. A Jewish printer, Jonathan Horowitz, brought the type for the first Hebrew Bible in America from Amsterdam and arranged for its publication in Philadelphia by Thomas Dobson in 1814. Although the two-volume set sold for nearly fourteen dollars, a high price at the time, Harvard and Andover Protestant divinity schools each bought forty copies for their entry-level students.

Meanwhile, American relations with England were deteriorating. War broke out in 1812 over free-trade issues, maritime rights, and the abduction of sailors into the British navy. English forces reached the capital and set fire to the White House. First Lady Dolley Madison lost her ball gowns, but saved her parrot and Gilbert Stuart's famous portrait of George Washington. Because many of the books in the Library of Congress were destroyed, Jefferson sold it his own collection, including seven volumes of Jewish interest. The invaders marched as far as Baltimore, but were driven back after a desperate fight in which bombs burst in air giving proof through the night that our flag was still there.

In 1813, President James Madison appointed one of his strongest supporters, Mordechai Manuel Noah, a twenty-eight-year-old journalist, politician, and playwright as consul to Tunis. But when James Monroe, then secretary of state, reported that "it was not known that the religion you profess would form an obstacle to the exercise of your Consular function," Noah was dismissed in spite of having saved American hostages from Berber pirates. He subsequently found careers as Tammany boss, newspaper publisher, sheriff, and acclaimed public speaker on behalf of his fellow Jews. On his becoming a judge, a detractor remarked "What a pity that Christians should be hung by a Jew." Replied Noah, "What a pity that Christians should have to be hung."

In 1819 he wrote *Travels in England, France, and Spain, and the Barbary States in the Years 1813–15*, the first book on overseas diplomacy by an American Jew. It included four etched views of the areas to which he had been assigned, in addition to Gimbrede's stipple portrait of the author (Ill. 9:1). He is chiefly remembered as a proto–Zionist visionary who, in 1825, dedicated himself to the establishment of Ararat—a Jewish homeland near Buffalo which he helped purchase—"until the Jews can recover their ancient rights and dominions, and take their rank among governments of the earth." Berated for assuming a quasi-messianic role, he was reminded that the Prophet was expected to lead Jews to "New Jerusalem and not to New York." However, an early seed for Jewish nationhood was planted; over seventy years later, others redeemed it.

Noah's first cousin, Uriah Phillips Levy, a cabin boy at the age of ten, later became the first American Jewish naval officer; in spite of his official duties, he remained a Sabbath observer and hung a mezuzah on his door. Challenged to a duel by an officer who taunted him with anti–Jewish slurs, he refused to return fire until slightly wounded; at that point he shot and killed his opponent. A pugnacious fellow, he was court-martialed six times; twice President Monroe reversed the charges. Although he eventually became commander of the Mediterranean fleet—the highest rank possible—the

Ill. 9:1. *Mordechai Manuel Noah.* Stipple engraving, 1819. By Gimbrede

secretary of the navy remarked that while he appreciated Levy's competence, he nevertheless held him guilty of "being of the Jewish persuasion." For the "improvement of the efficiency of the Navy" he was removed from service. Taking the case to a naval court, Levy demanded to know whether "my retirement will improve the smugness of certain officers and reinforce their prejudices." After a lengthy trial he was reinstated. For long years, he had opposed the brutal discipline meted out to sailors for infractions of duty. After much resistance, he finally succeeded in getting Congress to annul those measures, becoming widely known as the father of the law to abolish flogging and corporal punishment. In 1836 he bought Monticello, Thomas Jefferson's debt-ridden home, which he restored and willed to the government as a gift to the American people. His full-length portrait hangs there today. (Jefferson had assured Levy in writing that he decried anti–Jewish attitudes; in 1990, that note sold at auction for almost half a million dollars, breaking all records for autographed letters.)

By now, many Jews could feel with some satisfaction that they were being woven into the American fabric, not only because they had fought well against the British and had given financial support to the young country, but because they were moving into the mainstream of public life. Still, a sense of unease hung over them, and, although most remained privately Jewish, in public they adopted secular customs with such eagerness that rabbis feared the erosion of religious practices would put an end to established traditions. In many cases, they were right. Once romance insinuated itself, intermarriage moved Jews from the fringes of Gentile society right into Gentile bedrooms. But neither patriotism nor matrimony was enough to stunt a festering discrimination. The editor of *The New-York American*, Charles King, troubled by Jewish participation in communal affairs, accused Jews of dual loyalty, lacking "a single national attachment ... which makes them the exclusive patriot of their own country."

A spurt in the Jewish population to about fifteen thousand helped create a burgeoning English and Hebrew press. The myth of the Lost Tribes persisted in books such as Israel Worsley's *A View of the American Indians ... Shewing Them to Be the Descendants of the Ten Tribes of Israel*, 1828, and Mrs. Barbara Anne Simon's *The Ten Tribes of Israel Historically Identified with the Aborigines of the Western Hemisphere*, 1836. Joseph Aaron's *Key to the Hebrew Language*, 1834, the Christian Hebraist William L. Roy's *A Complete Hebrew and English Critical and Pronouncing Dictionary*, 1837, the first of its kind printed in the United States, and the leading Jewish Hebraist Isaac Nordheimer's *A Critical Grammar of the Hebrew Language*, 1838, were important aids to scholarship. Roy's work was particularly interesting, having received from Rabbi Enoch Zundel the first rabbinic approbation in a book published in America. Zundel had arrived in New York in 1832 from Eretz Yisrael carrying an appeal to Mordechai Manuel Noah, by then the most prominent Jew in America, to help the "wretched state of the children ... hungry, thirsty, and naked," as well as to raise fifty thousand dollars to pay off Turkish extortion demands. Roy translated the petition into English, and it subsequently appeared in several newspapers, including the *New York Christian Intelligencer*. Such was its reception that both Jewish and Christian congregations offered aid, while the artist, A. A. Hoffay, satisfied the call for Rabbi Zundel's portrait in 1833, the first published engraving of a contemporary Jew in the United States.

Solomon Jackson published the first successful Jewish monthly periodical, *The Occident and American Jewish Advocate*, 1843–1869, "devoted to the diffusion of knowledge in Jewish literature and religion," including social and secular information for Jews in widely scattered communities. It was founded by Isaac Leeser, an early exponent of Conservative Judaism and general factotum of the Mikveh Israel Synagogue in Philadelphia. It railed at the atrocities during the 1840 Damascus affair when charges of ritual murder were leveled against Jews. That incident mobilized intense cooperation among Jewish leaders, as well as an international protest by the U.S. State Department.

Leeser initiated the use of English in synagogue sermons, instituted afternoon classes in Jewish studies for children unavoidably attending missionary schools, fought for a public educational system that would affirm the doctrine of separation of Church and State, and self-published the *Instruction in the Mosaic Religion* in 1830 when he could find no one to undertake the financial risk; it was the first such manual prepared for American Jews. His edition of the Torah, a fifteen-year undertaking, was published in five volumes in 1845; it was the first translation of the Pentateuch into the English language by a Jew, and remained the American model until 1917 when the Jewish Publication Society issued its own edition. He had founded the society in 1845 with the expectation that Jews would "obtain a knowledge of the faith and proper weapons to defend it against assaults of proselyte-makers on the one side and of infidels on the other," as well as with the hope of "placing a mass of good reading within the reach of even the poorest families." (A fire closed down its building after six years; it reopened briefly from 1873 to 1875, and expanded its mandate in 1888 with the publication of literary, scientific, religious, and history books.) In 1848, Leeser published the first complete English translation of the Sephardic Siddur in America, and during the Civil War secured the appointment, against considerable opposition, of a Jewish chaplain. Congress had authorized only Christians.

Because many European Jews believed they would be included in the new human rights programs that Napoleon had initiated, immigration to America had fallen off in the period following the French Revolution, but his defeat in 1815 and the reintroduction of discriminatory laws cured them of that fantasy. With the outbreak of revolutions in 1830 and 1848, attacks against Jews in and out of the ghettos began once more; thousands gathered their belongings and turned to the West. Among the families and friends who encouraged their flight was the poet Penina Moise whose *Fancy's Sketch Book*, published in Charleston in 1833, was the first printed literary work by an American Jewess: "If thou art one of that oppressed race, Whose pilgrimage from Palestine we trace, Brave the Atlantic...."

Brave the Atlantic they did. While most settled in New York, thanks to the newly built roads, canals, and railroads, others found their way to Philadelphia, Baltimore, Cincinnati, Chicago, St. Louis, and a dozen other cities where they sometimes attracted unflattering attentions. Fortunately, wide open frontiers offered the opportunity to spread to less populated areas where they made themselves invaluable in international marketing and trade as well as in merchandising, peddling, and cotton jobbing. Some immigrants headed south, where small-town lifestyles seemed familiar; those finding homes in the North soon adapted to its commercial interests. When gold was discovered in California in 1848, a quarter of a million enterprising men went west to hack out boom-or-bust mining towns. Few Jews, however, were among the prospectors. Most opened shops or provided banking and other necessary services. Although some discarded their Jewish identification, many continued to observe religious customs despite the obvious difficulties. Alexander Isev's *California Hebrew and English Almanac*, 1851, helped locate congregations and kosher food in border towns and provided the correct time for lighting Sabbath candles. Until more suitable facilities came along, High Holidays services were observed in tents; circumcisions were performed in log cabins.

A few states were slow to grant Jews full-class citizenship, conveniently forgetting—or refusing to acknowledge—that Jews were equals under the Constitution. Not until 1826 did Maryland allow professing Jews to hold public office. Connecticut waited two hundred twenty years before Puritan resistance was overcome and Jews were able to form a synagogue in 1843; North Carolina and New Hampshire were the last to drop the oath "on the faith of a true Christian." before Jews could hold office. In 1849, Secretary of State Daniel Webster applauded "that extraordinary people who preserved through darkness and idolatry of so many centuries ... our own character and destiny as intelligent, moral and responsible people." With such

Ill. 9:2. *The Peddler's Wagon.* Wood-engraving, c. 1850

champions, it was no wonder that Jews remained grateful to America, building its assets in law, medicine, and education, and pursuing its development.

As the number of Jews increased across the nation, interest in Jewish matters generated markets for literary and religious texts. Business, commercial, and religious news items were featured in Robert Lyon's *The Asmonean*, 1849. Simon Tuska's *The Stranger in the Synagogue*, 1854, provided insights into Jewish customs and ceremonies. Joshua Falk's *Avnei Yehoshu'a*, a commentary on Pirke Avoth, 1860, was the first original rabbinic text written and published in America. The colophon by its typesetter, Naphtali ben Katriel Samuel, expressed thanks for the good fortune that enabled him to produce a trailblazing work.

The popular press, too, was invaluable in providing information and entertainment to outlying communities. Artist-correspondents were dispatched to chronicle the everyday experiences of interesting individuals. Sentimental or decorative wood-engravings of ethnic Americana—idealizing or demeaning—filled the books and news-sheets that were hauled to frontier towns on the weary backs of Jewish peddlers. Isolated settlers depended on these itinerant salesmen who supplied manufactured goods, reading matter, and small household items. A wood-engraving, *The Peddler's Wagon*, c. 1850, depicts such a tradesman with his cart and worn-out horse offering his wares to an eager family (Ill. 9:2). A few went on to establish large firms. During the 1850s and '60s, Levi Strauss made a fortune marketing canvas work pants; in the '70s he offered seam-riveted overalls guaranteed not to tear when packed with gold nuggets. Morris Rich opened the first department store chain in the South in 1867. Meyer Guggenheim developed metal polishes that he sold on his routes along with spices and lace; after switching to mining and metallurgy, his family became one of the wealthiest in America, establishing eponymous art museums in New York and Venice as well as funding numerous charities. A wood-engraving of 1859 explored the variety of goods to be had in L. J. Levy's shop

Ill. 9:3. *L. J. Levy's Shop.* Wood-engraving, 1859

in Philadelphia (Ill. 9:3). The Bloomingdale brothers opened their store in midtown Manhattan in 1886, followed by Adam Gimbel and the Straus clan (Macy's and Abraham & Straus), all of whom turned from peddling to building vast emporiums where milady and her gentleman could find the finest-quality goods available.

When the Civil War erupted, approximately nine thousand Jews, including nine generals, took up arms—some seven thousand from the North and two thousand from the South. They served with distinction and sacrifice on both sides of the struggle; geography generally was the factor that influenced conformity or dissent to the question of slavery. Impassioned speeches, mobs, and even murders attempted to sway those who stood either for or against the private ownership of human beings. Max Lilienthal, an abolitionist rabbi in New York, received a letter in 1861 from a Confederate captain, Jacob Cohen, stating that before he was aware of Lilienthal's anti-slavery views he had hung a lithograph of the rabbi on his home (Ill. 9:4). Now he mailed it to the rabbi, venting his feelings in a note written across the print: "Sir: Since you have discarded the Lord and taken up the Sword in defense of a Negro government—your picture which has occupied a place in our Southern home, we return herewith, that you may present it to your beloved Black Friends, as it will not be permitted in our dwelling ... I shall be engaged actively in the field and should be happy to rid Israel of the disgrace of your life...." Cohen was killed in the Battle of Manassas.

The Reverend Morris Raphall, author of an 1852 prayer book for women and the first rabbi to open a session in Congress, in 1861 addressed his well-to-do Ashkenazi New York congregation, B'nai Jeshurun, on the "Bible View of Slavery." Arguing that involuntary servitude was justified, he preached the only known pro-slavery Jewish sermon. Although his views were widely quoted to claim Jewish support for secession, David Einhorn, rabbi of Baltimore's Reform Har Sinai Temple, strongly censured him, pointing out that the variety of slavery practiced in America, where four million Negroes had virtually no legal rights, bore little resemblance to the ancient protections provided by Jewish law. It was a brave, but dangerous

Ill. 9:4. *Max Lilienthal.* Lithograph, c. 1860

rebuttal in that pro-slavery city; forced out by his congregation, he accepted the pulpit of Philadelphia's Keneseth Israel, where he continued to lecture about "defenseless human beings reduced to a condition of chattels"—particularly by a people having suffered that ignominy themselves. Einhorn and Rabbi Bernard Felsenthal were outspoken Abolitionists, but for the most part the rabbinate, uneasy as representatives of a controversial minority group, hesitated to appear assertive, and remained politically ineffective until the war was under way.

The most colorful Jewish politician of the time was Judah P. Benjamin of Louisiana, the first Jew to be elected to the United States Senate. Having earlier turned down the ambassadorship to Spain, he became Jefferson Davis' secretary of state in 1862. Widely known as the "brains of the Confederacy," Benjamin was the only member of the Cabinet who no longer owned slaves, although he branded abolitionists as "insane fanatics." When the North began to win battle after battle, Southerners, needing a scapegoat—and a Jewish one at that—blamed him for food shortages, inflation, and casualties. Senator (later, President) Andrew Johnson was quoted as saying that Benjamin would sell out either side if "he could in so doing make two or three millions." A Confederate congressman, Henry Foote, suggested that "if the present state of things were to continue, the end of the war would probably find nearly all the property of the South in the hands of Jewish Shylocks." Faced with accusations of treason, illegal money transfers to his personal accounts, causing the South's defeat, and even complicity in the assassination of Lincoln, he was branded with the epithet "Judah Iscariot." Although Benjamin was not a practicing Jew, when Senator Ben Wade of Ohio sneered at his race, he urged "the gentleman to please remember that when his half-civilized ancestors were hunting wild boar in the forests of Silesia, mine were the Princes of the earth." (Prime Minister Disraeli of Great Britain is credited with a similar remark in 1835 under similar circumstances.) *Harper's Pictorial History of the Civil War*, published in Chicago in 1866, claimed that "Mr. Benjamin, as is indicated by his name, and still more by his face, belongs to that keen and aspiring Hebrew race which for the last half-century has wielded an influence on Christendom altogether disproportionate to its numbers." Actually, his name and his face were already familiar, having been engraved on the Confederate two-dollar bill. When the South capitulated, he feared legal charges related to treason and Lincoln's murder and fled to England, where he established a distinguished law career.

Some military figures, as well as congressmen, shared anti–Jewish biases. Union General Henry Halleck linked "traitors and Jew peddlers," General William Sherman predicted that "the country will soon swarm with dishonest Jews," and General Ulysses S. Grant accused Jews in his encampments of speculating illegally in the cotton market. Lincoln had permitted limited cotton trade across the Mason-Dixon line since Northern textile mills were dependent on Southern cotton. Although a far smaller percentage of Jews than Gentiles were engaged in the profiteering, that didn't stop Grant from calling "Israelites" such "an intolerable nuisance that the department must be purged of them." Harassed by demands for licenses from everyone (probably including his own father), Grant, convinced that Jews were responsible for the black market in cotton, signed Order Number Eleven in 1862, expelling "the Jews, as a class ... from the department territory ... within twenty-four hours from the receipt of this order. Post commanders will see that all of this class of people be furnished passes and required to leave, and anyone returning after such notification will be arrested and held in confinement until an opportunity occurs of sending them out as prisoners, unless furnished with permit from headquarters. No passes will be given these people to visit headquarters for the purpose of making personal application for trade permits." When a howl of protest reached Lincoln, he immediately rescinded the order, although by then many had already been forcibly ejected. Jews recognized a great friend in the president and mourned his assassination. During the Passover holiday of 1865, black curtains hung in synagogues and memorial prayers were added to services. Grant later regretted his intemperance, and by way of apology appointed several Jews to important offices in his administration, and in 1869 successfully persuaded the Russian government to halt the banishment of some twenty thousand Jews.

Thanks to American commercial, industrial, and economic development following the war, Jews were able to share the boom in merchandising, banking, manufacturing, and import and export businesses. Congressional regulation of patents expedited dozens of inventions that changed the ways in which men grew their food and produced their necessities. Elevated railways built in the late 1870s moved people up and down the length of Manhattan, while the opening of the Brooklyn Bridge in 1883, spanning the East River and linking Manhattan to Long Island by way of Brooklyn and Queens, enabled many immigrants to relocate in Harlem at the northern end of Manhattan, as well as to the Bronx and Brooklyn. The reshaping of the economy brought about undreamed-of prosperity, often at the price of human mental and physical misery.

Jewish life, too, moved into uncharted areas. Some sixty congregations existed in New York City alone, competing for membership with fraternal orders and secular organizations such as Hebrew Benevolent Societies and B'nai Brith. Association with a synagogue was chiefly a personal decision. In a pluralistic nation, Jews of all denominations were able, if not to melt into the American pot, at least to form an important element in its variegated stew. It seemed as though they were finally becoming respected as a people who shared common interests and needs with their fellow citizens. Distinguished authors William Cullen Bryant, William Dean Howells, and Mark Twain wrote enthusiastically about them. Herman Melville, in his book-length poem, *Clarel*, 1876, expressed sympathy for Jews in Palestine. Henry Wadsworth Longfellow dealt with a talmudic legend in *Sandalphon*, 1858, included Jewish characters in his *Tales of a Wayside Inn*, 1863, and examined the conflict between Judaism and Hellenism in *Judas Maccabeus*, 1872. During his earlier travels to Newport, Rhode Island, in 1854, he wandered through its Jewish cemetery:

> How came they here? What burst of Christian hate,
> What persecution, merciless and blind,
> Drove o'er the sea—that desert desolate—
> These Ishmaels and Hagars of mankind?
> They lived in narrow streets and lanes obscure,
> Ghetto and Judenstrass, in murk and mire;
> Taught in the school of patience to endure
> The life of anguish and the death of fire.
>
> But ah! What once has been shall be no more!
> The groaning earth in travail and in pain
> Brings forth its races, but does not restore,
> And the dead nations never rise again.

Luckily, his crystal ball was clouded over.

Yet for many other individuals, the perception of Jews remained negative. The rabbinate tried to counter prejudice through education and social acculturation, beginning with the first Jewish day school in 1842 in the B'nai Jeshurun Synagogue on Manhattan's Elm Street. Not succeeding too well, they attempted at least to insure Jews a safe and secure place in society. The historian Henry Adams noted in 1879: "I have now seen enough of Jews and Moors to entertain more liberal views in regard to the Inquisition, and to feel that, though the ignorant may murmur, the Spaniards saw and pursued a noble aim." While Lew Wallace in his popular novel *Ben-Hur*, 1880, didn't advise harassing Jews, he saw in Judaism little more than the starting post to Christianity.

But with a determination to survive and grow, Jews continued to invest in a variety of synagogue institutions. The second oldest American congregation, Beth Elohim, had been dedicated in 1794 in Charleston, South Carolina by the city's four hundred Jews. Thirty years later it had become the largest, richest, and most discontented Jewish religious community in the country. When half of its members asked for, and were denied a more liberal constitution, they seceded in 1824 and set up the Reformed Society of Israelites. It was the beginning of denominational Judaism in America. English replaced Hebrew in most of the prayers, decorum replaced "disrespectful" behavior, the sale of honors or privileges gave way to formal dues, shorter services were instituted, and head coverings were abandoned; basic theological tenets,

Ill. 9:5. *Beth Elohim Synagogue.* Lithograph, c. 1838, after a drawing by Salomon Nunes Carvahlo

however, were not refuted. Ironically, the reformers dissolved their group nine years later when Beth Elohim adopted some of their practices. The trustees then commissioned the Sephardic artist Salomon Nunes Carvahlo to create a memento of the synagogue, but unfortunately, his drawings turned out to be memorials when it was accidentally destroyed by fire in 1838; a lithograph of the exterior after his drawing is all that remains of the graceful structure (Ill. 9:5).

When a new temple was erected in 1840, it boasted a Neo-Classical façade, joint seating for men and women, and a hotly contested organ, the first to be installed in an American synagogue. It is the oldest surviving Reform building in the world. Cantor Gustav Poznanski, in a burst of New World chauvinism, expressed its watchword: "This country is our Palestine, this city our Jerusalem, this house of God our Temple." Rabbi Leo Merzbacher provided the movement with a shortened prayer-book in 1855, and in the following year, the first German-language liturgical work, *Gesänge* (*Hymns and Psalms*) for Reform Jews was published in Philadelphia.

The Orthodox Beth Jeshurun congregation, formed in 1825 as an offshoot of the Sephardi Shearith Israel, was housed in a former Protestant evangelical church where, no longer dominated by Spanish-Portuguese leadership, the members followed the German tradition. Rabbinic authorities considered such recycled buildings a "sanctification of God's name."

Elaborate synagogues arose in the second half of the century wherever there was an affluent congregation. Many adopted the popular Moorish Revival style, often overlaid with a hodge-podge of Gothic, Byzantine, or Romanesque embellishments; the fashion evoked the glory days of medieval Spain, or perhaps the Oriental spirit that was considered quintessentially "Jewish."

Philadelphia's Romanesque-Moorish Mikveh Israel, 1860, resembled earlier European synagogues, as did the first Byzantine-Moorish Revival synagogue, B'nai Jeshurun, 1866, in Cincinnati. The bulbous-domed Emanu-El in San Francisco, completed in the same year, prominently displayed the Star of David and the Tablets of the Law until it was destroyed in an earthquake in 1906. New York's Emanu-El, 1868, at Fifth Avenue and Forty-third Street, was generally acknowledged as the last word in religious architecture with its five hundred gas jets lighting gilded and colorful ornaments; a wood-engraving in *Harper's Weekly* made at its dedication hardly exaggerated the soaring Romanesque-inspired structure (Ill. 9:6). It cost over eight hundred thousand dollars, but the congregation was in no mood to begrudge the visions of its famous architects, Leopold Eidlitz (a Jew) and Henry Fernbach. Twenty-three hundred seats accommodated the cream of New York's Ashkenazim until it was torn down in 1927 and replaced two years later by an even grander building on upper Fifth Avenue designed by Robert Kohn, Charles Butler, and Clarence Stein. When Fernbach's somewhat smaller Central Synagogue on Lexington Avenue was consecrated in 1872 with stained glass windows, Moorish twin towers, and thirteen golden domes, its fifteen hundred worshippers sat under a sixty-two-foot-high ceiling that echoed back the peal of its great organ.

The Sephardic community, having outgrown its earlier homes in lower New York, turned to Arnold Brunner, the first American-born Jewish architect of note, to reflect the aristocratic status of America's oldest congregation, Shearith Israel. Its lustrous marble and velvet interior and Greco-Roman exterior in the style of ancient Palestinian synagogues was dedicated in 1897 on Central Park West. Over two hundred synagogues served American Jews—only a small number were outside the Reform movement. But whatever the denomination, fewer congregants than rabbis had hoped for showed up, and many of those came for socialization rather than spiritual refreshment.

Rabbi Isaac Mayer Wise officiated for fifty years at Cincinnati's Reform B'nai Jeshurun beginning in 1854. America had hazzans, but few ordained rabbis until the latter half of the century. Wise listed their duties at the time: "Reader, cantor, ... teacher, butcher, circumciser, blower, gravedigger, secretary.... He read shiur for the departed sinners, and played cards or dominoes with the living; in short, he was a kol-bo, accepted bread, turnips, cabbage, potatoes as a gift, and peddled in case his salary was not sufficient."

Wise believed that "the object of Judaism is not political nor national, but spiritual," and that "doctrines inconsistent with reason are no longer tenable" because they hindered Jews from assimilating easily into American culture. He introduced mixed choirs and family pews, and championed the emancipation of women with the publication of the German-language weekly *Die Deborah*, 1855, the first Jewish magazine catering to their interests. He provided a platform for lectures by Ernestine Rose on women's rights, abolition, and public education. She had been influential in passing a bill in 1848 to allow married women to own property in New York, and had organized numerous campaigns on feminist issues. Born into an Orthodox rabbinical family, she married non–Jewish husbands. A portrait engraving of the free-thinking lady who spoke of herself "a child of Israel ... and the downtrodden and persecuted people called the Jews" made the rounds in 1857.

Wise's radical edition of the Siddur, *Minhag America* (*American Customs*), 1857, in English, German, and Hebrew was intended to invigorate and unify liberal congregations. In 1873, he merged thirty-four Reform temples into the Union of Hebrew Congregations, and crowned his efforts in 1875 by matriculating thirteen students in the rabbinical seminary Hebrew Union College; of the original group, which included an eleven-year-old girl, four graduated and went on to serve as the first American-trained rabbis in America. Unfortunately, his dream of reconciling the various denominational movements backfired at a HUC dinner in 1883 at which non-kosher food was served. Traditionalist rabbis walked out.

Ill. 9:6. *Temple Emanu-El.* Wood-engraving, 1868. From *Harper's Weekly*

His "Americanization" of Judaism at the Pittsburgh Conference in 1885 marked the principles that defined Classical Reform Judaism for the next fifty years. Its platform declared that Judaism was no longer a nation, but an evolving religious community. It denied the divinity of the Bible and the role of the Messiah, abolished sacrificial prayers, eliminated the practice of kashruth, and refuted the Zionist belief that the recovery of Palestine and the rebuilding of the Temple were the goals of all Jews. Morality and ethics were designated ultimate Jewish values; social justice, freedom of choice, and scientific progress were to take precedence over traditional observances. The platform was adopted by the newly formed Central Conference of American Rabbis in 1889.

Such unconventional views flew in the face of those who believed in the divine origin of the Torah and practiced the unchanging rituals of halachah. In 1885, Rabbi Alexander Kohut of New York's Ahavath Chesed Synagogue defined Reformism as "a skeleton of Judaism without ... spirit and heart." Others raised the question, "We know what they are against, but what are they for?" Not receiving a satisfactory answer, Orthodoxy continued to stress its own achievements, remained confident of its authenticity, prided itself on its exclusive devotion to God's word, and, unexpectedly, was fortified by Reform's extremism as well as the perception of a "forsaken" Judaism. The movement's weekly newspaper, *American Hebrew*, in 1879 introduced a modern American Orthodoxy in Yeshiva University in 1886 to teach both Jewish and secular subjects. But its constituency began to decline, unable to compete with permissive standards. Hoping to strengthen its forces, in 1898 it consolidated a variety of groups and institutions under the umbrella of the Union of Orthodox Jewish Congregations of America, a loosely bound organization that provided programs and guidelines for its affiliates.

A compromise filled the middle ground between the formalism of Orthodoxy and the progressivism of Reform. As early as 1853, Isaac Leeser had taken tentative steps towards the establishment of an intermediate position for those Jews who were willing to accept some changes in religious practices as long as they did not invalidate essential principles. He offered sermons and some prayers in English, excluding those he didn't consider mandatory. He established Maimonides College in 1867 as a rabbinic training center. It lasted only six years and failed to graduate a single student. Baltimore's Oheb Shalom, anchored with a strong Zionist policy, was among the first synagogues to accept Leeser's solution to religious dichotomy. Rabbi Benjamin Szold assumed the pulpit. (His daughter, Henrietta, founded the Zionist women's organization Hadassah.) He delivered a famous sermon memorializing Lincoln, edited a new Siddur in 1867 which was adopted by many synagogues, and published a commentary on the Book of Job in 1886.

Following his leadership, Rabbi Sabato Morais helped establish the Conservative Jewish Theological Seminary in 1887. Its rabbinical school in New York, with an initial enrollment of eight students, dispensed the "knowledge and practice of historical Judaism" unattached to the spirit of Orthodoxy or Reformism.

While competition between liberalism and traditionalism was divisive or even acrimonious, the well-loved Haggadah was esteemed by all denominations. In 1837, Leeser published its first translation into English by an American Jew as part of *The Form of Prayers According to the Custom of the Spanish and Portuguese Jews*. It was followed the same year by the first separate printing on the American continent, published by Solomon Jackson in New York, likewise for both Ashkenazi and Sephardi Jewry. But rather than an innovative example, it was actually no more than a Hebrew and English reprint of David Levy's London edition of 1794. L. H. Frank's *New Haggadah*, 1851, introduced a bit of sentimentality with a cover picture of a father and son holding each other's hands (Ill. 9:7). But such close relationships apparently were not very common—at least according to an 1883 Chicago edition by Chaim Lieberman. Disorder now entered the Jewish home. The Wicked Son smokes a cigarette and points a defiant finger at his old-world parents. The Simple Son compounds the insult by raising his thumb to his nose. Fortunately, the Wise Son, skullcap in place, carries on the tradition (Ill. 9:8).

During the Passover season, newspaper reporters, always on the lookout for an offbeat story, discovered the esoteric world of matzo. "A short chapter on some of the usages and observances of the strange people" was offered in *The Jewish Passover of 1858*, in *Frank Leslie's Illustrated Newspaper*, with wood-engravings detailing the stringently regulated manufactur-

Ill. 9:7. *Father and Son Holding Hands.* From *New Haggadah*, 1851. By L. H. Frank

הַגָּדָה שֶׁל פֶּסַח.

יְמֵי חַיֶּיךָ, הָעוֹלָם הַזֶּה. כָּל יְמֵי חַיֶּיךָ, לְהָבִיא
לִימוֹת הַמָּשִׁיחַ:

בָּרוּךְ הַמָּקוֹם בָּרוּךְ הוּא. בָּרוּךְ שֶׁנָּתַן תּוֹרָה

denotes this time only; but ALL the days of thy life, denotes even at the time of the Messiah.

Blessed be the Omnipresent; blessed is he, blessed is he who hath given the law to his people Israel, blessed be he: the

Ill. 9:8. *Four Sons*. Haggadah, 1883. By Chaim Lieberman

ing process and commercial distribution: *A Rabbi Checks the Flour* and *Preparing and Baking Matzes* (Ill. 9:9; Ill. 9:10). The paper went on to describe Jews as "quiet, law-abiding, good citizens; attentive and indefatigable in their various occupations, and among the very best of the adopted citizens of America." For more than fifty years, rabbis questioned whether machine-made matzos allowed fermentation and swelling of the wheat, disallowing its use. Their decision favored its practice.

Above: Ill. 9:9. *A Rabbi Checks the Flour.* Wood-engraving, 1858. From *Frank Leslie's Illustrated Newspaper. Below:* Ill. 9:10. *Preparing and Making Matzes.* Wood-engraving, 1858. From *Frank Leslie's Illustrated Newspaper*

Ill. 9:11. *Passover Seder*, 1889. From *The American Hebrew*. By Arthur Meyer

An unusual Passover Seder was performed by two dozen enterprising soldiers in the midst of Civil War battles. Having received matzos and Haggadot, they sent "parties to forage in the country while others stayed to build a hut for the services.... We obtained two kegs of cider, a lamb, several chickens and some eggs." Since they didn't know which part of the lamb was required, they cooked the whole animal, thus making sure they retained the paschal symbol. A brick served for the charoses, which, "rather hard to digest, reminded us, by looking at it, for what purpose it was intended." They found a weed whose "bitterness exceeded anything our forefathers 'enjoyed.'" It proved so fiery "that we forgot the law authorizing us to drink only four cups, and the consequence was we drank up all the cider." Quite tipsy, one soldier announced that he was Moses, another, Aaron, and another, Pharaoh; soon the three stalwarts "had to be carried to the camp, and there left in the arms of Morpheus.... In the wild woods of West Virginia, away from home and friends, we consecrated and offered up to the ever-loving God of Israel our prayers and sacrifice...."

Quite a different observance, depicted by Arthur Meyer in the *American Hebrew* during Passover, 1889, demonstrated that Jews were as public spirited as any other group in the celebration of George Washington's inaugural centennial; the father of his country was identified with Moses, the father of Judaism, who had also led his people to freedom and independence. A roundel showed the president keeping an eye out for Elijah (Ill. 9:11). And although the Four Sons did not appear at the table, Moses looked down with satisfaction at the assembled family.

The Jewish upper crust of New York, as ready for fun as for ritual, was always happy to find an excuse to dress up and forget cares. At the Academy of Music's *Purim Ball*, depicted in a wood-engraving of 1865, a merry time was had by all, including a reveler outfitted as a Chanukah dreidel (Ill. 9:12). But, true to the tradition of tzeduka, "Charity" was more prominently displayed than "Merry." The previous year's celebration had been given precedence over Civil

Ill. 9:12. *Purim Ball.* Wood-engraving, 1865

War news in the lead column of *The New York Times* with lengthy descriptions of the holiday's biblical history and an extravagant review of the festivities.

The public was entertained for better and worse with prints depicting the gamut of Jewish experiences around the country. *A. Levi's Feed and Livery Stable,* c. 1865, found Jews in the wild west of San Diego, California (Ill. 9:13). In 1872, *Harper's Weekly* printed an engraving by Sol Ettinge, Jr., *Sunday Morning in Central Park—Jews Drinking Mineral Water. Mansfield's Pioneer Newsstand,* c. 1875, a Jewish shop that also sold stationery and toys, appears to fit in comfortably in Tucson, Arizona (Ill. 9:14).

However, regardless of their desire to fit in, as more and more Jews arrived they began to be less and less welcomed. Derisive wood-engravings were regularly served up in *Judge, Harper's Weekly, Puck, Frank Leslie's Illustrated Newspaper* and other magazines that specialized in sharp-edged satire. Typical in its anti–Jewish tone was Ettinge's *Parting with the Wedding Ring,* 1872, in which a desperate Gentile mother bickers with heartless pawnbrokers. In *Taken In!,* the artist, Abbey, lapsed into a caricature of a Jew happily hoodwinking a naive customer (Ill. 9:15). A Southern writer, Cornelius Matthews, who frequented the center of the used-clothing business, compared Jewish high-pressure storekeepers to marauding Indians: "The old Redmen scalped their enemies, the Chatham clothesmen skinned theirs." Another print, *His Special Features,* 1894, describes a gentleman with a large nose derived from a percent sign and with dollar signs for eyebrows (Ill. 9:16). He knows the price of everything, the value of nothing.

The steady flow of printed images was so pervasive that Tammany's William "Boss" Tweed, whose minions effectively ran New York's ward politics, complained in 1871, "My constituents don't know how to read, but they can't help seeing those damned pictures." While most of those damned pictures were reproduced as wood-engravings, other printing techniques, some

Above: Ill. 9:13. *A. Levi's Feed and Livery Stable.* Wood-engraving, 1865. *Below:* Ill. 9:14. *Mansfield's Pioneer Newsstand.* Wood-engraving, c. 1875

TAKEN IN!

Above: Ill. 9:15. *Taken In!* By Abbey. *Below:* Ill. 9:16. *His Special Features*, 1894

"HIS SPECIAL FEATURES."

pioneered or popularized by Jews, were also available. In Philadelphia, Max Rosenthal was among the first to promote color lithography in America. Julius Bien, cartographer and president of B'nai Brith from 1854 to 1857, established a lithographic studio in 1870 that supplied maps and atlases to the United States Census Department. In 1877, Louis and Max Levy introduced photo-engraving to America; the technique unerringly replicated line drawings, almost immediately becoming the standard method of printing photographs, replacing hand-processed wood-engravings.

In 1877, the prominent banker Joseph Seligman was turned away from A. T. Stewart's Grand Union Hotel in Saratoga with the admonition that "no Israelite shall be permitted." (Had he not rejected President Grant's offer seven years earlier, he would have been the first Jewish Secretary of the Treasury.)

Henry Ward Beecher spoke for liberal Christians, as did Bret Harte (who had one Jewish grandparent) in denouncing the hotel's policy. *Harper's, The New York Times*, and other papers ran editorials and cartoons condemning the discrimination. But Mr. Seligman probably was pleased when an unrelated boycott, forcing the sale of Stewart's department store in New York, was followed by purchases of several Saratoga hotels by Jewish interests. The scenario was repeated when developers of Coney Island in New York and other areas attempted to exclude Jews because "we do not like Jews as a class."

Although many still found themselves on the outside looking in, entry to America remained open to millions of Russian, Hungarian, Austro-Hungarian, and Romanian Jews. A *Puck* wood-engraving by Frederick Opper and Joseph Keppler identified Uncle Sam as the Modern Moses; having parted the waters, he is perched on a high cliff welcoming new arrivers—including Jews with hooked noses. Hoping to counter the fear that the Jews would require unprecedented assistance, the American Committee for Ameliorating the Condition of Russian Refugees issued a broadside in 1891: "They do not come in quest of charity; they come not as paupers, seeking alms; they come in search of means to subsist by their own efforts...."

The newcomers had just endured two- or three-week crossings in the bellies of dilapidated, foul-smelling ships, rarely seeing daylight, rarely eating more than herring and potatoes because kosher food was not available. They had fled deprivations of every kind along with slurs that blamed them for the peasant uprisings following the assassination of Czar Alexander in 1881. The crush of refugees expanded to incredible proportions, exacerbating already resentful feelings. Those who were more or less solvent were charged with presumption or greed. An 1882 cartoon from *The Judge* commented on the events at *John Smith's Dry Goods Shop*; now that the bloated Jews had taken over what had once been a fine neighborhood, Mr. Smith quite properly decides to move his sign to choicer surroundings (Ill. 9:17). Anti-immigration prints such as *We Don't Need Imported Beggars*, 1889, became common. *The New York Dispatch* remarked that the stock exchange was filled with "descendants of Shylock."

Ill. 9:17. *John Smith's Dry Goods Shop*. Wood-engraving, 1882. From *Judge*

Such sneers mirrored the environment that denied jobs to Jews in certain professions and approved restrictions of housing and college applications. Signs announcing "No Jews or dogs admitted" were not rare. But, unlike dogs, Jews were demanding to be admitted.

Compounding their disillusionment was the attitude of their established German-American cousins who, embarrassed by their old-world mannerisms and Yiddish speech, kept them at arms length and even agreed that immigration should be limited. Nevertheless, from the comfort of their "up-town" residences and private clubs, the moneyed folks attempted, patronizingly but generously, to Americanize their "down-town" co-religionists and close the cultural gap. Bankers and merchants such as the Seligmans, Kuhns, Loebs, Strauses, Schiffs, and Lehmans opened their checkbooks. Professionally-run organizations oversaw health, education, and self-help agencies, outstripping almost all previous examples of welfare. Groups which drew their members from common cities or towns in Europe or Russia expanded at a tremendous rate, necessitating additional services. Many found them beginning in the 1890s at the Education Alliance, which taught language proficiency, social skills, and gracious manners. From the tot to the tottering, thousands took advantage of its free or low-cost classes. It provided training for a legion of creative artists such as Jerome Myers, Abraham Walkowitz, Jo Davidson, and Jacob Epstein, who worked well into the twentieth century.

Health care was a serious priority. Because doctors had a particularly hard time gaining acceptance in Catholic hospitals, the Jews' Hospital—forerunner of Mount Sinai—was established in New York in 1852, mostly by German Jewish immigrants. (Jewish patients in Catholic institutions were finding that nuns were as adept at missionary work as they were at nursing.) In 1881, the Jewish-run non-sectarian Michael Reese Hospital in Chicago opened with seventy patients. Ten years later, W. A. Rogers' wood-engraving *Home for Aged Hebrews* appeared in *Harper's Weekly* with an accompanying text describing the "beautiful and touching" treatment of the elderly: "I watch a rosy-faced old man who bustles about, notwithstanding he drags a

Ill. 9:18. *Home for Aged Hebrews*. Wood-engraving, 1891. By W. A. Rogers. From *Harper's Weekly*

stiff leg.... That is the happiest looking old man I ever saw" (Ill. 9:18). With the support of Jacob Schiff, Lillian Wald organized the Henry Street Settlement and Visiting Nurse Service in 1895 to provide aid for newcomers of all nationalities and to help the poor shed the "green-horn" stigma. Beginning in 1899, the National Jewish Hospital in Denver offered free medical care to anyone suffering from tuberculosis and chest diseases.

Regardless, the seemingly unstoppable deluge of cheap labor prompted Congress to pass legislation that year reducing the number of yearly immigrants from three hundred forty-six thousand to one hundred sixty-six thousand. Those with physical or mental impairments or who were thought likely to become public charges were returned home. *Indigent Russian Jews*

INDIGENT RUSSIAN JEWS DETAINED AT THE BARGE OFFICE, NEW YORK CITY.—DRAWN FROM LIFE BY MISS G. A. DAVIS

Ill. 9:19. *Indigent Jews Detained at the Barge Office,* 1891. By W. A. Rogers

Ill. 9:20. *The Frightening First Day in New York.* Wood-engraving, 1891

Detained at the Barge Office, 1891, mirrored that anxiety (Ill. 9:19). *The Frightening First Day in New York* was another barrier on the road to deliverance (Ill. 9:20). But once they were past these deterrents, relief organizations stepped in to help the new arrivals. They had paid ten to twenty dollars for their passage; now, with twenty-five dollars in hand, Sabbath candlesticks, a mortar and pestle, and one or two goose-feather pillows in a battered suitcase, they were ready for the golden land that awaited them. Very poignant was the wood-engraving of Jews sailing into the harbor, C.J. Staniland's *Entering a New World—Jewish Refugees from Russia Passing the Colossal Statue,* from *The Graphic,* 1892 (Ill. 9:21). Here was a view of hope and apprehension—bewildered Jews who could only guess at the future.

But by 1893, *Harper's Weekly* was featuring disillusionment on its front page—hope gone, expectations mocked. *Homes of the Poor,* a wood-engraving by T. de Thulstrup, looked in at that life in the one square mile that constituted Manhattan's Lower East Side (Ill. 9:22). The father is overwhelmed. Every apartment has become a factory where "the day isn't twenty-four hours long, it is stitching twelve coats." Elias Howe's invention of the lockstitch sewing machine in 1846, and its development by Isaac Singer and others, brought efficiency as well as the piece-work system and sweatshops to the Lower East Side district that clothed more than half the nation.

The struggle between workers and bosses, most of whom had only yesterday been sewing machine operators themselves, was joined. That an eight-hour day and reasonable working conditions were considered "outrageous and unjustified demands" led to the rise of unions and the proliferation of strikes. Unions fought to improve the state of affairs in the garment, cigar, cap, and shoe-making industries, with which Jews were familiar, having slaved in those jobs in the old country. The Hebrew Immigrant Aid Society (HIAS), the first international agency in America to help with refugee resettlement, was organized by Isaac Wise in 1881. The United Hebrew Trades, founded by Samuel Gompers and others in 1888, had likewise begun to improve the lives of thousands during the period of mass immigration. Nevertheless, parents as well as children as young as six were sucked into squalid lives, working sixty- to seventy-hour weeks for eight to fifteen dollars in deplorably overcrowded neighborhoods, sustaining themselves with meager stocks sold from pushcarts or baskets. *Harper's* in an 1890 issue provided a look at *A Friday Market in the Jewish Quarter of New York,* featuring W. A. Rogers' drawings of these enterprising street merchants: *The Dry Goods District, The Fruit Vender* (*sic*), *The Department*

ENTERING A NEW WORLD
"See the Daystar of Liberty Rise"
JEWISH REFUGEES FROM RUSSIA PASSING THE COLOSSAL STATUE IN NEW YORK HARBOUR

Ill. 9:21. *Entering a New World—Jewish Refugees from Russia Passing the Colossal Statue in New York Harbour.* Wood-engraving, 1892. By C. J. Staniland. From *The Graphic*

HOMES OF THE POOR.—Drawn by T. de Thulstrup.—[See Page 475.]

Ill. 9:22. *Homes of the Poor.* Wood-engraving, 1893. By T. de Thulstrup. From *Harper's Weekly*

of Small Wares, and *The Candle Merchant* (Ill. 9:23; Ill. 9:24). Other immigrants tumbled into prostitution, low-class indiscretions, and high-powered crime. A New York State committee in 1897 referred to Russian and Polish Jews as "the worst element in the entire make-up of New York life."

Whereas three hundred thousand Jews were living in all of the United States in 1878, by 1895 that same number were crammed into New York City's slums. Jacob Riis, author of *How the Other Half Lives,* 1890, commented that "nowhere in the world are so many people crowded together in a square mile," and expressed indignation at their filthy living conditions, poverty, and physical ailments. Those misfortunes were perhaps as great as those left behind, but on the whole they were far better off in their new home than in their old. Many were grateful for free public schools and libraries, Yiddish theaters and Socialist clubs, although some mourned that the traditions of holiday observances, religious training, and close family structures had been bent, if not broken. Children often resented their parents' efforts to maintain the old world culture, were ashamed of their appearance or their Yiddish speech. Parents were torn between resisting change or resigning themselves to situations they neither understood or nor liked.

The welcome mat was withdrawn. The economic depression in 1893, social anti–Semitism, and agitation about importing "cheap labor" from southern and eastern Europe again created a demand—politely rationalized as nationalism or the "American Way"—to restrict the inflow. An immigration bill intended to bar "illiterate undesirables" (i.e. Yiddish-speaking Jews) was vetoed in March, 1897, by President Grover Cleveland as he was about to leave office. Rabble-rousers spread the slogan "Down with the Jews." The dream of Enlightenment was fading. At the end of the century, Zionism became the ideal for many Jews, with over one hundred Zionist organizations in place.

THE DRY-GOODS DISTRICT.   THE FRUIT VENDER.

Ill. 9:23. *The Dry-Goods District; The Fruit Vender.* Wood-engravings, 1890. By W. A. Rogers. From *Harpers Weekly*

THE DEPARTMENT OF SMALL WARES.   THE CANDLE MERCHANT.

A FRIDAY MARKET IN THE JEWISH QUARTER OF NEW YORK.—DRAWN BY W. A. ROGERS.—[SEE PAGE 306.]

Ill. 9:24. *The Department of Small Wares; The Candle Merchant.* **Wood-engravings, 1890. By W. A. Rogers. From** *Harper's Weekly*

A dynamic and aggressive New York Jewish press percolated across the country, attracting readers to every avenue of Jewish interest. *The Jewish Record* appeared in 1868, proud to be the first English-language penny paper. The first Yiddish newspaper in New York, the *Jüdische Zeitung* (*Jewish Times*), 1870, reported on "politics, religion, history, science, and art." The first Hebrew periodical in America, *Ha-Zofeh ba-Erez ha-Hadasha* (*The Observer in the New Land*), was founded in 1871 by Zvi Hirsch Bernstein; it appeared irregularly for five years. *The American Hebrew*, published in 1879 by Philip Cowen, vigorously fought anti–Semitism and provided a public forum for such prominent Jewish leaders as Henrietta Szold, Israel Zangwill, and Emma Lazarus. Kasriel Sarasohn, known as the father of the Yiddish press, produced the first daily Yiddish paper with a wide circulation in 1881, *Die Tegliche Gazeten* (*Daily News*), but it was short-lived. Four years later he started the *Yiddish Tageblatt* (*Yiddish Daily Paper*) in New York, the first successful Yiddish daily, just in time to welcome the Conservative Jewish Theological Seminary, as well as the Yeshivath Etz Chaim, forerunner of Yeshiva University. The *Tageblatt* was followed by many Yiddish papers in addition to a number of secular radical periodicals in the '80s and '90s. Philadelphia's *Jewish Exponent*, 1887, has enjoyed a long history of documenting local news as well as international and Zionist concerns.

From 1885 to century's end, New York alone boasted the arrival and departure of some twenty Yiddish dailies as well as weekly and monthly periodicals with a combined readership of millions. These papers not only responded to the demand for world news and fiction, but for general information, amusement, and guidance as well. The Socialist *Forverts* (*Forward*), founded in 1897 by novelist, labor leader, and journalist Abraham Cahan eventually became the largest Yiddish paper in the world and one of the most interesting American dailies. Perhaps its most popular feature was the *Bintel Brief* (*Bundle of Letters*), the prototype of many advice and lovelorn columns. Thousands of problems were aired, ranging from orneriness to heartache, in-laws who gamble or want to be supported, husbands whose wives talk too much or not at all, lazy daughters who don't or can't cook like Mama, lonely fellows and girls looking for romance in the wrong places, distraught wives looking for wandering husbands, frightened old folks in a strange new world, and troubled people with no one else to turn to. Two of the country's largest general newspapers were *The New York World*, founded in 1883, owned and edited by Joseph (sometimes known as Jewseph) Pulitzer, whose father was Jewish, and *The New York Times*, founded 1896, headed by Adolph Ochs, the son of a volunteer rabbi and pioneer publisher. Their readers could opt for sensationalism (the *World*) or All the News That's Fit to Print (the *Times*).

When August Brentano emigrated from Austria in 1853, he was just another newsboy selling newspapers and magazines on New York streets. But by 1870 he had founded the Literary Emporium; expanded by members of his family, it became the world's largest bookstore. Its success encouraged authors as well as book dealers to solicit Jewish readership. Nathan Mayer's *Differences*, 1867, concerning Jews in the Civil War, was the first important novel by an American Jew. *The Origin of the Republican Form of Government in the United States*, 1885, by Oscar Straus, made the case for the Bible as a paradigm of the American political experience. Isaac Markens' *The Hebrews in America*, 1888, was the first work on that subject by a Jew, spotlighting American lifestyles and providing counter-arguments to anti–Semitic literature. Simon Wolf's *The American Jew as Patriot, Soldier and Citizen*, 1895, attempted to dispel the canard of Jewish disloyalty in the Civil War. In his German-language book *Jüdische Fragen* (*Jewish Questions*), published in Chicago in 1895, Rabbi Bernard Felsenthal of that city's Reform Sinai Congregation became one of the first to champion the Zionist cause in direct opposition to his movement's anti–Zionist position.

The most influential Jewish publishing house was the Philadelphia-headquartered Jewish Publication Society of America, founded in 1888 by Isaac Leeser after two unsuccessful earlier attempts. In its first dozen years it issued English-language texts such as Heinrich Graetz's comprehensive five volume *History of the Jews*, 1891 to 1895; Israel Zangwill's *Children of the Ghetto*, 1892; *The King of Schnorrers*, 1894; and the *American Jewish Yearbook*, 1899. The American Jewish Historical Society was founded in 1892 to promote "the collection, preservation, and publication of materials having reference to the settlement and history of the Jews on the American continent." Other works included Solomon Schechter's *Aspects of Rabbinic Theology*, Maurice Jacobs' *Jewish Ethics*, and Israel Abrahams' *Jewish Life in the Middle Ages*, all in 1896. It was a remarkable showing.

Other arts were not neglected. Moses Ezekiel, who fought in the Confederate army, is remembered as the country's first Jewish sculptor of note. Jewish theater arts originated in 1882 with Boris Thomashefsky making his acting debut. He, Jacob Adler, Jacob Grodin, and David Kessler became leading impresarios, overseeing dozens of quite awful comedies and tragedies which, fortunately, were often rescued by expert entertainers; audiences loved them. The first American exhibit of Jewish ceremonial objects was held at Chicago's 1893 Columbian Exposition, further spreading awareness of Jewish culture. Bernard Berenson, working in Italy, developed Renaissance connoisseurship to a high level of excellence beginning in 1894.

Mark Twain, no lover of organized religion, saluted Jewish achievements and business integrity in *Concerning the Jews*, published on 1899 by *Harper's Magazine*: "If the statistics are right, the Jews contribute but one per cent of the human race.... His contributions to the world's list of great names in literature, science, art, music, finance, medicine, and abstruse learning are also away out of proportion to the weakness of his numbers ... and he has done it with his hands tied behind him." It didn't stop Twain, however, from specifying how "Israelites" take economic advantage of former slaves, or from charging Jews with lack of patriotism and shirking military duty in America's wars—for which he apologized in *The Jew as Soldier*, 1904.

In general, however, the American community, Jewish and otherwise, was still too busy with political and economic expansion to be heavily involved in the world of fine arts. But although it was slow to develop, it did advance, despite the gloomy view of Alexis de Tocqueville, a young French aristocrat who had visited in 1831. In his book *Democracy in America*, 1835–1840, he observed that the country was too young to sharpen or refine its critical judgments. What he could not foresee, of course, was that rugged individualism and the drive for preeminence would soon make Americans—and its Jewish citizens—not only leaders of the industrialized world, but also significant achievers in the arts.

American achievements struck chords not only at home, but in ways that echoed across the ocean. France, dedicated to mutual friendship, sent Frederic Bartholdi's Statue of Liberty; its torch served as a lodestar to newcomers, symbolizing everything that was free and sheltering. The huge monument was unveiled on Bedloe's (Liberty) Island, October 28, 1886, in clear view of arriving ships. A contest was held to find a suitable inscription for its pedestal, with almost every prominent writer, including Henry Wadsworth Longfellow, Walt Whitman, and Mark Twain, joining the competition. It was won by a little-known American Zionist poet, Emma Lazarus, who devoted herself to "saving my own people." *The New Colossus*, 1883, was her inspiring answer to Longfellow's sympathetic but ultimately pessimistic *Jewish Cemetery at Newport* a generation earlier:

> Give me your tired, your poor,
> Your huddled masses yearning to breathe free,
> The wretched refuse of your teeming shore:
> Send these, the homeless, tempest-tossed, to me,
> I lift my lamp beside the golden door!

England in the Twentieth Century: Working Class to Upper Class

When Queen Victoria died in 1901 after a reign of sixty-three years, England had reached the pinnacle of its development and achievements. Although problems still resisted the advances and traumas of modernity, the period that had witnessed unchallenged ascendancy and unparalleled economic and social changes now drew to a close. Under Edward VII, efforts to eliminate some perquisites and powers of the House of Lords and to regulate commerce, tariffs, and trade unions moved to the political center. Overseas, vast native populations remained under the constraints of British imperialism although periodic calls were heard for self-rule. Louder voices, however, successfully argued that a looser grip on the colonies would mean a lessening of world influence, and that self-preservation and international leadership demanded a show of force in the provinces and a build-up of military forces at home.

Many had thought that major warfare would be rejected because the great controlling financial interests had imposed the necessary ingredients for the expansion of wealth and would not permit it; other than the conflict from 1899 to 1902 between Britain and the Boers (instigated, of course, by Jewish financiers), there had been no important military operations since 1870. The conflagration that erupted in 1914 therefore came as a shock to those who were unable to read beneath the calm. Britain's need to control the Eastern Mediterranean and maintain access to the Suez Canal clashed with Germany's demand for naval parity. England recognized not only the potential for the loss of trade routes to India but her responsibility for a free Europe. Since her standing army was relatively small, it took almost two years to pull together a viable force. The war was supposed to be short, but the sides were too evenly matched, and men are capable of sustained agony. Losses were so great that elderly men had to be recruited. Food shortages required rationing, prices rose precipitously for rapidly disappearing goods, and labor strikes threw normal government functions into disorder.

When Germany unleashed U-boat warfare in Atlantic waters, the United States was drawn into the battle, embroiling civilization in the first world-wide war. Fifty thousand British Jews served; a fifth of those died. Jews were urged to do all that they could for England; their casualties and honors for heroism were proportionately higher than that of the native population. However, since Russian-born immigrants were not required to serve, few of them did, much to the embarrassment of the larger community which found itself lumped together with those who avoided recruitment efforts.

When the fighting was over, four empires had disappeared from the map of Europe: Austria-Hungary, czarist Russia, Germany, and Turkey. England took the opportunity to begin a closer relationship with the continent. She mingled her culture with French art, Russian ballet, and Freud's celebration of the subconscious, while the Jewish community moved political Zionism to a new priority under the leaderships of Chaim Weizmann, Parliament member Herbert Samuel, Chief Rabbi Joseph Hertz, and Lord Rothschild. Partly in appreciation for Weizmann's chemical discoveries that helped defeat the German blockade, British Foreign Secretary Arthur Balfour facilitated the establishment of *a* (but not *the*) Jewish national home in Palestine in 1917; two years later Britain accepted a mandate to oversee the project. Nineteen hundred years had elapsed since the Jews first achieved a recognized connection with that ancient territory.

Zionism, which attracted the traditional immigrant population, had only ambivalent support from the upper classes who saw in it uncertain utopian ideals or Jewish ultra-chauvinism, both vulnerable to anti-Semitic pressures. Jews were a religious entity, they argued, not a political one. Nevertheless, the goal of wresting the Holy Land from Ottoman rule, as well as confirming historical and sentimental ties, led more and more Jews to favor the English invasion of Palestine in January 1917. Jerusalem was conquered that December, and Zionism became a bulwark of Jewish nationalism and pride, though not without last-ditch opposition from the League of British Jews, *The Jewish Guardian*, and some members of the Board of Deputies.

The Jewish population in England stood at about three hundred thousand, mostly an amorphous group of anglicized and Yiddish-speaking east Europeans. Manchester, Leeds, Liverpool, and Birmingham were home to some seventy thousand, but London's East End was by far the largest community. The district had once accommodated thieves, prostitutes, drunkards, and various other undesirables, but when the Industrial Revolution opened it up to commercial and manufacturing interests, a bohemian mixture of races and nationalities descended on the area, tamed most of its criminal activities, explored its welfare and social programs, and proceeded to live lives as moral or immoral as overcrowding and poverty might permit.

Most of the immigrants found precarious livings as small shopkeepers, making and selling clothes and cheap furnishings. Restructured lifestyles and newly-minted cultural attitudes upended their established norms. Women encountered unfamiliar situations outside the home and were liberated by newfangled appliances within. They frequented fur and jewelry shops when times were looking up, pawn shops when they weren't. Until they could afford middle-class lives, they stitched at home, took in boarders, or left the kitchen for pushcarts to help earn a living. Some found jobs in factories, studied shorthand, attacked typewriters, and soon outnumbered men in business and telegraph offices. Going and gone were tiers of petticoats, breath-defying waistlines, and the long skirts that concealed a well-turned ankle. Going or gone were the Jewish wigs, handmade dresses, and wrap-around shawls. Men worked as tailors, cobblers, glaziers, cabinetmakers, or peddlers, making do with bad housing, serious health issues, debt, and chronic unemployment. Sons and daughters had no trouble finding sources of entertainment, although not always the kind their parents or grandparents approved of. Six thousand children attended religious classes, learned English, and dreamed of leaving the neighborhood as soon as they could. Many eventually succeeded as teachers, professionals, merchant princes, and communal leaders. The industrialist Marcus Samuel, who founded the Shell Oil Company, became Lord Mayor of London in 1902. Michael Marks opened a store in Leeds in 1886 with the slogan, "Don't ask the price, it's a penny!" Two decades later the Marks and Spencer emporium arrived in London. Costs inevitably went up. Still, its working-class customers were pleased to find everything priced under five shillings.

The newcomers who had arrived at the turn of the century discovered important communal resources. They joined social and religious fraternal groups, attended English language classes, and visited the Yiddish theater. When necessary, they accepted local philanthropy. A wood-engraving of the period, *A Restaurant Where Synagogue Officials Packaged Kosher Food*, indicates that poverty was still an issue (Ill. 10:1). Many kept their Orthodox traditions as long as they could, as well as they could, and tried to become proper British citizens as soon as they could, for they knew they could not go back to the discrimination and bare lives they had fled.

And they read. In addition to Torah and Talmud, book shops, libraries, newspapers, and pamphlets provided intellectual stimulation. The Jewish *Evening News, Chronicle, Guardian,* and the Hebrew weekly *HaMeorer,* were hawked on busy street corners. Cecily Ullman, who

10:1. *A Restaurant Where Synagogue Officials Packaged Kosher Food,* c. 1900

published under her married name, Mrs. Alfred Sidgwick, wrestled with themes of inter-marriage and assimilation in *Scenes of Jewish Life*, 1904. Israel Zangwill's *Melting Pot*, 1909, suggested that Judaism's best choice to avoid disintegration was to deal with Christian ide-ology—hopefully outside of Zionist Palestine. Louis Golding's sizzling novel *Magnolia Street*, 1932, examined ambivalent feelings between Jews and Gentiles and explored the issue of inter-faith philandering.

And they communed with God, often visiting His institutions and heeding His repre-sentatives. Many were pleased when Rabbi Herman Adler, who served as Chief Rabbi, rep-resenting all of British Jewry on public occasions, was featured in a 1904 lithograph by Leslie Ward (known as Spy) in *Vanity Fair* proudly dressed in the clerical robe adapted from the Angli-can Episcopal Church (Ill. 10:2). Some of his constituents adopted *The First Prayer Book of the Jewish Religious Union*, 1902, which served the Jewish Religious Union, later known as the Liberal Jewish Synagogue. The United Synagogue's members rapidly embraced assimilation in their habits and professions, but remained committed to traditional Judaism. Manchester's Sha'are Tsedek Synagogue welcomed observant North African Sephardim as well as Egyptian and Iraqi refugees with a Middle Eastern style of worship. Liverpool, Leeds, and Birming-ham supported synagogues for Jews from exotic Baghdad, Turkey, and Greece.

But there were just too many Jews. An Independent Labour Party spokesman wrote that "Neither the principle of the brotherhood of man nor the principle of social equality implies that brother nations or brother men may crowd upon us in such numbers as to abuse our hos-pitality, overturn our institutions or violate our customs." Some Anglo-Jews, as well, resented the newcomers' willingness to work for low wages and charged them with jamming neigh-borhoods and introducing disease, immorality and crime. The Aliens Act of 1905 responded by temporarily halting the flood of indigent refugees. Although anti–Semitism wasn't phys-ically overt, it surfaced in rebuffs and sneers. Yet important Jewish leadership was soon in place, and Jews had become so much a part of English social and political life that the appointment of Rufus Isaacs as Lord Chief Jus-tice of Great Britain hardly raised an eyebrow.

Immigrants demonstrated that they were also assets to the theater, literature, and the art world. The Whitechapel Art Exhibition of Jew-ish art and antiquities, 1906, showed off unex-pected Jewish talent in painting and sculpture by such important post–Impressionists as Al-fred Wolmark, Sir William Rothenstein, and Simeon Solomon. The American-born sculptor Jacob Epstein startled viewers by adopting some abstract forms. The show, which hosted over one hundred fifty thousand viewers, was a great success. "Never before," gushed *The Jewish World*, "has there been a collection of pictures by Jewish artists, and we may say that the

10:2. *Rabbi Herman Adler*. Lithograph, 1904. By Leslie Ward (Spy). From *Vanity Fair*

Whitechapel Exhibition has definitely settled the place of Jews in the pictorial and plastic arts." In 1915, a Jewish art association and gallery named for the biblical Bezalel Ben Uri installed a permanent collection and sponsored exhibitions, lectures, concerts, and literary events for the Yiddish-speaking public.

Several English Jews participated in the New York Armory Show in 1913, which began to draw American and European art into a modern international school. David Bomberg, the first important native-born Jewish artist in England, was among those who picked up its radical thrust. The son of an immigrant Polish leather worker, he spent his early years in an East End lithographic studio before going to Paris in 1914 with Epstein to arrange for Jewish representation in Whitechapel's Twentieth Century Art Exhibition. As Bomberg told an interviewer from *The Jewish Chronicle*, his exposure to French post–Impressionist art altered his approach to design and composition: "I want to translate the life of a great city [i.e. London], its motion, its machinery into an art that shall not be photogenic, but expressive." His signature painting, *Ghetto Theatre*, 1919, met those guidelines. The same year saw the completion of his portfolio of six abstract lithographs, *Russian Ballet*, an impressive work of form, power, and movement in the Cubist-Futurist style. He visited Palestine under the auspices of the Zionist Organization, producing angular images of Jerusalem and Jericho. Unhappily, his brilliantly colored landscapes and portraits found little favor. His widow declared that he died "in a whirlwind of anger."

Relatively few Jews had turned to careers in art, possibly because they preferred the commercial and banking opportunities which were becoming available. Much like their non–Jewish colleagues, those who took up printmaking generally repeated rather than initiated new themes and motifs. Their work lacked the strength, dynamism and innovation found on the continent, relying on delicacy of finish, subtlety, and extraordinary skill. Most chose restrained or conventional subject matter and techniques, taking little part in such breakthroughs as Cubism or Expressionism that imposed a unique style or led in unexpected directions.

Painters were more adventurous. Like Bomberg, Jacob Kramer developed a mature manner that suggested Modernist influences. He remained close to the Leeds religious community, painting *Day of Atonement* in 1919 and illustrating Israel Cohen's *A Ghetto Gallery*. The city claimed him as a favored son and renamed its College of Art in his honor.

Mark Gertler admired the Paris avant-garde, but by 1913 he changed his mind. Writing to a friend that year, he concluded, "I don't want to be abstract and cater for a few hyper-intellectual maniacs ... I haven't had a grand education and I don't understand all this abstract intellectual nonsense." By 1924, he reversed himself again: "The less subject the better," he said, revealing an international style founded on basic design elements. But his moody paintings were slighted by critics. In 1939, despondent over ill health, reported Nazi terrors, and perceived artistic failure, he committed suicide at the age of forty-eight. The cliché of unrequited geniuses suffering apathy and snubs in their lifetime hung over the few forward-looking Jewish artists who chose Modernism over moderation; they faced ostracism and neglect based on general British hostility to abstraction. Nevertheless, the modernist movement in which they participated—but didn't lead—ultimately changed twentieth century art. Gertler is now honored among the finest British artists of the century.

Prints had become a rage bordering on obsession during the post-war period. Scurrilous roués were said to lure innocent maidens to their flats to view their etchings and who knew what else. However, those machinations were largely thwarted when the financial crash of the '30s terminated the etching boom. It didn't take long before resilient printmakers recognized that innocent maidens alone would not keep them in business, and they began to churn out fine lithographs, woodcuts and wood-engravings for limited edition books that were highly esteemed by collectors and libraries. Pearl Binder was a costume designer as well as a lithographer whose illustrations for Thomas Burke's *The Real East End*, 1932, captured the ambience of the old Jewish quarter. Barnett Freedman, born in the East End to Russian immigrants, created decorative lithographs for numerous volumes, including a 1939 edition of Dickens' *Oliver Twist*, and engraved the King George V Jubilee postage stamp.

Albert Rutherston illustrated a Haggadah in 1930, unremarkable in quality, but important Jewishly because it was one of only a few original editions produced in England in the twentieth century. Polish born Arthur Szyk luckily escaped the war and found refuge in London where his illuminated Haggadah, published in 1940, was a spectacular departure from the usual. It was hailed by *The Times Literary Supplement* as one of the "most beautiful books ever produced by human hands." A miniaturist in the tradition of the Middle Ages, with an inexhaustible supply of motifs and references, he was one of the few artists who clung to the human form in the '40s. Driven from his home by anti–Semitism, he construed the Exodus story in terms of Jewish suffering under the Nazis, depicting an arrogant Hitler as the Wicked Son (Ill. 10:3). The Haggadah was reproduced in lithographic editions to supply a wide-ranging demand.

The influx of about ninety thousand refugees from central Europe during the '30s did not materially affect the status quo of established Jewish life as much as the earlier eastern European immigration, since the later arrivals were mostly middle or upper-class Jews who brought much of their wealth, culture, and skills with them. Yet the German-Jewish Aid Committee, in conjunction with the Jewish Board of Deputies, was distressed by their manners and hoped they would keep a low profile. *Helpful Information and Guidance for Every Refugee* outlined a number of "duties which you are honour bound to observe: Spend your time immediately in learning the English language and its correct pronunciation; Do not talk in a loud voice; Do not make yourself conspicuous by your manner or dress...."

The pool of Jewish artists expanded with every group of Holocaust refugees who brought Europe's latest artistic wrinkles to their new home. Among them was Jankel Adler, who painted Jewish motifs and Hebrew lettering. Having been branded a "degenerate artist," he fled Germany in 1933, leaving and losing nine siblings. An Orthodox Jew, he imbued Hasidic themes with elements that can be traced to Chagall, although he eschewed that master's anecdotal emphasis. Josef Herman, from Poland, and Jacob Bornfriend, from Czechoslovakia, likewise were escapees, but their skills and styles were related to post–Cubism figuration. Herman settled in a Welsh mining town where his stark drawings and paintings of workingmen were acclaimed for their sculptural qualities. Bornfriend, who supported himself during the war as a factory worker, recreated early memories in a lithographic portfolio, *Jewish Festivals*, 1957. Most Jewish artists, commonly referred to as the "School of London," generally avoided Jewish themes. Leon Kossoff, Lucien Freud, and Frank Auerbach, Realists and Expressionists all, focused on the linear aspects of the human figure, repudiating what they considered the niceties and formalism of French art.

Unlike English art, English literature often was rabidly bigoted. Alfred Kazin said that if we were to stop reading all the anti–Semitic English writers, we would have to stop reading English writers. Beatrice Potter, Sydney Webb, Ezra Pound, Virginia Woolf, Hilaire Belloc, G. K. Chesterton, Graham Greene, D. H. Lawrence, Wyndham Lewis, John Galsworthy, Rudyard Kipling, and George Bernard Shaw were among the serious authors who, from time to time, disliked, feared, or loathed Jews. They were still perceived as conspirators, devils, outsiders, proper victims of massacres, but also as too loud, too emotional or too unemotional—characteristics often dressed up as "objective" descriptions. There were no Jewish artists or writers in England outspoken enough to make sufficiently apt or relevant rebuttals.

Except the expatriate American Ronald B. Kitaj. Perhaps the most complex figure in the world of contemporary art as well as the world of literature, he wrote with due modesty, "I draw as well as any Jew who ever lived." Searching for a Jewish dimension in his art and writings led to an exploration of the "Jewishness of Jewish art" and the history of "my people." His self-education of the Holocaust occurred "in the middle of my life when Jewishness and I bumped into each other ... I feel *more* human, *more* universal, *more* daring as a painter," he said, "if I can put the Jewish question to my art and to myself." Brought up in a strictly secular home, he abandoned his early environment and became confused as to where he is going. In his 1986 painting *The Jewish Rider,* he was still recording himself as the ever–Wandering Jew on his way to an unknown and fearful destination. In 2007 he committed suicide.

10:3. *Wicked Son.* Haggadah, 1940. By Arthur Szyk. Reproduced with the cooperation of Alexandra Szyk Bracie and the Arthur Szyk Society, www.szyk.org

Above: 10:4. *Jacob Epstein, No. 2*. **Etching, 1906. By Augustus John.** *Below:* **10:5.** *Desert Oasis.* **Etching, 1917. From** *First Palestine Set.* **By James McBey**

Non-Jewish artists who dealt with Jewish subject matter included Augustus John, whose emotionally tense etching, *Jacob Epstein, No. 2*, 1906, demonstrated his study of Rembrandt's prints (Ill. 10:4). James McBey's etching *Jewish Quarters, Tetuan*, 1912, recorded his visit to Spanish Morocco. Five years later, he went to the Middle East as an official war artist where he gathered material for his *First Palestine Set*, reminiscences of his travels from the Suez Canal to Beersheba. One of those etchings, *Desert Oasis*, suggests the bleak Roman ruins (Ill. 10:5). Frank Brangwyn worked as a tapestry designer for William Morris before taking up printmaking in 1900. He provided seventy-three etchings for Jerome and Jean Tharaud's French novel *L'Ombre de la Croix* (*The Shadow of the Cross*), 1931, depictions of east European Jewish types. Eric Ravilious, an industrial designer as well as a decorative illustrator, in 1933 made four engravings for Christopher Marlowe's sixteenth century *Jew of Malta*, the second of which depicts the evil Barabbas and his daughter Abigail

retrieving sacks of gold and jewelry hidden in his home to thwart its confiscation by the government (Ill. 10:6). The play bears similarities to the *Merchant of Venice*—Barabbas, like Shylock, is a despised Jew who seeks vengeance against his Christian adversaries, while his beloved daughter rejects her religion, much to his grief. Unlike Shylock, however, he is a psychopathic murderer who is undone by greed.

Sir David Muirhead Bone etched *The Jewish Quarter, Leeds*, in 1921 in the fine drypoint for which he was famous (Ill. 10:7). Dame Laura Knight etched *A Daughter of Israel*, c. 1950, in a submissive mood which perhaps no longer epitomized Jewish women (Ill. 10:8). Richard Hamilton introduced a Jewish theme in his etchings for James Joyce's *Ulysses*, 1922. In 1983, following thirty years of attention to the subject, Hamilton produced a portfolio illustrating the book, attempting to match Joyce's witty literary leaps with an equivalent artistic style. The etched, engraved, and aquatinted frontispiece depicts Leopold Bloom, a Jewish salesman of newspaper ads who, despite his alleged indifference to his Jewishness, sports a Star of David pinky ring, sings *Hatikvah* (*Hope*), and chats about Palestine. The story, a parable of two groups of outsiders—the Jews and the Irish—explores an eighteen-hour-day in the life of this Everyman figure recast as a Wandering Jew in an Irish society with few Jews. (Joyce explained why Ireland never persecuted Jews: "Because she never let them in.") Although Bloom represents the perpetual Jewish quest for identity in exile, he is less a Jewish type than a symbol of unease or discomfort.

Jews had been shaken by the publication in 1905 of *The Protocols of the Learned Elders of Zion*, the supposed minutes of a Jewish organization's design on world domination, in *The Morning Post* as well as in *The Times*. The following year, a *Times* reporter proved that the *Protocols* were a forgery taken from an 1864 pamphlet directed at Napoleon III. But proof or no proof, the Fascist ranting and threats of Sir Oswald Mosley, founder of the British Union of Fascists (BUF), introduced "Blackshirt" hate groups in 1932 which fueled abuses and vandalism in Jewish areas. Members of the Communist Party, as well as other anti–Fascist groups, undertook opposition to their strong-arm tactics, earning them gratitude of many voters. Concerned about the violence, the Board of Deputies and the *Jewish Chronicle* urged non-aggressive conduct in the face of harassment or provocation, warning Jews to avoid the Blackshirt marches. The perceived timidity angered one of the *Chronicle*'s readers: "Did Judas Maccabeus stay at home?" he asked. Nevertheless, it was clear that Blackshirts were not the only problem that faced the community. The Central British Fund for Jewish Refugees and other welfare organizations, overwhelmed by the needy and unable to care for the immigrants on their own, were forced to seek government subsidies. Another disturbing issue was the growing antagonism between Zionists and anti–Zionists. However, when a series of White Papers were issued from 1937 to 1939 limiting Jewish immigration to Palestine, many English Jews recognized the need to pull together. On the other hand, large numbers of Jews were pulling apart, going separate ways. Geographically and economically upwardly mobile Liberal or Reform-minded Jews, as well as German refugees and their well-trained rabbis, energetically resisted the traditional observances of their mainstream Orthodox brethren. Internal wrangling between them, of course, was as uncordial as their outward splits. Dislike and distrust of émigrés and their alleged bad manners and behavior resulted not only in private social discrimination, but in the government's interment of thirty thousand "enemy aliens." A year later, most were released under parliamentary urging.

In spite of setbacks and some unhappy policies, the march was forward. Many second- and third-generation Jews attended high school and college, found jobs outside of the sweating trades, and entered upper-class professions and service industries. Once arrived at middle- and upper-class status, they visited resorts, enjoyed swimming parties and kosher cookouts, diverted themselves with billiards, golf, and tennis, and won or lost bets on horses and prizefighters. The cultural scene was marked by a moderate literary upswing, including the

10:6. *Barabbas and His Daughter Abigail Retrieving Sacks of Gold and Jewelry.* Engraving, 1933. By Eric Ravilious. From *Jew of Malta.* ©2007 Artists Rights Society (ARS), New York/DACS, London

10:7. *The Jewish Quarter, Leeds.* **Etching, 1921. By Sir David Muirhead Bone**

arrival of the Soncino publishing house (no relation to the sixteenth century press of the same name). Among its editions from the '20s to the '40s were translations of Midrash Rabba, the *Zohar*, Rashi's commentaries, and, from 1935 to 1952 (with an interruption between 1938 and 1948 due to World War II), thirty-five volumes of the Babylonian Talmud, its first complete translation into English. Oxford University Press also published valuable liturgical books. Its Pentateuch and Haftorahs, 1938, edited by Rabbi Joseph Hertz with a Hebrew and English text, included scholarly explanations that were informative and occasionally even provocative. It rapidly became a fixture in almost every synagogue since congregants were able to follow the weekly portion service with interest and comprehension.

Failure of the post–World War I recovery and the subsequent depression had encouraged excessive nationalism and totalitarian governments in Europe. The threat of global war again hung over Britain. With the emergence of Adolf Hitler, international cooperation and negotiation turned into a cynical and hollow exercise. Troubled and fearful because she had fallen seriously behind in arms build-up and desperately playing for time, England arranged a naval agreement with Germany in 1935 and then dissuaded France from retaliating when Hitler moved into the Rhineland. Prime Minister Neville Chamberlain acted on the naive assumption that Hitler's objectives were satisfied and that his military operation was partly defensible in the light of the ill-advised Peace Treaty of 1919. "I believe that persecution arose out of two motives: a desire to rob the Jews of their money and a jealousy of their superior cleverness," he said. "No doubt Jews aren't a lovable people; I don't care about them myself; but that is not sufficient reason to explain the Pogrom." Perhaps if he had doubted less and cared more, World War II would not have been the fateful consequence.

10:8. *A Daughter of Israel.* Etching, 1950. By Dame Laura Knight. ©2007 Artists Rights Society (ARS), New York/DACS London

When Germany annexed Austria in 1938 and invaded Czechoslovakia and Poland in 1939 despite promises to the contrary, England went to war. Between May and August of that year a young Czech stockbroker, Nicholas Winton, attempted the rescue of six hundred sixty-nine Jewish children by requesting countries outside German influence to take them in. Sweden took some. So did Britain—but only those younger than sixteen. The last trainload from Prague, with two hundred fifty youngsters aboard, never made it. Scheduled to leave on September 3, 1939, the day Britain declared war on Germany, the children were forced to return to their homes, from which they were soon moved to death camps. None survived.

England moved rapidly to wartime status. Children were evacuated to safer areas to escape the incessant bombings that began in 1940. Able-bodied men and women entered the services. Civilians coped with food rationing and shortages of other items. Underground railway stations were turned into emergency bomb shelters. The Great Synagogue in Duke's Place, close to Bevis Marks, was lost to German bombs in 1941. The old East End community was bombed out of existence. British Jewry reinvented itself in the suburbs.

Fascist organizations swung into action, promoting radio broadcasts, pamphlets, and books that specialized in Jew-baiting. Although most British leaders and much of the public disapproved of such activities, the Labour government resisted efforts to ameliorate the situation through the creation of a Jewish state. Prime Minister Winston Churchill, sympathetic to the Jewish cause, sent a supportive message to *The Jewish Chronicle* in 1941 on the occasion of its one hundredth birthday: The Jew "has borne and continues to bear a burden that might have seemed to be beyond endurance. He has not allowed it to break his spirit; he has never lost the will to resist ... at the appointed time he will see vindicated those principles of righteousness which it was the glory of his fathers to proclaim to the world."

From 1939 to 1946 English unwillingness to help Jewish resistance efforts in Europe, in addition to the Foreign Office's refusal to implement Churchill's demand to bomb Auschwitz, continued to be severe disappointments. Nevertheless, Palestinian Jews fought courageously for the Allied cause and their own existence. Five thousand Jewish Brigade volunteers served alongside the British army in the war effort, urging enlistment and fostering patriotism through public relation lithographs. But the Jews recognized that the British were not going to abrogate the 1939 White Paper which restricted "illegal" immigration into Palestine, nor implement the Balfour Declaration which supposedly gave Jews the right to settle there. They demanded the establishment of their own independent state. Boatloads of European refugees heading to Palestine faced interception by the British navy, which forcibly removed them to detention camps in Germany and Cyprus. Serious clashes erupted between British soldiers and Jewish insurgents, climaxing with the 1946 blowup of the British military headquarters in Jerusalem's King David Hotel. Later that year the Jerusalem railway station and the Officer's Club were targeted, resulting in the death of a British engineer and twelve officers. The disasters were viewed as terrorism and cost the Jewish community much of its previous support. In the end, the turmoil proved too much. On May 14, 1948, the British high commissioner bowed to the inevitable and withdrew. The State of Israel was proclaimed that same day.

England was now very different from what it had been. The empire that had ruled a quarter of the world's population was dismantled. Economically strapped by the rebuilding of its cities and reduced in international prestige, it was immeasurably hard hit. Yet England's role in the twentieth century was pivotal to world peace. With American aid she twice led the defense of Europe against daunting odds. Churchill reminded the world that "England always wins one battle—the last."

The second Elizabeth had come to the royal throne in 1952, the Beatles to the musical throne in the 1960s. In between, the throne came to the Jewish community in the person of the Duke of Edinburgh when he attended a banquet celebrating the three hundredth anniversary of Jewish resettlement under Oliver Cromwell. The Victoria and Albert Museum in London commemorated the occasion with an exhibition of Anglo-Jewish art. Cecil Roth, who had co-founded the Jewish Museum at Woburn House in 1932, helped plan the show. He authored and edited several books on Jewish art and history during the '50s and '60s and was instrumental in such Jewish cultural outlets as *The Jewish Quarterly*, which in 1953 began publishing the latest news in literature and art.

England contributed to the commercial and military capabilities of Israel, her own interests benefiting along the way from the region's mobilized industrial economy. When Egyptian president Gamal Abdel Nasser seized the Suez Canal in 1956, cutting off English access to the Gulf of Aqaba—in effect choking off its trade and shipping—England, with French aid, helped Israel reopen the sea routes, thus maintaining control of the canal. Eleven years later, Nasser tried again and lost again after just six days. England provided reconditioned World

War II tanks and other military assistance which led to the successful conclusion of the war and established Israeli control of Jerusalem. But because of its long-standing dependence on Arab oilfields, England remained committed to the mideast policies, mostly inimical to Israeli interests. Three dozen of her best writers, however, announced that Israel had "a right to live." The London *Sunday Times* printed its manifesto on June 4, 1967: "Israel is a country the size of Wales. Today it is mobilized to prevent itself becoming another Auschwitz. The Arab states which surround it have declared their intention of exterminating it. There are two and a half million people whose right to live is threatened. Behind the political game, this is what the present crisis is about. This is the basic human fact."

By the century's end, there were about a third of a million Jews living in England—approximately the same number as at its beginning. Theological questions, problems of inter-marriage, outward migration, falling away from Jewish identity, minority status, and coping with a multi-racial, socially, politically, and economically diverse society, including an increasingly radical Muslim population, crowded earlier considerations of immigration and poverty. The community could not take great pride in either its secular or Judaic art or scholarship; there was a feeling of cultural and intellectual poverty. An ever-present anti–Semitism and anti–Zionism, both implied and explicit, hovered over the whole. Jews did their best to fit in and they did, but it came at a price; the need to do so was, in itself, demeaning, since they knew they were not always treated with the same dignity as were old-line Englishmen.

Yet compared to the situation on the continent, English Jews fared well. Discrimination was relaxed, enabling them to be represented in high government, educational, real estate and media positions and activities. They lived in the most sympathetic and integrated environment in all of Europe, were devoted to Israel and the campaigns to fund and protect Jewish causes. Many found it possible to achieve economic security, to care for their own, educate their children Jewishly in the denomination of their choice, maintain and honor their religious traditions, savor a Yiddish milieu, and provide an open forum for those who wished to explore the arts as significant issues in Jewish life.

11

France in the Twentieth Century: Grandeur and Loss

France had reason to feel proud. It was the cultural center of the world, its language still the choice of well-bred Europeans. Music, art, literature, science, the theater, all contributed to its glory and rejuvenation. A great world's fair had opened in Paris in 1900, parading achievements that represented the best the continent had to offer, including fifteen paintings by Jewish artists in the Hungarian pavilion. The energy and effervescence of the French art world was irresistible. But while *tout le monde* was still acclaiming the delights of Impressionism and the entrenched Romantic or Academic style, forward-looking masters were beginning to embrace liberating themes that no longer demanded descriptive or "truthful" reality. Former stylistic concepts were adjusted as a modern aesthetic replaced the decorative and emotive schools that had been French standards. The cords that bound artists to custom became untied, signaling a breach with the past and a pursuit of fresh ideals. Perhaps nowhere was this more evident than in the escapist, open, and brash atmosphere of Paris where hundreds of artists sought recognition and fortune.

An explosion of experimental isms—Primitivism, Fauvism, Cubism, Futurism, Expressionism, Abstractionism, Surrealism, Dadaism—launched fusillades of optic freedoms and confusions that became the hallmarks of twentieth century culture. Art, literature, and music were more whimsical, more radical, more spiritual, more symbolic and fantastic than ever before, scorning logical analysis, conventional forms, colors, and naturalistic representation. Art no longer demanded an outside reference system; it would be defined by the artist, not by the viewer. As the Jewish gallery owner Daniel Kahnweiler pointed out, artists "wanted to render the *essence* and not the appearance of objects." Actually, this was nothing new. Almost two thousand years earlier the consummate theoretician, Plato, wrote: "I will try to speak of the beauty of shapes and I do not mean what most people would expect such as that of living figures, but I mean straight lines and curves, and the plane or solid figures which are formed out of them; for these I affirm to be not only relatively beautiful, like other things, but they are externally beautiful...."

France's Jewish component got under way when Alsatian-born Max Jacob arrived in Paris from Brittany in 1901. Although he spent his time bouncing between riotous living and Catholic religious fervor, he soon became known as a capable painter as well as a critic and poet, achieving immortality when his friend Picasso contributed the first Cubist prints to his autobiographical *Saint Matorel* in 1911; the partnership produced strong links between the experimental natures of literature and the fine arts. Jacob's books were commissioned and published by Kahnweiler, who held the first Cubist exhibition in 1907.

Among the eighty thousand Jews who called France home was the theatrical sensation Sarah Bernhardt, daughter of a Dutch Jewish mother and an unknown Parisian father; her distracting charms graced a popular 1904 lithograph when she appeared as Princess Lointaine in a play by Edmond Rostand (Ill. 11:1). Other luminaries were the designer Leon Bakst, the half–Jewish authors Marcel Proust and André Maurois, the composer Darius Milhaud, and André Citroën, who supplied much of the allies' military ammunition during World War I, developed low cost mass-produced automobiles, introduced traffic signals, and dreamed up the floodlights that still bedazzle the Arc de Triomphe.

Ill. 11:1. *Sarah Bernhardt as Princess Lointaine.* Lithograph, 1904

As Jewish artists found their way to Paris, they acquired a group identity at La Ruche (The Beehive), a large dilapidated residence hall where Yiddish or Russian was more likely to be heard than French. Although most were east European by heritage, they became French by design and did their best work in Paris, kindling an efflorescence of activity after centuries of playing minor roles in the art world. Starving, brooding, or carousing in the cafés, they were alive to each other, relishing the opportunity to join in radical creative and political diversity unfettered by the academic or romantic references they left behind. Suddenly ready to express themselves secularly, suddenly accepted as creative individuals, suddenly exposed to the history of art in museums, and suddenly caught up in bohemian lifestyles, many in the blink of an eye dropped their familial Orthodox values and beliefs and discarded anecdotal or sentimental images for the colorful shapes of the avant-garde.

They were popularly known as the Circle of Montparnasse or the Jewish School of Paris. Their works incorporated folk art, the form and color innovations of Cézanne, the intoxicating Fauvist hues of Matisse, the Cubist fragmentations of Picasso and Braque, the convulsions of Van Gogh, and the moral—and immoral—prints of Toulouse-Lautrec. They differed generally from their French colleagues in an intuitive rather than cerebral manner. What they developed were various styles of modernism; what they did not introduce was a Jewish style—if such a specialty could be said to exist. With the major exceptions of Mané-Katz and Chagall, most consciously broke with distinctive or conventional Judaic subject matter which was considered dated or unfashionable. Although they produced "French" art, they were perceived by others as Jewish artists and certainly considered themselves as such, brought together by the need for community in an unfamiliar setting, concern for their families and friends back home, and common backgrounds, language, or cultures that transcended political or geographical frontiers.

The first wave of Jewish painters and printmakers was soon in place. Louis Marcoussis arrived in 1903, and within the next three years he was joined by Jules Pascin, Sonia Delaunay, and Eugène Spiro. Marcoussis, born in Poland to a wealthy family, became French to his fingertips. He moved smoothly into the select circle of Cubist artists producing, in addition to paintings, over two hundred technically elegant etchings, engravings, and woodcuts; many ranked him higher as a printmaker than as a painter. He differed from other Cubist masters in his more realistic and lyrical approach, remaining under their influence, although developing links to Surrealism. His undated etching of the Jewish expatriate author Gertrude Stein captures the strong, expressive force of her personality in spite of the fact that profile portraits generally delineate features rather then essence (Ill. 11:2). His forty etchings in 1934 illustrated an edition of Guillaume Apollinaire's *Alcools*, a poetical rendering of the Wandering Jew written twenty-one years earlier.

Very different from Marcoussis in graphic style as well as lifestyle was Jules Pascin, born to a Bulgarian Sephardic family. At age nineteen he made his first etching. His second attempt, executed with his typical economy of means, was a drypoint, *Au Balkans* (*In the Balkans*), 1904, perhaps a depiction of a small town or shtetl he visited on the way to Munich (Ill. 11:3). He was already popular there as a bawdy caricaturist for the sophisticated comic magazine *Simplicissimus*. Having heard of the wicked reputation of Paris, in 1905 he took off for the gilded city and soon lost himself in the excesses of brothels, alcoholism, and orgies. Although he was eventually repelled by the depravity and self-indulgence, he remained trapped in a life that was too fast to moderate and too decadent to resist. He took his art seriously, however, making woodcut book illustrations, including a few biblical scenes, but he never portrayed specific Jewish subject matter. His erotic and seductive forms carry parallels to Lautrec in the nervous urgency and grace of their sinuous lines, and to his good friend Chagall in the use of flattened space and facile distortion. He was only forty-five and restless, ill, and increasingly bitter when his habits finally took their toll. On the opening day of his one-man show in 1930, he hanged himself. The Yiddish novelist and playwright Shalom Asch spoke at his funeral, conducted at his request according to Orthodox Jewish law.

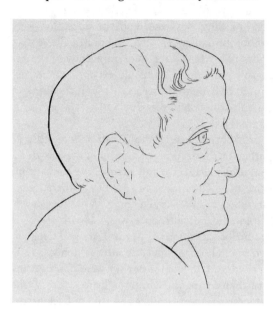

Born in 1885, the same year as Pascin, but more in tune with the ultra–Modernism of Marcoussis, Sonia Delaunay was one of the few women artists in Montparnasse. Russian by birth, she immigrated to Paris, where the sudden freedom from the cramped influences of her childhood led to innovative approaches to a variety of applied arts. She was among the first to break from the reigning Art Deco style by stressing abstract, rhythmic bands of receding and advancing structural planes. Having studied printmaking techniques with the Jewish engraver Rudolf Grossmann in the '20s, she and her artist husband Robert Delaunay examined the interaction between aesthetic form, light, and color harmonies. If anything relating to her Jewish background could be

Above: Ill. 11:2. *Gertrude Stein.* By Louis Marcoussis. ©2007 Artists Rights Society (ARS) New York/ADAGP, Paris. *Below:* Ill. 11:3. *Au Balkans (In the Balkans).* Etching, 1904. By Jules Pascin

extracted from her designs, it might be that the costumes and festivals of her Russian Jewish childhood were reincarnated in what she called "the infinite poetic combinations of color."

Eugène Spiro was the son of a German cantor, but chose a career in art over that of the synagogue. He lived in Paris from 1906 until 1914 before returning to his native home to produce war maps for the German army. When the Nazis later clamped down on his ability to work and exhibit, he fled to Paris until that city fell in 1940; in spite of serious illness he managed to get to New York, where he taught painting and printmaking until his death.

Amedeo Modigliani arrived in Paris in 1906, leaving behind a cultured family and a well-to-do uncle in Italy who helped sponsor him. He brought with him a handsome face, an engaging personality, and a love of classical decoration. Soon he picked up an appreciation for Catholic imagery (including a Catholic mistress), nude models, African tribal masks, contemporary design, and an addiction to alcohol and drugs. A committed but non-traditional Jew, in 1908 he titled the first painting he exhibited in Paris *La Juive* (*The Jewess*) and decorated it with Stars of David. He scribbled Hebrew letters on his drawing of the sculptor Chana Orloff and inscribed the Hebrew word for Jew on a portrait of the artist Moise Kisling, affirming that he and they were branches of the same stock. But he didn't live long enough to realize his potential. He died at thirty-five from tuberculosis, frustrated as an artist and perhaps as a Jew. As did Pascin, he squandered his gifts with eager impatience.

Jacques Lipshitz came from Lithuania in 1909 and developed into a leading Cubist sculptor and printmaker who explored socially relevant Jewish themes. After 1921 he spent most of his time in America. Mané-Katz was born to an Orthodox family in the Ukraine. In 1913 he went to Paris for a year, returned again in 1921 and remained there on and off between brief visits to Israel. Having been strongly influenced by the craftsmen of his hometown, he was one of the very few artists who identified strongly as a Jew in his work, painting biblical subjects as well as ghetto scenes. Twelve color lithographs depicting Shalom Aleichem's shtetl musicians, and sixteen moving lithographs of Holocaust victims for *La Revolte des Innocents* (*The Rebellion of the Innocent Ones*), 1961, secured his place as an artist of Jewish sensibilities.

Chana Orloff emigrated to Paris in 1910 and became a sculptor and popular portraitist— David Ben-Gurion and Shalom Asch were among her sitters—but she also favored less familiar subjects, as in her suite of portraits of French women. The woodcut *Mlle. Louise Marion*, 1919, effectively incorporates the grain of the plank as part of the design (Ill. 11:4). She fled occupied Paris in 1942, finding on her return that her studio had been ransacked. A frequent visitor to Israel, she died there in 1968 during an exhibition of her works.

After Moise Kisling arrived in Paris in 1910 from Krakow, he found a successful niche in Fauve and Cubist circles depicting rhythmically posed portraits and amply endowed nudes modeled after the work of Cézanne. For a time his work recalled his Polish-Jewish experience, but although he often chose models who, he believed, typified Jewish physical types, he avoided or ignored specific Jewish subject matter. During World War II he fled the Nazi regime, first serving with the French army, then escaping to New York. When Hollywood called, he supplied movie personalities with carefully composed portraits that paid his expenses until he was able to return to Paris. Like Orloff, he found that his studio had been destroyed.

Chaim Soutine was a sickly boy, abused and disowned by his family in Lithuania for taking a few cents from his mother to buy crayons. We are told that following a beating by the son of an Orthodox rabbi whose portrait he attempted to sketch, unaware of the family's strictures against it, he collected enough hush money to enable him to get to Paris when he was just seventeen. He worked there and in French villages for nine years before being discovered by the American collector Albert Barnes. Although none of his paintings contain Jewish motifs, his frequent representation of brutalized and bloody carcasses may carry attitudes involving biblical references to animal sacrifices. He was a mystic in the tradition of rebellious martyrs and traditionalists who simultaneously loved and hated God. For some, he was the archetypal Jewish artist, modern in his approach to existential suffering and despair. Others saw only violence and confusion in his predilection for the grim, hopeless aspects of Jewish life, a foreboding of the coming Holocaust in which he became trapped. He died of ulcers at forty-seven while trying to evade the Nazi police.

The first Jewish art journal in the twentieth century, *Machmadim* (*Delights*), 1912, focused attention on Jewish themes, although most Jewish artists preferred to work in an assimilated context based on their own unique attitudes and situations. Most, but not all. The artist who became the definitive exemplar of a positive attitude towards Jewish art was a young man recently out of his "sad-glad" Russian town, Vitebsk. With much of his imagery inspired by his Hasidic background, Marc Chagall sought God in the representation of love and joy—the very antitheses of Soutine. He studied with the Jewish designer for the Diaghilev Ballet, Leon Bakst, who filled his head with stories of Paris—the city of light where those hoping to paint could paint as they chose. Unlike his own Russia, there would be no burdensome restrictions concerning figurative art; unlike Russia, all neophytes were welcome.

He spent his formative years in Paris—1910 to 1914, the period of Cubism's development—honing the skills that turned him into the painter who stands perhaps just below Picasso in the innovative heritage bequeathed to the twentieth century. Although he sometimes adopted multi-angle fractured treatments and realigned three-dimensional planes with flat Cubist forms, he was no Cubist. "Let them eat their fill of square pears on their triangular tables!" he declared. In 1914, he returned to Russia, where, in remarkable breakthroughs, he wedded intellectual abstraction to a romantic sensibility. A year later he married Bella Rosenfeld of whom he said, "With her, love and flowers entered my room." In 1917, in the Yiddish journal *Shtrom*, he described his Jewish faith and artistic soul better than the dozens of critics who have since chewed over his works and explored his history: "If I were not a Jew (with all the content I put into that word), I wouldn't have been an artist, or I would be a different artist altogether. Is that news? For myself I know quite well what this little nation can achieve.... When it wished ... it showed Christ and Christianity. When it wanted—it gave Marx and Socialism. Can it be it won't show the world some art? Kill me if not!"

In 1920, he was selected to design and paint murals for the State Yiddish Chamber Theater in Moscow. He blended the town's shop signs with his own sense of illogic and fantasy, elements of Jewish daydreams and fables, and the celebration of life, color, and structure. He took Russian folk art, which was popularized by Bakst's Russian ballet companies, plus what he had learned in Paris, and threw them together in a mélange of mysticism and anti-rationalism. But the freedom he enjoyed didn't last long. The heady revolutionary spirit erupted into pogroms and, alarmed at the approaching storm, he and Bella left for Berlin and for Paris in 1923.

Ill. 11:4. *Mlle. Louise Marion*. **Woodcut, 1919. By Chana Orloff**

Ill. 11:5. *Fire in the Town.* Etching, 1923. From *Mein Leben (My Life)*. By Marc Chagall. ©2007 Artists Rights Society (ARS) New York/ADAGP, Paris

There his *Mein Leben* (*My Life*), a series of poignant reminiscences, was issued by Paul Cassirer, the Jewish publisher and art dealer. It contained twenty autobiographical etchings previewing his artistic sources in expressive, if somewhat ambiguous scenes of his homeland—funny, romantic, comforting, foolish, carnal, rueful. Among them is a *Fire in the Town*, undoubtedly painful given the frequency of such occurrences in the shaky wooden buildings, but the image of someone being carried out of the burning house in his bed injected a bit of whimsy even into that sorry event (Ill. 11:5). *The Grandfathers*, also from that series, depicts the morning prayers during which tefillin are donned by men to remind them of their religious obligations. The prints were intended to accompany his memoirs, but the book contained no text; not until nine years later did it appear in a French edition written by Bella.

His use of unrelated perspective and proportion, ecstatic interwoven figures, and changed angles of vision defy gravity and normal perspective. Floating projections were adopted as mystical symbols of mutability and the breakdown between body and soul. In the heyday of Freud, his art tended to release ids and oddities from customary restraints through free association in dream forms of the subconscious mind. "Our inner world," Chagall said, "is more real, perhaps, than the visible one." The melding of abstraction and humanistic tradition within a contemporary format addressed the nagging question of whether or not he had created a specifically Jewish style. His answer was yes.

In 1941 he and his family fled to America, where they lived until it was safe to return. After the mid '40s, in an effort to achieve even greater depth and movement he concentrated on color etching and lithography, producing some of his finest and most dynamic work in those media, although he seems to have lost or relinquished the unaffected qualities of his earlier works. He immersed himself as deeply in his prints as in his paintings, stained glass and tapestries. "When I held in my hand a lithographic stone or a copper plate," he wrote, "I believed I was touching a talisman." Chagall was considered the quintessential Jewish artist, and his bright prints, perhaps more masterly in color than in design, became the most sought after of all Jewish images, relating at least in part to the nostalgia that many Jews cherished of their own family traditions. He decorated synagogues, churches, Hadassah Hospital, the Vatican, Israel's Knesset, and the ceilings of opera houses in Paris and New York with exuberant messages of peace and paradise.

Visits to Israel were followed by Holocaust images. He wrote poetry in the '50s—*To the Martyred Artists*—a lament on the loss of friends who were unable to escape as he had done. Yet he chose to live in France rather than Eretz Yisrael because he feared he would be indelibly labeled as a ghetto artist rather than one whose vision spanned all cultures. His own formula was broader: "If a painter is Jewish and paints life, how can he help having Jewish elements in his work! But if he is a good painter, there will be more than that. The Jewish element will be there, but his art will tend to approach the universal."

Certainly universal in his approach was Theo Tobiasse. Born in Palestine in 1927, he was brought to France as a child and hidden from Nazis for two years in occupied Paris. He was a commercial artist before turning to a painting and printmaking style that embodied primitive, boldly colored images. His folio of eighteen lithographs, *Diaspora*, focused on the history of Jewish exile, a theme that he turned to again and again.

The Circle of Montparnasse lasted forty years—1905 to 1945—during which two great wars were fought, the stock market crashed, and the surrender of the French army put an end to the transcendent state of mind that was Paris. Side by side with the dynamism of the art world, the political life of France had been reshaped as a direct outcome of the Dreyfus Affair, guided in part by Emile Zola's *Vérité* (*Truth*), 1903, a fictionalized telling of the case. The final separation of Church and State had become law in 1905, permitting freedom of worship and freedom from Catholic imposed education.

But anti–Semitism wasn't to be rooted out by legislation, it was too institutionalized. Leon Blum, the first Jewish premier of France (elected in 1936), had commented in 1901 that Jews were imbued with the "spirit of Socialism." Those words helped raise the specter of Bolshevism among conservative voters, while those on the left saw financial and cultural takeovers by Jewish capitalists. Intensifying anti–Jewish sentiments, a French edition of *The Protocols of The Learned Elders of Zion* surfaced in 1905. It generated enough credibility so that three years later Charles Maurras' newspaper, *L'Action Française*, could be successfully established as the mouthpiece of resurgent race hatred. Even the Socialist paper *L'humanité* complained that Jewish schools fostered a "closed caste ... impenetrable by modern culture." As a plethora of newspapers and books were ready to attest, Jews were simply not Frenchmen. What were they? Aliens, Communists, beggars, manipulators, and crooks.

Shaky financial and political leadership brought the country only a step from anarchy. Germany, Austria-Hungary, and Italy renewed their Triple Alliance in 1902, challenging the combined strengths of Britain and France. They responded by signing their own entente the following year. Although some ingredients for stability and economic growth seemed to be in place, the rivalry helped precipitate World War I in 1914. As one nation after another took up arms, France, partly because of her preparedness, was able to field a strong military force. Fifty thousand Jewish soldiers and officers—immigrant and native—rallied to the cause in a broad show of patriotism. Ten thousand were lost. Among its acknowledged heroes was a Jewish chaplain, Rabbi Abraham Bloch, who sacrificed his life for a wounded Catholic soldier. Unable to find a priest, the rabbi offered the soldier a crucifix; in doing so he became a target himself. The incident was commemorated in a popular print, *Pour la Patrie (For the Fatherland)*, which was intended to emphasize the rapport between Christian and Jew. But it didn't help much.

France carried the brunt of the suffering for two years until England was fully able to mobilize and America could send reinforcements. However, the Treaty of Versailles, which concluded the war, did not satisfy her expectations of strong material guarantees or diplomatic pledges of security. The League of Nations received lukewarm support at best. French post-war governments locked horns with a resurgent Germany, tried to control corruption in high places and a runaway inflation, and attempted to reorganize and modernize its infrastructure. In spite of those efforts, political and economic chaos threatened the country with strikes, riots, and mass demonstrations; Jewish radicalism was blamed, particularly with the arrival of refugees seeking jobs and shelter.

French Jewry tripled in the twenty-five post-war years as part of the large migration. Thousands poured in from Mediterranean countries, Algeria, former Ottoman territories, central and eastern Europe, compensating the country for its huge manpower losses during the war. In spite of howls that these alien people were taking jobs from natives, France in many ways was a generous host. Typically, many native Jews, by now pretty well acculturated, were embarrassed by the lifestyle of large numbers who insisted on maintaining their east European manners and religious educational system which they declared was as good or better than what was available in France. Most settled in the Marais section of Paris where those who wished might adapt to the enlightened local culture, and those who could might achieve middle-class lifestyles. Discussions in cafés and living rooms often centered around support for Palestinian Jewry, but ambivalent attitudes or outright opposition towards political Zionism were heard as well. The Association of French Rabbis declared in 1923 that Zionism "cannot be reconciled with the principles of French Judaism" because it raised the question of dual loyalty, and because it competed with the view that French citizenship was reward enough. It wasn't until the Jews were scorched by the Nazi threat in the 1930s that the necessity for safety and independence was fully understood. Zionism received a new imperative, rekindling a deeply-felt, though submerged Judaism.

Essays on the "Jewish Problem" in art were beginning to appear in the press. German-Jewish artists, dealers, and collectors were accused of money-grubbing. They were too visible, they were not even able to speak the language properly, and, most important, they lacked the long tradition of French-born painters. In 1922, their "foreign" art was segregated to an annex in the Musée du Luxembourg. The following year the Salon des Independants arranged its exhibition space consistent with artists' country of origin. Only native-born Jews were lucky enough to be considered French; only Christian, neutral, or "nationalist" subjects by Jewish artists were accorded French School status. The literary magazine *Mercure de France*, 1925, sniffed that "... the day that painting became for the many a speculative business, the Jews came in...." The art critic Fritz Vanderpyl asked "Is There Such a Thing as Jewish Painting?" and then answered in the negative because, he argued, Jewish rapacity in an upward market nullified any aesthetic pretensions. Similar rhetoric followed, charging Jews with ignoring classical limits on representation and thereby eliminating themselves from consideration. The Jewish art critic Louis Vauxcelles, in a spasm of snobbery and self-loathing, wrote in *Le Carnet de la Semaine*, 1925, of the "barbarian horde" whose "culture is so recent! When they speak about Poussin, do they know the master? Have they ever really looked at a Corot? Or read a poem by La Fontaine? These are people from 'somewhere else' who ignore and in the bottom of their hearts look down on what Renoir has called the gentleness of the French School—that is, our race's virtue of tact."

An increasingly shrill tone appeared in a collection of articles by Camille Mauclair, who wrote for the popular newspaper *Le Figaro*. His book *Foreigners Against French Art*, 1930, appearing as it did in the wake of the stock market crash, not only exacerbated the issue of immigration among the working class, but reminded readers that Montparnasse was filled by "eighty percent Semites and every one of them a loser." And if being a loser wasn't punishment enough, he suggested that police raids and examination of their papers should be the next step. But in spite of his advice, Jewish artists, as well as the dealers and collectors who were important players in the art world, were determined to take advantage of whatever freedoms the country offered. As it turned out, most of them paid a heavy price for that privilege. They not only worked within a frequently anti–Jewish environment but faced social and artistic rejection as well. The anti–Dreyfusards had not been asleep. Anti-Semitism oozed out in ever-greater strength. Vicious street posters, mostly anonymous for obvious reasons, were pasted on accommodating walls. Jews retaliated by organizing marches protesting the election of the Nazi Party in 1933, by tacking up messages such as *Défendez les Juifs!* (*Defend Jews!*), and urging Frenchmen not to buy German goods. But too often their best efforts were useless.

Pierre Benoit was not a Jew, but, inspired by a visit to Palestine, he wrote of its heroic Jewish pioneers in *Le Puit de Jacob* (*Jacob's Well*), 1925. The Polish Jewish artist Arthur Szyk prepared its pochoir illustrations, one of which shows a principal character inquiring, "You are proud to be a Jew, Paul Elzear, isn't that true?" (Ill. 11:6). Perhaps a Jewish reader felt a surge of pride as well. Marcel Proust, whose mother was Jewish, wrote the nostalgic eight-volume *A la recherche du temps perdu* (*Remembrance of Things Past*), 1913–1927, revolving around the impact of time and memory, the love life of his alter ego, the Jewish esthete Swann, and the negative effects of the Dreyfus Affair. André Maurois was a prolific historian and biographer, whose novels *Bernard Quesnay*, 1926, and *Le Cercle de Famille* (*The Family Circle*), 1932, were reminiscences of his early life when he experienced anti–Semitism during the Dreyfus Affair.

Some Christian printmakers found Jewish subject matter attractive or interesting. Alexandre Lunois mastered the difficult technique of color lithography, which produced unusual translucent watercolor effects. Having won a prize in the Salon of 1887, he used the award to visit exotic places in Morocco. In that distant land, he heard about, but of course did not witness, the mikva ceremony. He did, however, compose a pastel-hued lithograph, *Le Bain de la Mariée Juive* (*The Bath of the Jewish Bride*), 1905–1906 (Ill. 11:7). According to the Sephardic custom, the prenuptial immersion was an opportunity for female friends and relatives to honor the bride, partake of delicacies, and admire the wedding presents which were displayed in the trousseau room. The bride's pose is that of a professional model.

Gustave Leheutre etched a delicate representation of his (and the eleventh century scholar Rashi's) native city, *La Rue de la Synogogue à Troyes* (*The Street of the Troyes Synagogue*), 1920, for Eugène Fromentin's novel *Dominique* (Ill. 11:8). The non–Jewish brothers Jean and Jerome Tharaud disseminated positive Jewish culture and tradition in their novels *Un Royaume de Dieu* (*God's Kingdom*), 1925, and *L'An Prochain à Jerusalem* (*Next Year in Jerusalem*), 1929. In the 1930s they switched to anti–Semitic themes. While never adopting Nazi extremism, they explained that since the current crop of Jews bore no relationship to their biblical antecedents, excluding them from the rest of humanity would insure a better world.

The "Degenerate Art" exhibit of 1937 in Munich spilled over into France and other countries where "non–Aryan" sentiments were exploited. Fascists took advantage of the internal weaknesses and challenged the Socialist and Communist Popular Front government under the leadership of the Jewish prime minister Leon Blum. As charges of Jewish clout and Zionist machinations flourished, anti–Semites stepped up their attacks; aside from political and social mayhem, thousands of artworks were stolen from Jewish homes, libraries, and museums. Although Blum attempted to curtail right-wing elements and was largely responsible for many working-class reforms, his nonintervention policies encouraged the Axis powers. Faced with fanatic

Ill. 11:6. *"You are proud to be a Jew, Paul Elzear, isn't that true?"* Pochoir, 1925. By Arthur Szyk. From *Le Puit de Jacob (Jacob's Well)*. Reproduced with the cooperation of Alexandra Szyk Bracie and the Arthur Szyk Society. www.szyk.org

anti–Semitism and thwarted in attempts to cope with the country's economic troubles, he resigned in 1937, leaving the government in the hands of radicals who harassed and deported the illegal refugees. Among his critics was the influential writer and doctor L. F. Destouches (Céline). Supported by a dozen organizations bent on the defamation or destruction of Jews, he gifted his audience with *Bagatelles pour un Massacre* (*Trinkets for a Massacre*), 1937, in which he accused Jews of sabotaging and raping France: *Le monde est un lupanar juif!* (*The world is a Jewish brothel!*).

The outbreak of war was inevitable. But what was inconceivable was the speed with which France was overrun. Paris, along with areas of the industrialized north and part of the Atlantic coast, fell in just a few weeks to the superior equipment of German armies. Marshal Philippe Pétain and Pierre Laval assumed command, toadying to the Nazi machine. Because Hitler was anxious to secure French cooperation before attacking Russia, he arranged a secret meeting with Pétain on October 24, 1940, in the town of Montoire where he agreed to a collaboration

Ill. 11:7. *Le Bain de la Mariée Juive (The Bath of the Jewish Bride)*. Lithograph, 1906. By Alexandre Lunois

between the two countries—in effect laying the groundwork for the pro–Nazi Vichy government in the capital of unoccupied France. Although Pétain at first defended Jews against physical violence, which he said was outside the domain of the military, he authorized the expropriation of Jewish property, denied exhibition space in the salons to Jewish and other foreign artists, introduced anti–Jewish legislation, and supervised the deportation of seventy-six thousand Jews to death camps in Poland.

Daniel Kahnweiler and other Jews went into hiding. Picasso, meanwhile, hadn't forgotten the encouragement he had received from the famous art dealer, acknowledging his gratitude in 1937 with a lithographed portrait of his friend and mentor (Ill. 11:9). Picasso never bought the anti–Semitic propaganda that Jewish agents and patrons destroyed the French market by ignoring the work of "true" Frenchmen such as André Derain, Maurice Vlaminck, and Dunoyer de Segonzac—all spokesmen for the Nazi ministry of culture—or that Jews were engaged in a conspiracy against the survival of a French art school. It was the sort of rhetoric that brought about fierce suffering and led to the murder of more than one quarter of the French Jewish population.

While some artists, such as Orloff, Chagall, and Lipschitz, escaped, some eighty Jewish artists perished. Max Jacob had hoped that his conversion to Catholicism in 1915 would provide him with a special status. Although all of his family were removed to concentration camps in the early '40s, Jacob assumed that as a Catholic he would be spared. He was wrong. To the Nazis he remained a Jew, pinned with a yellow star on which the word "Juif" was clearly displayed. He died of pneumonia in 1944 at the Drancy deportation camp after receiving Church rites, having first asked pardon of the Jewish prisoners there. Picasso memorialized him in his painting *The Charnel House*, 1944–1945, based on horrific photographs of piled-up cadavers.

Polish-born Walter Spitzer studied in Paris. His etching *Demain Ce Sera Mon Tour? (Will It Be My Turn Tomorrow?)* described the appalling image of hunger in the eyes of a camp inmate, and by extension, the bitter state of all European Jewry (Ill. 11:10). Many of those who survived owed their lives to Christian religious leaders and ordinary Christian families who protected and hid Jews at great risk to themselves.

During the war, General Charles De Gaulle escaped to England where he founded the Free French resistance and directed France's struggle against its enemies. Following liberation in 1943 and the creation of the State of Israel in 1948, he adopted some pro–Jewish policies, but they were short-lived. Because he sought a place in the hierarchy of the Arab world, he placed an arms embargo against Israel during the Six-Day War in 1967. Whatever rapport

Ill. 11:8. *La Rue de la Synagogue à Troyes (Street of the Troyes Synagogue)*. Etching, 1920. By Gustave Leheutre, from *Dominique* by Eugène Fromentin

Frenchmen might have had with Israel, he believed, was due to Jewish control of the media. It was his opinion that while Frenchmen elected Leon Blum and Pierre Mendes-France, they agreed with his own characterization of Jews as an "elite people, overconfident, and domineering." Although he later disavowed an anti–Jewish bias, his remark confirmed the government's leanings; several thousand French Jews headed for Israel and the United States. The majority of French Jews supported Zionism, although the left-wing students' movement—including some of its Jewish leadership—accused them of double loyalty and whipped up terrorist and pro–Palestinian demagoguery.

In 1954, anti–Zionists targeted the Jewish liberal prime minister Pierre Mendes-France, who extricated the country from war in Indochina only to involve it almost immediately in North Africa.

Above: Ill. 11:9. *Daniel Kahnweiler.* Lithograph, 1937. By Pablo Picasso. ©2007 Estate of Pablo Picasso/Artists Rights Society (ARS), New York. *Below:* Ill. 11:10. *Demain Ce Sera Mon Tour? (Will It Be My Turn Tomorrow?).* Etching, c. 1944. By Walter Spitzer. ©2007 Artists Rights Society (ARS) New York/ADAGP, Paris

Under Vichy, the Crémieu Decree, which had granted French citizenship to Algerian Jews, was revoked. De Gaulle refused to restore their rights until the Allies pressured him to do so. Algeria and other colonial possessions which had supplied France with profitable markets for over one hundred years initiated uprisings and bloody resistance from 1954 to 1962, resulting in the final recognition of their independence.

The pre-war number of Jews was almost doubled by a huge Sephardic immigration from former French and other predominantly Arab lands. Over three hundred thousand Jews lived in France in the 1960s, including many who migrated from Germany, eastern Europe and the former Ottoman countries. A decade later, the number had risen to five hundred thirty-five thousand. How did France deal with its moral conscience and the reintegration of Jewish survivors into French society? In his 1965 book *Anti-Semite and the Jew*, the non–Jewish philosopher Jean-Paul Sartre recalled the immediate postwar situation: "Now all France rejoices and fraternizes in the streets; social conflict seems temporarily forgotten; the newspapers devote whole columns to stories of prisoners of war and deportees. Do we say anything about the Jews? Do we give a thought to those who died in the gas chambers at Lublin? Not a word." Yet those who remained rebuilt their institutions and helped to resettle returning émigrés. The Jewish community came together around issues of the poor, the needy, and the rehabilitation of fifteen to twenty thousand orphans and abandoned children.

The '70s and '80s witnessed attacks on Jewish institutions and restaurants. The Rue Copernic Synagogue was bombed in 1980, killing four people. Anti-Jewish newspapers and journals such as *L'Action Française*, *Grigoire*, and *Le Franciste* disseminated Holocaust denial stories. Boycotts of Israeli goods were promoted. Dependence on Middle East oil reserves encouraged pro–Arab support, while right-wing assaults on "Jewish power" led to waves of violence. Issues of national identity were raised as both the Muslim and Jewish communities were accused of creating enclaves outside the centrality of the French state. Many Jews found themselves denationalized as "societies of foreign immigrants," or, at best, as "good foreigners." Having renounced the "right to be different" under Napoleon, they now demanded that right under the flag of multiformity.

Throughout the period, whether secular or religious, Socialist or right wing, many Jews continued to maintain the rituals that defined them. Earlier in the century, the dramatist and essayist Edmond Fleg, who rediscovered Judaism and Zionism following the Dreyfus Affair, translated the Haggadah into French in 1925 and accompanied it with four pochoir prints by Janine Aghion. When the Nazis silenced the Hebrew presses, Vichy prisoners created their own mimeographed Haggadot under horrendous improvised conditions. In the Gur Detention Camp at the foothills of the Pyrenees in southwestern France, thousands of Jews existing in almost indescribable conditions celebrated Passover in 1941 using copies of a handwritten Haggadah by Rabbi Leo Ansbacher, understandably incomplete since it was set down from memory over a period of months by an inmate, Aryeh Zuckerman. Prepared on stencils with a sharpened stone and duplicated outside the camp, the last page included hymns typewritten in Latin letters, which permitted participation by those unable to read Hebrew. Zuckerman escaped and joined the underground against the Nazis. Ansbacher ended his days in Israel. Another Haggadah was written and mimeographed in 1941 by Rabbi Leo Cohn in the Lautrec concentration camp. The Introduction explained that because "… there has been no famine greater than this … the normal observances, not possible under the current situation, could be abrogated, but … only in this year, a year of war." Cohn fought in the French Resistance and was killed while helping children reach Palestine. Yet another Haggadah, also mimeographed in 1941, was prepared in Toulouse by Rabbi S. R. Kapel. Its final line was inscribed in Yiddish: *Die Haggadeh zol zayn die letze in Goles!* (*May This Haggadah Be the Last in Exile!*)

At the end of the war, France, needing outlets for its goods, decided that Jews might be useful after all and that it was in her economic interest to supply Israel with major arms. Beginning in 1954 under the leadership of Mendes-France and continuing with the French-Israeli accord through the Sinai Campaign in 1956, there was further involvement in Israeli technology and science, as well as in intercultural projects. Relationships between France and Israel improved as tourism between the two countries gained ground. In spite of these symbols of cooperation, anti–Semitism showed few signs of abating. Conciliatory policies towards Israel waned dramatically as French relations with the Arab world waxed; embargos were placed on passage through the Straits of Tiran and on sale of arms to Israel. Although a unanimously adopted law in 1972 condemned anti–Semitism and all forms of racism, it didn't stop bombings or the desecration of synagogues and Jewish cemeteries. In spite of support from some prominent liberal Frenchmen and a nascent Jewish lobby, such incidents contributed to the decline of Jewish cultural life and the exodus of some Jews to Israel, although most remained.

Over half a million Jews lived in France at the close of the century; it had more than doubled its post–Holocaust size due to mass emigration from Egypt and North Africa. The government began to confront the excesses of the Nazi period, and church leaders tried to mend Catholic-Jewish relations. A human rights movement, open to all residents and not just the ethnically French, gained momentum. Newcomers were slowly absorbed into the economy thanks to communal organizations and resettlement programs. High schools, colleges, and universities included Hebrew language and cultural studies. Newspapers, books, and journals, including many in Yiddish, flourished along with Jewish radio and television programming. Jewish achievement was acknowledged when the prestigious Prix Goncourt was awarded to André Schwartz-Bart in 1959 for his novel *Le Dernier des justes* (*Last of the Just*). Nobel Peace Prizes were awarded to the jurist René Cassin in 1968 and the novelist of the Holocaust Elie Wiesel in 1986, while scholars Henri Bergson and Emile Durkheim were likewise accorded distinguished honors.

Ill. 11:11. *Personages: Three Figures*. Lithograph, 1957. By Ossip Zadkine. ©2007 Artists Rights Society (ARS), New York/ADAGP, Paris

Jewish artists meanwhile had drifted away from subjective material. The temperamental spirit that had defined much of the earlier work was apparently exhausted. The Russian-born painter and sculptor Ossip Zadkine, who had moved into La Ruche in 1910, worked chiefly in either a quasi-representational or abstract Cubist style, but on occasion dabbled in etching and color lithography. He had survived the Holocaust by escaping to New York, returning to Paris when it was safe once more. His Cubist-inspired studies, such as *Personages: Three Figures*, a seven-color lithograph created in 1957, made a transitional statement between intrinsic form and essential line (Ill. 11:11). This newer style, known as Informal Art in France and as Abstract Expressionism in the United States, offered artists freedom to deny materialism, and to some extent, human values in favor of attitudes that corresponded to personal sensations. Its graphic elements induced many painters to take up printmaking.

Pierre Soulages and Maryan S. Maryan, however, pioneered structural and calligraphic forms in their prints which carried spiritual rather than temporal significance. Soulages' works exclude the figure, but one can read emotional tensions in his deeply etched and aquatinted gestural strokes that stand out in heavy relief. *Eauforte No. 9*, 1957, was printed—and overprinted—with textured bars that move across the paper in interlocking three-dimensional surfaces (Ill. 11:12). He was deeply affected by the Holocaust experience, leading some observers to read hints of concentration camp walls in the image. Fortunately he escaped being a direct victim.

Not so Polish-born Maryan. There were few individuals who emerged from Auschwitz with as much disquiet and agitation. Imprisoned at age twelve and stripped of his family, he narrowly missed execution himself; severely wounded, he spent his

Ill. 11:12. *Eauforte No. 9*. Etching, 1957. By Pierre Soulages. ©2007 Artists Rights Society (ARS), New York/ADGAP, Paris

childhood in a displaced-persons camp. Haunted by those experiences, he moved to Israel where he studied at the Bezalel School, and then in Paris where he produced lithographs for Franz Kafka's *The Trial* in 1953. Two years later, he created a group of macabre lithographs based on the legend of the Golem. His not-quite-human nightmarish images embodied the horrors he witnessed, materializing as twisted, unnatural shapes. The fury that informed his monstrous creatures could have been produced only by someone who had actually had lived through the reality and anguish of the Holocaust and knew humans at their most depraved. Reality and anguish proved too difficult to exorcise and he ended his life as a suicide.

The stresses of two wars within just twenty-five years, the economic slump that made buyers scarce and the genocide that swept over Europe turned many artists inward and forced them to work more for themselves than for collectors. Some artists, like Soulages, were able to find an intellectual or affective direction of their own, but for others, like Maryan, the losses ruled out a significant artistic renewal, or even a meaningful life.

Although a Jewish museum was founded in Paris in 1948 to promote and revive cultural primacy, the Jewish art scene had passed its zenith. The cosmopolitan world moved across the Atlantic.

12

Germany and Austria in the Twentieth Century: Disaster and Renewal

The world population stood at almost two billion people in 1900. Of these, some ten and a half million were Jews; almost a million made their homes in Germany and Austria although their numbers were shrinking due to assimilation, intermarriage, birth control, and conversion. The drop would have been even steeper had not the arrival of almost one hundred thousand refugees from Galician and Russian pogroms balanced the losses. They turned up in strange clothes, speaking an embarrassing Yiddish and worshipping with an alarming lack of decorum. But thanks to their determination to lose their "greenhorn" status and thanks to the established Jewish population who supported them in spite of certain reservations, it hardly took two decades before they were indistinguishable from their more settled co-religionists.

On the whole, Jews believed they were accepted as part of the general community, and according to the constitution of 1871, they were. But as the Hapsburg Empire weakened, some of their privileges began to be challenged. Nevertheless, they found opportunities for success as artisans, proprietors of small and large businesses, and in the scientific and cultural explosions that rocked the early years of the new century. Among these luminaries were Kurt Weill, Otto Klemperer, Arnold Schoenberg, and Gustav Mahler in music; Samuel Hirschenberg, Max Liebermann, Hermann Struck, and Ephraim Moses Lilien in painting and printmaking; Paul Cassirer, Daniel Kahnweiler, and J. B. Neumann in the art market; Albert Einstein, Paul Ehrlich, and Sigmund Freud in the sciences; Hermann Cohen, Martin Buber, Otto Hirsch, and Leo Baeck in philosophy and religion; Heinrich Kohl and Carl Watzinger in archeology; Franz Werfel, Emil Ludwig, Arnold Zweig and Else Lasker-Schüler in literature; Walther Rathenau in economics and politics; Fritz Lang, Max Reinhardt, Ernst Lubitsch, and Lotte Lenya in the theater; Kurt Eisner, Rosa Luxemburg, and Karl Liebknecht in Jewish radicalism; and Albert Ballin in ship building. In addition, as patrons of modern experimental art, German Jews such as Oskar Reichel, Karl Wittgenstein, and Otto Benesch were notable for their great collections, as were the Austrian dealers Richard Lanyi and Otto Kallir. Jewish dealers were prominent players in the modern art market, bringing together artists and patrons.

Liberal newspapers and a substantial portion of book production were in the hands of Jewish firms, as were major department stores. Tietz's and Wertheim's were wonders of pageantry. "At one time the windows represented an Indian temple," an enthusiast wrote, "another time a Roman triumphal arch, or ships at dock, or waterfalls and cascades."

Many of these Jews lived double lives. Their confusion or discomfiture was frequently depicted in the satirical weekly *Simplicissimus* by the cartoonist Thomas Theodore Heine, who was of Jewish descent, but raised as a Christian. His spoof *Metamorphosis*, 1903, demonstrated that an upstart Jew cannot change his true identity as readily as he changes his garments and his name; and that neither Enlightenment nor Emancipation would confer respectability or hide his Jewish nose (Ill. 12:1). The captions tell of "Moishe Piss" who "deals in used clothes in Tarnopol. As Moritz Waterjet [!] he emigrates to Posen, where he sells fashionable Parisian dresses. Now he lives in Berlin as Maurice LaFontaine [the fountain] in Berlin, where he has created a new artistic fashion and deals in second-hand Parisian art." When *Simplicissimus* became a tool for Nazi propaganda in 1933, Heine, the "non–Jew," fled to Stockholm where he produced anti–German cartoons. The breakdown of conventional Jewish lifestyles was insinuated again in the humorous magazine *Schlemiel* (*Fool*), 1904. A cartoon by Fritz Levi captured the ambivalence of a young mother: "And because you're a member of a Zionist youth group, Father Christmas has brought you a menorah." From that same paper came *Metamorphosis of a Hanukkah Candlestick into a Christmas Tree*, 1906, yet another example of the weakening tradition (Ill. 12:2).

With anti–Jewish sentiments frequently lying very close to the surface, it didn't take much for the public to agree with the periodicals and lithographic posters that pointed out Jewish moral folly and negative characteristics. Together with highly popular lithographed post cards, such material reached virtually every person in the land. *Einst und Jetzt* (*Then and Now*) takes a snide look at a Jewish parvenu parading his newly acquired status (Ill. 12:3). In another card, Herr Muller "would like to know why all the Jews have German wet-nurses?" Responds Herr Schultze: "You mean you don't already know? That's how they learn how to drain us Germans dry." "Greetings from Borkum," shouts a card featuring a group of Jews being turned away from the anti–Semitic resort: "Whoever approaches with flat feet, with crooked nose and kinky hair ... must be shown the door. Get out!" And in a class by itself, *Gruss von Moorbad (Greetings from Moorbad)*, shows a Jew with a bald top and a gleaming bottom enjoying a mud bath (Ill. 12:4).

Clean or otherwise, they were living on the edge. Jews were kept out of high official positions in the government and military. Jewish doctors and lawyers were stonewalled in seeking advancement. University-trained teachers were denied full professorships on religious grounds. Nevertheless, there were reasons for German Jews to believe they were living in the best of times. Many lived in the best part of town and prayed in huge classical or Moorish-style synagogues.

Ill. 12:1. *Metamorphosis*, **1903. By Thomas Theodore Heine**

Above: Ill. 12:2. *Metamorphosis of Hanukkah Candlestick into a Christmas Tree,* 1906. From *Schlemiel* (*Fool*). *Below:* Ill. 12:3. *Einst und Jetzt (Then and Now).* Lithograph postcard. c. 1910

They were admired by world Jewry for their intellectual and economic accomplishments. Their legal and political self-help and welfare organizations worked to preserve Jewish rights and control class prejudice. Their schools taught modern Hebrew to students of all ages. In Frankfurt, the Christian Heinrich Frauberger laid the foundation for scientific studies of Jewish art in terms of its ethnographic contribution to German culture and was instrumental in the development of the city's Jewish museum. Determined to "rescue and collect," in 1901 he established a research society to document and publish material relating to Jewish artistic landmarks.

Adding to the flow of information were several art and literary publications: *Ost und West* (*East and West*) beginning in 1900; *Die Welt* (*The World*) in 1901; and *Mitteilungen der Gesellschaft fur Jüdischer Volkskunde* (*Journal of the Society for Jewish Folklore*) in 1902. A year later, the philosopher and author Martin Buber established the journal *Jüdischer Kunstler* (*Jewish Artists*), arguing that aesthetics and artistic creativity were normative, rather than atypical or irregular elements in Jewish culture. However, he denied that a true Jewish art was possible in his time. A national art, he insisted, "requires a national homeland, a heaven towards which to strive, and a unified body of people" in order to develop properly.

In 1902, the publishing house *Jüdischer Verlag,* began what would become the largest venture in Jewish and Zionist aesthetics in western Europe. Founded by Buber, Bernard Feiwel, and the Austrian-born print-maker Ephraim Moses Lilien, it sought to promote sound critical judgment. Lilien, the first important Jewish artist dedicated to the Zionist cause, believed that a Jewish identity could be shaped to parallel that of other nations by encouraging artists and poets to embrace Jewish themes. He set the pace by illustrating Morris Rosenfeld's *Lieder-Bukh* (*Song Book*), first published in Yiddish in New York in 1897, and translated into German as *Lieder des Ghetto* (*Songs from the Ghetto*) in 1903. *Sturm* (*Storm*) depicted an anguished Jew returning to Russia after being turned away from America for lack of money: "We are voyaging, but no one waits for us." No one except a hooded

Ill. 12:4. *Gruss von Moorbad (Greetings from Moorbad)*. Lithograph postcard. c. 1910

skeleton patiently biding its time for the wild ocean to deliver its hostage (Ill. 12:5). *Der Jud-ische May* (*Jewish May*) became a Zionist icon; its elderly Jew, restrained by barbed wire, stretches his arms towards the rising sun and a new beginning (Ill. 12:6). While former Mays were unhappy, the coming Springtime will surely be one of happiness: The message was clear—without a national home Jews would forever be insecure:.

> Nevermore of dread afflictions
> Or oppressions need ye tell;
> Filled with joy and benedictions
> In the old home shall ye dwell
> To the fatherland returning
> Following the homeward path.

Hermann Struck, the son of a prosperous Orthodox and ardently Zionist family, incorporated his religious beliefs into his widely collected prints. Following a meeting with Theodor Herzl in Vienna, he went to Palestine in 1903, the first such visit by a Jewish artist of note. Although his later works were distinguished more by skill than inspiration, for his 1902 etching *Havdala* (titled after the ceremony that closes the Sabbath), he relied not on a spurious sentimentality, but on genuine reverence (Ill. 12:7). The glow of the candles illumined the darkened interior of the room and perhaps, too, the spirit of the artist. Berlin's Paul Cassirer, the first dealer to exhibit the works of Europe's Jewish artists, was so impressed by Struck's technique that he commissioned *Die Kunst des Radierens* (*The Art of Etching*), 1908, which became a basic reference work for both students and experienced printmakers. During World War I Struck served in the German army as chief of the Department of Jewish Affairs where he had some success "convincing the authorities that the Jew is a positive element if his religious and national lives are unrestricted." Contacts with eastern Jews during that period led to a portfolio of twenty-two lithographs, *Skizzen aus Polen* (*Polish Sketches*), 1915, among which a dead Jew is a memorial to the harsh shtetl life (Ill. 12:8).

But nostalgia had had its day. Many artists turned to the more precise formal composi-

Above: Ill. 12:5. *Sturm (Storm)*. Etching by Ephraim Moses Lilien, c. 1900. From *Lieder des Ghetto (Songs from the Ghetto)* by Morris Rosenfeld. *Below:* Ill. 12:6. *Der Judische May (The Jewish May)*. Etching by Ephraim Moses Lilien, c. 1900. From *Lieder des Ghetto (Songs from the Ghetto)* by Morris Rosenfeld

tions of neo–Impressionism. Max Liebermann, born in Berlin to an upper-class Jewish family in the mid–nineteenth century, was
a transitional artist in that idiom, having
spent many of his eighty-eight years painting, printmaking, and directing the German
art world away from popular historical whim-
sies. His spare but descriptive images, his
flickering line and fidelity to nature placed
him at the head of the German school in
which graphics were prominently featured.
He was attacked for his early painting *The
Infant Christ Teaching in the Temple,* 1879,
with its reminder that Jesus was a Jew who
functioned in a Jewish setting surrounded by
rabbis. The slights made him uneasy and he
began frequent visits to Amsterdam, where
he felt more comfortable. In 1908, "very much
aware of belonging to the Jewish people," he
etched *Aus dem Judenviertel in Amsterdam*
(*The Jewish Quarter of Amsterdam*), views of
thrifty housewives, boisterous children, and
busy street vendors with pushcarts full of
tempting foods (Ill. 12:9). Leibermann felt

Above: Ill. 12:7. *Havdala.* Etching, 1902. By Hermann Struck. *Below:* Ill. 12:8. *Dead Jew.* Lithograph, 1915. By Hermann Struck. From *Skizzen aus Polen (Polish Sketches)*

Ill. 12:9. *Aus dem Judenviertel in Amsterdam (The Jewish Quarter of Amsterdam).* 1908. Etching. By Max Liebermann

physically safe in Germany; he argued that Zionism was appropriate only when Jews were threatened. But with the rise of Fascism after World War I, he became alarmed at the danger already in sight. He lived just long enough for the Nazis to divest him of his awards and the presidency of the Berlin Academy, but his stature as a pillar of art protected his life. When he died, no officials or notables, and only four brave artists from among the many he helped, came to his funeral. His widow committed suicide when her deportation became a certainty. Their home and art collection were subsequently ransacked.

Modeling himself after Liebermann as well as the French Impressionists, Lesser Ury was stimulated by the effects of natural daylight against the white of paper. Although his pastels and paintings were favored, he often relied on his prints to record his lonely wanderings. His Jewish instincts were expressed in large biblical themes and depictions of czarist refugees who had found a haven in Palestine. The Berlin National Gallery held a retrospective exhibition in honor of his seventieth birthday in 1931, an extraordinary tribute to a Jew given the virulence of the times.

Some artists, however, were denied their Jewish identity. Emil Orlik's parents baptized him as a child so that he would be acceptable to fashionable society. Nevertheless, he remained an unfashionable Jew to the Nazis, who destroyed many of his works. Among his surviving etchings, *Jules Pascin*, 1911, was an affectionate tribute to the Jewish artist (Ill. 12:10). Images of tailors like his father, shoemakers, and women mending suggest that Jewish story elements remained with him.

Max Pollak's *In Fluchtlingslager Nikolsburg-Auskammen (Hair Combing in the Nikolsburg Refugee Camp)*, 1914, was one of ten etchings of displaced Galician families made while he was on duty with the Austrian army (Ill. 12:11). Its story was blunt, its disillusion cutting. His

Above: Ill. 12:10. *Jules Pascin.* Etching, 1911. By Emil Orlik. *Below:* Ill. 12:11. *In Fluchtlingslager Nikolsburg-Auskammen (Hair Combing in the Nikolsburg Refugee Camp).* Etching, 1914. By Max Pollak

Ill. 12:12. *Sigmund Freud at His Desk*. Etching, 1914. By Max Pollak

etching *Sigmund Freud at His Desk*, 1914, theatrically pinpoints the doctor with dazzling light, capturing his troubled mood (Ill. 12:12). Freud has surrounded himself with pagan idols, perhaps as a challenge to the Second Commandment or as symbols buried in the unconscious mind. Although Freud claimed to be indifferent to religion, he preserved an attachment to his Jewish ancestry. Among his memorabilia were a medieval Chanukah lamp, his father's inscribed Hebrew Bible, and a copy of the Babylonian Talmud. He told the Vienna B'nai Brith organization in 1926 that although he was an unbeliever, "Yet much remained to make the attraction of Jewry and of Jews irresistible—many obscure emotional forces, which were the more powerful the less they could be expressed in words...." Pollak hoped that choosing prominent Jews as his subjects would elevate them in Christian eyes.

Karl Jakob Hirsch, great-grandson of the nineteenth century Orthodox rabbi Samson Raphael Hirsch, converted to Protestantism. As an author, he wrote fiction, poetry, and leftist political booklets. As an artist, he combined distortion with a kind of savage line. A small drypoint, *Wahnsinniger* (*Insane One*), 1922, records a figure literally scared stiff. In this image he apparently documented the confusion and chaos of his own life (Ill. 12:13). Hirsch's affinity for Christianity did him no good; when the Nazis came, he was one for whom they came. He escaped to America, but an emotional collapse resulted in his institutionalization.

While many artists were producing conventional images, Lovis Corinth, a non–Jewish contemporary of Liebermann, worked in a more Impressionist manner. For the portfolio *Der Kampf der Juden* (*The Struggle of the Jews*), 1910, he designed twenty-two lithographic illustrations for the apocryphal Book of Judith; they seem to question art's ability to mirror the human experience (Ill. 12:14). Three years before his death in 1925, he made a pair of lithographs of his longtime friends and patrons Erich and Senta Goeritz. They were just two of the many Jewish collectors and connoisseurs who helped preserve masterpieces through the heydays of post–Impressionism and Expressionism. Their wealth, derived from textile manufacture,

Ill. 12:13. *Wahnsinniger (Insane One)*. Drypoint etching, 1922. By Karl Jacob Hirsch

reflected the economic growth and industrialization of Germany which allowed the accumulation of great fortunes. Jewish patronage of the arts upgraded the Jewish image, although affluence often called unwanted attention to Jewish achievements and prestige.

Neither Liebermann, Struck nor any of their circle were to thrust German style into its greatest maturity. Following the lead of Picasso, others began examining African and South Pacific ritual crafts on display in ethnological museums. They looked back at sixteenth century masters who had likewise worked with subjective and spiritual imagery, particularly the human face. Those early influences were a latent source of capital which now paid off accumulated dividends in the emotional art of the Expressionist movement—an art based on exaggeration and externalized sensation which was largely represented through printmaking.

To understand its germinal influences, it is necessary to investigate the styles that preceded it, particularly Romanticism and Impressionism. The Romantic touchstones of spontaneity, excess, and freedom of choice in subject matter and pattern were distilled into an artistic adventure by German artists in the first quarter of the twentieth century. They reacted against the overt elegance of academic art, restored the emphasis on line which Impressionism had discarded, and concentrated on the enduring qualities of nature rather than the transient effects of light. Their politically and socially radical prints, characterized in part by slashing black strokes, in many ways determined their painting styles and were often of more significance. Their neurotic and intellectual approaches and defiance of authority alienated them from mainstream art and society.

The term Expressionism was first used in its art-historical meaning in 1911 when the Jewish art dealer Herwarth Walden opened the most important German Expressionist showcase in Berlin and bestowed that name in his magazine *Der Sturm*. Although he applied the term to the powerful works of Cézanne, van Gogh, and Matisse, in its wider sense Expressionism denotes German design from about 1905 until shortly before World War II. It was given

Ill. 12:14. *Der Kampf der Juden (The Struggle of the Jews).* **Lithograph, 1910. By Lovis Corinth**

dynamic form in 1905 by anti-academic, anti-intellectual, idealistic young crafts and architectural students in Dresden calling themselves *Die Brücke* (*The Bridge*), and by others in Munich who founded *Der Blaue Reiter* (*The Blue Rider*) in 1911. Desperation and cynicism as well as passion were conveyed through the immediacy of gesture and the grotesque. They discovered new truths in prosaic images and recorded a society that they believed was morally corrupt and betraying its own humanity.

Many Expressionists believed they were contributing to the betterment of a Socialist society, but in spite of their fervor they had only a modest impact. During their most active period, Germany was busy elsewhere, expanding the production of steel, electricity, dyes, and chemicals, and becoming caught up in grandiose long-range schemes of conquest through a naval buildup against Britain. When Archduke Franz Ferdinand was assassinated at Sarajevo in 1914, the delicate political balance that held Europe together collapsed in domino fashion. The major European powers enrolled in a system of mutually assured ruin; with the entrance of the United States, global war and mass slaughter became painful realities. When the hostilities ended in 1918, Europe was in eclipse, with the cost in manpower over twelve million dead and twenty million wounded; in Germany alone, two million died, four million were disabled. The imperishable monarchies were weakened or destroyed, generations of preeminence in the creative arts declined. It was the end of the civilization that had dominated Western life since the Renaissance and the onset of overstated nationalistic identities.

An unfortunate settlement imposed a situation that guaranteed another conflict. The short-lived Weimar democracy which followed the demise of the Kaiser's government existed roughly between 1919 and 1933. It was a period of Jewish influence and affluence in government, social life, and the economy. However, unrealistic reparations and heavy doses of collective guilt were forced on the entire population, a penalty that was beyond its power to cope with or repay. The humiliation of defeat, the loss of Germany's African empire and industrial areas, and a host of restrictions encouraged the rise of fanatic right-wing parties. Foreign trade fell, tariffs rose, the country ran out of credit and began to print paper money. It slid into debt and one of the deepest inflations ever known—the cost of a loaf of bread was billions of worthless marks. Almost everyone lost savings and security. The predictable reaction was to lay the onus on Jews, the universal scapegoat. The dark sides of capitalism and materialism were attributed to "Jewish power" which was duping the country through international conspiracies. Extremism and violence took over, marking the end of the Jewish utopian dream and the beginning of the depredations that uprooted multitudes and butchered and burned the Six Million.

Never mind that neither the pre-war government nor the arms manufacturers had included a single Jew. Ignored was the fact that twenty percent of the Jews had served in the German army as officers and soldiers, and that twelve percent of these had lost their lives. A poster, *An Die Deutschen Mütter*, addressed to the German motherland in memory of the Jews who died in the defense of their country, was disregarded by German nationalists (Ill. 12:15). Perhaps Admiral von Tirpitz had an answer: "The self-preservation of every individual, still more of every nation, is a duty, and since we need hatred for our self-esteem, we will instill it into the heart of every German and we will let it flame on every mountain-top of our Fatherland."

Some of this vexation and unrest was challenged by the Expressionist Brücke artists who dedicated themselves to sensibility in art and the elevation of the human spirit. One of their founders was a twenty-five-year-old Gentile artist, Ernst Ludwig Kirchner, who, with his fellow students helped to change the character of German art. His idealism shattered, his "untrained" or "primitive" paintings and prints renounced aesthetic tradition and took on discordant elements. In his 1918 woodcut *Head of Ludwig Schames*, he acknowledged the Jewish art dealer who helped popularize his work as well as that of Cézanne, van Gogh, Monet, and Manet (Ill. 12:16). The irregularly shaped plank of wood forced the image into a compressed space, while a flat, angular tribal nude wedged against Schames' head evoked a strong sensuality; estrangement is the controlling factor, as male and female avoid confrontation. Great black holes that pass for his eyes suggest a lost faith. When Schames died in 1922, Kirchner wrote, "In the noblest way he made it possible for me and many others to create and live."

A major influence on Kirchner was his teacher, the Jewish illustrator and type designer Hugo Steiner-Prag, creator of twenty-five lithographs for Gustav Meyrink's sinister novel *Der Golem*, 1916. It concerns an ancient legend about a clay monster that comes to life as an automaton able to perform good and terrible deeds through incantations of holy or magical names. In Jewish sources, it was associated by some scholars with the unformed substance of Adam, the "curiously wrought" original golem (Psalm 139:16) before he was invested with a soul (Sanhedrin 38b). The story grew over millennia in a variety of interpretations until it was connected to the sixteenth century Rabbi Judah Loew of Prague, who supposedly formed the creature and then destroyed it when it became intractable. Steiner-Prag cast his own magic in his interpretation of the brute haunting the old synagogue, *Die Hahnpassgasse* (*The Cock's Walk Alley*) (Ill. 12:17). *Im Ghetto* described the old Jewish quarter of Prague with its suffering inmates overwhelmed by the chaos of contemporary life (Ill. 12:18).

The Jewish artist Otto Müller, a member of the Brücke group, chose a ghetto setting for his lithograph *Polnische Judenfamilie* (*Polish Jewish Family*), 1920–21, associating it with the

Ill. 12:15. *An Die Deutschen Mütter (To the German Mother)*, c. 1918

Left: Ill. 12:16. *Head of Ludwig Schames.* Woodcut, 1918. By Ernst Ludwig Kirchner. *Right:* Ill. 12:17. *Die Hahnpassgasse (The Cock's Walk Alley).* Lithograph, 1916. By Hugo Steiner-Prag. From *Der Golem* by Gustav Meyrink

Christian Holy Family perceived as outcast Jews (Ill. 12:19). The print, dedicated to motherhood, envisioned the Madonna in Jewish terms. The crouching dog in the lower left corner may symbolize the fidelity of Jewish communal life. The artist must have felt close to the subject since it contrasted greatly with his typical elongated figures of naked young women and dark-skinned Gypsies. Shortly before the Nazi onslaught that most likely would have claimed him, lung hemorrhages resulting from his military service led to his early death.

Ludwig Meidner, together with Jacob Steinhardt and Hermann Struck, belonged to the so-called Independent school, yet another of the links between academic restraint and the spontaneous dynamism of Expressionism. Brought up in an observant Jewish home, Meidner dropped his religious traditions for the stimulation of Paris. Influenced by such disparate artists as Hieronymous Bosch and Vincent van Gogh, he shared their belief that sensitivity and social consciousness were lacking in art as in life. On his return to Germany in 1912 he joined his Jewish colleagues Richard Janther and Steinhardt in founding Die Pathetiker, a group which called attention to Impressionism's want of fellow-feeling or social sympathy. They described their work as an "affront to all unpathetic people," and adopted a style infused with a high degree of drama and emotion. In 1912, a mystical awakening convinced him of God's existence and the innate goodness of man. That revelation provided the impulse to express

Ill. 12:18. *Im Ghetto (In the Ghetto)*. **Lithograph, 1916. By Hugo Steiner-Prag. From** *Der Golem* **by Gustav Meyrink**

himself in prints and essays on Jewish themes in small, militantly leftist periodicals such as *Der Sturm* and *Die Aktion* which were supported by leading Jewish artists and writers like himself. Meidner excelled in an aggressive, agitated, explosive style of portraiture—a quintessential element of Expressionist art, which depended both on illusory convictions and on responses to the war's savagery. Portraiture, and especially self-portraiture, was a way of commenting, through agonizing or stressful images, on disconcerting situations. Frustration is evident in his drypoint of the idealistic Expressionist Jewish poet *Alfred Wolfenstein*, c. 1920 (Ill. 12:20). The portrait's slashing intensity is developed through nervous broken lines that vibrate across the page. The bulbous forehead speaks of intellect, the piercing eyes and pursed lips of inner pain. Critics complained that Meidner, like other Expressionist artists, disclosed his own personality more than that of his clients. His etched *Self-Portrait*, 1921, reflects a wariness and a psychological fear of light (Ill. 12:21). During the Nazi terrors, he fled to England where he barely made a living as a night watchman in a morgue, honing his skills by painting dead "clients." Returning to Germany after the war, he returned to Orthodoxy and finally recouped a successful career.

Jacob Steinhardt, one of a small number of artists whose interests, work, and spirit exemplified his Jewish heritage, found a middle ground between conformism and the revolutionary Brücke movement. After studying with Corinth and Struck, in 1909 he went to Paris where he joined Meidner and Janther. He was sent to the Eastern Front when war broke out, coming in contact for the first time with a community of shtetl Jews deeply faithful to God despite poverty and oppression. His drypoint *Der Trichter (The Funeral)*, 1921, conveyed their misery and the harshness of his war experiences (Ill. 12:22). In 1933, he left behind a threatening environment, choosing to settle in Palestine, where he taught printmaking and served as the director of the Bezalel Academy of Arts and Crafts.

Wilhelm (Willy) Jaeckel had been an early enthusiast of the war, but he was soon undeceived as horror stories from the front reached a stunned public. In 1915, his lithograph *Juden-Massaker (Massacre of the Jews)*, appeared in *Kriegszeit (Wartime)*, a nationalistic anti–Russian weekly published by Paul Cassirer between 1914 and 1916 that affirmed the anti-militarist sentiments of many artists (Ill. 12:23). In 1917, Jaeckel illustrated the Book of Job as a redemptive gesture following bestial attacks by the Russian army. Religious images drawn from the Bible were another aspect of German expressionist prints, reflecting spiritual attitudes that surfaced in times of devastation.

The malaise following the war was one of denial struggling against reality. In

Above: Ill. 12:19. *Polnische Judenfamilie (Polish Jewish Family).* Lithograph, 1920–1921. By Otto Müller. *Below:* Ill. 12:20. *Alfred Wolfenstein.* Drypoint etching, c. 1920–22. By Ludwig Meidner

1919, when the Weimar Constitution was adopted, the Socialist republic that emerged supported earlier achievements in the arts and sciences. A large part of the population, however, rejected those traditions, adopting decadent or bitter attitudes as they discovered that the problems of the world were intractable. The initial hedonism and sensationalism of the war degenerated into pessimism and economic upheaval, as right-wing military and industrial elements took control and exploited the frustration—much of which descended with appalling havoc on leftist radicals, including the liberal Jewish community. The naive expectation that social awareness might be awakened was shattered. The deterioration of older values left a vacuum. Not even the currency was spared. Ten, twenty, and fifty-pfennig notes issued by the anti–Semitic Bund showed the burning of Jewish-owned newspapers. The

Above: Ill. 12:21. *Self-Portrait.* Etching, 1921. By Ludwig Meidner. *Below:* Ill. 12:22. *Der Trichter (The Funeral).* Drypoint etching, 1922. By Jacob Steinhardt

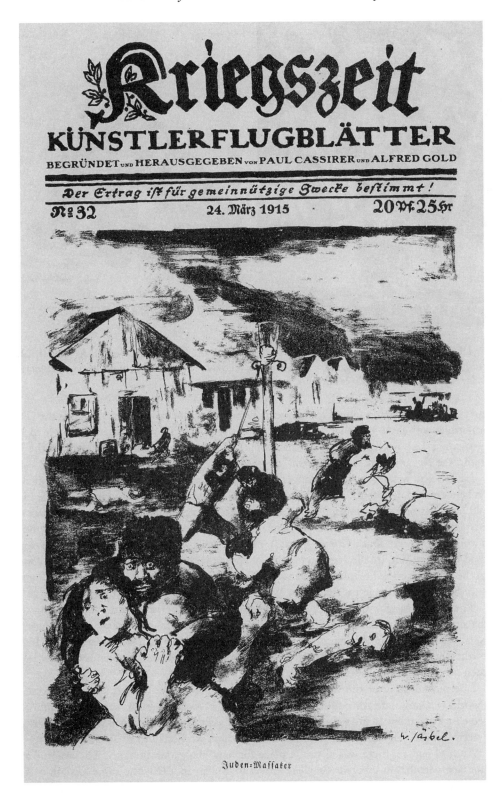

Ill. 12:23. *Juden-Massaker (Massacre of the Jews).* **Lithograph, 1915. By Wilhelm (Willy) Jaeckel**

Left: Ill. 12:24. *Betender Knabe (Praying Youth).* Woodcut, 1921. Lasar Segall. *Right:* Ill. 12:25. *Moving from the Shtetl.* Lithograph, 1922. By Rachel Szalit-Marcus. From *Mentshelakh und stenes (Little People and Scenes).* By Shalom Aleichem

twenty-pfennig coupon quoted Franz Liszt's opinion that "one day the peoples of all the Christian nations will come together to unite against the Jews." Those fortunate enough to have fifty-pfennig coupons could read "Germans of all political parties know the danger of the Jews and join the Aryan battle against them."

Lasar Segall was among those "dangerous" Jews who were disturbed by the bigotry and alienation he witnessed despite the avowed equality of the Weimar declarations. He hoped that his art would have a strong social impact on the general public but, like his fellow hopers, he was soon freed of the illusion. He often based his paintings and prints on melancholy childhood memories. His woodcut *Betender Knabe* (*Praying Youth*), 1921, shows a young man, his head overdeveloped, his body insignificant, intellectually incapable of coping with life (Ill. 12:24). He gets no comfort from the religious book he holds as he stares sadly at the viewer. Segall himself, gripped by fears of anti–Semitic buildup, left for Brazil in 1923, seeing nothing ahead but a grim future.

That future caught up with Rachel Szalit-Marcus, who perished in a concentration camp at the age of forty-six. But in 1922, still in her mid-twenties, she made seventeen lithographic illustrations for Shalom Aleichem's *Mentshelakh und stenes* (*Little People and Scenes)*. Images from the shtetl to the shores of America were tenderly represented by one of the few Jewish women artists working in Germany (Ill. 12:25).

Life picked up after the war. Like many people, Jews were buoyed by the thought that the world was now safe for democracy. An influx of Russian Hebrew writers and publishers raised educational levels and helped stem the tide of assimilation. Zionism was strongly rooted and active in the cultural and social institutions which worked hard to absorb the refugees.

And, of course, there was always a place for new Haggadah imagery. The graphic artist Menachem Birnbaum created his *Chad Gadjo* in Berlin in 1920, the same year that Adolf Hitler delivered his speech "Why We Are Against the Jews." Birnbaum's ten illustrations were horrendous omens of the coming doom. He begins peacefully enough with a kid bought for two zuzim, and ends violently with the execution of the Angel of Death, who has plunged his knife into the bloody carcass of an ox. The Angel, represented only by fingernails and wings, is killed by the Slayer who splits the black unknown with His presence (Ill. 12:26). Each survivor in turn represents brute power over the impotence of his victim. So it was all through history; so it would be when Birnbaum was destroyed in Auschwitz.

Joseph Budko's Haggadah, 1921, skillfully integrated the Hebrew text with illustrations. Budko was thought to be withdrawn and outwardly cold, but his art was warm in a style that permitted a melding of tradition with modernism, slavery with redemption. His faceless Jew trudges alone through history from a callous past to an unknowable future, moving over a snow-lined path, half-frozen, but determined and defiant. No signs or wonders for him—he knows he must make it on his own (Ill. 12:27). Like Steinhardt,

Ill. 12:26. *Angel of Death*. From *Chad Gadjo*, 1920. By **Menachem Birnbaum**

Ill. 12:27. *Faceless Jew*. By Joseph Budko. From 1921 Haggadah

Budko came from Poland. He settled in Berlin when he was twenty-two, illustrating books for a variety of publishers from 1917 to 1924. He made Palestine his final home where, until his death thirty years later, he was a teacher and mentor to a generation of young artists at the Bezalel School.

In 1923, encouraged by Erich Goeritz, Jacob Steinhardt produced the first woodcut-illustrated Haggadah since the Prague edition of 1526, and the first to combine woodcuts with a lithographic text, impeccably designed by Franziska Baruch. His misshapen but dignified figures recalled a Gothic style with their strong black and white contrasts, their emotional thrust and supernatural effects. Steinhardt lent an ominous note to the Passover story by providing the Wicked Son with a German uniform and spiked helmet.

A Haggadah of 1927 that was republished the following year with additional illustrations established a witty format of cavorting stick figures. The artist, Otto Geismar, produced an offbeat Four Sons, with the Wicked Son thumbing his nose at convention while the Wise Son studies his books, the Simple Son simply tosses a ball up and down, and the Unknowing Son apparently knows nothing at all. The inventive illustrations, employing the barest of lines and using white images on a black background as well as the reverse, lend a playful mood to the proceedings.

Erwin Singer created a unique Children's Haggadah, 1933, with five movable color illustrations activated by pull-tabs. It delighted children of all ages with pictures of matzo preparation and the Seder, during which the Afikoman is hidden in Papa's chair. To illustrate the Zionist theme "Next Year in Jerusalem," he contrasted a dark image of the Temple with a bright and sunny view of young people tilling the soil and tending its animal life. These Haggadot were among the last important editions to be produced in Germany before the Second World War.

Expressionism had spread rapidly for some twenty years, but its utopian ideals proved ephemeral, collapsing under the logic of economic recession, unemployment, war reparations, political strikes, and social upheaval. In its short life it had renounced Realism, flirted with Impressionism, developed new relationships of color and forms, and hatched new definitions and conceptions of aesthetics. Its cynicism contributed to Abstraction and Objectivity as viable alternatives.

In the early 1920s, *Neue Sachlichkeit* (*New Objectivity or Matter-of-Factness*) backed away from the idealistic manifesto which declared that if people learned to work together, they could make a better world. The derangement of the preceding years, as well as the excesses of Expressionism, led towards social criticism, chilling aloofness, realism, and clarity. At the head of this movement was Max Beckmann, sometimes mistaken for a Jewish artist because of his famous painting of a synagogue and his close association with a number of Jewish art dealers. When he was classed as "decadent" by the Nazis in 1937, he left for America where he worked for ten years until his death.

Otto Dix, another non–Jewish artist and a member of the "newly objective" group, produced nightmarish works so overloaded with bitterness and alienation that in the end they simply became incoherent. But in his 1922 drypoint of the art dealer and publisher J. B. (Israel Ber) Neumann, who encouraged and promoted many of the Expressionist artists, he produced a congenial image—but with exaggerated Jewish features (Ill. 12:28). Conrad Felixmüller also exhibited in Neumann's gallery. In 1914, he put together a portfolio of woodcuts inspired by Else Lasker-Schüler's *Hebraische Balladen (Hebrew Ballads)*, showing himself a master of insightful portraiture and demonstrating, along with Dix, "the free expression of personality." His woodcut portrait of Max Liebermann, 1926, was one of the many honors offered by painters and printmakers to the now elderly artist who had often championed their work.

Oskar Kokoschka was still another of the Christian artists in the *fin de siècle* Vienna Secessionist movement which promoted cooperation between arts and crafts. A powerful draftsman,

Left: Ill. 12:28. *I. B. (Israel Ber) Neumann.* Drypoint etching, 1922. By Otto Dix. *Right:* Ill. 12:29. *Paul Westheim.* Lithograph, 1922. By Oskar Kokoschka

master of undulant line, and dilettante jack of all trades, Kokoschka at twenty-one wrote the first Expressionist play, *Morder Hoffnung der Frauen* (*Women's Murdered Hope*), 1907; its frank treatment of the battle of the sexes expedited his hasty exit from Vienna. His affair with Alma Mahler, the widow of Gustav Mahler, was the scandal of the day. After she abandoned him in 1914, he moved her life-size, anatomically correct figure into his home and his bed. It accompanied him on his daily rounds until he destroyed it in a drunken frenzy. Fortunately, he continued to create prints. In 1922, he made a lithograph of his close friend Paul Westheim, emphasizing the Jewish art critic and publisher's warm personality (Ill. 12:29). Kokoschka was close to members of the Jewish community. He was one of the few prominent Christian artists to speak out vigorously against National Socialism and Fascism. After fleeing to London from Prague in 1938 at the height of the Nazi persecutions, he indicted his hosts as well as the Catholic Church as accessories to Hitler's rise through their policies of appeasement. Kokoschka was only one of the many radicals who submerged their psyches in the spirit of the era, the German *Zeitgeist.*

The art and publishing world afforded Jews one of the few avenues for inclusion at a time of exclusion from a variety of other professions or careers. A group of prominent and influential dealers honored their colleague Alfred Flechtheim on his fiftieth birthday with a special edition of his publication *Der Querschnitt* (*The Cross Section*), 1928, which included entries by almost every active painter or writer. Even Ernest Hemingway contributed a bit of doggerel to the collection in his typical extravagant style:

> God bless Flechtheim...!
> The age demanded that we sing and cut away our tongue.
> The age demanded that we flow,
> and hammered in the bung;
> The age demanded that we dance,
> and jammed us into pants
> and in the End the age was handed
> The sort of shit that it demanded—
> (But not by Flechtheim).

The early 1920s in Berlin had served as a meeting point for Jewish artists and writers. But when Paris called, many scattered to the City of Light; others found artistic and spiritual homes in the United States and Palestine. However, enough of the intellectual elite remained to support such enterprises as Fritz Gurlitt's publishing house committed to Jewish art and culture—the Verlag für Jüdische Kunst und Kultur—in which Meidner, Steinhardt, Struck, and Ury participated. During the few years in which the Weimar Republic flourished, a five-volume Jewish encyclopedia was published from 1927 to 1930 in Berlin by the Jüdischer Verlag, the first such undertaking in the German language. Russian Jews created a literary renaissance for Hebrew and Judaic works in Germany. Among the rapidly expanding Jewish presses was the Soncino Gesellschaft (no relation to the Hebrew printing firm of the fifteenth and sixteenth century), which functioned from 1924 until the Nazis closed it down in 1937. The ambitious *Encyclopedia Judaica* began publication in 1928, but only ten volumes were completed before it was muzzled by the Nazis. Dread portents had already been so unmistakably clear that when the Society of Jewish Bibliophiles' Bible was published from 1930 to 1933, it carried a secret code within its pages. The last to be issued before World War II, it printed certain passages from Deuteronomy in red ink, communicating warning messages as well as encouragement to the beleaguered Jews.

Nevertheless, book production and design remained key adjuncts to the art and culture of those perverse times. Newer forms of illustration infused fresh interest in prints and texts. Jewish innovators determined that good printing was no less important than it had been historically and went about demonstrating their technical and creative skills. John Heartfield and his brother Wieland Herzfelde had opened a publishing house in 1916, Malik-Verlag. It was generally acknowledged as the premier publishing event of the Weimar period. Malik-Vertag printed all kinds of revolutionary and Communist-inspired antiwar material and unleashed airy expectations that were fated for disappointment. Political and social conflict bound politics to art as the Modernist movement clashed with conservative elements. Heartfield developed original art forms and lithographic graphic designs. His photomontages and collages assembled from newspaper and other clippings were adapted for layouts and book jackets, propaganda posters, and radical journals with the potential of reaching an enormous audience.

He believed that unique and precious objects such as drawings and prints undermined "people's art" and were simply an expression of capitalist frills. Affected by the societal evils that he saw in the wake of the war, he concentrated on images of crippled soldiers, beggars, prostitutes, financiers, military, and bourgeois elements. As Jews and left-wingers, the brothers faced censorship, confiscations, and ultimately, forced exile, first to Prague in 1933 and, when that city was occupied by the German army, to London in 1938. Among Heartfield's anti–Nazi works was *Reservations: Jews Driven Like Cattle*, 1939 (Ill. 12:30). An unrepentant Communist, he made his final home in East Germany in 1950. Although he was never to know it, his work found a renewed expression in the American protest art of the 1960s and '70s.

But while the Left was immersed in social issues, on the Right the National Socialist German Workers' Party (Nazi) was rallying behind the ultranationalism of a young Austrian, Adolf Hitler. He revived Martin Luther's sixteenth century tirades and parroted the 1905 *Protocols of the Learned Elders of Zion*. A symbiotic relationship between a band of Nazis and a charismatic Hitler grew out of a painful political and economic situation in 1923. He had been convicted of attempting a government coup for which he received a five-year jail sentence. He served only nine months, time enough to write the first part of his manifesto, *Mein Kampf* (*My Struggle*), 1925–1927. He pointed out why it was necessary to exterminate the Jews: "Was there really anything foul or shameless anywhere, especially in the area of culture, on which at least one Jew had not cooperated? When I learned about the influence of Judaism in art, literature, film and the theatre, I understood how great the Jewish responsibility was for their present state ... because what was used here to destroy all human values was a pestilence with more fatal results than those the Black Death had had." In 1928 over seven million copies of the finished book, dubbed the Holy Writ by Hermann Goering, were distributed. The Nazi Party captured twelve seats in the Reichstag.

When the 1929 depression put about a third of the German population out of work or in need, fracturing the thin veneer of democratic processes, panic and lawlessness took over. People collectively turned to an authoritative leader (Führer). Rational behavior went out the door as Hitler strode in. The troubles were conveniently blamed on the Jews—they were "pacifist traitors" or Communists, had shirked their duty in the late war and fattened themselves on the scraps of the helpless middle class. Germany moved to a police state bent on world aggression and the death of Jews.

In 1932, A. P. Weber created a design for E. Niekisch's *Hitler—ein deutsches Verhangnis* (*Hitler—A German Disaster*), showing the life-blood of the country descending into a Fascist grave (Ill. 12:31). Hardly anyone seemed to care. After January 30, 1933, when Hitler was legally appointed chancellor of Germany, he took the country from a constitutional republic to total dictatorship in just a few months. Over eighty-eight percent of the electorate approved his regime. The façade of well-structured government turned out to be

Ill. 12:30. *Reservations: Jews Driven Like Cattle*. **Photomontage, 1939. By John Heartfield. ©2007 Artists Rights Society (ARS), New York/VG Bild-Kunst, Bonn**

superficial. Jews were barred from civil employment, their property was confiscated, assaults were either overlooked or encouraged. In May of 1933, the Nazis undertook a "new Spirit," aimed at the destruction of everything "non–German." Millions of books in Jewish libraries, synagogues, and private collections were burned or converted into pulp for paper mills. Torah scrolls, valued for their parchment, were used to make shoes, purses, and other leather items. Fortunately, some thousands of rare or valuable specimens did survive, but only because Brenn-Kommandos (arson squads), knowing their value, sold or ransomed them.

Brown-shirted Nazis learned the latest marching song:

> Crush the skulls of the Jewish pack
> And then the future, it is ours and won;
> Proud waves the flag in the wind
> When swords with Jewish blood will run.

That was the beginning. On April 1, 1933, a boycott of Jewish shops and professional offices was declared. Although fears of public opinion (still tenable) and economic resistance

Ill. 12:31. *Hitler—ein deutsches Verhangnis (Hitler—A German Disaster)*. Design by A. Paul Weber, 1932. ©2007 Artists Rights Society (ARS), New York/VG Bild-Kunst, Bonn

(still possible) forced a backdown, it was the herald of much worse to come. The perception of the Jew was back where it had been five hundred years earlier. The May 1934 issue of the anti–Semitic weekly *Der Sturmer,* under the editorship of Julius Streicher, reiterated the fifteenth century canard of ritual murder along with the 1879 slogan *Die Juden Sind Unser Ungluck (Jews Are Our Misfortune)*. The paper, published from 1923 to 1945, had by 1935 a circulation of four hundred thousand, and by 1940, six hundred thousand. Readership dropped when the absence of Jews made it less topical, although it remained Hitler's favorite magazine. It illustrated Jewish children and teachers being expelled from school, as well as *The Poisonous Mushroom*, which transformed the deadly vegetable into a Jewish nose. They and similar pictures were printed in classroom books issued by Streicher in 1938 where they contaminated an entire generation of German youth.

The Nuremberg Laws of 1935 subjected Germany's Jews to loss of citizenship, prohibited intermarriage and sexual relations between Jews and non–Jews, and eventually even legislated against their use of libraries, park benches, public transportation, automobiles, and telephones. Every kind of harassment, discrimination, and persecution was visited on the people accused of inventing Communism, exploiting capitalism, losing the war, controlling the liberals, ruling the conservatives, and infecting Christianity. Anti-Semitism exploded as racist nationalism, based on blood and soil, took hold. The state declared who was who. No German could be a Jew. No Jew could be a German.

Some tried. Lea Grundig, a member of the Neue Sachlichkeit group, was an idealistic Jewish Communist and anti–Fascist who challenged social and political injustice and championed endangered Jews. Primarily a printmaker, she remained in Germany until 1939, mocking the Nazi establishment with her etchings. *The Jew Is to Blame, Under the Swastika*, and other such works were issued clandestinely from her own press; though they reached only a limited number of people, those who saw them recognized the infinite courage of the artist. *The Flight Begins*, 1934, dramatized the pleasure with which young German men and women shoved and

Ill. 12:32. *The Flight Begins*. Etching, 1934. By Lea Grundig. ©2007 Artists Rights Society (ARS), New York/VG Bild-Kunst, Bonn

pushed helpless Jews until they were submerged into a void (Ill. 12:32). Following two arrests, Grundig managed to escape to Palestine where, unlike some other refugee artists, she kept the Holocaust images alive. Her husband Hans, an artist in his own right who had been forbidden to paint in 1934, survived internment in the Sachsenhausen concentration camp, and they were later reunited in East Germany.

Jews differed among themselves on many issues. Conservative Nationalists and liberal Zionists split the community. Orthodox and Reform congregations existed on separate levels, each vying for adherents. Conciliators such as Rabbi Leo Baeck and Otto Hirsch made valiant attempts to bridge the differences. Efforts to rescue children were undertaken by the Zionist Youth Aliyah movement which transported many to Palestine. General emigration was encouraged to develop its rural economy and to safeguard the community. But urging Zionism as a security measure or to stress unity and kinship was not what several hundred prominent leaders had in mind when they signed a proclamation in the Berlin *Vossische Zeitung*: "We profess the Jewish religion, but reject any sort of Jewish nationalism. We regard ourselves, along with the overwhelming majority of German Jews, as members of the German, not of the Jewish people." They were influenced by the combination of "better" behavior during the 1936 Olympic games, patriotism, inertia, and Arab riots, all of which contributed to the relatively small number of Jews willing to go while it was still possible.

Baeck survived Theresienstadt. Hirsch died in 1941 in the Mauthausen concentration camp. About two hundred thousand left between 1934 and 1939 when the doors slammed shut. In Austria, about half that number got out in time. Some fifty thousand more escaped during the following two years, leaving behind family, friends, property, and the wherewithal to begin life somewhere else. Unfortunately, many of them later found themselves once more under Nazi rule as their countries of refuge were conquered. When the Allies met in Evian, France in 1938 to address the ongoing problem of these stateless Jews, only tepid recriminations were heard; not one country was willing to do anything to help solve it. Hitler came to the very logical conclusion that the outside world would overlook the atrocities.

The Nazis declared war on Jewish culture in July of 1937 when an exhibition of "morally corrupt, Jewishly initiated" modern art opened in Munich's Archeology Institute. The spectacle celebrated the pernicious union of art and politics. About five thousand items by "radical progressive" artists were looted from thirty-two German museums; six hundred and fifty were destined for the *Entartete Kunst* (*Degenerate Art*) display. Only six of the artists were Jews, but that didn't prevent the exhibit from being designated a "Jewish-Bolshevik international conspiracy." The majority of the works were Expressionist and New Objectivity paintings, but prints, books, sculpture, music and other pre–1933 items by "charlatans and incompetents, pimps and perverts" were included as testimony to Bolshevik-Jewish manipulation and the "insults" sustained by the German "heroes of the Great War." Joseph Goebbels, the chief propagandist of the Nazi Party and holder of a doctorate in Jewish literature, spoke of the "horrifying and frightening forms" created by irascible Jews.

The *Entartete* show focused on Expressionist artists who had defied the corruption and oppressive nature of the totalitarian government and who were perceived as threats to stability. On view for four months, it attracted over two million visitors before going on a three-year tour to thirteen German and Austrian cities where it was seen by an additional million people. Never before had a nation gathered and denounced its artistic leadership on such a scale, burning about four thousand prints and drawings and selling the "garbage and dregs of degenerate art" to bring in needed cash.

Munich then organized a traveling anti–Semitic exhibition in November of 1937, *Der ewige Jude* (*The Eternal Jew*). Thousands of works portraying Judaism as a corrupt influence were burned in front of the main Berlin fire station on March 20, 1939. In order to undercut and invalidate all "harmful" material that represented the Jews in any form, art became the instrument of the state. Depictions of wholesome farm families, patriotic soldiers, heroically proportioned nude athletes, and Aryan craftsman and laborers in a debased neo–Classical style became the paradigm of a movement that emphasized subject matter or content over meaning; "racial ideals" were favored in order to promote the glory of the "Thousand-Year Reich." Hitler defined art as "the only truly enduring investment of human labor, more important than the satisfaction of daily needs." This from the pen of the frustrated architect and artist who had failed the entrance examination to the Vienna Art Academy in 1907.

On November 9–10, 1938, extensive and indiscriminate assaults terrorized thousands of Jews, destroyed hundreds of businesses, public buildings, and cemeteries, and looted, desecrated, or burned synagogues in Germany and Austria. The strategy of Kristallnacht, the Night of Broken Glass, had been planned well before, but the assassination of Ernst vom Rath, a secretary of the German embassy in Paris, by a young Jew avenging his parents' exile to Poland was used as an excuse to begin the violence. Horrendous penalties and reprisals were carried out.

Hitler challenged the European powers with faits accomplis, annexations, aggressions, and occupations without serious hindrance until France and Great Britain declared war after the invasion of Poland in September, 1939. By that time Jews faced even more restrictive laws.

More racist material was enlisted to "prove" the natural superiority of the Aryan people The Jewish badge returned. Jews lost professional and communal positions, were herded into concentration and death camps, forced to work in brutal conditions of starvation and sickness, labeled as parasites and grave-diggers of German institutions. The fatherland began the destruction of its own people and those of its neighbors. Extermination orders went out in 1941. In addition to hundreds of thousands of Catholics, Protestants, Communists, labor leaders, Gypsies, homosexuals, and "misfits" who were destroyed in the indiscriminate Final Solution, a third of all the Jews in the world perished. Once "racial purity" became the criterion for survival, the Jewish fate was sealed. Those with "Jewish blood," including eleven Nobel laureates, were suddenly contemptible "non–Aryans." The commandant of Auschwitz proudly announced that his five death chambers could kill sixty thousand Jews every day; between one and a quarter and one and a half million were gassed and burned there alone, a figure that doesn't include another half million who perished from starvation and sickness. Multitudes were blown out of smokestacks—but not before their wedding rings were confiscated and gold from their teeth was extracted, melted, and quietly shipped to supposedly neutral countries. (Along with millions of dollars of stolen artworks and "dormant" bank accounts, tons of looted gold reposed in the strongboxes of half a dozen greedy countries for fifty years and more until demands for restitution began to pry open the vaults.)

Insidious methods of medical experimentation, torture, rape, and slow starvation became acceptable procedures in a country with the highest cultural credentials and the basest humanitarian instincts. Not only were Nazi troops engaged in the murders, but vast numbers of civilians obediently, willingly, and enthusiastically tormented and murdered Jews because centuries of anti–Semitism had engrained the image of a hated people who deserved agony and death. Photographic evidence and personal testimony documented the participation of Germans who were aware of and indifferent to the scientifically directed slaughter. Hundreds of thousands of citizens served in the SS (Schutzstaffel, or Security Service); millions assisted them, others operated or controlled the trains which ran day and night carrying "those damned Jews." The genocide could not have succeeded without popular support.

While large numbers of refugees from 1933 to 1941 had managed to escape (many assisted by non–Jewish Germans, but only rarely by Austrians or Romanians), no one other than fellow Jews really wanted them. The British government admitted about forty thousand, mostly young children, but, as a result of Arab rioting in 1939, allowed only a trickle to reach Palestine. The Canadian minister for immigration, when asked how many his country would accept, replied that "none is too many." Although the United States had accepted some sixty thousand refugees by 1939, on orders from President Roosevelt, it refused admission to a boatload of Jewish exiles on the German ship *Saint Louis*. It was forced to return to continental Europe with six hundred and twenty passengers. Three hundred sixty-five survived. The others died in the Holocaust or from other war-related incidents. At the height of the Great Depression, eighty-three per cent of Americans answering a *Fortune* magazine poll indicated that they didn't want any more strangers competing for jobs. As a result, refugee quotas for Jews mostly remained unfilled.

The full military strength of the United States was added to the Allied forces in 1942. An unyielding Russian winter and Allied invasions in Europe finally checked German victories. Although Hitler's armies no longer dominated the continent, the liquidation of the Jews proceeded on schedule. In April and May of 1943, when Nazi tanks and Polish police faced an uprising in the Warsaw ghetto by underground forces armed with smuggled and other small weapons, they were forced to do the unthinkable—suspend their attack after suffering many losses. Almost half a million Jews made up the population at the start of the uprising—most of the world's Jews lived in Poland and two thirds of them died there, although the impetus came from Germany. Typhoid, starvation, suicides, and evacuations to other camps left about sixty thousand in the ghetto. Of those, seven thousand were shot and six thousand burned alive. Most of the rest were deported to concentration and death camps. The very few remaining victims were at the mercy of their former neighbors—a mercy that only occasionally knew compassion. What many Poles deduced from the annihilation was demonstrated in the vigilante pogroms in which fifteen hundred of the returning Jews were clubbed, tortured, and shot. Although several million Polish Christians were killed as well, war, not genocide, was the deciding factor. Few Jews chose to live in post-war Poland. Some scholars have thought that collective shame infiltrated the Polish psyche, making Christian Poles anxious to avoid those they wronged, and Jews recognized that that they would be less than welcome. Others have suggested that anti–Semitism was as rampant as ever and Jews wanted no part of it.

In April of 1945, Germany finally submitted to unconditional surrender and partition into Eastern and Western blocs. In the war-crimes trials that lasted from 1945 to 1951, over one hundred fifty thousand individuals were accused, many of anti–Jewish atrocities; in Germany, a dozen were sentenced to death, ninety-eight to life in prison, and six thousand to various prison terms. It was not what Hitler had envisioned. Savage to the end, he dictated his will on April 25, 1945: "Above all, I charge the government and the people to uphold the racial laws and to limit and resist mercilessly the poisoner of all nations, international Jewry."

The newly constituted West German government began serious efforts to revive Jewish life. In 1953, it signed a reparation agreement with Israel. Twelve years later formal diplomatic relations were established. The reintroduction of religious materials was among the first signs of recovery. A "Rainbow" Haggadah was printed by American Jewish soldiers in 1945 using a government press, its cover featuring nothing more than a crude table with a plate of matzos, a candelabrum, two eggs, a wine bottle and a cup. However, its eloquence lay, not in the unremarkable illustration, but in the introductory letter by the unit's chaplain, Eli Bohnen: "I am confident that this is the first Hebrew religious work printed in Germany since the beginning of the war ... the soldiers who did the actual printing told us that when they had to clean the press before printing the Haggadah, the only rags available were some Nazi flags, which for once served a useful purpose." A prayer for peace and the song "America" were added to the text.

In 1947, a Haggadah dedicated to the "Saved Remnant" was issued in the town of Landsberg. A group of displaced persons is depicted in a concentration camp encircled by a broken chain as the sun sets above a New Israel. And in a Munich Haggadah of 1948 published by the American Joint Distribution Committee, a wood-engraving showing forced labor in the camps once again reminded the reader that "they afflicted us, and laid upon us hard bondage." The mounting sun together with the barbed wire proclaim that "this Passover will be the last to be celebrated on the soil of Germany." Three weeks later the State of Israel was established.

Although printmaking was all but impossible in ghettos and camps because of the scarcity of materials and presses, prisoners of all ages left behind drawings on scraps of paper or fabrics describing conditions there. They recorded images of near-skeletons, not quite dead, agonized human beings and rotting cadavers, answering to an inner demand to tell what happened, to have a say over their own existence regardless of the risk, and to declare, "I was there and something of me remains." This need overcame fear of discovery since they clearly believed that if the works were rescued—and about thirty thousand were—future generations would cringe from a repetition.

Those who interpreted Holocaust material had to resolve personal feelings, sort out possible images and creative styles, and give sensitive expression to pictures still floating in their heads. Hermann Fechenbach, who lost his left leg from injuries sustained during World War I, didn't let his wounds stop him from expressing pain and misery in his painting and printmaking. It took the Nazis to do that; in 1933 his name was deleted from the official state register which meant he was no longer free to function as an artist. He managed to escape to Palestine and then to England where he was interned as a suspected alien for two years until a sympathetic art publisher arranged for his release. One of his woodcuts, *Barbed Wire*, shows an endless stream of prisoners—young, old, legless like himself—snaking their way through an enclosure flanked by bayonets pointing the way to almost certain death (Ill. 12:33). *Vio-*

Ill. 12:33. *Barbed Wire.* Woodcut, c. 1936. By Hermann Fechenbach. Courtesy Tobey C. Moss Gallery, Los Angeles

lence, perhaps a memorial for his twin sister who was killed in one of the slaughterhouses, recalls the torture in the camps (Ill. 12:34).

Herbert Sandberg was another of those artists who were able to recreate and extract meaning from stored-up memories. The son of Orthodox Jews, he had trained with Otto Müller. When Hitler came to power he attached himself to the Communist Party for which he worked underground in protest activities. Caught and sentenced to serve in a variety of prisons, he

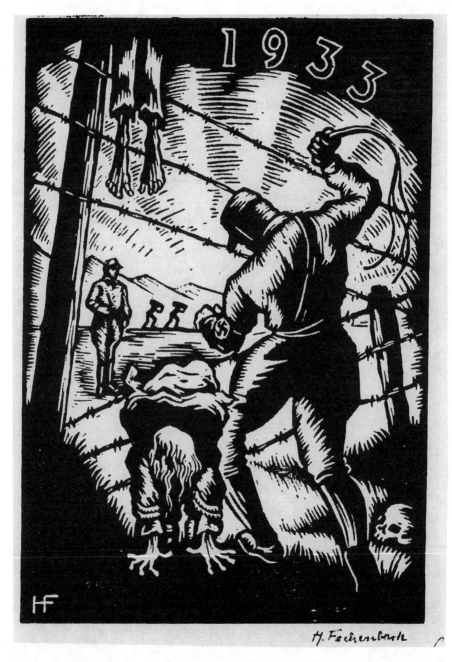

Ill. 12:34. *Violence.* **Woodcut, c. 1936. By Hermann Fechenbach. Courtesy Tobey C. Moss Gallery, Los Angeles**

ended up as a stonemason in the Buchenwald camp, a job that saved his life since bricklayers were in demand. Commissioned for the Buchenwald Museum, his *Stone Age*, from a series of seventy etchings titled *The Path*, 1959–1965, recollects a moment in the life of the men who shared his experiences (Ill. 12:35). The diagonal thrust of the club held in an outsized hand dominates the image, and catches the essence of brutality over the inmates' helplessness.

Italy's Jews had been well assimilated into Italian national life until 1938 when Benito Mussolini, pressured by Hitler, began to impose racial policies against Catholic-Jewish sexual relationships, Jewish teachers, and foreign Jews, and authorized Fascist control of the press. Four thousand Jews converted, five thousand fled. Italian strictures, however, were considerably milder than Hitler's because the average Italian not only refused to cooperate with deportation laws, but helped many Jews to relocate in safer areas. Mussolini was less warped than Hitler, refusing to set up extermination camps on Italian soil. However, when Germany occupied northern and central Italy from 1943 to 1945, eight thousand Jews were shipped to Auschwitz and other Nazi death camps. Nevertheless, Italian Jews had an eighty percent survival rate.

Primo Levi was born and died (possibly a suicide) in an apartment building in Turin following his liberation from Auschwitz. He was Italy's Jewish Holocaust voice, bearing witness to the atrocities in his memoirs and fictional accounts of his experiences. Originally trained as a chemist, he spent four decades recording the pain of his survival and contending with the

Ill. 12:35. *Stone Age*. Etching, 1959. From *The Path* by Herbert Sandberg. ©2007 Artists Rights Society (ARS), New York/VG Bild-Kunst, Bonn

collective sins of twentieth century man. Unable to discover rational meaning in good and evil in a transcendent power, he struggled without belief in a God he could neither fathom nor accept.

The Italian-Jewish artist Zoran Music said that art helped him to survive his two years in the Dachau camp for aiding the resistance movement. He produced works with a shock value that came from personal experience. The "heaps of bodies with their arms and legs sticking out ... had a tragic beauty," he wrote. "Some of them weren't quite dead, their limbs still moved and their eyes followed you around, begging for help. Then, during the night, a little snow would fall. The heap wouldn't move again." For years he refused to deal with those memories, painting instead pleasant scenes remembered from his boyhood days. But spurred by the Vietnam War and other fighting, he recreated his "death pictures" in a series, *We Are Not the Last*, as a protest and warning against universal "violence, arbitrariness, and injustice." One of those lithographs, *Cart of the Dead*, 1970s, depicting a mound of bodies anonymous in their nakedness, is sketchily drawn, as though threatening to fade from his inward eye (Ill. 12:36).

Leo Haas was born in Czechoslovakia at the turn of the century. He studied there and in Austria until deported to a concentration camp. Lucky to have survived, he documented his experiences in drawings and prints. Among the drypoints in his portfolio *Terezin-Theresienstadt*, 1945–1946, *Children on the Way to Auschwitz* depicts not only the youngsters themselves but their frightened friends at the window who know that they will follow very soon (Ill. 12:37).

An etching by Walter Spitzer, *Square in Front of a Barrack*, includes a view of an unknown camp (Ill. 12:38). The bleakness, the wasted figures, the dead being hauled off, and the vile smoke from the chimneys suggest that the artist was present and a witness. When his mother was killed

Ill. 12:36. *Cart of the Dead.* **Lithograph, c. 1970s. From** *We Are Not the Last.* **By Zoran Music.**
©2007 Artists Rights Society (ARS), New York/ADAGP, Paris

Ill. 12:37. *Children on the Way to Auschwitz.* Drypoint etching, 1945. From *Terezin-Theresienstadt.* By Leo Haas. ©2007 Artists Rights Society (ARS), New York/VG Bild-Kunst, Bonn

in the destruction of their town, the teenage Spitzer was deported to a camp near Auschwitz from which he survived a two-week death march to Buchenwald. After liberation he settled in Paris, illustrating books by Sartre and Malraux, still referring in his prints to Holocaust nightmares.

Two Austrian artists, Friedensreich Hundertwasser and Arik Brauer, remained alive in Nazi-controlled Vienna, basing much of their later work on childhood memories of dreamlike forms of devastation and death. Nazi troopers tracked down and killed sixty-nine of Hundertwasser's maternal relatives. Only he and his mother survived by hiding in cellars and trenches until the Russians freed Vienna in 1945. While his convoluted wavy drawings and serigraphs are filled with primitive color-saturated motifs, after the 1960s they were frequently metaphors for coping with death. Chimneys exude the black smoke of crematoria. Bloodstained gardens and earth washed by drops of blood cover his paper. Yet they offered him a spiritual renewal. "With graphic work," he said, "I can enter a paradise which I cannot reach with a painter's brush ... I can improve the world and make it more beautiful."

Brauer also extracted illusory castles in the air from his brutal childhood experiences in a Nazi labor camp. He enrolled in a Viennese art school in the 1950s, drawing portraits of people he had known and with whom he had suffered. His *Man in Gas* is plunged in deadly fumes. With a trickle of blood oozing from his mouth, he weeps bloody tears at the fate that he knows is to overtake him and that has already taken life from his child.

Ill. 12:38. *Square in Front of a Barrack.* Etching, c. 1938. By Walter Spitzer. ©2007 Artists Rights Society (ARS), New York/ADAGP, Paris

Germany's road back to respectability and responsibility in many ways was one of the most spectacular events of the post-war years. The infamous Berlin Wall that came down in 1989 was another. Many businesses admitted collusion with Nazi enterprises and agreed to billion-dollar settlements to hundreds of thousands of survivors. The giant Bertelsmann publishing group had produced at least nineteen million items that indoctrinated soldiers and Hitler Youth groups with anti–Jewish stereotypes. In an eight-hundred page report undertaken by its chief executive, the company expressed "sincere regrets ... we have learned that we cannot neglect our history."

Although the liberal community played a role in ameliorating Nazi value systems and moral climate, popular anti–Semitism still lingered at the end of the century. In 1997, Wolfgang Zeitlmann, a member of the Parliament, declared that because of Germany's high unemployment rate a quota system should be adopted: "The humanitarian intake of Jews can not go on forever; it will have to be brought to an end." Once more, foreigners wee held responsible for the country's ills.

The population of German Jewry grew very rapidly. As anti–Semitism and economic slowdowns were revived in Russia, Germany, physically close to the family and friends the refugees left behind, became for many Jews the preferred country for immigration. The arrival of over one hundred thousand former Russian and east European Jews in the 1990s who were granted full residential rights and work permits led to the rebuilding of the country. Jewish museums opened in Berlin, Vienna, and other cities. New synagogues appeared throughout the country; many, reflecting the Kristallnacht experience, utilized cracked glass in their ark and windows. No longer hidden from main thoroughfares, they were built directly on the street with bold Stars of David as decorative elements. And with bullet-proof glass and single entrances—just in case.

Like almost everyone else, Jews shared in Germany's remarkable social, political, and economic upswing. Many cooperated in a renewal of Jewish life, participated in Jewish organizations, and, although free to leave, chose to remain and rebuild. Yet, the spirit of the people seemed not to have made a comparable recovery. Generations not yet born will have to come to terms with their historical conscience. One aspect of the problem will be to define the boundaries of humanness. Another was suggested by the journalist Gunter Hofmann: "Germans will live unhappily with the confident 'We're regaining face'—and the uncertain 'Who are we'?"

13

Russia and Eastern Europe in the Twentieth Century: Radical Theories, Mass Migrations

The chief priority of the last Russian czar, Nicholas II, who ruled from 1894 to 1917, was to retain control over the peasantry, Church, and aristocracy. "I intend to safeguard the principle of autocratic rule," he said, "as steadfastly and unflinchingly as was the case with my unforgettable father." Any Jew who had suffered half a century earlier under Nicholas I would not be likely to forget him either for his harsh treatments against "non-useful" individuals. His son endorsed the policy of the Orthodox Church which called for assimilation or conversion, but the bulk of his Jews clung to their rabbis and yeshivot, zealously passing along their religious heritage. Others embraced the Haskalah movement which directed "westernized" students and intellectuals towards cultural and social revolution.

About five million Jews lived under Russian rule at the beginning of the twentieth century, double the number that had existed only fifty years earlier. Their culture and scholarship outclassed any other country in the world. Warsaw alone boasted five Yiddish dailies with a readership of over one hundred thousand. More than twenty thousand subscribed to Hebrew and Polish-Jewish papers. When not hampered by censorship, information concerning legal rights in freer lands was contrasted with the suppression of civil liberties at home. But oppression ballooned as the drive for political rights was perceived as a credible threat. A government-backed newspaper, *Bessarabetz*, had incited violence by depicting Jews as too rich and too revolutionary. Too rich they weren't, but many indeed were Socialists protesting their deplorable state. Mayhem erupted during Passover, 1903, in the city of Kishinev. With the shout, "Kill the Jews and save Russia," hundreds of police-backed rioters attacked Jews so viciously that responsible individuals—including Maxim Gorky and Leo Tolstoy—cried foul against "the most terrible outrages and atrocities of so-called Christians." When the bloodbath spent itself, forty-nine Jews lay dead, eighty-six were badly wounded, hundreds suffered other calamities, fifteen hundred homes and shops were destroyed, and Torah scrolls were desecrated. Reports of the carnage were picked up all over the world. *Frank Leslie's Illustrated Weekly* in New York illustrated *Jewish Massacre in Russia* on its front page: "The populace fell upon the Jews.... There are unpublishable tales of the most hideous atrocities.... A family of Jews barricaded themselves in their home, but the house was broken into by an infuriated mob, and they were overpowered after a courageous resistance. This is but one of many similar outrages perpetrated against the Russian Jews in this district" (Ill. 13:1).

Ill. 13:1. *Jewish Massacre in Russia.* Wood-engraving, 1903. From *Frank Leslie's Illustrated Weekly*

Chaim Nachman Bialik memorialized the torture and devastation in his poem *The City of Slaughter:*

> A tale of a belly stuffed with feathers,
> Of nostrils and of nails, of heads and hammers,
> Of men, who, after death, were hung head downward,
> Like these, along the rafter.
> A story of a suckling child asleep,
> A dead and cloven breast between its lips,
> And of another child they tore in two
> And many, many more such fearful stories...

Moved by these unhappy events, the Polish-Jewish artist Samuel Hirschenberg painted *Black Banner (or Funeral of the Tzadek)*, 1905, describing a group of Hasidic men bearing their dead leader to his grave. The implication, of course, was that the Jewish way of life was vanishing as well. The image, translated into an etching by Joseph Budko, was among the most affecting to reach the West (Ill. 13:2). Horrified Jews and Christians scrambled to organize protest meetings against the atrocities, indicating that Jews had allies, that others were willing to speak up and help them fight their battles.

Russia had other things to think about. She had gone to war with Japan in 1904 over expansionism and an outlet to the sea, conscripting some forty thousand Jewish soldiers; many were lost through forced conversions, warfare, starvation, or brutality. The Jews, living under constant threats, accusations of ritual murder, butchery, and expulsions, made every effort to escape

Ill. 13:2. *Black Banner (or Funeral of the Tzadek)*. Etching, 1905. By Joseph Budko

to whatever country would take them. Others learned to cope under incredibly difficult conditions. In spite of hardships, they organized self-defense agencies, workers' circles, and the Bund, all of which attempted to improve inhuman situations in factories or handicraft enterprises. These groups operated not only on the labor front but culturally and politically as well.

Jews were not the only ones to suffer under czarist despotism. The masses were picking up frightening revolutionary notions on their own. After decades of peasant ferment, the snail-pace of reforms by the autocratic government, and the collapse of the military forces in the Russo-Japanese War, revolution broke out in 1905. Repressive moves fell on much of the population, including the Jewish minority. Fearful of popular insurrection, in 1905 Nicholas II accepted constitutional limitations and a parliament (Duma). One result for the Jewish community was that some legal restrictions were softened, and some merchants, scholars, artists, and writers were permitted greater access to Russian cultural activities. Various parties, including the Zionist Socialists, and the *Po'alei Zion* (*Workers of Zion*), founded in 1906, took advantage of the moderate freedom while it lasted. This short-lived liberalism encouraged small numbers of Maskilim to favor Russian speech over Yiddish, secular over religious education, conversion over religious tradition, and Russian society over Jewish cohesion. A handful of these Jews moved into the middle class, working in the sugar, textile, timber, and shipping industries. Edifying societies sprang up to polish their minds, while a militant labor movement promoted their economic and nationalistic aspirations. Many chose the widely circulated Yiddish dailies and weeklies in Poland, Romania, Hungary, and Czechoslovakia which addressed both Zionist and assimilation issues, sports, humor, ladies' fashions, and youth movements. Shalom Asch, Ahad Ha-Am, H. N. Bialik, Shalom Aleichem, and I. L. Peretz were the stars of Jewish literature. Simon Dubnow wrote the three-volume *History of the Jews*, 1901, and helped edit a sixteen-volume Russian-Jewish encyclopedia which appeared from 1901 to 1913, while such publications were still possible.

None of these activities were lost on the Russians. As soon as it became apparent that Jews were participating in clandestine Socialist or revolutionary Zionist activities, or were casting eyes on bourgeois prospects, making inroads in areas where they were not wanted, vilification and abuse revived. Groups such as the Bund were outlawed by the government, while anti–Semitic newspapers spewed as much hate as they could muster. Terror was everywhere. A 1907 issue of the journal *Pliuvium* pictured a fiendish Jew with a knife in one hand and a revolver in the other aimed squarely at the face of every Russian reader.

The appearance of *The Protocols of the Learned Elders of Zion* in 1905, the supposed minutes of a Jewish organization's design on world domination, had gained widespread recognition. It had nothing to do with Jews, but was instead a forgery by a member of the Russian secret police based on a nineteenth century French pamphlet attacking the

Ill. 13.3. *Woman Lighting Candles*. Lithograph, 1910. From *Galut (Diaspora)*. By Wilhelm Wachtel

political ambitions of Napoleon III. It was designed to sway Nicholas' attitude against Jews, but he instead identified it as a fraud, writing that pernicious means did not justify the otherwise worthy objective of Jew-baiting. It was, however, turned against Jews, particularly after the Russian revolution in 1917 when the need to place blame for the deprivations during and after World War I fell on Jewish "revolutionaries." The *Protocols* infected Russia and Europe well into the twentieth century, and, through the backing of Henry Ford, much of America, too. It was exposed as spurious in 1921 by the *London Times*.

Blood libel and ritual murder charges were renewed in 1911 by the rightist press when Mendel Beilis, the manager of a brick kiln, was arrested on false evidence of killing a twelve-year-old boy. International outcries by alarmed liberals overcame the anti–Semitic arguments of the prosecutors. Beilis had been imprisoned for over two years when the all–Christian jury brought in a not-guilty verdict. But because many disputed the decision, assaults and massacres became wanton and out of control. For what it was worth—and it wasn't worth much to the authorities except for possible losses of international loans—Western reporters and governments indicted Russia as a stunted, easily taken-in feudal country. However, the agenda of the 1907 Triple Entente, which linked Russia, France, and England, made it clear that any anti–Russian boycotts or demonstrations by European powers to cut off economic assistance would precipitate a financial panic on the continent. No one was prepared to take such a risk. "What time has the world to trouble itself with the Jewish question?" asked Israel Zangwill. "We are coming into a period of history when the likelihood of other people fighting for us is getting less and less."

Nevertheless, a modern artistic and cultural creativity was stirring. As early as the 1870s, a non–Jewish art critic, Vladimir Stasov, encouraged Jewish artists to project a greater Jewish sensibility in their work. He urged Mark Antokolsky, the first Russian Jewish artist of note, to start a Jewish art school. Artist Leonid Pasternak, theatrical designers Natan Altman and Leon Bakst, and Joel Engel, who organized societies for Jewish folk music in 1908 and 1912, all became active. S. An-sky, author of *The Dybbuk*, and folk artist Solomon Yudovin led the first Jewish ethnographic expedition in 1912 to Polish villages in order to collect artifacts and codify them into a national archive for a projected Jewish museum. An-sky also persuaded Chagall and other progressive artists such as Isaac Levitan and Yehuda Pen that a folk-art idiom in conjunction with modern art would be useful in promoting a secular cultural identity. Following their lead, Eliezer (El) Lissitsky and Issachar Ber Ryback explored and recorded the motifs of about two hundred wooden synagogues in the heavily Jewish provinces along the Dnieper River in Belorussia. Exhibitions showcased in the Jewish Ethnographic Museum in St. Petersburg by the Jewish Society for the Encouragement of the Arts in 1916 and 1917 stressed Jewish rather than Russian identity.

Wilhelm Wachtel's *Galut* (*Diaspora*), 1910, a portfolio of fourteen Polish lithographs, was a mixture of romanticism and pathos. An Orthodox mother lights Sabbath candles as she prays for her son, unaware that he stands outside her window—inexorably separated from her by the walls of the house and by his assimilation into a contemporary way of life and dress (Ill. 13:3). From the same series, a few young men stand guard with little more than an ax and sticks and stones to ward off a rioting mob (Ill. 13:4). One can only imagine what followed.

With the onset of World War I, Jews focused on the thousands of desperate refugees forced back and forth across national borders without any means to protect themselves. Dislocation of families, food shortages, health problems, and persecutions on all sides were

Ill. 13.4. *Young Men Standing Guard*. Lithograph, 1910. From *Galut (Diaspora)*. By Wilhelm Wachtel

rampant. Publication of Hebrew books and periodicals was prohibited. French and English Jews who had poured money into the Russian war effort against German and Austrian armies pleaded that Jews from the eastern battle-front be permitted to move west. Jews who thought their contribution of four hundred thousand troops would be rewarded were sadly disabused; as the Russians fell back, they were blamed—this time as German spies. Retaliation came swiftly.

Whole towns were burned and their populations expelled to Siberia where they suffered and died in unspeakable circumstances. Russian-born Abel Pann, living in Paris at the time, recalled the horrors in his series of drawings *The Tear Jug*. From that set, *To Siberia* documented the abuse of families (Ill. 13:5). The contrast between the straight-backed arrogant soldier on horseback and the hunched figures of the Jews slogging through the snow was appalling. When the Russian ambassador saw the work, he asked the French government to forbid its publication. It was not issued as a lithographic portfolio in Jerusalem until 1926.

Having spent the war years from 1910 to 1914 in Paris, where he did his most lasting work, Marc Chagall returned to his Russian hometown, Vitebsk, occupying himself with sentimental shtetl scenes, while others promoted a more sophisticated approach as an alternative to provincialism. Lissitsky, who had joined Chagall at the Vitebsk art school, used Revolution-based motifs, but extended his vision to include fantasy, architecture, photography, and decorative typography. He discarded the realist styles of Antokolski, Gottlieb, Hirschenberg, and Lilien as old-fashioned and obsolete, lacking touch with the spirit of radical change and reform.

Ill. 13:5. *To Siberia*. Drawing, c. 1915. From *The Tear Jug*. By Abel Pann

He denigrated mawkish subject matter as "academic pseudo-art" expressed in content rather than in form. Looking for a new authenticity and aesthetic that included primitive spiritual and cultural qualities, he attempted a connection between secular contemporary art and authentic Jewish folk traditions in a specific Jewish national model, much as did Chagall at his best. However, he remained somewhat equivocal towards both Jewish and secular symbolism, having been exposed to a traditional upbringing in his early years and to Cubist-Constructivist concepts linked to Marxism as an adult. But the Communist Party's dim view of Zionism turned him away from nationalist images to a more esoteric frame of reference. His loyalty to Bolshevism, which he viewed as a liberation from Jewish persecution, brought him only meager patronage by the government he served.

By 1915, much had changed. The Pale of Settlement, where the Jewish masses had been confined as a temporary war measure, was abolished. (It was never reinstated because of the defeat of czarist regimes.) Democracy and full Emancipation were promised along with subsidies for literature, music, the Yiddish state theaters, and the Yiddish press. In addition, anti–Semitism would be suppressed. A two-year period followed during which Jews enjoyed almost unalloyed freedom. The abdication of the czar and the installation of a provisional government under Alexander Kerensky in 1917 offered hopes for a politically neutral Jewish value system within an independent, self-directed Jewish community. For a while, Jews believed that the new authorities would improve their situation, and for a short while they did. The text accompanying a lithograph, *Anti-Semitism Is Deliberately Anti-Revolutionary*, c. 1917–1918, demonstrated the type of vilification that the Bolsheviks promised to eliminate: "Comrades: A collection of vicious animals created anti–Semitism in Czarist Russia ... the czar, the clergy, the landlord, the rich peasant, the army, the police, the Black Hundred—all were organizers of Jewish persecution and pogroms" (Ill. 13:6). Enemies of the Jews, including the czar and czarina, contemptuously sniff daisies, while a Black Hundred gang member blows a shofar from which the heads of murdered Jews are disgorged.

True, anti–Semitism was frowned on, but it was resurrected soon enough. Waiting in the wings was Vladimir Lenin, who organized the Union of Soviet Socialist Republics (USSR). The "putsch" that followed dissolved the provisional government, thrust the Bolsheviks into power, and brought on a civil war in 1917. Jewish "enemies of the proletariat" were attacked by both the White and Red armies and charged with the economic chaos of the feudal system that had vexed the Russian peasantry for centuries. The symbolism of Lissitsky's lithographic poster *Beat the White with the Red Wedge*, 1919, challenged Jews to support the Bolshevik program—the play on words implicating the anti–Communist Whites as instigators of the pogroms (Ill. 13:7).

Lenin himself did not harbor anti–Jewish ideology although he felt that the Jews would have to assimilate and rid the country of any lingering capitalist notions. It was his executive agent for foreign affairs, the nominally Jewish Lev Davidovich Bronstein, who brought down horrendous consequences on the heads of Jews. Better known as Leon Trotsky, he guided Lenin's policies and successfully directed the civil war that followed the ousting of the moderates and put the Communists in control of vast territories and populations in eastern Europe. A 1917 poster published by anti–Bolshevik Whites, *Peace and Freedom in the Soviet Republic*, portrayed him with a Star of David on his chest and grossly "Jewish" features—a naked monster dominating the Kremlin while overseeing police brutality in a river of skulls. Trotsky, as well as other "internationalists," atheists, and self-hating Jewish revolutionaries, were largely responsible for some of the most destructive elements of the Revolution. Hundreds of thousands of Jews, victims of murderous peasant bands, were hounded throughout central and eastern Europe and Russia for their alleged rapaciousness and immoderate ambition. Having led an abortive attack on the leftist opposition to Joseph Stalin in the 1920s, he

Above: Ill. 13:6. *Anti-Semitism Is Deliberately Anti-Revolutionary.* Lithograph, c. 1917. *Below:* Ill. 13:7. *Beat the White with the Red Wedge.* Lithograph, 1919. By El Lissitsky

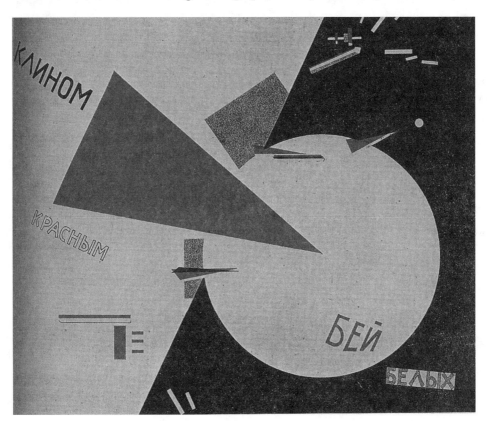

was removed from the Communist Party and exiled to Mexico in 1929. He was assassinated there in 1940.

Jewish hopes for equity were doomed. Shtetl life was systematically dismantled and its traditional economy destroyed. In 1918, the formation of a Jewish Section of the ruling Bolshevik Party, the anti–Zionist Communist propaganda organization Yevsektsiya, severed many Jews from their connectedness to the synagogue and Jewish educational and non–Communist labor affiliations; its function was to liquidate all Jewish communal property and transform Soviet Jewry into an assimilated proletariat. As industrialization reached Russia in the 1920s, Jews were encouraged to develop productive farming settlements, but that lasted only until Soviet agricultural collectivization was adopted, and Jews were forced out.

In the '20s, the Yevsektsiya played an important role in fostering Yiddish literature over works in Hebrew; in order to propagandize the Jews, it was necessary to appeal to them in their own language. Both the Socialist-oriented Bund and the Marxists, including many Jews, encouraged secular Yiddish culture, downgraded Zionism, and focused on eliminating discrimination, rooting out private property, and expunging religious practices. But those policies were soon abolished as part of Stalin's general retreat from all non-territorial nationalisms into his version of "Socialist content." In *The Old Cheder,* c. 1920, a lithograph published as a Soviet propaganda tool, an "enlightened" teacher points a young student towards the worthwhile elements gained in the up-to-date Soviet schools: healthful athletics, skilled well-developed workmen, and Russian language proficiency. He will learn to avoid his know-nothing fellows who boorishly spit on the floor. If he speaks Yiddish, he will gravitate to the intellectual and social defectiveness of common tradespeople and simplistic religious types (Ill. 13:8). Restrictions on Hebrew and Yiddish books followed once more and, with that, the exodus of the major Jewish artists to Berlin and points west. Those who remained, particularly those who adopted the official Realism style or worked for the Yiddish theater, fared better than other groups, possibly because more political attention was directed to literature and cosmopolitan culture than to art.

Because of its perceived relationship to bourgeois ideology, Realism had been out of favor before the war. But with the need to foster patriotic ties to the new government and to swing an unsophisticated populace to its political taste, readily understood naturalistic posters were marshaled to disseminate Marxist doctrines. Since most Jews were unable to read Russian newspapers—which were in very short supply anyway because of a shortage of good paper and distribution facilities—Communist teachings could easily be relayed through cheap persuasive prints with simple conventions. Anti-capitalist (read anti–Jewish) and anti–Revolutionary (read anti–Jewish) images were very much in evidence. Bigotry and fanaticism became valid expressions. Religious organizations and schools were banned, almost all synagogues were shuttered, property was confiscated by the government. "Reactionary" Hebrew education and publishing were outlawed again although, for a time, permission to print Yiddish (i.e. anti–Zionist) books was granted because they were thought to be ideal vehicles for Communist indoctrination. Most forms of Jewish activities, including the labor and Zionist movements, were dissolved. Everything aimed at total assimilation.

The Passover theme, however, survived as a symbolic vehicle of a once-flourishing community. Lissitzky designed ten zincographs after his watercolors for his *Chad Gadya Suite,* published in 1919. Inspired by the Passover song, he joined Russian folk images with fragmented Cubo-Futuristic elements, sweeping curves that dramatized movement, and a stylized border of Hebrew type, all of which marked a trend to Western abstraction. In *Then Came a Fire and Burned the Stick,* the image of a red rooster suggested arson, and the burnt Ukrainian synagogues recalled the destruction that he and Ryback had witnessed several years earlier (Ill. 13:9). The final episode depicts *God Smiting the Angel of Death* (represented by His all-seeing

Ill. 13:8. *The Old Cheder (School)*. Lithograph. c. 1920

Ill. 13:9. *Then Came a Fire and Burned the Stick.* **Lithograph, 1919. From** *Chad Gadya Suite.* **By El Lissitsky**

Eye). Communist elements, too, were introduced: the crown (symbol of the czar) on the head of Death, and the sword (symbol of the Revolution), implied that the victorious Russian Revolution had "killed" czarist rule. Occasionally the Passover theme was used simply to denigrate tradition. A Communist parody, *Haggadah for Believers and Atheists,* published in Yiddish in Moscow in 1927, was illustrated by the Jewish artist Alexandr Tyshler with an offensive text by the Jewish writer M. Altshuler: "May all the aristocrats, plutocrats, Bundists, Zionists and other counterrevolutionaries be consumed in the flames of the Revolution. May they never rise

Ill. 13:10. *Burning of Leaven*. Lithograph, 1927. From *Haggadah for Believers and Atheists*. By Alexandr Tyshler. Art ©Estate of Alexandr Tyshler/RAO, Moscow/VAGA, New York, NY

again." To depict the *Burning of Leaven*, a cheerful group of Russians shovel Jews into an oven, an eerie harbinger of Nazi crematoria (Ill. 13:10).

But when they could—or would—Jewish artists dealt with nostalgic or sympathetic subject matter as a funnel through which Jewish aspirations and folk histories could pass. Ernst Oppler's etching *Kleine Synagogue* (*Small Synagogue*), 1921, offered a view of east European worshipers quietly keeping faith with their rituals (Ill. 13:11). On the other hand, his portrait etching *Jacob Wassermann* captured the essence of the popular novelist who believed that the concept of Jewish chosenness was "plainly absurd and immoral," and that the prophetic vision made sense but Zionism did not; and that assimilation was inevitable, but conversion was repugnant. He lived until 1933, long enough to suffer the burning of his books and to seek a rapport with the eastern European Jewish ideology he had dismissed.

When Lionel Reiss, an American illustrator, traveled to eastern Europe in 1921 to "follow the trail of the wandering Jew," he discovered that while ghetto life had largely succumbed to destruction and modernity, he was still able to capture some of what was left of the old

Ill. 13:11. *Kleine Synagogue (Small Synagogue)*. Etching, 1921. By Ernst Oppler

traditions in etchings such as *Blessing the New Moon* (Ill. 13:12). Natan Altman, an active supporter of the Bolshevik Revolution, incorporated folk art into his geometric, asymmetric stage designs as well as a poster of a hunchbacked beggar, for *The Dybbuk*, 1920 (Ill. 13:13). Solomon Yudovin's *Man and Woman,* from his nostalgic series *Bygone Days*, 1921, depicted the tragic repercussions of the pogroms during the civil war (Ill. 13:14).

Issachar ber Ryback also chose to preserve and revitalize traditional Jewish life in his work. Born ten years after Chagall, he might have rivaled the master had his span been longer. While Chagall's memories were mostly positive, Ryback's were mixed. He had left a Russia of joyous occasions as well as of bloodbaths (in one of which his father was killed), and went to Berlin where he recreated a painful and irrecoverable past in a portfolio of thirty lithographs, *Shtetl: Mein Chorever Heim. A Gedenkniss (My Destroyed Home: A Memorial)*, 1917. In *A Woman Knitting*, the good housewife, having finished her preparations, quietly awaits the Sabbath in her comfortable home (Ill. 13:15). Unknowingly, with each stitch of her needles, life moves towards inevitable disaster, while down the street, *Tailors* bend their backs over an ironing board and sewing machine, turning out finery that no one will ever get to wear (Ill. 13:16). When Ryback moved to Paris the life and lights buoyed his spirit. There, many of the troublesome visions of his younger days were softened—the world he had left behind and could not protect. At the point of artistic recognition and financial security, he died, only thirty-seven years old. By 1922, El Lissitsky had become increasingly ambivalent over the value of Jewish folk art, sensing that it no longer represented a unique way of life or the flowering of a specifically Jewish culture. Along with other artists, he abandoned the idea that a national art form could be willed into being simply by the conscious resolve to produce one. The search for a meaningful "Jewish art" was over.

Above: Ill. 13:12. *Blessing the New Moon.* Etching, c. 1921. By Lionel Reiss. *Below left:* Ill. 13:13. *Hunchbacked Beggar*, 1920. From *The Dybbuk.* By Natan Altman. *Below right:* Ill. 13:14. *Man and Woman.* Etching, 1921. From *Bygone Days.* By Solomon Yudovin

Above: Ill. 13:15. *A Woman Knitting*. Lithograph, 1917. *Below:* Ill. 13:16. *Tailors*. Lithograph, 1917. Both from *Shtetl: Mein Chorever Heim. A Gedenkniss (My Destroyed Home: A Memorial)*. Both by Issachar ber Ryback

The year 1922 also noted the death of Lenin, followed by a bloody power struggle which eliminated challengers and marked the installation of Stalin as General Secretary of the Communist Party. Renewed attacks on Jews and on Jewish institutions prompted even Trotsky to recognize that "anti–Semitic agitation was being carried out with impunity." Stalin threatened so-called bourgeois decadence, fixing on the Jews who, in their attempt to create a distinctive Russian-Jewish style, had found themselves torn between alienation and adaptation, between their ethnic and national allegiance. State-sponsored and controlled Socialist Realism— "national in form, Socialist in content"—together with the ideals of the Communist Revolution became the measures of acceptable art, a style which was accessible to the masses and furthered the interests of rigid Soviet principles.

Unfortunately, "national in form" eliminated Jews who, by Stalin's definition, lacked the necessary qualification of having a national homeland and language (Yiddish didn't count). Art was required to support and reflect the cultural objectives of the state or it was muffled; political reality imposed a lid on any undertakings that touched on progressive Western aesthetics or that clashed with official dogma or ideology. But, having tasted freedom, many artists refused to cooperate and left. In 1924, the government placated Jews with an autonomous Jewish agricultural movement, OZED (Society for the Promotion of Jewish Settlement), to serve as an economic solution to the Jewish problem and a replacement for Zionism. A 1929 poster, *OZED*, by Mikhail Dlugach, addressed the Jewish farmer in Russian and Yiddish: "Every wheel the tractor turns helps the Socialist movement!" But the good times didn't last long. Yudovin, so zealous in his early representations of Jewish themes, fell into the Revolutionary spirit, bending art to mirror the party line. Jewish activists were directed away from the experiment of collective farming to staffing machine shops in the cities. But the yearning for freedom grew in proportion to the repression. Here and there a brave Jew bucked the system and somehow survived, particularly through opportunities to treat Jewish subject matter in book illustrations, portfolios, and stage design, where the suppression of independent ideas was moderated.

By 1936, purge trials began in Moscow. Bolsheviks and many others who defied the system—including many Jews—were murdered. Stalin had a choke-hold on every phase of Soviet life. He made moves to abolish Jewish status as a national entity, yet continued to have "Jewish" marked on their internal passports, which virtually guaranteed that they would remain a national minority. (Under Lenin, the Soviet passport designation was intended to recognize the Jews as a respected part of a multinational state. With Stalin, it became a badge of dishonor.) Savage restraints were laid on those thought to be inimical to the regime. Millions of Russians—thousands of Jews among them—simply disappeared, never to be accounted for, although horror stories of live burnings and other abhorrent torture seeped out of the gulags and prisons. In June, 1941, Germany's armies invaded Russia, its erstwhile ally, capturing city after city, advancing close to Moscow, and massacring two million Jews in a four-year period. According to Soviet estimates, one hundred thousand Jews, including seven hundred psychiatric hospital patients, were stripped, beaten, and machined-gunned in groups of ten as they were led down a column of Nazi executors at the Babi Yar ravine in Kiev. For years, blood leached out of the ground. Not until 1991 did the Russian government permit a memorial to be erected there.

The uprising of the Warsaw ghetto, which had held half a million Jews at its height and three hundred fifty thousand at the beginning of its liquidation in July, 1942, had been brutally put down by Polish troops. Some of the earliest descriptions of the disaster were preserved in a series of trading cards, *War News Pictures:* "Two Americans who had just made a tour of the ruined city of Warsaw, gave a heart-rending account of what they saw there. They estimated that forty thousand people had been killed, hundreds of thousands injured and thirty five per cent of the buildings destroyed...! The worst famine is said to have occurred in the crowded tenements of the old city and in the Jewish quarter. Nazi welfare organizations now distribute hot meals and bread to Germans and Poles, but the city's Jews, comprising thirty per cent of the population, have to live on their own resources." Only about sixty thousand Jews remained after the liquidation halted in September 1942; they were the ones who rose up in rebellion in April 1943.

German forces were defeated in the battle for Stalingrad in 1942. Russian soldiers liberated concentration and extermination camps as they marched west recapturing major areas. By 1945, the war was over. One hundred million soldiers had fought each other. Worldwide, fifteen million soldiers and some thirty million civilians died. Five hundred thousand Jews had served in the Soviet military, two hundred thousand were killed, many more were injured. In western and eastern Europe, Greece, and Yugoslavia, six million Jews were exterminated, almost one-third of the Jewish world. Were anti–Jewish feelings finally set at rest? Was something learned from all that waste? A pathetic few traumatized Jews, having survived Auschwitz, returned to Poland expecting to recover their homes and property which they assumed their friends and neighbors had kept in protective custody. Almost two years had passed, surely the worst excess of anti–Semitism had subsided, surely their neighbors and friends who were well aware of the death camp atrocities were prepared to make restitution. Instead, the level of vicious cruelty, torture, murder, and looting more than matched the Holocaust terrors. On the pretext of fleeing retaliation for the ritual murder of a Christian child, over two hundred Jewish survivors congregated in the Polish town of Kielce, waiting for emigration visas to Palestine. As they were ready to leave, a pogrom began, abetted by onlookers, police, and Soviet troops. Thirty-seven were murdered, eighty-two were wounded. Altogether, the last remnant of fifteen hundred Polish Jews, accused of seizing power and other fantasies, were beaten, gunned down, thrown out of windows and tossed from moving trains. The annihilation proceeded with measured intensity and with measured benefits to the executioners. They could blink at the shame and discomfort of bloodied hands and guilty consciences, dismiss the moral necessity of returning plundered possessions, and succeed in moving up to a middle-class society without having to confront or fear living victims.

Thanks to the decisive votes of America and the Soviets, the State of Israel was established by the United Nations in 1948. For aiding the fledgling country against the Arab armies, the Soviets received the applause of the Jewish world, but almost immediately Stalin reactivated anti–Zionist attacks. Many Jews who had defended Communist policies and had desired an Israeli connection to the Eastern Bloc were soon disenchanted. Leaders of the Jewish Anti-Fascist Committee as well as many scientists, doctors, writers, artists, musicians, and other "Jewish bourgeois nationalists" were accused of anti–Soviet "rootless cosmopolitanism" and were either executed, held incommunicado, deported to slave labor camps, or victimized in "show" trials. Six of the nine physicians who attended Stalin in his final illness were Jews who were accused of attempting to poison him. (He died before legal actions began, and the doctors were exonerated.) The satiric magazine *Krokodil* featured a cartoon, *Doctors Trial: Proof of the Crime*, 1953, in which a great hand shakes loose the mask of medical benevolence and integrity only to discover the malevolent Jew behind.

With a Jewish population in the USSR numbering two million, many of whom desperately hoped to emigrate, large numbers faced a variety of discriminatory practices, loss of jobs, isolation in Siberia, and a painful end to relations with the outside world. When Stalin died, expectations of good will and a Jewish cultural revival were floated. The reality, however, was expressed by a visiting Israeli newspaperman who brought back the discouraging news that no Jewish theater, school, library, bookshop, or restaurant existed. When emigration was finally permitted in 1968, attempts at reestablishing an active Yiddish press in Communist circles were mostly abandoned. A very few publications appeared after the demise of the Soviet Union, with the number of potential readers remaining small.

Although the terrors of the Stalin years were finally acknowledged, and control over the Soviet satellite countries began to fray, social and political life for Jews did not keep pace. They were barely referred to in the Soviet press, which passed over their persecution and murders in silence. Jewish activists were compared to Nazis, accused of participating in an "international conspiracy," and forced underground. Attempts at providing exhibitions for unofficial artists in the 1960s and 1970s were mostly unsuccessful, with the participants subjected to a war of nerves; nonconformists, some of whom included Jewish themes in their works, were reduced to showing their pieces furtively. Conformist art was the only art that was tolerated; abstraction, religious (and pornographic) images were repressed, as were human rights issues. Jewish libraries and art collections that had been confiscated were held hostage in spite of requests from religious leaders and heads of state to dislodge them.

In a vain attempt to rid the government of its most vocal counter-revolutionists, a few were permitted to go to Israel, France, and the United States. The dissident artist Alek Rapoport, charged with "formalistic distortion, ideological sabotage" and creating "religious, Fascist, and Zionist art," arrived in San Francisco in 1976. He recorded his departure the following year in a lithograph, *Farewell to the Shtetl*, taking leave from his friends, his paintings, and his synagogue on the hill. But the more that persecution and emigration restricted them, the more the protesters reacted to suppression by digging in their heels, secretly studying Hebrew, and professing loyalty to the spirit of Zionism.

When Nikita Khrushchev, currying favor with Arab world, threatened to destroy Israel "if she continues her present policy," Communism lost its appeal for many Jewish intellectuals as well as many of the Soviet masses. Although anti–Israel, pro–Arab politics persisted, the international "Free Soviet Jews" campaign focused attention on Jewish activists and refusniks. Repression was somewhat eased. Bits of encouraging news began to filter out from the porous Iron Curtain, some hopeful, some not. Some religious services and classes in Jewish learning were permitted and eagerly attended by thousands of reinvigorated Jews in Moscow, Leningrad, and other cities. By 1981 the gates were pried open for a quarter of a million Jews, more than half of whom went to Israel. The gates closed again three years later when fewer than a thousand were allowed to leave. By 1987, the Pushkin Fine Arts Museum in Moscow decided it was time to acknowledge the centenary of Chagall's works with an exhibit of ninety paintings and two hundred graphic works. Two years later a Jewish cultural center named for the Yiddish actor Solomon Mikhoels, who was murdered in 1948, opened in Moscow, followed shortly by a yeshiva with eighty students and a rabbinic faculty of five from Israel and America.

When economic stagnation began in the late 1980s, the government called for radical reforms, but by then it was too late. The Union of Socialist States effectively collapsed, unraveling within ten years. Forced to seek material help from its American enemy, it was further humiliated by the necessity of providing exit permits and opening new cultural opportunities for Jews as conditions for aid. The relatively liberal Glasnost and Perestroika movements had loosened economic and social vested interests, permitting greater freedom of information, but as soon as opinions could be expressed more openly, the Orthodox Russian ultra-nationalist anti–Semitic Pamyat activities became increasingly vocal. In drawing parallels between Zionism and Fascism, it accused the government of capitulating to Jewish interests, permitting too many Jews access to the professions, blaming the intelligentsia for "betraying the people," and allowing the Jewish exodus. In 1991, the mouthpiece newspaper *Moskovskii Komsomolets* showed a repulsive Aunt and Uncle Yid running off to America, trailed by Little Yid representing Zionist youth. A Fascist publication in 1993 caricatured the Russian heads of state,

Boris Yeltsin and Mikhail Gorbachev, as twin servile dogs under the leash of Jewish influence. The official *Pravda* and *Izvestia* newspapers condemned *Pamyat*, Polish bishops declared anti–Semitism a sin, and Polish president Lech Walesa addressed the Israel Knesset asking forgiveness for his country's treatment of Jews. Jewish museums and synagogues in Russia and eastern Europe were rehabilitated. Jewish agencies functioned, Jewish institutions were reactivated, advertisements for matzos appeared on television during Passover. Jewish artists found their voice, some their Jewish identity.

The demise of the Soviet Union was a challenge for Jews to reinvent their heritage and to ponder the role that their culture might play in a less restricted milieu. While many discovered and celebrated their Jewish roots, only about three hundred thousand "core" or practicing Jews, many of them elderly, described themselves as such in the Soviet census. Assimilation, falling birth rates, and mass emigration had taken a toll. Still, many of the one and a quarter million Jews within the former Soviet Union anticipated a renaissance. Given the liberty of open expression and renewed contact with world Jewry, they looked forward to generating a commitment to Jewish affairs as well as to Jewish art.

For all that, the head of the still active Communist Party, Gennady Zyuganov, warned the minister of justice in 1997 that Jews were responsible for the faltering economy and that the "spread of Zionism in the state government" was a cause of Russia's decline. The Anti-Defamation League's 1999 survey indicated that forty-four per cent of Russians held "strong anti–Semitic views." The question of whether Jewish life could evolve and mature in a postmodern Russian Western-style democracy remained unanswered at the close of the twentieth century.

14

America in the Twentieth Century: From the Immigrant Experience to Modernity

The world experienced enormous social, political, and economic changes after 1900, but nowhere were they as extravagant or vigorous as in America. Large corporations were spawned, frequently greedy and oppressive but instrumental in increasing the country's wealth and providing jobs for millions. Until their mutual needs could be balanced, there were fierce struggles between these monoliths and the recently formed labor unions. Department stores began to replace smaller establishments, offering labor-saving appliances and inaugurating innovative systems of family shopping. Powerful medical procedures prolonged life or at least made it less painful, while psychotherapy became the newest middle-class panacea. Prohibition came and went. The women's suffrage movement came and stayed. A storybook business evolved on the West Coast with Hollywood as its Mecca. Communication, transportation, and scientific enterprises slowly began to open closed or half-shut doors for many Jews. Good times had come, no doubt to linger.

But America had a flip side, too. Many Jews felt unconnected to the community at large—there was us and there was them. Promise coexisted with poverty; it also coexisted with assimilation, but not always with inclusion. Full acceptance in a completely equable society was—and still is—one dream away. Millions of immigrants experienced an acute sense of culture shock adjusting to a new language, new customs, and new ways of making or not making a living. Twelve- to fifteen-hour workdays were typical, sweatshop wages were impossibly low, chronic physical and emotional problems and dehumanizing social forces were hard truths. The *goldene medina* was turning out to be a mirage.

The Spirit of the Ghetto, 1902, a seminal study of Jewish life in the Lower East Side, gave readers a glimpse of that grimy corner of New York through the eyes of the Jewish artist Jacob Epstein and the pen of the non–Jewish author Hutchins Hapgood. *Working Girls Returning Home* portrayed the women, about one-third of the work force, who went out to work, becoming breadwinners (Ill. 14:1). Jewish labor leaders Sidney Hillman, Samuel Gompers, Lillian Wald, and David Dubinsky initiated strikes, raised funds, developed trade unions, and wrote muckraking articles berating the degrading conditions. They forced the garment industry, which employed perhaps half of the Jewish working population, to negotiate mutual concessions. But it took the 1911 Triangle Shirtwaist Company fire to shock New York into passing some of the country's first safety laws. The disaster occurred when one hundred forty-six people, mostly Jewish and Italian women, leaped to their death after being trapped behind a locked

389

WORKING GIRLS RETURNING HOME

Ill. 14:1. *Working Girls Returning Home*. By Jacob Epstein, 1902

door in the ten-story building. Arbitration legislation introduced by Justice Louis Brandeis finally gave exploited workers proper recourse to the legal system.

An etching and drypoint, *The Tenement, New York*, 1903, by Canadian-born Charles Henry White captured the dreary aspect of the congested airless flats in which whole families worked long hours sewing piece goods for meager wages. Shared toilets, filth, and noise were home to the three hundred fifty thousand Jewish "greenhorns" in the few square miles of the Lower East Side, an area more tightly packed than any city in the world. Pushcarts vied for space in street markets. Door-to-door peddlers climbed hundreds of stairs every day to wheedle or cajole housewives into buying necessaries or knickknacks. But while the disarray and poverty of their lives cramped their prospects, Jews also shared a unique sense of community. Holidays enlivened their existence. The wood-engraving by R. Levy *Passover Eve on the East Side*, 1905, signaling the onset of the most convivial days in the Jewish calendar, catches last-minute shoppers as they pick and choose the finest delicacies they could afford (Ill. 14:2).

To the poet Carl Sandburg, who didn't have to live there, Chicago's Jewish district had an almost sensual appeal. His *Fish Crier*, 1916, places the scene:

I know a Jew fish crier down on Maxwell Street with a voice like a northwind blowing over corn stubble in January.

Ill. 14:2. *Passover Eve on the East Side* by R. Levy. Wood-engraving, 1905

He dangles herring before prospective customers evincing a joy identical with that of Pavlova dancing.

His face is that of a man terribly glad to be selling fish, terribly glad that God made fish, and customers to whom he may call his wares from a pushcart.

But immigrant fish criers had not always been welcome in those neighborhoods. *Harper's Weekly* in 1902 noted that Secretary of State John Hay "expressed a strong disrelish of Roumanian Jewish immigrants," and then complained that "unlike valued citizens such as the Swedes or Germans ... these immigrants make very undesirable additions to our heterogeneous

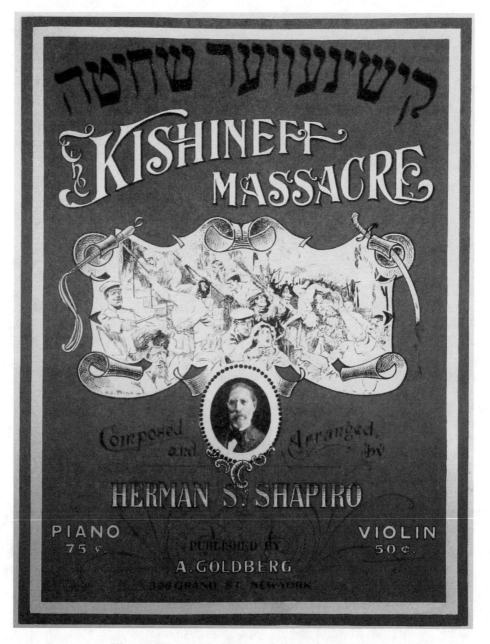

Ill. 14:3. *The Kishineff Massacre*. Lithograph, 1904

population.... They do not become Americanized. They do not learn English, and they preserve their own customs and ways, which are not in any sense American." President Theodore Roosevelt disagreed. In a 1906 letter congratulating Jews on the two hundred and fiftieth anniversary of their settlement in the New World, he wrote that Jews "have become indissolubly incorporated in the great army of American citizenship."

As new Americans, they shared concerns and pleasures that helped tie the old and new worlds into a single focus. Whenever friends got together for an evening of light harmony, lithographed sheet music was available. *The Kishineff Massacre*, 1904, which expressed horror at the Russian pogroms, played a part in bringing out one hundred twenty-five thousand New Yorkers, Jews and Gentiles alike, to protest the atrocities (Ill. 14:3). By contrast, *The Yiddisha Rag*, 1909, a popular nonsense song, signified nothing but dancing feet—"Wiggle and Jiggle when you hear that strain; everyone hollers please play it again" (Ill. 14:4). No wedding was official without the noisy congratulatory strains of *Choson Kale Mazol Tov* (*Joy to the Groom*

Ill. 14:4. *The Yiddisha Rag*. Lithograph, 1909

Ill. 14:5. *Choson Kale Mazol Tov (Joy to the Groom and Bride).* **Lithograph, 1909**

and Bride), 1909 (Ill. 14:5). And somebody's sister was sitting at the piano ready to bang out the 1911 hit tune *Long Live the Land of the Free.*

Lithographed greeting cards, too, were everywhere. The national eagle hovers over Miss Liberty's hat spelling *America*: "Open your gates that the righteous nation may enter" (Isaiah 26:2) (Ill. 14:6). But if that young immigrant family conducted itself as most newcomers did, the mother would soon doff her shawl, the father would shave his beard, and the children would dress like regular little Yankees. Rosh Hashanah "checks," payable to the recipient for "three

Ill. 14:6. *America.* Lithograph, c. 1910

hundred sixty five days of Health, Wealth and Happiness," miraculously came directly from the Bank of Heaven. Elaborate fold-out Valentine messages festooned with lovebirds and roses were pressed into Jewish service by the substitution of New Year messages and the addition of a colorful lithograph of family gathered around a festive table.

Recent immigrants, as well as those who were born in an industrialized America, were witness to a magical and restless world. Much of what they saw and what they shared turned up in splashy post cards. Did the first airplane take off in 1903? Before a dozen years passed, a lithograph for the Williamsburg Post Card Company in New York conjured up a Yiddish-speaking couple dispensing good fortune and cheer from an unlikely flying machine. Five years later the Model T automobile rolled out of the Ford Motor Company plant. Sure enough, three emancipated ladies drive along offering wishes for "a new year without pain and sorrow." Postcards of questionable humor regaled the market as well. Samuel Goldring's *Isador Gets His First 10% Cut* may not have been considered appropriate for a religious occasion but, judging by their ubiquity, circumcision jokes were quite acceptable.

These popular and expressive song sheets and cards were only one of the avenues to membership in the congregation of America. Classes and lectures of all kinds were widely available, offering parents hope that secular as well as religious education would give their children opportunities they only dreamt of. They couldn't know that such refinements would also break down households and hasten the drift from tradition and accepted values. The struggle to keep children tied to home and cheder too often clashed with the glitter of assimilation. In ritual, education, and marriage choices, young Jews were fleeing their own culture. Many saw nothing but discord and rebellion in the changing complexion of the Yiddish community. No longer were rabbis the ultimate authority. Writers, intellectuals, Socialists, and Zionists now defined the transformation of Jewish life. New ideologies soon won the allegiance of the large body of Jews who demanded something different from the ways of their parents, and something better than their current lives and working conditions. Catering to these needs were trade unions, organizations, synagogues, landsmanshaften, and civic associations. Their range of involvement stretched from overseeing social and religious considerations to helping the police catch bad guys looking for bargains in other people's pockets.

Higher education was not neglected. Wealthy German Jews funded the Jewish Theological Seminary of America, Yeshiva College (later University), and the Jewish Institute of Religion (later Hebrew Union College) to accommodate denominational needs. A collaborative effort produced the *Jewish Encyclopedia*, 1901–1906, and the first American Hebrew encyclopedia, *Ozar Yisrael*, appeared from 1907 to 1913. Louis Ginzberg began his seven-volume *Legends of the Jews* in 1909. Jewish publishers such as Alfred Knopf, Bennett Cerf, Richard Simon and Lincoln Schuster successfully gambled that the broad pursuit of information and entertainment would endure.

Newspapers and journals moved the topics of the day from the street to the kitchen table, where readers pored over advice columns, the latest gossip, or front-page scoops. In New York, the Yiddish press, by now the largest of its kind in the world, played an authoritative role in molding Jewish concerns, sustaining the immigrant culture and covering lifestyles across the ideological board and across the country. By its peak years in the '20s, the combined Yiddish dailies exceeded the circulation of *The New York Times*. When the century began, the Jewish daily *Forverts* (later *Forward*), which would be edited by Abraham Cahan for nearly half a century, was a widely read three-year-old Socialist phenomenon, publishing works by well-known authors and providing sympathy and advice to thousands of new immigrants in its *Bintel Brief* (*Bundle of Letters*) column. *Der Tog*, aimed at the "Yiddish intelligentsia," was less ideological, attracting readers inclined to "impartial" international news. The progressive Yiddish magazine *Schriften* was an outlet for literary articles and reproductions of paintings and prints by Jewish artists, while *La America* addressed Sephardim in Ladino. Communist sympathizers read the *Morgen Freiheit*. The Orthodox could choose between the *Tagblatt* and the *Morgen Journal*, according to their support of Zionism or a broader universalism. Some two dozen periodicals, including the influential *Boston Jewish Advocate*, were read by English speakers. Under the leadership of Jacob Landau, the Jewish Telegraphic Agency originally provided information concerning World War I; it later expanded to report Zionist concerns and Nazi terrors, and it remains a leading source of contemporary issues. The Annenberg family launched *The Philadelphia Inquirer* to "maintain the sanctity of personal liberty and the inviolability of human rights."

Wildly conflicting arguments for and against nationalism were expounded by Orthodox pro–Zionists, nonpartisan Zionists, labor Zionists, Communists, Secularists, and anyone else with a contentious agenda. Traditionalists maintained that God, not man, must intervene in history before a Jewish homeland could be established, while the Reform movement declared that Palestine was not its homeland—that "Jews in America are part of the American nation." Overarching these contentious views were defense agencies such as the American Jewish Committee, the Anti-Defamation League, and the American Jewish Congress, founded between 1906 and 1918 by prominent German-American Jews to deal with persecution, bigotry, accusations of dual loyalty, and troublesome civil rights issues.

Of course, getting away from weighty subjects from time to time was always welcome. Into that need stepped Maurice Schwartz, Jacob Ben Ami, the Jacob and Stella Adler family and others who mounted critically acclaimed—as well as piously maudlin—Yiddish plays, one of the few activities patronized alike by uptown parvenus and downtown locals. Florenz Ziegfeld and Billy Rose glorified the American girl and broadened the concept of glamor across the country. Theaters overflowed with Yiddish and English-speaking audiences laughing at Eddie Cantor, Fanny Brice, and Molly Picon, crying at Israel Zangwill's *Melting Pot*, or humming the tunes of Al Jolson and Sophie Tucker.

But Jews did a lot more than share compliments of the season, sing songs, or attend Yiddish shows. Wealthy individuals busied themselves for the benefit of the general community. They helped develop social agencies such as the Educational Alliance Art School, the Henry Street Settlement, the American Joint Distribution Committee (which was concerned with relieving the lives and misfortunes of Jews in Europe and Palestine), and the Hebrew Sheltering and Immigrant Aid Society (HIAS), which later saved hundreds of thousands of European lives from the Holocaust. Nathan Straus, co-owner of Macy's department store, was deeply involved in public health issues. Julius Rosenwald, president of Sears and Roebuck, acted in the interests of racial equality and personal liberties. For Jacob Schiff, Otto Kuhn, Solomon Loeb, Felix Warburg and others, the banking industry provided the opportunity to build great fortunes and to give them away with rare generosity. The highly successful attorney Louis Marshall set up effective arbitration boards for the labor movement.

The Educational Alliance Art School, founded 1889, took on the job of polishing unpolished immigrants. It hired Jewish and non–Jewish faculty to prepare exhibitions and teach general studies and art classes. It encouraged labor, political, and social institutions to bridge the way between "American" and immigrant culture. Step by step it served not only as a place to learn, but as a communal living room for musicians, actors, artists, anarchists, Socialists, and neighborhood pundits. True to form, not everyone was happy with the Alliance. Solomon Schechter, president of the Jewish Theological Seminary, resigned from its board in 1912, disturbed that while the immigrants were being Americanized, they weren't being sufficiently Judaized.

Meanwhile, hundreds of miles from New York City, ugly class and racial issues were brewing. Leo Frank, the Jewish manager of a pencil factory in Atlanta, Georgia, was accused in 1913 of killing a thirteen-year-old employee, Mary Phagan, on the testimony of a Negro janitor. Southern public opinion was against Frank, unusual given the fact that he was white and might lose his freedom to the allegations of a black man. However, as a local minister pointed out, "All the inborn prejudice against Jews rose up in a feeling of satisfaction that here would be a victim worthy to pay for the crime." The flimsiest evidence incited the judge, an all-white jury, and the local townspeople to convict the "Yankee Jew." When Frank's death sentence was commuted by the governor, a furious mob kidnapped and lynched him and left him dangling on a tree. He was still alive the next morning. No one was prosecuted or brought to trial for his murder. His name was finally cleared in 1986 when a former office boy admitted that he had seen the janitor carrying Mary's body, but had been threatened into silence. Not that the law found Frank innocent. He was pardoned posthumously only on the formal grounds that authorities had denied his right to further appeal.

In 1914, America turned its attention to the European war, sending its allies millions of tons of material and millions of dollars in loans. In the widely exhibited lithograph *Share*, 1915, produced by the Jewish Relief Campaign, the figure of America urged all to respond generously to European victims (Ill. 14:7). But patriotic efforts didn't help Jews who were attacked

Ill. 14:7. *Share*. Lithograph, 1915

as war profiteers. A United States Army manual alleged that "the foreign born, and especially Jews, are more apt to malinger than the native-born." When the pamphlet was brought to the attention of President Woodrow Wilson he recalled it, but its message was already deeply imbedded in the nation's consciousness. The Associated Press, ostensibly impartial in reporting the news, printed anti–Jewish caricatures until liberal social pressure forced it to reject racial or religious slurs. Heavy lips salivating over financial profits, large hooked noses, greasy hair, disreputable clothing, Yiddish jargon, and whatever could be interpreted as Jewish excesses found their way into newspapers and magazines. Attempts to defend Jewish sensibilities and offset prejudices were undertaken by many organizations and publications, including the *Menorah Journal*, the first literary magazine to explore Jewish opinion. But many people were still fearful of involvement in overseas troubles which they blamed in part on Jewish warmongers.

When America entered the war in 1917, the National Jewish Welfare Board, representing twenty-two agencies, stepped up to provide social and religious aid to the armed forces. One of its first efforts was a lithograph poster, *Brighten His Days Until the Homecoming* (Ill. 14:8). The United War Work Campaign joined the effort with a Yiddish broadside urging Jews to support the war effort: *Uncle Sam Sends Out the Call: 3,000,000 Boys Are Waiting for Your Answer. Life* magazine was not impressed. It printed a cartoon by Otho Cushing mocking dullwitted Jews who could not even recognize their country's fighting men, presumably because their clannishness ruled out any identification with their fellow citizens. Three soldiers—tall, posture perfect, conventionally featured, are inspected by Jewish yokels—short, slouching, thick-lipped: "Pretty goot lookers—eh, Ikey? Vot are they?" "Americuns."

The government as well as other agencies turned to poster art, among other media, to catch the eye through bold compositions and texts and to bring the war effort closer to the public. A lithograph by Charles Edward Chambers, *Shpeiz vet Gevinnen di Krig* (*Food Will Win the War*), 1918, issued in Italian and English as well as Yiddish by the United States Food Administration, was addressed to all recent immigrants, subtly demanding reciprocity for past favors: "You came here seeking freedom. You must now help defend it. Wheat is needed for the Allies. Waste nothing" (Ill. 14:9). The Statue of Liberty and a rainbow in the background represent freedom and anticipated good fortune. During the final week of the war, the Jewish Welfare Board, unaware that the struggle had just ended, issued Sidney Rosenberg's large poster rallying all Americans: *Civilians, When We Go Through This We Need All the Help and Comfort You Can Give.*

A quarter of a million Jews served in the armed forces; over fifteen thousand either died or were wounded. Altogether, over one hundred thousand American lives were sacrificed. With the coming of peace, America moved towards isolationism. The League of Nations, as the first world organization, was intended to promote internationalism, but it never achieved that goal. Alarms that subversives were about to invade America brought a demand for "real" Americans, not "Bolsheviks." A literacy test had been approved by Congress in 1917, over Wilson's veto, "as a means of further restricting and regulating immigration." Seven years later, the Johnson National Origins Act cut the influx of southern and eastern Europeans (i.e. Italians and Jews) to two percent of their representation in the census of 1890, which meant that Jewish immigration was reduced by over seventy-five percent. The spigot was all but turned off.

The mood of the times was captured in a popular song:

> Our flag they do not honor,
> Our rights they will betray—
> O! close the gates of our nation
> Yes, before that awful day.
> O! close the gates of our nation,
> Lock them firm and strong,

Ill. 14:8. *Brighten His Days Until the Homecoming*. Lithograph, 1917

Ill. 14:9. *Shpeiz vet Gevinnen di Krig (Food Will Win the War)*. Lithograph. By Charles Edward Chambers, 1918

Before that mob from Europe
Shall drag our colors down.

International economic and political isolationism, the Red Scare, and a rise in anti–Semitism prompted Henry Ford's Dearborn Publishing Company to issue four volumes of *The International Jew—The World's Foremost Problem*, 1919–1921. It consisted of almost a hundred articles that had appeared in *The Dearborn Independent*, including one that suggested the incinerating of "the whole fabric of Talmudic teaching." As a "partial record of an investigation of the Jewish Question," it disseminated the spurious *The Protocols of the Learned Elders of Zion* among other trumped-up and malicious fictions and forgeries. Those who read the articles discovered that Jews were responsible for the Bolshevik Revolution, the American Civil War, the assassination of President Lincoln, the plot to rid the marketplace of Christmas and Easter cards, and, by extension, the destruction of the entire Christian world. Many people believed it all. Lawsuits drafted by Louis Marshall in 1927 forced a retraction and apology, although Rabbi Stephen S. Wise argued, "Can any man be said to retract, who does not devote as much time and strength and substance to the *cancellation* of the results of his libels as he long devoted to the *publication* of them?" Nevertheless, blatant slander by "respected" scholars as well as polite social discrimination continued, resulting in such far-reaching antipathy that one-quarter of those answering a public opinion poll as late as 1944 agreed that Jews were a "menace" to America.

A downturn in the number of incoming Jews did not lessen anti–Semitism. The Ku Klux Klan, a hooded vigilante fellowship that had been organized following the Civil War, was reactivated in 1915 with a platform against Blacks, Catholics, and Jews. It was a dominant influence for a dozen years until it petered out under the weight of its own excessive venom. But in its palmy days it had the backing of several members of Congress, the FBI chief J. Edgar Hoover, and the attorney general of the United States, A. Mitchell Palmer, who expressed the view that "aliens on the steerage steamers were not of our sort."

The popular novelist Jack London had earlier defined Jews as a "miserable mass of weaklings and inefficients." He was not alone. Willa Cather attributed many anti–Jewish remarks to her characters. F. Scott Fitzgerald in *The Great Gatsby* described a Jew in demeaning terms. Jews moving out of the garment industry found it difficult to find jobs or to advance their positions elsewhere. Medical schools and universities adopted quotas as the number of Jewish applicants reached "unacceptable" proportions, necessitating the construction of equivalent Jewish institutions. President Wilson and over a hundred prominent Christian leaders protested this "organized campaign of anti–Semitism."

"Unacceptable" Jews were prominent contributors to American intellectual and cultural life. In science and medicine, Jews were at the forefront of research. The proportion of Nobel and other prizes awarded to Jews far exceeded their proportion in the population. The first Pulitzer Prize to a Jewish author went to Edna Ferber in 1924 for her novel *So Big*; similarly honored were Elmer Rice for *Street Scene*, 1929, and George Gershwin for *Of Thee I Sing*, 1931. Later Jewish writers—Saul Bellow, Philip Roth, Bernard Malamud, Chaim Potok—obsessed with guilt, anxiety, and men seeking Gentile ladies, swayed American fiction. The plays of Clifford Odets prodded American consciences by dramatizing festering social and economic problems. Concert halls hosted a bonanza of Jewish composers, instrumentalists, and conductors. Most of America's popular songs were written by Jews. Most of America's zany theatrical antics were performed by Jews. Jewish founders of Metro-Goldwyn-Mayer, Columbia Pictures, Warner Brothers, and many other large companies spearheaded the great expansion of the movie industry, although they mostly avoided stories of Jewish interest. David Sarnoff developed the first American radio chain, the National Broadcasting System (NBC) in 1926, which later became part of the Radio Corporation of America (RCA). Set designer Boris Aronson was Broadway's most influential stylist. Abraham Cahan, Sholem Aleichem, Anzia Yezierska, Sholem Asch, and other writers shared their rationalism, bitterness, or poignancy. Stephen Kayser, Alfred Werner, Joseph Duveen, and Bernard Berenson all confirmed the credibility and authority of Jewish scholarship in the arts, and, along with other Jewish dealers and curators, encouraged the newly rich to buy and donate many of the great works that now fill museums. Justices Louis Brandeis, Felix Frankfurter, and Benjamin Cardozo presided on the Supreme Court and, along with Bernard Baruch, advised presidents in war-related and civilian issues.

An era of prosperity and enhanced self-images permitted second-generation immigrants to move uptown and to the suburbs where they built imposing synagogues and community centers and became prominent or disreputable members of every profession they were permitted to enter. Their children and grandchildren were sent to Jewish camps that featured Indian crafts, schools where they studied anything but Hebrew curricula, and select colleges where they could meet Jewish marriage partners and insure Jewish survival. Families discovered to their gratification or surprise that they were conforming members of the white-collar middle class. As such, along with every household that boasted a *maven* of good taste, they comported themselves in the proper middle-class manner by decorating their homes in the latest fashion and hanging modern, newfangled pictures on their walls.

Jewish artists and their Jewishness did not always coexist happily in twentieth century America. The need or obligation to preserve traditional attitudes gradually faded once acculturation admitted newer conventions and styles. As parochial viewpoints were broadened to include the social, political, and economic changes, Jewish art lent itself to the corresponding issues of justice, idealism, industrialism, and alternate systems of beliefs. A significant number of Jewish painters and printmakers began to participate in a quiet revolution that was defining the American urban scene and the internationalism of modern art. The instruction of a non–Jew, Robert Henri, the most authoritative art teacher in the first half of the century, ushered in a contemporary American style. He broke with the Grand Manner tradition, announcing that "the big fight is on" against conventional subject matter. He encouraged artists to move away from musty formalism and towards describing what they knew best—their own neighborhoods, complete with grungy tenement buildings, garbage cans, corner saloons, and elevated trains. Blue-collar workers, immigrants, tired peddlers, hectic shopkeepers, and ordinary folks doing nothing much—all became grist for big-city "ash-can" art; much of it mirrored the Lower East Side.

Henri's followers chose the Armory Regimental Building in New York, with its particularly American identity, for an exhibition of Modernist European and American works. That landmark event in 1913, which signified the new principles that art would adopt, involved a number of Jewish artists and organizing members such as Jacob Epstein, Jo Davidson, William Zorach, Jerome Myers and Abraham Walkowitz. The departure from traditional representation was perceived by many critics and attendees as anarchic or ungodly at best, yet not only were cultural patterns in the United States changing, but American and European art was moving into a radical forward-looking school. Some three hundred thousand visitors were introduced to Modernism in its vitality, intensity, and directness, as well as in its subjective emotions and often startling designs. The exhibition catalogue tried to ease the shock: "Art is a sign of life. There can be no life without change, as there can be no development without change. To be afraid of what is different or unfamiliar is to be afraid of life."

Henri had already declared that those "who produce the most satisfactory art are in my mind those who are absorbed in the civilization in which they are living." A considerable number of young Jewish artists agreed with him, developing an authentic and unaffected style derived from the immigrant scene and their own family and ethnic background. Many who had come from eastern European backgrounds now grabbed the chance to work in the new manner, to engage freely in lifestyles of their choice, and to express themselves, if need be, through a sense of disquiet and dislocation. Many were already involved with each other through the Educational Alliance Art School, the People's Art Guild, the Yiddisher Kultur Farband, The Ten, and the Jewish Art Center. From the Yiddish press and visits to Europe, they had learned something about the work of Joseph Israels, Max Liebermann, Mark Chagall, Isaac Levitan, and Mark Antokolski. Now they were eager to strike out on their own, not necessarily as "Jewish artists" or as "religious artists," but with a social and political agenda that ranged over assorted international "isms." In most cases they remained responsive to their Jewishness, or at least to their common ancestry, even as they evolved as Americans. Within the parameters of Yiddish culture, many chose to express themselves in terms of everyday life, workplace drudgery, and unique selfhood.

The art community was moving in two directions. One offshoot, seemingly indifferent to grim social problems, adopted abstract elements which stressed balance, form, and color irrespective of content. The other deliberately chose not to remain "modern" or current. It was by far the more pervasive branch, maintaining close ties with the recognizable image because it appeared to have a connection with social justice and the class struggle through its sympathetic imagery of ordinary laborers and everyday life. In spite of the fact that many considered it more and more of an anachronism, Realism succeeded because a large number of people wanted pictures to which they could relate and which responded to what they expected of art. The devaluation of Modernism, together with the promotion of leftist politics, produced an outpouring of new themes. Ready and free to exploit social and moral issues, artists submitted their work to exhibitions and liberal magazines and newspapers. They were motivated by principles associated with "truth to nature" and social significance, as well as investigations into the psychology of the hidden and forbidden.

A few were disposed to identify themselves Jewishly. Abraham Walkowitz, a native of Siberia whose devout parents settled in the Lower East Side when he was a young boy, became a teacher at the Educational Alliance Art School and was one of the Jewish Expressionist artists who participated in the Armory Show, helping to convey European Modernism to America. Eager to interpret elements of his own life, he captured a contemplative mood in his *Self-Portrait*, etched about 1910 (Ill. 14:10). He was associated with both the radical Ferrer School, where Henri taught, and the People's Art Guild, both of them centers frequented by students for whom social relevance had become a prime focus. The Guild played an important role in bringing artists and audiences together by sponsoring lectures and exhibitions in locations where people were likely to gather. One of its goals was to link Yiddishkeit with familiar settings or existing conditions through the production of inexpensive but personally meaningful prints.

Ill. 14:10. *Self-Portrait*. **Etching. By Abraham Walkowitz, c. 1910**

William Meyerowitz was not only the son of a cantor and a cantor himself, he was also a member of the chorus at the Metropolitan Opera and a particularly fine draftsman, evoking atmospheric effects borrowed from French Impressionism. He and his wife Theresa Bernstein worked with a group of Jewish artists who taught in widely diverse styles, taking advantage of the opportunities offered by the Educational Alliance Art School and kindred art schools. Among them were Chaim Gross, Ben Shahn, Leonard Baskin, Louise Nevelson, Man Ray, Mark Rothko, Jennings Tofel, the Soyer brothers, Jerome Myers, Barnett Newman, Adolph Gottlieb, Elias Grossman, and Louis Lozowick.

The Educational Alliance prospered under the direction of Abbo Ostrowsky, whose artistic orientation had developed in pre-revolutionary Russia. His etching of the lofty Rivington Street Synagogue symbolized the search for concurrent Jewish and American ideals (Ill. 14:11).

Ill. 14:11. *Rivington Street Synagogue.* Etching. By Abbo Ostrowsky, c. 1915

He found them, not in the established uptown academies that promoted European Modernism, but in the coming of age of the Lower East Side. Perhaps the most gifted of the Alliance artists was Russian-born Max Weber, whose family immigrated to New York when he was a boy of ten. After a three-year study program in Paris where he picked up Cubist notions, he returned to New York in 1909 trailing clouds of abstraction and dramatic sensation. His interest in African culture and American Indian art, as well as in the flat patterns of Japanese prints, helped define an almost brutal style in his woodcuts and lithographs through the use of eccentric representations of space and form. He turned to printmaking because the equipment was relatively cheap and his financial situation relatively precarious. But by 1919 or 1920, when he printed the four-by-two-inch woodcut *Rabbi Reading*, he was already recognized for his ability to evoke natural Realism together with more progressive elements (Ill. 14:12). He confined the scholar in a compressed or isolated space, joining a sharp angularity with a mood of spiritual introspection. His Jewish works, which are among his most mature and deeply felt achievements, reflected the Hasidic mysticism of his native Bialystok, and sought as well to reinforce the religious values that he feared were being eroded in America.

Ill. 14:12. *Rabbi Reading*. Woodcut. By Max Weber, c. 1919

Peter Krasnow arrived in America from Russia in the early part of the century and concentrated on expressionistic Judaic themes. In his lithograph *Ritual Bath*, 1928, the immersing woman boldly confronts the viewer, erotically relating observance of a religious function to fertility (Ill. 14:13). During a Parisian interlude, he picked up Cubist and Fauve elements, and when California recalled him in 1934, he added wood sculpture to his other figurative art forms in a continuing exploration of harmonious volume.

William Auerbach-Levy was just eleven years old and already a gifted artist when he enrolled in the National Academy of Design, and already an apprentice in their etching class. He became a teacher at his former school and at the Alliance, turning out affective Jewish subject matter as well as caricatures of the intellectual and political smart set for New York papers. Like several of his colleagues, he warmed to the city's religious atmosphere, offering sensitive portrayals of rabbis and scholars.

Louis Lozowick emigrated alone to America at age fourteen hoping to find an atmosphere free of the anti–Semitic pogroms that followed the 1905 Russian revolution. After a period of study in Europe where he was influenced by the mechanistic style of Fernand Leger and others, he came home with a modernist outlook which he associated with the country's destiny—the dynamic power of machines in an industrialized and urbanized nation—and transmitted that force and energy into his prints.

After lecturing at the Alliance School and teaching at the American Artists School, he became an influential printmaker, extracting beauty from functional design, offering his beliefs in Jewish unity and social commitment to his students, motivating them to identify with their own community in the East Side shops, restaurants, and markets surrounding the elevated railroad tracks. His travels took him across America and to various cities in Israel where, shortly before his death in 1973, he created his last catalogued lithograph, *Unfinished Synagogue, Beersheba.*

The overhead train, so characteristic of New York, also exercised a fascination for Stuart Davis whose lithograph, *Sixth Avenue El*, 1931, decomposed a window view into a jumble of Lower East Side ingredients (Ill. 14:14). A non–Jew, Davis fused a variety of Jewish elements—a tenement building with its fire-escape ladders, a butcher's kosher sign, sewing machines, and a dress model. A small six-pointed star, seemingly unrelated to the image, ties together the ethnic qualities of the print.

America gave itself over to a binge that

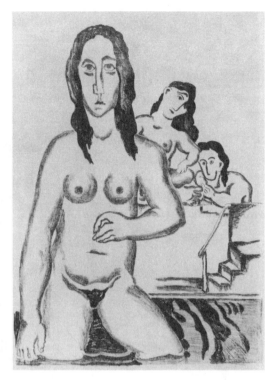

Ill. 14:13. *Ritual Bath*. Lithograph. By Peter Krasnow, 1928. Courtesy Tobey C. Moss Gallery, Los Angeles

lasted from the post-war period until 1929. Skyscrapers, bootleg whiskey, bobbed hair and the Charleston characterized those pre-depression years. Then the whole structure imploded. The collapse of Wall Street brought about the worst financial catastrophe in American history. Banks failed, work opportunities declined drastically, the market system faltered, and factories closed for want of customers. "Aggressive Capitalism," and by extension, the Jews, were blamed in part for the evils of homelessness, unemployment, underemployment, and foreign or external influences. In 1932, a piece of campaign literature for a justice of the Municipal Court in New York carried the slogan "Don't Vote for Pike, he's a kike. Vote for a real American."

Movie companies became an obvious target for mocking Jews as bloated plutocrats. A typical cartoon depicted a Judaized "Hollywood" pouring money into the pocket of an "alien refugee" while a "native American" is forced on the dole. A poster demanding a boycott of "every motion picture starring any member of the Pro-Communist Hollywood Anti-Nazi League" exhorted readers to "Destroy Jew Monopoly of the Motion Picture Industry with its Sex Filth Films and Jew-Communist Propaganda." Pamphlets blanketed the country addressed to "Christian Vigilantes," urging them to "Buy Gentile. Employ Gentile. Vote Gentile. Boycott the movies! Hollywood is the Sodom and Gomorrah where International Jewry controls VICE, DOPE, GAMBLING ... where young Gentile Girls are raped by Jewish producers, directors, casting directors who go Unpunished."

Some artists managed to find a bit of humor in the times, bleak as they were. Charles Laborde's drypoint caricature *New York—Quartier Juif* (Jewish Quarter), c. 1930, caught a storekeeper anxiously coaxing a prospect into Mandel's, one of the numberless Jewish-owned shops frantic to corral a live customer. In 1940, Saul Raskin turned to the ancient compendium

Ill. 14:14. *Sixth Avenue El.* Lithograph. By Stuart Davis, 1931. Art ©Estate of Stuart Davis/ Licensed by VAGA, New York, NY

of wise sayings *Pirke Aboth* for a whimsical look at one of its precepts: *Who is mighty? He who subdues his passions.* He illustrated the adage with an etching of an Orthodox young fellow vainly struggling to keep his mind on the Holy Book while his imagination flows towards the pleasures of sex, gluttony, and hubris. But flashes of wit were no match for the troubles of the prewar period.

Hitler had challenged America to accept European Jews in the '30s, but only about eleven thousand were admitted; the majority who were turned down were shipped to concentration and death camps. The Wagner-Rogers Bill of 1935 would have allowed an additional twenty thousand German children into the United States. President Roosevelt was later castigated for indifference to Jewish suffering in closing the doors to victims whose lives surely would have been saved had they been permitted entrance. But he apparently concurred with a 1936 *Fortune* magazine poll indicated that eighty-three percent of the population would reject the exiles of Nazi Europe.

Hardly anyone was willing to assist or retrieve Jews. The policy of Assistant Secretary of State Breckinridge Long, by his own admission, to "postpone and postpone and postpone" visas to bring refugees to America was endorsed by the president, certainly with the knowledge that such postponements would result in many further exterminations. Support and reinforcement was offered by Detroit's Father Charles Coughlin and his "Christian Front," which motivated and endorsed anti–Semitic individuals and organizations. Secretary of the Treasury Henry Morgenthau, Jr., encouraged by both concerned Jews and non–Jews, exposed Long's false claims that he had already admitted over half a million refugees. Fear of Arab reprisals, fear of foreigners, and fear of isolation sentiments dominated many government decisions. In 1938 an international conference took up the refugee issue, but not a single country offered any substantial aid. In spite of the pogroms in Poland in 1937 and the declaration of the governor-general of the Berlin Olympics in 1940 that "the Jews must vanish from the face of the earth," opposition to immigration persisted. Politics and the nation's paranoia prevented rescue. By 1939, the Hitler-Stalin pct and the onset of the European war drew many Americans into the anti–Nazi effort, but nothing they could do stopped the horrors. In 1941, when the United States was attacked by the Japanese at Pearl Harbor, it was too late to prevent the obliteration of most of Europe's Jews.

The War Refugee Board, established in 1944, was mandated to "aid the victims of Nazism while pressing the Allies and neutrals to take forceful action in their behalf," as well as to set up emergency shelters in Oswego, New York. Board director John Pehle claimed that while bombings of concentration camps would have killed many inmates, more would ultimately have been saved because enough death machines could not have been rebuilt at that time. He admitted that had these objectives been implemented, "things might have been different."

Nevertheless, American Jews did their best to move on. Some demonstrated recuperative powers in the job market, thanks in part to the pool of academics who were able to find work in certain white collar, nonprofit, and government agencies. Others profited when Roosevelt established his New Deal to cope with the problems of agricultural subsidies, taxes, deficit spending, and banking reform. It was a "Jew Deal" according to some. (Eighty-two percent of the Jewish vote went to Roosevelt in the presidential election of 1932, and ninety percent in 1940.) In a cartoon of the period he was identified as the leader of Jewish conspirators, including Bernard Baruch, who helped organize New Deal legislation and protect the country's economic reserves; Henry Morgenthau, Jr., in charge of the war effort; civil libertarian Felix Frankfurter of the U.S. Supreme Court; justice of the New York Supreme Court Samuel Rosenman; and Benjamin Cohen, who put together a good part of the New Deal program. "How long will the American people continue to tolerate this hysteric, degenerate JEWISH PLOT, with their phony EMERGENCIES?" the caricaturist asks. A legitimate question, considering that "Jews are the cause of high taxes—slavery—starvation and death." Yet their leadership helped the country to come back from economic collapse through broad legislative programs designed to benefit the jobless, to build new projects, and to help the farmers feed a demoralized nation whose president declared that one-third of its people were "ill-nourished, ill-clad, and ill-housed."

The shock of severe unemployment and economic crises affected the whole spirit and focus of reality, including the arts. Fortunately, the federal government initiated a series of projects which remained in effect from 1933 to 1943, alleviating some of the hardships. Art became a propaganda tool for government agencies which harnessed the supply of creative talent in the cause of patriotism and unity. Relief programs such as the Works Projects Administration (WPA) underwrote job opportunities, established community art centers, and awarded commissions for decorating federal buildings. Over five thousand struggling artists—many of them Jews—helped New York leapfrog to the forefront of the art community with politically inspired works. Under those circumstances it was no surprise that "ash can" Realism replaced Social Realism. Large cities were viewed more as adversaries than as sources of vigor and excitement.

Artists worked for the standard ninety-five dollars a month, taking advantage of various support programs, among which the printmaking tradition was kept alive and given official recognition. Thousands of images, mostly representational in the prevailing social-realist mode, were churned out at reasonable prices, frequently describing poverty and loneliness with compassion, occasionally with cynicism. Jewish and non–Jewish artists alike took their perceived moral responsibilities seriously, addressing regionalist issues, cultural ferment, labor problems, and racial and political inequities. Jews promoted Yiddish as well as proletarian culture as they dealt with the garment industry, contemporary social matters, Nazi dangers, and the eastern European experience.

Although only a handful of the WPA artists ever made much noise in the world, William Gropper carved out a prominent place for himself first as a cartoonist and satirist and then as a class-conscious Social Realist. He was born in 1897 on the Lower East Side, but his spiritual home was within the leftist movement, as was Louis Lozowick's and Max Weber's, all of whom sought political or militant solutions to labor exploitation, Fascism, anti–Semitism, and the perception that creativity was stifled by American capitalism. These themes became ideological symbols to many twentieth century Jewish artists for whom Communist internationalism—or supra-nationalism—was a foil against repression in general and anti–Semitism in particular. Frustration and confusion had drawn many liberals to Communism during the 1930s. Some leftist artists refrained from any expression of Jewish themes; occasionally they manifested an antipathy towards the Jewish establishment. Interest in the working class represented for them the chief priority.

Gropper's lithograph *Sweatshop*, 1934, confronts the viewer with tired wage slaves confined in an ill-lit, ill-equipped room. It was a harsh commentary on the needle industry, dominated by Jews whom he viewed as exploiters, although the "bosses" were often as poor as their workers. He remembered how night after night as a youngster, he carried home bundles of cloth from the workshop for his mother to sew; at fourteen he was a factory drudge himself, earning five dollars a week for twelve-hour days, six days a week. But he knew how to draw, and that was his passport out of the slums and into the Ferrer School where he studied under the direction of Henri. "Right then I began to realize that you don't paint with color," he said, "you paint with conviction, freedom, love, and heartaches—with what you have." Those words came back to him after World War II when he reexamined his Jewish identity in the darkness of the Holocaust. "In 1947, I was invited, with brother artists from all over the world," he said, "to the unveiling of the Warsaw ghetto monument. I'm not Jewish in a professional sense but in a human sense; here are six million destroyed. There is a ritual in the Jewish religion of lighting a candle for the dead, but instead of doing this, I decided to paint a picture in memory, every year. In this way, I paid my tribute, rather than burning a candle." His lithograph *Holocaust*, 1967, was that year's recognition of the Polish Jew who ended his days in a bloodied coffin surrounded by Nazi soldiers traumatizing, lacerating, and taking life.

Like Gropper, Ben Shahn was another of the WPA's beneficiaries. He was committed to the leftist cause at an early age and helped kindle the American conscience by boldly confronting moral issues. Born in Lithuania, he grew up in New York's poorest neighborhoods, already a junior scholar in biblical studies. Stirred by the misery he saw around him, he dedicated much of his talent to challenging urban blight, injustice, and destitution. He explored his Jewish identity through designs for a number of synagogues as well as in paintings and prints. A lithographic poster, *This Is Nazi Brutality*, 1942, was an anti–Fascist propaganda effort to support the Graphic Arts Division of the Office of War Information (Ill. 14:15). Following the alleged killing of a local police officer by a Jewish youngster in Lidice, Czechoslovakia, a ticker-tape flashes news of the retaliatory massacre that destroyed all its men, women, and children. On behalf of the collective victims, a hooded figure stands resolutely beneath a threatening sky, his hands shackled. The Germans claimed that "all the buildings of the village were leveled to the ground, and the name of the village was immediately abolished." Not quite; in several countries, towns were renamed to memorialize the fallen community—and Shahn's poster refreshes its ashes.

His serigraph *Warsaw, 1943*, bitterly commemorating the twentieth anniversary of the razing of that city, again employed the powerful symbolism of clenched hands. He added the Hebrew prayer "These victims I will remember for my soul is torn with sorrow. There is no one to help us in the time of our disaster" (Ill. 14:16). His Haggadah, published in 1964, "reflecting the images that were always invoked in my fancy by the majestic and meaningful ritual," was influenced by Chagall and by the costumes of the turbaned Jews of Tunisia whom he visited in 1927–1928. But above all, it was the biblical message of human rights and dignity which he linked to the upheavals of the depression years that lent authority to his lithographs.

Raphael Soyer was born in Russia—along with his twin, Moses— to a learned Hebrew teacher and writer one week before the turn of the century. The family, enlarged by the arrival of Isaac seven years later, was suspected by the czarist government of intellectual (i.e. radical Jewish) leanings, and was forced from their home.

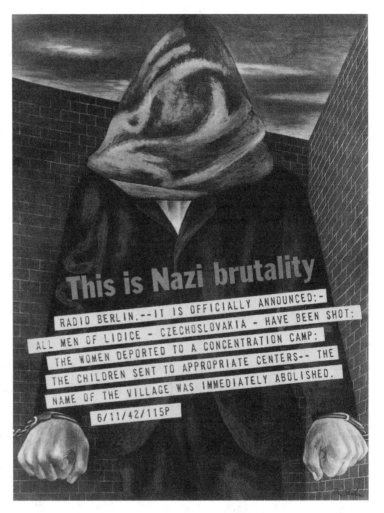

Ill. 14:15 *This Is Nazi Brutality*. Lithograph. By Ben Shahn, 1942. Art ©Estate of Ben Shahn/Licensed by VAGA, New York, NY

Finding political refuge in America in 1912, they became cultural rather than practicing Jews, discovering their vocations in the struggles of working men and women. Pessimism and fear found their way into an etching of *The Artist's Parents*, 1963–1964. Derived from Raphael's 1932 painting of the same subject, it paid tribute to those whom Roosevelt called the forgotten people at the bottom of the economic pyramid. The image interpreted a Jewish sensibility despite his assertion that his art wasn't "Jewish."

Soyer and other artists who established themselves in the international leftist movement believed that radical secularism rather than ethnic cultural influences would prevent intolerance. But it didn't always work out that way. When the respected journalist Dorothy Thompson visited Germany in 1933 and wrote that the Jews suffered from an "outbreak of sadistic and pathological hatred," the news media either ignored or suppressed much of her information. Hoping to stem the indifference and bigotry, Rabbi Stephen Wise and the American Jewish Congress called for an anti–Nazi demonstration that filled New York's Madison Square Garden. Street parades protested Hitler's book-burning frenzy, while boycotts of German goods were supported across the country. But Secretary of State Cordell Hull had his own agenda—an apology to the Nazi government when someone tore down a swastika flag from the *Bremen* passenger steamship.

America found itself facing new problems. Nations were choosing up new sets of allies and adversaries and continued to threaten their own survival. In 1942 twenty-six countries, including America, Britain, and the USSR, banded together against the Axis powers—Germany, Italy, and Japan—to form the United Nations. The organization was headquartered in New York City, and its charter, drafted in 1945, was designed to insure international peace and security and to maintain friendly relations among world bodies. Mutual distrust, however, almost immediately created a cold war that represented a great divide between Western democracy and a Communist-controlled Russian and east European dictatorship.

Perhaps an effort to move away from painful realities, led to the interest in less disturbing abstract designs. Some critics believed that wars, bombs, and the threat of self-annihilation were enough to move artists away from the flawed human spirit. Others suggested that artists simply rebelled against imitating nature or had exhausted the representational vein. Content-free shapes, spectacular in size, impersonal in appearance, and idiosyncratic in technical methods now emerged as the dominant artistic school and defined modernity. In 1943 Barnett Newman, Mark Rothko, and Adolph Gottlieb addressed a letter to *The New York Times* heralding a new art movement: Abstract Expressionism.

Yet, the Soyers, Shahn, and Gropper stuck with the individual personality. So did Arthur Szyk. Born in Poland, driven to Paris by anti–Semitism, invited to Europe's capitals to exhibit his work, he ended his career in America. His cartoons appeared in dozens of posters, magazines, and newspapers, and in two war-related books, *The New Order,* 1941, and *Ink and Blood,* 1946. In the latter, he depicted the Nazi leadership surveying a report indicating that two million Jews had already been murdered. *"We're running short of Jews,"* they comment (Ill. 14:17).

The post-war art experience that led to an upsurge of interest in lithography occurred in New York when Tatyana Grosman opened the Universal Limited Art Editions (ULAE). Her first venture was the suite *Stones,* 1957–1959, by the Jewish artist Larry Rivers. Shortly thereafter, the Ford Foundation funded the Tamarind Lithography Workshop in Los Angeles under the direction of June Wayne. As global nonprofit institutions, ULAE and Tamarind, both founded by Jewish

Ill. 14:16. *Warsaw, 1943.* Serigraph. By Ben Shahn, 1963. Art ©Estate of Ben Shahn/Licensed by VAGA, New York, NY

women, had an enormous influence on the aesthetic and technical understanding of the medium. Together, they developed experimental and creative workshops, prodded their colleagues and students to stretch their imaginations and talents, and provided studios where artists could find distinguished teachers and enthusiastic patronage as well as the tools and equipment to execute intricate, high-quality prints.

Innovative Haggadot were slow to appear in the early years of the century although several later specimens were extraordinary. The Union Haggadah, 1907, was the first standardized American Reform edition; mostly in English, it included photographs, musical notations, explanations and commentary. Other versions, designed for youngsters, included brightly colored illustrations. Nondescript models were offered by

Ill. 14:17. *"We're Running Short of Jews."* From *Ink and Blood.* By Arthur Szyk, 1946. Reproduced with the cooperation of Alexandra Szyk Bracie and the Arthur Szyk Society. www. Szyk.org

commercial companies promoting kosher products. Mordecai Kaplan published a Haggadah for the Reconstructionist Movement in 1942 illustrated by Leonard Weirgard. A useful edition for members of the armed forces appeared in 1943. Ben Shahn's superb 1964 work featured hand coloring and gold leaf. A unique Haggadah by David Moss, commissioned by an American family and subsequently produced as a facsimile in 1987, is remarkable for its illuminations, calligraphy, paper-cutting, fold-aways, mirrors, and moveable components. He chose a card game and a psychological perspective for depicting the Four Sons: "As a game of chance, we have no control over the children dealt us. It is out task as parents, as educators to play our hand based on the attributes of the children we are given. It is the child not the parent, who must direct the process."

Leonard Baskin's Orthodox background was a source of ambivalence—on the one hand he was a "born-again atheist," on the other, his brain was "serried with ... the sound and smell

of shul, of home, of Yeshiva, of the nearly all–Jewish street." The Holocaust tragedy was reflected in his 1952 woodcut *Man of Peace*—the flayed "physical presence of our common humanity ... our common suffering." His themes, as demonstrated in his 1974 Haggadah, ranged
from talmudic questions and the meaning of man's role in the universe to the fundamental cor-
relations between creation, freedom, and the great questions of life and death. Bypassing Abstraction, he remained tied to the figure and the angst of German Expressionism.

At first, there was a surprising dearth of Holocaust-related art by Jewish artists, possibly
because there seemed to be a need or desire to distance themselves from the tragedy and from
the "Jewish artist" label. Adolph Gottlieb, Louise Nevelson, Philip Guston, and Sam Francis
defined themselves primarily as universalist rather than as exponents of Jewish tradition. According to that definition they were free to examine structure, harmony, color and energy from
their own determinate and complex views of the world, much as is possible in architecture or
music. In 1966, Harold Rosenberg addressed the issue of whether or not the apparent anonymity
of Abstraction results in a barren or fruitful art—particularly a Jewish art. He argued that it
"constitutes a new art by Jews ... which is a profound Jewish expression.... To be engaged with
the esthetics of self has liberated the Jew as artist by eliminating his need to ask himself whether
a Jewish art exists or not."

Not everyone agreed, claiming instead that Jewish artists—abstract or not, like it or not—
were connected to Jewish culture. Barnett Newman was deeply affected by "man's natural
desire for the exalted" expressed though Jewish culture and mysticism although he did not
perceive himself as a member of any organized religion. The metaphysical qualities infusing
his work were related to his claim that "Jews can paint abstract art because they believe in an
abstract God." His huge canvases and graphics in the '60s, characterized by subtle gradations
of color slashed by vertical rays of light, influenced minimalist and conceptual art as well as
affirming transcendental experiences. Mark Rothko favored horizontally separated glowing
color fields that have been interpreted as spiritual altars relating to the biblical void. Some
critics objected to these explanations and interpretations, convinced that any attempt to represent or render a manifestation of God (or any sublime image) goes beyond the capability or
role of art.

By the time the full realization of the Holocaust atrocities became known, some artists
began to understand and represent the calamity as unequalled in scope or numbers. Harold
Paris, the son of a Yiddish actor, was barely out of his teens in 1945 when he learned of the
Buchenwald extermination camp. Although he was primarily a sculptor, in 1948 his engraving *Where Are We Going?* asked and attempted to answer the profound question of evil. Leon
Golub's lithograph *Charnel House*, 1946, was an early post-war indictment of a humanity cursed
by inhumanity (Ill. 14:18). His frightening evocation of fire and destruction grew from the horrors of the death camps as well as from the devastations of Hiroshima and Nagasaki.

Jack Levine, a self-styled curmudgeon, rasped, "I come of people who do not even
acknowledge Jesus Christ. Why am I supposed to acknowledge Abstract Expressionism?" He
was born in 1915 to an Orthodox family in a poor immigrant section of Boston, and as a young
artist he portrayed the Sodom and Gomorrah lifestyles of the army elite, politicians, and high
society. Following the death of his beloved father in 1939, however, he turned to Jewish subjects. "The gas ovens were too horrible for me to face," he said, but his lithograph *Warsaw
Ghetto*, 1969, became an icon and symbol of Nazi evil (Ill. 14:19). He dedicated it to the
unknown German photographer who had snapped pictures of Jews being forcibly removed from
their homes.

Some pundits proved to their own satisfaction that the Holocaust had never taken place.
Denial surfaced almost as soon as statistics were made public. But from the mid–'50s through
the '60s, spearheaded by the 1952 publication of Anne Frank's diary and continuing through

Above: Ill. 14:18. *Charnel House.* Lithograph By Leon Golub, 1946. Art ©Estate of Leon Golub/Licensed by VAGA, New York , NY/Courtesy Ronald Feldman Fine Arts. *Below:* Ill. 14:19. *Warsaw Ghetto.* Lithograph. By Jack Levine, 1969. Art ©Jack Levine/Licensed by VAGA, New York, NY

the Arab-Israeli conflicts, concern for the truth demanded accurate information. For those who rejected its existence, no argument was convincing. For those burdened with memories, the misrepresentation and refutation of facts was harrowing. For the Jewish people the ultimate response occurred when the State of Israel was recognized on May 14, 1946. Just eleven minutes after David Ben Gurion announced its launching, President Harry Truman, defying his own State Department, led most of the international community in acknowledgement of the new country. (In his 1947 diary he expressed a common type of anti–Semitism: "The Jews, I find are very, very selfish ... when they have power, physical, financial or political, neither Hitler nor Stalin has anything on them for cruelty or mistreatment to the underdog." It was an uncharacteristic note.)

Popular posters such as the United Jewish Appeal's *Their Fight Is Our Fight: Give Today,* 1946–1947, kept Jewish issues in the forefront. In 1948, the Procurement Division of the United States Army, in cooperation with Rabbi Phillip Bernstein and the American Jewish Joint Distribution Committee in Munich-Heidelberg, supervised and published a remarkable nineteen-volume set of the Talmud, using a press that had once turned out Nazi material. The bottom of each title page carried a chilling picture of a concentration camp; the top, an image of Eretz Yisrael: *"From Bondage to Freedom, from Darkness to a Great Light."* It was dedicated to the United States Army: "This special edition of the Talmud, published in the very land where, but a short time ago, everything Jewish and of Jewish inspiration was anathema, will remain a symbol of the indestructibility of the Torah."

Mauricio Lasansky, an émigré from Argentina, was a charismatic teacher and artist who turned to Jewish history for subject matter in many of his prints. Following the 1961 trial of the Gestapo officer Adolf Eichmann for "crimes against humanity," he created the portfolio *Nazi Drawings*, thirty life-size Holocaust images. Completed between 1961 and 1966, they possess a violent intensity and great dramatic effect in the portrayal of battered skeletons, brutalized and tortured children, raped women, indifferent bishops, and even self-castrated Nazis.

The '50s and '60s brought new or revised aesthetic systems, including a greater predilection to line and form. When Pop (Popular) Art made its gaudy appearance with flat, linear, and hard-edged images, it not only rejected Abstraction but focused on instant recognition, which was one reason why it attracted wide public interest: art could be anywhere and everywhere. Pop was generally accepted as a legitimate style of urban consumerism taking its inspiration from the cheerful primary colors of soup cans, comic strips, or photographs. Its prints were clever examples of reproductive work with precedents reaching back to the 1930s when a similar interest in commonplace or real-world images represented a popularist aspect of the American experience.

In an attempt to coordinate aspects of vision and technology, these mechanically reproduced prints denied strong feeling or outward structure, examining instead the impact of commercial media on popular culture. The affinity of the public for such works hinged on their lack or absence of emotional content, perhaps a way of drawing back from the American tragedies of the assassination of President John Kennedy in 1963 and his brother Robert five years later. Racial tensions flashed between blacks and whites as Dr. Martin Luther King's 1968 boycott of the bus company that denied Rosa Parks a "white" seat heralded the end of overt segregation and led to his death. Anti-Vietnam War passions led to mass demonstrations. Societal upheavals spread as America's youth challenged almost any form of traditional or contemporary authority; the pervading mood came close to destroying the country's spirit. The moon landing in 1969 raised it, the Nixon scandal of the '70s depressed it.

Like some other Pop figures, Andy Warhol learned his craft in New York's commercial art centers. He was the best known of this phenomenon, and through his self-promotional highjinks, the flashiest of the lot. As a cult devoted to celebrities, Pop lent itself to portraiture, although its treatments had more to do with surface pattern than with the human situation. In 1980, he completed a silkscreen portfolio in his typical electric colors, *Ten Portraits of Jews of the Twentieth Century,* among whom were Golda Meir, Martin Buber, George Gershwin, and Marilyn Monroe. He referred to the series as the Ten Jewish Geniuses. The publisher, Ronald Feldman, had been concerned that the decade which had seen an Arab-Israeli war, an oil embargo, and a United Nations which charged Zionism with racist doctrines, was eroding Jewish hopes and expectations; he believed that the celebration of Jewish luminaries by a Gentile superstar (with one Jewish great-grandparent) would encourage interfaith relations.

But throughout those difficult times, ambitious undertakings even in the art world continued to shape the texture of experience. Jim Dine also believed in an art that used everyday materials to reflect the wide influence of commercial advertisements. Born in the midst of the depression, he started working as early as 1960 in Grosman's ULAE, but it wasn't until 1970 that he began to concentrate seriously on printmaking. Although his work included few Jewish images, in an early lithograph, *Purim,* 1966, he playfully scattered elements of the holiday's symbols—Queen Esther's crown, Haman's tricorner hat (which ripens into the delicacy Hamantasch), and a grogger which noisily erupts whenever the villain's name is mentioned during the reading of the Megillah (Ill. 14:20). His most characteristic image, an empty dressing gown, neatly belted, drawn with arms akimbo, was first introduced in his prints in 1965. The idea of entirely withdrawing his person became a sign of lost presence and individuality in a lonely and bankrupt culture. *Yellow Robe,* 1980, a self-portrait lithograph, commented

Ill. 14:20. *Purim.* Lithograph. By Jim Dine, 1966. ©2007 Jim Dine/Artists Rights Society(ARS), New York

on nonattendance at his own life, a Surrealist approach in which he concealed himself inside an otherwise straightforward object (Ill. 14:21). His later prints helped spark a transition away from Pop's detachment to the restoration of the expressive, if hidden, human personality.

Larry Rivers left behind a Jewish home in the Bronx, blaming Jewish guilt and being white for his sexual, alcoholic, and drug addictions, and for exploiting his role as art's bad boy. But he was serious about his work. Renouncing Abstract Expressionist and Pop styles, he found his own way with realistic figurative paintings. He returned to his Jewish identity with a huge three-panel narrative painting, *The History of Matzoh*, 1982–1984, which traced Jewish history over millennia. Having been introduced to Isaac Bashevis Singer, he agreed to illustrate the 1984 edition of the author's *Magician of Lublin*. Set in Poland in the late 1800s, the story tells of Yasha Mazur, adrift in a spiritual vacuum, who sentenced himself to life imprisonment as an Orthodox Jew. The lithograph of the former libertine avoiding the "ever-assailing temptations of the flesh" shows him donning a prayer shawl and phylacteries featuring the Hebrew words Tallit and Tefillin (Ill. 14:22).

The magician's retreat from the world mirrored the loss of the meaning and emotional impact of the post–Holocaust world as it inevitably began to recede from the late twentieth century consciousness—although the welfare of Israel remained paramount. More and more, the lure of secular Jewish lifestyles questioned the durability and even the survival of American Jewry. With the move away from concentrated Jewish environments and ritual observances, comfortable suburbs regulated the degree of Jewish commitment. While synagogues, organizations, federations, and community centers went up everywhere, gathering Jews together in spiritual or commodious settings, they were not able to derail the vexing issues of intermarriage, the large percentage of children not being raised as Jews, or a declining population.

The good news was that intolerance and prejudice apparently were on the decline. The Roman Catholic Second Vatican Council in 1965, *Nostra Actate*, and other subsequent conferences rejected deicide, renounced anti-Semitism, and warranted that Judaism was a living religious organism. Mainline Protestantism, while not quite as sweeping, accepted responsibility and regret for its own anti-Semitic practices. The confrontation by Christians of their past violence and dogma was valued and accepted as sincere expressions by many Jewish leaders, but it was less successful in filtering down to those Jews who stressed the discrepancy between official statements and the frequent countenancing of radical pro-Palestinian movements. (Jews, on the other hand, fell short of acknowledging

Ill. 14:21. *Yellow Robe*. Lithograph. By Jim Dine, 1980. ©2007 Jim Dine/Artists Rights Society (ARS), New York

Christian efforts to mend fences or to educate themselves on positive Jewish–Christian achievements.)

A particular sore point was the missionary effort to convert Jews. Some Christian groups refrained, seeing in Judaism an ongoing covenant with God; others, such as the Lutheran Church Missouri Synod in 1977, maintained that since evangelizing is fundamental to their belief, "We repent of our past neglect in evangelizing Jews." The Conservative Baptist Seminary in Denver stated that there is "no atonement, no forgiveness, no salvation, and no eternal hope in Judaism as a religion." Some Catholic guidelines acquiesced in the belief that Catholicism was the only road to union with God. Most Jews found it offensive and disrespectful to be specifically targeted for conversionary activity, even though the statements ostensibly rejected anti–Semitism. Textbooks in some schools still encouraged negative attitudes towards Judaism as a dead religion, as well as assigning blame and eternal suffering to Jews for the death of Jesus. Nevertheless, leaders in all religious groups expressed hope and expectation that new generations of ecumenically trained teachers would create more positive and accepting situations.

Art, literature, and religious continuity in the twentieth century defined American Jewish culture and was defined by it. Many Jews found that the ties that bound them to heritage and history were stronger than those which had lapsed or been severed. Despite occasional intolerance, fear of the extreme political right, the lack of intra–Jewish communication, or concerns about the "Vanishing American Jew," in no other country were

Top: Ill. 14:22. *The Magician,* Lithograph. By Larry Rivers, 1989. From *The Magician of Lublin.* By Isaac Bashevis Singer. ©Estate of Larry Rivers/Licensed by VAGA, New York, NY. *Bottom:* Ill. 14:23 *Dusk.* Etching, 1990. By Richard Pantell

opportunities or rewards as possible. To the extent that those issues represent a crisis in American Judaism, the challenge of redefining Judaism for the next century will remain fundamental issues for Jewish leadership.

Richard Pantell's *Dusk*, a 1990 etching of a family on its way to the synagogue suggested that regardless of irresolution, withdrawal, or disjunction, basic Jewish traditions—at least for some—would be carried on (Ill. 14:23). By and large, the *goldena medina* had kept its promise.

15

Israel in the Twentieth Century:
The Dream Projected,
Fulfillment Deferred

From 1517 to 1917 Jews lived under Ottoman rule in what the world called the Holy Land. For Jews, it represented their Home Land which God had bequeathed to them following the biblical Exodus. Jerusalem was the capital toward which they prayed and hoped to return in the days of the Messiah. But while they waited, quarrels between them and Arabs who resisted the very notion of a non–Muslim Jewish state, as well as differences between Zionists who favored immigration and land purchase and Jews who wanted to build relationships and coexist peacefully with Muslims, were already joined.

In the course of time, lesser but nonetheless significant events had been underway in that remarkable place. After a hiatus of over two hundred years, Hebrew printing returned to Palestine. Israel Bak had brought his presses from the Ukraine to Safed in 1831, and during the next two years he published a Sephardic Siddur and the Book of Leviticus; the latter's title page bore his self-description as "eminent and wise." (Arab printing began in Beirut in 1834.) But having lost his printing equipment in a peasant insurrection, an earthquake, and a Druze uprising, Bak moved his stock to Jerusalem, determined to produce Hebrew works that would raise the city's cultural level and call attention to its ethical principles. In 1841, he issued a compilation of moral treatises, *Avodat HaKodesh*, by Hayyim Yosef David Azulai, the first of about one hundred thirty books he would print during the course of twenty-two years. Readers also had access to two rival newspapers—the Orthodox *HaLevanon* and the somewhat more liberal *HaVazzelet*, which began publication in the early 1860s; both were concerned less with ideology than with topical political and agricultural problems.

Beginning in 1881 with the assassination of Czar Alexander II, for which the Jews received a good part of blame and a large part of violence, a wave of Zionist immigration (the First Aliya) arrived in Palestine. About seven thousand Jews made their homes in Jerusalem, comprising a majority of its population at the end of the nineteenth century. Most lived in scruffy primitive housing, but tourist potential cleared the way for more upscale quarters. Permission had been granted to rebuild some of the ancient synagogues and holy sites. Christians saw opportunities for missionary activities. European countries took notice and opened consulates. Thanks also to Sir Moses Montefiore, Baron de Rothschild, and other philanthropists the city grew in prestige and influence, spreading out in a dozen Zionist settlements beyond the old walls. In 1901, the Fifth Zionist Congress established the Keren Kayemet

LeIsrael (Jewish National Fund) to purchase the swampy and rocky land that had little to recommend it other than the principle that all of Judea was sacred and indispensable. With this
incentive, the Second Aliya (1903–1914) brought new infusions of Zionist pioneers.

Theodor Herzl determined to revive the concept of unity in native Jewish surroundings.
Goaded into action by intolerance and bigotry during the Dreyfus Affair, his prophetic *Der
Judenstaat* (*The Jewish State*), 1896, proposed that the world's Jews should create a modern
democratic national home where they would no longer suffer as aliens or pariahs. The book
was translated into eighteen languages in at least eighty editions. At first it received a negative response, both from the world powers who suggested locations other than Palestine and
from Jews themselves on both sides of the issue—the ultra-religious were willing to wait for
the Messiah, the assimilationists wanted a dispersed Jewry, and most of the rest were comfortable where they were. In his novel *Altneuland* (*Old-New Land*), 1902, he predicted that a
viable Socialist utopia with a majority Jewish population would come into being as a secular
state. "If you will it," he declared, "it is no dream."

After futile attempts to persuade Kaiser William II and the Ottoman government to permit Jewish colonization under German protection, Herzl considered and then rejected pro-
posals to settle Jews in the Sinai Peninsula, Cyprus, or Uganda. ("We will not go to Egypt,"
he remarked wryly, "we have been there.") When atrocities against Russian Jews in Kishineff
flared in 1903, Herzl turned to England, whose twenty-year history of admitting persecuted
Russian Jews raised hopes of continued sensitivity to refugee problems: "England—whose
greatness sweeps over all the seas—free England will understand and sympathize with the aims
and aspirations of Zionism." But Rothschild and others in free England were resistant to the
movement's political ideology, unwieldiness, secularism, and perceived incitement to anti–Semitism. However, steadfast ties with the Land of Israel, concern for the impoverished pioneers,
and the hope of securing Jewish survival in the aftermath of the massacre overcame much of
the opposition. It was clear that for those Jews who yearned for a country with rights guaranteed by law, a geographic entity of their own was essential. Agricultural equipment, medical
supplies, as well as provisions for technology, banking, small factories, and religious institutions began to flow in. Although the early settlers learned to farm, much of the required labor
was provided by the competing Arab population which had greater practical skills and worked
for lower wages.

Herzl, like Moses, was not meant to see the Promised Land under Jewish stewardship.
He guided his dream for seven years, but the vision prospered at the cost of his health. On
July 4, 1904, at age forty-four, the dreamer died. He had predicted that "God breaks the vessels which He used." However, he did not operate in a vacuum. A group of immigrant Jews
had already established the Hibbat Zion (Lovers of Israel) movement which provided an orga-
nizational base for agricultural settlements.

With Herzl's death, Jewish return became a mission across five decades of opportunity
and conflict. He had single-mindedly pursued the political components of Zionism; now its
cultural aspects were getting needed attention as well. As early as the 1870s, the Russian scholar
Vladimir Stasov had begun exploring Jewish art and ceremonial artifacts. He believed that every
nation should develop its own indigenous art, and that Jewish artists should concentrate on
Jewish subject matter. His studies were welcomed by Martin Buber, who declared that the only
Jewish art possible was that which originated on Jewish soil. Only in Palestine, he insisted, could
Jewishness be adequately nurtured. Buber, who had been trained in the arts, urged that both
the ghetto mentality and the Jewish School of Paris artists be relegated to an artistic limbo.

The idea of promoting Jewish culture had also occurred to Boris Schatz, a young artist
who had trained in Paris and later served as court sculptor to Prince Ferdinand of Bulgaria.
He had approached Herzl in 1903 with the idea of developing an art program in Palestine.

Having received encouragement, he rounded up a small staff and a few students, opened a miniature biblical zoo, and organized the Bezalel School of Art and Crafts with the goal of melding past and present into a fresh artistic experience. It says something about the Jewish psyche that the first important educational institution in Jerusalem was not a yeshiva, a university, or even a technical training school, but an academy of art designed to make objects that looked "Jewish," reflected Jewish traditions, and were dedicated to the "rebirth of the ancient Jewish nation." Through the development of a museum and a system of exhibitions in European and American cities, Schatz took Stasov's ideas further, creating a school that would produce handmade goods able to compete favorably in the international marketplace, arouse national and religious feelings, encourage settlement, and affirm and preserve what he perceived as authentic Judaism. In addition to arts and crafts, Schatz's curricula included the study of music, Hebrew, biblical themes, and Oriental and Diaspora elements.

At the peak of the school's existence, over five hundred students and thirty-five different classes turned out ceremonial objects, postcards, rugs, silver, metal knick-knacks, picture frames, cane furniture, paintings, illustrated books, graphics, and other folk items. But Schatz soon lost some of his best teachers and students, who rejected his academic Realism and anti–Modernism in a period that coincided with Cubism in France and Expressionism in Germany. Art could no longer be defined by geography, his detractors insisted, but must be identified with universal standards. He was frustrated as well by lack of public support, Orthodox objections to the school's secular nature, and the fact that more Christians than Jews bought his wares. In *The Comedy and the Tragedy*, a 1914 cartoon, the artist S. Maud consoled him: "Professor Schatz, don't worry. For every president of a synagogue who buys a Torah crown in Tiffany's, there is a church president who will buy one from you."

The opening of Technion in 1924 in Haifa, and Hebrew University a year later in Jerusalem, challenged Bezalel's "unprogressive" activities, while his difficult relationship with his executive board, unreasonable expectations for his products, inability to develop an indigenous "Hebrew" style, and concentration on a classical tradition rather than on the current pioneer life resulted in a financial fall-off and the demise of many of the workshops. He managed to keep the school operating through appeals in Europe and America, but by the time he died on a fund-raising tour in Colorado in 1932, his original conception was passé, and many of his artists began to borrow from and then blend in with more universal styles. Yet he certainly wasn't a failure. He put Palestine on the map as a place dedicated to the arts and provided an environment for students who might never have had such opportunities. He inspired European-trained teachers to immigrate and create works that have since become treasured collectibles of the religious and secular alike. For twenty-five years his school and museum persevered in fostering artistic sensibilities dedicated to a unique and distinctive ideal.

His was not the only voice. The publication of the *Complete Dictionary of Ancient and Modern Hebrew* by Eliezer Ben-Yehuda enabled readers to keep up with current ideas and events. Begun with the encouragement of Chaim Weizmann and others in 1904, its eight thousand pages in seventeen volumes were completed in 1959 by his widow and son. It was due to their efforts that everyday spoken Hebrew once again was heard in the land through the introduction of hundreds of newly coined words in periodicals and daily newspapers.

Other distinguished cultural and educational institutions were formed in the '20s: the Eretz Yisrael Opera, the Ohel Theater, and the Habimah Theatre, newly arrived from Russia. Museums and dozens of galleries which showcased local and refugee artists testifying that the pursuit of talent and aesthetic expression was very much alive. An early Bezalel student, Russian-born Nachum Gutman, affiliated himself with the Modernist movement as a painter, scenery designer, writer, and illustrator of children's stories. Gutman lived for a time in the Arab quarter, and he idealized Arabs as the authentic children of Zion—close to the soil, earthy, healthy—more representative of the biblical land than were east European Jews. Although he was not so naive as to underestimate the inherent danger of romanticizing the Arab, he proposed a "Hebrew" art and morality drawn from what he perceived as their inherently natural rights. In a nostalgic mood shortly before he died in 1980, he reinterpreted a painting from the 1920s with the screenprint *Bygones: A Train in Herzl Street*. It depicted Arab women relaxing in the orchards, unaware that a train, riding north from Jaffa into the new city of Tel Aviv, would bring, not only modernity, but a strong and forceful secular Jewish presence, inevitably displacing them and altering the nature of the country (Ill. 15:1).

Romanian-born Reuven Rubin, perhaps the most impressive of Bezalel's students, served only a year with Schatz in 1912. He was one of the first to meld a sensuous, romantic national style drawn from east European folk themes and a modern ideology that explored new forms of expression. Having studied in Paris, he rebelled against the school's conservatism, adopting instead something of the primitivism and flat colors of Paul Gauguin and Henri Rousseau. But by ignoring the cynicism of German Expressionism, the angst of French Surrealism, and the wit of Cubism, he furthered utopian images of Palestinian laborers and pioneers, reflecting the illusions of those who longed for positive, heroic images in a new country. From his woodcut portfolio *The God Seekers*, 1922, he offered a bearded, submissive east European scholar trapped in an environment he barely understood; he is being deposed by a reborn Adam and Eve who will regenerate and reclaim the biblical land (Ill. 15:2). "It seems to me now that I always knew instinctively that there was a country where I would develop as a Jewish artist,"

Ill. 15:1. *Bygones: A Train in Herzl Street*. Screenprint, c. 1980. By Nachum Gutman. Courtesy the Israel Museum, Jerusalem

Ill. 15:2. *East European Scholar Contemplating a Reborn Adam and Eve*. Woodcut, 1922. From *The God Seekers*. By Reuven Rubin. Courtesy the Israel Museum, Jerusalem

he wrote. "I don't mean a painter of Jewish subjects, but one whose roots are embedded in the soil of his own homeland, Zion...."

Bezalel artists Ze'ev Raban, Abel Pann, and Ephraim Moses Lilien likewise shared a partiality for Zionist motifs which they interpreted in decorative figurative styles. Raban's illustrations of children's books taught holiday observances to thousands of youngsters, while his lithographic posters in the late 1920s promoting *"Lord" Jaffa Oranges, Finest for Flavor* and *Come to Palestine* encouraged a sense of national identity as well as offering tranquil images to Jews who were vitally important to the tourist industry.

Abel Pann was born into a Latvian rabbinical family. At bar mitzvah age he left home with high hopes, five rubles, and the decision to choose art over Talmud. Schatz hired him in 1913 to form the school's lithographic workshop. (It was only after 1919 that suitable lithographic stones and paper became available in Palestine; earlier work was executed in Europe following Bezalel designs.) He made graphic records of czarist pogroms that shocked and demoralized believers in human progress, and in 1926 he created a portfolio of twenty-five biblical themes beginning with the creation of the world. He never approved of Modernism, calling its artists and promoters uncouth, fawning, and ignorant.

The conflicts that arose between the "joyless" contemporary style and Bezalel's more genial outlook coincided with the rising secularism of young intellectuals in the new artistic center of Tel Aviv. Founded in 1909, it was the first city in Palestine with a majority Hebrew-speaking Jewish population. Because it lay at some distance from religious Jerusalem, its citizens felt free to develop an aura of self-sufficiency and self-confidence. The Tel Aviv art community's interests revolved around post–Impressionism, Constructivism, and other prevailing fashions; Bezalel's days were numbered. After Schatz's death, the Tel Aviv Museum, which opened with a one-man show by Reuven Rubin, attracted a number of Modernists who had already broken from conventional Western Classicism for the subjective values of design, light and color. (The "New Bezalel" School reopened in 1935 with a strong German Expressionist slant under the direction of Joseph Budko who, along with Jacob Steinhardt, attempted to bridge the old and the new.)

The leadership of Zionism in the West had passed to Chaim Weizmann, who during World War I developed chemical breakthroughs in the processing of grain alcohol into badly needed rubber and the production of acetone for making gunpowder. Through these patriotic efforts, he gained friendships with the foreign secretary Arthur Balfour, the colonial secretary Winston Churchill, Prime Minister Lloyd George, and the first professing Jewish member of Parliament, Sir Herbert Samuel, and was thus in an enviable position to further Zionist interests. His mediation skills helped secure a letter on November 2, 1917 from Balfour to Lord Rothschild, president of the English Zionist Federation, acknowledging that "His Majesty's Government views with favour the establishment in Palestine of a national home for the Jewish people...." Yet it was a disappointment to Zionists that the declaration specified *a* national home of the Jewish people in place of an earlier draft designating Palestine as *the* national home. While Balfour genuinely favored the concept of a Jewish state, he also expected that Jewish interests would recruit American backing for British control of the trade routes through the Suez Canal, wresting Palestine from Turkish jurisdiction. President Woodrow Wilson, recognizing American pro–Zionist sympathies, "concurred in the formula" suggested by London as well as by the Jewish ambassador to Constantinople, Henry Morgenthau, Senior, and Louis D. Brandeis, the first Jewish appointee to the Supreme Court.

Britain gained control of the area, a trophy she had craved for generations. On December 10, 1917, after sixteen months of conflict with Turkey, England's General Edmund Allenby, aided by the founders of the Jewish Legion, Vladimir Jabotinsky and Joseph Trumpeldor, liberated Jerusalem and occupied most of Palestine in time to prevent a major deportation of Jews, and set in motion a series of political and educational operations that transformed the Middle East. For two years the British military ruled the area. From 1919 to 1924, an additional thirty-five thousand immigrants, mostly from eastern Europe, brought the total Jewish population close to one hundred thousand. In 1920 Britain accepted a mandate to create a Jewish national home, dispatching Sir Herbert Samuel to serve as high commissioner. After two years of wrangling, the mandate was approved by the League of Nations. Henrik Ibsen, in his play *Peer Gynt*, had declared that "the Jew has taught me how to wait." Indeed, Jews had spent nineteen hundred years learning how to wait for a politically and geographically recognized connection with their ancient home.

But Arab and Jewish hostility was already festering. An early effort to establish Arabic points of view was undertaken by a Palestinian journalist, Najib Nasser, in his book *Zionism: Its History, Objectives, and Importance*, 1911. That year, a Palestinian newspaper, *Filastin*, cautioned its "Palestinian" subscribers to be wary of Zionism. In 1913, the First Arab Nationalist Congress met in Paris. No longer were Muslims, Christians and Jews living as reasonably friendly neighbors. Palestinian Arabs demanded full rights, a national identity, and Syrian control of Jewish Palestine, demands that the Zionists were not willing to grant. Samuel's problems were exacerbated by the struggle between Jabotinsky's right-wing Revisionist party and David Ben-Gurion's Labor government. The former wanted the "slow moving and unimaginative" Zionist leadership to aggressively encourage mass immigration (the third Aliya, 1919–1923) to actively support the paramilitary struggle against growing Arab terrorism with the clandestine Haganah defense source, to develop agriculture, and to secure Jewish sovereignty in all of Palestine through swift political action. On the other hand, the opposition Mapai laborites led by Ben-Gurion in the '30s believed that buying land for the national control of agricultural and industrial resources was paramount in order to reduce dependence on Arab labor and to insure a viable stable Israel. Immediate colonization was not his priority; civil and economic self-restraint within a Democratic Socialist structure was. The difficulties of that situation, however, paled against the ongoing brutality, sabotage, and strikes that convinced Britain of Arab strength and Jewish weakness, and of the impossibility of establishing order, let alone harmony.

When a partition scheme proved unworkable, Churchill issued a White Paper in 1922 narrowing the intent of the Balfour Declaration which, he claimed, "did not contemplate that Palestine as a whole should be converted into a Jewish National Home." Jewish rights would be extended only to the land *west* of the Jordan, although the mandate included the territory *east and west* of the Jordan River and the Dead Sea; under that ruling three-quarters of the territory mutated into the Hashemite Kingdom of Transjordan (later known as Jordan), leaving one quarter of the promised area to the Jewish entity. Churchill emphasized that "economic absorptive capacity" would be the measure by which immigration would be determined, a policy that actually had the approval of some Zionists who feared that inundation by Jewish immigrants would overwhelm the country's resources. He also assured the Arabs that they would not be dominated by the Jewish population; the Jews already in Palestine, he acknowledged, were there "as of right and not on sufferance." This did not sit well with those Arabs who wanted every Jew out. Jabotinsky left the Zionist organization in 1923 believing that its acquiescence to British positions represented a renunciation of the Balfour policy; he predicted that "an iron wall of Jewish bayonets" would be necessary to compel Arab acceptance of a Jewish presence on both shores of the Jordan.

From 1924 to 1931, eighty thousand newcomers, mostly from eastern Europe, were added to the settlements, creating an urban life with small businesses, but worsening an economic crisis in 1926 and the worldwide depression three years later. Much of what had been a fascination with Arab culture was eradicated when dozens of Jews were killed by Arab violence in 1929. England again began to restrict immigration and prohibit land sales, arguing that riots would erupt with every intake of refugees. These cutbacks, outlined in the anti–Zionist British White Paper of 1930 under the authority of labor leader Sidney Webb, were denounced as a further abrogation of the mandate and a painful watering down of the Balfour Declaration. When Weizmann resigned his leadership of the Jewish Agency in protest, public opinion forced Prime Minister Ramsay MacDonald to soften the terms of Webb's position.

While reports of anti–Semitism in Europe added to a revived emotional linkage with ancestral land, political developments in England cooled off some unrealistic dreams. Confrontations between economically sufficient Jews and immigrants from underdeveloped areas, between the Orthodox who knew who was Jewish and the Secular to whom God had not yet given that information, divided the public. Yet none of those issues persuaded Zionists that the dream was a mirage. Orange groves were planted, city roads were constructed, homes and factories rose from the ground, hospitals were established, music and literature flourished. Hebrew periodicals and daily newspapers such as *Ha'aretz*, *Hadashot*, and *Hashahar* mushroomed to serve every conceivable variety of literary, labor, Zionist, political, religious, and nonreligious philosophies.

Agricultural reform and social equality in the kibbutzim became watchwords for the "young worker" movement Ha-Po'el ha-Tsa'ir, and the utopian "young guard" Ha-Shomer ha-Tsa'ir, inspiring paintings and prints that elevated nationalism and labor to extraordinary levels of significance and dignity. Landscape art, the primary style in the '20s and '30s, was initiated by Yosef Zaritsky, Avigdor Stematzky, Yeheskel Streichman, Anna Ticho, and Leopold Krakauer, who focused on the tranquility of the Judaean hills. David Rose, an American artist who spent a year studying with Hermann Struck in the Bezalel School, documented the reclamation of the countryside in 1932; his etchings captured young *chalutzim* (pioneers) baling hay or struggling with the obstinate soil under an enervating heat. "It was a queer union of East and West," he wrote, "with long outstretched strings of freight-laden camels jaunting slowly along, and here modern houses with many machines and strangely garbed figures at work."

But it was difficult during those anxious years to focus on idealized agricultural or Socialist views during the perils of Hitler and worldwide depression. Almost two hundred thousand German and central European Jewish refugees, legal and otherwise, had poured into the country by 1936, bringing a sophisticated culture and economic vigor. The Jewish presence was raised to forty percent of the population; in Jerusalem the figure rose to sixty percent. Among the newcomers was woodcut artist Jacob Steinhardt who, moving away from his "Pathetiker" mode, brought the Expressionist tradition to Palestine. He evoked dreary corners of the towns, oppressive in their dehumanizing squalor, lit only where the sun could find a slit between the dilapidated houses. Steinhardt's attention to the Jewish experience was later sharpened through his series of woodcuts that related biblical incidents to the simmering conflict between Jew and Arab. In *Jacob and Esau*, 1950, a woodcut prompted by the War of Independence, he marked the fratricidal hatred between the scriptural brothers, hoping that the peaceful reconciliation achieved by those ancient enemies might be echoed in his own time.

It was a futile hope. The Balfour Declaration died a dishonored ruin in 1939 with the publication of a revised White Paper. London bowed to Arab nationalism as well as to the hundred million Muslims living in the British Empire who demanded the establishment of an independent Palestine state and the curtailment of Jewish immigration and land sales. Issued by British Colonial Secretary Malcolm MacDonald in 1939 at the height of Nazi slaughter, the declaration ruled that "expansion of the Jewish National Home by immigration [would occur] only if the Arabs are prepared to acquiesce in it," and limited Jewish immigration to seventy-five thousand, after which "the gates would be permanently closed." The Arabs were furious, having expected all Jewish immigration to be stopped; the Zionists felt betrayed. The paper was only partially enacted because the League of Nations—encouraged in particular by Germany and Italy—judged that it violated the interpretation which the commission had placed on the mandate. But by then events in Europe had unraveled Palestinian aspirations and much of Jewish life.

Forty-two years later MacDonald acknowledged that hundreds of thousands of lives might have been saved had Britain carried out its original charge. Reminiscing on public television, he confessed, "We were very sad ... that we had to take this decision because of ... the certainty of war.... We knew the Jews would be on our side ... whatever happened.... Therefore we probably made more concessions to the Arabs than we would otherwise have done." Britain's continued policy of placating the Arabs led to the development of a militant national movement and a diminution of Jewish influence—oil and Middle East power struggles taking precedence over other considerations. The concessions, intended to secure Arab loyalty, accomplished nothing. MacDonald was right about one detail, though. When war broke out, one hundred and thirty-six thousand Jews in Palestine joined the Allies, while the hope of destroying Jewish Palestine guided the Arabs straight into the Nazis' iron grip.

In December, 1941, the "illegal" Romanian refugee ship *Struma*, a decrepit wooden cattle barge with but one freshwater tap and bunks piled ten high, set out for British Palestine. When the engine almost immediately failed, a passing boat made some repairs, but not before its crew helped themselves to all the valuables aboard, mostly gold wedding bands. Two weeks later (after what should have been a fourteen-hour trip) the *Struma* crawled into Istanbul's harbor, where it remained for more than two months. Despite freezing weather, almost no sanitary conveniences, dysentery, and infestations of lice, the neutral Turkish government refused shelter or supplies. English authorities looked away. Finally set adrift six miles from shore, it was torpedoed the next day by a Soviet ship. Seven hundred and seventy-nine passengers and crew—including one hundred and three children—went down. Only one nineteen-year-old man was recovered alive after spending twenty-four hours clinging to a scrap of wreckage, while dozens of people around him sank beneath the Black Sea's icy waters.

Other boatloads of refugees had similar fates or returned to Europe with predictable consequences. Fifty-one ramshackle ships, however, did manage to bring almost twenty-seven thousand survivors to Palestine by slipping through blockades; some gained entry by eliciting world sympathy through hunger strikes; some were forced to deposit their human cargo in detention camps while the Jewish Agency was denied certificates that would have rescued one hundred thousand inmates.

Conflict between the Orthodox and other groups involving the mingling of the sexes and other religious observances were disruptive. The Russian-born and American-educated artist Elias Grossman's drypoint *The Wailing Wall*, 1943, depicted both men and women together at the Temple Mount in the pre-statehood period. Many images of concurrent prayer at this remnant of the Second Temple are known since at least the sixteenth century, although the rabbinate no longer permits it. While Jews of different persuasions confronted and affronted each other, one unifying element that tied people to the tradition was the printing of the Haggadah, central to all.

Whether experienced as a Spring Festival narrative, a religious or secular document, or even as a painful response to Nazi terror, the Haggadah appeared in one form or another on the Seder table of almost every Jewish home or kibbutz. The earliest Jerusalem edition was a Judeo-Persian translation printed in 1904 by Samuel Zuckerman for the benefit of Bukharian Jews. Although it was just another copy of the 1695 Amsterdam prototype, its title page proclaimed that the "like of its pure Persian rendition has never yet existed." Not to be outdone, a year later a Calcutta Jew, David Hai Eini, commissioned a trilingual Jerusalem Haggadah with a Hebrew, English, and Arabic text, intended for the variety of Jews living in India. Although Calcutta had had its own Hebrew press for over sixty years, the cachet of a Jerusalem imprint was important.

Ze'ev Raban illustrated an (unpublished) Haggadah in 1925; his figures gracefully flow in Oriental settings adapted from ancient Assyrian friezes. (The first printed edition appeared in 1955.) The Four Sons share a tableau with symbolic animals including a wise old owl in the tree. The satirical *Haggadah shel ha-Bayit ha-Le'ummi (Haggadah of the National Home)*, 1930, noted the betrayal of the mandate directives. Published by the Dead Sea Publishers in Tel Aviv, it was written by "Afarkeset"—who judiciously withheld his identity. Its title page by Ze'ev

Ill. 15:3. *Lord Balfour and Theodor Herzl.* **From** *Haggadah shel ha-Bayit ha-Le'ummi* (*Haggadah of the National Home*), 1930. **By Ze'ev Navon. Courtesy the Israel Museum, Jerusalem**

Navon conjured up a meeting between Lord Balfour and a winged Herzl in the Garden of Eden (Ill. 15:3). Lamenting Britain's biased investigation of the 1929 riots and massacres in Hebron and Safed, the author's bitter parody of the thanksgiving poem *Dayanu* (*Sufficient*) declared: "With how many kindnesses has John Bull benefited us: Had he given us the Balfour Declaration and not added a second part that invalidates it, it would have been sufficient. Had he added a second part that doesn't invalidate the first part and not given us a foreign military power, it would have been sufficient..."

When Palestinian Jewish Brigade soldiers volunteered for service with British occupation forces in the 1942 North African campaign, they printed a mimeographed Haggadah declaring that "Egypt has not ended for Israel. For us, the whole world is Egypt. With burning grief and vengeance let us remember in our celebration tonight the Jewish homes throughout the world in which the holiday is so fearfully observed.... Next year in Jerusalem!" Echoing that hope was Tel Aviv's imprint for the refugees in Cyprus, 1947. The cover featured a sailing ship which they believed would take them to Eretz Yisrael.

A militant Haggadah illustrated by Arie Alweil in 1948 depicted Haganah soldiers bristling with weapons (Ill. 15:4). The message was clear: neither faith nor tradition alone could insure security. A lavishly illustrated edition printed in Tel Aviv by the Sinai Publishing Com-

Ill. 15:4. *Haganah Soldiers.* **Haggadah, 1948. By Arie Alweil. Courtesy the Israel Museum, Jerusalem**

pany in about 1950 carried an early English translation. Two years later, an Independence Day Haggadah from the same city caused alarm in Orthodox circles for its attempt to replace the traditional liturgy with irreverent and controversial material. Because it was officially issued by the publicity branch of the Israel Defense Forces, it was roundly attacked by the rabbinate which forced its removal from circulation. The efforts of its disparaged author, Aharon Meged, a magazine editor and cultural attaché in London, were then supplanted by a more acceptable 1956 version.

Haggadot increasingly focused on contemporary political issues such as war and peace, Russian Jewry, and the Holocaust, creating a bond between past and present and affecting secular as well as traditional observers. A children's book, *Medinati Yisrael (My State Israel)*, published in 1959 and illustrated by Levin Kipnis, included a Haggadah with specially conceived ceremonies for Independence Day, in addition to an alternative text for the Passover Seder. A warlike example, strongly Zionist in tone, it represented the Four Sons as a general, captain, sergeant, and private and was dedicated to the victorious army of the Sinai Operation. No longer filled with traditional religious imagery, it depicts refugees approaching the Holy Land, hoping to share a glorious future with its brave citizens.

Kibbutz Haggadot were in a separate class, often in modified or deviant formats, frequently omitting customary passages and absenting God from their pages. The charming story of the Four Sons no longer seemed apt for those whose children had seen too much hardship and war; the Ten Plagues almost paled before the reality of their experiences. Along with the bitter herbs were hard questions: "Why is the situation of the Jews different from that of all the nations?" asked the Na'an Haggadah in 1942. "Every nation dwells in its own house and homeland, but the Jews are scattered around the world, hated, persecuted, and even restrained from entering Eretz Yisrael, their own country." There was a logical answer. Neither anti–Semitism nor the struggle for a homeland had died.

Seven years later, in what may have been the first time a Haggadah was printed in a sovereign Israel, Na'an's members once more sat around the festive table, this time celebrating independence, this time remembering and honoring the friends and family lost in Israel's wars. And with the establishment of the State, a new set of questions and answers became relevant: "Why is this night different from all other nights? In past years we carried out the Seder in spite of the oppressors who ruled over us and who hindered our growth and ability to immigrate. Now we are free in the State of Israel, the gates welcome the refugees from exile, and all the land is ours."

Hundreds of kibbutz Haggadot have been produced, many of them poorly mimeographed, stenciled, or lithographed, and awkwardly decorated by home-grown artists. No matter. They wrote and drew as they felt, influenced by Socialist and seasonal agricultural themes or expressing through ancient rituals a shared religious, nostalgic, or folk tradition. Professionally printed versions were turned out as well. The 1952 "Zim" edition, illustrated by Jacob Zimberknopf in Tel Aviv, offers a unique impression of the *Wicked Son*—a chubby, smoking purse-snatcher with an attack dog in tow (Ill. 15:5). That Haggadah ends happily as a dove of peace flies triumphantly towards a redeemed city, modifying the traditional "Next year in Jerusalem" to "Next year in a *rebuilt* Jerusalem!"

But it took a long time before a rebuilt Jerusalem would become a reality. Six years earlier, with the intensification of underground operations, the Irgun opposition under the command of Menachem Begin initiated devastating attacks against British installations. Following British refusal to admit one hundred thousand refugees, and the arrest, hanging, and flogging of over twenty-five hundred Jewish leaders, the Irgun blew up the British military headquarters housed in Jerusalem's King David Hotel, killing dozens of Britons, Jews, and Arabs. It claimed an evacuation warning was given; the British denied it. Although the Haganah, too,

Ill. 15:5. *Wicked Son.* Haggadah, 1952. By Jacob Zimberknopf. Courtesy the Israel Museum, Jerusalem

participated in some anti–British strikes, it was partially successful in curtailing the Irgun fighters who were denounced by Churchill as well as by many Jewish agencies and individuals.

On orders from Prime Minister Clement Attlee, Foreign Secretary Ernest Bevin rejected the Anglo-American Committee's recommendations to increase Jewish immigration to Palestine, and arrested members of the Jewish Agency. The Haganah *Exodus 1947* ship, carrying some forty-five hundred deportees, was captured and escorted to Haifa where the injured were hospitalized. Under Bevin's orders, the passengers were then taken to France where the refugees refused to disembark, remaining aboard the fiercely hot and congested ship for three disastrous weeks before being returned to Germany. (Eventually most found their "illegal" way to Palestine.) British warships, now freed of wartime duties, rounded up every evacuee vessel they could find and dropped off the strays in barbed-wire camps in Cyprus, the island most of the world had forgotten.

But not Naphtali Bezem. He had survived his early teen years in a Polish concentration camp, lost his parents at Auschwitz, and came to Palestine when he was fifteen years old and already a competent draftsman. In 1947 he headed for Cyprus, where he taught printmaking to some thirty-five inmates. Although conditions for the fifty-five thousand souls who spent time in the camp from 1946 to 1948 were abominable, with armed guards poised to spot escapees, study groups were formed. With the support of Diaspora and Palestinian Jews under his instruction, *The Exiles in Cyprus* was published in 1947 with twenty-seven woodcuts describing the three-year incarceration. *Wedding,* a linocut by the prisoner Moshe Bernstein, showing the bride and groom protectively covered with a tallit, takes place in front of a barbed-wire watchtower, reestablishing the tradition that the family endures under the most trying situations (Ill. 15:6). "Cyprus is one station on our sorrowful road to Israel," they reported, a road of "enforced inactivity and a destiny of paralysis."

The General Assembly of the United Nations was remarkably unmoved either by those conditions or the status of the Jews. Later that year it voted to partition Palestine into Arab and Jewish states, with Arab control of the West Bank and Transjordan. Over seventy-five percent of the area offered to the Jews was desert. They accepted the decision, but the Arabs rejected it, electing instead to stage massacres in Yemen and Syria as well as murderous attacks in Jerusalem. They rebelled against housing and job shortages and political inequities that infected some elements of the government, but most of all because they insisted on complete political control. Britain turned down the partition plan, ignored Arab insurgency, washed her hands of the whole problem, and announced plans to bow out of her mandate.

The Union Jack was lowered. The White Paper of 1939 was nullified. Ben-Gurion delivered the Declaration of Independence on May 14, 1948. Against the combined wishes of American and English oil interests, the Departments of State and Defense, and the British War Office, President Harry Truman redeemed his pledges to American Jewry. With a need of Jewish votes in the coming 1948 elections, and a little push from his Jewish friend Eddie Jacobson, he recognized the sovereign state of Israel. (Some believed that had Roosevelt been president, the results would have been otherwise; during the Yalta Conference King Ibn Saud reputedly persuaded him to abandon his already lukewarm policy to Zionism.) The Soviet Union, after thirty years of pro-Arab support, but in hopes that its action would lead to the breakup of colonialism and Britain's supremacy in the Middle East, followed America's lead.

It was during the period following 1948 that the Arab world—whose cultural and tribal ties were linked with the artificial constructs of Syria, Jordan, and Iraq—adopted the concept of Palestinian nationhood despite the fact that Palestine had generally been synonymous with the Jewish population. The misnomer "West Bank" likewise came into existence when the Jordanians, themselves only a recent British creation, captured Judea and Samaria, renamed them, and announced they were part of an "ancestral" homeland. These areas—including the Gaza Strip—had been under the British mandate and before that, the Turkish Empire. Since that whole area had been officially designated as a Jewish National Home, Israel was, in fact, "occupying" its own soil. War came once more in 1955 when guerrilla activity in the Gaza Strip brought retaliation. A year later Israeli forces moved into the Sinai Peninsula to put down further attacks. With French and British support but American opposition, an Egyptian blockade at the Straits of Tiran that effectively prevented shipping of

Ill. 15:6. *Wedding.* Woodcut, 1947. From *The Exiles in Cyprus.* By Moshe Bernstein. Courtesy the Israel Museum, Jerusalem

strategic material through the port of Eilat and the Suez Canal led to an invasion of the Canal Zone. The Egyptian air force was destroyed in a hundred-hour campaign.

With Chaim Weizmann as its president, Israel became one of the United Nations. Not that most of the delegates were kindly disposed to its newest cardholder. Of the one hundred eighty-five member nations—including Iraq, Iran, Cuba, Libya, North Korea, Sudan and Syria—only Israel was denied the right to belong to a "regional group" which would make it eligible to serve a term on the Security Council or other important bodies. In an acerbic lithograph in June, 1948, Arthur Szyk's handcuffed Israeli soldier is informed of the Security Council's deliberations: "We agree with you on every point, except your stubborn insistence on surviving" (Ill. 15:7). Survive they did. In spite of boycotts, raids, landmines, and sabotages, the "ingathering of the exiles" was a reality. The Law of Return, July 5, 1950, gave every Jew the right to immigrate as a citizen. Nearly three quarters of a million did so in just four years. Later that year the "Magic Carpet" airlifted Yemen Jews to Israel.

Some forty years had to pass before twentieth century Jews, much like their ancestors in the Sinai desert, achieved access to the land. But euphoria was short-lived. Access did not mean security or peace. The Arab world hardly waited to draw a breath before invading the new-made country. Egyptian air attacks began at once. Seven Arab armies swept across the land,

Ill. 15:7. *We Agree with You on Every Point, Except Your Stubborn Insistence on Surviving.* Lithograph, 1948. By Arthur Szyk. Reproduced with the cooperation of Alexandra Szyk Bracie and the Arthur Szyk Society, www.szyk.org

capturing and looting the old Jewish quarter of Jerusalem, precipitating the death of thousands of Jewish and Arab soldiers as well as many civilians in the War of Independence. It was only the first of many attempts to destroy the Jewish state. The Six Day War in 1967 witnessed Israeli occupation of the West Bank, the Sinai Peninsula, and the Golan Heights between millions of Arabs and six hundred thousand Jews, swinging much of the world's sympathy in favor of a Jewish return to its biblical home.

At least a million refugees, rescued from Romania, Yemen, Syria, Ethiopia, Egypt, Iraq, Russia and other countries swelled Israel's population, strengthening its resources. Cultural strides soon followed. The discovery and decoding of the Dead Sea Scrolls and the dramatic excavations at ancient Masada were spectacularly impressive. The opening of the Israel Museum provided a showcase for international artworks. Scholars were examining historic documents which had been found at the turn of the century in the genizah of an ancient synagogue in Egypt. Newspapers, magazines, and publishing houses offered information on almost any subject and manner of expression, and lent credibility to the image of a potent and energetic country. New cities, medical centers, and universities popped up from Dan to Beersheba.

The country now concentrated on its domestic problems, founding settlements, integrating immigrants from the Arab world and displaced-persons camps, coping with discontent due to the social and economic gap between European and non–Ashkenazi Jews, and developing its resources. Compulsory army service and educational programs helped; anger expended on religious issues didn't. Efforts to encourage both Zionist and leftist ideologies became a priority. The Shamir brothers, the foremost graphic designers of stamps, paper money, and logos, who had created propaganda art as far back as the '30s, were called on to deliver upbeat messages of opportunities and sporting chances. Their poster, *Min Ha'ir el hacaphar*, c. 1950 (*From Town to Settlement*), urges a Jew, whose profile is imposed over a productive farming area, to help feed a growing nation (Ill. 15:8).

Moshe Gat, who came from a poor Haifa family, aimed at formulating a Marxist social tool that would speak directly to wage earners, not as plodding or inferior drudges, but as capable and proud citizens. His woodcut *At Work*, 1953, was an example of the protest art directed at industrial and manual laborers who were perceived as unjustly exploited (Ill. 15:9). Such prints, he said, not only "communicated with the masses," but gave workers an opportunity to buy art at "non-bourgeois cost." Time almost totally reversed those sentiments. Hardly two decades later only a small percentage of Israelis believed that the proletariat rep-

Ill. 15:8. *Min Ha'ir el hacaphar (From Town to Settlement)*. c. 1950. By the Shamir Brothers. Courtesy the Israel Museum, Jerusalem

resented the most consequential element of society, or that workers were unable to defend their economic status. The leftist movement was mostly forsaken as disillusionment with radicalism and Soviet Communism erupted in the late sixties; communities, while steeped in idealism, were at the same time moving rapidly from the past to the future tense.

From the late '40s to the early '60s a conflict developed between a provincial Israeli art based around street scenes, city views, and landscapes, and the more seasoned artists who banded together to form the country's first avant-garde art movement. Joseph Zaritsky, Avigdor Stematsky, and Yeheskel Streichman, having moved past their earlier content-related styles, were influenced by European Modernists Marcel Janco and Mordecai Ardon. Janco was active in the irrational Dada and post–Expressionist Cubist movements in France and Switzerland. Ardon was a Bauhaus-trained artist whose lyrical, amorphous shapes are among Israel's most important works. The shift to contemporary art was helped by Arie Aroch and others who were stimulated by Abstract Expressionism. This style, centered in Paris and New York, found a fer-

Ill. 15:9. *At Work*. Woodcut, 1953. By Moshe Gat. Courtesy the Israel Museum, Jerusalem

tile soil in Israel as it did in other parts of the world, inspiring artists such as Leah Nikel, Raffi Lavie, and Aviva Uri. Perhaps the emphasis on light, space, mass and geometric shapes, having little or no figurative representation, offered a respite from disquieting reality.

A wide range of original graphic techniques, developed in America in the 1960s by the trailblazing Jewish teachers and patrons June Wayne and Tatyana Grossman in the Tamarind Lithography Workshop in Los Angeles, and the Universal Limited Art Editions (ULAE) in New York, were adapted by Israeli printmakers. Yet despite the examples of contemporary American art, Jerusalem's attachment to a passing era of nationalistic or provincial tradition remained. But as more artists began to divide their time between New York and Israel, the modernistic Tel Aviv model prevailed.

Life in Israel moved on. Adolf Eichmann was abducted from Argentina by Israeli agents for crimes against the Jewish people and humanity. He was hanged in 1962, and his ashes spilled in the sea. In the religious world, contention reached a new high as Orthodox leaders demanded unswerving control over traditional practices, while Conservative and Reform rabbis lobbied for their own brands of observance. Scholarship, archeology, and productive enterprises turned Israel and its three million Jews into a competitive, energized social, economic, and military power.

Political issues were less satisfactory. The Palestine Liberation Organization (PLO) took root in 1964 under the Arab League with the goal of setting up an Arab state. Yassir

Arafat, former chief of the terrorist Fatah, a faction of the PLO which hoped to liberate Palestine, pledged the destruction of Israel. Hopes for peace faded as Egypt's Gamal Abdel Nasser
accused Israel of aggression against its ally Syria, and declared his intention to "totally
exterminate the State of Israel for all time." Following the shelling of the Golan Heights (territory east and north of the Sea of Galilee donated by Britain to the Syrian French Mandate
in 1923), he closed the Straits of Tiran. An Egyptian cartoon in *Al Jarida* portrayed him kick-
ing out a repulsive Israel, as Iraq, Lebanon, and Syria hover nearby. When Nasser set up a
blockade cutting supply lines on May 22, 1967, a vulnerable Israel, fearing terrorist attacks
and even a second Holocaust, opened hostilities on June 6, pulling off an incredible
victory virtually annihilating Egyptian, Jordanian, and Syrian air power and quadrupling
its territory. Six days later Israel's third war with Arab states was over. (It was supposedly
called the Six Day War to resonate with the Six Days of Creation.) The liberated Western
Wall was the first object that Jewish soldiers sought out. The shofar was blown. Jerusalem
was Jewish again. The Golan Heights, the Straits, and the Wall were in Jewish hands. The
peace process would surely begin. And the people raised their voices in Naomi Shemer's
Jerusalem of Gold.

The euphoria didn't last. The miracle was one thing; governing an occupied Palestine and
settling the land was another. A worrisome economy and anxieties over political leadership
created spasms of self-doubt. Many asked if diplomacy would have been more successful in
establishing peaceful coexistence. The United Nations Security Council adopted the inten-
tionally vague Resolution 242 in December, 1967, calling for Israeli "withdrawal from territories," not "*the* territories," and a "just settlement of the refugee problem." Neither side agreed
with nor completely understood that mandate. Nor did the Six Day War or the attacks on El-
Al planes in Athens and Beirut, or Egyptian artillery assaults along the Suez Canal which followed over the next two years, establish the intended peace. The accumulated antagonism,
however, did bring on the fourth Arab-Israeli conflict, lasting from 1967 to 1970 when the
"War of Attrition" was ended with a cease-fire.

Satirist Ephraim Kishon and cartoonist Kariel Gardosh (Dosh) took up the pen in a
humorous "apology" to Israel's enemies—*So Sorry We Won*, 1970. They depicted the state
through the eyes of a child—the innocent "Israelchik" Srulik in floppy sun hat, shorts, and
sandals. But their humor had a cynical bite. "Anyone who believed that our government would
take so many provocations without reacting was damn right!" recalled Kishon, who with Dosh
produced the comic feature *Wunderkind*. A triumphant caption read: "The Israel army proved
that you can avoid a two-front war by fighting on three fronts" (Ill. 15:10). Like his predecessor in France Henri Daumier, Dosh was an important caricaturist, exercising considerable
influence through his cartoons in the daily newspaper *Maariv*, lampooning political events and
skewering vulnerable politicians.

Pop Art took off in Israel as elsewhere in the '60s and '70s with mundane images and
hard-edged forms. Like other movements of the time it was motivated in part by the New
York school and the collages of Robert Rauschenberg. Israeli artists Benni Efrat, Yair Gar-
bouz, and Raffi Lavie, among others, promoted the style, mixing images and collage to express
some of the most bizarre and disturbing viewpoints in the genre. Pop Art reflected an environment that eschewed traditional boundaries of propriety or decorum, so it was only a question of time before the underbelly of Israeli life would emerge as viable artistic subject matter.
Spiritual loss, disillusionment, and almost continuous warfare pointed the way to the chaos
between Israeli and Arab populations, which was frequently interpreted through the lens
of Jerusalem artists as they drew together for mutual support. In 1974, a group of teachers,
artists, and professional printers under the leadership of Arik Kilemnik founded the Jerusalem
Print Workshop to further collaborative relationships in a central establishment. Promi-

Ill. 15:10. *The Israel Army Proved That You Can Avoid a Two-Front War by Fighting on Three Fronts.* From *So Sorry We Won*, 1970. By Ephraim Kishon and Kariel Gardosh (Dosh). Courtesy the Israel Museum, Jerusalem

nent visitors shared their visions and talents, providing Israelis with a significant contemporary presence.

Israel was no longer a pioneer society. It was forced to cope with a militant Islam, disorder, and violence, including an attack against Israeli Olympians in Munich, Germany on September 6, 1972 in which eleven athletes were murdered. The irascible Pulitzer Prize–winning American cartoonist Paul Conrad, not known for Jewish sympathies, joined much of the free world—though not the United Nations Security Council—in condemning the terrorists with his lithograph *O, Israel, Thou Bleeding Piece of Earth,* in which he depicted a Star of David leaking blood.

But spilt Israeli blood on the playing field was not enough of a deterrent to prevent another war on the battlefield. Goaded by anti–Jewish fervor, neo–Nazi clubs and Arabic publishing houses found new life centered in Damascus and Cairo where they helped whip up intense hatred against the state. On Yom Kippur, October 6, 1973, Egyptian and Syrian troops using Soviet-supplied missiles launched a surprise attack that almost cost Israel its life. By the time a shaky cease-fire was enforced, Israel had again paid heavily—two thousand five hundred fifty-two of its people dead, over three thousand wounded. Prime minister Golda Meir resigned, bringing down the government and establishing Yitzhak Rabin as prime minister. Did the UN General Assembly now reexamine the record of Jewish persecution and the right of Jews to establish themselves in a homeland that reflected their national aspirations? Seventy-two of its members in 1975 decided that Zionism was nothing more than "a form of racism and racial discrimination"; sixty-seven nations either voted against the resolution or abstained. Negotiations between Israel and the Arab nations moved to the front burner as the General Assembly recognized Arafat as the voice of the Palestinian Arabs and endorsed their right to national independence and sovereignty.

In 1973, the Gentile German painter and printmaker Oskar Kokoschka, whose works had been confiscated as degenerate art by the Nazis, came to Israel, aged eighty-seven. Hoping to encourage positive interactions between Arab and Jew, he produced and donated a lithographic portfolio, *Jerusalem Faces*, to the Jerusalem Foundation, choosing as sitters four Jews, a Muslim, and the Greek Orthodox Patriarch. With few but deft lines, his portrait of Moshe Dayan summoned up the rakish eye patch, shrewd grin, and jaunty air of the controversial minister of defense (Ill. 15:11).

Innovative images were created in the kibbutzim (founded in 1909 in Degania), where the early pioneers came together in self-sufficiency to form economic, social, and agrarian associations. The egalitarian spirit that helped make the movement the bulwark of the Israel state was founded on the principle that men and women worked according to their ability and were paid according to their needs. Yohanan Simon's lithograph *Kibbutz*, 1976, shows two trees sprouting regenerating branches; perhaps they represent the parallel growth of the two antagonists, Jew and Arab. He had been a Social Realist in the '50s and '60s, promoting the working classes and the labor movement, hoping that artists would take their cue from "the people." But in his later years he sought the tranquil life of the kibbutz, its amicable way of living, its peace and contentment, and its moments of relaxation and play between parents and children.

Although Israeli culture had lost, for better or worse, much of its overt "Jewish" content, it continued to maintain its creative capacity. Adult education, youth programs, and study groups were geared towards intellectual and aesthetic achievement. Important and authoritative works established the country's right to legitimate comparison with the best international production. Proud of the many accomplishments of its citizens, the young country published its first *Who's Who in the State of Israel* in 1949. The eight-volume *Encyclopedia of Israel in Pictures* with Hebrew, French, and English texts, followed in 1950. Nelly Sachs shared the Nobel Prize in literature with Shmuel Yosef Agnon in 1966. Rabbi Adin Steinsaltz's monumental transcription of the Babylonian Talmud, initially in modern Hebrew (beginning in 1970) and then in English (beginning in 1989), was an enormous contribution to a clearer understanding of its literary sources. *The Encyclopedia Judaica*, completed in 1971, was a boon to almost every branch of learning. *The Journal of Jewish Art*, begun in 1974 by Bezalel Narkiss, gave new credibility to Israeli scholarship. A comprehensive examination of printed and illustrated Haggadot from the fifteenth century to 1975 appeared in 1975 by Yosef Hayim Yerushalmi.

Ill. 15:11. *Moshe Dayan*. Lithograph, 1973. From *Jerusalem Faces*. By Oskar Kokoschka. ©2007 Artists Rights Society (ARS), New York/ProLitteris, Zürich

Threats of war and terrorism, however,

remained a daily obstacle to stability and unity—but not necessarily to artistic output. The hostile Syrian and Israeli armies facing each other across the Golan Heights became for Polish-born Joshua Neustein an analogy for contested borders. In his mixed-media experiment *Territory*, c. 1975, he utilized a photograph of his German shepherd dog emptying its bladder—in effect staking a claim to the area. A pebble-like texture glued over the lower half of the photo-etching and collage called attention to the divided pictorial space and raised questions regarding the negotiability or inviolateness of boundaries.

Yosl Bergner grew up in Warsaw but fled to Australia at seventeen to dodge his parents' fate in Auschwitz. Although he did not witness the Holocaust personally, by the time he moved to Israel in 1951, the atrocities had become fixed in his mind. His Surrealist serigraph *The Butterfly Eaters*, from the late 1970s, depicts a group of children apparently engaged in an ordinary picnic (Ill. 15:12). But the table sits in an

Ill. 15:12. *The Butterfly Eaters*. Serigraph, c. 1977. By Yosl Bergner. Courtesy the Israel Museum, Jerusalem

abandoned space lit only by a dying source of energy, and the children, detached and isolated from their normal environment, are occupied in snuffing out the lives of an innocent and harmless species. Young as they are, their impassive and empty faces are devoid of personal interaction, expressing not so much evil as indifference, not so much brutality as lack of moral concern. The theatrical setting conjures up bareness, exile, and the end of being.

Moroccan-born Pinchas Cohen-Gan was caught in the dilemma of what art is and what man's place is in society. Combining issues of personal isolation with a sense of human dignity and welfare in his lithograph $A_1=f(NC)$, 1976, he responded to the figure while at the same time hiding the face of a young man (Ill. 15.13). According to the artist, the significance of the formula is: A_1= a segment of art; f=function; N=nature; C=Culture. Therefore, a segment of art is equal to the function of the multiplication of Nature and Culture. By disavowing Minimalism's generally accepted higher rank in art, he reduced, but did not eliminate, decorative abstraction in a formal approach to social topics.

Jacob Steinhardt's strong influence on Moshe Hoffman's black-and-white woodcut technique is unmistakable, although their subject matter is very different. Hoffman studied at the Bezalel school, then moved on to a dramatic Expressionist style. A series of stark images reflecting the concentration camp experience combine a maximum of horror with a Japanese interest in Minimalism. As an endless procession of boxcars tunnels into an extermination depot, there is no suggestion of their human contents other than one small sealed window. Once Israeli art began to free itself from Holocaust imagery, it moved towards a cosmopolitan search for universality along with a broader political and social agenda. The display of sexual fantasies was one aspect of that trend, but Hoffman's work had broader implications. His

$$A_1 = f(N.C)$$

Above: Ill. 15:13. $A_1=f(NC)$. **Lithograph, 1976. By Pinchas Cohen-Gan. Courtesy of the artist.** *Below:* Ill. 15:14. *Self-Portrait.* **Woodcut, 1976. By Moshe Hoffman. Courtesy the Israel Museum, Jerusalem**

Self-Portrait, 1976, places him between the legs of a voluptuous nude whose pubic region does double duty as chest hair. (15:14) The inconsistency and confusion represented, perhaps, the inconsistent and confused behavior internalized in the national psyche.

Ambiguity was manifest not only in art but in the events that shaped Israeli life. The demands of international diplomacy made it necessary for the country to have a pragmatic voice in its dealings with international governments. When Israeli hostages were held at the Entebbe Airport in Uganda in 1976 the government staged a spectacular recovery. It proved that a military strong Israel that put its chief trust in man's ability to control his fate was indispensable if it was to secure a safe place for endangered Jews. With shrewd understanding of the issues, in November 1977 President Anwar Sadat of Egypt startled the world with a visit to Jerusalem and an address to the Knesset. Optimism was expressed with the founding of the Peace Now movement. One year later, American president Jimmy Carter officiated at the historic Camp David, Maryland, meeting between Prime Minister Menachem Begin and Sadat with the signing of "A Framework for Peace in the Middle East." Having established that "the Jewish people are entitled to one place on this earth where they can have their own state, one given to them from time immemorial," Carter set a rosy course; the Nobel committee, caught up in the fervor, awarded Begin and Sadat its coveted Peace Prize.

During the latter half of the century, peaceful negotiations and solutions appeared possible. Egypt and Israel exchanged ambassadors in 1980; the assassination of Sadat a year later in Cairo brought sincere eulogies from Israel which praised his peace negotiations. In a gesture of accord the Sinai Peninsula was returned to Egypt in April 1982. Operation Moses two years later was hailed for the mass rescue of Ethiopian Jews.

But peace didn't follow. The Security Council continued to condemn Israel. Arab "rights" to self-determination, West Bank settlements, military buildups, and border warfare hampered efforts at conciliation and economic recovery.

Naphtali Bezem,"Big People, Little Houses"

Ill. 15:15. *Big People, Little Houses*, c. 1980. By Naphtali Bezem. Courtesy of the artist

Naphtali Bezem was one of the few members of the New Bezalel School who openly honored Jewish culture, equating spirituality with idealism and the renewal of religious life through traditional motifs such as the shofar and Star of David. His serigraph *Big People, Little Houses*, c. 1980, with rigid Byzantine-like images, addresses the tensions of an overly large immigrant population faced with congestion and an alarming shortage of adequate living quarters (Ill. 15:15). Modernistic style and Surrealistic references to cultural and sexual objects are manifest in a totem pole integrating notions of fertility and sustenance; the rebirth and survival of the country is suggested in the context of the Lion of Judah, and religious expression in the symbolism of Sabbath candles.

Free market approaches, foreign competition, and dwindling and aging membership forced reconsideration and reforms of core Socialist and communal values that marked the fading pastoral image of the kibbutz and the eroded "myth" of a "normal" Zionism. Escapism, the elevation of nature, and rejection of devastation and warfare increasingly became points of reference. Menashe Kadishman turned to the natural world and sheep images, which represented sacrifice and a forfeited innocence. Larry Abramson was concerned about the natural world, as opposed to the cultural that he viewed as imperiled. Asaf Ben Zvi explored reality, imagination, and myth in landscape, animal, and plant life. Figurative art, or at least the fragmentation of human and animal figures, appeared in the work of Hila Lulu Lin and Dudu Mezah who, also deploring the stresses in contemporary life, suggested that human forms and personalities were no longer holding together.

Ilan Hasson's enamel-like lithograph *Sabbath Eve*, 1985, on the other hand, reflected the pleasant sentimental spirit of tourist art, evident in the mixture of Israeli setting, flat Oriental aspect, and decorative medieval patterns (Ill. 15:16). Yet its images remain interesting, set as they are against a backdrop of terrorism and the stylistic diversity of Tel Aviv's environment. David Gerstein, a painter and sculptor, also kept a wary eye on the Tel Aviv scene. In an etching from his *Balcony Series*, c. 1980, a harmlessly eccentric lady takes her ease (Ill. 15:17). He contrasted the sharp angularity of the terrace and shutters with the ovals of her face and the rug beater hanging on the wall. Both wait patiently to be put to a useful

Ill. 15:16. *Sabbath Eve.* Lithograph, 1985. By Ilan Hasson. Courtesy the Israel Museum, Jerusalem

Ill. 15:17. *A Lady Takes Her Ease*. Etching, c. 1980. From *Balcony Series*. By David Gerstein. Courtesy the Israel Museum, Jerusalem

service. Likewise offering a bit of high-spirited whimsy is Russian immigrant Yuval Mahler's serigraph *Sunday*, c. 1980 (Ill. 15:18). Swinging from the treetops, sharing a picnic, or just taking a welcome day off, a cheerful group of family and friends invites the viewer to share a fleeting moment.

Moshe Gershuni, a vigorous supporter of Peace Now, expressed antiwar passions when the 1982 Lebanon incursion against terrorist forces was followed by a large Israeli invasion and heavy casualties among Jews, Arabs, and Christians. Pent-up anxieties and anger brought down the government of Prime Minister Begin in 1983. Rather than viewing objects in terms of their external forms, Gershuni internalized the conflict in deeply subjective symbols. He used the *Kaddish* prayer recited by mourners for a series of eight nightmarish etchings based on his paintings of dead flowers, birds, and other decaying objects that meld beauty with death, the agony of war, and destruction. It was no surprise that the intifada erupted in 1987 with Palestinian uprisings and that the radical Hamas guerrilla groups were founded a year later.

The political tensions seemed to awaken interest in figurative art laced with edgy stresses, though not generally through a "Jewish" lens. Women artists such as the Sabra Aviva Uri and the American-born Pamela Levy protested the loss of Jewish and Arab lives in war after war. Levy, along with other '80s artists, saw in Israel a potential land of milk and honey although she recognized the realities of war, contention, and loss of national aspirations. Her serigraph *A Girl of Jerusalem*, early 1980s, depicts a youngster clutching her mouth in nervous tension as she stands frozen against a backdrop of ominously prying windows (Ill. 15:19). The gesture of desperation presaged a series of tragic episodes just as the country was preparing to celebrate

Ill. 15:18. *Sunday*. Serigraph, c. 1980. By Yuval Mahler. Courtesy the Israel Museum, Jerusalem

half a century of nationhood. Cultural and religious polarities between Tel Aviv and Jerusalem were exacerbated while spiritual vexations threw the country into a political convulsion.

But better times were anticipated when Arafat announced his recognition of Israeli's right to exist and renounced terrorism at the end of 1988. Two years later freed Russian Jews were arriving in Israel, a year before Israel and the Soviets began diplomatic meetings. The United Nations General Assembly repealed its "Zionism is racism" resolution on the eve of 1992, but trouble was brewing. President Saddam Hussein of Iraq emerged as the latest threat to peace. Warnings of nerve gas, long-range weapons of total destruction, and crippling of oil installments in Arab states were directed at Western countries which Hussein accused of "strangling" his people. To his chagrin, the intimidation resulted in a Security Council oil embargo. He responded by firing thirty-nine Scud missiles towards Israel during the Gulf War in 1991. But all attempts at peace floundered when violent outbreaks were staged in contested

Ill. 15:19. *A Girl of Jerusalem*. Serigraph, c. 1982. By Pamela Levy. Courtesy Samantha Budiselich and Yuval Levy

territories in 1993 following the signing of the Oslo I agreement which provided some withdrawal areas and the establishment of a Palestinian autonomous authority. Once again, an American president hosted a White House celebration as Rabin and Arafat shook hands with Bill Clinton as matchmaker. Rabin, Peres, and Arafat received the Nobel Peace Prize in 1994.

But terrorism escalated. Baruch Goldstein killed twenty-nine Palestinians and wounded dozens more in 1994 as they were praying in their holy Tomb of the Patriarchs in Hebron. On November 4, 1995, the prime minister of Israel, Yitzhak Rabin—who had participated in secret negotiations with Arafat's organization—was gunned down at a peace demonstration by Yigal Amir, a fervently Orthodox Israeli Jew, who decided that a government supporting compromise on Palestinian issues should be defeated by murder. Foreign minister Shimon Peres succeeded Rabin, and was himself succeeded by Benjamin Netanyahu and Ehud Barak. None was able to eliminate security lapses, accusations of prisoner brutality, budget scandals, influence peddling, bungled covert operations, or rigidity by the religious and Socialist leadership—all dangerous cracks in the body politic. In the final months of the millennium, Barak and Arafat signed a land-for-peace agreement that offered Arab Palestine a further eleven percent of the West Bank in addition to freeing three hundred and fifty prisoners accused of security-related offenses. But in a clear challenge to the "peace of the brave," Arafat reiterated his old demands to "build our independent Palestinian state with its capital in Holy Jerusalem" and to stop "all [Jewish] settlement activity" in the West Bank and Gaza. The world held its breath.

The chasm between older and newer settlers, and between the secular or modern Orthodox and the ultra-zealous, had grown so visibly that relationships which once were merely incompatible became xenophobic. By century's end Israel withdrew from southern Lebanon and suffered the second intifada beginning on September 28, 2000. The country had absorbed two and a half million Ethiopian, Russian and other immigrants, yet partisanship often defeated hopes for a melting pot environment. The small nation continued to seek a political and religious status quo, but the myth of inclusiveness, of cooperation or even of fellowship between Arabs and Jews, as well as among all Jews regardless of origin or beliefs, was fast being dispelled. Many dreams proved empty and ephemeral; perhaps they had always been unrealistic. A serious drop in the birth rate remained problematical, as did issues of assimilation, intermarriage, emigration, equality of civil liberties for Jews and non–Jews, the autonomy of the Palestinian entity in some form, Hezbollah rockets, Hamas radicals, and the fate of Jerusalem as an undivided capital. The Jew had returned home, but it was not yet his Promised Land.

For some, Israel's light among nations appeared to have dimmed. Israeli author Yossi Klein Halevi suggested that independence means "taking the dream out of the realm of the ideal and into the realm of the concrete, and that in turn means living with a certain amount of disappointment." Nevertheless, every Jew knew there was a place of refuge and welcome in times of trouble, and every Jew knew that there was a place that conferred a sense of belonging whenever opportunity or inclination refreshed the memory. Given its economic and political constraints, no country developed its infrastructure, commercial links, computer innovations, or medical advances with greater ingenuity. Israel's gross national product was larger than that of all the nations around it. The state's vast accomplishments in technology, science, scholarship, commerce, the arts, and self-defense have had no parallel in modern times. No country was more generous or prompt with its resources to nations stricken by disaster. Despite acknowledged weaknesses, no country of its size ever absorbed such enormous numbers of diverse immigrants; there were more foreigners than natives, more secularists than religionists, perhaps even more skeptics than idealists. The society evoked by Herzl and Buber along with their followers and detractors developed in radically new ways. Less thought was given to the once-burning question of how to foster a national Jewish identity in the historical homeland and more on basic survival, control of the environment, and the ways in which liberal social structures impinged on traditional values.

The art community likewise confronted change and ambivalence. Motivated at first by the Bezalel paradigm of Jewish identity as a national experience, animated by battles for independence and acceptance, grappling with the reality of European losses, artists seemed driven by either nostalgia or pessimism. Nevertheless, they succeeded in creating a post-modern aesthetic, sophisticated, universal, pluralistic in design and style, inevitably linked to television, video, photo and other forms of quirky or fantastic imagery. Still committed to a restructured future, still imbued by a particular "Israeli" vision, there remained the will to carry their artistic and political integrity into the new century and the hope that there would still be time to jump from the fire back into the frying pan.

Glossary

Abstract art Forms independent or apart from specific subject matter

Afikomen Matzo eaten at end of Seder

Aliyah Moving to Israel; honorary reading from Torah

Aquatint A printmaking method creating tonal, rather than linear, passages

Ashkenazim Jews from France, Germany, and eastern Europe and their descendants

Balbatim Upstanding citizens

Bar/Bat Mitzvah Ceremony marking coming of age for thirteen-year-olds

Bauhaus A twentieth-century school of architecture

Bimah Pulpit

Challutzim Early pioneers in Palestine

Charoses Mixture of fruit, wine, and nuts eaten during Passover Seder

Chasidim Orthodox Jews who share certain pious tenets

Cheder Elementary Hebrew school

Collage Picture formed from various materials stuck on canvas

Colophon Inscription giving information about publication

Constructionism A twentieth-century Russian movement based on collage

Cubism A twentieth-century abstract movement

Dada A twentieth-century anti-art movement

Diaspora Life outside land of Israel settled by Jews; Yiddish: Galut

Dreidel A game using a spinning top, played during Chanukah

Drypoint An engraving method that prints as a soft and rich velvety tone

Dybbuk Soul of a dead body inhabiting a living person

Engraving A printmaking technique creating a sharp and clear line

Eretz Yisrael Land of Israel

Etching A printmaking technique using a mordant to incise a design into metal

Etrog Citron fruit used during Sukkot holiday

Genizah Repository for sacred books

Goldena Madina Golden Land

Haftorah Readings from the Prophets

Haganah Jewish fighting force in Palestine

Haggadah Book read during Passover Seder

Halacha Rabbinic laws incumbent on Jews

Hasidism Jewish mystical religious movement

Haskalah Secular nineteenth-century Enlightenment movement

Hazzan Cantor

Hozen Bridegroom

Impressionism Nineteenth-century Modernist movement

Intaglio Lines incised below the surface of a metal plate

Irgun Retaliatory army against Arab and British attacks

Kabbalah Mystical tradition

Kaddish Mourners' prayer

Kashrut Jewish dietary laws

Kibbutz Commune of pioneers in Israel

Kiddush Blessing over wine or bread

Kol Bo Encyclopedic jack of all trades

Kosher Jewish dietary laws

Ladino Language of Sephardim based on Spanish

Landsmanschaften Immigrants from same town or region

Linocut Relief cutting on linoleum

Lithography A printmaking technique that retrieves drawings from a stone

Lulav Tree branch or frond used during Sukkot holiday

Machzer Prayer book for High Holidays

Maskilim Followers of the Haskalah

Massorah Commentaries on Hebrew Bible

Matzo Unleavened bread eaten during Passover holiday

Megillah Purim Scroll

Menorah candelabrum, seven or eight-branched

Mezzotint A printmaking technique creating tonal effects through burnishing

Mezuzah Scripture inside small case attached to doorpost of Jewish home

Midrash Moral tales interpreting and derived from the Bible

Mikvah Ritual bath

Pentateuch First five books of the Bible; i.e., Torah

Phylacteries Small boxes containing quotations from Hebrew scriptures worn on the head and left arm by observant men during morning prayers

Pirke Aboth Ethics of the Fathers

Pochoir Printmaking technique using stencils

Printmaking A technique for reproducing identical images by cutting designs into wood, engraving on metal, or drawing on stone or other matrixes, then inking and transferring them onto paper

Purim Holiday commemorating the delivery of Persian Jews

Sanhedrin Supreme court of ancient Jewish nation; convoked by Napoleon in 1807

Sephardim Jews from Spain, Portugal, and North Africa and their descendants

Serigraphy or Silkscreen A printmaking technique involving a stencil process whereby ink is forced through a screen

Shiur Talmud lesson

Shochet Kosher slaughterer

Shofar Ram's horn blown as way of repentance

Shtetl Small town in central or eastern Europe

Shul Synagogue

Siddur Daily prayer book

SS Schutzstaffel, Nazi group which carried out Jewish destruction

Stipple A printmaking method using incised dots to create soft tonal patterns

Sukkah Temporary structure built during Sukkot, feast of Tabernacles

Tallit Prayer shawl

Targum Aramaic translation of Hebrew scriptures

Tefillin See Phylacteries

Torah Five books of Moses.

Tsitsis Fringed garment worn by observant men

Tzeduka Righteousness; charity

Wood-engraving An intaglio process in which lines lying below the wood's surface are inked and printed

Woodcut A printmaking method using raised designs that are inked and printed

Yeshiva Upper-level Hebrew instruction

Yiddish Language spoken by Ashkenazi Jews

Zincograph A printmaking technique that retrieves images from zinc

Bibliography

Abrahams, Israel. *By-Paths in Hebraic Bookland*. Philadelphia: Jewish Publication Society of America, 1920.

Abrams, Elliott. *Faith or Fear: How Jews Can Survive in a Christian America*. New York: Free Press, 1997.

Abramson, Lillian. *Hanukkah ABC*. New York: Shulsinger, 1968.

Adler, Miklos, and Saul Touster. *Beyond Words: A Holocaust History in Sixteen Woodcuts Done in 1945 by Miklos Adler*. New York: American Jewish Historical Society, 2001.

Aleichem, Sholem. *Inside Kasrilevke*. Trans. Isidore Goldstick. New York: Schocken Books, 1965.

_____. *The Old Country*. Trans. Julius Butwin and Frances Butwin. New York: Crown, 1946.

_____. *Tevy's Daughters*. Trans. Frances Butwin. New York: Crown, 1949.

Altman, Sig. *The Comic Image of the Jew: Exploration of a Pop Culture Phenomenon*. Rutherford, N.J.: Fairleigh Dickinson University Press, 1971.

Altshuler, David A. *The Precious Legacy: Judaic Treasures from the Czechoslovak State Collections*. New York: Summit Books, 1983.

Amar, Ariella and Ruth Jacoby. *Ingathering of the Nations: Treasures of Jewish Art: Documenting an Endangered Legacy*. Jerusalem: Center for Jewish Art, 1998.

American Jewish Committee. *The Jews in Nazi Germany: A Handbook of Facts Regarding Their Present Situation*. New York: H. Fertig, 1935.

Amichai, Yehuda, and Lynne Avadenka. *I Am Sitting Here Now*. Huntington Woods, Mich.: Land Parks Press, 1994.

Amishai-Maisels, Ziva. *Depiction and Interpretation: The Influence of the Holocaust on the Visual Arts*. Oxford: Pergamon, 1993.

Amram, David Werner. *The Makers of Hebrew Books in Italy: Being Chapters n the History of the Hebrew Printing Press*. Philadelphia: J.H. Greenstone, 1909.

An-Ski, S., A. M. Efros, A.S. Kantsedikas, V. Rakitin, Andrei Dmitrievicj Sarab'ianov. *The Jewish Artistic Heritage: An Album*. Moscow: RA, 1994.

Antin, Mary. *The Promised Land*. Boston: Houghton Mifflin, 1912.

Arab Office. *The Future of Palestine*. London: Arab Office, 1947.

Aston, Frederick A. *A Challenge to Every Jew*. New York: s.n., 1932.

Ausubel, Nathan. *The Book of Jewish Knowledge: An Encyclopedia of Judaism and the Jewish People, Covering All Elements of Jewish Life from Biblical Times to the Present*. New York: Crown, 1964.

_____. *Jewish Culture in America: Weapon for Jewish Survival and Progress*. New York: New Century, 1948.

_____. *Pictorial History of the Jewish People: From Bible Times to Our Day Throughout the World*. New York: Crown, 1953.

Bacon, Josephine. *Illustrated Atlas of Jewish Civilization: 4000 Years of Jewish History*. Enderby, U.K.: Silverdale Books, 2003.

Bahat, Dan. *Twenty Centuries of Jewish Life in the Holy Land: The Forgotten Generations*. Jerusalem: Israel Economist, 1975.

_____, and Shalom Sabar. *Jerusalem, Stone and Spirit: 3000 Years of History and Art*. New York: Rizzoli, 1998.

Baigell, Matthew. *Jewish-American Artists an the Holocaust*. New Brunswick, N.J.: Rutgers University Press, 1997.

Baldwin, Neil. *Henry Ford and the Jews: The Mass Production of Hate*. New York: Public Affairs, 2001.

Bandes, Susan J. *Abraham Rattner: The Tampa Museum of Art Collection*. Tampa, Fla.: The Museum, 1997.

Barkley, Harold. *Likenesses in Line: An Anthology of Tudor and Stuart Engraved Portraits*. London: H.M.S.O., 1982.

Barnavi, Elie, and Miriam Eliav-Feldon. *A Historical Atlas of the Jewish People: From the Time of the Patriarchs to the Present*. New York: Knopf, 1992.

Barnett, C. Z. *The Dream of Fate, or, Sarah, the Jewess: A Melodrama in Two Acts*. London: J. Duncombe, 1838.

Barnett, Richard David. *Catalogue of the Permanent and Loan Collections of the Jewish Museum, London*. London: Harvey Miller, 1974.

Baron, Stanley, and Jacques Damase. *Sonia Delaunay: The Life of an Artist*. New York: H. N. Abrams, 1995.

Barquist, David L., Myer Myers, Jon Butler, and Jonathan D. Sarna. *Myer Myers: Jewish Silversmith in Colonial New York*. New Haven, Conn. Yale University Press, 2001.

Barron, Stephanie, and Peter W. Guenther. *Degenerate*

Art: The Fate of the Avant-Garde in Nazi Germany. Los Angeles: Los Angeles County Museum of Art, 1991.

_____, Sabine Eckmann, and Matthew Affron. *Exiles + Émigrés: The Flight of European Artists from Hitler.* Los Angeles: Los Angeles County Museum of Art, 1997.

Bartlett, Samuel Colcord. *From Egypt to Palestine: Through Sinai, the Wilderness and the South Country.* New York: Arno Press, 1977.

Belth, Nathan C. *Fighting for America: An Account of Jewish Men in the Armed Forces—From Pearl Harbor to the Italian Campaign.* New York: Jewish Welfare Board, 1944.

Ben-Asher, Naomi, and Hayim Leaf. *The Junior Jewish Encyclopedia.* 9th ed. New York: Shengold, 1979.

Benoschofsky, Ilona and Sandor Scheiber. *The Jewish Museum of Budapest.* Trans. Joseph W. Wiesenberg. Budapest: Corvina, 1989.

Berger, Natalia. *Jews and Medicine: Religion, Culture, Science.* Philadelphia: Jewish Publication Society, 1997.

Bergner, Yosl. *Illustrations to I. L. Pertetz.* Montreal, Quebec: Hertz & Edelstein, 1950.

Berkeley University Art Museum. *Human Image in German Expressionist Graphic Art from the Robert Gore Rifkind Foundation.* Berkeley, Calif.: University Art Museum, 1981.

Berlin, Charles, and Joshua Block. *Hebrew Printing and Bibliography.* New York: New York Public Library, 1976.

Berman, Colette, and Yosef Miller. *The Beautiful People of the Book: A Tribute to Ethiopian Jews in Israel.* Jerusalem: Millhouse, 1988.

Berman, Nancy M., and Vicki Reikes Fox. *The Art of Hanukkah.* New York: Hugh Lauter Levin, 1996.

Bermant, Chaim. *The Walled Garden: The Saga of Jewish Family Life and Tradition.* New York: Macmillan, 1975.

Bernstein, Philip Sidney. *Rabbis at War: The Canra Story.* Waltham, Ma.: American Jewish Historical Society, 1971.

_____. *What the Jews Believe.* New York: Farrar, Straus and Young, 1950.

Bialer, Yehuda Leib, and Estelle Fink. *Jewish Life in Art and Tradition: Based on the Collection of the Sir Isaac and Lady Edith Wolfson Museum, Hechal Shlomo, Jerusalem.* New York: Putnam, 1976.

Bilski, Emily. *Berlin Metropolis: Jews and the New Culture: 1890–1918.* Berkeley: University of California Press, 1999.

_____, Peter Junk, Sybil Milton and Wendelin Zimmer. *Art and Exile: Felix Nussbaum (1904–1944).* New York: Jewish Museum, 1985.

Birmingham, Stephen. *The Grandees: America's Sephardic Elite.* New York: Harper and Row, 1971.

Birnbaum, Pierre. *The Anti-Semitic Moment: A Tour of France in 1898.* New York: Hill and Wang, 2003.

Blatter, Janet, and Sybil Milton. *Art of the Holocaust.* New York: Rutledge Press, 1981.

Blau, Joseph L., and Salo Wittmayer Baron. *The Jews of the United States, 1790–1840: A Documentary History.* New York: Columbia University Press, 1963.

Bleiberg, Edward. *Jewish Life in Ancient Egypt: A Family Archive from the Nile Valley.* Brooklyn, N.Y.: Brooklyn Museum of Art, 2002.

B'nai B'rith. *Anti-Semitism in the Egyptian Media: A Report by the Anti-Defamation League.* New York: Anti-Defamation League, 1997.

Bober, Jonathan. *The Etchings of William Meyerowitz: Archer M. Huntington Art Gallery, College of Fine Arts, University of Texas at Austini, 22 March–19 May 1996.* Austin, Tx.: Huntington Art Gallery, 1996.

Boulton, William Biggs. *The Amusements of Old London: Being a Survey of the Sports of Pastimes, Tea Gardens and Parks, Playhouses and Other Diversions of the People of London from the 17th to the Beginning of the 19th Century.* London: J. C. Nimmo, 1901.

Burgess, Gelett. *The Maxims of Noah. Derived from His Experience with Women Both Before and After the Flood as Given in Counsel to His Son Japhet.* New York: Frederick A. Stokes, 1913.

Burke, Thomas, and Pearl Binder. *The Real East End.* London: Constable, 1932.

Burstein, Abraham. *The Ghetto Messenger.* New York: Bloch, 1928.

Butler, Elizabeth, Lady. *Letters from the Holy Land.* London: A. & C. Black, 1906.

Calimani, Riccardo. *The Ghetto of Venice.* Trans. Katherine Silberblatt Wolfthal. New York: M. Evans, 1987.

Calmet, Antoine Augustin. *An Historical, Critical, Geographical, Chronological, and Etymological Dictionary of the Holy Bible in Three Volumes.* Vol. 3. London: Knapton, 1732.

Chagall, Marc. *My Life.* New York: Orion Press, 1960.

Cheney, Sheldon. *A World History of Art.* New York: Viking Press, 1937.

Cohen, Arthur Allen.. *The Unknown Steinhardt: Prints by Jacob Steinhardt Produced Between 1907 and 1934: The Jewish Museum, New York, January 20–April 19, 1987.* New York: The Museum, 1987.

Cohen, Richard I. *Jewish Icons: Art and Society in Modern Europe.* Berkeley: University of California Press, 1998.

Cohen, Steve. *That's Funny, You Don't Look Anti-Semitic: An Anti-Racist Analysis of Left Anti-Semitism.* Eds. Libby Lawson and Erica Burman. Leeds, U.K.: Beyond the Pale Collective, 1984.

Cohn, Emil Bernhard, ed. *Juedischer Kinder-Kalendar.* Berlin: Juedischer Verlag, n.d.

Cohn-Sherbok, Dan. *The Blackwell Dictionary of Judaica.* Oxford: Blackwell Reference, 1992.

Colodner, Solomon. *Jewish Education in Germany Under the Nazis.* New York: Jewish Education Committee Press, 1964.

Comay, Joan. *The Diaspora Story: The Epic of the Jewish People Among the Nations.* New York: Random House, 1981.

Congress for Jewish Culture. *The Warsaw Ghetto Uprising.* New York, 1974.

Cooper, Abraham. *Portraits of Infamy: A Study of Soviet Antisemitic Caricatures and Their Roots in Nazi Ideology.* Los Angeles: Simon Wiesenthal Center, 1986.

Cowen, Anne, and Roger Cowen. *Victorian Jews Through British Eyes.* Oxford: Oxford University Press, 1986.

Cox, Jane. *London's East End Life and Traditions.* London: Weidenfeld & Nicolson, 1994.

Darton, William, and Thomas Darton. *London Cries*. Tokyo: Holp Shuppan, 1996.

Debre, Moses. *The Image of the Jew in French Literature from 1800 to 1908*. Trans. Gertrude Hirschler. New York: Ktav, 1970.

De Lange, Nicholas, ed. *The Illustrated History of the Jewish People*. New York: Harcourt Brace, 1997.

Diehl, Gaston. *Pascin*. Trans. Rosalie Siegel. New York: Crown, 1968.

Dimont, Max I. *Jews, God, and History*. New York: Simon and Schuster, 1962.

Diner, Hasia R. *Jewish Americans: The Immigrant Experience*. New York: Hugh Lauter Levin Associates, 2002.

Disraeli, Isaac. *Curiosities of Literature*. Ed. Everett Franklin Bleiler. New York: Dover, 1964.

Doré, Gustave. *The Doré Bible Illustrations*. New York: Dover, 1974.

_____. *The Legend of the Wandering Jew: A Series of Twelve Designs*. London: Cassell, Petter & Galpin, 1800.

Duda, Eugeniusz. *A Guide to Jewish Cracow*. Warsaw: Jewish Information and Tourist Bureau, 1990.

_____, and Marek Sosenko. *Dawna Pocztowka Zydowska Ze Zblorow Marka Sosenki: Old Jewish Postcards from Marek Sosenko's Collection*. Krakow: Muzeum Historyczne Miasta Krakowa, 1998.

Duff, E. Gordon. *Early Printed Books*. London: Kegan Paul, Trench, Trubner, 1893.

Eis, Ruth. *Twenty-five Years, Judah L. Magnes Museum*. Ed. Nelda Cassuto. Berkeley, Calif.: The Museum, 1987.

Eisenstein, J. D. *Hagadah: The Narrative of Israel's Redemption from Egypt*. United States of America: Hebrew Publishing, 1928.

Elzas, Barnett A. *The Jews of South Carolina: From the Earliest Times to the Present Day*. Philadelphia: J. B. Lippincott, 1905.

Endelman, Todd M. *The Jews of Georgian England, 1714–1830: Tradition and Change in a Liberal Society*. Philadelphia: Jewish Publication Society of America, 1979.

_____. *Radical Assimilation in England Jewish History, 1656–1945*. Bloomington: Indiana University Press, 1990.

_____, and Tony Kushner, ed. *Disraeli's Jewishness*. London: Valetine Mitchell, 2002.

Evans, Eli N. *The Provincials: A Personal History of Jews in the South*. New York: Atheneum, 1973.

Falla, P. S., and Susan Lambert. *French Popular Imagery: Five Centuries of Prints: Catalogue of an Exhibition Held at the Hayward Gallery, London, 26 March–27 May 1974*. London: Arts Council of Great Britain, 1974.

Feinstein, Steve, Yehudit Shendar, and Matthew Baigell. *Witness and Legacy: Contemporary Art About the Holocaust*. Minneapolis, Minn.: Lerner Publications, 1995.

Felsenstein, Frank. *Anti-semitic Stereotypes: A Paradigm of Otherness in English Popular Culture, 1660–1830*. Baltimore, Md.: Johns Hopkins University Press, 1995.

_____. *The Jew as Other: A Century of English Caricature, 1730–1830: An Exhibition, April 6–July 31, 1995*. New York: Library of the Jewish Theological Seminary of America, 1995.

Finkielkraut, Alain. *The Imaginary Jew*. Trans. Kevin O'Neill and David Suchoff. Lincoln: University of Nebraska Press, 1994.

Finzi, Roberto. *Anti-Semitism: From Its European Roots to the Holocaust*. New York: Interlink, 1999.

Fischer, Klaus P. *The History of an Obsession: German Judeophobia and the Holocaust*. New York: Continuum, 2001.

Fischer, Yona. *Expressionism in Eretz-Israel in the 'Thirties: And Its Ties with the Ecole de Paris: Exhibition at the Israel Museum, Jerusalem, Spertus Hall, Autumn 1971*. Jerusalem: The Museum, 1971.

Fishof, Iris. *Jewish Art Masterpieces from the Israel Museum, Jerusalem*. Southport, Conn.: H. L. Levin Associates, 1994.

Fleg, Edmond. *Why I Am a Jew*. Ed. Louise Waterman Wise. New York: Bloch, 1929.

Flint, Janet A. *The Prints of Louis Lozowick: A Catalogue Raisonne*. New York: Hudson Hills Press, 1982.

Fluek, Toby Knobel. *Memories of My Life in a Polish Village, 1930–1949*. New York: Knopf, 1990.

Foa, Anna. *The Jews of Europe After the Black Death*. Berkeley: University of California Press, 2000.

Fontaine, Laurence. *History of Pedlars in Europe*. Trans. Vicki Whittaker. Durham, N.C.: Duke University Press, 1996.

Fraser, James Howard, Steven Heller, and Sibylle Fraser. *The Malik-Verlag, 1916–1947: Berlin, Prague, New York: An Exhibition*. New York: Goethe House, 1984.

Freed, E. *The Silence of the Good People*. Los Angeles: Southern California Committee Against Neo-Nazism and Anti-Semitism, 1962.

The French Connection: Jewish Artists in the School of Paris, 1900–1940: Works in Chicago Collections, October 24–December 31, 1982. Chicago: Maurice Spertus Museum of Judaica. 1982.

Friedrich, Otto. *Before the Deluge: A Portrait of Berlin in the 1920's*. New York: Harper & Row, 1972.

Front Page Israel: Major Events 1932–1979, As Reflected in the Front Pages of the Jerusalem Post. Jerusalem: Palestine Post and Arno, 1979.

Gamzu, Haim. *Painting and Sculpture in Israel: The Plastic Arts from the Bezalel Period to the Present Day*. Tel Aviv: Eshcol Publishers, 1951.

Gay, Ruth. *The Jews of Germany: A Historical Portrait*. New Haven: Yale University Press, 1992.

Geffen, David, and Moshe Kohn. *American Heritage Haggadah: The Passover Experience*. Jerusalem: Geffen Publication House, 1992.

Gergel, Belinda. *In Pursuit of the Tree of Life: A History of the Early Jews of Columbia, South Carolina, and the Tree of Life Congregation*. Columbia, S.C.: Tree of Life Congregation, 1996.

Gersh, Harry. *The Story of the Jews*. New York: Behrman House, 1964.

Getlein, Frank, and Dorothy Getlein. *Christianity in Modern Art*. Milwaukee, Wis.: Bruce Publication, 1961.

Gilbert, Martin. *The Illustrated Atlas of Jewish Civilization*. London: A. Deutsch, 1990.

_____. *The Jews in the Twentieth Century*. New York: Schocken Books, 2001.

Gilman, Sander L. *Jews in Today's German Culture.* Bloomington: Indiana University Press, 1995.

Gitelman, Zvi Y. *A Century of Ambivalence: The Jews of Russia and the Soviet Union, 1881 to Present.* New York: Schocken Books, 1988.

Glassman, Bernard. *Anti-Semitic Stereotypes Without Jews: Images of the Jews in England, 1290–1700.* Detroit: Wayne State University Press, 1975.

Gold, Leonard Singer. *A Sign and a Witness: 2,000 Years of Hebrew Books and Illuminated Manuscripts.* New York: New York Public Library, 1988.

Goldberg, M. Hirsh. *The Jewish Connection: The Incredible—Ironic—Bizarre—Funny—and Provocative in the Story of the Jews.* New York: Shapolsky, 1986.

Gombrich, E. H. *The Story of Art.* 14th ed. Oxford: Phaidon, 1984.

Goodman, Abram Vossen. *American Overture: Jewish Rights in Colonial Times.* Philadelphia: Jewish Publication Society of America, 1947.

Goodman, Philip. *The Passover Anthology.* Philadelphia: Jewish Publication Society of America, 1961.

Goodman, Susan Tumarkin. *After Rabin: New Art from Israel.* New York: Jewish Museum, 1998.

Gordis, Robert, and Moshe Davidowitz, eds. *Art in Judaism: Studies in the Jewish Artistic Experience.* New York: National Council on Art in Jewish Life, 1975.

Gottesman, Milton M. *Hoopskirts & Huppas: A Chronicle of the Early Years of the Garfunkel-Trager Family in America, 1856–1920.* New York: American Jewish Historical Society, 1999.

Grafman, Rafi. *The Israel Museum Guide.* Jerusalem: The Museum, 1983.

Greenberg, Sidney. *A Modern Treasury of Jewish Thoughts.* New York: T. Yoseloff, 1960.

Gribetz, Judah, Edward L. Greenstein, and Regina Stein. *The Timetables of Jewish History: A Chronology of the Most Important People and Events in Jewish History.* New York: Simon and Schuster, 1993.

Grinstein, Hyman. *The Rise of the Jewish Community of New York, 1654–1860.* Philadelphia: Porcupine Press, 1976.

Gross, Jan T. *Artists of Israel, 1920–1980: The Jewish Museum/New York, February 19–May 17, 1981.* Detroit, Mich.: Wayne State University Press, 1981.

_____. *The Emergence of Jewish Artists in Nineteenth-Century Europe.* New York: Merrell, 2001.

_____ *Fear: Anti-Semitism in Poland after Auschwitz: An Essay in Historical Interpretation.* New York: Random House, 2007.

_____. *In the Shadow of Conflict: Israeli Art, 1980–1989.* New York: Jewish Museum, 1989.

_____ *Russian Jewish Artists in a Century of Change, 1890–1990.* Munich: Prestel, 1995.

Grossman, Cissy. *A Temple Treasury: The Judaica Collection of Congregation Emanu-El of the City of New York.* New York: Hudson Hills Press, 1989.

Grossman, Grace Cohen. *Jewish Art.* New York: Hugh Lauter Levin, 1995.

_____. *New Beginnings: The Skirball Museum Collections and Inaugural Exhibition.* Los Angeles: Skirball Cultural Center, 1996.

Grossmann, Emery. *Art and Tradition.* New York: T. Yoseloff, 1968.

Grubel, Monika. *Judaism.* Hauppauge, N.Y.: Barrons, 1997.

Gruber, Ruth Ellen. *Virtually Jewish: Reinventing Jewish Culture in Europe.* Berkeley: University of California Press, 2002.

Gursan-Salzmann, Ayse. *The Last Jews of Radauti.* New York: Dial Press, 1983.

Gutmann, Joseph, ed. *Beauty in Holiness; Studies in Jewish Customs and Ceremonial Art.* New York: Ktav Publication House, 1970.

_____, ed. *No Graven Images: Studies in Art and the Hebrew Bible.* New York: Ktav Publication House, 1971.

Gutstein, Linda, *History of the Jews in America.* Secaucus, N.J.: Chartwell Books, 1988.

Hapgood, Hutchins. *The Spirit of the Ghetto: Studies of the Jewish Quarter in New York.* New York: Funk & Wagnalls, 1902.

Harby, Isaac. *Daily Prayers (Reform, Reformed Society of Israelites).* Columbia, S.C.: R. L. Bryan, 1974.

Hatefutsoth, Beth. *Beth Hatefutsoth: The First Years.* Tel Aviv: Nahum Goldmann Museum of the Jewish Diaspora, 1983.

Hayter, Stanley William. *New Ways of Gravure.* Revised ed. London: Oxford University Press, 1966.

Hebrew Union College. Skirball Museum. *A Centennial Sampler: One Hundred Years of Collecting at Hebrew Union College: [Exhibition], Hebrew Union College Skirball Museum, February 22–October 31, 1976, Los Angeles, California.* Los Angeles: The Museum, 1976.

Helzel, Florence B. *Narrative Imagery: Artists' Portfolios.* Berkeley, Calif.: Judah L. Magnes Museum, 1991.

_____. *The Print and Drawing Collection: Judah L. Magnes Museum.* Berkeley, Calif.: The Museum, 1984.

_____. *Shtetl Life: The Nathan and Faye Hurvitz Collection.* Berkeley, Calif.: Judah L. Magnes Museum, 1993.

_____ *Witnesses to History: The Jewish Poster, 1770–1985: A Selection from the Judah L. Magnes Museum.* Berkeley, Calif.: The Museum, 1989.

Hertz, Joseph H. *A Book of Jewish Thoughts.* London: Oxford University Press, 1920.

Hertzberg, Arthur. *The French Enlightenment and the Jews.* New York: Columbia University Press, 1968.

_____. *Jews: The Essence and Character of a People.* San Francisco: HarperSanFrancisco, 1998.

Herzog, Hanna. *Contest of Symbols: The Sociology of Election Campaigns Through Israeli Ephemera.* Cambridge, Ma.: Harvard University Library, 1987.

Heschel, Abraham Joshua. *The Earth Is the Lord: The Inner World of the Jew in East Europe.* New York: H. Schuman, 1950.

Heuberger, Georg, ed. *The Rothschilds: A European Family.* Sigmarigen, Germany: Thorbecke, 1994.

Heyd, Milly. *Mutual Reflections: Jews and Blacks in American Art.* New Brunswick, N.J.: Rutgers University Press, 1999.

Hinz, Berthold. *Art in the Third Reich.* Trans. Robert Kimber and Rita Kimber. New York: Pantheon Books, 1979.

Hirschler, Gertrude. *Ashkenaz: The German Jewish Heritage.* New York: Yeshiva University Museum, 1988.

Howe, Irving, and Kenneth Libo, ed. *How We Lived: A Documentary History of Immigrant Jews in America, 1880–1930.* New York: R. Marek, 1979.

Hundert, Gershon David. *The Jews in a Polish Private Town: The Case of Opatow in the Eighteenth Century.* Baltimore, Md.: Johns Hopkins University Press, 1992.

Hyamson, Albert Montefiore. *The Sephardim of England; A History of the Spanish and Portuguese Jewish Community.* London: Methuen, 1951.

Hyman, Paula. *The Jews of Modern France.* Berkeley: University of California Press, 1998.

Into the Arms of Strangers: Stories of the Kindertransport. Deborah Oppenheimer and Mark Jonathan Harris. Warner Home Video, 2001.

Isaacs, Ronald H., and Kerry M. Olitzky, eds. *Critical Documents of Jewish History: A Sourcebook.* Northvale, N.J.: Aronson, 1995.

Jacobowitz, Ellen S., and George H. Marcus. *American Graphics, 1860–1940: Selected from the Collection of the Philadelphia Museum of Art.* Philadelphia: Philadelphia Museum of Art, 1982.

Jacobs, Janet Liebman. *Hidden Heritage: The Legacy of the Crypto-Jews.* Berkeley: University of California Press, 2002.

Jacobs, Joseph. *The Jews of Angevin England.* New York: Gordon Press, 1977.

Jagielski, Jan. *A Guide to Jewish Warsaw.* Warsaw: Jewish Information and Tourist Bureau, 1995.

Jay, Robert. *The Trade Card in Nineteenth-Century America.* Columbia: University of Missouri Press, 1987.

Jerusalem and the Israeli Printmaker. Jerusalem: Ministry of Education and Culture, 1980.

Jewish Museum, New York. *Jewish Experience in the Art of the Twentieth Century: Exhibition, October 16, 1975 Through January 25, 1976,* New York: The Museum, 1975.

Jewish Themes/Contemporary American Artists. New York: Jewish Museum, 1982.

Jewish Themes/Contemporary American Artists II, The Jewish Museum, New York, July 15–November 16, 1986. New York: Jewish Museum, 1986.

Johnson, Paul. *A History of the Jews.* New York: Harper & Row, 1987.

Juhasz, Esther, ed. *Sephardi Jews in the Ottoman Empire: Aspects of Material Culture.* Jerusalem: Israel Museum, 1990.

Julius, Anthony. *Idolizing Pictures: Idolatry, Iconoclasm, and Jewish Art.* New York: Thames & Hudson, 2001.

Kacyzne, Alter. *Polyn: Jewish Life in the Old Country.* New York: Metropolitan Books, 1999.

Kahn, Ava Fran. *Jewish Life in the American West: Perspectives on Migration, Settlement, and Community.* Los Angeles: Autry Museum, 2002.

_____. *Jewish Voices of the California Gold Rush: A Documentary History, 1849–1880.* Detroit: Wayne State University Press, 2002.

Kampf, Avram. *Chagall to Kitaj: Jewish Experience in 20th Century Art.* New York: Praeger, 1990.

_____. *Jewish Experience in the Art of the Twentieth Century.* Hadley, Ma.: Bergin & Garvey, 1984.

Kaniel, Michael. *A Guide to Jewish Art.* New York: Philosophical Library, 1989.

_____. *Judaism.* Poole, U.K.: Blandford Press, 1979.

Kanof, Abram, and Tom L. Freudenheim. *The American Jew in the Visual Art of America.* New York: American Jewish Historical Society, 1966.

Karp, Abraham J. *From the Ends of the Earth: Judaic Treasures of the Library of Congress.* Washington, D.C.: Library of Congress, 1991.

_____. *The Jews in America: A Treasury of Art and Literature.* New York: Hugh Lauter Levin, 1994.

Karshan, Donald H. *Prints.* New York: Cooper-Hewitt Museum, 1980.

Katz, Alexander Raymond. *A New Art for an Old Religion.* New York: R.F. Moore, 1952.

Katz, Jacob. *Tradition and Crisis: Jewish Society at the End of the Middle Ages.* New York: Free Press of Glencoe, 1961.

Kaufman, Isidor. *American Jews in World War II; The Story of 550,000 Fighters for Freedom.* New York: Dial Press, 1947.

Kayser, Stephen S., ed. *Jewish Ceremonial Art: A Guide to the Appreciation of the Art Objects Used in Synagogue and Home, Principally from the Collections of the Jewish Museum of the Jewish Theological Seminary of America.* Philadelphia: Jewish Publication Society of America, 1955.

_____, and Isidore S. Meyer. *Early American Jewish Portraiture.* 1952.

Kedourie, Elie, ed. *The Jewish World: History and Culture of the Jewish People.* New York: H. N. Abrams, 1979.

Keen, Michael E. *Jewish Ritual Art in the Victoria & Albert Museum.* London: HMSO, 1991.

Keller, Sharon R., ed. *The Jews: A Treasury of Art and Literature.* New York: Hugh Lauter Levin, 1992.

Kishon, Ephraim. *So Sorry We Won!* Tel Aviv: Ma'ariv Library, 1967.

Klagsbrun, Francine. *Jewish Days: A Book of Jewish Life and Culture Around the Year.* New York: Farrar, Straus, Giroux, 1996.

Kleeblatt, Norman, ed. *The Dreyfus Affair: Art, Truth, and Justice.* Berkeley: University of California Press, 1987.

_____, ed. *Mirroring Evil: Nazi Imagery/Recent Art.* New York: Jewish Museum, 2001.

_____, ed. *Too Jewish?: Challenging Traditional Identities.* New York: Jewish Museum, 1996.

_____, Gerard C. Wertkin, and Mary Black. *The Jewish Heritage in American Folk Art.* New York: Universe Books, 1984.

_____, and Susan Chevlowe, eds. *Painting a Place in America: Jewish Artists in New York, 1900–1945: A Tribute to the Education Alliance Art School.* New York: Jewish Museum, 1991.

_____, and Vivian B. Mann. *Treasures of the Jewish Museum.* New York: Universe Books, 1986.

Klein, Dennis B. *Hidden History of the Kovno Ghetto.* Boston, Ma.: Little, Brown, 1997.

Klemig, Roland, and Gabrielle Bamberger. *Jews in Germany Under Prussian Rule.* Berlin: Bildarchiv Preussischer Kulturbesitz, 1984.

Klinov, Yeshayahu. *Herzl, Seer of the State.* Tel Aviv: s.n., 1950.

Kokoschka, Oskar. *Jerusalem Faces.* New York: Marlborough Graphics, 1974.

Kolb, Leon, ed. *The Woodcuts of Jakob Steinhardt Chronologically Arranged and Fully Reproduced.* Philadelphia: Jewish Publication Society of America, 1962.

Korn, Bertram Wallace. *American Jewry and the Civil War.* Philadelphia: Jewish Publication Society of America, 1951.

Korn, Irene. *A Celebration of Judaism in Art.* New York: Smithmark, 1996.

Krajewska, Monika. *Time of Stones.* Warsaw: Interpress, 1983.

Kuhnel, Bianca. *The Real and Ideal Jerusalem in Jewish, Christian and Islamic Art: Studies in Honor of Bezalal Narkiss on the Occasion of His Seventieth Birthday.* Jerusalem: Hebrew University of Jerusalem, Center for Jewish Art, 1998.

Landau, Paul. *Art and Women Artists in Israel.* Tel Aviv: Women's International Zionist Organization, 1949.

Landsberger, Franz. *A History of Jewish Art.* Cincinnati, Ohio: Union of American Hebrew Congregations, 1946.

_____. *The Jewish Artist Before the Emancipation.* Cincinnati, Ohio: Hebrew Union College, 1941.

_____. *Rembrandt, the Jews and the Bible.* Philadelphia: Jewish Publication Society of America, 1946.

Laub, Morris. *Last Barrier to Freedom: Internment of Jewish Holocaust Survivors on Cyprus 1946–1949.* Berkeley, Calif.: Judas L. Magnes Museum, 1985.

Lawrence, Eugene. *The Jews and Their Persecutors.* New York: Harper & Brothers, 1877.

Lehrmann, Chanan. *The Jewish Influences on European Thought.* Rutherford, N.J.: Fairleigh Dickinson University Press, 1976.

Leiser, Joseph. *American Judaism, the Religion and Religious Institutions of the Jewish People in the United States.* New York: Bloch Publishing, 1925.

Lenin, Vladimir Il'ich. *Lenin on the Jewish Question.* New York: International Publishers, 1936.

Levitte, Georges, and David Catarivas. *Les Juifs.* Paris: R. Delpire, 1964.

Levy, Jane, and Florence B. Helzel. *The Jewish Illustrated Book: A Selection from the Judah L. Magnes Museum.* Berkeley, Calif.: The Museum, 1986.

Lewbin, Hyman. *Rebirth of Jewish Art: The Unfolding of Jewish Art in the Nineteenth Century.* New York: Shengold Publishers, 1974.

Linder, Willy. *Classic Jewish Postcards for All Occasions.* New York: Schocken Books, 1996.

Livni, Zvi. *Landscapes in Israel: Eight Original Lithographs.* Tel Aviv: Yavneh Publication House, 1957.

London, Hannah Ruth. *Portraits of Jews by Gilbert Stuart and Other Early American Artists.* New York: W.E. Rudge, 1927.

Lowenthal, Marvin. *The Jews of Germany: A Story of Sixteen Centuries.* New York: Longmans, 1936.

Luckert, Steven. *The Art and Politics of Arthur Szyk.* Washington, D.C.: United States Holocaust Museum, 2002.

Luczynska, Zofia. *Jewish Kazimierz: A Short Guide.* Krakow: Studio Zebra, 1993.

Malenczyk, Jerzy. *A Guide to Jewish Lodz.* Warsaw: Jewish Information and Travel Bureau, 1994.

Mamet, David. *Bar Mitzvah.* Boston: Little, Brown, 1999.

Mann, Louis Leopold. *Glimpses of the Jewish Exhibit in the Hall of Religion: A Century of Progress 1933 and 1934.* Chicago: s.n., 1933.

Mann, Vivian B., ed. *Gardens and Ghettos: The Art of Jewish Life in Italy.* Berkeley: University of California Press, 1989.

_____, ed. *A Tale of Two Cities: Jewish Life in Frankfurt and Istanbul, 1750–1870.* New York: Jewish Museum, 1982.

Marcus, Amy Dockser. *Jerusalem 1913: The Origins of the Arab-Israeli Conflict.* New York: Viking Press, 2007.

Markowski, Stanislaw. *Krakowski Kazimierz: Dzielnica Zydowska: 1870–1988.* Krakow: Wydawn, 1992.

Martin, Bernard. *A History of Judaism.* Vol. 2. New York: Basic Books, 1974.

Mason, Philip P., ed. *Directory of Jewish Archival Institutions.* Detroit, Mich.: Wayne State University Press, 1975.

Mayer, A.L. *Bibliography of Jewish Art.* Ed. O. Kurz. Jerusalem: Magnes Press, 1967.

Mayer, Eugen. *The Jews of Frankfurt: Glimpses of the Past.* Frankfurt am Main: W. Kramer, 1990.

McCabe, Cynthia. *The Golden Door: Artist-Immigrants of America, 1876–1976.* Washington, D.C.: Smithsonian Institution Press, 1976.

Meek, H. A. *The Synagogue.* London: Phaidon Press, 1995.

Meidner, Ludwig, and Donald J. Brewer. *Prints, Drawings and Watercolors of Ludwig Meidner: The Earnst and Lilly Jacobson Collection: University of Southern California Art Galleries, January 4 Through February 2, 1973.* Los Angeles: University of Southern California Art Galleries, 1973.

Meltzer, Milton. *A History of Jewish Life from Eastern Europe to America.* Northvale, N.J.: J. Aronson, 1996.

Merian, Matthaeus. *Great Scenes from the Bible: 230 Magnificent 17th-century Engravings.* Mineola, N.Y.: Dover Publications, 2002.

Meron, Michal, and Neville Alexander. *The Jewish Festivals and Holy Days: Full Colour Reproductions of 12 Original Paintings.* Old Jaffa, Israel: Studio in Old Jaffa, 1995.

Mihailovic, Milica. *Judaica in Yugoslavia.* Beograd: Proex Prosveta, 1990.

Milton, Sybil, ed. *Art of Jewish Children Germany: 1936–1941: Innocence and Persecution.* New York: Philosophical Library, 1989.

Minear, Richard H., Theodor Seuss Geisel, and Art Spiegelman. *Dr. Seuss Goes to War: The World War II Editorial Cartoons of Theodor Seuss Geisel.* New York: New Press, 1999.

Mintz, Sharon Liberman, and Elka Deitsch. *Kehillat Ha-Kodesh: Creating the Sacred Community: The Roles of the Rabbi, Cantor, Mohel and Shohet in Jewish Communal Life: An Exhibition, December 18, 1996–April 17, 1997.* New York: Library of the Theological Seminary of America, 1997.

_____, and Elka Deitsch. *Precious Possessions: Treasures from the Library of the Jewish Theological Seminary: An Exhibition May 14, 2001–August 20, 2001.* New York: Commonplace Publications, 2001.

_____, and Lisa Anne Rotmil. *Text and Context: The De-*

velopment and Dissemination of Medieval Sephardic Culture: An Exhibition, October 28, 1992–February 5, 1993, the Library of the Jewish Theological Seminary of America* New York: Library of the Jewish Theological Seminary of America, 1992.

Miron-Michrovsky, Issachar. *Eighteen Gates of Jewish Holidays and Festivals.* Northvale, N.J.: Jason Aronson, 1993.

Mohr, Gordon. *The Satanic Counterfeit: A Review of* The Protocols of the Learned Elders of Zion, *the Communist Textbook* Psychopolitics, *and Henry Ford, Sr.'s* The International Jew, *Placed in Historical Perspective.* United States: s.n., 1982.

Mohrer, Fruma, and Marek Web, ed. *Guide to the YIVO Archives.* Armonk, N.Y.: M.E. Sharpe, 1998.

Moore, Clare, ed. *The Visual Dimension: Aspects of Jewish Art.* Boulder, Co.: Westview Press, 1993.

Moore, Deborah Dash, and S. Ilan Troen. *Divergent Jewish Cultures: Israel and America.* New Haven, Conn.: Yale University Press, 2001.

Morgenstein, Susan W., and Ruth E. Levine. *The Jews in the Age of Rembrandt.* Rockville, Md.: The Museum, 1981.

Mosk, Stanley. *Democracy in America—Day by Day.* New York: Vantage Press, 1995.

Murphy, Bruce Allen. *The Brandeis/Frankfurter Connection: The Secret Political Activities of Two Supreme Court Justices.* New York: Oxford University Press, 1982.

Naggar, Betty. *Jewish Pedlars and Hawkers, 1740–1940.* Camberley, U.K.: Porphyrogenitus, 1992.

Namenyi, Ernest. *The Essence of Jewish Art.* New York: T. Yoseloff, 1960.

National Museum of American Jewish History. *The American Jewish Experience.* Philadelphia: National Museum of American Jewish History, 1989.

Noah, M. M., and Abraham J. Karp. *Mordecai Manuel Noah: The First American Jew.* New York: Yeshiva University Museum, 1987.

Nochlin, Linda, and Tamar Garb, ed. *The Jew in the Text: Modernity and the Construction of Identity.* New York: Thames and Hudson, 1996.

Ofrat, Gideon. *One Hundred Years of Art in Israel.* Boulder, Co.: Westview Press, 1998.

Okun, Rob A., ed. *The Rosenbergs: Collected Visions of Artists and Writers.* Montague, Ma.: Cultural Forecast, 1993.

Ouaknin, Marc-Alain, and Gerard Garouste. *Haggadah: The Passover Story.* New York: Assouline, 2001.

Outwater, Myra Yellin. *Judaica.* Atglen, Pa.: Schiffer, 1999.

Palgrave, Francis Turner. *The Golden Treasury.* Chicago: Row, 1915.

Pann, Abel. *The Bible.* Jerusalem: Palestine Art Publication, 1923.

Paret, Peter. *"The Enemy Within"—Max Lebermann As President of the Prussian Academy of Arts.* New York: Leo Baeck Institute, 1984.

Parkes, James William. *The Jew in the Medieval Community; A Study of His Political and Economic Situation.* London: Soncino Press, 1938.

Parnes, Stephan O., ed. *The Art of Passover.* New York: Hugh Lauter Levin, 1994.

Pennell, Joseph. *The Jew at Home: Impressions of a Summer and Autumn Spent with Him in Russia and Austria.* London: W. Heinemann, 1892.

Petropoulos, Jonathan. *Art as Politics in the Third Reich.* Chapel Hill: University of North Carolina Press, 1996.

Philipson, David. *Old European Jewries.* Philadelphia: Jewish Publication Society of America, 1894.

Picciotto, James. *Sketches of Anglo-Jewish History.* London: Trubner, 1875.

Pilch, Judah. *Jewish Life in Our Times.* New York: Behrman House, 1944.

Pohl, Frances K. *Ben Shahn.* San Francisco: Pomegranate Art Books, 1993.

Posner, Raphael, and Israel M. Ta-Shma, eds. *The Hebrew Book: An Historical Survey.* Jerusalem: Keter Publication House, 1975.

_____, Uri Kaploun, and Shalom Cohen, eds. *Jewish Liturgy: Prayer and Synagogue Service Through the Ages.* Jerusalem: Keter Pub, 1975.

Prague Ghetto in the Renaissance Period. Prague: Published by Orbis for the State Jewish Museum, 1965.

Prescott, Emma-Stina, and Kenneth Wade Prescott. *The Complete Graphic Work of Jack Levine.* New York: Dover, 1984.

Prescott, Kenneth Wade. *Ben Shahn: A Retrospective, 1898–1969.* New York: Jewish Museum, 1976.

Raban, Ze'ev. *The Song of Solomon in Coloured Plates.* Jerusalem: Song of Songs, 1930.

Raban Remembered: Jerusalem's Forgotten Master: Essays and Catalogue of an Exhibition at the Yeshiva University Museum, December 1982–June 1983. New York: The Museum, 1982.

Rabinowicz, Tzvi. *Treasures of Judaica.* South Brunswick, N.J.: T. Yoseloff, 1971.

Radin, Max. *The Jews Among the Greeks and Romans.* Philadelphia: Jewish Publication Society of America, 1915.

Raphael, Chaim. *A Feast of History: Passover Through the Ages as a Key to Jewish Experience.* New York: Simon and Schuster, 1972.

Rashell, Jacob. *Jewish Artists in America.* New York: Vantage Press, 1967.

Reiss, Lionel S. *My Models Were Jews: A Painter's Pilgrimage to Many Lands, A Selection of One Hundred and Seventy-Eight Paintings, Watercolors, Drawings and Etchings.* New York: Gordon Press, 1938.

_____. *New Lights and Old Shadows: New Lights of an Israel Reborn, Old Shadows of a Vanished World; A Selection of Two Hundred and Ten Paintings, Watercolors, Drawings and Etchings.* New York: Reconstructionist Press, 1954.

Rembaum, Joel Edward. *The Jews, the Bible, and the Talmud: A Problem in Christian Tradition.* Los Angeles: University of Judaism, 1982.

Robertson, Bruce. *Representing America: The Ken Trevey Collection of American Realist Prints.* Santa Barbara, Calif.: University Art Museum, 1995.

Robinson, Andrew. *Paper in Prints.* Washington, D.C.: National Gallery of Art, 1977.

Romero, Elena, and Uriel Macias Kapon. *The Jews and Europe: 2000 Years of History.* New York: Henry Holt, 1994.

Rosen, Robert N. *The Jewish Confederates*. Columbia: University of South Carolina Press, 2000.

Rosenberg, Jakob. *On Quality in Art: Criteria of Excellence, Past and Present*. Princeton, N.J.: Princeton University Press, 1967.

Rosengarten, Theodore, and Dale Rosengarten. *A Portion of the People: Three Hundred Years of Southern Jewish Life*. Columbia: University of South Carolina Press, 2002.

Roth, Cecil. *A History of the Jews: From the Earliest Times Through the Six Day War*. New York: Schocken Books, 1970.

_____. *Jewish Art: An Illustrated History*. New York: McGraw-Hill, 1961.

_____. *The Jews in the Renaissance*. Philadelphia: Jewish Publication Society of America, 1959.

_____. *Personalities and Events in Jewish History*. Philadelphia: Jewish Publication Society of America, 1953.

_____. *A Short History of the Jewish People*. Hartford, Conn.: Hartmore House, 1969.

Rubens, Alfred. *A History of Jewish Costume*. New York: Funk & Wagnalls, 1967.

_____. *A Jewish Iconography*. London: Jewish Museum, 1954.

_____. *Some Aspects of Jewish Iconography. Based on a Lecture Delivered to the "Friends of the Jewish Museum" on December 1954 to Mark the Publication of A Jewish Iconography*. London: Jewish Museum, 1955.

Rubin, Louis Decimus. *My Father's People: A Family of Southern Jews*. Baton Rouge: Louisiana State University Press, 2002.

Rubin, Susan Goldman. *L'Chaim! To Jewish Life in America! Celebrating from 1654 until Today*. New York: Harry N. Abrams, 2004.

Sabar, Shalom. *Ketubbah: Jewish Marriage Contracts of the Hebrew Union College Skirball Museum and Klau Library*. Philadelphia: Jewish Publication Society, 1990.

Sachar, Howard Morley. *Dreamland: Europeans and Jews in the Aftermath of the Great War*. New York: Vintage Books, 2003.

_____. *A History of Israel: From the Rise of Zionism to Our Time*. New York: Knopf, 1996.

Sack, John. *An Eye for an Eye*. New York: Basic Books, 1993.

Salamander, Rachel, and Schalom Ben-Chorin. *The Jewish World of Yesterday, 1860–1938*. New York: Rizzoli, 1991.

Sanders, Ronald. *The Lower East Side: A Guide to Its Jewish Past with 99 New Photographs*. New York: Dover, 1979.

Schappes, Morris U. *The Jews in the United States; A Pictorial History, 1654 to the Present*. New York: Citadel Press, 1958.

Schauder, Wendy Bernstein. *The Jewish Book Guide: Your Comprehensive Source for Books of Jewish Interest*. Northvale, N.J.: J. Aronson, 1990.

Scheindlin, Raymond P. *The Chronicles of the Jewish People*. New York: Smithmark, 1996.

Schiff, Zeev, Ehud Yaari and Ina Friedman. *Israel's Lebanon War*. New York: Simon and Schuster, 1984.

Schoener, Allon. *Jewish Life in America: Fulfilling the American Dream: A Documentary Exhibition from Colonial Times to the Present*. New York: Anti-Defamation League of B'nai B'rith, 1983.

_____. *The Lower East Side: Portal to American Life, 1870–1924*. New York: Jewish Museum, 1966.

Schreckenberg, Heinz. *The Jews in Christian Art: An Illustrated History*. New York: Continuum, 1996.

Schreier, Barbara A. *Becoming American Women: Clothing and the Jewish Immigrant Experience, 1880–1920*. Chicago: Chicago Historical Society, 1994.

Schroeter, Daniel. *Morocco: Jews and Art in a Muslim Land*. Ed. Vivian B. Mann. London: Merrill, 2000.

Schwab, W. M., and Julia Weiner. *Jewish Artists: The Ben Uri Collection: Paintings, Drawings, Prints and Sculpture: A Catalogue of Works by Jewish Artists and of Jewish Interest in the Possession of the Ben Uri Art Society, London*. London: Ben Uri Society, 1994.

Schwartzman, Sylvan D., and Jack D. Spiro. *The Living Bible*. New York: Union of American Hebrew Congregations, 1962.

Schwarz, Karl. *Jewish Artists of the 19th and 20th Centuries*. New York: Philosophical Library, 1949.

Sellyei, Anna, Laszlo Muller, and Agnes Takach. *The Jewish Face of Budapest: Guidebook*. Budapest: B'nai B'rith, 1995.

Seltzer, Robert M. *Jewish People, Jewish Thought: The Jewish Experience in History*. New York: Macmillan, 1980.

Sevillias, Errikos. *Athens, Auschwitz*. Athens: Lycabettus Press, 1983.

Shachar, Isaiah, and R. Grafman. *Jewish Tradition in Art: The Feuchtwanger Collection of Judaica*. Jerusalem: Israel Museum, 1981.

Shahn, Ben. *Prints and Posters of Ben Shahn: 102 Graphics, Including 32 in Full Color*. New York: Dover, 1982.

Shamir, Ilan, and Shlomo Shavit, ed. *Encyclopedia of Jewish History: Events and Eras of the Jewish People*. North Ryde, New South Wales: Angus & Robertson, 1986.

Shiloh-Kohen, Nurit. *Bezalel, 1906–1929*. Jerusalem: Israel Museum, 1983.

Silberman, Charles E. *A Certain People: American Jews and Their Lives Today*. New York: Summit Books, 1985.

Silver, Kenneth E., and Romy Golan. *The Circle of Montparnasse: Jewish Artists in Paris, 1905–1945*. New York: Universe Books, 1985.

Singer, Isaac Bashevis. *Lost in America*. Garden City, N.Y.: Doubleday, 1981.

_____. *The Magician of Lublin*. New York: Noonday Press, 1960.

Slesar, Henry, and Mel Crawford. *Kosher Comics*. New York: Parallax Comic Books, 1966.

Smith, Gerald L. K. *The Roosevelt Death: A Super Mystery: Suicide? Assassination? Natural Death? Still Alive?* St. Louis, Mo.: Christian Nationalist Crusade, 1947.

Sola Pool, David de. *Portraits Etched in Stone: Early Jewish Settlers, 1682–1831*. New York: Columbia University Press, 1952.

Soussloff, Catherine M. *Jewish Identity in Modern Art History*. Berkeley: University of California Press, 1999.

Soyer, Raphael. *Raphael Soyer: Fifty Years of Printmaking, 1917–1967.* Ed. Sylvan Cole. New York: Da Capo Press, 1967.

Spencer, Charles, and V. D. Lipman. *The Immigrant Generations: Jewish Artists in Britain, 1900–1945: Essays.* New York: Jewish Museum, 1983.

Stauben, Daniel, and Rose Choron. *Scenes of Jewish Life in Alsace.* Malibu, Calif.: Joseph Simon, 1991.

Stav, Arie. *Peace—Arab Caricature: A Study in Antisemitic Image.* Tel Aviv: Zmora-Bitan, 1996.

Stern, Norton B. *Mannie's Crowd: Emanuel Lowenstein, Colorful Character of Los Angeles, and a Brief Diary of the Trip to Arizona and Life in Tucson of the Early 1880s.* Glendale, Calif.: A.H. Clark, 1970.

Sweibocka, Teresa, Jonathan Webber, and Connie Wilsack. *Auschwitz: A History in Photographs.* Bloomington: Indiana University Press, 1993.

Szyk, Arthur. *The New Order.* New York: Putnam's, 1941.

Taller, Stephen Lee, and Frances K. Pohl. *Remembering Ben Shahn: Selections from the Stephen Lee Taller Collection.* Berkeley, Calif.: Judah L. Magnes Museum, 1998.

Tammuz, Benjamin, ed. *Art in Israel.* London: W.H. Allen, 1965.

Tenney, Jack B. *Zionist Network: A Tenney Report.* Tujunga, Calif.: Standard Publications, 1953.

Tharaud, Jerome, and Jean Tharaud. *The Chosen People: A Short History of the Jews in Europe.* Trans. Frances Wilson Huard. London: Longmans, Green, 1929

Tobias, Thomas J. *The Hebrew Benevolent Society of Charleston, S.C., Founded 1784, the Oldest Jewish Charitable Society in the United States.* Charleston, S.C.: Hebrew Benevolent Society, 1965.

Trachtenberg, Joshua. *The Devil and the Jews: The Medieval Conception of the Jew and Its Relation to Modern Antisemitism.* New Haven, Conn.: Yale University Press, 1943.

Trzcinski, Andrzej. *A Guide to Jewish Lublin and Surroundings.* Lublin: Hotel Unia, 1996.

Twain, Mark. *Concerning the Jews.* Philadelphia: Running Press, 1985.

Ungar, Irvin. *Justice Illuminated: The Art of Arthur Szyk.* Chicago, Ill.: Spertus Institute of Jewish Studies, 1998.

Unterman, Alan. *Dictionary of Jewish Lore and Legend.* London: Thames & Hudson, 1998.

Vishniac, Roman. *A Vanished World.* New York: Farrar, Straus and Giroux, 1983.

Vital, David. *A People Apart: The Jews in Europe, 1789–1939.* Oxford: Oxford University Press, 1999.

Volavkova, Hana. *The Pinkas Synagogue, A Memorial of the Past and of Our Days.* Praha: Statni Pedagogicke Nakladatelstvi, 1955.

Walker, John. *Portraits: 5,000 Years.* New York: Abrams, 1983.

Weinstein, Jay. *A Collector's Guide to Judaica.* New York: Thames & Hudson, 1985.

Weizmann, Chaim. *The Jewish Case Against the Palestine White Paper; Documents Submitted to the Permanent Mandates Commission of the League of Nations.* London: Jewish Agency for Palestine, 1939.

Wigoder, Geoffrey. *Dictionary of Jewish Biography.* New York: Simon and Schuster, 1991.

_____. *Jewish Art and Civilization.* New York: Walker, 1972.

Willett, John. *Heartfield Versus Hitler.* Paris: Editions Hazan, 1997.

_____. *The Weimar Years: A Culture Cut Short.* New York: Abbeville Press, 1984.

Williams, Robert H. *The Anti-Defamation League and Its Use in the World Communist Offensive.* Flesherton, Ontario: Canadian Intelligence Publications, 1947.

Winograd, Henryk, Jacob Rosenbaum, and Belle Rosenbaum. *Chronicle of Jewish Traditions: A Sentimental Journey Exhibition, Yeshiva University Museum, March 8, 1992.* New York: Yeshiva University Museum, 1992.

Winter, Irene, and Stephanie Rachum. *Ingathering; Ceremony and Tradition in New York Public Collections.* n.p.: Sequoia Graphics, 1968.

Winter, Naphtali. *The High Holy Days.* New York: Leon Amiel, 1973.

Wischnitzer, Rachel. *From Dura to Rembrandt: Studies in the History of Art.* Milwaukee, Wis.: Aldrich, 1990.

Wolf, Simon. *The Presidents I Have Known from 1860–1918.* Washington, D.C.: press of B.S. Adams, 1916.

Wurmbrand, Max, and Cecil Roth. *The Jewish People: 4000 Years of Survival.* Tel Aviv: Massadah-P.E.C. Press, 1966.

Zangwill, Israel. *Dreamers of the Ghetto.* New York: Harper & Brothers, 1898.

_____. *The Melting-Pot: Drama in Four Acts.* New York: Macmillan, 1914.

Index

Titles of prints appear in *italics*, followed by artist's name where known. Titles of books or portfolios appear in **bold**. The Haggadahs are listed under their publication area or designer as they are known.

463